CW00408090

Silent Conversations

Anthony Rudolf. 2005. Photograph by Sonia Rouve.

Silent Conversations

A Reader's Life

Anthony Rudolf

LONDON NEW YORK CALCUTTA

Seagull Books, 2013

© Anthony Rudolf, 2013

ISBN   978 0 8574 2 080 0

British Library Cataloguing-in-Publication Data

A catalogue record for this book is available from the British Library

Typeset in NewBskvll BT and Adobe Garamond Pro by Seagull Books, Calcutta, India

Printed and bound by Maple Press, York, Pennsylvania, USA

For Paula Rego, at home, in the studio, in the Prado

What is reading but silent conversation?

—Walter Savage Landor, *Imaginary Conversations*

Contents

Contents

Contents

Contents

Contents

Contents

Contents

Contents

Contents

Contents

Acknowledgements

Regular interlocutors by phone:

> in particular Alan Wall, whose snapshot reactions helped clarify thought/feeling processes,
>
> as did the reactions of Clive Sinclair, Paul Buck, Musa Moris Farhi, Elaine Feinstein and Paula Rego.

Regular interlocutors by email:

> in particular James Hogan, whose paced reactions helped clarify thought/feeling processes,
>
> as did the reactions of Michael Heller, Richard Berengarten, Deryn-Rees Jones and Howard Cooper.

Occasional interlocutors:

> Julia Farrer, Paul Coldwell, David Hare, Christopher Ricks, Susannah York (RIP), Michael Pinto-Duschinsky, Z. Kotowicz, Yves Bonnefoy, Daniel Weissbort, Judit Kiss, Inge Elsa Laird (RIP), Michael Hamburger (RIP), Michael Sheringham, Michael Moorcock, Mark Hutchinson, Margaret Hogan (RIP), R. B. Kitaj (RIP), Jason Wilson, Jane Augustine, Norma Rinsler, Valentina Polukhina, Michael Schmidt, Claude Vigée, Stan Smith, Anne Serre, Lisa Russ Spaar, Stephanie Lafferty, Tom Rosenthal, Bill (W. D.) Jackson, Rosanna Warren, John Naughton, Steven Jaron, Stephen Romer, Jon Glover, Owen Lowery, Ros Schwartz and Tracy Bartley.

Also, those who answered specific questions, as named throughout the book. Any mistakes are the author's.

To Bruce Ross-Smith, who, in addition to being a regular email interlocutor, read the entire book in draft and acted as devil's advocate, thereby forcing me to clarify my thoughts, sometimes against my will. Sally Mercer, too, for second-reading her husband.

Acknowledgements

To John Taylor, touchstone and guardian of the flame.

To Mark Hutchinson who early on encouraged me to carve rather than to mould and who, on hearing how long the first draft was getting, reminded me of the last sentence of Emmanuel Hocquard's *The Library at Trieste*: 'Writing is also about knowing when, at any given moment, to stop.'

To Ivor Sherman, who kept my computer going in good times and bad.

To Bethan Roberts: see note at the beginning of the bibliography.

A few subsections or parts of subsections—adapted or verbatim or in draft—have appeared in journals (print or online) or books. My thanks to the respective editors: *The Reader, Modern Poetry in Translation, International Times, Jewish Chronicle, Stand, London Magazine, Jewish Quarterly, Poetry Nation Review (PNR), Poetry Review, Big Bridge, Temporel, Peut-Etre, Bow-Wow Shop, Ready Steady Book, Menard Press 40th Anniversary Keepsake Catalogue Carcanet Blog, Normblog; Yves Bonnefoy: poésie et dialogue; Random House/Faber Book of 20th Century French Poetry.*

I would like to thank Elaine Lustig Cohen for permitting me to use a letter from Arthur Cohen and Jean Crozier for a letter from Andrew Crozier; also, Hugo Williams and Judith Herzberg for permission to quote from their own private letters to me. Thanks too to the following: Anne Beresford for permission to quote from a letter from Michael Hamburger; Marilyn Kane for permission to quote Carl Rakosi; Catherine Fried and Hilde Gill for permission to quote Erich Fried; John Glad for permission to quote his translation of a poem by Anatoly Steiger; Stephen Stuart Smith of Enitharmon for permission to quote David Gascoyne; Peter Jay of Anvil Press for permission to quote Ruth and Matthew Mead's translations of Johannes Bobrowski, and his own co-translation of Janos Pilinszky; Hana Amichai and Miriam Neiger-Fleischmann for permission to publish Yehuda Amichai's 'The Jewish Time Bomb'.

Acknowledgements, too, to the other authors and publishers whose copyrighted works have been quoted, according to fair usage in terms of length (prose) and percentage (poems). A few attempts to achieve contact with copyright holders have been unavailing. Please advise any omissions or mistakes. Unintended, they will be remedied in future editions.

And to everyone at Seagull Books for their friendliness, forbearance and professionalism.

Preliminary Note

Some French books are discussed with reference to English translations, some not. Where translations have not been mentioned, Google can be consulted concerning possible availability.

Where a translator from any language is not acknowledged, the translation is almost always by me.

With very rare exceptions, and I name them, all books were on my desk at the time of discussion.

The final drafts of this book were made in late 2011 and mid-2012, a year to eighteen months after I completed the previous drafts, which began in 2006 or even 2005. In a book of this kind, it is impossible to keep 'up to date'. Since everything I read could, in principle, feed back to the text, many recent books have gone unrecorded or virtually unrecorded, for example the novels of J. M. Coetzee, which I have finally got round to reading over the last few months, or the essays of Arthur Krystal, culminating in his fine book, *Except When I Write*, as well as more books by J.-B. Pontalis (RIP) than I do in fact discuss.

Another example: thanks to a new tradition—the annual trip to New Zealand, where my grandson Charlie and family live—I have begun exploring and enjoying the country's literature and art; too late, however, for the present work, apart from the rare sneak preview. I look forward to constructive engagement in an essay one day.

I am sadly aware that many fine books, even by friends, have slipped through the net, but the book grew organically rather than systematically, and I can only apologize where necessary.

Preface

I am seventy. I have spent more than six years writing this book.

The book has given new meaning to my life. Equally, my life has given old meaning to the book.

Here are my books.

Here is my grandfather. Here are my grandchildren.

Here is Europe. Here I was born, during a world war. Here I will die . . .

Why do I read, why do I engage in these silent conversations?

I read because the forms of life and the structures of experience, the energy and beauty of the mind and its double, the body, are explored, incarnated and traced in the best literature.

And you, why do you read?

Introduction

1

My book, like many literary works, involves excess, desire and the controlling hand of absolute possession, certainly where reading and rereading are concerned. Subject matter and form are dialectically interrelated, and out of that interrelationship is born the book's deep content, which is the love child of conscious and unconscious longings for healing and wholeness, for unity and redemption. Such longings are widespread, if not universal, in our condition of finitude. When I was a child, reading either completed the world, or, better yet, *was* the world. Now that I am approaching seventy, when I am supposed to have put aside childish things, the experience of literary time and its double, literary space, remains a major consolation. Is this what Marcel Proust meant when he wrote that ideas are substitutes for sorrows? On the other hand, when it comes to a reading of our only world, I hope my practice will improve, despite the chaos and darkness reflected in that world's mirror. Roland Barthes argues somewhere that the reader becomes a new character or new characters in the book that he or she is reading. *La Foule*, my late friend Raymond Mason's bronze in the Tuileries Gardens in Paris (behind the Jeu de Paume and also at 527 Madison Avenue in Manhattan), is said to contain one hundred figures. However, if you count them, there are only ninety-nine: you yourself, participating in this wonderful work, are the hundredth . . . I hope readers will be drawn into my book in a similar manner, but have no fear, I'm not George Eliot's spider, still less a praying mantis. Barthes's erotics of reading can be taken too far.

One of the impulses behind the present book is inventory and classification. My categories, however, as listed in the contents of the book, are neither impermeable nor sacrosanct. Intoxicated by anamnesis, like Walter Benjamin, I have to be, want to be, flexible: 'The rags, the refuse—these I

1

will not inventory but allow, in the only way possible, to come into their own: by making use of them.' When Benjamin does that, when we too—with luck—make use of 'the rags, the refuse', then, in words taken from 'Harmonie du soir', a beautiful poem by another of my tutelary spirits whose name begins with the letter B:

> Les sons et les parfums tournent dans l'air du soir;
> Valse mélancolique et langoureux vertige!

> Sounds and perfumes dance in the evening air;
> Melancholy waltz and vertiginous languor!

I like to think that Charles Baudelaire, Benjamin's poet of poets, would have enjoyed my reversal of the last two words of this short quotation for the sake of a half-rhyme in English, *g_air/guor*, which, out of context, incarnates the meaning that is differently conveyed when you read the full stanza.

The eponymous hero of Italo Calvino's *Mr Palomar*, having decided he must pay close attention to the things of this world, realizes, after failed attempts, that 'he has to face each time problems of selection, exclusion, hierarchies of preference; he soon realizes he is spoiling everything, as always when he involves his own ego and all the problems he has with his own ego.' Readers already aware of Oulipo, the rule-based group founded by Raymond Queneau, will not be surprised that Calvino—author of such wondrous books as *The Castle of Crossed Destinies* and *Invisible Cities*, *If on Winter's Night a Traveller* and the aforementioned *Mr Palomar*—was a member. The patently Oulipoan rule-clarifying index of the latter gives the game away. Calvino, like Queneau—who wrote a preface to *Bouvard and Pécuchet*—was a great admirer of Gustave Flaubert's posthumous eponymous masterpiece.

2

It would be interesting to study the bibliophile as the only type of collector who has not completely withdrawn his treasures from their functional context.

—Walter Benjamin, *Arcades Project*

A few years ago I completed a long journey round my apartment, pulling a geographical, to take a resonant phrase out of context. I visited each room in turn and wrote down the 'infra-ordinary' contents and their local history, in the spirit of Georges Perec's endotic anthropology, an anthropology partly inspired by Queneau. While on my travels, I kept my beloved library at arm's length. 'In great matters, it is enough to have had the intention,' as John Dee wrote of Archimedes. Perhaps it would be more accurate to say I put off investigating the library till last, for the excellent reason that its phenomenology is more complex than that of the other elements which make up the periodic table of my apartment. Even as I crossed a frontier of the mind into a land of found content, I still had not decided whether an account of the books in the flat where I had lived for more than quarter of a century should be condensed into the final chapter of an intended 'travel' book or whether the account required a whole book to itself. In either case, the intention was to show my books the way into the new text. The decision would depend on the length of the eventual book. Meanwhile, obliged, like Buridan's donkey with its equidistant piles of hay, to choose between two equally deserving options, I had to get off the mental fence or starve. After weeks of indecision—shifting from ham to ham in a bath of unknowing—over whether to continue my long interrupted book about my grandfather or embark on the text about my library, I chose the library, partly because I could not find things (books, folders, papers, maps) I needed to consult in order to resume work on Grandfather. Perhaps they would turn up while I went through my books. Finally, it became clear that I had a whole book in my sights, not merely a chapter in the 'travel' book.

Walter Benjamin in 'Unpacking my Library' (*Illuminations*): 'Habent sua fata libelli'. These words may have been intended as a general statement about books. So books like Dante's *The Divine Comedy*, Spinoza's *Ethics* and Darwin's *The Origin of the Species* have their fate. A collector, however, interprets this Latin saying differently. For him, not only books but also copies of books have their fates. As so often, Benjamin supplies a proof text. I am not, strictly speaking, a collector of, say, first editions of a particular author. Long ago, it's true, I collected literary periodicals in a desultory way but the word 'desultory' proves that even then, despite being a bibliophile, I was not serious about collecting. I have a complete set of the *Review* edited by Ian Hamilton and need only one issue of Jon Silkin's *Stand* for the jackpot. But that's about it.

Some of my friends have or have had extensive working libraries. The painter R. B. Kitaj, for example. Musa Moris Farhi, epic writer and epic person, donated his twenty-five thousand books to his alma mater in Turkey. Possession of a serious library has to do with one's appetite for reading, one's professional needs, one's reader-/writer-specific version of retail therapy and other causes that may emerge in the present work. But a large library has no necessary link with the hobby, or obsession, of book collecting. Tom Rosenthal is a collector, the real McCoy. Rick Gekoski sells association copies to wealthy collectors out of his book rooms. If you collect T. S. Eliot signatures or autographs or Virginia Woolf associations and would like to own the copy of the first edition of *The Waste Land* as hand-printed by Woolf and signed by Eliot to her (or the other way round), Rick Gekoski is your only hope. Gekoski has written lovingly and wittily about Rosenthal in the latter's seventieth-birthday book which I edited and then published at Menard Press. [Memo to collectors: *Life in Books* contains specially written texts by Rosenthal's friends, including Salman Rushdie and Gore Vidal, henceforth claimed, in order to shift the stock, as Menard Press authors. Among the Menard titles which became collectors' items in their day was Paul Auster's first UK book, *The Art of Hunger*, published before he was Paul Auster (as in 'I knew Doris Day before she was a virgin').]

You would expect a publisher to possess a number of books with personal inscriptions to him but I also own a few with personal inscriptions to others. Thus, as Jonathan Griffin's literary executor, I inherited about two hundred of his books, including Volume One of Charles de Gaulle's *Memoirs*, which Griffin translated. Here too, pages uncut, is the second volume of the French edition, whose inscription makes it a classic association copy: 'en témoignage de ma grande et bien cordiale estime, Charles de Gaulle 7.11.59'. Mind you, when I was in Lille, de Gaulle's birthplace, while waiting to change trains for Charleville and the Rimbaud trail, I went to a book fair in the old town centre and mentioned the treasure to a dealer. Resounding silence. Prophets and homeland are the words I am looking for.

Here too are inscribed copies to Griffin of books by Henry de Montherlant, whose plays the English poet translated, and two volumes of the *Carnets*. Tucked into the earlier one is a clipping of the French author's *Times* obituary and a cutting from the same day announcing that he shot himself because he was afraid of going blind.

The other side of the coin is face up, and with egg on it, when a book you yourself wrote and signed with a message to someone, perhaps even a friend, turns up in a second-hand book dealer's catalogue (and, in my case, for not very much money). Inscriptions are one of the themes I shall be exploring later on, now that I have got off the fence and begun this text. Other themes shall be unread books, books read many years after they were bought, the interaction of writing and reading and so on. More will doubtless emerge during the writing, as structure and theme interact dialectically and with luck, perhaps a little judgement too, transmute each other.

My books are in several rooms, mainly the sitting room. Specialized collections are on shelves in my study, namely books by and/or about certain writers of particular importance to me: Yves Bonnefoy, Edmond Jabès, Claude Vigée, Yevgeni Vinokurov, Primo Levi, Franz Kafka, Lord Byron, Honoré de Balzac, all witness to past or ongoing or future projects in my writing life. There is also the question of whether I should classify books by French and Russian authors independently of English-language books. Some cases are difficult: Jeremy Reed's book on Arthur Rimbaud, *Delirium*, which—focusing on London in 1873 and *Une Saison en enfer*—is as good, given its perspective, as Edgell Rickword's *Rimbaud* and far better than Henry Miller's *The Time of the Assassins*, a weak effort by the old 'rogue' (George Brassai's word for him in *The Paris Years*, his unexpected memoir of Miller), especially when compared to his best works like *The Colossus of Maroussi* and *Quiet Days in Clichy*. Reed's critical works include a book on sexuality and poetry and a book on Lautréamont. *Madness: The Price of Poetry*, a study of Hart Crane, Rainer Maria Rilke, Robert Lowell, Friedrich Hölderlin, John Clare and others, begins with a deeply moving exploration of the agon of a marvellous and terrible (in the proper sense of the word) poet, Gerard Manley Hopkins. This is a serious phenomenology of the life's work and work's life of his great poets. Perhaps of all poets who approach the edge even once, Reed himself has been in that place. But the madnesses of his exemplary geniuses are never romanticized. So, does *Delirium* go under 'French' or 'Biography'?

3

The Oxford philosopher R. G. Collingwood, in his austere *Autobiography*, writes: 'I taught myself to read Dante and made the acquaintance of many other poets, in various languages, hitherto unknown to me. These unauthorized readings (for which, in summer time, I used to perch in a willow tree overhanging the Avon) are my happiest recollection of Rugby [school].' This recollection would have touched a chord with Proust, and reminds me of the outdoor episodes in the French writer's beautiful and haunting essay on reading which started life as an introduction to a volume of John Ruskin (although not *Praeterita*, which Proust claimed to know by heart). Moving indoors, Proust plays 'the proprietor in a room filled to overflowing with the souls of others and which preserves the imprint of their dreams . . .' As a proprietor myself, I intend to begin sorting out the books in my sitting room. One of many reasons for the disorder is that I helped myself to about three hundred books from my father's library and inherited the ones already mentioned from Jonathan Griffin. There was no room for them on my shelves, already packed to bursting point. A number of my father's books move me greatly and almost entirely because of their provenance, a different example of Benjamin's gloss on Terentianus Maurus. Many of these I shall never read or reread, but they serve as icons of the gone world of my childhood, of a gone man (twice over, the young father and the man who died too soon aged seventy-one) who did not read as many books as he would have liked, partly because he had a demanding day job—his professional reading was tax returns, balance sheets and reports. In later years, his out-of-office work as a magistrate required a different kind of professional reading, and there were the *Times* and the *Economist* and the *Jewish Chronicle* (and other newspapers and periodicals at different times), not to mention the long letters I used to send him when I was engaged in my nuclear obsession and too cowardly or unsure of my position to engage in a face to face discussion. (Not sure I trust those explanations.)

Perhaps the very process of sorting through my books will generate a high conceptual framework, a meta-narrative for the story I want to tell. More at home among my books than anywhere else, I have always been struck by the profound interiority evoked in paintings where someone is reading. He or she is as involved with the book as we are while looking at the painting. Indeed, there is a sense in which we are that person. Yes, I know it's a good excuse or device—the painter needs 'that painted countenance' (Robert Browning's phrase which I offered the late Michael Podro when he was still seeking a title for his magnificently learned and fascinating book *Depiction*) not to be looking out or at us, and yet does not want to have the back of the person 'in your face'. Paula Rego tells me that prints or paintings with a figure facing away from the viewer, especially if the figure is looking out of a window, are always the most popular in her various series, such as the *Father Amaro* pastel paintings or the *Jane Eyre* lithographs. As her main male model, I wonder why. Are they less demanding? Less threatening?

In pictures, letters being read are less interesting than books being read, for letters psychologize our reading of the painting, or, at least, introduce a third-party mystery. They never incarnate interiority, since a letter is intimately personal to the recipient by virtue of its alterity. It suggests love or betrayal or something imported by the agency of an unknown power broker or a known intimate. It has not been *chosen*—unlike a book, which is an extension of the reader's own interiority rather than an intrusion, whether sought or unsought. Maps could be said to inhabit terrain somewhere between books and letters. A map suggests future or past pleasure, and travel often connotes a companion. But the book, haven of private reading, matrix of interiority, trigger of dream, is the only extension of human presence that works in a painting to deepen our awareness of self-reflexivity and thus feeds back to the viewer of the painting, who is willy-nilly drawn into the picture, as in a mirror or through a glass. Whereas a mirror in the picture itself distances the viewer just as its always self-conscious deployment works against the interiority of the character looking in the mirror. (Think *Las Meninas* by Diego Velázquez or *The Music Lesson* by Johannes Vermeer.)

One of the most fascinating paintings in a show of self-portraits I saw at the National Portrait Gallery was of Johannes Gumpp, loaned from the Uffizi. In this strikingly modern conception, we are as if standing behind the painter whose image is reflected in the mirror to the left while the self-portrait is well on the way to completion on the easel to the right. How right Gumpp was to leave the self-portrait on the easel unfinished! The lonely mirror shall have the last 'word', he seems to be telling us. Only a mirror is objective; a mere picture cannot attain that kind of perfection; and to prove it, the picture we are looking at shows us only his back. And yet, of course, he has painted himself into the mirror, and I shall be painting myself into a corner—a very enjoyable one, admittedly—if I continue wandering round these perceptual and conceptual paradoxes. Still, it was the perfect picture for the cover of my book *Zigzag*, although the reproduction is too dark.

4

'I, in a hurry to find the place and the formula', as Rimbaud wrote in his *Illuminations*, this title to be pronounced, according to Verlaine, in English— easy, imagine the word spoken by Inspector Clouzot. While continuing to seek my high concept, my meta-narrative and the story beneath the threshold, I'm easily sidetracked by new connections or reminders of old ones. Here is George Oppen's *Selected Letters*. So special was the man and so remarkable were his letters that for sure all his many correspondents kept them. The book has two notes concerning Yves Bonnefoy: the opening section of one of George Oppen's most important poems 'Of Being Numerous' alludes to Bonnefoy's work as quoted by Mary Oppen. George's friend Stephen Schneider (the poet Samuel Klonimos) had translated Bonnefoy's *Du Mouvement et de l'immobilité de Douve* and reignited Oppen's prior interest in the French poet. Peter Nicholls, in *George Oppen and the Fate of Modernism*, gives a fascinating account of parallels between the two poets. Later, and independently, Yves Bonnefoy became interested in George Oppen. What a thrill that this textual link exists between two writers who mean so much to me.

Emmanuel Levinas wrote that 'discourse is violence', for discourse involves classification and classification involves high risks, in particular when groups of people are threatened, threatened solely because they are different, because they are other. Fortunately, I am dealing with books—not with people. So let me enter the fray and embark on their classification, with all due respect. This is an opportunity, a unique opportunity, to tidy up, not merely for the purposes of the current text but also for me to live and work with less frustration and more comfort. Add all the units of ten minutes I spend looking for something specific and you have a tidy (*sic*) amount of wasted time over my working life. During the four years in the 1990s when I was seeing a psychotherapist (Deryck Dyne, who sadly and prematurely died), one of the themes that came up, while I was trying to think/feel my way through a labyrinthine *folie à deux*, was the way I made my writing life so difficult for myself, thanks to untidiness and self-sidetracking. I suspect too that the reason I am at my best writing texts that do not require research, such as miniature fables (and sometimes poems), is that I write first drafts at white-hot speed—no time to make life difficult for myself. Was I so bad or so wicked that I had to punish myself? As with people, so with books—reading itself is a *folie à deux*. Barthes says that if a book is bad, he stops reading it; if the book is good, he stops reading and thinks about what he's read so far, makes notes and picks up the book again. Nothing is straightforward, when it comes to reading. It is an activity, not a passivity.

'The Circus Animals' Desertion' is one of the key statements about artistic process since Stephané Mallarmé and Arthur Rimbaud. Here on their 'painted stage', representing 'heart-mysteries', are all my books merely a way 'to engross the present and dominate memory'? W. B. Yeats' self-command at the end of that wondrous poem ('I must lie down . . .') remains a categorical imperative if I am not to perish, like some J.-K. Huysmans character, amid thousands of books, enchanted by a dream. The ones piled under the computer table—my first thought is that, unlike those on the shelves, they are there by accident. That is to say, their being-in-the-world is not collective—if some of them are poetry books, or autobiographies, so what? Furthermore, I do have a poetry section in this room but the shelves were filled up long ago. Perhaps I don't have to decide on categories yet. In which case, I should make notes about the books and then construct my thoughts before I return to the computer with specifics to be tailored into paragraphs. My initial impulse is to reorganize the books by genre. And yet, the first two I pick up are by Rilke: *The Book of Hours* and *Diaries of a Young Poet*, which I used as the basis of a Rilke trail in Florence one afternoon, when Paula went shopping—Mandarina Duck was on the menu—before returning to the Uffizi, where she fed on or off Giovanni Bellini, Masaccio and Antoine Watteau. The two Rilke books by one principle belong together—that is, the organizing principle should be centred on author rather than genre, especially when the author is, surprise surprise, in my pantheon. I offer a silent prayer to the masters of the universe, or rather of this particular universe, or, even more modestly, of a constellation, the necklace of Bs that graces my *imaginaire*: Beckett, Baudelaire, Barthes, Benjamin, Butor, Bachelard, Blanchot, Bataille, Bonnefoy, Boulez, Bergman. Reading this list, my friend Z. Kotowicz sardonically proposed that I add one more—Bardot; then, as an afterthought, Bush, Blair and Berlusconi.

I must press on in my attempt to match books to categories and vice versa. It's called research, and there is much to do. Yes, 'engrafted in the tenderness of thought' (*The Prelude*), I have miles to go before I wake. Sometimes I think my existence has been one long fugue, an unearned reverie, 'a fiction . . . a dream of passion' (as Hamlet says) in order to escape the responsibility I lay claim to—being a writer. No longer a translator or editor or literary critic—a writer, that is, one who tells his story to the best of his ability. How much time I have spent wandering in my mind to the four corners of the earth (that biblical phrase beloved of the Flat Earth Society), segueing round the mountains like a dancer, dancing through the seas like a merman draped in seaweed, taking every possible detour in order to avoid settling in one corner of England, there to write. After all, the name Angleterre was one of the mystical reasons adduced by Menasseh ben Israel from biblical texts to persuade Oliver Cromwell to allow the Jews back into England, although some scholars see the Dutch rabbi diplomat's messianism as purely opportunistic.

5

Two days later. A (temporary?) accommodation between the books on the floor and categories has been reached, and I am faced with a dilemma. At a guess, there must be five thousand books in this room alone. I have sorted not more than a few hundred into dedicated piles. Am I going to spend the entire summer going through the books? Where do I begin? Soon I must turn my attention to the subject-ordered books on shelves; they are not entirely disorganized, despite my chronic inability to put them back in the right place. The chronic inability extends to cassettes and CDs and floppy disks which are often in the wrong case or gathering dust in no case at all. Nor must I forget the randomly shelved books in the hall and elsewhere. They too belong in this book. I am in trouble. Back to basics, back to the books. There they stand, as if alive. I await a miracle—either my story or my high concept. Are they one and the same thing? Dream on.

In 'Le Reniement de Saint Pierre', Baudelaire tells us he would have no second thoughts about leaving a world where action was not sister to the dream. Or, in Rimbaud's words, 'Poetry will no longer submit action to rhythm. Poetry will be ahead of the game.' As Max Weber wrote, 'nothing is gained by yearning or tarrying alone.' I have an idea, which is what passes for action when I'm in this frame of mind: I could embark on the writing without having constructed an overarching biblio-taxonomical structure in advance. I could write an allotted amount every day on any aspect that takes my fancy (captures my imagination is a fancier way of putting it), say five hundred words. If I do *all* the sorting first, I will lose the habit of a daily stint of writing. Let me find the story, the high concept, in the very process of writing, which is also the writing of process.

Yes, it is time to dive into the waters of oblivion and rescue my dead since, as Pascal Quignard writes in *Sur le jadis*, 'language is the *only resurrection* for what has disappeared' (his emphasis), something Paul Celan would have seconded. For the Jews, the soul remained with the body until the latter had wholly decomposed. For the ancient Greeks and Romans, as described in Fustel de Coulanges's classic study *The Ancient City*, the souls of the dead remained buried with the body. But Fustel de Coulanges makes no mention of the Jewish statute of limitation. The dead remained alive, hence the need for libations. He quotes Euripides, a speech by Iphigenia: 'I pour upon the earth of the tomb milk, honey and wine; for it is with these that the dead rejoice' (translation revised). Let this writing yield a reunion with the dead, as I drink with my eyes to the books on my shelves. Let Jove's nectar nourish writer and reader. Meanwhile, one of my favourite poets, George Seferis, in 'Stratis the Mariner among the Agapanthi', asks the relevant question:

> There are no asphodels, no violets, no hyacinths;
> How then will you talk to the dead?
> For the dead know only the language of flowers
> That is why they keep silent—
> They journey, and keep silent, they endure and keep silent
> In the assembly of dreams.

The present work is, among other things, a dialogue with the dead (Jean Genêt reports that Alberto Giacometti had the idea of burying one of his sculptures as an offering to the dead), perhaps including my younger self, the younger self who more than forty years ago annotated some of the books under consideration. Revisiting my past, how can I fail to be reminded of *Krapp's Last Tape*? My dialogue takes place in what Martin Heidegger, quoted by Celan, called a Zeithof, a time-court: 'The now-point gives consciousness a time-court, borne out in what memory continually apprehends.' Inspired by this word, Celan coined his own, 'Zeitgehöft', translated by John Felstiner in his *Selected Poems and Prose of Paul Celan* as 'Homestead of Time', which 'tries for a sense of poems as places where time is at home'. Shall I then call this book a *timestead*—where I conduct the dialogue with my dead . . . and with my living? Celan:

> Leap-centuries . . .
> leap-
> births, . . . Leap-
> deaths
> . . .
> Stations of reading in the late word.

Such a *timestead*, station of reading, is the remarkable book about Celan, *Sous la Coupole*, by Jean Daive whose *Décimale blanche* was translated by Celan and who himself translated Celan's *Strette*. Although writers like Edmond Jabès and André du Bouchet turn up in *Sous la Coupole*, this atmospheric, obsessive and centripetal book is written as a record of many conversations between Daive and Celan, albeit reconstructed and conflated from memory (unless Daive had a hidden tape recorder). By the strangest coincidence, while I was reading Daive's book (twelve years after publication, shame on me), I received an email from Rosmarie Waldrop which mentioned in passing that she was translating *Sous la Coupole* and asking me if I had read it.

6

The thrill, or recollection of the thrill, obtained when reading, or as a result of reading, certain books, particularly when young. By thrill, I mean the sensation that the book in question is already or about to be or will later be of major significance in one's life. I think of *Tristes tropiques* and *To the Finland Station*—Claude Lévi-Strauss is in the list of pantheon authors I originally intended to make and then abandoned, so it is not surprising that one of his books engendered the thrill. Edmund Wilson is not on my list (although he would have certainly been on my father's list) and yet *To the Finland Station* remains in my mind as a book that utterly captivated me as a young man. When I told my late friend Professor Chimen Abramsky that I was reading Jules Michelet's journals and that I had first encountered Michelet in Wilson's book, he replied that *To the Finland Station* was a very fine book indeed. We agreed, or, more modestly, I agreed with Abramsky that Wilson was completely engaged with his theme and carried the reader along on a great swell of prose.

Then there are the books I read in what I shall risk calling my maturity, books which I like to recommend to friends who may not have come across them, just as they recommend books to me. Thus, three exceptional books which, in my experience, embody and generate insight into creativity beyond the specifics of the author or the subject: David Sylvester's *Interviews with Francis Bacon* (the third edition is best, with its account of the way Sylvester edited Bacon's words); *Notes of a Cinematographer* by Robert Bresson; Igor

13

Stravinsky's *Poetics of Music* ('the more art is controlled, limited, worked over, the more it is free'), introduced by George Seferis. I had planned to draw up a full list of best books. Then I shifted to the idea of a pantheon of dead writers before abandoning it as simplistic:

Non-Fiction: Primo Levi, Walter Benjamin, Georges Perec, Robert Antelme, Claude Lévi-Strauss, Ludwig Wittgenstein

Fiction and drama: Anton Chekhov, Franz Kafka, Samuel Beckett, Joseph Roth, Marguerite Duras, Tillie Olsen

Poetry: Charles Baudelaire, Emily Dickinson, Arthur Rimbaud, Laura Riding, George Seferis, Czesław Miłosz, Charles Reznikoff, Wallace Stevens, Paul Celan, George Oppen, Marianne Moore, Octavio Paz

Unclassifiable: Roland Barthes, W. G. (Max) Sebald

However, the idea is worth a moment of reflection for it involves magical thinking, talismanic identifications, ghostly demarcations. Perhaps a distinction should be made between writers I continue to read seriously and closely such as Barthes or Oppen, and writers like Lévi-Strauss or Riding whom I read closely in the past. All four would have been in my pantheon but the first two remain in my working library. The distinction between the two is useful rather than profound. Over my long life as a reader/writer, members of the dual category have moved back and forth between the two modes, though it is possible that, as one grows older, the working library contains fewer names. The real question is: What does one mean by 'reading closely and seriously'? I suspect it connotes at least four things: intellectual affinity, psychic need, emotional feedback and bio-rhythmic kick-starts. When, one day, I return to my own poems, it may well be that I shall need Laura Riding again. For, I tell myself, if she is a poet, which she is, perhaps I am, whereas if Robert Duncan is a poet, which he is, perhaps I am not. This should not be pursued too far. As I said, on this level of need and self-perception, one is in the realm of magic and talisman. There is a sense too in which Riding, famous for the wrong reasons but not widely read, and even Duncan, need me—all books are completed by their readers. If in doubt about this, summon up for yourself the name of a forgotten writer. And act upon the summons.

'For the wrong reasons'—this knowing phrase raises and begs various questions. Unglossed, and given Riding's colourful escapades with Robert

Graves and others, the phrase can only imply that the right reason for a writer to be famous is for his or her writings alone, not for the matrix of the life that generated the work, or, more nuanced, the matrix of the lived life in dialectical relationship with the mind that reflects on the life and the world and out of which matricial triangle the work is generated. This attitude, allied to the idea once associated with New Criticism—that the work can be explained without reference to the life or, indeed, anything outside the poem itself—is hopelessly simplistic and puritanical. While it is self-evidently true that the work cannot be reduced to the life, it is equally true that it was not made in some kind of sterilized echo chamber of the mind. Here are Riding's *Collected Poems* and *First Awakenings: The Early Poems*. There is no way that her extraordinary life bears no relationship to her work, no way that knowledge of the life cannot generate insight about the work and vice versa. Bring on the biographies. Bring on the correspondences. Tell me more about her. Felix Arvers, a contemporary of Balzac, was the author of many plays and one book of poems. He is remembered for one sonnet, 'L'amour caché', an inferior variation on 'When you are old and grey', Yeats' version of Pierre de Ronsard's most famous poem. Who knows, perhaps the mystery and secret of Arvers' forgotten life deserves a glance? When I mentioned his poem on a visit to Bonnefoy in rue Lepic, he immediately quoted some lines from it.

What about Albert Mérat, admired by Paul Verlaine? Mérat was the only poet apart from Verlaine that the seventeen-year-old Rimbaud, in his 'Lettre du Voyant' of 15 May 1871, had a word of praise for. Mérat refused to be included in 'Coin de table', the famous group portrait of the Vilains Bonhommes by Fantin-Latour, now in the Musée d'Orsay, which contains the oft-reproduced image of Rimbaud looking like a cherub, or, more accurately, a *putto*, because he, Mérat, feared contamination by the bad boys. Graham Robb in his biography of Rimbaud suggests that a handful of Mérat's poems are worth a first look. That's a perfect sidetrack project the next time I feel the need to wander from the straight and narrow.

The lives of William Carlos Williams and Wallace Stevens are well documented. Williams was a paediatric physician in general and hospital practice, although he would sometimes make notes for a poem, in his car, between patients or stay up after an emergency night call. Stevens who, unlike

Rilke, was not subsidized by wealthy ladies, composed his poems walking to work, dictated them to his secretary, and spent the rest of the day in the business of insurance. In the case of writers, perhaps we are, after all, talking about lifestyle options. And yet, the relationship between lifestyle and identity is not necessarily a function of economics. Nor is the visual aspect of style an optional extra. True, it can be left to default or convention ('Mr Eliot in his four-piece suit'—Virginia Woolf) but it must involve the mindset of the creator, the deep structures of his or her *imaginaire*. Once again, Rilke comes to mind. Enough, what counts is the end product, not the life that once pulsated through the Prague-born German-language poet, now buried 'under so many eyelids', words from his self-epitaph engraved on the tombstone in a Swiss churchyard, an epigraph surely echoed in Celan's 'niemandsrose'.

7

Edward Dahlberg's *The Sorrows of Priapus* (with drawings by Ben Shahn), *The Leafless American* ('A true writer is a learned reader'), *The Flea of Sodom* and *The Carnal Myth* are on my desk. He is sententious, aphoristic, highly coloured, an overwriter rather than an underwriter, like Robert Burton in *The Anatomy of Melancholy*, one of Dahlberg's ancestors. I open *The Carnal Myth* at random and find: 'There is much confusion abroad, and our poets are no wiser than the street urchin.' Dahlberg likes generalization: 'When man is in doubt regarding his soul or the strength of his character, he will labour for his destiny, which is what the Greeks did.' We think we know what he means. *The Leafless American* contains a wonderful essay on Spain, 'the most Jewish of all the countries in Europe'. Another essay, 'The Sandals of Judith', is a flight by a sexual man who believes that 'all knowledge, and what we call the intellect, is only the wisdom of the body'. The prose here and elsewhere is instinct with a deep, almost carnal knowledge of the rhythms of the King James Bible—psalms and prophets, proverbs and the Song of Songs. A treat from *The Sorrows of Priapus* —we learn that the 'merciful licence' of alcohol was permitted only to the old men and women, 'heavy with desolation'. And another classic thought which, with any luck, one only assents to on rare occasions: 'It is difficult to know whether the tongue or the phallus is more harmful to men.' And this, to demonstrate again that the rhythms of the Bible and Jewish liturgy were lodged in his ear: 'Man pines to live but cannot endure the days of his life.'

Let me pause for reflection. There is a world of difference, a time world of difference, between categorizing and naming a large number of books. Do I want to name all those books? Ruthlessness is called for. There is no place for sentimentality or whimsy of the kind that even a great critic like J. Hillis Miller indulges in, in his *Versions of Pygmalion* which I would retitle *The Coronation of Prosopopoeia* (not a bad description of his theme). He says that to read and respond to one book betrays his responsibility to all the other books. With my worries about authors I have neglected, about priority and time, I know what Hillis Miller means but, essentially, his observation is an upmarket postmodern version of the old ontological question: Why is there something instead of nothing? He knows very well that he would read more if he wrote less. Ah, but given his vocation as a critic, he would read less closely if he read more widely. This weak reading of Hillis Miller is a projection of my sentimentality.

As a child, I approved of the custom (and still remember it fondly) that when you dropped a sacred Jewish book you were supposed to kiss it. I learnt early that words and not images were at the heart of my ancestral religion. Now, as a non-practising liminal Jew, I still believe in books, and in commentary. A question for Hillis Miller (author too of *Illustration*, a pioneering exploration of hypertextuality), who stands in for all readers, if I may flatter them/us and him at the same time. The question has to do with writing on a computer: Is it a fruitful metaphor to argue that such writing involves moulding rather than carving?

8

A recent article in *Le Monde* about the library of the writer Bernard Frank tells us that he now surrounds himself by Pléiade editions to the exclusion of all his other books. In other words, in his seventies, he has made a choice to spend the rest of his life reading classics, ancient and modern. On the question of quantity, some people start out travelling light, and stay that way. They include my friends, Z. Kotowicz and James Hogan (aka Augustus Young). They are not surrounded by thousands of books, in the way that Kitaj was and Farhi was (until recently) and Alan Wall is. Me too. Do I really think I will reduce my library to the essentials? It is no accident that Kotowicz and Hogan move house frequently. They are sailors rather than farmers, nomads rather than nesters. Kitaj was exceptional among painters—he had a huge library of non-art as well as art books that many of his colleagues, including Paula, possess. Painters are more open about their influences than writers. They are always saying of other painters: 'You can tell he's been looking at so and so.' Even those who, unlike Kitaj and Avigdor Arikha, Frank Auerbach and Jonathan Leaman, have not been great readers (about art or anything else), dip into their libraries of catalogues and monographs, including the old black-and-white ones from Phaidon beloved of Kitaj and Paula, and the catalogues of friends and rivals. A clue to Kitaj's taste is contained in the lines from Auden's 'Letter to Lord Byron' in Auden and MacNeice's *Letters from Iceland* from which the painter took the title of an exhibition he curated in 1976, *The Human Clay*: 'To me Art's subject is the human clay, / And landscape but a background to a torso; / All Cézanne's apples I would give away / For one small Goya or a Daumier'.

As someone who lives on the word processor, I have no doubt that the reading of books (unlike the writing of books) has not been overtaken by the use of a computer screen or by Kindles and iPads, partly because if I spend all day at the screen I want my reading of books to be on the page. True, I download articles from the Internet, and friends send drafts of texts. Paula sends JPEGs. Nommi in Jerusalem sends photographs. Patrick in Vigo sends jokes. I went through a long phase of circulating political texts whenever I felt the need to make a futile gesture. Yet the book, even a decently bound paperback, has a special place, a special space, where safety and danger merge—an objective correlative for the life of the mind. My books are well behaved on the outside (safety in numbers?), lined up like good or, at least, obedient children. With the wrong glasses on, I cannot make out their titles but the shapes are familiar. I discern the essays of Max Weber (in the old familiar Routledge and Kegan Paul pale blue dust jacket); three biographies of the prematurely deceased grandfather of Anglo-Jewish poets Isaac Rosenberg; a Soviet edition of the poems of Alexander Tvardovsky, whom I translated; John Holt's *How Children Learn*. Every captain, sad or not, has his thunder, and every book its fate. And a fair number of my books are bound up with my fate as a reader, that is, as a person with a mind and a character. I had problems with Weber when I was a social anthropology student; now, however, I find that some of his essays speak to our condition in a cruel world.

A book bought to be read later (I have many of those) involves a flirtation with deferred danger—the book could demantibulate my given structures, make demands I won't find easy to live with. Or a book I've already read—what if I have been misquoting it or misreading it after many years? That may not be a great crime but it is surely a little sin. And yet, to know the books are there, hundreds of mini-worlds full of energy and excitement and life, is profoundly reassuring. This is where I belong, here in this room, with its unending supply of altogether otherworldly goods—ready to be brought into my sphere of influence at the snap of an impulse's finger, or, quite the opposite, at a summons from my heart's deep core.

So, we arrive at the question of whether to reread or not reread well-/ill-remembered books from long ago, most of which were not annotated, even if the copies survive. The words on the pages of a book remain the same, yet we bring to books we reread a greater experience of the world, of the word, for now we have our own past for testing against the present, not only the pasts found in the books we loved. On the other hand, every book reread steals time we could have spent on the first reading of a good book. Spent? Don't I mean 'saved'? I have serious gaps in my reading of English literature, partly because, when university friends—John Barrell, Andrew Crozier, Terry Eagleton, Richard Berengarten, Angus Calder, John Tyler and others—were reading books in and out of F. R. Leavis' 'great tradition', I was reading French and Russian fiction and poetry, even after I had changed subjects from modern languages to social anthropology. Years later, I read *Jane Eyre* (and *Wuthering Heights*) when Paula asked me to pose as Mr Rochester. Perhaps you saw Rochester on two of the Rego postage stamps, including the second-class one, where he is sitting on a horse rented from the BBC props department (and very uncomfortable it was too). Posing for Paula is the nearest I shall get to being a real actor, apart from the occasion I read a Hebrew prayer in a Radio Four play by Elaine Feinstein. I make a solemn vow to read George Eliot before I die. That has to be a greater priority than rereading any of the Dostoevsky novels I read with passion when I was young. Or is it?

9

Not all my books are lined up like obedient children; others are like drunken soldiers, some leaning to the left, others to the right (unlike Dombey's books, also soldiers). They don't fall down because they are propped up by their neighbours. Each one is at once the middle panel and left hand and right hand of a triptych. Some have been put back horizontally, on top of other books. If they were soldiers, they would be from different regiments. Look, ahead of me, are the 'teach yourself' Que Sais-Je? platoon, recalling the days of my autodidacticism; the Gallimard/NRF company, the Poètes d'aujourd'hui regiment, the squad or, if you like, constellation, of Pléiades. Permanently on parade, they stand there awaiting my command. Their spatial configuration is a joy to behold. But they are unusual in their being ordered. Most shelves suggest a projection of the primordial chaos of my mind. I glance to the right, and look at the wall covered in pictures, with more propped up against the central-heating radiators in summer. How the energy and power of Paula's paintings and etchings reveal themselves 'at a glance'. In no way do the limits of her spoken language (for we all have our spoken limits) mean the limits of her visual world. She's looking for the world she had before the space was made, as Yeats almost wrote.

What would be the logical, the rational way of proceeding? If the intention is to meditate on the categories poetico-taxologically, I shall have to sift through *all* my books. But that is logistically impossible—I would need an empty room. The children's former rooms are stuffed with unsorted rubbish. I am stuck in the lounge. Keep moving. Attack the pile of books heaped high behind the television. So far I have only come up with two new categories, and have added them to the contents list. Books go straight to their designated pile, unless a fatal attraction summons me and its old black magic has me in its spell once more.

Just so: What have we here?

Answer: A French anthology with resonant words as its title—part of a line from a late poem by Hölderlin, 'Bread and Wine': *Wozu dichter in durftiger zeit?* What use are poets in hard times or in a time of dearth or in 'a destitute time'? The latter phrase is John Felstiner's, in *Paul Celan: Poet, Survivor, Jew*, a masterwork of translation as literary criticism and vice versa. Felstiner generates new and important insights into Celan through his meta-critical readings of his own translations of the poet. *Wozu Dichter*—dates from 1980 when I became involved in the nuclear issue. Paul Schmidt's American translation of Bonnefoy's *Rimbaud par lui-même* (the most profound exploration of Rimbaud I have read) is un-annotated by me because the original French edition contains my marginalia. If Bonnefoy's short meditation of 1961 is my all-time favourite book by one poet on another, then my favourite autobiography, an intellectual and affective meditation on the highest level, is Barthes's *Roland Barthes par lui-même*, in the same series as Bonnefoy's and the only one whose author and subject are the same, negating the paradox of the publisher's concept. I open *Roland Barthes* and find a meditation on his two work spaces or places, in Paris and in the country, which are, he says, identical, even though he never takes anything from one place to the other. They are identical because the disposition of their elements is identical—'c'est la structure de l'espace qui en fait l'identité'. The structure of the space constitutes its identity. Another meditation makes me wince—*la compulsion de programme* (his emphasis), the hypomania of list-making writers with too many projects to complete.

'There is a sense in which the work in progress is never anything but a meta-book, a temporary commentary on the work to come. The whole of Proust is a prospectus. The work is a rehearsal (the idea works better in French: répétition). The work is an endless moving staircase,' writes Barthes. I would add that it feels like walking up the down staircase, although Benjamin used this particular figure differently. I could quote endlessly from

21

Roland Barthes, whose narrator is sometimes 'I', sometimes 'he'. I did not obtain my mental structures from Barthes. I found him and elected him mentor because his way of being on the page corresponded or responded to my deepest needs. I'm sure Max Sebald knew this book well, with its photographs and quotes and fragments, but it's too late to ask him. Yes, Barthes sits at the top table, a member of my now-abandoned pantheon and, more important, my working library. Favourite writers, living and dead, are witness to one's attempts 'to invent and to prove true . . . to live . . . and not to formulate . . . [H]e [the poet] will formulate only incidentally,' as Bonnefoy writes of the poet's task in *Rimbaud*. As for the reader, I agree with Georg Lichtenberg: 'To read means to borrow; to create out of one's readings is paying off one's debts.' Here ends the 'inaugural space' (Emmanuel Hocquard) of my introduction.

France and French Literature

It seems obvious to me that the writing of my books influences my life, deranges it, modifies it. Whence, perhaps, the desire, sometimes, to modify my life, to influence my writing in the sense I desire.

—Mathieu Bénézet, *Ceci est mon corps*

Now all roads lead to France
And heavy is the tread
Of the living; but the dead
Returning lightly dance
—Edward Thomas, 'Roads'

Death is the wall where we face the firing squad
No pity for the soldiers
—Alain Jouffroy

Introduction

The first French book I read voluntarily (that is, not as a school text) was Georges Sand's *François le Champi*, which I found on the shelf in my bedroom while on an exchange holiday in Royan with André Both, a French contemporary, and his family in 1959. Not having read Proust yet, I could not know the important connection but later I would make the happiest of discoveries: this was one of the books given to Marcel by his grandmother as a birthday present and read aloud to him by his mother in the early pages of *A la Recherche du temps perdu*. Sand's book, of whose contents I remember nothing, is also the subject of an intense and wondrous meditation on reading and memory towards the end of *A la Recherche*: the narrator recalls that he contemplated the book 'for the first time in my little bedroom at Combray, during what was perhaps the sweetest and saddest night of my life'. The decline in his 'health and willpower' dates from that very night.

What is the conceptual force of 'French' in the taxonomy revealed by my contents pages? It would be legitimate and indeed natural to include Graham Robb's brilliant, unsolemn and entertaining biography *Rimbaud* under 'Biography', to take a book that happens to be on my desk while I have been translating a prose poem by Rimbaud for Lisa Russ Sparr's anthology of London poems. Even though Rimbaud is a presence throughout the book you are reading, a dedicated French section is essential to my empirical designs, by which I don't mean a matter of convenience but something that has emerged from the way the book has been composed.

Among my Que Sais-je volumes are several by the linguistician Pierre Guiraud, all carefully annotated. Evidently he had an impact. I remember writing to him, pointing out a mistake, probably a misprint, or showing off in some other way, and that he replied, politely conceding my point. The dozen or so Classiques Larousse books, with their familiar blue and white covers, date back to the Modern Sixth Form at school. The Ecrivains de Toujours series was useful to me in the days when I backed up my reading of favourite or significant writers with at least one critical book on each of them. Here are the Jean-Paul Sartre and Albert Camus volumes. These two writers are part of my heritage as a reader of a certain generation, as are, to a lesser extent, André Malraux and André Gide.

What is this thing with France? After all, I entered the Modern Sixth for a severely practical reason—I was more likely to get into Oxbridge, said the school, than if I entered the Classical Sixth. The thing with France has something to do with personal dialectics—France, especially Paris, became the other of the other (my own country), a mental construct, like Sartre's hell and Rimbaud's I, a literary space but not (yet) a topographical place. My reading of and about French writers was sporadic and unsystematic for many years, so I need to figure out a way of making sense of my French library. I would read what grabbed my fancy, but fancy has its parameters, parameters of need—need for what? A matrix, a springboard.

Older readers of French fiction will remember that Thomas Nelson and Co. was based in Edinburgh and Paris. Their editions of French fiction were easily available, as were translations such as *Trois Hommes dans un bateau*. Here is *Trois contes*, which Flaubert took time off from *Bouvard and Pécuchet* to write, proving that he was, finally and thank goodness, less obsessed than his two heroes. Here are editions of two of Balzac's greatest novels, *Cousine Bette* and *Le Père Goriot*. The statue in the garden of the house in rue Tournefort where Mark Hutchinson's friend Eric Walbecq of the Bibliothèque nationale lives—one of two houses Balzac combined to create Maison Vauquer (the lodgings of Eugène de Rastignac and Le Père Goriot)—is still there. You can see the house in a photograph by Eugène Atget, no less. 'Pension bourgeoise des deux sexes et autres' was the sign at Madame Vauquer's establishment.

I vividly recall the study/bedroom in the Jewish students' hostel, rue Guy Patin, which for six months in 1961 I shared successively with Larry Schwartz, Henri Béhar and, briefly, the future international cellist Raphael Sommer. On the bookshelves above my desk were thirty or forty books which I bought either because they were on the reading list of my course at the British Institute, then at 7 rue de la Sorbonne, or as part of my self-education programme. Many of these titles were the old poorly bound Livres de Poche, with their garish covers (perhaps the latest fashion in book design?). I still cherish them as memory boosters: *Journal d'un cure de campagne* by Georges Bernanos (made into a film by my favourite director, Robert Bresson); *Pitié pour les femmes* by Henry de Montherlant; *Vol de nuit* by Antoine de Saint-Exupéry; *Thérèse Desqueyroux* by François Mauriac; and, especially, Jean-Paul Sartre's *La Nausée* and André Malraux's *La Condition humaine*.

Twentieth-Century French Prose
Jean-Paul Sartre and André Malraux

Sartre's *Réflexions sur la question juive*, another of my surviving Livres de Poche, influenced many of us at one time. The young Dannie Abse's remark that Hitler rather than Moses made him a Jew has its origin in a specific history and culture, and it was Sartre who presided over one session of the endless debate. Written in 1944, the book now strikes me as naive in its exploration of Jewishness, although my marginalia and scraps of paper with their scribbled reactions to that first reading, in 1961, of this much-thumbed edition testify to the author's Socratic power and intellectual passion. A useful recent book, *The Jew in the Text*, contains Susan Rubin Suleiman's gloss on the third section of the writer's reflections, where it is clear that he hadn't done his homework and that most of what he knew about Jews was from the antisemites he hated. Claude Lanzmann, after emerging from the Resistance, offered high praise: 'We could compare Sartre's *Reflections on the Jewish Question* to Zola's *J'accuse*.' Later, after visiting Israel, he realized that Sartre had oversimplified the question of Jewishness and told Sartre, who said he should write a book about it. The theme is implied in Lanzmann's films and the issue continued to preoccupy Sartre throughout his life.

On the first page of my copy of Simone de Beauvoir's *Adieux: A Farewell to Sartre*, I note a list of numbers in my handwriting, enabling me to turn at once to pages where I have marked a passage or underlined a sentence. As so often, I am struck by Rilke, or someone's use of Rilke. Thus, de Beauvoir's quote from the master: 'Every man bears his death within himself, as the fruit bears its stone.' She continues: 'Sartre's decline and death were those that his life had called for. And perhaps that is why he had accepted them so serenely.' Some of these concerns are explained or mirrored in his poised and focused short memoir, *Les Mots*. I have always been delighted by the very long sixth footnote in *Qu'est-ce que la littérature?* of 1947: Sartre quotes Bonnefoy a touch ironically but approvingly, impressed by certain thoughts the young (shortly to be ex-) surrealist expressed. Bonnefoy's 'name seems to predispose him to speak with absolute sincerity'.

My copy of Malraux's *La Condition humaine* still contains notes about a number of writers which I must have copied down during a lecture by our inspirational teacher, Gilbert Quénelle, at the British Institute: here is the decisive clue that these are Quénelle's words, not my own: 'His works develop—compare Mauriac, one book always.' I could not have held that opinion on Mauriac since I had only read one book by him, *Thérèse Desqueyroux*, which sadly remains true to this day.

La Condition humaine, first published in 1933, conveys its existential thought in a prose which retains its power to move but the book feels less subtle, less compelling in its characterizations and micro-observations than Sartre's *La Nausée*, which came out in 1938. This wondrous novel (much admired by Levinas) stays with you, always. No reader forgets its haunting leitmotif: 'Some of these days you'll miss me honey', a blues—from a country Sartre admired at that time—sung on a cafe phonograph and played by a pianist. Sartre venerated Charlie Parker. David Miller in his *Dorothy and Benno Stories* recounts that the novelist went backstage to meet Parker after a gig in Paris. 'I have all your albums,' said Sartre. 'And I have all yours,' replied Parker. Claude Vigée recalls meeting Sartre at Gershom Scholem's house in Jerusalem. After gefilte fish made by Mrs Scholem (Sigmund Freud's niece), they discussed poetry, which Sartre dismissed on the naive grounds that truth is more important than beauty. I would have liked to discuss this proposition with Pier Paolo Pasolini, of whom Balthus said he died like a Christian martyr. The strength of *La Nausée* comes from the charged beauty of the prose, notwithstanding the high literality and metafictionality of the writing. There will always be rain over Bouville tomorrow. There will always be Sartre over his faithful readers tomorrow. I shall not, however, be rereading the stories in *Le Mur*, let alone his plays. It is enough that his work is part of my patrimony, as is that of Camus.

After reading Susan Sontag's discussion of Francisco Goya's *Disasters of War* in *Regarding the Pain of Others*, I made my way slowly through *Goya*, Bonnefoy's book on the Black Paintings, a remarkable speculation and uncharacteristically tentative. I could borrow Paula's school prize copy of Malraux's famous book on the painter, and thus kill two birds with one stone, having neglected the novelist for years, but suspect I will have to be satisfied with my ancient memories of *La Condition humaine* and *L'Espoir*, and more recent ones of *Antimémoires* and *Les Chênes qu'on abat*, the novelist's conversations with de Gaulle. In Martine de Courcel's *Malraux Life and Work*, we learn from Isaiah Berlin that he discussed with Malraux whether Plato would have snubbed Dante had they met at a dinner party. 'Anti-Critique', Malraux's essay in that book, is brilliantly Borgesian at two moments: 'If we have read Rimbaud and Mallarmé, "Recueillement" appears differently to us than it did to its author, Baudelaire.' And: 'We cannot separate an important work from its metamorphosis . . . It only exists within the framework of a dialogue, and it cannot be for us what it was for [the painter], as he had no knowledge of the works of art that were to follow his own.'

In *Anti-Memoirs*, Malraux evokes one of his great heroes, Fyodor Dostoevsky: 'those words that have haunted our century; the only reply, since the Sermon on the Mount, to the holy barbarism of the Book of Job: "if the order of the universe must be paid for with the torture of one innocent child . . ."' I shall never forget my teenage reading of that very passage in *The Brothers Karamazov*, which Philippe Forest too quotes in his painful book about the death of his child, *Tous les enfants sauf un* (you will recognize the allusion to Peter Pan), and which J. M. Coetzee refers to in *Diary of a Bad Year*. Dostoevsky would have agreed with Benjamin Constant, who wrote in *Adolphe* as quoted by Roger Martin du Gard in his *Notes on André Gide*: 'I detest that fatuity of mind which believes that what is explained is also excused; I hate that vanity which finds it interesting to describe the harm that it has done, and asks to be pitied at the end of its recital, and, as it patrols with impunity among the ruins for which it is responsible, gives to self-analysis the time which should be given to repentance.' Enter Friedrich Nietzsche, to whom Dostoevsky, as a psychologist, was even more important than Stendhal, according to the epigraph which precedes Gide's short study, *Dostoievski*. G. W. Ireland in his *Gide* reminds us that, after his death in 1951, Sartre wrote that the whole of French thought in the previous thirty years 'was obliged to determine its position with regard to Gide'. He went on: 'Gide is an irreplaceable example because he chose . . . to become his own truth.' Malraux and Camus held him in the same high regard. For Jean Genet, the older writer was 'of a dubious immorality' (if he actually made this perceptive and witty remark, otherwise 'ben trovato'). Today, I would guess that Camus and Sartre are far more widely read than Malraux and (apart from the *Journals*) Gide, whose *La Symphonie pastorale* and *La Porte étroite* I have in school editions, covered with annotations. On the other hand, Margaret and James Hogan are reading him down in Port-Vendres, prompting me to take another look at *Les Nourritures terrestres*. The hero's name Nathanael could well have been the source for the pen name of Nathanael West, born Nathan

Weinstein, whose brilliant collected short novels, including *Miss Lonelyhearts*, I read in my father's copy long ago. Gide misquoted Jean Racine, his favourite poet—there is hope for us all.

I ask myself whether a person of Malraux's depth and quality could have become minister of culture here. The answer is no, for two reasons: (1) such a person would not be entrusted with the job in the first place and (2) there is no equivalent of Malraux in our culture, a great creative artist who can and would want to run things on that scale, although we have had actor-managers (Laurence Olivier would have been the *perfect* person to play Malraux in a film). Malraux, in addition to being a major writer, fought in the Spanish civil war (*L'Espoir*) and was commander of the brigade that liberated Strasbourg. I met one of his sons, who came to the publication party for my book on Piotr Rawicz, *Engraved in Flesh*, at the Montparnasse flat of Count Christoph Schwanenberg von Schwerin, whose father was one of the leaders of the bomb plot against Hitler. Christoph told me he was glad the bomb plot failed, because it was essential that Nazi Germany should be completely destroyed. Philippe Labro, a brilliant French journalist, paints a striking portrait of Malraux in *Je connais gens de toutes sortes*, which James Hogan sent me on learning about the nature of the present work. Labro reprints his newspaper articles verbatim and then comments on them in postscripts: 'Death transforms life into destiny': I emailed that quote from Malraux to Jamie Fergusson, when he was still boss (and my *patron*) at the obituary page in the *Independent*. Against this, Labro is reminded of lines from Guillaume Apollinaire's 'Marizibill':

> I know people of all kinds
> They do not match their fates
> Indecisive like dead leaves
> Their eyes are fires almost out
> Their hearts move like their fates

Marguerite Duras

Now that the 'patrimonialization' of her work is assured, Marguerite Duras enters the Pleiade, so says her editor in an interview in *Le Monde*. I possess and am possessed by Duras' prose fiction. Here too are *L'après-midi de*

Monsieur Andesmas (which I am astonished to find I bought as early as 1963, almost certainly after seeing *Hiroshima, mon amour* at the Rex cinema in Cambridge with the three Johns—Barrell, Butt and Tyler); *L'Amant* (*The Lover*); and *The North China Lover*, an elaboration of the earlier book, drawing on an even earlier screenplay and including some of the directions. Beautiful, unsparing and lethal prose with some unexpected affinities to Coetzee. *La Douleur* is an autobiographical account of the final year of the war and the return of her partner Robert Antelme from the camps. Graham Greene's remark that every novelist must have a sliver of ice in his heart (was he glossing Kafka's celebrated remark: 'a book must be an ice axe to break the sea frozen inside us'?) could be truer of Duras than of any other writer before Coetzee. Her gaze is unnerving, her eye a camera or a laser.

I do wonder whether conventional taxonomy helps or hinders an understanding of such a great and singular writer. The drafts printed in *Wartime Writings* often segue from fiction to autobiography; either way, the writing could not be more literary. I have on my desk a book of her essays, *La Vie matérielle* (*Practicalities*). The first draft, she says, consisted of spoken remarks on topics such as alcohol, the pleasures of the *sixième arrondissement*, theatre, writers' bodies, photographs, eating at night, to name the chapters I started with, because they mean a lot to me too. Playwright, screenplay writer, novelist and, not least, occasional essayist par excellence, she is the most direct, the most pure, the most sharp, the most tender, the most cruel, the most melancholic, writer of all. She took what she needed from the *nouveau roman*, not least from Nathalie Sarraute (Antelme, says Duras in the *Notebooks*, 'operated through tropisms and I'm not displeased with that turn of phrase'. Is this forgetfulness or an implicit homage to Sarraute's great and influential book of 1939, *Tropismes*?), and wrote herself into the mainstream without sacrificing the essence of her vision. Sometimes one disagrees with her: 'No other human being, no woman, no poem or music, book or painting can replace alcohol in its power to give man the illusion of real creation. Alcohol's job is to replace creation.' There speaks the alcoholic and also the drinker, and what she is saying is a spectacular half-truth about herself, Francis Bacon and, indeed, people I know. 'Death, the fact of death coming towards you, is also a memory. Like the present' (from a prose poem, 'The Star'). And on

Racine: 'I've found you have to look for a long while for the sacred in writing: but the wind of the sacred does blow through the great forests of Racine. Through the tops of the trees in the great Racinian forest. That's Racine. Not in detail, not as he's read and thought about. It's his music. It's music speaking.' Near the end of the book is a beautiful paragraph, a prose poem called 'Eating at Night'. It ends: 'In the evening and at night, talking, we sometimes throw caution to the winds. In these conversations, we tell the truth however terrible, and we laugh as we used to do when we still drank and could only talk to one another in the afternoon.' That extract, perfectly pitched, has the piercing power of absolute honesty. Truth and beauty are one.

In her discussions with Xavière Gauthier, *Woman to Woman*, after mentioning in passing Jules Michelet's book on women and his eroticized view of menstruation, Duras talks about another of his thematic books, *La Sorcière* (a book Rimbaud absorbed), and recounts a story she finds sublime. Apparently, during the high Middle Ages, while the men were away at the wars or the crusades, the women got so bored and hungry (does she mean for food or for sex?) that they went to the woods and talked to the squirrels and the foxes, to the birds and the trees. And when the husbands came back to empty houses, they would go to the woods and find their wives still talking to the birds. Gauthier, a radical feminist scholar, replies: 'the men must have said: they're completely crazy; this is really woman's foolishness.' Duras: 'That's right. And then they burned them. To stop it, block up the madness, block up feminine speech.' The two women then discuss Joan of Arc who, according to Duras, 'had a political mind equal to Saint-Just', a judgement which would have astonished Luis Buñuel but not Carl Dreyer. According to Duras' biographer Laure Adler, Antelme, when in his cups, would say that he preferred Jules Michelet to Karl Marx. *La Sorcière* demonstrates that we must not derive Michelet's views on women entirely from his journals, a subject I discuss later.

Albert Camus/Louis-René des Forêts

Camus lives! I was nervous about revisiting him after my passionate reading of his books when young. Here are four works of fiction: *La Chute* (*The Fall*),

La Peste (*The Plague*), *L'Etranger* (*The Outsider*) and John Barrell's copy of *Exile and the Kingdom*. Here too are *Youthful Writings* and *L'Homme révolté* (*The Rebel*), and *Le Mythe de Sisyphe* with the famous opening sentence that I no longer agree with, having long reflected on the deaths of friends such as Primo Levi, Piotr Rawicz and, more recently, R. B. Kitaj: 'There is only one really serious philosophical problem: that of suicide.' I am due to reread *La Chute* for the fourth or fifth time but this time I will read it 'against' the English version, partly out of professional curiosity, partly because a translation can serve as literary criticism, as French readers of Proust in English have testified. It is a mysterious and disturbing monologue by a self-styled *juge-penitent*, a man with a bad conscience who attempts to create a space, in language, where he can review his past and move on. *La Chute* was written by a man in his early forties. Here comes the plaint: Oh, the books we lost through Camus's death at forty-eight in a car crash, something we only know thanks to the books already written and, therefore, as with Schubert, we are grateful for what we have. The book cries out to be read 'against' in a different way, that is, against a beautiful book which, so Maurice Blanchot argues in *L'Amitié*, influenced it, although some critics manage to reverse the influence despite the fact it came out earlier: I am referring to Louis René des Forêts's *Le Bavard*, which is included in a collection of four stories, *The Children's Room*. John Naughton's eponymous book on des Forêts takes us carefully through this great writer's prose and verse, culminating in *Ostinato* and *Les Poèmes de Samuel Wood*. Following Naughton, we may want to compare *Samuel Wood* with *Pour un tombeau d'Anatole* of Mallarmé (available in excellent translations by Paul Auster and Patrick McGuinness), in their telling of the death of a child, their refusing all consolation and transcendence, their resisting the temptation of nothingness or non-being—even though the living, unlike the dead, have not yet finished dying. The posthumous sequel to *Ostinato* came out in 2006, *Pas à pas jusqu'au dernier*, written at the very end of des Forêts's life: 'Do not watch yourself age in the mirror death holds up to you, nor defy death with big words, but if possible welcome it in silence like a child in its cradle smiling at its mother.' I wonder if Camus read Ralph Ellison's *Invisible Man*, published in 1953, three years before *La Chute*. He read closely Dostoevsky's *Notes from Underground*, as did des Forêts and

Ellison, not to mention Malraux and Sartre. (Vladimir Nabokov, however, despised it, we learn from his 'Memoirs from a Mousehole'.)

Had Albert Camus lived into old age—his centenary approaches—I suspect he would have sounded like a mild version of Emil Cioran, that arch pessimist and cynic. Politically, I wonder where Camus, and say George Orwell, would stand in respect of, say, Iraq. Would they argue that we have to oppose terror and fanaticism irrespective of those who may be opposing it for the wrong reasons, and, at the same time, that we have to oppose the USA's policies when they are aggressive and retrograde ditto? The two writers would insist that anyone who only supports one of these two positions is guilty of a new treason of the clerks. Raymond Williams in *Orwell* quotes a passage by Camus, and what the French writer said about 'Europe' remains painfully relevant. Orwell himself asks what we would do if we had to choose between Russia (i.e. the Soviet Union) and America: 'We are no longer strong enough to stand alone, and if we fail to bring a Western European union into being, we shall be obliged, in the long run, to subordinate our policy to that of one Great Power or the other. And in spite of all the fashionable chatter of the moment, everyone knows in his heart that we should choose America.' That is a powerful argument for some version of the European Union but, right from the start, the UK has been too bound up with the USA to heed it. Britain's indefensible posture is linked to the nature and provenance of our nuclear and non-nuclear military intelligence, which, unlike France's, entirely dovetails with the USA's. On 18 October 1947, around the same time as Orwell, Léon Blum, quoted by Jean Lacouture in his biography *Léon Blum*, wrote: 'We want neither to be Americanized nor Sovietized. The majority of French citizens, like the majority of the citizens of the world, want to be neither American protégés nor Soviet subjects.' Typically, Blum has chosen his words carefully and cannot be accused of equating the two great powers. Earlier, as Lacouture insists, France, under huge pressure from London, ended up with sympathetic non-intervention in Spain while Britain maintained a position of hostile neutrality.

Certain passages in des Forêts haunt the reader's memory forever, writes Bonnefoy, 'because they illuminate as much as they disturb, exalt as much as they rupture'. Like the *bavard* and the *juge-penitent*, two of my favourite characters in twentieth-century fiction, I find myself entering the spirit of the text. That is an understatement in the case of the former, for the bavard *is* the very spirit of the text. *Le Bavard* is all voice, goes with the 'grain of the voice' as Barthes would say. 'All voice' conveys much of the impact of *La Chute* too, the last book published in Camus's lifetime. Ronald Aronson's fine *Camus and Sartre* contains fascinating accounts of the intimate interaction between many of their texts. In his opinion, the *juge-penitent* is based on Sartre. The novel is a satire on left-wing politics and associated philosophy such as existentialism, emphasized by the addition (according to Adele King in her study *Camus*) of an epigraph in the English edition taken from Mikhail Lermontov's *A Hero of Our Time*, long a favourite book of mine: '*A Hero of Our Time*, gentlemen, is in fact a portrait but not of an individual; it is the aggregate of the vices of our whole generation in their fullest expression.' Aronson oversimplifies a little, for the passage in *La Chute* which ends 'the portrait which I show to my contemporaries becomes a mirror' suggests to us that Clamence, the *juge-penitent*, is a representative collage of figures; one of these is undoubtedly Sartre, another is Camus himself. Perhaps one could reconfigure Clamence as Camus/Sartre imagined by des Forêts's anti-hero, known only as *le bavard* (chatterbox or telltale). Early in the novel, Clamence even says 'je suis bavard', probably not a deliberate allusion. *La Chute*, like *The Rebel*, is not a comfortable book for older left-wing intellectuals.

[Coda: Peter Hoy, co-founder of Menard Press, dear friend, great teacher and bibliographer *extraordinaire*, never wrote the literary criticism everyone knew he had in him to write. Here are two bibliographies by this serial sidetracker, *Julien Gracq* and *Camus in English*. The Camus is inscribed optimistically: 'à Tony, camarade bibliographe, fidèlement, Peter, 22.XI.71.' The following gives an idea of the organized mind you need to have in order to master such detail, and why I, no mean sidetracker myself, never did embark on the Bonnefoy bibliography he proposed: *An Annotated Bibliography of Albert Camus's Contributions to English and American Periodicals and Newspapers (1945–1968)*, Second (Revised and Enlarged) Edition. The publisher is Minard, only one letter different from Menard, but a letter contains a world.]

French Poetry

INTRODUCTION

I cannot overstate the importance of French poetry in my life, even more than in my work, if the distinction can be made. I 'used' France and its poetry as a cover story for my early attempts to experience life as a writer and poet, even as I endured boring day jobs. I went to Paris as often as possible and made friendships; I learnt much and discovered who I was, or, more modestly and accurately, who I wasn't. Ever since I came upon Bonnefoy's *Hier régnant désert* by chance, in a bookshop, nearly fifty years ago, I have explored the signs and wonders of French poetry, encouraged by French poets: Yves Bonnefoy himself and three younger friends then living in London—Claude Royet-Journoud, Anne-Marie Albiach and the late Michel Couturier—and, after them, Claude Vigée, Edmond Jabès and Michel Deguy. English, American and other French friends had their own preferences and discussions took place over wine or, sometimes, on the telephone. The fixtures on my radar in the early years were many, and included Peter Hoy, Jonathan Griffin, Keith Bosley, Anthony Barnett, Paul Buck and Paul Auster. Later, Harry Guest, Mark Hutchinson, Steven Jaron, Stephen Romer, Anne Serre, Anne Mounic, Michèle Finck, Jennie Feldman, John Taylor and others entered the fellowship.

In his introduction to the work of that wondrous sixteenth-century poet Maurice Scève, the poet Jean Tortel deploys a Borgesian gambit concerning precursors: 'Mallarmé justifies Scève: it is because we have integrated Mallarmean utterance into our sensibility that we can endure the rigour and burning coldness of Scève.' The poet Louise Labé, beautifully translated by Rilke, was a friend and associate of Scève's unless, that is, as has been suggested, she was either (a) a courtesan, La belle Cordière, whose poems were written by Scève and his friends; or (b) entirely invented by them as a kind of pre-Pessoan heteronym. It's a good thing the poet is not running in the Olympics . . . What matters is that her passionate sonnets are remarkable; and, if a man wrote them, he was well in touch with his anima. Duras, in one of her best books, *The North China Lover*, has the child's teacher, in a lesson on Labé, refuse 'to call her by her epithet, La belle Cordière', thus implicitly rejecting the legend.

I have three complete bilingual editions of François Villon: Galway Kinnell's ('But where are the snows of last year?'), Anthony Bonner's ('But where are the snows of bygone years?') and Peter Dale's ('Where is the drift of last year's snow?'). Bonner has an introduction by William Carlos Williams which does not mention the translations but reminds us that 'only a Frenchman could have had the special feeling for the cocotte, for women, tender but daring.' 'By my mother's memory,' he writes, 'there is nothing sacred but the truth.' The great Baroque poet Jean de Sponde's sequence *Theorems* has been translated with typical authority and verve by Keith Bosley, the de Sponde of Slough, as I once jokingly named him.

NINETEENTH-CENTURY FRENCH POETRY

Victor Hugo (with Vigny)

> These things have passed
> Like shadows, like the wind

It was quite something to meet the painter Marie Hugo (the great-great-granddaughter of Victor Hugo) at the private view of Paula's print show in Nîmes in 2008, as well as Jean Leyris, sculptor-son of Pierre Leyris, the illustrious translator of Hopkins and Eliot. Yves and Lucy Bonnefoy were there too, since Paula's latest prints illustrated the fable at the heart of *Les Planches courbes*, a recent volume by Bonnefoy. Nearly fifty years ago, in one of my first conversations with Yves, I asked him a direct question: 'Who are the greatest nineteenth-century French poets?' 'Baudelaire, Nerval, Mallarmé and Rimbaud,' came the reply and he presented me with his book on Rimbaud. I noted that his list did not contain the four grand Romantic poets: Hugo, Lamartine, Vigny or Musset. Bonnefoy did, however, mention in passing Vigny's 'La Maison du berger' ('a great poem'). My old undergraduate *Poésies complètes* is here, with the poem heavily annotated, including the line 'I love the majesty of human suffering' and the famous lines addressed to the dedicatee of the poem, a faithfully married Englishwoman, Eva Holmes: 'Do not leave me alone with mother Nature, / For I know her too well not to fear her now', which is a possible echo, doubtless unconscious, of Hermione in Racine's *Andromaque*: 'I have loved him too much not to hate him now.'

Many years later, I reminded Bonnefoy of our conversation and he said I had 'improved' the story, for 'Hugo is certainly a great poet, although many poems are damaged by facile effects, and there is more to Vigny than one great poem.'

Hugo, as you would expect, was on the modern languages syllabus at Cambridge—I still have my copies of *La Légende des siècles* and *Les Feuilles d'automne*, the latter a phrase which, until this moment, I had not noticed translates as 'Autumn Leaves', the English title of one of my favourite songs, Jacques Prévert and Joseph Kosma's 'Les Feuilles mortes'. (The online audio-website Spotify has twenty-six versions. I select the one by Miles Davis, which is by far the longest.) Another book, *Les Contemplations*, contains a sad, sad poem, all the sadder for its understatement, even without making allowances for this particular poet's tendencies in the other direction: 'Demain, dès l'aube . . .' ('At dawn, tomorrow'). The poem is dated 3 September 1847, the eve of the fourth anniversary of the death of Leopoldine, Hugo's beloved daughter who drowned, aged nineteen, with her husband (Charles Vacquerie) of a few months. After the tragedy, Hugo wrote almost nothing for ten years. But of the more than four thousand drawings made by this most fecund of writers, many were done during that period. Vincent Van Gogh and Eugène Delacroix much admired his achievements as a visual artist. I saw an exhibition of his works on paper in dark pen-and-ink wash at his house in the Place des Vosges and it is no surprise to learn that the surrealists and abstract expressionists considered him a precursor. Max Ernst's frottage and grattage owe something to his example, and at one remove the same applies to Henri Michaux, who was obviously influenced by Ernst. When I told Yves that Paula admired Hugo, he replied that he was not surprised given her own pantheon in which Goya is prominent, and that one could pursue the comparison between Goya and Hugo.

A parable about communications, ancient and modern: Leopoldine and Charles died at Villequier on 4 September 1843. Hugo and his first and lifelong mistress Juliette Drouet (whom he took up with only after his wife renounced pregnancy, that is, renounced sex) arrived at Rochefort in southwest France on 9 September after a trip to Spain. At an inn in the nearby village of Soubise, he ordered a beer and newspapers; he gave a scream—it was from the account in *Le Siècle* that Hugo learnt about the catastrophe of Villequier. He left at once, but the first leg of the Paris carriage was full. So he—alone, one infers from a tender letter Juliette wrote him on 13 September—had to sit on the top until La Rochelle, reaching Paris on 12 September. On 4 September, Madame Hugo wrote a letter to the poet, presumably *post-restante*, saying the couple 'is at Villequier. They left me the day before yesterday and return this evening.' She herself learnt of their death the next morning from their son-in-law's brother. What happened was that the Vacquerie family had bought a large boat and decided to organize a trip on the Seine to inaugurate the new arrival. In a strong wind, Leopoldine was blown overboard and not even her husband, who was an excellent swimmer, could save her. He took her in his arms and chose to die with her. Later, it turned out that another newspaper, *Presse*, contained an article by Alphonse Karr who, knowing Hugo read this paper, attempted to attenuate his grief by writing about Charles' heroism—a thoughtful act but hardly likely to help, even if Hugo had read *Presse* before *Le Siècle*. Ten years later, however, in exile in Jersey, after consulting a medium, Hugo wrote a memorial poem addressed to his son-in-law; it draws on Karr's article: 'Unable to save her, he wanted to die'. This is a weaker poem, a case study for Mario Praz's *Romantic Agony*, although Praz does not quote it.

The elegy 'A Villequier' is something else: one painful line—'Grass must grow and children must die'—heads a significant meditation on life and death in the final section of Proust. A long and rhetorically public poem written one year after the deaths, 'A Villequier' is placed immediately after 'At dawn' in 'Pauca meae', the section of *Les Contemplations* devoted to his daughter and consisting almost entirely of a pre-wedding poem, a wedding poem and fourteen poems of mourning. There are allusions to happy days—'daddy, come here / we'll bring you your chair / tell us a story . . . / I was Ariosto and Homer'—as well as table-turning attempts to make contact with the dead. One of the poems was written immediately after the death of Drouet's daughter but it has a different tone, as if he is keeping his distance, lest his mistress' tragedy enflame his own. 'A Villequier' explicitly speaks of his broken heart, but the poet makes his peace with God and destiny. Death, he writes, is a beginning not an end. There are echoes of Job, Pascal, Kabbalah and

Genesis. On rereading the poem, I find it profoundly moving, a prayer for the dead on behalf of life, and oh-so-different in all respects from Mallarmé's devastating and devastated 'Pour un Tombeau d'Anatole'.

Consider this, and in our time, how long everything, physical journeys and communication, took in those days, a few years before the commercial application of telegraph, let alone telephone (and landlines, let alone mobiles) and some years before a train would have been possible for Hugo. (The young Rimbaud, heading for Paris and Verlaine in 1871, will miss Hugo by ten minutes at Charleville Station). Think how speeded up news, good and bad, is today. Although such a tragedy is the same in any age, the structure, if not the nature, of feeling cannot but have changed, given the radical acceleration of information.

Alphonse de Lamartine

The poet Peter Mayer, whose chrestomathy, *Alphabet Poems*, Menard brought out long ago (it contains a previously unpublished poem by Coleridge), presented me with a seventeenth-century *Handbook of Proverbs*, reissued in 1855 by H. G. Bohn, a distinguished Victorian publisher. As usual, the preliminary and end pages list in-print titles, yielding treasures for the likes of me. I was not surprised to find Horace's Odes, Cary's Dante, books by Michelet as well as works by Schiller, Goethe and Schlegel, but I was astonished at the presence of five books by Alphonse de Lamartine, including literary works and volumes of contemporary political history—parts were written in English, doubtless with the help of his English wife—as well as his *Three Months in Power*. Let me explain my astonishment. Lamartine was on the syllabus of French A-level and university degrees in modern languages. However, he, along with Musset, Vigny and Hugo, do not speak to us in the way Hölderlin, Coleridge and Leopardi do. When I was young, and perhaps nothing has changed, Lamartine was the poet who wrote 'Le Lac' (which Paula too remembers from school) and one or two other poems. We knew nothing about the relatively progressive politician (constitutional monarchist and a liberal), who was foreign minister and briefly and bravely in charge of the government in the incredibly difficult circumstances of 1848. He was heavily defeated in the presidential elections that year. Three years later, when

President Louis Napoleon established his dictatorship, prompting a great text by Karl Marx, Lamartine abandoned politics.

Literary and artistic figures are marginal to politics in the USA, UK and Germany. In France (including its former colonies), however, they order things differently and/or better. Apart from Lamartine, think of Léon Blum, Jacques-Louis David (who may have signed Marie Antoinette's death warrant), Leopold Senghor (*Poems of a Black Orpheus*), Aimé Césaire (*Return to My Native Land*), Saint-John Perse, André Malraux. Marc Chagall was a commissar in the USSR in the 1920s; Jorge Semprun was minister of culture in Spain; Vaclav Havel was president of Czechoslovakia and then the Czech Republic. But, apart from the secretary for foreign tongues under Cromwell (John Milton), Benjamin Disraeli (just about) and Archibald Macleish (who served in Roosevelt's wartime administration), one is hard put to think of a successful Anglo-Saxon equivalent. Lamartine must be the highest-ranking poet in politics after Samuel Hanagid in Spain and John Milton, and before Leopold Senghor.

Gérard de Nerval

I own ten complete versions of Gérard de Nerval's *Les Chimères* in English. One translator, Robin Blaser, offers a classic *apologia pro vita sua*—defending his liberties (i.e. his liberty-taking), he writes, 'These translations required that I become Nerval and yet remain my own poet.' He argues too (given his poetics, he has no choice) that people have placed too great an emphasis on the biography, 'when we are meant to depend upon the poems'. Well, it all depends on what you mean by 'depend', as C. E. M. Joad and William Carlos Williams both understood. We learn from *The Disinherited*, Benn Sowerby's life of Nerval, that Nerval's most famous phrase, 'the black sun of melancholy', is already found in a letter written on his trip to the Orient.

One version of *Les Chimères*, made by the poet Will Stone, was published by Menard Press on our thirtieth anniversary in 1999. The sequence is irresistible to translators, partly because the endlessly reverberating modalities of its imbricated mythography permit multiple readings, encouraging translators of these great poems to face the challenge of what, fortunately, is a short work. It was Bonnefoy who, while insisting on Nerval's greatness as a poet, alerted me to the writer's wondrous prose, as enigmatic and luminous as that tragic sentence in the letter to his aunt on the eve of his suicide: 'Do not wait up for me, the night will be black and white'. Would that Nerval could have heeded Celan's lines in 'Speak, You Also', as translated by Michael Hamburger: 'Speak— / But keep yes and no unsplit. / And give your say this meaning: give it the shade'. *Aurélie* is a remarkable account of the poet's mental state, which he was encouraged to write by Dr Blanche in the latter's clinic in Passy (near Balzac's house and Vigée's apartment; other patients included Guy de Maupassant), now the Turkish embassy. It is his spiritual diary, his *Vita Nuova*, as Rosanna Warren suggests.

> And at the moment when, tired of this life,
> One winter evening, his soul at last took off
> And he departed saying, 'why did I come?'

These are the last three lines of Nerval's sonnet 'Epitaphe' which, according to Norma Rinsler, was enclosed with a letter to his friend Princesse Marie de Solms and only published years after his death.

Robert Duncan's version of 'El Desdichado', not him at his best, reads as though it has been cobbled together from other versions. The rare spelling of 'melancholia' suggests that the image is derived from Albrecht Dürer's great engraving, as does the use of the definite article in front of it:

> I am the dark one,—the widower,—the unconsoled,
> the prince of Aquitaine at his stricken tower:
> my sole *star* is dead, and my constellated lute
> bears the black *sun* of the *Melencolia*.

Théophile Gautier's early poem 'Melancholia' refers to Dürer's engraving and its 'soleil tout noir' (which it isn't), and Nerval surely knew this poem by his school friend. Nerval also refers to the engraving in *Aurélie*. Rinsler suggests other possible sources for the image: Hugo's 'Ce que dit la bouche d'ombre' (the image later used by Rimbaud to describe his mother), the German writer Jean-Paul and, possibly, Milton's 'darkness visible'. Corneille's 'cette obscure clarté qui tombe des étoiles' from *Le Cid* also springs to mind. Michelet had a copy of the engraving in his study.

41

'Studies have shown that light during the night interferes with melatonin, "the hormone of darkness", which is secreted by the pineal gland at night. Melatonin both impedes cancers and boosts the immune system' (*The Independent*). That mysterious and evocative phrase, 'the hormone of darkness', would have interested Georges Bataille, who would have agreed with Francisco de Quevedo that 'the ass is like the face of the Cyclops', alluded to by Octavio Paz in his essay on metaphor in *Conjunctions and Disjunctions*. The 'prince d'Aquitaine' at his broken, lightning-struck, stricken, ruined, riven, doomed, torn-down tower, represents the very ruins, and the fragments shorn against the ruins, which we revisit in the line immediately following the quote from Nerval at the end of *The Waste Land*. Once again, a major poet elects his precursor (the great prince of Aquitaine in misprision lies) and once again the history of literature is rewritten.

Charles Baudelaire

> I was like a child agog to see the show,
> Hating the curtain as you hate an obstacle.
> At last the cold truth stared me in the face:
> I was dead—no surprise there—and the dreadful
> Dawn embraced me. So what! Is that all?
> The curtain had risen and I was still waiting.
>
> ('Le Rêve d'un homme curieux')

You gave me your mud, and from it I made gold—proud and true, although it never made the final cut of *Les Fleurs du mal*. Baudelaire looms over the writers I love. He is, in short, a key presence, even now, in any unveiling of the *pathétique* of serious readers of European literature, thanks not only to his own genius but also to that of his most influential readers: Walter Benjamin, Rainer Maria Rilke, T. S. Eliot, Yves Bonnefoy, Paul Celan, Jean Starobinski, to name only a few. My Enid Starkie student edition of *Les Fleurs du mal* is heavily annotated in a conventional way. The verses or phrases I have underlined were discussed by our lecturer Alison Fairlie, whose monograph *Baudelaire: Les Fleurs de mal* I read carefully, judging by my notes. Fairlie's name triggers memories of other lecturers in the French faculty: Douglas Parmée and Odette de Mourgues, Dorothy Colman and Rhiannon

Goldthorpe. Rhiannon—ah, there was a beauty, and hardly ten years, perhaps five years, older than the students—many of us testosterone-laden male virgins—surrounding her. As if on cue, the page falls open at 'Le Beau navire'. Speaking of the 'soft enchantress', the poet writes: 'I want to paint your beauty for you / Where childhood is in alliance with maturity'. And I recall a line from 'Le Voyage': 'Et toujours le désir nous rendait soucieux' ('And desire always made us anxious'). The penultimate stanza was recited by Jorge Semprun in Buchenwald while Maurice Halbwachs was dying, an episode I discuss in another section of this book. 'Le Voyage', one of the most important poems in *Les Fleurs du mal*, also contains a stanza I wanted to live up to and never could. My heart was not light enough, unlike the travellers Baudelaire compares to hot-air balloons:

Truly, travellers are those alone who part
For parting's sake; air-borne, light of heart,
They never wander from their destiny,
And always say: let's go, not knowing why.

As I indicated in the introduction to this book, I have long been haunted by the final stanza of 'Le Reniement de Saint-Pierre', for I have tried and failed to motor a life in which dream and action are synchromeshed, in which inner and outer bear some resemblance to each other, in which literature and politics enable a serious engagement with the self and with the world. In my student edition, I have underlined a line from 'Le Cygne': 'Et mes chers souvenirs sont plus lourds que des rocs' ('And my dearest memories are heavier than rocks'). This line is so heavily freighted with significance for me that I am having second thoughts about the generation of the underlinings. Perhaps some of them were not mimicking professorial suggestions but were, after all, my own.

I used a line from a poem with a daunting title, 'L'Héautontimorouménos', 'Je suis la plaie et le couteau' ('I am the wound and the knife'), as an epigraph in one of several draft poems I sent Donald Davie in 1973. Despite some reservations, he liked the drafts (influenced by his own verse line) and, in a lengthy letter, explained why, but he rightly told me to remove the epigraph. In truth, even at the time I knew that its deployment was a classic example of Sartrean bad faith, a charge Sartre naively flung at Baudelaire himself in

Baudelaire, his study of this poet who, Sartre thought, paid more attention to the driver's mirror than the road in front of him. My epigraph wasn't even a darling to be murdered, rather the remnant of a half-discarded pose, *Romantic Agony* stuff, detracting from my own truth which, as Levinas writes somewhere, runs the risk of holding one hostage.

How true it is that the poetry we learnt by heart when we were young, we still remember when we are old, how easy it was to memorize. On the way home from school on the Northern Line, my classmates (Ralph Ullmann and Richard Hyams) and I and would commit to memory 'To be or not to be?' or 'Once more unto the breach' or 'The Listeners' by repeating one line and then adding the second and the third and so on. By the time we reached our stations (in my case, Golders Green), we had stored them in our minds. Baudelaire's 'L'Invitation au voyage', one of the perfect lyric poems in Western literature, the acme of a classic romantic theme, was one of the texts Madame Peyrollaz, our phonetics teacher at the British Institute in Paris, used. The poem, which I still know by heart, has a flowing song-like sound which must have resonated with Paul Verlaine, a later poet who carried such musicality to unprecedented virtuosity without, in his many best works, displaying facility or poetical effects for their own sake. The poem has been set to music by at least ten composers, notably Henri Duparc. It was one of the seventeen songs that constitute the composer's entire *oeuvre*, but let me not be sidetracked by my obsession with those great artists who have left only a tiny amount of work, for reasons of mental anguish.

Repeatedly, in the margin of the Starkie edition, I have written 'Romantic Agony'. The eponymous book was not on our official reading list, but I read it closely. Mario Praz was a Bachelardian reader of poetry, which is not always a compliment. He piles up examples of a particular trope, giving equal weight to all of them. Yet we are grateful for his dictionary of quotations, which such discourse amounts to. On my desk are Francis Scarfe's bilingual versions of Baudelaire, *The Complete Verse* (with prose translations) and *The Poems in Prose*. Himself a 1940s' poet, Scarfe was director of the British Institute in Paris for many years, and as a student I met him there in 1961. Little did I know that only a few years later I would become friends with people like the late Michael Hamburger, who signed his own Baudelaire selection, *Twenty*

Prose Poems, for me on 26 March 1968. Michael's introduction, written when he was nineteen and now revised, is typically lucid and informative, drawing on his scholarship as a critic and his inwardness to poetry as a practitioner. Quoting Baudelaire's brilliant pun, syphilization, Hamburger explains in passing that this great poet is a crucial link between romanticism and symbolism; but let us leave the literary history to one side, as Michael himself does, and proceed to 'L'Invitation au voyage', Baudelaire's prose version, grabbing the French in Scarfe's bilingual edition or Henri Lemaître's Garnier edition, *Petits poèmes en prose* (*Le Spleen de Paris*). We learn from Lemaître that, in an earlier version, the poem contains a reference associating the Land of Cockaigne with Goethe's most famous Mignon poem 'Kennst du das Land . . .', translated in Hamburger's *Goethe: Poems and Epigrams*. Is there a rare infelicity or inaccuracy in this translation (cf. HD's version discussed elsewhere)? Would the protagonist address the father as 'my beloved', even if the word 'father' is silently present? 'My dearest' is surely more appropriate. How I wish I could phone Michael and shmooze over these matters, as we would once have done. Kitaj too, partly because 'Kennst du das Land' is one of his important paintings. But, like our mutual friend Michael Hamburger, this marvellous painter, rooted in European romanticism, is dead. I salute their memory.

Comparing the two Baudelaire translations of 'L'Invitation au voyage', I note that Hamburger's is as accurate as Scarfe's and more fluent, more idiomatic. Scarfe's versions betray their origins in his earlier Penguin edition, where the project was to supply a crib. I note too that the first edition of Hamburger's translations appeared when he was only twenty-one. He was translating from French and German and writing English poems only a few years after arriving here from Germany without knowing a word of English, Hamburger being one of Hitler's gifts to British culture. His introduction is better too. While both translators mention *Gaspard de la nuit* as a French precursor, Hamburger rightly points out the influence of Thomas De Quincey and Edgar Allan Poe; Scarfe only mentions them in passing, preferring to compare Baudelaire's texts to those of William Hazlitt and Charles Lamb and even eighteenth-century writers such as Oliver Goldsmith and Joseph Addison, which seems mistaken. Furthermore, Hamburger, unlike

Scarfe, points out that, before the establishment of *vers libre*, the prose poem was a medium where French poets could escape the rules and regulations English poets were not subjected to. Even Baudelaire, whose verse poems are innovative in ways that are no longer obvious—since he himself, influenced by Vigny, created the post-Romantic and post-Hugo aural climate in which metre was re-heard by later innovators such as Rimbaud—felt the need for the prose poem. A valuable insight is that 'Baudelaire was his own guinea-pig; and in his experiments he made ample use of masks, of what Yeats called "the anti-self".' Many years later, Hamburger would develop these and other themes in that essential book, *The Truth of Poetry*. Sartre, according to Hamburger, recognized the poet's 'nobility and greatness as a man', even though he freely chose his own hell.

Baudelaire died three years before Duparc composed his setting of 'L'Invitation au voyage'. How poignant that the poet writes in the prose version: 'A musician [Weber, one of Baudelaire's "beacons"] has written "The Invitation to the Dance". Where is he that will write "The Invitation to the Voyage", which one may offer to the woman he loves, to the sister of his choice?' (The verse poem, as you know, begins: 'Mon enfant, ma soeur / songe à la douceur'.) A search on the Internet reveals that one of the ten known versions was written in Baudelaire's lifetime—by Jules Cressonnois. Was it performed? Did Baudelaire know? It is true, as Hamburger says, that nothing in the prose poem matches the first two lines of the poem, but the prose poem is a wondrous text in its own right. One of its themes is that of Matthew Arnold's poem, 'The Buried Life', written a few years earlier. Arnold's poem is heart-rending because, in his mind and perhaps in ours, it makes plain his feeling that he had underachieved, whereas the same cannot be said of the French poet: 'to be, *above all else, a great man* and a *saint* in one's own eyes'. And yet, here is an extract from Baudelaire's text in which he shows how we attempt to escape 'ennui' and 'spleen' in our search for an unrealizable ideal:

> Dreams! Always dreams! And the more ambitious and delicate the soul, the farther dreams remove it from what is possible. Every man carries within him his dose of natural opium, incessantly secreted and renewed, and, from birth until death, how many hours can we count that are filled with positive joy, with successful and decisive

action? Shall we ever live, shall we ever pass into that picture painted by my soul, the picture that resembles you?

I don't agree with Lemaître that the natural opium includes art. Yes, there are many references in this prose poem to Dutch interiors but Baudelaire does not want to accompany his 'sister' to an art gallery, nor does he want to be in a painting. This is a dialectical poem: art and life are allegorical of each other. As I said, he is exploring the 'buried life' of Arnold's poem:

> But often, in the world's most crowded streets,
> But often, in the din of strife,
> There rises an unspeakable desire
> After the knowledge of our buried life;
> A thirst to spend our fire and restless force
> In tracking out our true, original course.

The title of Baudelaire's posthumously published *Mon cœur mis à nu* is taken from Poe, whom he famously translated and, according to Eliot, improved. Poe invited writers to live up to the challenge of the text, for then they would have written a masterpiece. Christopher Isherwood's translation of this and the intimate journals has an introduction by W. H. Auden. Baudelaire's reflections provide a kind of matrix (perhaps Hart Crane's 'matrix of the heart') to the poems in prose, which in turn can be read as a matrix to the great sequence of verse poems. These in turn cast their aura back on the matrices and deepen their significance. Certainly, taken out of context, there are weak aphorisms and crude judgements but there are also profound insights. Overall, it is a marvellous book of revelation. When it comes to depth charges of the kind associated with Kierkegaard or Nietzsche, Baudelaire may not always deliver, but I think we can say he is always working his passage as a poet (drawing primarily on experience and imagination, as Hamburger says) rather than as a thinker, a theologian or a philosopher. I'm glad I thought of that before discovering Auden's statement that the entries require to be read (I paraphrase) as the observations of a human spirit who is a poet, a French poet, a nineteenth-century French poet. Auden discusses Baudelaire's observations in terms of the Greek concepts of *arêté* and *hubris*, and what he calls the Jewish concept of the hero, Job and Abraham. By the time of the New Testament, the religious hero is revealed to faith as the suffering servant. He goes on to say that 'Poe and Baudelaire are the fathers of modern poetry in that they were the first poets (with the possible exception of Blake) who, born into the modern age . . . revealed what a decisive change this was.' Baudelaire worries away about what it means to be a gifted individual in a world where his gifts cut him off and arrives at a paradox: 'God is the most prostituted individual of all beings, because he is the closest friend of every individual, because he is the common inexhaustible reservoir of love.' Love, that is, as *agapé*, not the eros of the dandy.

Auden thinks, and Bonnefoy tells me he agrees with him, that the 'terrifying and pathetic' passages at the end of *My Heart Laid Bare*, where Baudelaire abandons the dandy self and comes down to earth, reveal a more radical change of heart than Rimbaud's, who merely became a different kind of dandy, demonstrating the same hubris and desire to be unique, the same lack of humility as before. Too late, but in all honesty, Baudelaire genuinely wants to be a better man and a better poet. *Uncle Vanya*-like, we find: 'To heal all things, wretchedness, disease or melancholy, absolutely *nothing* is required but an inclination for work.' And 'I believe that I stake my destiny upon hours of uninterrupted work' and 'To sit down at once and write. I reason too much.' This is painful for a serial sidetracker to read.

'Do not forget Verlaine!'

Verlaine 'is hidden in the grass', wrote Mallarmé in a memorial ('tombeau') poem. That is, Verlaine is immortal, not buried in a tomb. Jorge Luis Borges too rated the French poet highly. '*N'oubliez pas Verlaine!*'—this was how the Argentinian writer bade farewell to Bonnefoy and Starobinski from his hospital bed in Geneva. Verlaine was a great songwriter in words, a great lyric poet. That 'feuille morte', in 'Chanson d'automne', which resembles him while 'le vent mauvais' ('ill wind') carries him off, is an ancestor of the song by Prévert I mentioned while writing about Victor Hugo and which, even as I write, sounds from my computer player because I typed 'Prévert' into Google and found that Kosma's music, endlessly recycled, plays along with the words. 'Autumn Leaves' is one of my talismanic memories, taking me back on the wing of nostalgia to John and Gisèle Tyler's house on Tenison Road in Cambridge. Gisèle, a teacher, and John, the only married undergraduate in our circle, would occasionally invite friends to dinner and I would cycle there with a bottle of plonk (five shillings as I recall) bought at the wine merchant's (Thatcher's?) in Market Square, and Gisèle would French-cook and we would talk in French, and sometimes Terry Eagleton or John Barrell would be there too, and Tyler would play records of French songs and I, in my virginal innocence, would be carried off by the *chansons* (as Verlaine was carried off, but in my case it was a 'vent bon' not a 'vent mauvais') to a place where one day, if I was lucky, I would not be lonely, to a place of joy, albeit melancholy joy, because that was my understanding of love, as I discerned it in poetry and music. Now, fifty years on, the poem conveys its eternal truth: 'Je me souviens / Des jours anciens / Et je pleure'. Suddenly I even have fond thoughts for a woman who hurt me (and whom I hurt). Every time the Kosma music ends on the website, the song starts up again and I wallow in my *souvenance* of ancient days.

My edition of *Poèmes saturniens/Fêtes galantes* comes with a long preface from that remarkable *chansonnier*, Leo Ferré, although he appears never to have sung Prévert: 'The life of Verlaine is a misunderstanding. Man, he loved Woman, woman he loved men. In between, he wrote.' So begins Ferré's belatedly romanticized rejection of details I unashamedly provide in my discussion of Rimbaud below. Even now, Verlaine's life has only interested me insofar as it impinges (and how!) on Rimbaud's. Ferré's preface ends beautifully if absurdly: 'In the grumblings of poets, as in those of dogs, there is something of that innocence which puts into question the human condition, for, in truth, poets are not men. Angels? . . . Why not? Angels, up there, sleep with other angels, and one imagines this is not forbidden in that land where the stars have no gender, where the underworld has no seasons, where an engagement ring turns the head of Saturn.' I browse the pages of *Fêtes galantes*, which owes more to Watteau than Ferré allows and which appealed enough to that early and pioneering genius of modern music, Claude Debussy. Here is 'Colombine' which Georges Brassens sings; here too is 'Colloque sentimentale', which Madame Peyrollaz made us recite in the British Institute phonetics class in 1961.

James Hogan is interested in the figure of Scaramouche—because Pascal evokes the clown as the patron saint of savants—so I have emailed him

'Scaramouche et Pulcinella'. 'Nevermore', in *Poèmes saturniens*, is another reminder of the eternally surprising importance of Poe the poet in France. The English ear with enough French to discern the sounds of French poetry knows that Mallarmé, who translated Poe's verse into prose, and Baudelaire, who translated only his stories, were greater poets (as was Verlaine) than the American, whose portrait Manet painted and poem 'Le Corbeau' he illustrated, and whose 'Fall of the House of Usher' Debussy wanted to set to music. The musicality of Verlaine, who is to Whistler what Rimbaud is to Gauguin, to Tennyson what Rimbaud is to Hopkins, is several orders more subtle than that of Poe. For us, it is Poe the prose writer who counts.

Joanna Richardson's *Verlaine*, like her Baudelaire, is not a success. For example, she deploys archaic diction ('tis and thou, and various inversions), and the three simple lines quoted above become: 'I then recall / Time's funeral / And I shed tears', the word funeral introduced for the sake of a rhyme, because the French rhymes. The poet Alastair Elliott is or was in charge, appropriately enough, of special collections at the University of Newcastle (i.e. pornography). His translation of *Femmes/Hombres* is remarkable in every respect. I don't know what Richardson would have made of the rude subject matter, but Elliott offers a master class in verse translation. Another of my Verlaine volumes contains *Jadis et naguère*, where we find the beautiful dream poem 'Kaleidescope', written in his prison cell in Brussels after he shot Rimbaud in the hand. I like to think that the city evoked in the poem is London. In my third volume, which includes *Sagesse*, there is a remarkable autobiographical poem 'Du fond du grabat', in which Rimbaud is described as the 'shipwreck of a dream / that never goes on strike', a possible allusion to 'Le Bateau ivre'.

Stéphane Mallarmé/Arthur Rimbaud

Stéphane Mallarmé writes: 'Every method is a fiction and good for demonstration.' That fiction is what I am looking for as I try to make sense of my books, but what I am doing appears to reverse Mallarmé —my demonstration is a fiction, and, with luck, good for method. 'Fiction,' Mallarmé continues, 'is the very process of the human mind.' Responding to a request from Harrison Rhodes, one of his Tuesday guests, concerning his links with Rimbaud (see *Divagations*), the poet says something wonderful about his younger contemporary: 'the sumptuous disorder of a passion that can only be described as spiritually exotic. Explosion of a meteor alight with no other cause than its presence, the only issue and then extinguished.' He tells Rhodes that he saw Rimbaud on one occasion only, at the famous Dîner des Vilains Bonhommes in 1872, almost a quarter of a century earlier. He did not speak to him but noticed his hands and later learnt that they had autographed—written—'some fine lines; unpublished; his mouth, with his pouting lip and sly smile, did not recite a single one'. He had 'the perverse and haughty puberty' of an 'adolescent demon'.

Bonnefoy wrote the prefaces to the Folio editions of Mallarmé's *Poésies*, *Vers de circonstance* and the correspondence, all three books superbly edited by Bertrand Marchal. *Vers de circonstance* contains a section of quatrains the poet wrote as addresses on or for envelopes. I wonder if the postman-artist known as Facteur Cheval ever delivered a Mallarmé letter, a *pomenvylope* anticipating the dozens Nicholas Moore sent me. Here's one Mallarmé sent to Edgar Degas, who happened to live at the same address as Émile Zola, followed by a free translation. (The two neighbours were on opposite sides concerning Alfred Dreyfus. Zola put some paintings of Degas into *L'Assommoir*.)

Rue, au 23, Ballu.
        j'exprime
Sitôt juin à Monsieur Degas
La satisfaction qu'il rime
Avec la fleur des syringas.

Compayne Gardens, 59,
Mister Weissbort, friend of mine,
This parcel is a box of tricks:
The latest work by Doctor Ricks

Mallarmé wrote a charming letter to Debussy after the first performance of Prélude à l'après-midi d'un faune:

Paris, Sunday, [23 December 1894]

My dear friend,

I have just come out of the concert. I was greatly moved: your illustration of *Afternoon of a Faun* is a marvel! It exhibits no dissonance with my text, save that, in truth, it goes deeper into nostalgia and light, richly, subtly, uneasily. Debussy, I clasp your hands with admiration.

Your, Stéphane Mallarmé

A footnote by Marchal tells us that, shortly afterwards, Mallarmé made a revealing witticism, perhaps to his friend Degas: 'I thought I had already set it to music.' This is not necessarily incompatible with the letter to the composer, but it is telling. It reminds me of comments by Paul Valéry and Maurice Blanchot; first, Blanchot in *L'Espace littéraire*: 'André Breton disavows music, because he wants to preserve within himself the right to hear the discordant essence of language, its non-musical music, and Kafka, who never stops seeing himself as a person more closed to music than anyone else in the world, nonetheless finds in this defect one of his strong points: "I am really powerful, I have a certain strength and, to characterize it briefly if obscurely, it is my non-musical essence."' And Valéry in *Analects*: 'Adding music to a good poem is like using a stained-glass window to light a painted picture.' Another note by Marchal reminds us that, after having been rejected by the magazine *Parnasse*, *Afternoon of a Faun* was first published in an *édition de luxe*, with wood engravings by Édouard Manet, in 1876, the same year that he painted Mallarmé's portrait. They were close friends and lived on the same street, conveniently enough if together you are going to inaugurate modernism in the visual arts, which I discuss later on in this book.

Henri Mondor usefully quarried Mallarmé's letters for his views on poetry, published as *Propos sur la poésie*. Thus, we find the French poet telling Swinburne that he is pleased to learn he is translating Villon, for 'you are penetrated by Baudelaire as only you know how to be, at the times when you are not getting on with your own work; for they are two visionaries from two different epochs'. Apart from the unintended innuendo, the interest in this remark is the implication that translating poetry is what you do when you are not getting on with your own work, perhaps the kind of self-sidetracking with which I am only too familiar. I'm not sure where Henry Weinfield drafted his complete Mallarmé, but Keith Bosley's equally but differently remarkable versions started life during quiet times on the night shift in Bush

House where, for many years, he worked as a presenter, just as Bonnefoy drafted Shakespeare translations on the 80 and the 21 buses while travelling from his home in Montmartre to the Collège de France in the Quartier Latin, changing at the Gare Saint-Lazare.

I am pleased to have the same initials as Arthur Rimbaud, this 'marvellous boy', to quote Wordsworth on Thomas Chatterton, although whether the famous lines beginning 'We poets . . .' can be applied to Rimbaud is a moot point. Whether, indeed, it is a moot point about any poet is itself a moot point, most keep on keeping on. Despondency is one thing, madness another, an early death something else again. Had Rimbaud lived no longer than sixty-five, that is, survived until the end of World War I, you can be sure that Breton would have sought him out and encouraged him to write again. The abandonment of poetry was *then*, this would have been *now*, when he, like Stendhal in this respect if no other, at last found his readers many years after writing his path-finding works. Some years ago, at the French Institute, I attended the launch of a book by Alina Reyes, *Politique de l'amour*. As I requested a signature on my purchased copy, I commented that her initials, Rimbaud's initials, my own initials and, stretching a point Rimbaud's 'l'*a*mour est à *r*éinventer', which she had quoted in her spiel, were the same, although there is no word for this linguistic phenomenon. If 'AR' was a word, one could coin the neologism 'homo-acronymic', but it isn't.

On my desk, apart from Bonnefoy's books on Rimbaud and Robb's biography, are two Pléiade editions of the poet (1954 and 1972), which have recently been overtaken by a third. René Char, who famously wrote 'tu as bien fait de partir, Arthur Rimbaud' (cf. Rimbaud: 'on ne part pas'), makes implicitly high but baffling claims for him in a preface to an old paperback edition. When it comes to Rimbaud, he writes, 'poetry ceases to be a literary genre, a competition. Before him, Heraclitus and a painter Georges de la Tour had constructed and revealed the House above all others where human beings should make their home: at once a dwelling place for breath and meditation . . . If I could really explain what Rimbaud means to me, I would know what poetry lies ahead of me, and I would no longer write.' Compare Bonnefoy's straightforward assertion: 'One of the four or five greatest French poets'. I remain obsessed by those who abandon prematurely a life of creative distinction, from Rimbaud through Duchamp to Lubetkin. Some go silent and then return—George Oppen and Artie Shaw, both of them for around twenty-seven years.

I have taken another look at *Flagrant Délit*, Breton's famous polemic of 1949 about Rimbaud, a time when Rimbaud was still widely thought of as an adjunct to Verlaine. Part of Breton's agenda was to remedy this. He demotes Verlaine but promotes the almost-forgotten figure of Germain Nouveau, with whom Rimbaud lived in 1874 at the now-vanished 178 Stamford Street near Waterloo station (after living with Verlaine in Camden Town) and near the Lambeth potteries which produced 'painted plates', the original subtitle of the *Illuminations*, and which Verlaine wrongly took to mean coloured plates as in engravings. Breton saw Nouveau as Rimbaud's peer: 'two geniuses . . . two natures', 'two heavenly stars'. He sends us to Nouveau's 'Savoir aimer', which he says is a marvellous work, with echoes of Gregorian chant. He speaks of a wonderful letter Nouveau addressed in 1893 to the dead Rimbaud, 'over-hidden in the tomb' (cf. Mallarmé on Verlaine) and tells us that their relationship is the key to Rimbaud's life's work. Were I younger, I would open a folder labelled Germain Nouveau and research him. Robb seems to have overlooked this text of Breton, only quoting a remark from the French writer's *Anthologie de l'humour noire* to the effect that Rimbaud's final piece of doggerel (I'm the Roquefort, I'm the Gruyère, I'm the Brie, etc.) can be seen as his 'poetic and spiritual testament'. This surprises me and I ought to check out the context to see if Robb has missed an irony. Later in life, Nouveau became a wanderer. According to Georges-Emmanuel Clancier, there is a legend that, during the Belle Epoque or 'Belle Epoque', when Nouveau was in Aix-en-Provence, Cézanne would give him a hundred sous every Sunday. Recently, Paul Buck went to Patti Smith's Rock and Rimbaud concert. He'd met the singer before and took her a message from me about the house at 8 Royal College Street which we (the Rimbaud–Verlaine committee) have sought to safeguard, seeking a Maecenas who would enable the use of the house for artistic purposes or, at least, preserve its original features. Smith, like Bob Dylan and so many others, have loved the house, love that it is still there, as atmospheric in its own way as Poe's house in Philadelphia.

[Coda: I have been reading Nouveau's *Savoir aimer*. It has its moments.]

TWENTIETH-CENTURY FRENCH POETRY

Paul Valéry (and Georges Brassens)

The inclusion of a songwriter like Brassens in the *Poètes d'aujourd'hui* series (number 99) is equivalent to that of Bob Dylan or Leonard Cohen (*Flowers for Hitler* and *Poems 1956–1968*) or Cole Porter in an English-language series. The words were written to be sung but it does not follow that none of the songs can be read as poems without the music. After (before) all, thousands of years ago, poetry started life in song, in recitation, in the spoken word. Even so, when I turn to a favourite Brassens song, 'Une Jolie fleur' or 'Je suis un voyou', it is impossible not to hear the much-loved melancholy tune behind the words, whereas some I know only from the page do seem rather simple verses. This is not a problem to worry the head. I like the fact that Brassens and Valéry are both natives of Sète. The singer, however, unlike the poet, is not buried in the cimitière marin, the marine cemetery, and therefore rests further from the sea than the poet. In the Brassens volume is a photograph of him at the grave of the poet. And there is a room devoted to Brassens in the Paul Valéry museum: the songwriter has a room (a stanza) in another's house (poem). I wonder what the poet would have made of the presence of the songwriter. One Brassens song, respectfully ironic, alludes to Valéry and 'Le Cimitière marin', the poem and the cemetery:

> Déférence gardée envers Paul Valéry,
> Moi l'humble troubadour sur lui je renchéris,
> Le bon maître me le pardonne.
> Et qu'au moins si ses vers valent mieux que les miens,
> Mon cimetière soit plus marin que le sien,
> Et n'en déplaise aux autochtones.
>
> I bow my head before the master poet,
> But I the humble troubadour outdo him,
> May Paul Valéry forgive me;
> And even though he is il miglior fabbro,
> Let my cemetery be more marine than his,
> With all due respect to the natives.

A rough calculation reveals that Valéry's poetry amounts to between two and three per cent of his published and consecrated work. Is this a record low in a poet of such renown? What, if anything, does it tell us about him? There is a revealing text about his last visit to Mallarmé: 'I was standing beside this person. There was nothing to suggest I would never see him again. In the gold of day, there was no raven charged with making predictions. Everything was calm and safe . . . But while Mallarmé was speaking to me, his finger pointing to a page, I recall that my thinking began to dream *of that very moment*. Distractedly, it invested it with a quasi-absolute value. Standing next to the living man, I thought of his destiny as having been accomplished . . . He only needed a few poems to throw into question the very purpose of literature.' Pierre Bayard quotes another revealing text, the poet's homage to Proust: 'I well recognize from the little I have had occasion to read what an exceptional loss, etc., etc.'

Guillaume Apollinaire

The title of the late John Adlard's short study of Apollinaire's London phase, *One Evening of Light Mist in London*, is taken from the first line of 'La Chanson du mal aimé', a wondrous love poem for Annie Playden, the one woman known to have escaped the old rogue's embraces, by emigrating to Texas from Landor Road in Stockwell, south London. (Had Apollinaire heard of Walter Savage Landor? He would have been struck by the irony of a street named after a poet one of whose most famous poems includes the lines: 'A night of memories and sighs / I consecrate to thee'. Mind you, one night is quite a short period. And what if it is named after a different Landor?) There are other poems about Playden: 'L'Emigrant de Landor Road' and 'Annie'. I inspected 75 Landor Road some years ago, when attending a session at an acupuncturist's, three doors away. Half a century after she fled, Playden, interviewed by Professor Leroi Breunig, said: 'Kostro [he was born Kostrowicki], what became of him?' Here is my copy of Oliver Bernard's Apollinaire versions. Folded into it is a long letter, dated 17 March 1986, in his beautiful italic hand, about a poem we had both translated, and the letter I wrote him after reading a review of his translations. We would meet years later on the Rimbaud–Verlaine London house committee and at Michael

Hamburger's funeral. Running to catch the Métro which would take me to the Eurostar after Yves Bonnefoy's daughter's wedding reception at the Maison de l'Amerique latine in the summer of 2007, I saw again the plaque marking Apollinaire's apartment in boulevard Saint-Germain and made a mental note to return to the wonders of his poetry, although I am ashamed to say I did not realize (until put right by Claude Vigée) that there is a pun on Loup in the ferocious love poems addressed to Lou.

Max Jacob/Edmond Jabès/Guy Lévis-Mano

The poet Marcel Béalu was proprietor of a bookshop, Le Pont traversé, on the corner of rue Saint-Séverin, at the Luxembourg end of rue de Vaugirard, the longest street in Paris. I visited him with my friend Michel Couturier while researching the background to Max Jacob's *Advice to a Young Poet*, which Menard eventually published in the translation by John Adlard. Béalu identified the poet not as Jacob's friend Edmond Jabès (the rumour) but as Jacques Evrard, a surgeon and—ironically enough, given Jacob's fate at the hands of the Nazis—a former collaborationist. Here too is a book by Béalu himself, *D'où part le regard* and signed 'Pour Anthony Rudolf, qui sait traverser le pont, Marcel Béalu, 5 Nov 1972'. Couturier and I met Evrard near his hospital. After talking frankly about his youthful errors, Evrard agreed to write an essay for the book and said we could reproduce the original notebook cover in the Menard edition. I managed to sell all five hundred copies of the book fairly quickly and without a single review, thanks to word-of-mouth recommendations by Jacob fans such as the poet Lee Harwood.

Lettres de Max Jacob à Edmond Jabès, edited by Steven Jaron, contains a poem-letter from Jacob, with an appropriate reply from Jabès:

Saint Benoît-sur-Loire (Loiret), 20 January 37

Dear Edmond

Write me your life *hour by hour*. Yes

your city *street by street*. No!

your house. Yes

your apartment. Yes

your work table. Yes

your friends *one by one*. No!

the people you visit (at what time?) yes
what do you eat? Where?
what do you drink? Where?
which are the political parties?—No
what do you think about the war? About Germany? No
is Egypt pro-Soviet Russia? No
what do you think of Cocteau's descriptions of Egypt?
Yes
is the sphinx in a bear pit?—yes
let's play at which of us will love the other more: yes.

Max Jacob

I await twelve closely written pages

Reply:

Cairo, February 4, 1937

23, rue Kasr el-Nil

And why not?
You are happy at St. Benoît.
Here, I push forward with my early life.
You are ageless and I'm a few years old.
And on my table dreams your photograph.
We love each other, both are involved with each other
And you write to me laughing. When you pray
Angels come down to gaze on you. Alas!
No one had that idea with me;
Only love paid me a visit. Glory, pursued
By me you've abandoned it. My room is quiet, the sun
Shines.
How do we describe what's left?
I try my luck at futures,
I plunge an eye in mystery.
If I wake while dropping off
I rotate the world with my finger—
Reading you I perforate a sail

In the sun I play with my skin.
If my mood greys the sky,
My wit claps with a knife.
                    Your friend,
                    Edmond Jabès
As for Cocteau, let him go . . .
His world tour
            Is quite amusing

The affectionate, yet sometimes tense, close relationship between the much younger francophone Egyptian Jewish poet and his mentor ('Reb Jacob, mon premier maître' Jabès would call him thirty years later in *The Book of Questions*) is described in Jaron's scholarly introduction. Jaron, who is married to Jabès' granddaughter, shows how Jabès' early work is clearly defined as those poems and texts written before the announcement of Jacob's death aged sixty-seven at Drancy in 1944, when Jabès himself was thirty-two. It was clear to Jacob that Jabès, gifted as he was, had not yet found his voice. Indeed, he said Jabès' very early work was good enough to be put in the wastepaper basket which, according to Marcel Cohen's report of a discussion with Jabès, is what the older man is supposed to have done. *Je bâtis ma demeure*, the Gallimard collection of the poet's mainly verse poems, contains work from 1943 to 1957, after which date—having had to leave Egypt in the wake of the Suez crisis—he began work on *The Book of Questions*, for which he is best known. Sadly, only one of Jabès' letters from this correspondence survives, the one I have translated above. Jabès sent Jacob some 'closely written pages' with his reply, identified by Jaron as the poem 'L'Eau non potable', which was published as a pamphlet in Paris in 1936 by Guy Lévis-Mano, the poet, printer, publisher and typographer whom I had the good fortune to meet in his Montparnasse print shop (6 rue Huyghens) in the 1970s, where he worked alone, in artisanal overalls and a socialist or republican beret, seemingly shorter than some of his machines. Jonathan Griffin was one of his subscribers. Lévis-Mano reminded me of my friend Asa Benveniste, an American-born writer who lived his entire adult life in the UK. Like Lévis-Mano, Asa was a Sephardi Jew, poet, printer, publisher (Trigram Press) and typographer. He was a descendent of early printers of the Talmud in Venice. Perhaps Lévis-Mano was too. In an article on prisoner poets published in 1944, Jean Starobinski quotes Jean Garamond: this was Lévis-Mano's *nom de guerre* and a clue that he was a printer.

Louis Aragon

Louis Aragon published 'Le Musée Grevin' in clandestinity in 1943 under the *nom de guerre* of François la Colère. The following stanza is surely one of the earliest references in literature to the dread place named in it. Aragon, a senior member of the communist resistance, would have known what was going on in the East. I checked the question of dates with Claude Vigée, who himself was a junior member of the Jewish resistance, centred on Toulouse.

> Auschwitz Auschwitz oh bloody syllables
> Here you live and here you die by inches
> It's called slow execution. Little
> By little, a part of our hearts dies there

Vigée agrees that this is likely to be the first published literary reference to Auschwitz, certainly in French. By 1943, he and his group already knew the cruel facts from their superiors, including the Russian-born poet Dovid Knout (married to Ariadne, the daughter of the Russian composer Alexander Scriabin. She had converted to Judaism), thanks to intelligence supplied by the Irgun in Palestine. An email to Starobinski elicits interest but no further information, since he does not have access to his books. As for Hebrew, the Holocaust writings from the 1940s of a major poet, Uri Zvi Greenberg, were not published until 1951.

Arthur Koestler's *Arrival and Departure* contains a description of Jews murdered in a gas truck, the predecessor of the gas chambers, deployed by the Einsatzgruppen on the Eastern front. The novel was published in 1943, the same year as 'Le Musée Grévin'. A further conversation with Vigée reveals that, in July 1942, Pierre Emmanuel, a Christian member of the non-communist resistance, presented him with his new book, *Jour de colère*, published in March 1942. This contained a poem entitled 'Camps de concentration'. The title but not the poem itself was censored by the Vichy regime in Algeria, where the publisher was based. The poem is reprinted facsimile in Vigée's *Etre poète pour que vivent les hommes*, with the title in Emmanuel's handwriting as inserted by the poet when they met.

Aragon Poet of Resurgent France contains a selection of poems by translators including Stephen Spender and Louis MacNeice, and an important essay by Peter Rhodes on Aragon as a Resistance leader. We learn that he edited a first-aid manual for the use of resisters, which he was as proud of as any volume of poems. Among the translators of poems from Aragon's *Les Yeux d'Elsa* is John Hayward with 'More Beautiful than Tears'. The book was first published under another title in 1945; Hayward and Eliot began sharing a flat in 1946 but they already knew each other. Did this fine translation have any input from Eliot?

René Char/Pierre Reverdy

René Char saw his *Feuillets d'Hypnos* (*Hypnos: Notes from the French Resistance 1943–1944*—newly and masterfully translated by Mark Hutchinson) as a kind of fiction in fragments but, great text though it is, I cannot read it that way. We know what Char was doing behind the scenes and between the lines of his text—he could have saved his friend, the poet Roger Bernard, from a German firing squad. He and his men in the Resistance in the Vaucluse had the Germans in their sights. But had they done so, the Germans would have killed the entire village in reprisals. *Alors?* A great poem in the same moral territory is George Oppen's 'Route' in *Of Being Numerous*, set in Alsace.

When I was young, I fell in love with the work of Pierre Reverdy, a great poet and recognized as such by his peers—painters and poets—in the heady world of Paris before and after World War I. I translated about twenty of the poems. More recently, I copied out and translated a complete poem displayed in the Char exhibition at the Bibliothèque Nationale, which ends:

> I speak beautiful
> poems to you
> cherished Char searching for
> hard stones beneath the earth
> You know now
> how to place them
> in the sun
> to turn them into words
> of purer matter

1955 with all the best
things it could have within

This poem addressed to 'Cher Char chercheur' is not contained in *Sable mouvant*, a small collection of later work; perhaps it only appeared in a limited edition. Like his friend and contemporary Max Jacob, Reverdy converted to Catholicism in the 1920s. Jacob became a Benedictine monk, Reverdy a lay member of the Benedictine abbey of Solesmes. Unlike the Jewish-born Jacob, Reverdy survived the war. Given his association with the visual arts and with cubism in particular (Juan Gris and Reverdy were close), it comes as no surprise that John Ashbery, Ron Padgett, Frank O'Hara and others have translated him.

André Frénaud (and the hands of a pianist)

Poésie/Gallimard is a valuable collection, reprints for the most part, of essential poets. The two *Poésie* volumes by André Frénaud sit alongside individual collections which he sent me after we became acquainted, having met via his close friend Yves Bonnefoy. Eventually I translated and published a few poems in magazines, and reviewed his one and only—and superb—prose book, *Notre inhabileté fatale*, the title taken from Rimbaud's *Illuminations*. But you cannot translate too many people in great quantity, and I was already overbooked with my main poets. After translating a considerable number of Bonnefoy's poems, I translated work by various people as the fancy (or preferably the imagination) took me; the 'faithful' translator of YB felt like an adulterer when turning his attention to certain poets in quantities beyond the occasional. I have published books of Jabès and Vigée and the Russian poet Vinokurov, and have almost enough work for a book of Deguy. These were my other and concurrent major affairs throughout the Bonnefoy marriage (which is still going strong, I'm pleased to say).

Here are two pamphlets of Frénaud poems, *November* and *A Round O*, translated by John Montague and Keith Bosley. For a long time these were the only works by this distinguished figure available in English outside magazines, until Keith's bilingual edition of *La Sorcière de Rome*. The original French edition is on my desk now, along with *Les Rois mages* and *La Sainte face*, the latter containing a warm dedication, dated the day Frénaud, his wife

Monique and Augustus Young came to dinner in 1973, after we had visited Rimbaud's house in Camden Town. Of the major twentieth-century French poets, Frénaud is the least well served by translators, in terms of quantity that is. I visited him 'in the land of his apartment / in the shadow of himself', rue de Bourgogne, close to the Rodin museum. Reverentially he handed me a rare original copy of Rimbaud's *Une saison en enfer*—the only book published in Rimbaud's lifetime—and I equally reverentially held it in my hands.

Hands: Rimbaud's poem of 1871, 'The Hands of Jeanne-Marie', celebrates the women of the Commune and parodies certain sentimentalists. 'Have they rolled cigars / or trafficked in diamonds?'—the first of these two lines is suggestive of Prosper Merimée's *Carmen* as well as his other masterpiece *Colomba* ('une belle vengeance est belle'). My friend Richard Berengarten has completed a poem sequence about hands, which Paula says are the most difficult thing of all to paint. I have met Stephen Bishop Kovacevic two or three times at the house of Marina Warner and could not take my eyes off the hands of this great pianist. When I apologized for my stare, he said that he too stole a glance at Vladimir Horowitz's hands when the master was not looking. On another occasion, Kovacevic told me that Dinu Lipatti's version of the Chopin waltzes were used to offset his own in a Radio Three programme; I had to admit that Lipatti was my favourite pianist and the waltzes my favourite Lipatti. But I also told him what he already knew: it's not a zero-sum game. One can love several different versions, although surely not all the versions, even all the good versions. In any case, the me who listens to Stephen's wondrous CD of Chopin and Ravel waltzes is not the me who bought the Lipatti LP around forty years ago. Kovacevic cheerfully agreed that there wasn't only one way to play something, and he would be interested to learn how I characterize the difference between his and Lipatti's interpretation of the waltzes. There's a challenge to fear and to relish.

Edmond Jabès (and Paul Celan)

Rosmarie Waldrop's *Lavish Absence: Recalling and Rereading Edmond Jabès* is a wonderful meditation on translation and friendship and poetry by his major English-language translator. Having myself translated verse poems he wrote before he embarked on the great prose sequences he will be remembered by, and having known Jabès as a friend, I find myself deeply moved by the quietly eloquent *Lavish Absence*, which joins Marcel Cohen's *Du désert au livre* (a book of interviews) and Steven Jaron's *The Hazard of Exile* as the best way into an *oeuvre* that has yet to reach its full flowering of influence and love.

Like Bonnefoy, Jabès was a friend of Celan who, we learn, kept insisting he would not translate *Le Livre des questions* into German while its author kept insisting he hadn't asked him to. So, via Edmond and Yves, I have personal links at one remove to Celan, not forgetting too my friendship with Celan's late wife Gisèle Celan-Lestrange. That this matters to me is magical thinking gone mad, and yet the life of a person is so imbricated in their work that it is not trivial to want to be party to the life, however vicariously. Indeed, it is necessary. But it is not sufficient. What counts is work. Maybe it is not too late for me to learn that one must concentrate and work hard if one is to get to square one, which is to produce an *oeuvre* at all, let alone a good one. One day, in a few years' time, if I survive that long, all my heroes and mentors will be dead. And within the wider family, as the oldest grandchild, I will be the oldest living member. How is it possible that I am on the brink of old age? My greatest fear and shame as I look at my CV at seventy is what it proclaims: 'Not bad for a man of fifty'. The wasted minutes and hours spent sidetracking myself through correspondence and boy-scout behaviour, the books I failed to write because I was too lazy to keep the kind of notebooks that would make them possible, the cowardice in personal relationships that often led me to go round the world rather than say what I really thought—I cannot recover those years but, who knows, perhaps I shall yet produce a *récit* incarnating the tension between, let us say, writer and translator, right brain and left brain, Dionysus and Apollo, warring over my soul.

Poets discovered through Yves Bonnefoy

I have already touched on Bonnefoy's *Hier régnant désert* (1958) and his 1961 book *Rimbaud par lui-même*. Those two books and *L'Improbable* (1959) changed my life fifty years ago, and remain potent, as transformative elements in life always do. I knew I must have a life on the page, because the page is where the forms of life speak to us most deeply. More than any other books, they helped make it possible for me to find a way forward while recovering from the academic failure which ensured that I, unlike my college friends, had no future as a professional scholar. *L'Improbable* contains an essential essay on that singular figure, the poet and leading Marquis de Sade scholar, Gilbert Lély. Here is Lély's *Oeuvres poétiques*, inscribed to me. Folded into it is a carbon copy of a letter I wrote him, mentioning our mutual friend Bonnefoy and asking Lély if he would send me his book of poems; also folded in are copies of translations I made of a few of his poems in the early 1970s, some of which were published by Paul Buck in *Curtains*:

'The Young Witch'
Your love shocks me like the middle ages.
You knock on horrible and lovely doors.
Already the inquisitors and hangmen
Disguised as foreign students, labourers,
Were getting impatient, gnawing at you,
Poking at you, tearing you apart . . .
You open up. Tomorrow
Thanks to you, they'll put up scaffolds.

Curtains was a little magazine set single spaced on a typewriter with a fading ribbon but which, in the fine tradition of obsessed editors with a mission, had a greater influence on serious readers than people sometimes realize. Buck and I have always had parallel and occasionally overlapping concerns—the mutual passions being French literature, art and cinema. Broadly, while I was exploring Breton and Bonnefoy, he was exploring Bataille and Bernard Noel. While I was discovering Balthus (after reading *L'Improbable*), Paul was discovering Klossowski. While I succumbed to Truffault, he succumbed to Godard.

Back in 1963, when we first met, Bonnefoy spoke to me about his friends André du Bouchet, Jacques Dupin and Philippe Jaccottet. Over the years, all three have built up formidable bodies of work and have been widely translated. I myself translated a handful of poems by each of them. I have never met Jaccottet, the only survivor of the three, but du Bouchet was in England for the Cambridge Poetry Festival one year. The author of *Dans la chaleur vacante* was rightly cross with me for describing him (naively intending a compliment) as a 'disciple of Giacometti' in the introduction to an anthology issue of *Modern Poetry in Translation* (*MPT*) which I edited. It has a previously unpublished Giacometti drawing on the cover, and the artist's work remains an obsession of mine. Books on him by Yves Bonnefoy, James Lord and Jean Genet, among others, encourage one to think harder and feel more deeply about this great artist and 'to investigate the biography of his work', in the phrase of Bonnefoy.

Dupin came to London where Couturier interviewed him at the French section of the BBC overseas service. Before the poet took us to dinner at Luigi's in Covent Garden, we had a drink at the Coal Hole in the Strand, by the site of Fountain Court where Blake spent the last few years of his life. The translators of this powerful poet include John Taylor, Paul Auster and Stephen Romer. Auster published his first Dupin selection as *Fits and Starts*, at his own Living Hand Press in a trade edition and also in a limited edition with an original lithograph by Alexander Calder, which I am pleased to own, courtesy of the publisher. Romer quotes Barthes's characterization of modern poetry as 'existential geology'—the elemental quality manifest in Dupin reminds me of Ponge and early Char. John Taylor has published a first-rate selection of Jaccottet (*And Nonetheless*), who has also been translated by Derek Mahon and, as a prose writer, by Mark Treharne, one of Menard's French series.

I have a number of books by a haunting lyric poet Jean-Paul Guibbert, whom I translated and with whom I struck up a correspondence over a number of years after Bonnefoy drew my attention to his work. One of his books, *Haut lieu du coeur* (aurally also 'au lieu du cœur'), is illustrated by a member of Bonnefoy's circle, my late friend Nasser Assar, a painter of mysterious and evocative landscapes and brother of the singer, the late Shusha Guppy. There is an earlier book with the same title but different text illustrated by Pierre Fournel. This is one of sixty copies with three original drypoints, which Paula found 'very thirties', not a pejorative comment. Guppy, whom I knew for years before discovering she and Nasser were siblings, wrote *The Blindfold Horse*, a lovely autobiography about her childhood in Iran, as well as *A Girl in Paris*, a self-indulgent second volume. Her 2007 *Guardian* article on monarchy (one of many subjects we disagreed about) concluded with the statement that she had terminal cancer and would write no more.

Here is Guibbert's *Le Second cercle*. Folded into it are two letters from 1965 addressed to me at my parents' house, where I was still living, a year after graduating. Jean-Paul Guibbert tells me he likes Georges Seferis, René Char, Pierre Jean Jouve and Jean Joubert, the last-named a poet translated years later by Denise Levertov (whom I discuss on other pages) and Ruth Fainlight, whose recent collected poems merits close attention. Here too are other books by Guibbert culminating in *La Chair du monde*, a collection of his work up till 1982. A glance at the editorial note reveals the occultation of the Fournel-illustrated *Haut lieu du coeur*—it is as if it had never existed. 'Some texts,' a note tells us, 'which were written to praise or name a person, a place, a moment or an event, still survive, in the original slim publications.' I fix my eyes on the two envelopes—41 Middleway, London NW11—and the souvenance of ancient days briefly works its magic.

Michel Deguy

In general, translated contemporary poetry available in book form is a function of personal friendship and love of a body of work, and that is as it should be. Jacques Dupin is available in English because Paul Auster and Stephen Romer and John Taylor loved his work, Edmond Jabès because Rosmarie and Keith Waldrop and others loved his work. In the early days, translation, mainly of Bonnefoy and, to a lesser extent, Vinokurov, was my cover and mask, a plausible explanation for my involvement with literary matters since I didn't want to own up to my writerly ambitions, even as I endured my day jobs. And it supplied me with a workshop education until I discovered who I was or, more modestly and accurately, who I wasn't. Also, I met some very interesting and gifted people, one of whom was Michel Deguy. I have enough translated poems of his, as I said earlier, to make up a pamphlet or small book. A few have appeared in magazines and anthologies, including Auster's *Random House [Faber] Book of Twentieth-Century French Poetry*, to which my 1973 French issue of *MPT* was a kind of prequel. Inscribing his *Poèmes 1960–1970*, Deguy flatters me by saying that I know these pages better than the few French readers do and in a more friendly way than many of his friends. 'There is nothing wrong with them save their excuses,' as he writes in another context. Somehow we never took off, as a translation marriage, that is. Perhaps he came on my scene too late; perhaps his language was, ultimately, beyond my ken as a translator. I don't know.

Deguy is a philosopher poet *par excellence*, and how appropriate it is that we have to use the French phrase. By philosophy, however, I do not mean that he has 'a philosophy of life' which can be extrapolated from the poetry, nor even that he has a philosophy of poetry, that is, a poetics, which can be extrapolated. Rather, philosophy and poetry are virtually coextensive for this extraordinarily brilliant and sometimes proudly difficult writer, although the process is the reverse of Wittgenstein's 'Philosophizing should be like writing poems'. In a short, dense preface to Jean-Pierre Moussaron's study of Deguy, Jacques Derrida calls the poetry 'Poématique babalienne', babel symbolizing the bewildering registers and modalities of discourse of this 'penseur poétique', rather than foreign languages in the usual sense. The best essay on Deguy in English is by John Taylor. He quotes the title of Deguy's *Poèmes en pensées* (poems in thought or poems in thinking), which is as good a sound bite or thought bite to characterize his work as one could find. And, if I may gloss Taylor, it means that Deguy's imagery is meta-imagery, since feeling and experience are mediated via conscious projection of thought and concept. Yves Bonnefoy's agon concerning conceptual thinking is not for Michel Deguy, whom I last met when he arrived jet-lagged from the USA in time for Bonnefoy's eightieth-birthday reading in Paris. Reading Deguy's work can be a roller coaster of conflicting senses, since it demands speed and meditation all at once. The experience is like driving a car in top gear with your foot constantly on the brake. In 1994, Michel's wife Monique died, and during the course of the next few months he wrote the texts which ended up as a book, *A ce qui n'en finit pas*. Reading this heart-rending threnody generates the familiar paradox of pleasure and enchantment out of the narration of grief. I translated around ten of the poems for *MPT* and dedicated them to the memory of Monique.

The three volumes in the Gallimard *Poésie* series reprint many of the books which Deguy gave me over the years, such as *Fragment d'un cadastre*, inscribed to me with the line 'ce premier livre qui naît de la rive d'en face (petite Bretagne)', that is, as opposed to Grande-Bretagne. *Fragment d'un cadastre*, his first poetry book, opens with a poem called 'La Vigie' (the look out), and so he begins, as he will go on, mixing verse and prose, interweaving poetry and a meditation on it, in a way that allows one to call him a dialectical poet, perhaps the dialectical poet, again. 'The poet wanders in search of sites of essence. What does he want? To listen to the precipice, the hillside, the storm, the slope, the hill, harbingers of being, and which announce to him his own way of being in the world.' *Actes* has an inscription in Deguy's familiar scrawl—'cette contribution au marché . . . non: sur les marches communes de la poésie'. One section of *Gisants* begins with a prose poem called 'Dedication': 'I cannot write your name. Laws forbid it. Having written your name, I would say that I shall never speak it and thus I shall conceal it. You are my oracle. It is written that your wish should be fulfilled that I write a *recumbent figure*' (or *gisant*, which also exists in English). Three translations (now revised) from *Oui-dire*, which I sent Paul Auster for his anthology in 1980 or thereabouts:

1

The tree lights up the temples of the sky
The horse swallows the spring
Colour draws on the animals
Leaving a man
My life
The mystery of as
Then shadow turns into light

2

Days are not counted
Learn to form a convoy of singing deportees
Trees flanked by entreaties
Ophelia in the river-run of time
Assonances guiding a meaning towards the poem's bed
How shall we name what gives the tone?
Poetry like love risks all on signs

3

The swan trained
Begins to speak again

Poet who prefers
To tell it like it is
Through the fingers of the genitive
Sorites of the poem

The last line of the second poem is surely wonderful—a blazing truth about literature and life. The last line of the third poem contains a technical term from logic. Non-philosophers have to check out its meaning and then read back into the poem what Deguy is getting at. Some thirty-five years after translating the poems, I well remember looking up *sorites* in my *Harraps* 'Mansion' French–English dictionary and, having found, of course, the same word in English, going to the *OED* and then phoning my friend the philosopher David Pole. Revising the translations today, I decided, out of curiosity if not necessity, to look up three or four words in my long-serving dictionaries. As if it were yesterday, I found myself back in the field of force, in the cat's cradle woven from meanings and sounds. 'Entreaties' is an improvement on my earlier 'prayers', and not only because it contains the sound of the word tree and yields a para-rhyme with 'deportees'. And so it goes on, the endless dialectic of sound and sense, the recreation of rhythm rather than its reproduction. I concur with John Taylor's view of this poet's work: 'ce n'est pas rien', 'it is not nothing', that French phrase of understated high praise. Perhaps 'it's quite something' conveys the tone. Deguy edited with Jacques Roubaud an anthology of American poetry. Once again, we realize that an intelligently edited and well-translated anthology can serve as a powerful intervention in the target culture, in terms of how one particular foreign literature is perceived—at the heart of the anthology are members of the Objectivists, Black Mountain and New York schools. No Beats on the one hand, no confessional poets on the other. The book leads off with Gertrude Stein, and this choice points us in the direction the editors want us to go.

Here finally are prose books: firstly, Deguy's religious meditation, *Un homme de peu de foi*, is one of a number of texts where he continues his obsessive and fascinating reflexion on Judaism, Nazism and related questions concerning universalism. Thus the greatest indictment of the Nazi war against the Jews is that it was a crime against humanity even more than it was a specific genocide. This sounds like terminological quibbling and some Jews won't like it for other reasons. Yet Deguy is right. Two more volumes: an alphabet book, *Le sens de la visite*. Under R, for example, we find Raison, Rêve, Rue, Rodin, Résurrection, Relique, Racisme, Référence, Religieux, Retenue. Deguy even found time to write a whistleblowing account of *Le Comité*, Gallimard's reading committee, on which he served for twenty-five years.

Claude Royet-Journoud (and company/et cie)

> The metaphor is far more intelligent than its author, and this is the case with many things. Everything has its depths. He who has eyes sees something in everything.
>
> —Georg C. Lichtenberg, *Aphorisms*

Born in Lyons, like Maurice Scève, Louise Labé and two writers he championed, Roger Laporte and Roger Giroux, Claude Royet-Journoud, in the rigour and purity of his post-Mallarmean quest to write a book that is not a series of discrete poems, sets the face of his hyper-intelligence against metaphor, except of course the substratum of etymology that is inescapable. He quotes Mallarmé: 'Comment échapperons nous à l'analogie?' If ever there was a 'literalist of the imagination' (Marianne Moore), it is Claude, my exact contemporary, and despite our sporadic misunderstandings and squabbles— trivial stuff resulting from my insecurities—my friend. His work involves composing and then destroying hundreds of pages of prose until he is left with a *book* which is to be read *as* a book and not as a collection of minimalist poems. If there is an analogy, it is with certain painters or composers, who reduce rather than build up. Wittgenstein's propositions in *Tractatus Logico-Philosophicus*, one of my own talismanic books, are a pretext to Royet-Journoud's work. After his return to Paris from self-exile in London, it was typical of this exceptional individual to turn up at my quondam regular haunt, the grandiosely named but cheap Hôtel des Grands Balcons in rue Casimir-Delavigne, with a gift of a book, Blanchot's appropriately titled *L'Amitié*. First at rue du Dragon then in rue de la Harpe, I would visit him, and we would chat about the old days, go out for a meal, discuss the miserable ongoing failure of Michel Couturier's literary executor to do anything about his work.

71

I have loved the work of Roger Giroux for years. Somewhere in this apartment is a multicoloured letter to me eventually reprinted in a book. Neither book nor letter is to hand, but it contains his friendly critique of one of my translations, and I recall diagrams as well as words. This was an intimate and authentic 'texte' in the best French style of deadly serious yet playful engagement with a reader, a text pleasing enough to him to reprint. I remember visiting him at his office near the Odéon, in rue de Condé, two minutes from my hotel, in the 1970s when he worked for the famous Série noire published by Gallimard. My 1973 *MPT* anthology contains versions of Giroux by Peter Hoy, Paul Buck, Jonathan Griffin, Paul Auster and myself—an unusually large range of translators for a single poet, which I instigated to honour one who was neglected, one of the many brought to my attention by Claude. Some years later, Anthony Barnett would make the largest selection from Giroux to date.

I challenge readers with good French to get hold of at least one of the Royet-Journoud quartet, say *Le Renversement*, and read as they have never read before, perhaps even as they have never been read before. Or find English translations of parts of them, mainly by a master of the art, Keith Waldrop, as put out by small presses, including *Objects Contain the Infinite* and *The Crowded Circle*. A fine book about Claude's work has been gathered by Michèle Cohen-Halimi and Francis Cohen: *Je te continue ma lecture*, which is a syntactically incorrect phrase from Couturier's *L'Ablatif absolu*—I'll continue to you reading—used jokingly by Claude and Michel when reciting texts to each other on the phone. Michele Cohen-Halimi has also written a book, *Seul le renversement*, on the first volume of Royet-Journoud's sequence. Her suggestive interpretation ends: 'Such was the lived thickness of *my* reading: a precision filled with frenzy in which the hand (which writes) and the eye (which reads) always suppose, enigmatically, a silent and intimate exchange: Jeu de Paume'.

The young Royet-Journoud, whom I met through Anthony Barnett or Alberto de Lacerda in 1968, had some of the attributes of the young Ezra Pound. In London, and later in Paris, Claude was a tireless propagandist and proselytizer for the poetry and poetics he believed in. The first book he gave me was his early Rimbaldian chapbook with its English title *Way Out*. It no longer appears in his lists of publications. He would read you poems over the phone, encourage you to translate poets from his circle and their precursors, and seek help in promoting *Siècle à mains*, a magazine he edited with his wife Anne-Marie Albiach and Michel Couturier. Claude, well aware of what he was doing, introduced me to his quondam father figure Edmond Jabès, who later became the oldest poet in my *MPT* anthology. Royet-Journoud met Auster through me, and Paul met Jabès through Royet-Journoud. I remember the day before Jabès' funeral at Père-Lachaise in 1990. His widow Arlette was shocked that the American had not been in touch. I said he must be away or he would have made contact, no question. We phoned New York from the little apartment in rue de L'Epée de bois, but there was no answer. Sure enough, it emerged later he had been on holiday, out of reach in those pre-mobile phone (let alone email) days.

A few years ago, I sent Royet-Journoud my book on Piotr Rawicz, whom he had met in Greece, and by return he sent me his two most recent books, *Théorie des prépositions* (inscribed 'pour faire entendre le récit des articulations' with 'Llan' printed on the official dedication page, an allusion to *Llanfair* . . . , published by Peter Hoy in Oxford and edited by CRJ—a serious little magazine, whimsically named after the longest Welsh word) and *La Poésie entière est préposition* (with the inscription 'for Anthony, who perhaps knows that' preceding the title on the title page). Here too is Waldrop's immaculate translation of the first book, *Theory of Prepositions*. The title connects explicitly with Louis Zukofsky's book of essays, *Prepositions*, Zukofsky being a poet Albiach translated with extraordinary skill and sensitivity. Anne-Marie's second book *Etat*, which Bonnefoy persuaded his own publisher to bring out after encouragement from me (says yours truly modestly), has a touching inscription from 1971. If you look closely on the spine of the cover of this classically austere production from Mercure de France, you will see that the H of her surname has been 'letrasetted', the one and only mistake in a book of utmost typographical complexity, especially in those pre-computer days. Here too are her books *Figure vocative* (described by Paul Auster on the cover of Anthony Barnett and Joseph Sima's translation *Vocative Figure* as achieving 'a sublime lyricism') and *Mezza Voce*, dedicated to Claude, and indicative of the separated couple's enduring dialectical interaction as poets. As I write, I have received from Claude Waldrop's translation of her *Figurations de l'image*, *Figured Image*, and a magazine full of homages to Anne-Marie, of which the shortest and simplest in its acknowledgement of singularity is, once more, Paul Auster's: 'The astonishing work of Anne-Marie Albiach resembles that of no other poet in the world today', and that is the truth of the matter.

[Coda added at proof stage: Anne-Marie died on 5 November 2012, aged seventy-five. Rest in peace, dear Anne-Marie.]

In 1969 I was sent a novel 'de la part de Claude Royet-Journoud avec l'amitié de Jean Frémon', *Le Miroir et les alouettes*. Frémon is a distinguished writer who, in later years, followed Dupin as head of a major Paris gallery Maeght Lelong. We met at the international art fair in Madrid one year, and I invited him to Paula's private view at Marlborough Gallery in Madrid the same evening. Here is his *La Vraie nature des ombres*, a cunningly constructed book of memories and reveries. His *Le Singe mendiant* encodes in short prose and verse illuminations the work of writers he admires. Here too is a big book of his writings on art, *La Gloire des formes*, whose remarkable first section, 'Le Double corps de l'image', I would like one day to translate and bring out as a short book. Pascal Quignard too, I met through Claude, at a flat in the Place de la Contrescarpe, along with Jean Daive and others. Quignard's *Le Nom sur le bout de la langue* is a short, intense novel:

> Before the female sphinx, one must know how to reply or die. Presence of mind confronts staircase wit. How reply to the enigma and, somehow, return the mirror? Having the time of return for each word which is on the tip of your tongue, that has become a piece of paper: this is what it is to write. To write is to assume the time of what is lost, assume the time of return, associate oneself with the return of the lost. Then emotion has the time to revive memory: memory has the time to come back; the word has the time to be found again; origin has the time to destroy again; the face rediscovers a countenance.

Anthologies

The Oxford Book of French Verse, chosen by the now-forgotten St John Lucas, was published in 1907. There was a second edition in 1925. By 1951, it had been reprinted fifteen times. This, my first anthology of French poetry, I purchased from the school's second-hand bookshop on 16 September 1958, the date I entered Modern Sixth Junior. (I checked this memory of purchase with Julian Barnes, who confirms it.) The book's previous owner, according to the name inserted in the date stamp above mine, was Champness—he did not give himself an initial, thus internalizing or ironizing or short-handing his name, since we boys were known to masters, sometimes even to each other, by our surnames. I have rarely opened this book in recent years but, seeing his name again, I remember his initials: J. H. Champness. I never spoke to him; nor am I interested enough in him or his destiny to check him out in Google or wherever, but how names do furnish a past. How the names of fellow pupils coalesce to resonate with a modicum of significance in the reconstruction of earlier versions of the poem, otherwise known as the self of an ageing man!

[Coda: Today, reading the *Guardian*, I find a death notice for John Champness of Lancaster, aged seventy-one, a couple of years older than me. Now I do google and find that this Champness wrote a history of Lancaster Castle. Do I really care if it is the same Champness? And yet the ontological poem enters another revision.]

The Oxford anthology itself is poorly edited—there are no table of contents and no proper index; only a list of poets identified by poem numbers, and, even more uselessly, a list of first lines identified again by poem numbers. No page references whatsoever, so this reader cannot make a swift comparison of the weights given to different poets and will have to turn the pages manually. Nor, like Champness, are the poets given initials, neither fore like gentlemen nor aft like players (arcane cricket reference making sense only to cricket lovers, and then only if they are cricket lovers over a certain age). We are not told if the poor introduction was written for the first edition or the second. Only one remark in it can be said to offer food for thought: 'No man of genius was less of an innovator than Corneille, except, perhaps, Dryden.' However, credit is where credit is due—the editor draws our attention to the significant fact that a major influence on all the Romantic poets (including the English ones—AR) was François-René Chateaubriand of whom Alain Robbe-Grillet writes in *Préface à une vie d'écrivain* that when Chateaubriand lies he lies in good faith. However, although, in the words of Claude Vigée, 'the first great French poetry since

Racine's plays more than a hundred years earlier was written by Chateau-briand and it was in prose,' typically, all we get is a single and feeble poem.

Returning to the weight of my muttons—there are twenty-six pages of Lamartine, twenty-nine of Vigny, forty-one of Hugo, forty of de Musset. Totalling more than twenty-five per cent of the entire book—and, perhaps you can guess where this is leading: two pages of Nerval, ten of Baudelaire, five of Verlaine, five of Mallarmé, five of Rimbaud, one of Corbière and three of Laforgue. The subtitle of the anthology is laughable ('thirteenth century–twentieth century'), considering the last and most 'modern' poet included is Charles Guerin, a minor and unreadable symbolist, who was born in 1873 and died in 1907. I shall not insult the reader's intelligence by pointing out more than one poet—let's say Apollinaire—whom a half-way alert and qualified editor could have included even as early as 1925 (the equivalent would be to omit Thomas Hardy from an English anthology that year), but I shall not blame St John Lucas. Clearly Oxford University Press was going through one of its bad phases, keeping a book in print that was already inadequate in the year of the first edition, 1907, rather than commissioning a successor volume.

The next anthology I bought was *La Poésie française*, a 'panorama critique' of the new French poets written and edited by the late Jean Rousselot. About fifty of the more than three hundred poets he discusses are listed on the cover, ending alphabetically with Claude Vigée who, however, has been included in a section of Christian poets, which suggests Rousselot had not read his work very carefully. The anthology, which went through a number of editions, is cognate with the uneven *Poètes d'aujourdhui* series from the same publisher, Seghers, and reflects that unevenness. I bought it in Paris in 1961. Vigée was forty at the time and his first book had been published by Camus at Gallimard five years earlier. Eight years later he would become a friend of mine, thanks to Yves Bonnefoy's address book, produced as always when I was travelling, in this case to Jerusalem. Rousselot was a schematic, old-fashioned and somewhat superficial critic. But if you reckon up the poets, nobody is missing, to misquote John Berryman. Claude tells me that this civil servant (as he is described in biographical notes) was a police inspector, which immediately makes him more interesting.

By the early 1970s, I felt ready to edit my own anthology of twentieth-century French poetry, which was published as a special issue of *MPT* and has already been alluded to. I looked at a number of existing anthologies, as you do, two of which were by the pioneering Rimbaud scholar, C. A. Hackett of Southampton University, a friend of F. T. Prince. I cannot lay my hands on his first volume, but it certainly ended with Yves Bonnefoy (born 1923) and André du Bouchet (born 1924), since his *New French Poetry* begins with Robert Marteau, born two years later. My intent was more polemical than his: I wanted to establish a teleological line from my earliest poets such as Jabès to Royet-Journoud and company. Sam Hackett chose the poets he liked best. His notes on them are first class, reflecting close reading and serious thought, as well as personal involvement with France and the poets themselves. Fifteen of his twenty-two poets are in my much larger collection, reflecting an overlap of taste, as you would expect with a man who wrote four books on Rimbaud, the first of which was published in 1938.

Fats Waller, in 'A Porter's Love Song for a Chambermaid', tells us he is 'the happiest of troubadours'. Here are two excellent anthologies of the time/place/language where all the ladders of Western poetry start: Occitania or Oc. First, the superb Occitan/French bilingual *Les Troubadours* edited by Jacques Roubaud, a poet whose range and depth of scholarship equals that of our mutual friend Deguy. Here, for reasons he gives in his introduction, it is essential to have the two languages, close cousins (like Yiddish and German, I would say), face to face. One has the impression of understanding Langue d'oc, thanks to Roubaud's labours in producing a kind of syncretic verse/prose paragraph as the translation of a stanza. One of the poems which is in Roubaud's anthology and also in Alan Press' *Anthology of Troubadour Lyric Poetry* is by Bertrand de Born, a contemporary of Marie de France, the twelfth-century French poet on whom Paula's university-professor cousin Ana is an expert. Ana spent a sabbatical at All Souls College in 2007 and worked on original manuscripts in the Bodleian. An extract from de Born's work is used by an early translator, Ezra Pound, as an epigraph for his crucial poem, 'Near Perigord'. There is a famous image by Doré in which de Born is carrying his own head (*Inferno*, Canto XXVIII), a posthumous misfortune caused by his love of war albeit, as he saw it, in a good cause, that of Aquitaine.

Si tuit li dol e.lh plor e.lh marrimen
E las dolors e.lh dan e.lh chaitivier
Qu'om anc auzis en est segle dolen
Fossen ensems, sembleran tot leugier
Contra la mort del jove rei engles,
Don rema Pretz e Jovens doloros,
E.I. mons oscurs e teintz e tenebros,
Sems de tot joi, ples de tristor e d'ira.

If all the grief, the tears, the distress, the suffering, the pain and the misery which one had ever heard of in this grievous life were put together, they would all seem slight compared with the death of the young English king, for which Merit and Youth are left grieving, and the world dark and sombre and gloomy, empty of all joy, full of sadness and sorrow.

Si tous les deuils et les pleurs et les malheurs et les douleurs et les
pleurs et les misères qu'a connu ce monde douloureux étaient
mis ensemble ils sembleraient légers devant la mort du jeune roi
anglais dont restent prix et jeunesse douloureux le monde
obscur éteint et ténébreux privé de joie plein de tristesse et de peine

Later, I acquired more specialized or narrowly focused anthologies, including the fourth edition (1958) of the huge *Poètes de la NRF*, with a preface by Paul Valéry. Nowhere are we told when the first edition appeared. My inscription tells me I bought this in Cambridge in 1963, after I had abandoned modern languages for social anthropology: I was anticipating my long parallel life of day jobs and literary activities, the latter with France as its centre. Here is *Mille Neuf Cent Quarante Quatre*, published twenty years later in 1964 as a memorial to the clandestine publishing activities of Les Editions de Minuit during the French Resistance. Poems by Jacques Destaing (Louis Aragon), Roland Mars (Francis Ponge), Benjamin Phélisse (André Frénaud), Maurice Hervent (Paul Eluard) and Serpières (Eugène Guillevic) are contained in *L'Honneur des poètes* on 14 July 1943, 'a day of oppressed liberty' and, on another significant date, 1 May 1944, in that important quarterly, *Europe*: Isaac Lacquedem (Benjamin Fondane, the *nom de guerre* being one of the names of the wandering Jew), Jean Noir (Jean Cassou), Hugo

Vic (Michel Leiris) and the only woman, Anne (Edith Thomas). One recognizes some contributors from their poems, for example Guillevic:

The wine ration
He allows himself
Is not enough
In the bitter days.

His wine ration—
Ah! we know who rules.

Death counts for nothing,
Wine not yet.

The eloquent Aragon, in his 1964 introduction, writes:

Let us remember (and a fig for the Nazis!) that for there to be a Europe, it was necessary that Goethe and Schiller were citizens of the French Revolution, that Byron and Shelley like Manzoni spoke our language of liberty, that Petofi sang like Rouget de Lisle; let us remember that from Pushkin to Mayakovski, without whom the Europe of poetry is amputated, the same heart beats as in French poetry from Agrippa d'Aubigné to Victor Hugo; let us remember that the same monster killed Federico Garcia Lorca, Saint Paul Roux the Magnificent and Max Jacob; let us remember that France, Europe and poetry are indivisible and bonded in the same blood.

A Visit to Paris

The official reason for the trip, in 2006, was an English Faculty conference on poetry translation at Paris 3 Sorbonne nouvelle. My role was to engage in a dialogue with Claude Vigée on his Eliot translations and my Vigée translations. Off I went to the Eurostar with books in my bag, since you must never go anywhere without reading matter. Yes, I knew I would be buying books in Paris, some already listed in my new notebook, others to be discovered in favourite bookshops. But what if the train were to break down? Heaven forbid that I risk sitting there and introspecting or entering into a reverie. Looking out of the window! (extrospecting, Keith Douglas might have said), yes, but what is there to look at if the train stops in the Channel Tunnel? I settled down with *The White Cities*, Joseph Roth's atmospheric reports from France, having read all his novels over the years: '[Arles] basks in the sun like an evening, mossed with the green of many memories' (cf. Jules Renard's *Journal*: 'the green waters of memory'). To celebrate Roth, I shall have a drink in one of his haunts, the Café de Tournon.

Sensible visitors to the city always boycott the overpriced standard-issue hotel breakfasts. Next morning, I went out in search of a decent place. Sure enough, for less than half the price of the two-star hotel offering, I found an old-fashioned cafe near Saint-Sulpice serving good orange juice, delicious coffee, a fresh croissant and a tartine with jam and butter. As usual, I popped into the great church (favoured by Simone Weil) to take a look at Delacroix's mural of Jacob and the Angel. Gauguin, well acquainted with Delacroix's work, surely did the same before embarking on his revolutionary painting, *The Vision of the Sermon*. Now I was all set up, like the victim of a plot, although in this case the plot was to follow the trail and, entering the present tense more favoured by the French, if you follow me or if you were following me, we begin at the Foyles of Paris, Joseph Gibert on Boul' Mich, but only to buy a square-ruled notebook from the *papeterie* department, before heading, where else?, to La Hune on boulevard Saint-Germain by the Deux-Magots and L'Ecume des Pages next door.

I ask for two important books I'd read about in *Le Monde des livres*: I am so behind with my reading, to coin a phrase, that I no longer phone Grant and Cutler in Great Marlborough Street to place orders for new French books. The first was Paul Celan's *Correspondance*—with his close friend and lover in Israel, Ilana Shmueli. I looked through it that evening, my hands atremble with the anticipation of excited reverie, which always accompanies the first encounter with a new book by one of the handful of writers about or by whom I must read everything. 'Ich trinke Wein aus Zwei Gläsern' catches my eye, the line of Celan that supplied the title for the published version of my Adam Lecture at Kings College London, *Wine from Two Glasses*, some years ago. In a letter to Siefried Unseld, Celan wrote: 'my poems are not ciphers, they are language.' In a letter to Ilana, he explains that 'Jener' (the Other) refers to Hölderlin, a rare example of self-exegesis on the part of this poet who, Michael Hamburger always insisted, is difficult rather than hermetic. The notes, prepared by the translator Bertrand Badiou, are impeccable. When Celan went to Israel on his one and only visit, he was, Hamburger wrote to me, 'at his wit's end, desperate and ill—mainly because his marriage to Gisele . . . had broken down. That marriage had been his matrix and anchor. I experienced his paranoia in later years—directed at me because of a book review I did not write, as I told him repeatedly'. Yves Bonnefoy already has the book. Claude Vigée, who knew Ilana in Israel, is about to buy it.

My second request in La Hune is Gérard Genette's *Bardadrac*. This is an alphabet book 'harvested', according to the preface, rather than 'made', and a treat in store for the train journey back to London. The preface alerts us to a book that is lighter in tone than the brilliant works of this author on rhetoric, diction, poetics and so on. It includes, Genette tells us, the following objects: 'contingent epiphanies, good or bad ideas, true and false memories, aesthetic points of view, geographical reveries, clandestine or apocryphal quotations, maxims . . .', etc. Alphabet books, like other compilations, are suspiciously easy to confect, but when the quality of the mind subscending the writing is that of a Genette or a Miłosz (for example, the latter's *ABC*, in which he compares Rimbaud in Africa to Conrad's Kurtz, an appealing thought), all doubts and unease melt into air. As with Miłosz, Genette has found a way of writing personally, autobiographically if you like. This suggests that elsewhere the French critic writes impersonally, which he doesn't, although naturally one learns more about Miłosz from his poetry than about Genette from his criticism (see, for example, Genette's afterword to Robbe-Grillet's *Dans le labyrinthe*). Bardadrac is a treasure chest, a rattle bag, a cornucopia. The word 'impersonal' is stupid in this context. No writer is impersonal, except as a rule of the game: Levi in *If This Is a Man* explicitly affecting scientific experiment; Marianne Moore; Reznikoff. Here are two of Genette's items. They are inscribed in an old and recognizable French tradition.

'Port'

Traditionally, sailors have a woman in every port. The truth is, rather, that every man, sailor or not, seeks a port in every woman.

'Scorn'

Be economical with your scorn. Few people are worthy of it.

Other short texts are twenty-five Perecian 'I remember's. As Genette says, everybody's doing it. Perec via Joe Brainard inaugurated a *genre* taken up by myself, and Genette has a lot of fun remembering things, which, as he says, one had never forgotten only collected or harvested through an act of conscious and organized anamnesia. Involuntary it is not. After about one hundred and fifty memories, he ends: 'I shall remember dying: I have made a knot in my handkerchief.'

I spot three more books in La Hune, two about a writer who means much to me, the third by a writer Mike Heller recommended I should read. The first is Levinas, and the books are *Méditations érotiques* by Marc-Alain Ouaknin and *Entretiens avec Emmanuel Levinas* by Michael de Saint-Cheron, where the intellectual dialogue between Malraux and Levinas is discussed. There has been no Jewish thinker of such distinction in the UK, and by Jewish thinker I mean someone who engages in Jewish religious and philosophical thought within the context of the wider culture, not merely a thinker who happens to be Jewish. It is one reason why I am in this country, in this bookshop, buying this book. The other author is Giorgio Agamben, and the book *Profanations*. I open it at random and find a chiasmus, a rhetorical trope often over-valued and often under-earned, but not in this instance—'to communicate one's imagined desires and one's desired images is the most arduous task of all.' When I read this out to Alan Wall he said it was not an example, then changed his mind when I expressed disappointment and attempted to mollify me. 'It's a very mild chiasmus, just about a chiasmus, but you may be upbraided by expostulating rhetoricians'.

I left La Hune and went to L'Ecume des Pages close by, where I bought a book for Samuela, the little great-grandchild of Edmond Jabès and the daughter of Steven Jaron and Brigitte Crasson, at whose flat I am dining tonight. On to Librairie Gallimard in boulevard Raspail. I do not enter. I am not the man I was. I am not the buyer I was. Continue along Raspail, turning into boulevard Montparnasse, for Tschann. This too I pass. Zigzag east to the bookshop at the bottom of rue Mouffetard, where I find Pierre Assouline's *Rosebud*. These are biographical essays, including one on Celan and one on

Balzac and his *Chef d'oeuvre inconnu*, and one on Orson Welles, whose cinematic masterpiece Assouline considers to be 'the matrix of modern biography', a strong, even reckless, statement.

Before the conference, I installed myself in a cafe opposite Notre Dame—having popped into Shakespeare and Company for an atmosphere fix which lasted all of thirty seconds, surely my last visit—and wrote in French a brief statement on translation, not trusting myself to improvise. I find it enthralling to be in dialogue yet again with people who work from French to English, my opposite numbers indeed. 'Bottom, thou art translated,' cries Snug in *A Midsummer Night's Dream*, Paula's favourite Shakespeare play. Such a cruel play, Alberto de Lacerda told her. The conference is being held in a former dissecting theatre, enabling me to get an easy laugh by quoting Wordsworth: 'we murder to dissect.' After the round-table discussion between Vigée and myself chaired by Anne Mounic, a unique worker in terms of quantity while retaining quality, I move into the audience and sit next to Stephen Romer, who whispers to me that he is not in agreement with Claude's comments on Eliot and philosophy. We stay for the next event, a talk on Bonnefoy as translator of Keats and Leopardi. Someone catches my eye and hands me a note alleging a mistake in one of my translations of Vigée. I scribble back to him that I shall look into the matter and slip out to clear my head before dining with the Bonnefoys in the Chinese restaurant across the road from their flat in rue Lepic. Yves always orders the same things, just as my son Nathaniel always had numbers 29a and 46b from the Chinese takeaway in North Finchley.

Jewish Worlds

Whenever I have to go abroad for a short time, I put two books in my bag. One, a work of Kafka, and the other, chapters of the mystics or a Hasidic text.

> —Aharon Appelfeld, *A Table for One: Under the Light of Jerusalem*

A cage went in search of a bird

> —Franz Kafka, *Reflections*

For me, especially in a poem, Jewishness is sometimes not so much a *thematic* as a *pneumatic* concern.

> —Paul Celan, in John Felstiner's *Paul Celan: Poet, Survivor, Jew*

Introduction

Many of my Jewish books are in the classic Globe Wernicke bookcase between the two windows in the sitting room, where I used to work. In the days when books did furnish a room, such handsome stackable mahogany bookcases with sliding glass fronts were *furniture*, and the books were hardbacks. Those were the books, my friends. My parents had five or six Globe Wernicke units, and this is the sole survivor, eidetic evidence of childhood. It houses some of my Jewish books—memoirs, history, theology, fiction, biographies, anthologies, literary criticism and so on. I also keep here, propped up against books behind the glass, a few treasures not on my dedicated treasure shelf elsewhere in the room: an old-style penny dated 1862 (you could buy a 'flying saucer' sherbet lemon in rice paper for a penny when I was a child and you always hoped the penny was dated 1933—worth a fortune because so few were struck); a bus ticket the conductor would clip and ping in the days before Gibson machines; and a Dutch yellow star the late Rabbi Michael Goulston gave me. You can tell it is Dutch because the word *Jood* is printed on it. What's more, the letters look like Hebrew script. This, according to the Jewish Historical Museum in Amsterdam, was a sick and vicious Nazi joke rather than an act of defiance by Jews ordered to prepare yellow stars for their own use. Goulston was given it by our mutual friend Johan Polack, the gay publisher and bookseller in Amsterdam, who had been in the same class as Anne Frank at school and survived the occupation in hiding because he had rich parents. He always admitted this and later used his wealth to publish serious Jewish literature and the magazine *European Judaism* as a small return for his privileged situation. Dear Johan, he turned up, wearing his eternal hypochondriac's scarf, with his 'nephew' at the bar mitzvah of one of the Goulston boys. After a few drinks, the status of the nephew changed several times. Everybody knew the score and nobody minded. On display too are the menus from my bar mitzvah celebration in 1955, from my son's in 1987, and from my daughter's bat mitzvah in 1989, all signed by the guests.

It is time to find out what story, personal to me, is told by the hundreds of Jewish books awaiting my attention. Perhaps the story is the search for the story. 'Jewish' is a different kind of category, synthetic rather than analytic, from the classic subject matters of this book such as cinema, social anthropology and music, but the wind bloweth as it listeth, the point of view shifts when it must, and that is the only way this text can play. The subsections overlap to some extent, and so do the sections. There was no way they could not, as you will discover.

The psychotherapist Eugene Heimler was a close friend of mine but, as with another touchy and powerful personality, Jon Silkin, I would sometimes get the impression we were having a quarrel even when we weren't, and I would back off for a few weeks or even months, only to return to the fray when feeling less frayed. I always had a problem with uncle figures and older brother figures (avoiding the 'f' word here), all the more so with a camp survivor who had plans for me. According to Heimler's German-born widow and third wife, Birgitta (now a deeply devout ultra-orthodox Jerusalemite known as Miriam), there is to be a memorial plaque to Eugene (also known as John and Jansci) on their house in the main square of his hometown, Szombathely. This, it turns out, will be a few yards from a plaque to Rudolf Virág, who was also born in Szombathely. He, I remind you, is the father of Leopold Bloom, a more marginal Jew than Heimler. Another character in *Ulysses*, Moses Herzog (better known as the eponymous hero of Bellow's novel), has his own plaque on a house in Dublin, which I found while on a trail there, Jewish or literary, I forget. Heimler's memoir of Auschwitz, *Night of the Mist*, is a classic. A pioneer in the two worlds conjured up by the title of his book, *Mental Health and Social Work*, he founded the movement known as Human Social Functioning, essentially a rapid-fire technique for documenting and analysing people's feelings and needs without extended therapy. I attended a training course and became the editor of the movement's newsletter for a short period.

Human Social Functioning is designed for use in situations (e.g. prisons) where there are large numbers of people and restricted resources, including the time of therapists, although for many of the inmates time, if not of the essence, is of the existence. 'Do not ask why pain / Only what is to be done with it', Heimler wrote in his verse play *The Storm*, which I translated with him and published at Menard Press. These words are on his tombstone, very close to those of my friends Felek Scharf, Jakov Lind and Nina Farhi, as well as Rabbis Albert Friedlander, Michael Goulston and Hugo Gryn, in Hoop Lane Jewish cemetery, across the road from the famous crematorium. Visit this cemetery next time you go to a cremation in Hoop Lane. You will see vertical tombstones on the left, horizontal ones on the right. This is because the right-hand side houses a Sephardi (Spanish and Portuguese) cemetery and the left-hand side an Ashkenazi one, with their different traditions.

Heimler was the unofficial rabbi to Goulston, whose last words at the age of forty were spoken to Heimler in hospital; Goulston weighed four stone. I have often wondered what Michael said, but Heimler would never tell me. The celebrated Rabbi of Kotzk (the Kotzker Rebbe) is said to have gone silent for years. Legend has it that he had lost his faith. Unwilling to lie or tell the truth, he kept silent, not unlike the rabbi in a camp who was asked by a man in extremis what he should do after a Nazi officer had said he must decide which of his two sons shall be handed over and murdered. Although we are not told that this rabbi lost his faith, nothing in the tradition could generate an answer to the Nazi officer's question. Nothing in any religious tradition could. This tells us a lot about Nazism and about religions. As Jean Améry rightly says in *At the Mind's Limits*, the essence of Nazism was torture, physical and mental, predicated upon absolute power over the victims, which is close to the behavioural definition of evil proposed by Paul Oppenheimer in his book *Evil and the Demonic*. Had Michael Goulston, like the Kotzker Rebbe, lost his faith? Michael loved associating with secular or irreligious Jews like Silkin, who in turn found this deeply sympathetic man a source of information and understanding and a symbolic presence of community, if not faith. At Goulston's funeral, I vividly remember Rabbi Lionel Blue saying during his eulogy that there was someone in the congregation who should study for the rabbinate and take Michael's place, and he looked hard at me. But it was not to be, and could never be. After Goulston died in 1972, I was appointed managing editor of *European Judaism*, having been literary editor for two years. This lasted for three years, during which time I published texts by Jabès, Derrida, Starobinski and other European masters. Then there was a quarrel involving my role, as a result of which the editorial board and I parted company.

On one occasion I accompanied editorial colleagues to Paris for a conference with the editors of *Nouveaux Cahiers* and for one of the colloquiums that were a feature of our magazine. Paul Auster and I served as interpreters and translators. Emmanuel Levinas came to the non-kosher dinner after the meeting but did not eat, thus honouring us by turning up, and honouring himself by not compromising his religious practice. During the visit, I met people whose books I had read—Albert Memmi, Robert Misrahi, Roger Ikor, Richard Marienstras and Arnold Mandel. There was also Manès Sperber, that old Jewish radical and unbeliever from a Hasidic *shtetl* in my ancestral patch of East Galicia, ten years younger than Joseph Roth and an exact contemporary of Elias Canetti. Sperber, a friend of Malraux, Koestler and other senior figures in the ex-communist intelligentsia, was editorial director at Calmann-Levy, where I visited him in an office above a small shop in a Benjaminian arcade near the Opera. His three-volume autobiography *All Our Yesterdays* is the work of a powerful intelligence (as befits a close collaborator of Alfred Adler) and a valuable contribution to our understanding of the background to the vanished geo-intellectual world of Freud and Zweig, ranging from the shtetl, via Berlin and Vienna, to Paris. He also wrote a fiction trilogy, *Like a Tear in the Ocean*. I read them in the Wiener Library while working on material about the Holocaust; they do not measure up to his memoirs.

Writings of the Disaster

Memoirs, etc.

Let me begin with a book I have presented to my old friend Richard Berengarten. I bought it at the Jewish Community Centre in Belgrade in 1972, en route to the Struga Poetry Festival in Macedonia. Edited by Zdenko Löwenthal, and better known as the *Black Book*, its full title is *The Crimes of the Fascist Occupants and Their Collaborators against Jews in Yugoslavia*. Richard lived and taught in Belgrade from 1987 till 1990, and went native, later becoming deeply involved in polemics about Serbia. One of his best poems is 'The Blue Butterfly', which draws on the wartime experiences of Jews and others in occupied Yugoslavia. The German army and their collaborationist allies in the Yugoslav federated countries played their part in the final solution, murdering or deporting eighty per cent of the country's Jews. The *Black Book*, which Berengarten had read in a library, was a key source for his poem, and my copy belongs on his shelves, mute witness to atrocity, one more reminder of our responsibility to fight all varieties of fascism and to be on guard against symptoms of dictatorship in our imperfect democracies.

I also gave Richard *Destruction and Survival* by Charles W. Steckel, containing detailed information about the destiny of Jewish communities in Yugoslavia during the war. In turn, he sent me Cadik Danon Braco's *The Smell of Human Flesh*, the most gruesome and cruel book I have ever read, and there is plenty of competition. It is an account of the Bosnian Jewish author's time spent in the infamous Croatian Ustashi concentration camp at

Jasenovac. 'Don't read this unless you're feeling strong,' wrote Richard. I ignored his well-intentioned remark. My sense is that if someone has had the courage to write such an account, we owe it to those who were tortured and murdered for their ethnicity or religion by psychopaths and gangsters unleashed by fascist ideologues to read about their torment, whatever state of mind we are in. To ignore them is to allow them to die a second death, still in despair, still alone. To read about them is to accompany them on a different and better journey, a journey which implicitly connotes a promise that we shall seek to build a world in which such behaviour will have become impossible.

One of the strangest books on my shelf is *Shivitti: A Vision*, signed 'To Tony by Y. Denur', upside down on the inside back cover because the author forgot it was the English-language edition and not the original Hebrew which, as you know, reads from right to left. Yehiel de-Nur was the Israeli Hebrew name adopted by the Polish-born writer Yehiel Feiner, who wrote under the name of, indeed was reborn as, Ka-Tzetnik 135633, his number in Auschwitz, a literal pen-name tattooed on his arm at the camp, where he had survived being eyeballed by Josef Mengele himself, the SS officer and doctor who specialized in selections and experiments on human beings. The author of *Shivitti* wrote at least one international bestseller, *House of Dolls*, about his sister's experience in an SS brothel, as well as later books such as *Sunrise over Hell* and *Star Eternal*. Apart from his appearance at the Eichmann trial (which I discuss later), he was the most secretive of men, and did not even turn up in Jerusalem for the inaugural award of the literary prize he endowed, which was awarded to Aharon Appelfeld. When in Tel-Aviv I would visit KZ at his modest apartment in the north of the city, and we would also meet in London.

His memoir's title, *Shivitti*, taken from psalm number sixteen, which was also important for Paul Celan, means 'I have set . . .': I have set before you a vision. He describes his treatment for nightmares by a controversial Dutch psychiatrist, Professor Jan Bastiaans of Leiden University, whose specialized therapy involved controlled doses of LSD. I remember, as a child on holiday in Holland, that above the university gates are the Latin words for 'abandon all hope ye who enter here', the inscription at the entrance to Dante's hell. I wonder now if this was some kind of scholarly joke at a university which (like Edinburgh University, its exact contemporary, whose postgraduate students had to study at Leiden) was founded in the late sixteenth century without a chapel, a bastion of tolerance fit for a man like Baruch Spinoza. Yehiel Denur relived his Auschwitz horrors in the care and company of Jan Bastiaans, returning freer than when he entered the therapy. He was no longer plagued by nightmares. More this Jewish Orpheus could not ask. But when he died he weighed, his daughter told me, thirty kilos. The survivors I have been privileged to know: Primo Levi, Ka-Tzetnik 135633, Piotr Rawicz, Aharon Appelfeld, Dan Pagis, Eugene Heimler, Ana Novac (whose French plays I translated), Elie Wiesel, Jean Samuel (Primo Levi's Pikolo), Rudi Kennedy and others inspire in me a sense of awe. They were/are glamorous in the proper sense of the word, and it is all I can do not to become completely obsessed with the world that they succeeded in telling and therefore, in one sense, defeating. That Levi and Rawicz and, in slow motion, Ka-Tzetnik 135633 killed themselves, only reinforces the sense of courage and lucidity one associates with the great writers of the Shoah.

Miriam Peleg-Marianska and Mordecai Peleg's *Witnesses* and Adina Blady Szwajger's *I Remember Nothing More: The Warsaw Children's Hospital and the Jewish Resistance* are particularly powerful books. Blady Szwajger, a medical student, tended children in circumstances almost as dire as those of the starving doctors conducting experiments while tending the starving. Piotr Rawicz, in his novel *Blood from the Sky*, wrote a scene set in a ghetto based on his native Lvov: '. . . a nurse armed with a syringe. Several mutilated children were still suffering. The nurse went around distributing death, like portions of gingerbread stuffed with darkness.' This was one of Blady Szwajger's responsibilities. *Witnesses* is a fascinating account of a Jewish couple who were able to work in the Polish underground because they didn't 'look Jewish'. Revisiting the testimonies I read and wrote about years ago is having the effect, at last, of reconfiguring my default setting, which is to obsess about persecution and resistance, especially in Poland and Ukraine, where members of my family who had not left for Britain, the USA or British mandate Palestine (later Israel) were murdered. I need to spend more time looking to the future, for example by keeping tabs on the implications of government policies towards minorities in countries that elect their governments. As Rabbi Abraham Joshua Heschel, who practised what he preached, wrote: 'In a democracy, some are guilty, but all are responsible.'

Last Letters from Stalingrad is a deeply sad book. These letters were never delivered to the soldiers' loved ones, since the German High Command impounded them in order to research morale on the most important front line of all. Joseph Goebbels said of the letters that they were 'untragbar', unacceptable or—a stronger word—unbearable, which was also said of the Jews. Unbearable and therefore to be suppressed. The letters are often unbearable to read. James Schevill's fine book of poems *Stalingrad Elegies* draws on them.

Reflections

Pierre Vidal-Naquet's *Assassins of Memory: Essays on the Denial of the Holocaust* raises important questions. In the title essay, he insists that many aspects of the past, including genocides and lesser massacres, 'are part of our culture, not of our memory'. *At the Mind's Limits* by Jean Améry was already a classic when Primo Levi devoted a chapter of *The Drowned and the Saved* to engaging with the shade and arguments of this exceptional individual. The importance of Améry's testimony derives from his stringent perspective and passionate argumentation, which in turn derive from his status as a German-language intellectual and radical, a man who was not only tortured by the Nazis but also worried away about the nature and implications of totalitarianism. I remain haunted by his recollection in Auschwitz of Hölderlin's poem 'The Half of Life', when he had no one to share his recollection with. Max Sebald's essay on Améry, in *On the Natural History of Destruction*, deals sensitively, as we would expect, with the anguish of memory in the heart and mind of the writer. It was as if 'every fragment of memory touched a sore point'. Sebald reminds us of the extraordinary example of irony with which Améry concludes the 'curiously objective' description of his torture (he was hung by his arms from a hook until they were dislocated) in *At the Mind's Limits*: 'Torture, from Latin *torquere*, to twist. What visual instruction in etymology!' It is impossible not to think of Torquemada, given that observation.

91

Sebald argues that Améry's restraint enables him to put forward his theory that torture is not an optional or marginal extra but at the very heart of totalitarianism. Améry believed in resistance not because it might be effective but out of solidarity with the victims of aggression. In the end, he agreed with Emile Cioran that the ability to continue living is made possible only 'by the deficiencies of our imagination and our memory'. Sebald's essay 'Between History and Natural History' in *Campo Santo* is an early working out of the ideas in *On the Natural History of Destruction*. There is a fascinating note (whether by Sebald or by the book's editor is not clear) about my old mentor and Menard author, Lord Zuckerman. The note refers to Zuckerman's autobiography *From Apes to Warlords*, in which the author discusses the uselessness of carpet or 'area' bombings on civilian targets, whether in Germany or Vietnam, and how it does not break the spirit of people. During the war, when Solly Zuckerman was on Eisenhower's staff, he wanted to write an article entitled 'The Natural History of Destruction' for Cyril Connolly's *Horizon*, but it never happened. Irène Heidelberger-Leonard discusses Levi and Améry in her biography of Améry, *The Philosopher of Auschwitz*. The discussion is not entirely satisfactory partly because the only biography of Levi she has read is Myriam Anissimov's flawed *Tragedy of an Optimist*, and in general she does not take enough issue with Améry. But she explores his life thoroughly and sheds light on his day jobs such as journalism, his influences (notably Sartre), his Jewishness and his thoughts on *ressentiment*, torture and 'self-murder'. When Améry writes 'the limits of my body are the limits of myself', he is glossing Wittgenstein out of the depths of personal experience.

A particularly troubling book is Caleb Perechodnik's *Am I a Murderer?* This is the testament of a Jewish ghetto policeman in Otwock near Warsaw. Such policemen were the ghetto equivalent of being a Jewish kapo in the camps. In Jacob Neusner's *Understanding Jewish Theology*, Emil Fackenheim discusses one of the diabolical antisemitic policies of the Nazis which worked against even the minimal efficiency of having the strongest Jews survive long enough to provide work fodder before they died: two work permits would be supplied to each family. One was for the able-bodied man to whom they gave it; the other was in the gift of the man himself, thus forcing him to select who shall live and who shall die. This dilemma would be institutionalized in the Jewish Councils, the Judenrats, about which Primo Levi wrote with such depth and understanding in *Moments of Reprieve* and elsewhere. Here are Elie Cohen's *Human Behaviour in the Concentration Camp*, Otto Friedrich's *The Kingdom of Auschwitz* (Ka-Tzetnik 135633 saw it as another planet) and Terrence Des Pres's *The Survivor*. How many books can one read in this (killing) field without going numb? Why does one put oneself through it? For me, that question is now in the past tense. These days, as already suggested and as will emerge elsewhere in this book, I am more concerned with what happens next, what lessons are to be learnt from the catastrophe.

An exemplary cultural history, *Prisoners of Hope: The Silver Age of the Italian Jews, 1924–1974* by H. Stuart Hughes discusses Svevo, Moravia, Bassani, Ginzburg and the two Levis, Primo and Carlo (brother-in-law of Primo's mother's cousin). I read Carlo Levi's *Christ Stopped at Eboli* in my teens, long before I had heard of Primo Levi. This study of oppressed people made a great impression and the theme remains a permanent component of my world historical view. Dan Bar-On's *Fear and Hope* investigates the three-generation phenomenon as manifested in Israel. Survivors of camps and ghettos were notoriously and understandably buttoned-up. They did not speak about their experiences to their children, who grew up either in ignorance of what their parents went through or sensing a dark secret in an atmosphere of repression and suffering. In many cases, however, this changed when the grandchildren came along: now the youngsters asked their parents about 'over there' and 'the hitlerite beast' (common phrases at the time and used by David Grossman in *See Under: Love*, which I discuss later), partly because that is what children do when not discouraged and partly because the mood and, reflecting this, educational policy in the country, changed after the Six Day War. Suddenly diaspora history and life were not something to be ashamed of, something to be bracketed between the end of Jewish sovereignty two thousand years ago and its rebirth in 1948. Teachers encouraged young students to find and adopt and tell the story of a survivor. Lo and behold, some of the children had one in their own family.

Primo Levi and Jakov Lind

In many respects, Primo Levi is the writer who has touched me most deeply; certainly he is *primus inter pares*. *If This Is a Man* is a noble and luminous book, a supreme masterpiece on the topic which, for many years, preoccupied me more than any other. He combined his productive writing life with a demanding non-literary day job (as a top industrial chemist). He is the source of my greatest pride as a publisher, for Menard brought out his earlier collected poems, *Shema*, in English, the first book-length translation of his verse into any language. That was back in 1976. When, a decade or so later, *Shema* went out of print, I knew it was in his best interests as a poet to move on to a big publisher. I recall a telephone conversation with the then poetry editor at Faber and Faber, Craig Raine, who said they couldn't do it, since the policy originally implemented by Eliot was only to publish translations by poets already on their list (e.g. Eliot's own version of Saint-John Perse). But I persuaded Raine—or he persuaded himself (and his colleagues)—that this was ridiculous in the case of Levi. It was reissued with the title *Collected Poems*, first as published by Menard, and later in an expanded version.

Levi took up a good and robust position on Israel, which got him into hot water in America: audiences were not used to a Jewish writer who was neither religious on the one hand nor uncritically pro-Israel on the other. In 1986, he came to London where I interviewed him in public at the Jewish cultural centre in Hendon, Yakar. Another evening I took him and his wife to dinner at Daphne's in Camden Town where he said he had not enjoyed himself so much for a very long time. After he returned home, we corresponded for about a year, as we had, around ten years earlier, when I published his poetry. In April 1987 he killed himself. Rabbi Artom of Turin gave a classic ruling that the writer's suicide was 'delayed homicide', which meant it was permitted to bury him in consecrated ground. The following year I found myself, all nerves, on a television book programme chaired by Jill Neville and on Radio Three's *Night Waves*, discussing *The Drowned and the Saved*, the remarkable sequel, forty years on, to *If This Is a Man*.

Here are his books in English, many of which I reviewed, as well as the Italian original of his collected poems, *Ad ora incerta* (with a cherished dedication: 'A Tony Rudolf, con amicizia e riconoscenza'), and the French edition with a preface by Jorge Semprun. Here too is Simon Wiesenthal's *The Sunflower*, an exploration of his dilemma faced with a dying Nazi who wanted to confess terrible crimes to him: the book is completed by the comments of several writers including Levi. Jacques Presser's account of Westerbork transit camp in Holland, *The Night of the Girondists*, is introduced by Levi: 'A debatable book, then, maybe a scandalous one; but it is good that scandals should come, for they provoke discussion and make for inner clarity.' Levi's two British biographers, Carol Angier and Ian Thomson, both learnt Italian and spent ten years doing the research, which included picking my brains in the days, long ago, when I counted as a UK expert on Levi and wrote a short book on him. I have been asked several times which of the three biographies to read. My advice: avoid the French one, read Thomson's if you want an account where the biographer keeps himself at a distance from the story, read Angier's if you are curious to read a biography where the author is explicitly part of the story. I am grateful for both books.

I published *The Stove*, a minor book by the Viennese-born Jakov Lind, who died a few days after his eightieth birthday. As I said in the eulogy I delivered at his funeral, he was a trickster, a bad boy like Kosinski and Rawicz, unlike Appelfeld and Levi. If you were to read Lind's neglected fiction—on my desk are two of his major novels, *Landscape in Concrete* and *Soul of Wood*—and autobiographies, you would obtain some idea as to what kind of teenager he was and how his daring and self-confidence (linked to his sexual precocity) helped him survive in the open, as a Dutch sailor or bargee in Germany, having left Holland because, as he explained to me, you were safer inside the mouth of the monster than between the teeth. Tom Maschler of Jonathan Cape told me that Lind was one of those writers you have to publish even if they make a loss, because they honour the house. This approach, sadly, is no longer possible. I shall spare you the riff on the book trade.

Michel Borwicz

In a number of writings, I have touched on the Jewish presence in the underground and armed Resistance movements, where they were not always welcome, for reasons to do with why the Final Solution took place where it did. A controversial book in its day was Reuben Ainsztein's *Jewish Resistance in Nazi-Occupied Eastern Europe.* I read too *They Fought Back*, accounts of Jewish resistance in the same part of Europe, edited by Yuri Suhl, and Lucien Steinberg's *Not as a Lamb*. The title of the latter alludes to a view (see, for example, Arendt and Bettelheim), which was widespread until the late 1960s, when these books came out (the historiography has progressed since then), that Jews in effect colluded in their own destruction and, rather than 'roar like young lions', were taken 'like lambs to the slaughter', to quote Jeremiah. One of Steinberg's lions is the writer Michel Borwicz. Like Primo Levi, who had been captured as a partisan rather than as a Jew, Borwicz owned up to being Jewish and was sent to the infamous Janowska camp (written about by Leon Weliczer Wells in an important testimony—*The Janowska Road*), rather than shot on the spot as a Polish partisan. But life in Janowska was, as they say, no picnic. Borwicz was brutally tortured and then hanged for some minor offence against mindless regulations: 'You will drink coffee with schnapps,' as a guard described the verdict.

En route to the scaffold, Borwicz remembers an anecdote about a public execution in the Middle Ages: at the same point in the proceedings, the condemned man, seeing his guards clear the path amidst the gaping throng, says to them: 'Take your time, gentlemen. The spectacle yonder cannot commence before I arrive.' I don't know about that poor devil, apocryphal or not, but in the case of Borwicz, the rope broke and he was not re-hanged. Thus was his life spared a second time. Officially, this was because, as in England, if the rope breaks (three times?), German law or custom said the condemned man should be spared. The commandant, on trial for his crimes twenty years later, tried to cite Borwicz, who later became a senior Resistance leader, as a witness for the defence. According to Borwicz's own essay, which serves as a prologue to his remarkable book, *Ecrits des condamnés à mort sour l'occupation nazie*, the rope did not break by accident but may well have been tampered with by someone (the prescient commandant?), who had his reasons to show mercy occasionally. The full story, already amazing enough, will never be known. For Borwicz, it was enough that, after the 'reprieve', he could continue with his Resistance work in the camp (helping people escape, etc.), albeit in the form of long-term planning, since it was advisable for him to lie low.

Jiri Weil

Jiri Weil's *Life with a Star* is a masterpiece of European literature. Like Rawicz's *Blood from the Sky*, it is 'a dazzling and profound novel, one of the great works in that category of Holocaust literature concerned with Jewish survival outside the camps in occupied territory', as I wrote in a review of the English translation. I drew attention to its irony and sardonic humour: 'They [yellow stars] were of high quality and cheap, a real bargain. Only one crown for a star made of fine pre-war material. In fact, they were practically giving them away.' And its haunting lyricism, in this extract from the section where he is working in the Jewish cemetery in Prague: 'whenever leaves touch the rake they change into words. And these words live, even after the bones of martyrs are scattered, even after their bodies change to dust and ashes.' A major theme, as in *Blood from the Sky*, concerns the actions of the local Judenrat. The controversial role of these Jewish Councils across Europe, which negotiated with the Germans and often did their dirty work for them, was not discussed by scholars and writers in a nuanced and objective way until long after Weil died in 1959. Strangely, Philip Roth's prefaces to *Life with a Star* and a later novel *Mendelssohn Is on the Roof* are identical. He summarizes the opening of *Mendelssohn*: 'An SS man has orders to remove the statue of the Jewish composer Mendelssohn from among the statues of musicians that ornament the roof of the Prague Academy of Music. Since he does not know which one is Mendelssohn, he decides to take down the one with the biggest nose. This turns out to be the statue of Wagner.'

Children

Understandably, people have wanted to contradict various discourses about Jewish behaviour (including one strand of pre-1967 Zionist propaganda, with its vested interest in portraying diaspora Jews as feeble and pacific), by demonstrating that 'we fought back'. Sadly, most often circumstances were such that you could not fight even if you wanted to. Resistance, however, does not have to be armed. I agree with Martin Gilbert against Lawrence Langer—whose *Holocaust Testimonies: The Ruins of Memory* is an important book about survivors but marred by a personalized attack on Gilbert—that there was such a thing as spiritual or inner resistance, and this, with the required modicum of luck, could keep you going against the odds although, in the end, it could not save my cousin Jerzyk (whose diary I discuss below).

An affecting and important work, and one which takes issue with what the author sees as the 'ideology' of Reuben Ainsztein and others who, by concentrating on armed Resistance, completely ignore the other kind as well as the lives and deaths of children in general (one and a half million were murdered), is Deborah Dwork's *Children with a Star*. I thought she should have made more allowances for the pioneering Ainsztein, as I pointed out to her in an otherwise complimentary letter. In *The King of Children*, Betty Jean Lifton tells the story of the world-famous educationist Janus Korcak, a hero of the Warsaw Ghetto, who went to his death with the orphans in his care, refusing all possibility of escape. Wajda's controversial film *Korcak* is essential viewing.

Criticism

A significant literary critic in the field of Jewish and Holocaust literature is James Young, whose books include *Writing and Rewriting the Holocaust*. This book put me onto the essential work of Hayden White and also got me thinking more seriously about video and photography, modalities of remembrance that Young has touched on at greater length in later books. He is the most generous of writers, and therefore kinder, even if implicitly, than I am to Yaffa Eliach (later in this section), for he sees the territory as sacred and cannot bear to make negative judgements. For the most part, however, he deals with masterpieces and writes with deep understanding of rhetorical strategies and narratological modes. Sidra DeKoven Ezrahi's *Booking Passage* contains crucial readings of canonical texts such as 'Written with a Pencil in a Sealed Wagon', the best-known poem by Dan Pagis. Along with Celan and Appelfeld, Pagis is one of the great Jewish writers of former Bukovina. Menard took over Stephen Mitchell's translations from Carcanet. The book was later expanded and published in the USA as *Points of Departure*. Pagis was not only a leading Hebrew poet, he was also a distinguished scholar in the field of mediaeval Hebrew poetry (*Hebrew Poetry of the Middle Ages and the Renaissance*) and yet he did not learn Hebrew until his teens! Here is the Pagis poem I translated with the help of the poet Miriam Neiger-Fleischmann:

'Written with a Pencil in the Sealed Wagon'
Here in this transport
I am Eve
With Abel my son
If you see my older son
Cain son of Adam
Tell him that I

Jonathan Wilson sees the poem as the apotheosis of an earlier one by Avraham Sutzkever, 'Written on the slat of a railway car', not included in Seymour Mayne's translation of the Yiddish poet's *Ghetto Poems*; there is also the poem by the émigré Russian poet Anatoly Steiger, who died in 1943:

We believe books and music,
We believe verse and dream,
We believe words . . . (Even when
They're said to us in consolation
From the window of a railway car) . . .
　　　　—Translated by John Glad

Gabriel Levin thinks that we are confronted by an unsurprising affinity of immensely resonant subject matter for the three poets rather than any question of influence of the two older poets on Pagis, whose poem has become the canonical one.

Diaries and letters

The Diary of Adam's Father is a long letter addressed to the brothers of Aryeh (Adam) Klonicki (Klonimus), in which Adam's father apologizes for writing in Hebrew rather than his first language Yiddish but predicts, rightly, that Hebrew will be more accessible in the future. He kept this diary in the West Ukrainian town of Buczacz for two weeks in July 1943, during the final phase of the ghetto. The book also contains documents about Adam, whom his father affectionately calls by the Yiddish term *bubele* (the boy was born on 8 July 1942 and is, therefore, my exact contemporary almost to the month) and who had been named Adam for the symbolic reason implicit in line five of Dan Pagis' poem above. Shmuel Yosef Agnon, the most famous son of

Buczacz and the major Hebrew novelist of the twentieth century, had hoped to write an introduction: he died before achieving this, leaving only a note. Adam was hidden with a Christian peasant family. The diary-letter tells of a period in hiding when a father refused to strangle his own crying child; of children being thrown from the top floor of our former family mill, Rudolf's Mill, in my ancestral Stanislawow or being buried alive in order to 'save bullets', a very praiseworthy counter-example to the disgraceful charge that the Nazis wasted resources in their war against the Jews. After the war, when the diary was recovered by family survivors, the peasant family claimed that they had taken Adam to a nunnery and that he had survived, and may still be alive somewhere in Ukraine. On the other hand, this could have been a cover-up. Adam's parents were among the many murdered. The book was published by Kibbutz Lochamei Hagetaot (Ghetto Fighters), which has an important museum. When I visited the kibbutz in 1969, the survivors of the ghetto would have been in their late forties. One of the commanders of the Warsaw Ghetto, the legendary Itzik Zuckerman, author of a significant testimony, *A Surplus of Memory*, lived there. Today, even the youngest living survivor among the child smugglers would be in his or her late seventies. The last surviving leader of the Warsaw Ghetto uprising was the Bundist Marek Edelman. I kept putting off a trip to Poland to visit him and now it is too late.

A fascinating diary, much less famous than *The Diary of Anne Frank*, is on my desk. It was written by an older Dutch contemporary of Anne, sixteen-year-old Moshe Flinker, and, unlike her, a member of a religious family: this is *Young Moshe's Diary*, written in Brussels, and in Hebrew not in Dutch. The last dated entry is 6 September 1943: '. . . I am absolutely sure that all the sufferings we have undergone have given us certain rights, and by the general spiritual elevation of our people we have managed to raise the question of the Jews to the status of a problem for all mankind . . .'. He can be forgiven for not alluding to duties as well as rights at that moment of supreme danger but, nonetheless, one could spend hours and pages deconstructing the theological and political implications of this comment, both with and without hindsight. Here too is *The Diary of David Rubinowicz*, which the twelve-year-old Polish boy kept for two years from 21 March 1940, before being shipped off to a death camp—probably Treblinka—in 1942. David's entry for 8 January 1942: 'In the afternoon I learned that there were two more Jewish victims in Bodzentyn. One was killed outright and the other wounded. They arrested the wounded man and took him to the local police station in Bieliny, and there they'll probably beat him to death.' The tone is matter of fact, like that of a boy at boarding school writing home to his parents about routine happenings. David didn't have to read books involving murder. There was more than enough at home. It was routine.

The last dated entry—one day after Moshe's last—in Etty Hillesum's *Letters from Westerbork* was not written in the camp but thrown from the train taking her to Auschwitz, where she died on 30 November. The card to her friend Christine begins: 'Opening the Bible at random I find this: "the Lord is my high tower",' a literal translation from the Dutch, if one looks at the facsimile in the photograph. A swift phone call to my Judaism expert Howard Cooper elicits the information that 'high tower' occurs in a number of places in the Bible: the wording of the English translation suggests that she was reading Psalm ninety-four. It is touching that her Bible should have opened to the words Jews traditionally read for consolation in times of danger and sorrow, unless the Psalms were her main reading in the camp, which could explain why her Bible opened there. In a letter of July 1943, she writes to Maria that the only way you could survive in Westerbork was to follow the advice in the Gospel of Matthew: 'Sufficient unto the day is the evil thereof.' Etty had various Bibles in the camp as well as the Koran and the Talmud. Her favourite writer was Rilke and her lover was Julius Spier, the founder of psychochirology, the study of palm prints. So insightful was he, that Jung himself persuaded Spier 'to turn the talent into a full-time profession'. Ethel Spector Person, in *Love and Fateful Encounters*, discusses Jung's affair with Sabina Spielrein (a personality and intelligence equal to Lou Andreas-Salomé) and that of Etty with Spier, 'another dramatic story in which transference love appears to be the prime catalysing agent in a young woman's psychic transformation.'

My cousin Jerzyk kept his diary for a few weeks in October/November 1943 in Drohobycz where one of his uncles met Bruno Schulz—a hundred and fifty miles west of Adam Klonicki-Klonimos' father in Buczacz. Jerzyk killed himself with cyanide, wrongly assuming that a knock on the door was the Gestapo come to get him, his parents, his uncle and grandmother after a tip off about their hiding place. It was a tragic error of judgement but also an act of heroic resistance on the part of the eleven-year-old, who had sworn never to be taken alive. 'I'm not a writer, I'm not even a grown-up,' he wrote in his diary, but in some respects he was a premature adult. I edited and translated the diary, having obtained a transcript from Yad Vashem in Jerusalem, and published it as *I'm Not Even a Grown-Up*. The entry of 10 September is the only one written on the same date as an Anne Frank entry and it moves me that they both reacted optimistically to the news of the capitulation of Italy. Anne had been listening to the Dutch service of the BBC and Jerzyk may well have learnt about it from the BBC Polish service. I have the original diary here, a family heirloom par excellence given to me by Jerzyk's mother, Aunt Sophie, in Tel-Aviv, after it was thought lost. She and her husband Izydor survived the war and I consulted them before and after visiting the sites of Jerzyk in Drohobycz and Stanislawow. Imagine, surviving your own child who committed suicide. They, at least, were not among the hundreds of thousands of East Galician Jews herded into ghettos and shipped off (trained off, one might say) to Belzec and other death camps.

[Later, during final revision: Jerzyk's sister Irit has found and sent me Sophie's own war diary. I have commissioned Antonia Lloyd-Jones, a distinguished translator from the Polish, to translate it for me.]

Jerzyk's grandfather, Fabian Urman, was the headmaster of the Baron de Hirsch School in Tlumacz, in what is now western Ukraine, East Galicia as it was. My grandfather at one time was a Baron de Hirsch forester. (Hirsch was one of the greatest Jewish philanthropists of all time. Among his main concerns were education of Jews in impoverished Galicia and emigration from Russia to the USA and Argentina.) Here is the *Memorial Book of Tlumacz*, in English and Hebrew, given to me by Jerzyk's father Izydor. It is one of many such books commemorating murdered communities, whose remnants live in Israel and other countries. I dwell enough on death and sorrow in these pages, so let me begin by reporting an unexpected detail from the history of this small town: its name ultimately deriving from the Turkish tilmaç—Tlumacz in Polish, Tolmacz in Ukrainian, Tolmycz in Yiddish—means 'translator' or 'interpreter'; apparently the name derives either from the fact that many translators lived there or from the gratitude felt by locals for a military interpreter who dissuaded Tatars from pillaging the town. In Tlumacz, there was a (too?) pious rabbi who, when praying, always wore white and put on two pairs of *tefilin* (phylacteries) simultaneously. I remember Tlumacz, a sad, broken place. A typical episode from the Nazi occupation: the Gestapo declared that three hundred Tlumacz Jews would be killed if three men, in hiding because brave leaders had warned them they were on a list of wanted men, were not delivered to the SS. 'When this became known, the three at once turned themselves over to the Ukrainian militia.' That was the last that was heard of them. Another section of the book refers to people from the town being taken to nearby Stanislawow, and 'being put to death, along with hundreds of Jews, in Rudolf's Mill'—which I mentioned earlier and which was owned by my great-uncle Samuel Rudolf before he left for Haifa; it became known after the war as Devil's Mill.

Reference books

Serge Klarsfeld has shown that in World War II in France, protestant villagers were the best protectors of Jews. He has also shown that the French people in general (as opposed to the Vichy regime, which amazed the Nazis with its zeal) had the best record in occupied Europe. *French Children of the Holocaust*, edited by Klarsfeld, and *The Auschwitz Chronicle*, edited by Danuta Czech, a former member of the Polish resistance and later head of research at Auschwitz, are enormous reference books that I consult from time to time. They are part of my life as a humble remembrance of victims in these particular killing fields. The passion and rationale of Klarsfeld's book is to give the deported children a local habitation and a name. They are Jewish and they are children. They are my older brothers and sisters. If they are not everybody's brothers and sisters, and if today other child victims everywhere are not our brothers and sisters, then we are nothing and the world is dead. The book contains biographies of a quarter of the eleven thousand deported Jewish children and the names and addresses of all of them. Here is the angelic, almost pre-Raphaelite, figure of Albert Kaczka, born on 22 April 1933, in Paris. He was arrested with his parents Szmul and Rywka, at 8 rue des Panoyaux during the Vel d'Hiv roundup, and deported on convoy twenty of 17 August 1942. His father was sent to Auschwitz on convoy thirteen and his mother on convoy fourteen. Patrick Modiano, who must have studied Klarsfeld's work, is an evocative and haunting novelist: *Ring Roads, Night Rounds, Dora Bruder* and other books explore Paris under the occupation, the Paris of the deported children, all of whom are photographed in Klarsfeld's book.

The Auschwitz Chronicle is an invaluable record of daily life, that is to say, daily death. It records all the transports and selections and enables researchers to pinpoint any of the estimated one and a half million Auschwitz murders more closely. According to the chronicle, two transports, one from Berlin and one from the Sosnowitz ghetto, arrived in Auschwitz on 5 August 1943. The men were given the numbers 135373–135367. Cross-reference this to the database of the International Tracing Service (which can be consulted in Yad Vashem in Jerusalem and whom I emailed) and we find what I knew we would find: a Polish Jew called Ichiel Feiner was given the number 135633. Feiner, on arrival in Israel, adopted the name Yechiel Denur, also on the ITS database, and later the pen name which you will recognize from earlier references in this book: Ka-Tzetnik 135633. His new name had literally been engraved in his flesh. There is one discrepancy between the chronicle and the ITS database: ITS dates his arrival as 6 July: presumably a clerical error on their part. Daniel Weissbort's father, too, was from Sosnowitz. If he had not left for Belgium before the war . . .

Albert Kazcka must have arrived on 23 or 26 August 1942 (probably the former, unless there were long delays) on one of two transports from Drancy containing many children aged under fourteen, all gassed on arrival. Primo Levi's biographers tell us Levi's number—174517, which I saw with my own eyes when we met in London; and his date of arrival in Auschwitz—26 February 1944, having left the camp at Fossoli on 22 February. Sure enough, the details of the transport of six hundred and fifty people from Fossoli are given in *The Auschwitz Chronicle*. Liberated on 27 January 1945, Levi was one of only one hundred and twenty-four survivors of the *selektion*: Kafka finds his way even into that single terrible word. Grete Bloch, Kafka's close woman-friend and intermediary between him and his fiancée Felice (see, among other books, Canetti's brilliant study of Kafka's letters to Felice, *Kafka's Other Trial*), was on one of the last transports from Fossoli. Bloch did not survive Auschwitz.

During the final revision of this book I learnt from Anny Dayan Rosenman (a fellow Piotr Rawicz devotee) that Rawicz's camp number has been identified: 102679. I immediately contacted the Auschwitz Archives and explained that he was using a false name and asked whether they had any information. The archive director, Woijchiec Plosa, asked for my email address and a couple of days later informed me that this was the number given to Jurij or Jura Bosak (Bosiak, Bosiek, Boziac or Boszek). He was allegedly born on 4 August 1920 (my book on him tells the reality: 12 July 1919) in Sopocin (the reality: L'vov) and was deported to Auschwitz in the transport from the Cracow district. This transport arrived in Auschwitz on 16 February 1943. On 18 September 1944, Jurij Bosak was transferred from KL Auschwitz to KL Flossenbürg.

I have exchanged emails with my close friend Miriam Neiger-Fleishmann, a painter and writer living in Jerusalem. Miriam, whose poems I have co-translated with her over the years, was born in Komarno, Slovakia, after the war. She writes:

> My sister was deported to Auschwitz. She was born 23.9.1934 in Komarno and died less than 10 years later on 30.6.44. She had the same name as me. She was the daughter of my father. My father married my mother after the holocaust. Life continues & I am happy with my grandchildren. How are you and your grandson? Shana Tova and the best, love Miriam.

I replied:

> She had approximately the same life span as my cousin Jerzyk. I looked in *The Auschwitz Chronicle* and find that on June 29 1944 there was a selection from a transport from Hungary. That is the date she arrived. I shall scan the page and send it to you . . . Where did you find the details of your sister? My grandson is wonderful. I shall see him tonight. I wish you too Shana Tova, a good year. Love, Tony

To which, Miriam replied:

> It is for sure the same deportation where my paternal grandparents
> were sent and probably my cousins. It might also be the one my
> mother's family were on. Both my grandfather Samuel Perlman and
> his wife (and the sister of my grandmother Rachel-Rose who died
> before the war) were killed about the same time. My mother and
> her sister were both in Auschwitz for about two months, but they
> were sentenced to life instead and sent to Germany to work in
> ammunition factory in Lippstadt.

Jacques Derrida and Maurice Blanchot

I spent much of the 1970s worrying about the Holocaust and much of the
1980s worrying about nuclear war. Now I worry about the lamentable failure
of our leaders to address the problems facing humanity with humility,
determination, intelligence and lucidity. Today, with climate change on top
or underneath all the other problems facing the world, one must *think and
write disaster* differently, but, as Primo Levi sadly and angrily noted in *The
Drowned and the Saved* in 1986 and in the last letter he wrote me a year later,
the lessons of the past have not been learnt.

Some readers will have recognized my phrase 'write disaster' as a
borrowing from Maurice Blanchot's *L'Ecriture du désastre*. The English-
language edition, *The Writing of the Disaster*, benefits from a brilliant
translation by Ann Smock. This major work belongs on the same shelf as
Levi's *If This Is a Man* and Antelme's *The Human Race* (both first published
in the same year, 1947) and the poems of Celan and Radnoti, as does
Blanchot's *The Instant of My Death*, a kind of postscript to *The Writing of
the Disaster*. The former is a brief, powerful, elliptical and apparently
autobiographical text completed by Jacques Derrida's characteristic and
brilliant essay, *Demeure*. Another book involving Derrida is Hélène Cixous's
Portrait of Jacques Derrida as a Young Jewish Saint. I yield to no one in my
admiration of both writers, but this ultra-sophisticated and ironically self-
aware hagiography, by a writer not at her considerable best, does Derrida no
favours. Circumcision is one of its themes. And the circumcision of the word
(in Celan's phrase) is the theme of Derrida's short and wondrous meditation

106

on Celan, *Shibboleth*, which begins: 'Once: circumcision takes place only once.' Hitler had an opinion on this subject: 'Conscience is a Jewish invention; it is, like circumcision, a mutilation of man' (quoted in Jean-Pierre Faye's important book, *Migrations du récit sur le peuple juif*).

Among the many thoughts and aphorisms that combine to form Blanchot's slow-burning meditative masterpiece are, firstly, a paradoxical and haunting phrase that encapsulates the entire enterprise of reflecting on atrocity—'*Keep watch over absent meaning*' (emphasis in the original), and, secondly, 'Philosophy, which puts everything into question, is tripped up by poetry, which is the question that eludes it.' This is the ultimate examination question for philosophy and literature students and, more broadly, for anyone who worries about these issues, that is to say any reader that my book may find. It is a question Celan could have put to Heidegger when they met, indeed the very meeting that Celan sought with the flawed master—unlike Blanchot, the German philosopher never redeemed himself for earlier political flaws—implied or even incarnated Blanchot's assertion.

Politics

Israel and Palestine

At the end of 2008, Operation Cast Lead began in Gaza, the name taken from a Chanukah poem by Hayyim Nachman Bialik. Israel/Palestine has important parallels with Ireland and Algeria. Israel's tragedy is that it has not produced a Charles de Gaulle. David Ben-Gurion was no longer in a position to practise what he preached when, after the Six Day War in 1967, he said all the territories apart from East Jerusalem should be given back in exchange for peace. Would he have implemented this, or would he too have presided over the colonial occupation of another people? It is worth reading the chapter entitled 'The Creation of Israel' in Nahum Goldmann's *The Jewish Paradox*, the follow-up to his autobiography, *Memories*. Goldmann was vain without being pompous or self-important, and was influential behind the scenes in all kinds of ways. I met this 'important Jew' (as Auden said of Freud) a few times at private meetings in London, when he would flatter insider dissidents with unpublished stories about the great and the bad and encourage us to continue fighting the good fight from within. He foresaw what would happen if Israel failed to be proactive in the search for peace and he knew there would be trouble if the USA failed to lean on Israel when necessary. He would have been proud of Itzhak Rabin, who broke out of the inflexible hard line associated with all Israel's leaders while in office, apart from the second prime minister Moshe Sharett. I want to believe that Rabin would have grown in stature had his assassination attempt not succeeded, unlike those that de Gaulle survived. These days I feel a terrible sadness and lack of hope concerning Israel.

I have a shelf of books about the conflict in the Middle East. I read them long ago in order to educate myself about something that was beginning to obsess me. If you are going to obsess, obsess on the basis of knowledge. The only other political matter I have obsessed about to this degree is nuclear weapons. In the 1960s and 1970s, I was a member of the London branch of Mapam, a group of socialist Zionists, now as defunct as Old Labour. Its headquarters were in Broadhurst Gardens, border of Swiss Cottage and West Hampstead. Mapam had an English-language magazine *New Outlook*, edited by Israeli old-timers including Simha Flapan, who taught us that Israel, or his version of Israel, was a member of the coalition of causes right-minded (i.e. left-minded) persons could support without contradiction. British-born Dan Leon was another editor, and addressed meetings when he was in London. His 1964 book *The Kibbutz* has an introduction by Anthony Wedgwood Benn. It is a paeon of praise to a vanished phenomenon, the Hashomair Hatzair kibbutz movement. As an RAF pilot stationed in Egypt, Tony Benn visited Kibbutz Sha'ar Hagolan in 1945 on the day Germany surrendered. I stayed there as the guest of the poet Avraham Shlonsky's daughter in 1970. The Hashomair Hatzair kibbutzim were run according to socialist principles and they inspired people all over the world. The kibbutz members were frontier pioneers and, in Benn's words, were not a 'land elite living off the labour of native workers like the settlers in South Africa or the colons in Algeria'. This is the Israel of Claude Lanzmann's 1972 film *Pourquoi Israel*, the first of his trilogy of films of which the best and best known is *Shoah*. The aim of *Pourquoi Israel* was to portray Israel firmly in the anticolonial and postcolonial mould that was so important on the French left, a mould that Sartre had pioneered. Camus, by contrast, was ambiguous about his native Maghreb, for the well-known reason that he would put his mother before his ideals, echoing a famous equivalent remark by E. M. Forster.

This was my Israel until disillusion and disenchantment set in over many years, and it was Benn's Israel too on his three visits to Sha'ar Hagolan in 1945, 1956 and 1963. I don't think Benn would take back what he wrote about the kibbutz movement, but one thing he would no longer find acceptable is that he wrote about Israel without mentioning the Palestinians. His only mention of non-Jews is to Arabs in general (or possibly Israeli Arabs) and, poignantly enough, he expresses the hope that it might be on the basis of the socialist ideology of the kibbutz that 'Jew and Arab can find their common destiny within a united and peaceful Middle East—freed from exploitation and nourished in unity by the soil in which both communities have such deep roots.' This was before the fateful Six Day War of 1967, following which Israel complicated its victory by settling the West Bank and occupying Gaza, thereby storing up trouble. The earlier dream of Moshe Sharett, Israel's most radical and progressive prime minister, died with the failure to capitalize wisely on the military victory. A memory stirs of meeting Jacobo Timerman in London on the publication of *The Longest War*, an indictment of Israel, written in the immediate wake of Israel's 1982 war of choice in Lebanon, from the perspective of a brave Ukraine-born Jewish journalist who left Argentina for Israel after surviving the most intimate attentions of the fascist Junta (see his classic *Prisoner without a Name, Cell without a Number*), a regime which was bound to resent the editor of the country's leading liberal newspaper. In 1984 he returned to Argentina.

The tone of that autodidact George Brown's autobiography *In My Way* is strangely affecting. The book contains a section on the Middle East conflict, which makes interesting reading today. The then foreign secretary was rightly proud of Resolution 242, which he fathered in or on the United Nations following the Six Day War. He did not for one moment fantasize, as Tony Blair would later, that you can mediate in this intractable conflict without leaning on Israel. The UK's imperial attitude towards nationalists like

President Nasser of Egypt and, very relevant today, Prime Minister Mossadeq in Iran, has not served us well.

Our group at London Mapam rightly had a bad conscience about the Palestinians, a state of mind which was more moral than other boxes you could tick but still required rationalizations to enable an apparently coherent position. For forty years, I have understood that Israel will never be free and secure and, given certain policies, not deserve to be free and secure until there is a viable Palestinian state. Only then, in the words of Isaiah, will 'Zion be redeemed with justice'. Until that time, it will remain a colonial power, and all its considerable achievements in science, medicine and non-military technology will be less appreciated than they should be because of the systemic failure of humanity, imagination and intelligence in respect of another people. How can one not be deeply pessimistic about Israel, which has hitched its star to a self-defeating neoconservative vision? A few years ago, my own cousins in Jerusalem called me 'traitor' and 'suicide bomb lover' for arguing a case fairly close to that of Yossi Beilin, Avraham Burg and other doves on the Israeli left, but I take comfort from the knowledge that there is a minority in Israel which understands the need for a civilized solution and, crucially, wills the means as well as the end. 'Those to whom evil is done / do evil in return', wrote Auden in 'September 1, 1939', a poem widely circulated after 9/11, and a thought echoed by Burg in his critically important book *The Holocaust Is Over*. Daniel Barenboim, whose attitude and practice serve as a beacon of enlightenment in a benighted world, would agree with Auden: the pianist's book *Everything Is Connected* represents music as a paradigm of political decency. The argument from enlightened self-interest has had no effect on Israel. Of American presidents, only Eisenhower and Bush Senior, both Republicans, have ever put serious pressure on Israel. Obama has talked tough but failed to put pressure—the worst of both worlds.

Hannah Arendt

From Michael Hamburger's powerful sequence 'In a Cold Season', written after the Eichmann trial: '. . . / To number words that did not sob or whimper / As children do when packed in trucks to die / That did not die two deaths as mothers do / Who see their children packed in trucks to die'. Here are

Hannah Arendt's *The Jew as Pariah* and her hugely influential and controversial book *Eichmann in Jerusalem*, with its famous subtitle *A Report on the Banality of Evil*. Arendt made important enemies for her thesis, not least Gershom Scholem—although she and he were not dissimilar as scholarly *yekke* intellectuals—and Reuben Ainsztein, who contended she misunderstood the nature of the situation the Jews and their leaders found themselves in. When I studied the Eichmann trial after Arendt's book was reissued in 1968, I had not yet heard of Ka-Tzetnik 135633, let alone read his books, written about him or got to know him. KZ fainted during his cross-examination and was one of many witnesses who failed to impress Arendt. She implies that KZ is a downmarket author of 'human interest' stories on sensationalist subjects; she does not understand that what he does as a writer is deploy the conventions of such books, and of pornography too (the sexuality of violence rather than the violence of sexuality), in order to recount his truth about the perpetrators. It was not until the Yom Kippur War of 1973, when KZ was serving as a war correspondent, that we were finally in touch: he wrote to me on the back of a cigarette packet from the Golan Heights, thanking me for my review of his books in *Stand*, which I had sent him.

A note on socialism and Judaism

Two prizes from childhood Hebrew classes (also known as Sunday School and cheder) have turned up: S. M. Lehrman's *The Jewish Festivals* and *The Jewish Design for Living*. In the latter, we find this interesting quote from a sage of yore: 'If you minimize your merits, others will minimize your faults.' There is also what is for me a heart-wrenching section on 'Judaism and socialism' in this book published in 1951, a time when social democracy was at its apogee and looked set to conquer the world. Today the argument leaves a bitter taste in the mouth, twice over. Lehrman sees Fabian-style socialism as compatible with and influenced by Jewish teachings and indeed by Jewish individuals. He says that this version of political economy guides 'the policy pursued, more or less, in the State of Israel today; a policy which, if undisturbed by war and faction from within and without, bids fair to become the model of enlightened statecraft. The new Jewish state can teach the world that Socialism has a spiritual background behind its economic and political doctrines . . . The reconciliation between Judaism and Socialism is important in life today, and especially in our national homeland, Israel. Both have so much in common that it is a pity a gulf has been erected in partisan minds between them . . . In Jewish social ethics, God is revealed . . . as the father of *all* his created beings. This, in fact, is the most prized contribution of Judaism towards the advancement of civilisation and towards the unfolding of the divine plan on earth. All mean are equal; all are entitled to a fair share of the good things in this life.'

History

Introduction

Apart from what happened in Central and Eastern Europe during World War II and what led up to it—on my desk is *The Last Years of Austria–Hungary*, edited by Mark Cornwall—the period of history that most interests me, in detail rather than broad brush, is the long first half of the seventeenth century (ending with the Restoration), with its remarkable interaction between Jewish, Portuguese, Dutch and English history: the emblematic figure in this fourfold nexus has to be Rabbi Menasseh Ben Israel, encircled by Uriel Acosta, Rembrandt van Rijn, Baruch Spinoza, Oliver Cromwell, Peter Paul Rubens and others, with a glance forward to the later part of the century as the drama of Jansenism, Huguenots and persecution is played out in France, not least in Racine's last two plays, *Esther* and *Athalie*. My uses and abuses of history can be found in my stories. I have Pascal and Spinoza playing chess on a visit of the latter to Port-Royal even though we know they never met, either in France or in Holland. But we want them to have met.

Jean Racine/Queen Esther

The Secret Jews by Joachim Prinz enthralled me, as did Cecil Roth's *A History of the Marranos* and *Menasseh Ben Israel*: these were three of the books I read for background to my short stories set in seventeenth-century Lisbon, London and Amsterdam. The phenomenon of a Marrano Jew or indeed anyone living an 'official' or life-saving double life serves as a metaphor of the universal human condition, for there is always a relative disjunction between our inner and outer lives, even to ourselves, never mind our nearest and dearest. John Docker in *1492: The Poetics of Diaspora* reads the personality of Leopold Bloom as that of an Irish-Hungarian Marrano. Queen Esther, understandably, is a hero to all Marranos. As children, growing up with the cycle of Jewish festivals, we loved her because the Purim story is elemental, the goodies and baddies so plainly evident. I saw a rare and beautiful production of Jean Racine's musical drama, *Esther*, at the Comédie française a few years ago, and once upon a time had designs on it (or for it) as a translator, before deciding to write a story about Racine instead.

Following what is perhaps the greatest of his plays on a classical theme, *Phèdre*, poorly received on its first appearance in 1677, Racine fell silent for twelve years, certainly because the authoritarian political and theological environment in France had become incompatible with the free expression his great powers required. Nor did his Port-Royal Jansenism help, however discrete and Marrano-like he was. But in 1689 he was commissioned to write a play on a biblical theme by someone he could not refuse, namely the king's wife Madame de Maintenon, for the girls to perform at her school at Saint-Cyr. She wanted a moral tale without the dodgy passions of the plays on classical themes like *Phèdre*, and it had to have songs and music and plenty of choruses to increase the number of performers. Racine's subject and treatment were ideal from Madame's point of view, and the theme suited him for his own reasons. However, despite affinities with *Iphigénie*, the play, a kind of libretto, was never going to be one of the masterpieces by the poet of genius who is France's greatest playwright.

Here are my *Théâtre complet de Racine*, François Mauriac's *La Vie de Jean Racine*, Geoffrey Brereton's *Jean Racine* (excellent on the extent to which the royal characters reflect their French opposite numbers at the court Racine knew so well), Vanessa Ochs' study of biblical women titled *Sarah Laughed*, and a sumptuous book about *Esther* bought at the Comédie française. Harold Bloom in *The Shadow of a Great Rock*, his new book which I have only had time to dip into, quotes his colleague Herbert Marks as saying that the Book of Esther is the inaugural text of diaspora Judaism 'since Purim seems to have begun as a celebration among those who chose to stay in Babylon'. This is true if we discount prophetic texts such as Isaiah.

There were a number of reasons why I believed that a translation of *Esther* was one of the few projects in the winter garden of my fantasy with a snowball's chance of success. Its biblical subject matter—the dastardly plan of the Persian king's grand vizier, Haman the Amalekite, to destroy the Jews and Haman's eventual defeat thanks to Esther's courage—cannot fail to remind one that in Racine's France it was dangerous to be a Huguenot or a Jew. In 1685, four years before the commission of the play, Louis XIV's Revocation of the Edict of Nantes removed the rights of Protestants, so that Huguenots had to flee the country, some coming to London, hence the French street names in the East End: my mother Esther lived in Fleur-de-Lys Street. Louis was planning the expulsion of the Jews and it is somewhat surprising that he loved Racine's version of the biblical story, although admittedly it could only be performed privately until Madame's death in 1719. It entered the Comédie française repertoire in 1721. Racine's play, as Christian as you would expect, is wittingly and fascinatingly philosemitic and, which is something else, proto-Zionist, nearly two hundred years before *Daniel Deronda*. The playwright, possibly taught by a Marrano at Port-Royal, had many books on Judaism in his library, according to a list reprinted in Lucien-Gilles Benguigui's fascinating *Racine et les sources juives d'Esther et Athalie*. The play speaks to our time, as one could tell from the excitement and buzz at the Comédie française a few years ago. Indeed, *Le Monde*'s reviewer saw the production as making a post-Holocaust point.

The eventual production of a modern English translation could use music from Handel's, indeed England's, first oratorio *Esther*, which was based on Racine's play (the libretto was co-written by Alexander Pope) and produced in 1732. Handel also wrote an oratorio based on Racine's final play *Athalie*, the writer's second commission from Madame de Maintenon; Felix Mendelssohn wrote beautiful incidental music for the play. The Old Testament theme (see Kings and Chronicles) enabled Racine to return to his theological roots and write something as powerful, in its own way, as *Phèdre* or *Andromaque*. (The latter's second act, according to Samuel Beckett, is 'the best bit of dramatic construction ever made'). The hidden God of the Jews and the hidden God of the Jansenists and Calvinists are to all intents and purposes the same. I wonder if there has been an English-language performance of *Esther* since the eighteenth century.

According to the writer Naim Kattan, Lucien Goldmann was surprised when told that his Marxist studies of Racine, including *Le Dieu caché* and *Racine*, possessed a Jewish dimension. *Athalie*, a much finer play than *Esther*, was far less successful and only had two performances. Madame de Maintenon cannot have liked it. We must, however, be grateful to her as catalyst, for without the commission of *Esther*, Racine would not have returned to the stage. *Esther* was, in effect, the warm up for *Athalie* after the long silence. Goldmann thinks the English Revolution may have affected the two sacred dramas: 'The English revolution strengthened Racine's opposition to the world and revealed to him the possibility of a victorious rebellion which was the expression of the divine wrath against the wicked kings.' Later writers, including Emily Dickinson, Herman Melville and R. S. Thomas and many Hebrew poets, worry their heads and their verses about the hidden face of God, or *hester panim* as it is called in Hebrew. This very question is at the heart of the short, powerful and intense story by Zvi Kolitz, *Yosl Rakover Talks to God*, which is accompanied by an essay by Levinas that Leon Wieseltier takes issue with in his afterword.

(Mrs) Beth-Zion Abrahams, Sir Martin Gilbert, Cecil Roth

On the cover of Martin Gilbert's *First World War*, we find Paul Johnson quoted: 'Martin Gilbert: our greatest living factual historian'. While it is too easy to say that a non-factual historian sounds to the untutored ear like an oxymoron, let me take the phrase at face or ear value and say that I do not read enough history to know whether this is quite the compliment the publisher took it as, but presumably it implies that Gilbert does not write interpretative history or conceptual history. Be that as it may, I have benefited considerably over the years from his historical geographies in the form of maps, for example *The Arab-Israeli Conflict*. His truly masterful chronicle, or factual history, is *The Holocaust* in which he traces the Jewish tragedy across time (World War II) as the Germans move across space (eastwards). This book was essential background reading while I was researching the life and death of my cousin Jerzyk.

Back in the 1970s, when I began to be interested in my ancestors, I devoured Werner Keller's post-biblical history of the Jews, *Diaspora*. Rereading the short chapter on the return of the Jews to England in 1656, I have been reminded that under Charles the First the unofficial Jews in London worshipped in the house of the Portuguese ambassador, himself a Marrano, Antonio de Suza. His son-in-law Antonio Fernandez Carvajal was 'virtually the treasurer of the kingdom'. Norman Cohn's magnificent and beautifully written *Warrant for Genocide* is a critically important book whose main material on revolutionary messianism in the Middle Ages has early Jewish apocalypse as its prequel, and modern fanaticisms as its culmination. Cohn is best read immediately before J. P. Stern's *Hitler*, which helps us understand, if help is needed, why people like Raoul Wallenberg were so important. As late as 1982, John Bierman, whose *Righteous Gentile* tells the story of Wallenberg, thought it was possible that Wallenberg could still be alive in the Gulag. Varien Fry, Sousa Mendes, Chiune Sugihara, Oskar Schindler, Nicholas Winton and others are only the most famous of the not inconsiderable number of people who were mensches (se questo è un uomo . . . : 'in a place of no men, strive to be a man', as the Talmud says in *Ethics of the Fathers*). The fate of Wallenberg arouses one's pity and outrage. Could he have lived on for decades? Perhaps gone mad? Would that be a mercy? His fate does not bear contemplating.

Cecil Roth's *Short History of the Jewish People* was presented to me and inscribed by two school friends, Michael Pinto-Duschinsky and Richard 'Specs' Hyams, on the occasion of my bar mitzvah in 1955. It perches alongside a 1953 Hebrew classes prize (according to the book plate), *The Jews in England* by '(Mrs) Beth Zion Abrahams', the brackets round her title doubtless a leftover from the Victorian convention of women authors known as Mrs Beeton or Mrs Gaskell or even Mrs Humphrey Ward. Keeping these books among other Jewish books rather than with my tiny 'History' collection elsewhere in the room reminds me that *history*, British, that is to say English, history, was what I 'did' at school. One year the teacher was Joe Hunt, whose name is memorialized in *The Sense of an Ending* by Julian Barnes, also taught by Hunt. I knew that this history had nothing to do with the world of my ancestors who were elsewhere in 1066, 1656 and 1832. Jewish history supplied and still supplies me with an origin narrative, given that my immigrant grandparents, while eventually naturalized as British, were not English. But if origin has its roots on my Globe Wernicke shelves, the routes of destiny calls upon other narratives, other bookshelves, for I no longer buy into teleological stories, and I do not belong in Israel itself. Thanks to the quality of the translation, the King James Bible remains a resource for all anglophone readers. But the fact that there were Jews in England a thousand years before Julius Caesar (recalling Disraeli's reply to an antisemitic taunt in Parliament: 'Yes, I am a Jew, and when the ancestors of the Right Honourable Gentleman were brutal savages in an unknown island, mine were priests in the Temple of Solomon.') and some came over with William the Conqueror, does not in any way relate to the world of my grandparents, who were products of centuries of Ashkenazi Jewish settlement in Central and Eastern Europe.

Saul Friedländer

The Prague-born Saul Friedländer is a distinguished historian. I have here not his major historical works but his fascinating memoir of childhood in occupied France, *When Memory Comes*, as well as his short *Reflections of Nazism*, which sits alongside a short, sharp book by Philippe Lacoue-Labarthe and Jean-Luc Nancy, *Le Mythe nazi*. The memoir contains interesting thoughts about Israeli mentality and Jewish history which are not irrelevant to the situation thirty years after he wrote the book: 'Peace initiatives are going to bring to light the hidden contradictions of our society' comes a few pages after 'Will we ever believe in peace? Will we ever be able to envisage our future from a perspective of peace? Since the beginning of its history, this people has seen itself as alone and surrounded by enemies, and has been incapable of having faith in anything save its God, and then its destiny. For centuries misfortune and catastrophe have always seemed to be the most imminent eventualities, though the trust in ultimate deliverance has never entirely disappeared.' Friedländer was deeply affected by his first proper Passover celebration: 'It is the holy words, repeated over the centuries, that give the general symbol its particular force, that mark the sinking of roots in a group, the sinking of roots in history and time. Because they have never been entirely clear, and always open to exegesis and explanation, it is the holy words that open the doors of imagination and allow the humblest of participants to understand, in his own way, the story of feeling and liberation, knowing that these traditional words are his anchor and foundation within the community.' Rereading *Reflections of Nazism* (subtitled *Essay on Kitsch and Death*), a study of the way Nazism has been mythologized in films and books, I remain struck by words I underlined many years ago on a return flight from Israel, where I bought the book: 'The issue is one of *indiscriminate word and image overload of topics that call for so much restraint, hesitation, groping*, on events we are so far from understanding' (his emphasis). Friedländer continues: 'In Nazi eyes, the extermination of the Jews was a vital necessity. It represented a sacred mission . . . . No documentary proof allows the conclusion that at any time—except for the last months of the war—was exploitation of Jewish slave labour considered more important than the extermination of the Jews.'

Friedländer's remarks, in particular the residual 'trust in ultimate deliverance', can be related to the conclusion of *Red Rising in Bavaria*, Richard Grunberger's history of the short-lived People's State set up after the revolution in which the Kingdom of Bavaria broke away from the German Reich. It survived for a few months in 1919 before being brutally crushed by German troops. One minor figure involved in the uprising was Ret Marut, later known as B. Traven, whose 1927 novel *The Treasure of the Sierra Madre* was made into a terrific film by John Huston, starring Humphrey Bogart. The leaders of the uprising, the poet and playwright Ernst Toller, Kurt Eisner, Gustav Landauer and Eugen Leviné, prefigure Alexander Dubcek and the Prague Spring. It was Leviné who said at the trial in 1919, which resulted in his execution: 'We communists are dead men on leave' (Proust generalized this to all of us, in his 1905 essay on reading). Grunberger, discussing the idealistic, even religious side of Leviné, writes: 'What motivated his near-suicidal persistence in proclaiming the Second Soviet Republic was a messianic urge to make the idea manifest here and now so as to secure the constant renewal of its reality in future times.' The historian quotes Martin

Buber's funeral tribute to his mentor Landauer, in which the philosopher depicts this 'tendency towards realisation' as the most precious heritage of classical Judaism: 'The renewal of the earth is the advent of the Kingdom of God.' This is heady stuff, and it motivated many Jewish secularists in the old progressive and radical traditions of pre-state Zionism. Arthur Cohen, discussing Buber's essay 'Plato and Isaiah' in his *Martin Buber*, makes a suggestive remark: 'Where Plato is disillusioned by failure, Isaiah is emboldened. Failure confirms truth. Though the truth may fail in the historical moment, the message of truth is preserved and borne through history.' One Jewish secularist with his own ideas on these matters was the man of whom an old rabbi, who knew him as a boy before he changed his name, said: 'The Trotskys make the revolution and the Bronsteins pay the bill.' In 1938 Trotsky wrote: 'It is possible to imagine without difficulty what awaits Jews at the mere outbreak of the future world war. But even without war the next development of world reaction signifies with certainty the physical extermination of the Jews.' This prophecy is cited by that multilingual polymath Robert Wistrich in his *Trotsky: Fate of a Revolutionary*. Even though I don't always agree with my old friend's politics, I am grateful for books like *Revolutionary Jews from Marx to Trotsky* and *Weekend in Munich*.

Milton Hindus/Irving Howe and Bill Fishman

Here is my late friend Milton Hindus' anthology *The Old East Side* and a parallel cultural history, Irving Howe's labour of scholarly love, *The Immigrant Jews of New York*. The books make a good pair, dealing with the mass immigration across the Pond from Central and Eastern Europe that also brought my grandparents to London around the middle of the period between 1881—which saw the assassination of the reforming Czar Alexander the Second and the consequential surrender to the forces of reaction, antisemitism, etc.—and 1914. Millions entered the land of the free, while a smaller but still large number came to the UK of Britannia and the France of Marianne, and to Ottoman Palestine: my mother remembered her mother tying her hair with a Union Jack ribbon before she rushed the few yards to Spitalfields Market to cheer the King on Empire Day. In her old age, Esther Rudolf told me she would ban all faith schools—Christian, Jewish and

Muslim—in the name of integration, while instructing children out of school hours in their ancestral heritage, to prevent assimilation. Bill Fishman's *East End Jewish Radicals 1875–1914*, covers the same period, but focuses on anarchists and socialists in Whitechapel, often on their way to the USA and in effect serving their radical apprenticeship in London. The hero is the much-loved Rudolf Rocker, a German gentile who carried out his social, educational and organizational work in Yiddish, the language of the workers. Rocker's son Fermin became an artist whom I regularly visited over the years and would eventually commemorate in an obituary. Fermin, who died at ninety-seven, was perhaps the last living person to have met Prince Peter Kropotkin, having sat on his knee when he was a small boy.

Religion and Theology

The Jewish way of questioning and answering gets into the very marrow of my being. But how can I be open to everything else if I become too absorbed with that which I already am.

—Elias Canetti, *Notes from Hampstead: The Writer's Notes, 1954–1971*

Introduction

I have always enjoyed reading theology, in particular Jewish theology. For me, theology works like poetry. The key terms (e.g. God) serve as an infrastructure equivalent to metre and rhyme in poetry. Within that framework, great minds like Emmanuel Levinas and André Néher, Franz Rosenzweig and Leo Baeck, Martin Buber and Arthur Cohen, Yeshayahu Leibowitz and Emil Fackenheim make their moves. I find their ways of thinking spellbinding and one need not share the writers' beliefs or faith to be educated by their insights. They are not limited by their Jewishness. We all have particularist elements in our make-up, but we are one species and share one destiny on this our only planet, which we will destroy if we do not acknowledge our universal brotherhood and sisterhood and act upon this recognition. Some years ago, Tony Blair as prime minister acknowledged that carbon emissions by air travel could destroy the planet but, instead of showing real leadership and calling for radical measures in terms of rationing, redistributive taxation, etc., asked us to redouble our efforts in terms of technology. It beggars belief that cowardice and complacency will destroy us, but they will if we fail to put in place the necessary remedial measures. 'At the last judgment, only tears will be weighed,' writes Cioran in *Des Larmes et des saints*. The credit-crunch crisis of 2008 briefly made radical (i.e. common sense) measures fashionable, possible and indeed necessary, but the political will (and power?) was not sufficient to reform our social, economic and political life. Will the Labour Party embrace the necessary policies? Will the USA?

Prayerbooks, etc.

Here is my copy of Danby's *Mishnah*, a bar mitzvah present which still contains the visiting card of Solomon Taylor, the headmaster of my Hebrew classes at Hampstead Garden Suburb Synagogue, offering his best wishes for the future. The phone number on the card is SPEedwell 8126; today, more than half a century later, the phone number is 020-8455-8126—after intermediate stations, 455-8126, 081-455-8126 and 0181-455-8126. Why, indeed, should it completely change? Yet, such continuity moves me. I cannot resist taking a look at a famous section in the *Mishnah*: on women's purity. The main topic is menstruation. Such dialectics and detailed descriptions are about as opposite to the Christian image of a woman—idealized in the Virgin Mary and transgressed by Jules Michelet—as can be imagined. It is no wonder that Paula Rego's Mary in her Life of the Virgin series in the chapel of the Portuguese president's palace at Beleym created problems for the devout when the paintings were unveiled. Paula's Mary is a real woman, a fertile woman, a pregnant woman, a 'fully ripe fig' in the phrase of the *Mishnah*, the Oral Law compiled and redacted at the end of the second century anno domini, as Jews are not supposed to call it, preferring to say CE, the Common Era. (BC, cleverly enough, is known as BCE, before the Common Era.) The archbishop of Lisbon defused the row over Paula's pictures: 'The aesthetics are not to my taste, but there is no doctrinal objection.'

Here are my prayerbooks, long unopened except to check liturgical references for my short stories. The first is a Passover *Machzor* (prayerbook) that my father was given on his bar mitzvah. On the title page it says 'Wien 1926' and 'Made in Austria'. No publisher is given but there is a 'sole agent', namely Shapiro and Vallentine of 81 Wentworth Street, close to Petticoat Lane. The book is inscribed 'with best wishes to Henry from Buba and Uncle Isaac', *buba* being the Yiddish word for grandmother. This grandmother was the second wife of my great-grandfather (and sister of the first wife, who died young) and, strictly speaking, was my great-great-aunt not my great-grandmother; these details trigger an enjoyable mystery: I have seen a photo of my great-grandfather holding me in 1943. It follows (as it were) that he was alive in 1927. How come, therefore, that he did not participate in this gift from his wife and youngest child, Ike, who was only a few years older than my father? The only possible answer is that he gave my father a different present, now lost (perhaps a pair of *tefilin*, phylacteries, which doubtless, like mine a generation later, were never worn).

Here too are Reform and Liberal prayerbooks, acquired in the days when I was actively involved in their making, to the point of proofreading and even contributing: one of my Jabès translations was used in the study anthology at the end of the quondam Daily and Sabbath prayerbook of the Reform movement edited by Rabbis Lionel Blue and Jonathan Magonet, answerable to a committee chaired by the late Rabbi Hugo Gryn:

On the side of the road
there are leaves
so tired of being leaves
they have fallen.

On the side of the road
there are Jews
so tired of being Jews
they have fallen.

Sweep away the leaves.
Sweep away the Jews.

Will the same leaves
grow again in spring?
Will there be spring
for the downtrodden Jews?

In the 'martyrology' section of the Reform movement's High Holy Days prayerbook from that time (and now overtaken by a new or even two new editions) is something I wrote at the height of my preoccupation with Auschwitz and Hiroshima. Earlier, Ka-Tzetnik 135633 associated the two, and rightly so, as harbingers of our destiny as a species. He was less concerned than Richard Rubinstein with the First Great War, which led to both.

> The Nazi genocide of Jews (and gypsies) was a *disaster*. It can only be redeemed into *tragedy* if a meaning is read out of it (I avoid the blasphemy 'read into it'): it was—with Hiroshima—the *penultimate disaster*, the final warning to do all we can to prevent the *ultimate disaster*: nuclear war—the end to civilization and life on this planet.

And here are two prayerbooks I used when young: the legendary *Singers Prayerbook*, named after its translator, with my name and address in my mother's handwriting at the front and Chief Rabbi Hertz's *Authorised Daily Prayerbook*, a gift from the synagogue, presented to me on the day of my bar mitzvah. The bookplate is signed by Rabbi Dayan Dr Lew and three top-hatted honorary officers—Asher Fishman, Max Fulder and Harry Landy. It is almost beyond belief to me that these solemn dignitaries of my father's generation—whose names conjure a world lost and gone forever—were then only about ten years older than my son is now.

Hertz's prayerbook was first published in 1941. A 1946 note states: 'The Chief Rabbi, Dr J.H. Hertz, C.H. *zatsal* [in Hebrew letters, meaning "may his memory be blessed"], was not spared to see the completion of this one-volume edition of his Prayer Book. He had, with impeccable timing, carried out all the proof corrections until page 1064, "Confession on a Deathbed", which happened to be the last page he corrected; closing there his great Jewish leadership.' Before the morning and night prayers for young children which end the book, there is a selection 'from the Jewish moralists' for congregants to mull over: 'It is not the iron, but the force that moves the iron, that fells the tree' (*The Ways of the Righteous*, fifteenth century) reminds one of a famous line by Dylan Thomas.

Kaddish

Two books on mourning have moved me, as they should: Leon Wieseltier's long and belated first book, *Kaddish*, a word generally associated with Allen Ginsberg's strong poem for his mother. The late Isaiah Berlin told me he thought Wieseltier was overrated as an intellect, but then he thought that of himself too, or so he said, on more than one occasion. *Pace* Berlin, *Kaddish* is a remarkable book. It is the journal of a grief year by a secular intellectual who returns to his people for the duration: it is about the Kaddish said three times a day after his father's death, about his need to ritualize the grief, and make sense of the ritualization. The book was preceded by Esther Broner's *A Kaddish Journal*. Hers is chattier, more about the departed, and also about her own situation as a woman not counted in for a *minyan*, a quorum of ten adult Jewish males, without which there can be no service and therefore no Kaddish.

Messianism and socialism

One matrix of a writer is his language, another is his religious or ethno-cultural background, a third is his ideology or worldview. Socialism remains part of my worldview even though I was never a full-blooded Marxist, just as I draw on Jewish values although I do not hold to the fundamental tenets, as in Mamonides' Thirteen Principles of Faith, the nearest thing we have to a catechism, which is incarnated liturgically in the Yigdal hymn. There is a link between the two, already touched on by S. M. Lehrman, namely the idea of socialism as a secularization of Jewish messianism, and indeed there is a famous Midrash to the effect that when mankind creates a world fit for the Messiah, the Messiah will no longer be needed. The house of Rav Kook, the first chief rabbi of Palestine, was in Princelet Street in the East End, opposite where my grandparents and my aunt Fan lived, as described later. Kook, stuck in London for the duration of World War I, was the *sandek*—the man who had the honour of holding the child about to be circumcised—of my late Uncle Phil. Once installed in Palestine, the rabbi welcomed the socialist atheist workers on the kibbutzim into the fold, which was an inclusive and visionary if patronizing gesture, and not to be compared to the retrospective conversion by Mormons of dead Jews that has been going more or less simultaneously with their allowing us to use their records for genealogical research. Kook's reasoning, faced with fundamentalists appalled by his attitude, was that kibbutzniks were the equivalent of the Temple workers who built the Holy of Holies, even though the high priest alone was allowed into it and then only on Yom Kippur. Today, I would describe myself as a writer, citizen and grandfather. These are my templates and inform the way I think and feel. Language, religion and ideology are backdrop.

Mysticism

In his poem 'The Golem', Borges makes an easy yet cunning rhyme: Golem and Scholem, an association which doubtless led him to his poem in the first place. Here are books by Gershom Scholem and others on Jewish mysticism and Kabbalah. In my copy of Perle Epstein's autobiographical *Pilgrimage of a Wandering Jew*, she inscribed the following message: 'from a Semite to an Ethnic', which was how she characterized us long ago. Here are books on Zen and Kabbalah that Perle (now Besserman) gave me twenty years after our previous meeting, including *A New Kabbala for Women* and *A New Zen for Women*, an entertaining account of what Zen has done for women and also, contrary to popular belief, of what women have done for Zen. She is properly doubtful about Madonna and other devotees of popular or populist Kabbalah. My copy of Scholem's *Major Trends in Jewish Mysticism* (inscribed 'Tel-Aviv, March 1970') is well thumbed, with underlinings and marginalia such as 'Borges' and 'Wiesel'. Several books by the latter are here, including *Legends of Our Time* and his first and most famous book, *Night*, whose French preface by Mauriac I discuss later. Scholem's *Major Trends*, as Sandor Gilman in his short and valuable study *Kafka* reminds us, is insistent about the importance of Kafka for a modern understanding of Kabbalah. Gilman quotes Brecht as writing as early as 1934—only a year after the first camp, Dachau, had been set up—that Kafka is worth studying to see how he foretold the 'Dantesque' making of the concentration camps.

In *Redemption and Utopia: Jewish Libertarian Thought in Central Europe*, Michael Lowy tells the story of an intellectual world that I love and where I belong. Gershom Scholem has written: 'the blazing landscape of redemption has concentrated in itself the historical outlook of Judaism. Little wonder that overtones of messianism have accompanied the modern Jewish readiness for irrevocable action in the concrete realm, when it set out on the Utopian return to Zion. It is a readiness which no longer allows itself to be fed on hopes. Born out of the horror and destruction that was Jewish history in our generation, it is bound to history itself and not to meta-history; it has not given itself up totally to Messianism.' According to Lowy, Scholem's objective historiography was not incompatible with his religious anarchism. Scholem, the intimate friend of Walter Benjamin (see *Walter Benjamin* and *From Berlin to Jerusalem*), was one of the major figures in Jewish thought since Spinoza. The long quote comes from Scholem's critically important essay, 'The Messianic Idea in Judaism', in the eponymous book. There you will also find 'Redemption through Sin' and 'Revelation and Tradition as Religious Categories in Judaism'. It is astonishing how ignorant and unhistorical many accounts of modern Israeli politics are, whether hostile or friendly. It is as if Zionism, even political Zionism, began sometime between the liberation of Auschwitz on 27 January 1945 and the day the United Nations voted for partition (29 November 1947, Claude and Evy Vigée's wedding day) or perhaps 14 May 1948 when Israel declared itself an independent state (and the day my anti-Zionist ultra-orthodox maternal grandfather died). In fact, it was one of the last late-nineteenth-century movements of national liberation, building on centuries of religious fervour directed (*le mot juste*) towards Jerusalem. (And lately building on land in occupied territory.)

Harold Bloom, in *Kabbalah and Criticism*, pays proper tribute to Scholem: 'Kabbalah is essentially a *vision of belatedness*, and I would praise Scholem above all for having transformed his own belatedness, in regard to the necessary anteriority of his own ancient subject, into a surprising earliness. Kabbalah is an extraordinary body of rhetoric or figurative language, and indeed is a theory of rhetoric, and Scholem's formidable achievement is as much rhetorical or figurative as it is historical.'

INDIVIDUALS

Arthur A. Cohen and others

Understanding Jewish Theology, mentioned earlier for its essay by Emil Fackenheim, is edited by Professor Jacob Neusner, who has written/edited more books than any other scholar in his own or perhaps any discipline: estimates range from four hundred to nine hundred. The book sits alongside the best scholarly Jewish reference work for the general reader, *Contemporary Jewish Thought*, edited by Paul Mendes-Flohr and Arthur A. Cohen, which contains well over a hundred authoritative and often brilliant mini-essays including Geoffrey Hartman on 'Imagination' ('There is no imagination without distrust of imagination'), Emil Fackenheim on 'Holocaust', Arthur A. Cohen himself on various subjects including 'Eschatology' and 'Redemption', Adin Steinsaltz on 'Talmud' and Gershom Scholem, no less, on 'Judaism'. Hartman quotes Karl Kraus on Nazi language: 'A bloody dew clings to the flowers of speech' (Which poet does that bring to mind?). Cohen, with whom I had a warm epistolary friendship, was a distinguished scholar, theologian, novelist, publisher and book dealer, in the last capacity assisted as a cataloguer by the young Paul Auster, who needed day jobs until his novels took off and he could live from his pen.

Here are Cohen's short and brilliant study *Osip Emilievich Mandelstam*, his three novellas collected in *Artists and Enemies* and his novel *An Admirable Woman*, whose heroine, according to the cover, was 'suggested to me by the remarkable personality and intellectual career of an old friend, Hannah Arendt'. And yet, a postcard from the early 1980s states: 'It ain't Hannah, although I knew her and admired her.' Another card from that time touches on matters that still concern me:

> Dear Anthony, thanks for the card and the two pamphlets. I know I have promised you a Menard pamphlet on nuclear warfare, but frankly I have been waiting for a hook that will enable me to tie my thinking to certain positions I have already developed in *The Tremendum*. If you would allow a frankly theological inquiry into the relation of God to the nuclear terror and the ethnical issues that tie God to our history I might undertake it for you. I would like you to bill me for the following: Simha Flapan, Senghor, Jabès, Gilboa, Winkler, Moshe Dor, Pagis, Amichai, Levi, Leah Goldberg, Kleist, Max Jacob, MenCards series Two, Suarès. I am sorry you are no longer publishing [i.e. literature]. It's always been a secret passion of mine. I still think of self-publishing a monthly newsprint sheet

with no subscription List, but only those I choose to receive it. Ever best, Arthur

Giving up Menard Press has been a regular trope in my life as a publisher, and that was neither the first nor the last time I cried wolf. At the time of writing, I am, at last, deadly serious about taking this step: the Menard Press fortieth-anniversary-keepsake catalogue, published in 2010, is a valediction to the familiar compound ghosts of my poets and friends. When I reread Cohen's card for the first time in more than twenty years, I fixed on the phrase: 'the nuclear terror and the ethnical issues that tie God to our history'. Did he mean to write 'ethical'? Given (a) the position of the word at the mid-point of a perfect three-point statement ('the relation . . . our history') and (b) that the author is a distinguished Jewish theologian, I believe he intended what he wrote, namely 'ethnical'. On the other hand, why did he use this relatively rare synonym of the word 'ethnic'? The second meaning of 'ethnical' is: 'of or relating to ethnology', which does not fit here, although if you replace 'ethnology' with 'ethnicity' it does. Not that Cohen would talk of ethnicity if he meant nationality or peoplehood. No, either he means 'ethnic' or, oh dear, is it, after all, a typing mistake for 'ethical'?, I asked Bruce Ross-Smith, a brilliant polymath who teaches anthropology and who features prominently in the acknowledgements to this book: 'Yes, I agree ethical would seem to fit, but can't help but feel ethnical was exactly what Arthur Cohen intended and that this could be deciphered, rather along the lines, perhaps, though distantly, of Evans-Pritchard's theo-ethnography and moral identities, in his case mediated by a Catholic God and the subtexts of history. In *Culture as Praxis*, Zygmunt Baumann comments favourably on the subtlety of the Evans-Pritchard position. Ethnical was surely a deliberate usage, which only AC could have elaborated. What a pamphlet Cohen could have written for you!'

I have found another text by Cohen in *Confrontations with Judaism*, edited by Philip Longworth. Cohen's essay, 'The Jewish Intellectual in an Open Society', defines, indeed confronts, the situation Rabbi Michael Goulston was addressing during the last years of his short life when he used the magazine he founded with Lionel Blue, *European Judaism*, as a way of engineering a dialogue between scholars and rabbis on the one hand and secular intellectuals on the other. Cohen discusses and praises Franz

Rosenzweig (*European Judaism* published an essay on Rosenzweig by Jonathan Sacks, then not yet a rabbi, let alone chief rabbi) for charging 'Judaism with the burden of an almost Erasmian revolution, a humanist counterpoint to both Christianity and Marxism, which avoids both traditional obscurantism and the tedious litanies of Jewish self-hatred, which exposes . . . what is unqualifiedly best [in Judaism], precisely because its concern is to afford the world a vision totally disconnected from the instrumentalities of power, sacerdotal or secular. At least, this is the direction of my own humanism, no less messianic for being humane, no less conservative for being apocalyptic, and no less original for being tied in all things to the archetypal Jewish Sage, Saint and Prophet.' I first read this essay in 1971, more than ten years before Cohen and I were in touch with each other. Were he alive today, I would ask him what he meant by 'Saint'. Today too, one would expect him to write 'counterpoint to Christianity and Marxism and Islam', or even 'Christianity and Islam'. As for Cohen's 'monthly newsprint sheet', today this would be a blog, and what a blog he would have written.

Outside the writings of Rabbis Ignaz Maybaum and Lionel Blue, a rare non-academic mention of Islam by a Jewish writer forty years ago can be found in a fascinating and heavily annotated essay in Longworth's book by Henri Baruk, a distinguished French psychiatrist who 'recognised a remarkable correspondence between the methods propounded in the Talmudic treatise *Sanhedrin* and those he had used to bring peace to the Charenton', a famous clinic torn apart by intrigue. Baruk believed and argued that all Jewish tradition is linked to the concept of *tsedek*, generally translated as 'righteousness' but which he understood to mean the justice that derives from a person's empathy with what Buber would call the Thou and Levinas the Other. Baruk makes a strong statement: 'Faith in the principle of redress, defending what is just, is the very essence of the Hebraic faith, a faith which is as far from the glorification of sacrifice found in Christianity as it is from the fatalism of Islam.' I infer from the notes that Baruk wrote this essay in 1966, that is to say before the Six Day War, when everything changed forever, certainly for diaspora Jews, who could no longer avoid thinking about the implications of Israeli actions which were at odds with the imperatives of the Jewish religion. His only reference to Israel is the wish that its penal policy should be based on *tsedek*. I do not blame him for failing to touch on the Palestinian issue at that time; perhaps he addressed it later, for he lived till he was more than a hundred, dying in 1999. Given recent history in the Middle East, there is an unintended irony in Baruk's final sentence: 'Judaism is above all centred on history, the final end of which remains—in spite of its harrowing setbacks—the march towards peace, and understanding between nations in the Messianic era.' Israeli leaders regularly implicate the diaspora in their policies by insisting that they speak for all Jews. This devastates the ridiculous argument often flung at diaspora Jewish radicals that to speak out in criticism is treacherous.

Theodicy: Why evil in God's world? Rabbi Ephraim Oshri's *Responsa from the Holocaust* is a significant and interesting book by a creative interpreter of the law who rose to the occasion. Oshri was a man to whom devout Jews brought their problems in a time/place where 'the lesser of two evils' was not on offer for, as in William Styron's *Sophie's Choice*, any choice was predicated upon a system of absolute evil, designed to humiliate and destroy, even at the expense of efficiency and sense. The theology implied by Yaffa Eliach's *Hasidic Tales of the Holocaust* is not acceptable. It amounts to a combination of Polyanna, of the Jewish version of Candide's philosophy summed up by the Hebrew phrase 'Gam zu letova' (This too is for the good) and an implication that piety and 'ancestral merit' will see you through the worst evil that can be thrown at you. Cohen's *The Tremendum* is possibly the most powerful and eloquent book I have read in this fraught territory. Particularly valuable is his deployment of the concept of 'subscend', which speaks volumes to me and is a permanent fixture in the lexicon of my *imaginaire*. Did he invent this neologism? When I typed the word into Google sixteen hits were registered, as opposed to 'transcend', for which there were nearly twenty-three million. 'If there is no transcendence beyond the abyss [of the death camps], the abyss must be inspected further . . . The abyss must be *sub-scended*, penetrated to its perceivable depths,' and he proceeds to the atomic bomb. *If Not Now, When?* is a record of Cohen's conversations with his former teacher Rabbi Mordecai Kaplan, the founder of the radical Jewish movement Reconstructionism. Kaplan, unlike Cohen, saw Judaism as an evolving 'religious civilisation', a humanistic approach at odds with Cohen's trans- and, indeed, subscendency.

Emmanuel Levinas, Gillian Rose, Moris Farhi and others

Jonathan Rosen's *The Talmud and the Internet* is a fascinating and brilliant little book, written after a computer crash in which he lost a journal he was writing about his aged grandmother, and in which he comes to terms with his loss. In respect of the Talmud and the Internet, the author, like me, is 'proficient in neither' but 'a child of both'. He is not the first person to notice the visual and other parallels between a page of the Talmud and the home page of a website, though he may be the first to explore their poetics and benefit from their synergy. He quotes a passage by Donne which I like to think was known to Borges: 'God's hand is in every translation, and his hand shall bind up all our scattered leaves again for that library where every book shall lie open to one another.'

One reason for the widespread scholarly interest in Emmanuel Levinas in recent years—the philosopher emerged from Lithuanian Talmud studies rather than Galician Hasidism, the world of Buber and his *Tales of Rabbi Nachmann*—is that the intertextual techniques of the Talmud, the imbrication of commentary and source, quotation and text, are intrinsic to poststructuralist discourse. You don't have to be Jewish, as the old Levi's rye-bread advertisement had it—featuring Native Indians and other minorities on deservedly famous posters in the 1960s—to find the style of Levinas relevant to your work in the age of Barthes and, later, Derrida, whose *Adieu to Emmanuel Levinas* contains two of his most profound and beautiful texts, including the funeral oration. More important, a meditation on what Levinas is thinking and worrying about reveals that he has much to say to us in this day and age. Here are *Textes pour Emmanuel Levinas* (including Derrida, Ricoeur and Jabès) edited by François Laruelle and a book of interviews, *Ethique et Infini*, both from the early 1980s. In the latter book, I see a marginal comment, the single word 'Musa', beside these words of Levinas, in my translation: 'Alterity and duality do not disappear in love . . . . The pathos of an erotic relationship resides in the fact that there are two people, and that the other participant is absolutely other.' Musa is my friend Moris Farhi, distinguished epic novelist (*Journey through the Wilderness* and other books) and poet of the elemental (*Songs from Two Continents*); he has always argued for a merger, an aspiration encouraged by personal experience.

I deeply admired Gillian Rose and learnt from her essays, *Judaism and Modernity* and *The Broken Middle*, impassioned meditations, liminal and aporetic at once. We began a dialogue after I wrote a short notice of *Love's Work*, only for our contact to be broken by her death. Its optimistic epigraph is one I try to live up to, and pass on to friends when things are going badly: 'Keep your mind in hell, and despair not' (Staretz Silouan). It was thanks to Z. Kotowicz, who introduced me to Gillian Rose's close friend and literary executor Howard Caygill (author of *Levinas and the Political*), that I published her posthumous and moving *Paradiso*. This is a key text, but *Mourning Becomes the Law* is a more profound book and her masterpiece. In it, she ticks off Derrida for what she calls his logophobia and, in passing, helps us understand a little better Walter Benjamin's demanding text, *The Origins of German Tragic Drama*. She wrongly dismisses Levinas as a 'Buddhist Jew', although she never lets Simone Weil, whom she opposes to him, off the hook.

'Buddhist Jew', applied to Spinoza, recurs in Rebecca Goldstein's brilliant and exciting study *Betraying Spinoza*, which takes issue with the religious teachers and philosophy teachers of her youth, and deploys her skills as philosopher and author of three novels which live up to their ambitious titles (*Thirty-Six Arguments for the Existence of God*, *The Mind–Body Problem* and *The Late-Summer Passion of a Woman of Mind*) to explore the mind and work and life of this genius, one of my great heroes. Ironically enough, 'Buddhist Jew' could also be used of Lévi-Strauss, although he and Levinas had little or nothing to say to each other in public discourse and may never have met. One remark by Levinas I know by heart is his comment about Israeli colonial occupation of another people and its territory, a comment which should be branded on the minds and hearts of senior Israeli politicians: 'Next to a person who has been affronted, this land—holy and promised—is but nakedness and desert, a heap of wood and stone.' I was privileged to read the unpublished memoir by Lynn Rose, mother of Gillian Rose and her sister Jacqueline Rose. Rarely have I read a more painful account of parental love than the chapter where Lynn has to face and endure her daughter's anger, the entirely understandable consequence of mental anguish emanating from awareness of mortality in the wake of terminal illness.

Gillian influenced and was influenced by Rowan Williams, archbishop of Canterbury at the time of writing, to whom I introduced myself at Abbot Hall gallery in the Lake District during a private view of a show of his sister-in-law, that wonderful painter and friend of Paula's, Celia Paul. He was in mufti, so I asked him if he would prefer not to talk shop, but he didn't mind, and we did. I dropped the name of his friend Jonathan Sacks, with whom I had had a sporadic correspondence over the years. I then told Williams that I would like to send him my essay 'Everything is Prepared for the Feast', which Sebastian Barker, Menard poet of distinction, published in *London Magazine*. This has led to a second sporadic correspondence with a religious leader. Rowan Williams, who is among other things a poet (*The Poems of Rowan Williams*) and a great reader of David Jones (see *Grace and Necessity*) and Dostoevsky (*Dostoevsky: Life, Faith and Fiction*), appeared to be nailed to an eternal cross within the Anglican Communion. Whether he likes it or not, Williams, like the chief rabbi, was a politician, and there is no escape from considerations of the lesser evil. No wonder he reads Gillian Rose. His moving and beautiful sequence, 'Winterreise', was written in her memory. 'Dying by degrees, perhaps, is a winter journey.' I sent Williams a copy of Geoffrey Hill's plain-speaking elegy to Gillian. Published in *Poetry Chicago*, it had been forwarded to me from New York by a sharp-eyed and thoughtful friend Michael O'Brien (author of a wondrous book of poems, *Sleeping and Waking*) because Hill mentioned *Paradiso*.

Abraham Joshua Heschel, Joseph Soloveitchik, I. F. Stone

In *Halakhic Man*, Rabbi Joseph Soloveitchik's utterly fascinating book about the nature of Jewish belief and practice (specifically the highly intellectual Lithuanian tradition of which he was the most illustrious survivor or practitioner in the USA), the author reminds us that Judaism abhors death and bids one, in a famous Biblical phrase, to choose life and to sanctify it. He tells us that whenever his illustrious grandfather feared death, he would study the laws of corpse defilement and this would calm him down. 'The act of objectification triumphs over the subjective terror of death.' Is this not a kind of psychological vaccination? Soloveitchik also tells us that the Halakha 'is not particularly concerned with the metaphysics of time': the time that his classical tradition approves of 'is fixed and determined', not 'a flowing stream'. This segues nicely to the remark of someone he respected but disapproved of, the Hasidically inclined Rabbi Abraham Joshua Heschel, author of that ecstatic hymn to a destroyed world *The Earth Is the Lord's*: 'The Jews in Eastern Europe lived more in time than in space.' This striking thought explains the unworldliness of people like my maternal grandfather. It is cognate with Lionel Kochan's equally striking assertion that Judaism is a religion of the ear, Christianity a religion of the eye, which I discussed in a National Gallery catalogue essay on Kitaj. Kochan's *Beyond the Graven Image* is a demanding study of the Jewish attitude to graven images, and the limits on the famous prohibition. Kitaj's *Second Diasporist Manifesto*, which friends received a day or two before he died by his own hand is an obsessional exploration of art and Jewishness: 'Depart this world dumb-founded by art and Jews,' states paragraph or verse 442. He wrote from five in the morning until it was time to go to the studio, with its north light, in the former garage of his house in Westwood near UCLA (once owned by Peter Lorre), where he would work until evening, when he would read. The writing primed his mind, cleansed the left brain, freeing him up to make paintings. His death, the manner of it, shocked and distressed his friends, who emailed each other, circulating obits and flinching in the powerful light which death—any death, but suicide in particular—always casts on the lives of those affected. As to why he killed himself, one of the causes was the onset of Parkinson's. But the self-slaughter was, as it always is, more complex than that.

Heschel's hymn to a destroyed world is simultaneously a hymn to an idealized people who perceived themselves, Shekhina-like, to be living in exile from Zion, to which they would return with the Messiah. Rabbi Heschel writes: 'Study was a technique of sublimating feeling into thought, of transposing dreams into syllogisms, of expressing grief in formulating keen theoretical difficulties and joy in finding a solution to a difficult passage in Maimonides.' Soloveitchik, whose grandfather's way with death exemplifies perfectly Heschel's sublimation, has an interesting footnote to his remark about objectification in *Halakhic Man*. He quotes Stefan Zweig as saying that Tolstoy conquered the fear of death that had seized hold of him through an act of objectification, that is, transforming death into an object of his artistic creation. It is characteristic of Soloveitchik to honour the reader's intelligence by leaving us to infer what is unsaid, namely his opinion that persons who live their lives according to Jewish religious law have a weapon as powerful as the making of a work of art, or at least the reading of a work of art, in this instance presumably *The Death of Ivan Ilyich*, one of the greatest works of fiction ever written. In his essay on 'Culture' in *Contemporary Jewish Religious Thought*, Paul Mendes-Flohr quotes Soloveitchik as calling for a dialogue between the man of faith and the man of culture; cultural endeavours, he acknowledges [as with Tolstoy—AR], have a potentially majestic, blessed quality. Culture, by which Soloveitchik means that which the secular Jew lives by, deserves a dialogue, and yet encoded into *Halakhic Man* is a polemic against Christianity and, differently, against non-orthodox Judaism. No dialogue would appear to be possible. The polemic against the latter comes at the end of the first of the two sections of the essay where, speaking of what he calls liberal (i.e. any form of non-orthodox) Judaism, he states that when it 'expelled the *Shekhinah*, the divine presence, from the broad arena of Jewish life, it set aside a special place for it in the synagogue. As a result, according to the liberal Jewish outlook, the synagogue stands at the heart of religion. The Halakhah, the Judaism that is faithful to itself, however, which brings the divine presence into the midst of empirical reality, does not centre on the synagogue or study house. These are minor sanctuaries. The true sanctuary is the sphere of our daily, mundane activities, for it is there that the realisation of the *Halakhah* takes place. The true Torah giants, the halakhic men par excellence, were indeed champions of truth and justice. They glowed with a resplendent ethical beauty.' In his eulogy for Soloveitchik (see *Memories of a Giant*, edited by Michael Bierman), Jonathan Sacks quotes Soloveitchik as telling him that 'Professor' Heschel's description, in his 'beautiful book' *The Sabbath*, of the Sabbath as 'a sanctuary in time' was a 'lovely idea' but that it is from 'Halakhah [and 'the thirty-nine categories of work'] not from poetry that you have to create a theory of Shabbat'. Note that Soloveitchik could not bring himself to call Heschel 'rabbi' because the latter's rabbinic status had been bestowed by orthodox *and* non-orthodox religious authorities. Unlike *Halakhic Man*, *The Halakhic Mind*, Soloveitchik's other major book aimed at the general reader, comes as a disappointment: it is pedantic, even scholastic, the aspect of Lithuanian Judaism the Hasidic movement rebelled against long ago.

Abraham Heschel was above all a preacher, activist and teacher. This was a man, a mensch. Much of the writing (English was his fourth language) in his many books is too exhortative for my taste. Nor am I as impressed as I used to be by thoughts like the following: 'for the pious man, it is a privilege to die'. However, he has a doughty and subtle champion, Edward Kaplan, who explains and defends Heschel's rhetorical strategies and networks of tropes in a study of his 'poetics of piety', *Holiness in Words*. Heschel is seen in a famous and iconic photograph from 1965, marching alongside Martin Luther King in Selma-Montgomery, Alabama. As Kaplan explains in an essay on Heschel in Grayston and Higgins' *Thomas Merton Pilgrim in Progress*, the rabbi was in dialogue with the influential Christian poet and pacifist, who sought to understand the Jewish prophetic tradition but whose contemplative tendencies led him to Buddhism. There is no rest for the wicked and no file is ever closed: as always with key figures, the postman brings a new book when one has to move on, in this instance *Spiritual Radical*, the second and remarkable volume of Kaplan's biography of Heschel. Edmond Jabès told me that Heschel was an admirer of his work, especially *The Book of Questions*, and used to send him books, but that unfortunately he did not reciprocate the admiration. Here, finally, are Heschel's *Man's Quest for God*, *Man Is Not Alone* and that strange book *A Passion for Truth*, a curious reflection on three radical spirits—the Baal Shem Tov, Kierkegaard and the Rabbi of Kotzk.

Heschel had a soul brother in another old Jewish radical, a secular one, I. F. Stone, whose famous weekly I began reading in the USA and subscribed to when I returned home after my six months in Chicago in 1966, which I touch on elsewhere in this book. Every embassy in Washington subscribed too. Stone avoided press conferences and what we would now call spin-doctors like the plague and instead studied closely all the government documents he could lay his hands on. *The Best of I. F. Stone* is a monument to his far-sightedness, historical awareness and radicalism. The essay he wrote after the Six Day War remains a key text, and should be required reading, even now, when Israel appears to have lost the will and perhaps the desire to go the extra mile for peace. His essays on the USA imply the possibility as well as the necessity of a progressive coalition for change. Sadly the high hopes and deep commitment implied by the solidarity between Heschel and King, two of the greatest religious figures of the last hundred years, have been severely damaged by developments in his homeland since 9/11.

S. H. Bergman

Thanks to an introduction from Rabbi Albert Friedlander, I was able to meet Samuel Hugo Bergman, the retired rector of the Hebrew University, on my first visit to Israel in 1969. I was invited to his house in the attractive Jerusalem suburb of Rehavia, not far from the apartments of my friends Dov Noy, Claude Vigée and Robert Friend. After his wife had offered me tea, Bergman presented me with his introduction to modern Jewish thought, *Faith and Reason*, and inscribed it in Hebrew. Then the unforgettable moment: he allowed me to clasp the high-school-keepsake album of 1901 in which his classmate Franz Kafka (not yet our Kafka of course, and so all the more moving) had written a message, an experience for me only equalled by the occasion when André Frénaud handed me his Rimbaud first edition. The fantasy of meeting Kafka or, say, Isaac Rosenberg is, of course, different from the fantasy of meeting someone who had died before it would have been possible to meet them, Flaubert or Dostoevsky, or indeed Rimbaud—even if he had lived a long life. To ruminate on meeting Kafka, one has to engage in fantasy: let's say Kafka was not a sick man and had not died aged forty in 1924 and that he had immigrated to Palestine and that one met him, aged nearly ninety, in Tel-Aviv, on one's first visit to Israel in 1969. But had his health been good, he would have had a different psyche-soma and he would not have been the man and written the books that make one want to have met him in the first place, and which are the reason why I felt that frisson of *proximity-in-distance* when holding the high-school-keepsake book in Bergman's house, the same frisson I felt in George Steiner's Cambridge house, where he showed me one of the handful of books that survived the pillage of Kafka's library.

John Rayner and Ignaz Maybaum

My friend and neighbour the late Rabbi John Rayner, who came to Britain on a Kinder-transport, admired Abraham Joshua Heschel and was as outspoken on contemporary issues as Heschel was. Here is Rayner on Margaret Thatcher and the Pharisees in one of the last sermons included in the collection published as *An Understanding of Judaism.*

> Unlike the Prophets, and unlike Jesus, the Pharisees did not content themselves with merely preaching concern for the weak: they actually legislated for an equitable social order. So whether the leader of a government under whose legislation the gap between rich and poor has grown ever wider, and the problem of homelessness ever graver, is in a strong position to criticise the Pharisees for their supposed lack of concern for the unfortunate is a question to which it is not easy to think of a polite answer.
>
> The historical truth is that the Pharisees were champions of freedom, champions of democracy, champions of neighbourly love, and champions of social justice . . . If this country, during the 1980s that are now about to end, had made a serious attempt to live up to the ideals they taught and practised it would undoubtedly be a more just, compassionate and humane society than it is.

As Rabbi David Goldberg writes in his preface, Rayner was the finest exponent of the lost art of homiletics in Anglo-Jewry. Albert Friedlander could be uniquely inspired when the mood took him during the delivery of unscripted or semi-scripted sermons, but he did not and could not maintain the endless flow of meticulously prepared high-level sermons. Rayner sometimes used to send me drafts of his texts on Israel and if I toned him up on occasion, he toned me down when I went over the top. He could not have been further removed from the folksy wisdom of an East End boy like Lionel Blue who, like John Rayner, also moved to this part of North London in later life. Blue was the first UK Jewish cleric to come out as gay, perhaps the first UK cleric of any denomination. It's not that one can't imagine John as gay, rather that one can't imagine him telling Yiddish jokes and publishing cook books.

Another theologian whose work I have dipped into is a well-nigh forgotten figure, Ignaz Maybaum, the teacher of Lionel Blue and other senior Reform rabbis. He understood earlier than most that Islam was a significant part of the religious landscape of Europe. Here are his *Creation and Guilt,*

The Jewish Home and *Jewish Existence*. He argues that in Christianity love is supposed to rule supreme, in Islam law is supposed to rule supreme, while Judaism, involved in a dialectical relationship with the two world religions for centuries, in principle marries the two. There is no escaping the fact that if Israel defines itself as a Jewish state as opposed to a state where the majority of the population are Jews (even though, in constitutional terms, it is not strictly speaking a Jewish state, since a sovereign secular parliament voted powers to the religious authorities which it could take back), then it cannot complain if it is measured and found wanting against the highest standards: democracy and social justice are incompatible with fundamentalist religion, where fundamentalists are in a majority. What's more, as I wrote elsewhere: 'Fundamentalist Judaism is necessarily incapable of surviving in the modern world without deploying a host of devices (and rationalising their use by means of legal fictions) such as *Shabbat* lifts and time switches. These ultimately derive from a scientific praxis that is under-pinned by a worldview rejected by Jewish fundamentalists.' Jonathan Sacks, master of the soundbite and a humane and intelligent man, should be ashamed of his *bon mot*: 'I am the acceptable face of Jewish fundamentalism.' As for Buddhism, it makes the differences between the other three traditions seem minor. By implication, Maybaum calls for a synthesis of humanism and religion. Maybaum would be better known if his writerly qualities matched his religious insights.

Maybaum's last two books were *Trialogue between Jew, Christian and Muslim* and another study of the three traditions, *Happiness outside the State*. Here he is very rude indeed about the Lubavitcher Rabbi, describing him as a guru and his followers as pious fools in Polish headgear. For Maybaum, Torah involves prophecy and transcendence. To understand it, or rather to misunderstand it, as *law* is to adopt a Pauline and Islamic attitude towards Judaism: Paul who would reject the law, Islam which would expand its terrain. Both attitudes are the source of hundreds of years of misunderstanding by Christians, by Muslims and, above all, by orthodox Jews. A rabbi is neither priest nor ulema, he insists. Again, for Maybaum, famously rejected by orthodoxy in England when he arrived from Germany on the grounds that he was too theological in his approach, the holiness of the moral law is what it is all about. Like Freud, he quotes a famous remark of Kant with approval:

'the eternal stars above me and the moral law within me' and equates this with Micah's famous words ('do justice, love mercy and walk humbly with your God'), in short he equates it with Judaism.

Folklore and Humour

FOLKLORE

Howard Schwartz and others

I have a whole bunch of books written, edited or translated by my old friend Howard Schwartz, an immensely productive poet, storyteller, editor and scholar living in St Louis. Nothing can bring back (thank goodness) or equal the intensity and scope of our early collaboration on *Voices in the Ark*, a giant anthology of twentieth-century Jewish poetry from all languages, published in 1980, just as nothing can bring back other 'joint ventures' of the 1970s and 1980s when, to all appearances 'infiniment disponible', like the character in Cyril Connolly's *The Rockpool*, one had the time and energy to work on several fronts at once, juggle different parts of the brain in a way that becomes impossible for persons of a certain age. Here are Schwartz's tales of the supernatural, *Lilith's Cave*; *Miriam's Tambourine*, an international anthology of Jewish folktales; *Elijah's Violin*, a collection of Jewish fairy tales; and *Gabriel's Palace*, his collection of Jewish mystical tales. *Gates to the New City* contains twentieth-century 'modern Jewish tales': Babel, Bialik, Jabès, Kafka, Agnon, Appelfeld, Lind and other members of the family of my ancestral *imaginaire*, an *imaginaire* that feeds into and is fed by Muslim, Christian and other *imaginaires* in our only world, our threatened, plundered, dangerous, wondrous world. I spend time briefing myself on political developments in the Middle East and elsewhere, arguing with people for whom Israel can do no wrong and others for whom Israel can do no right, so it warms my heart to linger awhile in Howard's land of Jewish dreams, various and beautiful, while on a darkling plain, ignorant armies clash by night, 'swept with confused alarms of struggle and flight'. Sadly, the roar of Matthew Arnold's 'Sea of Faith' is neither withdrawing nor retreating and 'The turbid ebb and flow / of human misery' abides eternal. *Imperial Messages* is Schwartz's collection of parables: Kafka, Borges, Dostoevsky, Gogol, through to our late friends, Larry Fixel and Cecil Helman. Among his written rather than edited works are poetry—*Gathering the Sparks* and *Vessels*—and stories: *The Captive Soul of the Messiah* incorporates one of the most physically beautiful of all Menard books, *Midrashim*, with illustrations by John Swanson, whose old testament screen prints adorn my bedroom.

The doorbell rings. It's the postman with *Tree of Souls*, Schwartz's new book, described on the cover as the first anthology of Jewish mythology in English. I start thumbing through this latest cornucopia: here are favourites to revisit—Shekhina, Lilith, Azazel—and hundreds of other myths to draw on. I learn that there was even a Jewish Icarus at the time of the Temple; the story, according to one commentator, is an anti-Christian polemic. Who knows, maybe I'll find something Paula can use. So far, the only specifically Jewish fable she's been inspired by is the Dybbuk, making two prints after seeing the classic Yiddish film with me some years ago. Schwartz is one of the scholar children of our mutual friend, the legendary Zeida and Grand Duke of Jewish folklore studies, Dov Noy in Jerusalem, who lives in the Rehavia apartment of the former prime minister, Moshe Sharett. Merely glancing at *Voices in the Ark* reminds me of the giant effort involved in editing a twelve-hundred-page anthology, editorially and administratively. All those permissions: there can never be a second edition, for reasons of copyright finance, energy and priorities. The book exhausted us and tested our friendship, which, however, survived, although we went on to pursue different interests. If Howard had not moved into folklore, I would not be learning from *Tree of Souls* that every midnight in a palace in Paradise, presided over by the prophetesses Miriam and Deborah, righteous Jewish women and righteous Jewish men copulate, and that the fruit of these unions 'are the souls of those who become converts to Judaism'.

Howard Schwartz's *Reimagining the Bible: The Storytelling of the Rabbis* has affinities with Dan Jacobson's *The Story of Stories: The Chosen People and Its God*. Robert Alter's *The World of Biblical Literature* is a good reminder, like Gabriel Josipovici's *The Book of God*, of the Bible's status and nature as a great work of literature, irrespective of the reader's religious perspective. A book that, by definition, could be filed under 'Reference Books' but has made a special request to sit here alongside the other two is Robert Alter and Frank Kermode's *The Literary Guide to the Bible*. Nor should I forget Erich Fromm's earlier meditation on the Old Testament and freedom, *You Shall Be as Gods*. David Curzon's *Modern Poems on the Bible* (Paul Celan, Zbigniew Herbert and so on) and *The Gospels in Our Image* are major anthologies of modern Midrashim on, respectively, the Old Testament and the New Testament.

Here are two classic anthologies I regularly dipped into when I was young: Nathan Ausubel's *A Treasury of Jewish Folklore* and *A Treasury of Jewish Humour*. The former is inscribed '1953. To Anthony with love from Grandpa and Grandma Rudolf', in the handwriting of my paternal grandmother, who was more at ease in English than my other grandparents, having arrived here from Poland at the age of two, unlike her husband, who was in his early twenties when he reached the docks. A sticker tells me that the book was bought at Jack Mazin's shop in Berwick Street, which was the main specialist Jewish bookshop in London, along with Shapiro and Vallentine in Wentworth Street in the East End, run by the scholar, bibliophile and future professor of Hebrew at University College London, Chimen Abramsky.

A curiosity

The Friday Night Book, aimed at children of immigrants, dates from 1933. Its sections include Magic, Jewish Wit and Humour, Mathematical Problems (in the Talmud) and Palestine Scenes/Songs. Even religious Jews among the parents of the children at whom *The Friday Night Book* is aimed would not necessarily be acquainted with Astronomy, which the ancient rabbis had to understand because of the complexities of the Jewish calendar. The beautiful statement found in the Talmud that 'Sleep is one sixtieth part of death', is derived from the Babylonian sexagesimal system adopted by the Jews.

A related and sublime statement is reminiscent of Borges' 'Avatars of the Tortoise': 'Anyone visiting a sick person relieves him of a sixtieth part of his illness . . . If that be so, then let sixty people visit the patient and cure him of the whole of his illness.' However, 'each visitor removes a sixtieth of what is left, and not of the whole illness. In this way there is left, after the first visitor, 59/60ths of the original illness, so that the second visitor removes only one sixtieth of 59/60, i.e. $59/60^2$, leaving 59/60 minus $59/60^2$, which is equal to fifty-nine-sixtieths of 59/60, i.e. $(59/60)^2$ of the original illness. Similarly, the third visitor leaves $(59/60)^3$ of the original illness, and so on. After the sixtieth visitor, there would still be left $(59/60)^{60}$, which is still approximately one-quarter of the original illness.' My friend Michael Rowan Robinson, astrophysicist, mathematician and poet, tells me that one-quarter is wrong: it should be 0.365. When it came to pi, the rabbis appear to have been satisfied with a very rough approximation of 3, which was no better than that of the Babylonians, inferior to the Hindus and Chinese (3.16), which in turn was less accurate than Archimedes.

The 'Songs' section includes Psalm 51. This wondrous poem was written by King David—who has some claim to being the most interesting figure in the Bible—after he was reproached by the prophet Nathan for his affair with Bathsheba, the wife of Uriah. You had to recite the first verse, the Neck Verse, if you wanted to obtain benefit of clergy, a privilege whose preservation Thomas a'Beckett died for. It saved the life of Ben Jonson, who recited it in Latin after killing an actor in a duel in 1598. As we know, in earlier days, the only people who could read in England were at court or associated with the church or educational institutions, apart from the handful of Marranos living here before the unofficial Return of the Jews under Cromwell in 1656.

HUMOUR

Hyam Maccoby and others

Humour! Ah, the famous Jewish humour: by actual persecution out of perceived superiority. A superiority complex served as a defence mechanism, because if you introjected what the Other thought of you, you were finished. Therefore if he treated you like that, it was because he was too stupid to know anything else. The humour was related to the intellectuality which was driven by a religious faith that required literacy, and this in turn led to great achievements in fields (other than Talmud studies) requiring verbal skills—comedy, psychoanalysis, the law—after the emergence of Jews from the ghetto and the ending of quotas (e.g. at Harvard and Yale), with all those words and ideas begging for a good home if they were not to waste their 'sweetness on the desert air'.

Berel Lang's valuable book *Writing and the Holocaust* contains the last essay of Terrence Des Pres: 'Holocaust *Laughter?*'. He discusses *Maus* by Art Spiegelman (surely a perfect combination of names for such an artist) and *This Way for the Gas, Ladies and Gentlemen* by Tadeusz Borowski (a key book and well covered/uncovered in *This Way* edited by Marco Sonzogni). Here are George Mikes' *The Prophet Motive*, a book about Israel by a man who, unusually for a humorist, was not politically reactionary, and Steve Lipman's *Laughter in Hell: The Use of Humour during the Holocaust*: there is a raid on a Jewish home at breakfast time. 'Who are those men?' a frightened boy asks his grandmother: 'SS, mein kind.' The Yiddish reply involves a pun on the normal everyday request of a grandmother: 'Eat, eat, my child.' Kurt Vonnegut's ferocious satire *Mother Night* has the main character, a double agent (Nazi and American) who is about to stand trial in Israel, being asked by Eichmann in jail if he would like to borrow a few Jews for the book he too is writing.

Here too is Hyam Maccoby's *The Day God Laughed*, an entertaining collection of Talmudic and other byways. For example: 'These are compelled to give their wives a divorce, if the wife so desires: One who is afflicted with boils; one who has polypus, which causes bad breath; one who collects dog's excrement for a living; a coppersmith; a tanner.' And: 'Rav Kahana once went in and hid under Rav's bed [Rav was a great third-century rabbi] to see how his teacher conducted himself in intercourse with his wife. He noted that Rav chatted and joked with his wife before having intercourse with her. Said Rav Kahana: "It is as if the mouth of Father had never tasted such food before!" Said Rav: "Kahana, are you here? Go out, for it is not good manners." Said he to him, "It is Torah, and I have to learn." ' A parallel story tells of Rabbi Akiva following Rabbi Joshua into a privy and ending 'It is Torah, and I have to learn.' This is a potential defence against almost any charge.

Literature

Introduction

Ilan Stavans' anthology of Latin American Jewish stories, *Tropical Synagogues*, which includes such interesting writers as Clarice Lispector and Moacyr Scliar from Brazil, also has three marvellous tales by Borges: 'Emma Zunz', 'Death and the Compass' and 'The Secret Miracle', but, surprisingly, not 'Deutsches Requiem'. Stavans tells us that Borges, by far the most interested in Jewish matters of the great Latin American writers, tried to learn Hebrew, as did Kafka and Benjamin. He says that, like them, Borges was unsuccessful. This is unfair to Kafka, who made good progress in his lessons with Puah Mencel, the Zionist emissary to Prague. I had to pinch myself years later when I corresponded with her; Clive Sinclair even met her. We both met Kafka's niece and, as already related, I met Kafka's school friend, Shmuel Bergman, in Jerusalem. Clive and I are one handshake away from Kafka!

S. Ansky, Mark Twain and Herman Melville

As a loyal groupie of the late Susannah York, I drove to Stratford-on-Avon some years ago to see her in *Camino Royal* and have dinner with her afterwards. Browsing round the theatre bookshop during the interval, I bought a remainder copy of *The Dybbuk and Other Writings* by S. Ansky. What attracted me was not only the text of this wondrous play but also the extract from his Galician diaries, written during World War I—a few years before Babel wrote his own diaries of the Polish–Soviet War—when the world of my grandfather was already in its death throes. The Nazis delivered the *coup de grâce* a generation later. *The Dybbuk* was the first film Paula and I saw together, back in 1996. Earlier that afternoon, I had gone with my mother to another Yiddish classic, *Yiddle with a Fiddle*. I thought that the neutral territory of a cinema foyer would be as good a place as any for them to meet for the first time. In Mandelstam's *The Noise of Time* there is a charming portrait of Ansky: 'He preserved everything, remembered everything . . . In a house where everyone was . . . cracking the tough agrarian nut, Semen Akimich gave the impression of a gentle haemorrhoidal Psyche.' Ansky was the exact contemporary of Sholom Aleichem, whom he despised. Aleichem's daughter, Marie Waife-Goldberg, does not even mention Ansky in her biography *My Father Sholom Aleichem*. She does, however, tell the well-known story that Aleichem was introduced to Mark Twain as 'The Yiddish Mark Twain', to which Twain replied graciously, 'I am the American Sholom Aleichem'. I learnt from Henry Tobias' *The Jewish Bund in Russia* that not only did Ansky write the Bund hymn, 'The Oath', he had once been the secretary of the famous populist Peter Lavrov. The playwright wrote *The Dybbuk* in two versions, Russian and then Yiddish, before it was translated into Hebrew by his contemporary, the great poet Bialik.

We learn from Hilton Obenzinger's *American Palestine: Melville, Twain and the Holy Land Mania* that Mark Twain was not in favour of Zionism: 'it will not be well to let that race find out its strength. If the horses knew theirs, we should not ride any more.' Melville believed that the idea of Jehovah was conceived in the Pyramids, an echo of a later view, Freud's. Obenzinger writes: 'The Pyramids provide the supreme example of man-made sublimity, of "doing violence to the imagination" in Kant's formulation, but Melville locates their power, beyond both man and nature, in that "supernatural creature, the priest",' from whom Moses derived his inspiration. Melville's greatest poetry was in *Moby Dick* but he was no mean poet in verse. 'Clarel' contains a fascinating section called 'Concerning Hebrews'. It seems likely he visited London's East End: 'The Houndsditch clothesman scarce would seem / akin to seers.' The section deals quite consciously with the crisis of faith among post-Enlightenment Jews as they experienced a world in which their ancestral heritage was becoming a religion independent of lineage and peoplehood. The Christian or gentile perception of this crisis in Melville comes across as anti- and philosemitic all at once (although Obenzinger tells me he prefers 'Judaic' to 'Semitic'). Obenzinger's latest book, *New York on Fire*, is a multivocal poem, a collage of cityscapes probably inspired by Charles Reznikoff. Surprisingly, perhaps, given Obenzinger's interest in Melville, it does not touch on the fire at the office of the New York publisher Harper that destroyed most of the remaining copies of the first edition of *Moby Dick*.

Bible translation

In a memorial article on George Oppen, Hugh Kenner wrote that the poet 'once interrupted some blather about Biblical translation by remarking that what they needed for that job was a carpenter: no, better "a Jewish carpenter"'. There are many translations, including Donald Davie's *The Psalms in English* (translated by various hands) and Peter Levi's *Psalms*, not his best book. Essential reading are *The Wisdom Books* (Job, Proverbs and Ecclesiastes) and *The Book of Psalms*, Robert Alter's versions: 'And I shall dwell in the house of the Lord for many long days.' Here too is Everett Fox's remarkable version of the *Torah*, the five books of Moses, which Ted Hughes argued for strongly and Robert Alter praises highly on the cover. No one should be without Alter's differently remarkable version, *The Five Books of Moses*, which Ted did not live long enough to see. My default Bible, if that is the word, is the second translation of the Masoretic text by the Jewish Publication Society of America, published in 1985. The original 1916 edition, with different books allotted to different translators (as in 1985), was the first to be translated into English directly from the Hebrew, rather than indirectly, as with the King James Bible. The King James is, to some extent, a revision of the Geneva Bible which itself incorporated most of Tyndale, who translated from the Latin and from Luther's German.

Many English writers have the authorized version in their ink. Once upon a time, I had the mad idea of comparing Tyndale, Geneva and King James line by line and seeing if I could spot a verse with Shakespeare's imprint, for I wanted him to have been involved in some capacity: a Borgesian fantasy! Indeed a mere list of my many unfulfilled projects would make a Borgesian prose poem in its own right. On the other hand, Shakespeare himself quotes from the Geneva Bible, so that's full circle. Here is the Soncino *Pentateuch*, which I received as a prize at Hebrew classes. Its commentary by Chief Rabbi Hertz is now a fascinating historical curiosity: he seeks the truth 'wherever it is to be found' and therefore also quotes non-Jewish sources, one reason the book has been replaced by the fundamentalist and therefore inferior Artscroll edition; yet Hertz remains a valuable resource, a learned idiosyncratic guide for perplexed of North Finchley.

[Coda: Two years earlier, in 1954, I received a Soncino *Pentateuch* as a prize. I had completely forgotten about this until a recent phone call from my childhood synagogue: the book was in the synagogue office; it had been returned to them from Hampstead Synagogue. The only time I visited Hampstead Synagogue was in 1958 for the bar mitzvah of a cousin; perhaps I had taken the book with me. More than half a century later, the book has come home.]

147

After Robert Alter's version, I like reading Robert Gordis' commented translation of one of my favourite works from the Bible, Koheleth or Ecclesiastes, supreme 'wisdom' book, great poem and source of book titles for Henry James and Ernest Hemingway. My largest unfulfilled project was the Menard Bible, a grandiose ambition that could never have been funded and even if it could, would have required full-time attention for the rest of my life. A new translation of the Book of Job, which Jonathan Swift read every year on his birthday—that would have been something. But it was not to be. 'I have other plans,' as Alberto de Lacerda said to the American woman who wished him a nice day.

Literary Essays and Reviews by A. M. Klein, the Canadian poet silent for the last twenty years of his life, was published after he died. Of the significant Jewish poets writing in English, he is up there with Reznikoff as a writer deeply preoccupied, although not exclusively, with Jewish themes and concerns. The first text in his prose collection discusses a Yiddish *vers libre* translation of Koheleth. He finds an affinity between the philosophy of the great preacher—'Vanity of vanities, sayeth the preacher'—and the Jews of the diaspora. This, in his opinion, renders the translation into Yiddish easier than most books of the Bible. Let me conclude with Gordis' version of verses from the final section of the book and send you to Alter and King James for comparison:

> When the almond-tree blossoms,
> The grasshopper becomes a burden,
> And the caper-berry can no longer stimulate desire.
> So man goes to his eternal home,
> While the hired mourners walk about in the street . . .
> Before the silver cord is severed,
> And the golden bowl is shattered,
> The pitcher is broken at the spring,
> And the wheel is shattered at the pit.
> The dust returns to the earth as it was,
> And the spirit returns to God, who gave it.
> Vanity of vanities, says Koheleth, all is vanity.

Memoirs/Fiction

Benjamin Wilkomirski; Jerzy Kosinski; Bruno Schulz; David Grossman and Amos Oz

If you were, say, ten, when you were liberated from the camps you would now be in your late seventies. Fiction is beginning to take over from memoir. Not only that, in recent years we have become aware of how constructed even testimonies are, especially the best ones. In fiction, of course, we automatically expect construction. Benjamin Wilkomirski claimed that his book *Fragments* was autobiographical. Had he admitted he invented facts and presented his text as a novel, he would not be in trouble as an impostor, as someone who 'softens historicity', in James Wood's phrase. One defence, which Eva Hoffman and others indignantly reject, is that he genuinely persuaded himself he had been in Majdanek else he could not have found the resources to write the book. That proposition conflates two points: the first concerns his mental state and the second involves a literary judgement. Those who think it is a good book have to be saying that a mad empathy generated the writing; those who think it is a bad book must mean that he was a wicked fraud. Would someone who could perform the mental operation involved in recovering a false memory be able to write a good book, one that was good enough to win the non-fiction Jewish book of the year award? Would it have won the fiction award? Maybe, after all these years, the contamination Hoffman felt (as one of the judges of the award) has faded. Jerzy Kosinski's *The Painted Bird*, supposedly based on his own experience, was published as a novel, and that makes a difference. Today, Kosinski is best known for *Being There*, thanks to the film starring Peter Sellers. Both are far better books than *The Hermit of 69th Street*, with its sexual pun in the title and cod footnotes, although a spot check of unlikely notes revealed them to be factual. In his selected essays, *Passing By*, Kosinski quotes his spiritual guide Abraham Joshua Heschel as saying that the eight centuries of Jewish life in their native Poland 'was the golden period in Jewish History, in the history of the Jewish soul'. Given how the period ended, this is possibly a counter-intuitive thought, though one well worth reflecting on.

One of the most fascinating writers emanating from that world was Bruno Schulz, whose early death in the Drogobych ghetto deprived us of many works. Schulz had a 'protector', an SS officer called Landau, for whose house he painted murals (which were removed in the dead of night by Israeli agents many years later, supposedly protecting the Jewish patrimony), and was murdered by a rival protector whose Jew Landau had murdered: 'you shot my Jew, and now I'm shooting yours.' Sadly, we have to be content with the wondrous short stories, *The Street of Crocodiles* and *Sanatorium under the Sign of the Hourglass*: '. . . the Book, without precise details or epithets and in this very restraint there is a sigh of powerlessness, a silent capitulation before the immensity of transcendence, for no word, no allusion, could shine, perfume or vibrate with this shudder of fear, this presentiment of the nameless thing whose sole foretaste on the tip of one's tongue exceeds the limits of wonder'. *The Booke of Idolatry*, which collects Schulz's strange drawings, was edited and introduced by his biographer the poet Jerzy Ficowski, who chased round the world in an unsuccessful search for Schulz's lost manuscript novel. Cynthia Ozick deals with the subject in her novel, *The Messiah of Stockholm*.

In 'Books That Have Read Me', the first essay in David Grossman's *Writing in the Dark*, the author explains that his novel *See Under: Love* is an attempt to 'write about a *Jewish* existence in an *Israeli* idiom. But it also attempts the opposite: to describe Israel in a "diasporic" language'. *See Under: Love* rightly caused a great stir when it appeared in English. Grossman's extraordinary book incarnates a 'guerrilla war with words', to quote a phrase from the novel itself. His obsession with what happened 'over there'—part of his motivation was to avenge the murder of his tutelar Bruno Schulz, rescued from death in the novel and turned into a salmon, a 'journey clothed in flesh', as Clive Sinclair remembers Grossman saying—has to the author's great credit become intimately related to his concerns about Israel's colonial occupation of the West Bank, as described in *The Yellow Wind* and *Sleeping on a Wire*, and in his first novel, *The Smile of the Lamb*.

Grossman's is an Israeli voice from a later literary generation than the widely translated Aharon Appelfeld, A. B. Yehoshua (*The Continuing Silence of a Poet*) and Amos Oz. It is two generations later than three distinguished writers who are, sadly, less well known abroad: Aharon Megged (*The Living on the Dead* and *Foiglman*), Yoram Kaniuk (*His Daughter*) and Sami Michael, whose *Victoria* is set in his native Baghdad. Among the many books by Oz I have on my shelf are *The Hill of Evil Counsel* (a big influence on Grossman), *Don't Call It Night*, an atmospheric short novel set on the edge of the desert, and his fabulous memoir, *A Tale of Love and Darkness*. Oz's work is blessed, as he well knows, by the stellar translations of Rabbi Nicholas De Lange, professor of Semitics at Cambridge.

Isaac B. Singer, Solomon Maimon, Clive Sinclair, Bernard Malamud and others

Clive Sinclair's memoir, *Diaspora Blues*, is an entertainingly brilliant exploration of the inevitably complex relationship intelligent and reflective Jews have with Israel, *whatever* their opinion of its government. That relationship has become more complex than it was twenty years ago when Clive wrote his book, and today the tone would be different. In *The Brothers Singer*, Sinclair introduced us to their sister, Esther Kreitman, whose remarkable novel *Deborah* should not be neglected. Isaac Singer must have relished the fascinating *Autobiography* of Solomon Maimon (highly recommended by John Gross, now sadly gone, when he took me to tea in Wolseley's). Maimon, an eighteenth-century Polish wunderkind who mastered the Talmud by the age of seven, tells of his visits to Hasidic groups as well as the more congenial enlightened rationalist Jews of Berlin. He finally abandoned the world of what would later be called fundamentalism when he witnesses a Jewish fellow being whipped solely because his wife gave birth to a daughter. Later, having met Moses Mendelsohn and been praised by Immanuel Kant, Maimon died a secular Jew, like Spinoza. He ends with a line from Virgil: 'Quo fata trahunt retrahuntque sequamur'—wherever the fates drag and drag us back let us follow. Maimon would have liked the singular and prodigiously learned Guy Davenport and enjoyed discussing his introduction to Burton Raffel's translations of Greek poetry, *Pure Pagan*: 'The West has two sources, seemingly inexhaustible: the Hebrew dialogue with God and the Greek dialogue of mankind with itself.'

When Sinclair's close friend the late Cecil Helman went to visit Isaac Bashevis Singer in New York (Bashevis is a masculine version of Bathsheba, his mother's name), the lecherous old vegetarian pointed at the settee and said: 'You know whose *tochus* was there before yours? Barbara Streisand's; I

151

told her no, you can't have the rights to *Yentl*.' Presumably on some future occasion she charmed Singer with her *tochus* (metaphorically speaking), for she made the film, although he is said not to have liked it. Here are two collections of his stories, *Old Love* and *Gimpel the Fool*. The title story of the latter volume is one of Saul Bellow's rare translations. Gimpel is a lineal descendent of Bontsche the Silent, Isaac Leib Peretz's little man in the eponymous story. Here is a letter from Eve Roshevsky, Singer's editor at Doubleday. It accompanied his memoirs, *A Little Boy in Search of God*, *A Young Man in Search of Love* and *Lost in America*, sent 'with regards from the author and editor both'. I had been introduced to Roshevsky by my friend Perle Epstein with a view to interesting Doubleday in my 'documentary poem' about my grandfather. Roshevsky asks me to forgive Singer for not answering my letter: 'he adores receiving letters and hates writing them' and anyway 'he has had a very hectic year since receiving the Nobel Prize.' Singer was a prolific writer of fiction, his best work being his short stories and two of the novels—Sinclair agrees—*The Slave* and *Enemies*.

The finest of Singer's memoirs is *Lost in America*. This book and *A Young Man in Search of Love* have classic illustrations by Raphael Soyer, a figurative artist of the generation of Firmin Rocker. The illustrations in *A Little Boy in Search of God* by Ira Moskowitz are less subtle and also less solid than Soyer's, a judgement confirmed by Paula. Singer explores mysticism, including the sexual variety, as when the young writer meets a woman old enough to be his mother, Mrs Gina Halbstark, granddaughter of rabbis, who rents him a room ('you'll pay whatever you can afford') and they embark on what turns out to be his first fulfilled love affair. 'She kissed and bit me' could happen anywhere but 'I know you from an earlier life' sounds more Hindu or Buddhist than Kabbalistic. He has a dream in which a pious ancestor admonishes him: 'You've desecrated your soul. You are defiled! You've copulated with Lilith, Naama, Machlat, Shibta!', the last three being spirits and whores far less well known than Adam's first wife. We are not surprised when he informs us that in bed 'she spoke both like a holy woman and a whore . . . called herself Rahab the harlot.' Having reincarnated him as David and herself as Bathsheba, she, the older woman, tells him that after her funeral he must sleep with another woman and think of her. Howard Cooper has come up with more details:

'Lilith and Na'amah are often paired as "female devils". In the Zohar, Lilith, Na'amah and Machlat are named as three of the four 'mothers of the demons', the other being Agrat. Shibta seems to be a demon mentioned in the Talmud. She pounced if someone didn't wash and say a blessing before eating.'

I wonder what Singer made of Bernard Malamud's conclusion to a story in *Pictures of Fidelman*, where the Jewish hero is in bed with his Catholic lover: 'She clasped his buttocks, he clasped hers. Pumping slowly, he nailed her to his cross.' The erotic power and beauty of this quasi-blasphemous image is shocking. Sinclair reckons that it is Yiddisher triumphalism, but for all we know the girl's orgasm is triumphant too. Somehow you cannot imagine Singer pumping slowly, or at least not with Gina Halbstark. When I suggest to Clive that, compared to Bellow, Roth and Mailer, Malamud is neglected, he replies: 'Oy, is that an understatement.' Malamud's daughter Janna Malamud Smith has written a memoir about him (which I have not yet read and which had mixed reviews), *My Father Is a Book*. It joins three fine books by daughters about their fathers, all of whom were born within two or three years of each other: Judy Golding's *The Children of Lovers*, Susan Cheever's *Home before Dark* and *Night Studio* by Musa Mayer (Philip Guston's daughter).

[Later: I have much enjoyed two more contributions to the genre: *Major/Minor*, Alba Arikha's memoir of her father, Avigdor Arikha, and *Reading My Father* by Alexandra Styron, in 2011. The subjects are half a generation younger than the other four.]

Joseph Roth

Joseph Roth, a favourite writer of mine, is from the Austro-Hungarian world of Mahler, Freud and others who left the provinces of the empire for Vienna and, in Roth's case, also Berlin and Paris. He has affinities with Gustav Mahler and Stefan Zweig, none with Robert Musil, something I allude to in a brief discussion of Michael André Bernstein later. It is interesting to reflect on writers who have been influenced by Roth and difficult to come up with names. Maybe another Jewish son of Austria Hungary, Jakov Lind, maybe the Italian writer Claudio Magris, born in Trieste in 1939, about twenty years after it ceased being part of the empire—because the empire ceased to exist.

I discuss them on other pages. Sinclair suggests the Appelfeld of *Badenheim 39*, whom I also discuss elsewhere. Roth's exact contemporaries were Bruno Schulz, Walter Benjamin and Osip Mandelshtam, great Jewish writers, all very different from each other and from him. Roth, among other things, is a lucid, undeceived chronicler of Europe's dispossessed, symbolized by the empire's Jewish minority—he came from Brody in their heartland of East Galicia now West Ukraine, which I visited twenty years ago when it was still part of the Soviet Union. He creates a distinctive and grounded mythography of imperial decline—as befits a major novelist who was also a great journalist job—coloured by an elegiac tone and bittersweet feeling as heart wrenching and melancholy as Mahler, a son of the empire from a previous generation. The empire itself went after World War I, the Jewish communities during World War II. The elegiac nostalgia on the part of this master who wrote several great novels, in particular *Radetzky March*, is steeped in observation and thought and only occasionally tumbles into sentimentality, as at the very end of Job. My great-uncle Zygfryd Rudolf could have walked out of a Roth novel. He, like Isaac Babel, visited Brody, a hundred miles from his and my grandfather Josef Rudolf's town, Stanislawow. Later, Zygfryd and Roth, both born in 1894, and students in Vienna at the same time could have met in the famous Cafe Museum or at the Opera. On the other hand, Joseph Rudolf, another Roth character, was too poor and uneducated to move in those circles except, on the margin, as a waiter in a cafe in Budapest or a steward on a boat plying on the Danube between Vienna and Budapest, before heading for London and a family life which would eventually produce the author of this book.

Chaim Raphael and Alexander Baron

Two old timers I remember fondly are the novelist Alexander Baron and my good friend Chaim Raphael, a truly learned Jew of the old school: essayist; thriller writer under the name of Jocelyn Davey (*The Undoubted Deed*) with a detective based, he told me, on Isaiah Berlin; popularizer (*Minyan: Ten Jewish Lives in 20 Centuries of History*), don, senior civil servant and best modern editor of the Passover *Haggadah: A Feast of History*. When Raphael was old and lame he would invite younger friends to 'dinner' (delicatessen from Waitrose downstairs, ex-John Barnes department store) at his Finchley Road flat. He wanted to know what was going on in the younger generation, while I was keen to learn from an old-timer who was a class act. Now I too am entering the ranks of the old-timers. Here are Raphael's autobiographies *Memoirs of a Special Case* and *A Coat of Many Colours*, the latter dedicated to 'the *kinder* and *einiklach*', Yiddish words for children and grandchildren. It contains a valuable chapter on the Vilna Gaon, the most learned rabbi of the eighteenth century, and a sworn opponent of Hasidism.

Alexander Baron was a modest and retiring figure. In my teens I read my father's paperback of *From the City from the Plough*. Musa Farhi gave me a replacement copy of this famous book about the battle for France, set in August 1944. The author was in the army for six years, being twenty-two when the war broke out. The reading of the book, but not the details, I remember vividly, now that I have a booster in my hands. According to the blurb, the book 'took a year to write; the author worked on it between midnight and 8 a.m., for during the day he was assistant editor of a theatre magazine and had to spend most evenings seeing plays'. I regret bitterly not having taken up the author's invitation to come for tea, around 1982, when we would meet at editorial meetings of the *Jewish Quarterly*. Baron had been neglected for years until, some years later, Iain Sinclair relaunched him, writing an introduction to that classic London novel, *The Lowlife*. One assumes Baron's assistant editorship was an afternoon job, and that he got some sleep in the mornings. In Mike Moorcock's opinion, he was a great working-class Jewish writer who, with Gerald Kersh and others, has slipped out of the public consciousness because he focused on unfashionable subjects and issues.

Aharon Appelfeld

No Israeli novelist has been more important to me since the death of Ka-Tzetnik 135633 than Aharon Appelfeld. I had the chance to bring out the UK edition of his essays *Beyond Despair*, but the arrangements fell through. He is as far removed from Ka-Tzetnik 135633—along the spectrum of Jewish remembrancers in the age of the Shoah—as it is possible to be. Like Primo Levi and Robert Antelme and unlike Ka-Tzetnik and Rawicz, Aharon is a chaste and 'pure' writer. He writes what the French call *récits* rather than novels; these are stories or fables which, however psychologically acute, are not primarily driven by character or plot but by a meditative voice of great intensity and profundity. I learnt from a friend in Jerusalem, Aloma Halter, that she had translated two autobiographical books by Appelfeld. She kindly sent me a proof copy of the first one, which is an account of his life as a cafe writer. Along with my late friend Alberto de Lacerda, Appelfeld is the truest example of the species since Elias Canetti and Joseph Roth, Jean-Paul Sartre and Simon de Beauvoir. The moment *A Table for One* arrived, I sat down and began reading it over a mug of Turkish coffee. It is a handsome book, with paintings by his gifted son Meir, apple-blossom time, in the field of their surname. Appelfeld knows. 'X or Y *knows*' is one of the highest terms of praise in Paula Rego's kitty. Yes, Aharon Appelfeld knows: he not only knows, he knows better. You will find many of his novels listed in the bibliography. I cannot improve on the Gabriel Josipovici's assessment in his introduction to an early book, *The Age of Wonders*: 'Appelfeld shows how people use words and their imaginations to deny reality and themselves; the truth, when it comes, is silent. With this book, indeed, post-war writing has come of age, for it has grasped and made palpable for us the relation of the great modernist tradition of Kierkegaard, Nietzsche, Proust and Kafka to the crucial events of modern times, and it has done so not by being clever but by being wise, not by numbing us with images and ideas but by looking quietly and steadily at what is central to our lives.'

Poetry/Film

Jerome Rothenberg

If Jerry Rothenberg's books, *Poland/1931*, *Khurbn*, *Gematria* and others listed in the bibliography, are not full of Jewish poems, then the genre does not exist. Gematria is traditional Jewish numerology (Hebrew letters linked to numbers) and has been given a bad name by numerous Jewish and non-Jewish 'readers' of the Bible who deploy codes to reveal prophecy, or make connections between 9/11 and Leonardo da Vinci, between Dan Brown and Madonna, between Hitler and the founding of Israel. However, it has been shown by mathematicians that anything can be proved in this way, that the codes are corrupt, and it is all a load of rubbish. Rothenberg, though, uses numerology as it cries out to be used (when not sleeping the sleep of the terminally bored), playfully, unteleologically, as one might use the I Ching or the Fibonacci sequence, to generate hyper-modern aleatory poems, and it is no accident that one section of the book is dedicated to John Cage. Yet his text is no more random than the best automatic writing by surrealists. *Gematria* is dedicated to Rothenberg's friend and mine, Edmond Jabès, with whose work it has affinities, as it has with Armand Schwerner's and Charles Bernstein's. In the final section, 'Beyond Gematria', Rothenberg, via Celan, arrives at a new incarnation of his restlessly inventive and endlessly driven voice at the interface of antiquity and the messianic future. *Khurbn* contains the poems Rothenberg heard after visiting his ancestral Polish town only a few miles from Treblinka, and therefore not that far from my maternal grandfather's town, Lomza. 'Khurbn' is a Hebrew synonym for 'Shoah'— destruction—both words some people use in preference to the widely disliked 'Holocaust', a word which may have first obtained wider currency in this context via Mauriac's 1958 preface to the French first edition of Elie Wiesel's *Night*, although earlier uses of it are recorded in the OED. Rothenberg, an eloquent and very American post-Black Mountain poet, shows that it is impossible to drink black milk without reading Celan. You can climb the highest mountain in Europe, you can walk round the mountain, you can dig a tunnel through the mountain; you cannot ignore the mountain.

Rothenberg's *A Big Jewish Book* (and its later revised edition, *Exiled in the Word*) is an extraordinary in-gathering of exilic writers. It ends, as it must, with Celan's poem to Nellie Sachs, written at the Stork Inn, Zurich. It is perfectly clear that what I have written about Rothenberg has been slanted to the Jewish section of my book and he might prefer, and with good reason, to be included in the poetry section. I discussed the problem in my introduction: unfortunately, bilocation is impossible, given my framework.

Muriel Rukeyser and Rose Drachler

Abraham Chapman's anthology *Jewish-American Literature* is pleasantly strong on poetry, with George Oppen, Muriel Rukeyser, Denise Levertov, Louis

Simpson, Ed Field and Harvey Shapiro. Rukeyser, inspiration for later feminists, political radical, single mother and bisexual, was one of the translators and also, I have heard, the lover of Octavio Paz: there is a book to be written on translation and love affairs. I have touched on the theme in an essay on cooking in my translation of the Slovene poet, Ifigenija Simonovic, *Striking Root*. Chapman reprints from Rukeyser's book *The Life of Poetry*, an autobiographical essay, which—such are the collage-collegialities of anthologies—finds itself positioned between essays by Groucho Marx and Elie Wiesel. Following her famous poem 'To be a Jew in the 20th century', Chapman includes 'For my Son' which ends with a strange idea and yet one which I understand in my bones as a son and a father:

> like all men,
> you have not seen your father's face,
> but he is known to you forever in song, the coast of the skies, in
>   dream, wherever you find man
> playing his part as father, father among our light, among our darkness,
> and in your self made whole, whole with yourself and whole with
>   others,
> the stars your ancestors.

An older American and very Jewish poet was Rose Drachler; her *Collected Poems* rightly impressed John Ashbery, whose workshop she attended for a year. Published extracts from her diary reveal, to my surprise (shame on me), that she read Bronk, Jabès and Levinas; she also quotes Bonnefoy several times. In Israel in 1980, when she had nothing else to do—presumably on a beach holiday—she spent two weeks reading and rereading Ashbery's *Three Poems*. She has an insight into the hostility so many reviewers show Ashbery: they hate the fact that 'his poems are intransitive'. And then: 'poetry is bread', she writes. 'I live in a house of bread. I eat very plain food on a very plain level. It is good.' She is talking about her own poems, and she is right. Her lyric impulse is mediated by high intelligence and close reading.

Claude Lanzmann/Claude Vigée (with Dannie Abse)

Susan Rubin Suleiman's anthology, *Contemporary Jewish Writing in Hungary*, contains an excerpt from Imre Kertész's *Fateless*, but not from his *Kaddish for an Unborn Child*, a disturbing monological projection that rivals those of Thomas Bernhard and Louis René des Forêts. Apart from Claude Lanzmann's *Shoah*, which is *sui generis*, the best of many films about the camps may well be Kertész's *Fateless* and Arnot Lustig's *A Prayer for Katerina Horovitzova*. Significantly, the screenplays of both films are adapted from their own books by the two novelists, both true literary and cinematographic professionals.

The original French text of the subtitles of *Shoah* was never published in England because it is laid out as a recitatif and Lanzmann refused permission for the English publisher to reset it as prose in order to save space, and therefore cost. A few months after I had interviewed him in public in London, he took me to dinner chez Lipp in boulevard Saint-Germain and there, during an argument, which he provoked with a man at the next table (a senior figure in the French Jewish community), I saw him eyeball the poor fellow, forcing him to back off, and indeed leave. It was a display of macho power that shed light both on his years in the Resistance and the eleven years spent making his masterpiece against opposition and indeed resistance on the part of persons who should have supported him. *Shoah*, ninety per cent of whose footage ended up on the cutting room floor, is a supreme *oeuvre*, a universal masterpiece, so cunningly constructed that people come away thinking they have seen newsreel footage of bodies, which they haven't. It is not a documentary about survivors; it is not a documentary. It is a film about a death machine, about a decision-making machine, about the dead: a profound exploration of radical evil, a film about responsibility. Its nine and a half hours pass almost as quickly as a film of normal length. It should be seen together with its postscripts, *Sobibor*, which Paula and I caught at the ICA on its only English appearance, and *The Karski Report*. Lanzmann was aggressive to a member of the audience during questions. The next day he asked me who the person was: I said it was a friend of mine, Michael Kustow; there was a silence and then, recalling that Kustow had helped make possible the showing of *Shoah* on Channel Four, Lanzmann expressed regret for his over-reaction.

159

Au Sujet de Shoah contains valuable essays by several people, including my friend Michel Deguy, a distinguished poet-philosopher who worries away at 'Jewish' issues without ever infantilizing his Jewish colleagues by ring-fencing aspects of the argument to protect easily offended sensibilities, so often paraded as a defence against painful truths. In his later book *Aux heures d'affluence*, characteristically segueing from prose to verse and back in a manner pioneered by Claude Vigée (although we may be talking affinity rather than influence here), Deguy has reprinted his Shoah essay and added a postscript where he argues for the singularity of what has become known as Auschwitz (a rhetorical trope in the post-memoir age) and warns against metaphoricity, the using of the trope where it is not appropriate. We have two responsibilities, he says: to raise a monument to what happened, and to teach, worry about, meditate, discuss, *write the disaster*, so that it remains forever singular, forever unrepeatable. He ends: 'The elaboration of the *vision* of *Shoah* deprives the *revisions* of their proof of the non-existence of the unbelievable through absence of trace.'

Pourquoi Israel and *Tsahal*, the first and third films in the triptych of which *Shoah* is the centrepiece, are respectively historical and political curiosities where Lanzmann's private views about Algeria and Israel particularize the content and lower the quality. (I am the only person I know who has seen the first one, and few have seen the third.) But *Shoah* set Lanzmann free as an artist, his private views, like that of its viewers, omnipresent, as air is omnipresent—invisible. It is astonishing how many people insist on reading the film as a documentary or as propaganda (albeit propaganda they think they favour), but it is neither one nor the other, as I have already explained. The mainly Jewish audience divided that way during questions after my public interview of the *auteur* in London, and he was rightly annoyed for it is, he rightly insisted, an *oeuvre*, a highly wrought work whose construction has designs upon and works its passage on our unconscious. Its theme, as I said, is the dead, and the survivors he interviews talk about the dead, not about themselves. Some years later, I showed Lanzmann the last letter I received from Primo Levi, in which he praised *Shoah*. Praise from such a quarter counts for something and Lanzmann was duly impressed.

Evelyne Vigée, wife of the poet Claude Vigée, died on 17 January 2007. She was buried in Claude's ancestral village, Bischwiller, a few miles from Strasbourg. The 'pregnancy of death' (as Alsatian Jews say) began with her burial and ended nine months later (according to the custom of Alsatian Jews), when the 'matseva' (the tombstone) was consecrated. Death, as Pasternak says somewhere, is a second birth. My friendship with Evy and Claude Vigée began when I met them in Jerusalem in 1969—armed with an introduction from Yves Bonnefoy—on the first of my visits to Israel over the following twenty-five years. Claude and I had an immediate rapport as fellow Jewish poets and for me, as a translator from the French, it was and remains natural and appropriate to translate his verse and prose, so close to my own concerns, not least the poems about Evy in verse and prose written in the months since she died.

I integrated Claude's texts into a sequence and they have now been published. Books of mourning for a loved one belong in a tradition inaugurated by Dante's *Vita Nuova*, that wondrous work in verse and prose by the 'chief imagination of Christendom' (Yeats). Roland Barthes alludes to Dante in his posthumously published and lacerating *Journal de deuil*, a diary of mourning for his mother. Dannie Abse, who is to the UK what Vigée is to France—namely the senior Jewish poet—also lost his wife and wrote a strong book of prose and verse, *The Presence*, about the aftermath of her death, but, unlike Claude, not about her dying, for she was killed in a car crash. Dannie, like Claude, is a poet of great distinction. More than most, he writes directly out of his lived life. He is a national treasure, but which nation? For Dannie is not only British and Jewish but Welsh, just as Vigée is not only French and Jewish, but Alsatian. 'Abse', as I was reminded when typing his name into Search and Find, forms the first four letters of the word absence. One episode in his book recounts a meeting with Musa Farhi and me in Michael Joseph's Temple Fortune bookshop/cafe. He writes that I winced when, in response to my question, he told me the truth about his feelings. I, however, recall trying to convey with my face a sense of sorrow and sympathy. It goes against all my experience of grief to wince at the truth of an old friend. Yet it came across as a wince, and I regret that. In Paris, Claude Vigée continues to write poems. Here are the two most recent:

Anthony Rudolf

A Sign of Evy

'The Time that Remains'

At the end of the day,
in the forgotten ditch
by the obliterated road,
the black reflection
of the tree with broken arms,
its hands twisted, no bark, no strength,
still shines in the black water
of the silent puddle:
my little winter music

Paris, 27 December 2011

'Slow Extinction'

Life of a woodlouse,
life of a dead nettle
burning, withered,
life shrivelled up
in luminous ashes
less and less visible,
life ends slowly
and my brief time on this earth
gives way to darkness
in the cold wind
bright and dry
at noon.

Paris, 15 January 2012

Poetry

(1) In the small hours on the other side
     Of language . . .

(2) . . . We make up a different language for poetry
     And for the heart . . .

(1) —W. S. Graham, *Malcolm Mooney's Land*

(2) —Jack Spicer, *Language*

Introduction (1)

I have no idea if W. S. Graham and Jack Spicer read each other's work, but the two quotes merge into a found poem that evokes the shades watching over me: they will not tolerate loose thinking or sentimentality. When I started writing this book about my reading, about my books, about my life in books and books in my life, I found myself working on several sections simultaneously. When it came to poetry, there were books all round me, but I left for later the ones on the shelves behind my piano, that is to say the vast majority. The time finally arrived to confront that majority. The question was whether the categories which emerged from the preliminary engagement would survive the onslaught. I had to press on and hope that the dialectic would ride to my rescue: if the material reality of fourteen long shelves of books did not force an adjustment of my draft categories, then perhaps the earlier taxonomy made a kind of sense.

A preliminary cull enabled me to put on one side books never opened, for whatever reason. Accumulation of such books is normal when you have spent your life as a book person. Let them be sold or given away. Nonetheless, they deserved that I light the candle of a passing thought in their memory, for each of them contains a life. Now I had to push on with my exploration of the unculled books. Maybe, in the words of Yeats, I would find 'the face I had before the world was made' (a clean slate, with *my* own face on, to adapt a line by Sylvia Plath), that is to say, the world of books. Or was it my need to reconstruct, symbolize and jettison the shards and debris of a gone world? The question abides: all my books, especially the best ones, are they the royal road to lucidity concerning mortality ('In the play of language death disappears,' writes Canetti in *Notes from Hampstead*) or a bunch of by-ways to protect me from reality? Ah, to pose the question that way is to think undialectically. The story of one's life is made up as one goes along.

There is another reason for my nervousness: the longest component of this book turns out to be the poetry section, and yet in recent years poetry has fallen away in terms of my existential involvement and psychic need. For most of the three and a half years I was working on the first draft, I postponed paying full attention to this particular modality of my taxonomy, for the simple reason that since the mid-1990s I have become more involved in fiction and autobiography, both as writer and reader. Now I have to make an effort of recovery from the hollows of memory to discover why I own so many poetry books—read or unread, remembered or forgotten, loved or rejected—and to decode the concomitant subtext: why I abandoned poetry as my *recherche primaire* (to use the French word), having embraced it as a student thanks to my accidental involvement—neighbours in the same college—with John Barrell and Terry Eagleton, and why I put on the (real) mask of translator of Yves Bonnefoy and, later, of other poets to cover the face of my own attempts at writing poetry. The mask stayed on for years.

Germane to this was my simultaneous discovery, aged nineteen, of writing and sexuality, after an unusually long period of latency. This phenomenon (see the essay which ends *The Arithmetic of Memory*) is crucial to my self-understanding. Elsewhere I have written that my political involvement in the early 1980s took me entirely away from poetry; that, however, was a self-dramatizing exaggeration. I was trying to draw attention to the fact that poetry mattered greatly but the world had survived for poetry to matter greatly in. The truth is, I dipped into many poetry books at great speed in the 1980s. I was trying to keep in touch with something that had been important to me and might again become important.

I was fascinated by the long silence of three American writers I had the privilege of knowing personally, poets George Oppen and Carl Rakosi and the fiction writer Tillie Olsen, and I was deeply affected by the implications of Karl Kraus' last poem, written in the year of his death, 1936.

Jean Améry quotes it in *At the Mind's Limits*. I first translated it back in the 1960s:

Don't ask what I've been doing all the time
I hold my tongue;
and I shan't say why.
And there is a stillness when the earth cracks.
No word fitted;
I speak only in my sleep,
and dream of a laughing sun.
It will all pass;
afterwards it makes no difference.
The word passed away when that world woke up.

I bought or acquired or kept poetry books in order to stay warm. I was reborn outside the womb, plonked down beside alpha-males and real poets, and had to create my own matrix, a place where I could be initiated into the community of letters, worded or maybe reworded. My father wanted me to be a lawyer. I did not want to go down the expected road and he had enough sense not to press the point. His own ambition to study for the bar was not fulfilled because his father could not afford the premium then required. (Guess what my son's profession is. What's more, he has co-authored a definitive study on international money laundering.) I ended up putting my spare-time efforts into a literary life. There was not much in the way of income, but I was able to top up the money earned from day jobs for which I was overqualified. (Federico García Lorca's letters to his father on the subject of literature and day jobs are fascinating.) The answers to the eternal questions about life, death and the universe were blowing in the wind of what I perceived to be freedom, defined as keeping options open while committing to a desired goal. In other words, it was about questions, as Gertrude Stein is supposed to have said on her deathbed, not about answers.

I was not a 'natural' poet like the Russian I translated, Yevgeni Vinokurov, or Tom Clark, whose *Stones* is here, with its wicked parody of Wallace Stevens, 'Eleven ways of looking at a shit bird'. Rather, as Donald Davie would write in a note to his collected poems, poetry went or came against the grain of a natural inclination for abstraction and ratiocination. And indeed poetry can and does happen in those circumstances—provided one keeps the antennae open—just as, on occasion, conceptual art transcends the literature and anthropology with which it has such affinities and generates an authentic visual construction: think Susan Hiller and Sophie Calle.

Introduction (2)

Now it is time to sort the books, following the first cull. As I have already explained, my thoughts on poetry are not restricted to this section alone, since the taxonomy has to some extent been a matter of convenience, a surface structure, and the overlapping categories are porous. The deep structure of lived experience contains intertwinings and imbrications: Rainer Maria Rilke, for example, will be found in other sections too.

A second cull is required. To the right of my desk are dedicated groups of books: war poets, Objectivists, UK avant-garde, etc., and separate heaps for the poets of whom I have several or even many works, quantity being a self-evident index of interest and affection. To the left of the desk are two large groups, British and American poetry, that were not rejected in the first cull. I must go through them and make inroads into my intended writing. Some of the books will end up in the heaven of perpetuated ownership, the rest in a hell of rejection: the latter deserve a ceremony of adieux, in the phrase of Simone de Beauvoir already quoted, for many of them are good books whose only fault is not to fit my narrative.

For some time now, the books (and I) have been in a purgatory of indecision and the time is fast approaching to put them (and myself) out of their (and my) misery. Perhaps I am trying to remember or discover where I belonged, or wanted to belong. My early and intense reading of English-language and French poetry, of French and Russian literature in general, had something to do with learning how to escape from 'a world I never made', in Housman's phrase, as no young person's ever is, in order to return to it disabused but free, free to cherish what that world could give me and, who knows, free to give something back. That may be the deep structural link between the different sections and subsections of the book. I mentioned Rilke. Another, deeply pertinent, example consists of two Francophone Jewish poets, Claude Vigée and Edmond Jabès, who belong in at least three sections—French, Jewish and poetry. When yet another translation of the *Duino Elegies* turns up, the Find and Replace facility will reveal references throughout the book to Rilke, and then I shall have to make an executive decision: where to insert the gloss or story generated by the sight of the latest version. I trust I have made these incisions neatly and woven the tapestry seamlessly.

Some of the piles by my desk contain authors whom I read but did not want to explore at greater length, both in terms of time and text. It reflects badly on me that I did not give some of them sufficient time of day. But life is finite, and the time for reading is an important part of life. One final point: I may discover a pattern in this group of books, though I doubt it. It looks as though I was more eclectic than some of my public pronouncements suggested. I was trying to pass myself off as a modernist with his own slant when I was nothing of the sort. I was attention-seeking, inventing a gap whose filling would henceforth be associated with me. One critic, Peter Riley (who had published my work in *The English Intelligencer*), saw through me when he attacked the French poetry issue of *MPT* which I guest-edited in 1973. Not content with my genuine knowledge of the French contemporary scene and passing it on to interested readers, I wrote a ridiculous, ill-informed and overheated polemic, which impressed no one. Some of the books in these piles are very good, but I doubt that I did justice to all the ones I read. The American books suggest to me that I made an effort over a period of time to cover the waterfront—The USA loomed large in my *imaginaire*. But however good the poets were, mostly they did not become part of my life. We shall come to those who did and perhaps discover why.

'Our intentions slip through our days,' writes Jenny Joseph in her brilliant and unclassifiable prose book *Extended Simile*, and I feel that my own intentions are in danger of slipping as a result of my anxiety to pinpoint and classify and discover explanations. And yet, worrying my way through this difficult section—so much more trouble to write than the French and Jewish sections—I have no doubt that reading these books, in whole or in part, played a serious part in my formation. Poetry is brought into the narrative throughout the book—not only in the poetry section—and quoted or alluded to where it feels right. This is as it should be. That's all I need say on the subject.

I do not think it is necessary to signal which books were given to me and which I bought, assuming I can remember. That particular modality of recollection is not significant. What is true is that within the poetry subculture—that the phrase can be used is already a giveaway about our times—if the book is brought out by a small press, sometimes one wants to support the publisher and buy the book at a launch. Sometimes, since many of us (publishers, I mean) know each other, we swap, possibly in the hope of a review. Sometimes, if I'm given a copy, I buy more to give as presents. Sometimes, the poet concerned is a good or close friend who wants to present me with a copy, perhaps as a past publisher or, more subtly, as a future one.

At the time of writing, my New York friend Mike Heller is rereading Yeats' long prose text 'Per Amica Silentia Lunae' and that encourages me to do the same, for one of the pleasures of modern life is to revisit the work of a favourite author in the immediate (email) company of someone else. On my desk, as you would expect, are Yeats' *Collected Poems*, *Collected Plays*, *A Vision* and *Autobiographies*. Special favourites ought not to need trigger mechanisms, they *are* trigger mechanisms, but sometimes one needs reminding. There are many books here that I have read or dipped into once and once only but remember liking and perhaps learning from. All the same, one cannot like every writer equally and I am beginning to think that the great loves of one's reading life, the touchstone figures, are those one has encountered early, and still needs, sometimes for extra-literary reasons. I have only so much time to read and must return to the matrixial breast of psychic nourishment supplied by the favourites whom I continue to reread, drinking at source the milk, white and black, generated from the depths of human feeling and the heights of human thought. It is my loss if I do not go back to the other books. But when I reread Yeats, Oppen, Celan, Dickinson, Stevens, Machado, I know this is time well spent.

Introduction (3)

Out of these nothings / —All beginnings come
—Theodore Roethke, 'The Longing'

(A) VIVID MEMORY

There was a time, long ago, when I would sit down and read through, passionately and carefully, the collected works of a particular poet. I recall three: Keith Douglas, Theodore Roethke and James Wright. I read Douglas' *Collected Poems* and *From Alamein to Zem-Zem* with Desmond Graham's biography *Keith Douglas* to hand, having been introduced to the poet by Ted Hughes' pioneering selection. I made my way to World War II literature after immersion in the poetry of World War I, the latter an inevitable and benign consequence of friendship with Jon Silkin. Keith Douglas, who died at twenty-four, had such a mastery of craft and radical access to his vision that he bears comparison with Isaac Rosenberg whom he apostrophizes in 'Desert Flowers': 'Rosenberg, I only repeat what you were saying.' Watch out for the poems of Owen Lowery, an unknown (at the time of writing) and gifted poet who loves the work of Douglas and, to some extent, identifies with him.

'I have known the inexorable sadness of pencils': in addition to Roethke's *Collected Poems*, I have *Words for the Wind* (bought while I was a student) and *The Far Field*. I read Roethke's poems, helped along by *Selected Letters*, selected prose (*On the Poet and His Craft*), essays on the poetry (*Theodore Roethke*) and notebooks (*Straw for the Fire*). Many notebook statements I annotated seem now to be wind in the straw, but I remain struck by a handful, including: 'Every poet must be, has to be, his *own* mother' while 'Form acts

169

the father: tells you what you may and may not do.' Painful for me is his thought that 'One form of the death wish is the embracing of mediocrity: a deliberate reading and rereading of newspapers.' The following, too, strikes a chord in this chaotic writer: 'I have a jumbled mind that only achieves clarification at times and then under pressure, as in a classroom. Then the material [presumably in or of the poem] provides the unity; the random insights.' David Gascoyne referred to Ted Roethke as a teddy bear whose honey was alcohol. Dipping into his poetry after many years, I know the inexorable sadness of a work I no longer rate highly.

Having discovered that wondrous lyric poet James Wright through his *Shall We Gather at the River* in the early 1970s, I read his *Collected Poems* in a concentrated way a few years later. I remember with gratitude the charge I received from Wright and from Roethke. Wright also made beautiful translations of Herman Hesse's *Poems*, as well as the prose and verse sketches of Hesse's *Wandering*, the best of the German writer's four non-fiction books on my shelf.

In a letter to the young Claude Vigée, the poet's admirer Gaston Bachelard wrote: 'J'ai mis votre livre dans le rayon des livres inoubliables.' He was not pretending to be polite, nor was he being sarcastic. On the contrary, the letters to Vigée and the references to him in Bachelard's books are very complimentary. But, on the other hand, 'I have placed your book on the shelf of unforgettable books' suggests he will never read the book again. Bachelard read poetry books carefully and selected, often naively, images that fed his themes. He was a busy man, with a huge agenda of professional reading.

(B) BARREN LEAVES

Where did these books come from? Some, as suggested earlier, were given to me by small-press editors, perhaps in exchange for Menard books, some by authors. Some I would have bought second-hand or new, during a session of retail therapy. Perhaps the present work involves re-tale therapy. Some of the books are in languages I cannot read. Ah, the languages it is too late for me to master, or be mastered by. I would need to take a sabbatical of three months to improve significantly my Russian (and a year for my Hebrew), although it is still possible for me to revise my published and draft translations of Vinokurov, my sole remaining Russian ambition. But this pile of unread or unreadable books it would be otiose to name: they, like Thom Gunn's sad captains, do not 'remind me, distant now'. Doubtless, I dipped into some of the books, out of perceived obligation, only to abandon them. Some of these unread and/or unreadable books may have cost their authors as much effort as the good or best books, although I doubt it. But here, on the receiving end, they are junk, and should end up in the modern equivalent of the junkshop, namely the charity shops on my High Street. If they are junk, am I a junkie (pun courtesy of William Burroughs)? Yes, I, and people like me, are junkies. We need our fix. And yet the pun has to apply to the good books as well and if it doesn't, it is unearned.

British Poets: Inscriptions and Other Memories

Introduction

When I told Steven Jaron that I was writing this section of the book he mused that what the author inscribes in your book is, in law, copyright (in the same way that a letter is), and was I going to seek permission to quote? I replied that I would be working on the assumption that any colourful or significant message was sincere and if ever there was a case where permission could be taken for granted, it was this.

David Gascoyne

My copy of David Gascoyne's *Early Poems* is affectionately inscribed. I have folded into it a long chatty letter he sent me with a request to send Menard's catalogue to the wife of his local MP on the Isle of Wight: 'she runs a nice small bookshop called Mr Micawber.' Here too are his various poetry books culminating in *Collected Poems* and *Existential Writings*, as well as *Selected Translations* and *Collected Verse Translations* (I write about his journals on another page). *Selected Translations* is an anthology of his favourite French poets plus Giacomo Leopardi and Friedrich Hölderlin. Hölderlin's 'The Walk' was, in turn, a favourite poem of Samuel Beckett's. When Alan Clodd of

Enitharmon Press invited me to edit a sixty-fifth birthday book for the poet, I asked David to translate the poem, which contains these lines:

> You beauteous forests on the slope
> Painted against the wall of green,
> Where I make my random way
> Rewarded by the sweet respite
> From every hurt my scarred heart's had
> When the insight's been made dark,
> For the price of such insight and of art
> Must ever by suffering be paid.

My introductory homage ended: 'On his sixty-fifth birthday we give thanks for his beauty and the beauty of his poems. The shades of the poets say thou to David Gascoyne.'

Gascoyne was only nineteen when his *Short Survey of Surrealism* was published in 1935. This book and Sir Herbert Read's *Surrealism* of 1936 (the year of the London International Surrealist exhibition, in which Gascoyne was a key player) mark in print the moment when the movement finally arrived in the UK, explicitly that is, for according to André Breton (and to Gascoyne himself), Lewis Carroll, Edward Lear and other English figures were forbears of this great revolution in the arts. In his introduction to the 1982 reprint of the survey, Gascoyne quotes from Samuel Beckett's translation of Octavio Paz's essay, 'Poetry and History': '*The poet* [Rimbaud] *and his word are one*' (Paz's italics). Paz continues: 'Such has been, during the last hundred years, the motto of the greatest poets of our civilisation. Nor has the meaning of that last great movement of the century—surrealism—been any different.' Well, on the one hand, this is a truism; on the other hand, Eliot, a poet Paz considered among the greats, would dispute it. And where does it leave Rimbaud's 'Je est un autre'?

In Gascoyne's translation of André Breton and Philippe Soupault's so-called automatic writing, *The Magnetic Fields*, I keep a letter from David, dated 20 June 1986, that is, about two weeks after the death of my father: 'I am most sorry to hear [about this]. I know that the death of one's father is always a deeply disturbing event, whatever one thinks one's feelings about him to have been.' He then tells me about a poetry conference he is to attend in Florence, whose participants include Eugène Guillevic and Czesław Miłosz. 'It is particularly sad that Borges has not lived long enough to represent Argentina.' Borges died on 14 June, ten days after my father. I remember visiting David and Judy Gascoyne on the Isle of Wight after attending F. T. Prince's funeral in Southampton. Among the topics we discussed were Breton's *Nadja* and *L'Amour fou*. In *Arcane 17*, Breton followed up those earlier explorations of love with an evocation of 'bonté' (kindness, goodness) as a source of salvation for a damaged world, quoting Apollinaire's last and wondrous poem, 'La jolie rousse': 'We wish to explore goodness, a vast country where everything is silent.' David and Judy were dear friends, and I cherish memories of meetings in London, Cowes and Paris, and the phone calls David would make out of the blue.

F. T. Prince and Henry Reed

In his mid-twenties, F. T. Prince was published by Eliot at Faber and Faber and later by Rupert-Hart Davis. Then, as happens, he was picked up by small presses—Fulcrum, Menard, Anvil and Carcanet—where he has come to rest. It meant a lot for the Menard list that Frank Prince consented to be published by me, although he himself saw it as a rescue. I have all his poetry books from before and after my own direct involvement, including the American collected poems published at Sheep Meadow Press by that redoubtable editor, poet of quality and art dealer, Stanley Moss. I recall long ago, late one evening, going up to Moss' suite in the Savoy hotel, Monet's old room. Opening the door in a dressing gown, he smiled and said: 'Anthony, I have just sold the last remaining Piero Della Francesca in private hands,' and called for champagne and steak sandwiches. Here are Prince's editions of *Comus* and the Arden Shakespeare *Poems*. Here too is that remarkable critical book *The Italian Element in Milton's Verse*, inscribed for me in April 1976, that is, around the time I published the second of Menard's three Prince titles. In the final months of Frank's life, I edited with Anthony Howell a special section of *Poetry Nation Review*, with essays by Geoffrey Hill, John Hall, John Ashbery, Mark Ford and the two editors. After Prince died, I published a version of my essay as an obituary in *The Independent*. Later still, I rewrote it for the *Dictionary of National Biography*: contributors are under a strict contractual obligation not to plagiarize their own published work, an almost impossible requirement. I list those three published works as an example of the post-publishing process, completed many years later by my participation in 2012 in Prince's centenary conference at the University of Southampton where he taught for many years. The officiating Catholic priest at Frank's funeral in Southampton had married the Princes long ago. It had been the priest's first wedding. I expressed the hope that this would not be his last funeral: 'Oh no,' he said with a smile, 'that will be my own.'

Henry Reed and F. T. Prince, exact contemporaries, are best known for their much anthologized poems written during World War II: Prince's 'Soldiers Bathing' and Reed's 'Naming of Parts', the first of three poems in 'Lessons of the War'. I inscribed Reed's 1946 book, *A Map of Verona*, with my name and the date of purchase, 'June 1965'. Above my name, he has written 'Signed with fortitude for' and below the date: 'by Henry Reed'. The explanation is that I visited him while he was a patient at the National Hospital in Queen Square in 1975; I hope I phoned in advance and that it was his idea: I was chasing him to write a poem for an event in Southwark Cathedral I was organizing for Sam Wanamaker, which would eventually become a book: *Poems for Shakespeare IV*. Reed never did write the Shakespeare poem. On separate occasions, he and Prince began a reading at the Poetry Society as follows: 'I *have* written other poems, you know.'

Nicholas Moore

Nicholas Moore entered the *Sunday Times* poetry translation competition in 1968 with thirty-one versions of Baudelaire's 'Spleen' ('I am like the king of a rainy country'), which the judge George Steiner delighted in drawing attention to, although Moore did not win. I wrote to the poet, offering to publish the versions at Menard Press; after all, if this did not meet Menard's translation remit, what did? *Spleen* finally appeared in 1973 under the joint imprint of Menard and Black Suede Boot Press run by two poets, Barry MacSweeney and Elaine Randell. Menard brought out a revised and expanded edition in 1990. Moore, who had once been almost as famous as Dylan Thomas, disappeared from view between the publication of *Recollections of the Gala* in 1950 and his rediscovery with *Spleen* in 1973. But he never stopped writing, an object lesson in Chekhovian stoicism. We maintained correspondence over many years; there was gallows humour from the hospital ward when he noticed that every time a patient died the survivors were moved along, towards the door. Many of the letters came in (or indeed on) what he called *pomenvylopes*. Although I have given some away as gifts to deserving persons, I still have a stockpile of these marvellously inventive and sometimes crazy texts with their multiple provenances and targets. Thanks to his exemplary literary executor Peter Riley, Moore's reputation and visibility were enhanced during his final years, and more work was published. This has been helped by increased interest in the poetry of the long neglected and indeed despised 1940s, now that the template placed on it by a successor generation has lost its potency.

Menard co-published, with the Covent Garden Bookshop, another of Moore's books when I was working in the basement of the shop as manager of the periodicals department: *Resolution and Identity*. Similarly, I published Barry MacSweeney's own pamphlet on Chatterton, *Elegy for January*. It was in the bookshop basement that I introduced Barry to my colleague Elaine Randell, which led to their marriage. Later books culminated in Peter Riley's posthumous selection, *Longings of the Acrobat*. Riley's note in *Spleen* informs us that Moore had an influence on the New York 'school' of poets, which is not to say that he had anything in common with F. T. Prince, another Menard poet whom the New York poets, not least Ashbery, admired, and who was bemused if flattered by the attention. Moore's books pre-dating his long absence from the scene, and which are on my desk now, include *The Island and the Cattle* from the notorious Fortune Press and *The Glass Tower*, with Lucian Freud's drawings. Here too is a one-volume reprint of the eight issues of the impressive little magazine *Seven* Moore co-founded in 1938 when he was a Cambridge undergraduate. His final issue contained Wallace Stevens and Elizabeth Smart and an editorial taking issue with *Horizon* for saying its 'politics are in abeyance'. Moore was a brave and admirable man, a far better poet than he has been given credit for, and, as a world expert on irises, another of those splendid gardener-poets like his fellow Menard authors, my friends Geoffrey Dutton (of the famed nine-acre marginal garden in Scotland, a romantic creation at the opposite pole to Ian Hamilton Finlay's Little

Sparta) and Michael Hamburger, both now deceased. (Franz Kafka, Ludwig Wittgenstein and Raymond Mason worked as gardeners for a time, but they were labourers.)

Donald Davie

Donald Davie, in the first of his *Collected Poems* (signed 'with love' to Brenda, my then wife, and me, 'Tours 6.viii.73', where and when we visited him and his wife Doreen en route to Saint-Paul de Vence) has a long endnote which I've already touched on. It spoke volumes to me:

> It is true that I am not a poet by nature, only by inclination; for my mind moves most easily among abstractions, it relates ideas far more readily than it relates experiences.
>
> I have little appetite, only profound admiration, for sensuous fullness and immediacy;
>
> I have not the poet's need of concreteness . . .

But, he continues,

> . . . a true poem can be written by a mind not naturally poetic— though by the inhuman labour of thwarting the natural grain and bent. This working against the grain does not damage the mind, nor is it foolish; on the contrary, only by doing this does each true poem as it is written become an authentic widening of experience—a truth won from life against all odds, because a truth in and about a mode of experience to which the mind is normally closed.

Davie died before I could bring myself to renew our dialogue after a serious quarrel about the miners' strike in 1974. He, like George Steiner, influenced me more than I've previously admitted to myself. He, again like Steiner, was a mercurial and curiously vulnerable personality. He went public on himself in his poetry, more so than in autobiographical prose, and that was right and proper for him. I found a copy of a letter I wrote Doreen Davie after Donald died: '. . . I suspect you spotted the father-figure situation, and doubtless I was not the only person who set him up that way . . .'

Davie has made a considerable contribution to translation and approaches to translation. *The Psalms in English* I mentioned earlier in this book. His Mickiewicz 'travesty' (in the technical sense), *The Forests of Lithuania*, can be read in the latest and definitive *Collected Poems*. Among his translations, I like best *Poems of Doctor Zhivago*. Published separately, these remind the reader of the central fact that Doctor Zhivago himself is a poet and that this wondrous novel is a prequel to the poems which conclude the book. Prose and verse in a novel or novella, as in C. K. Stead's fascinating *My Name Was Judas*, enjoy a dialectical relationship. It is therefore essential that translations of the poems 'work as poems' (as we say) and Davie's do, far better than the versions at the end of the well-known English edition of the novel I devoured as a teenager. I have not yet consulted the new translation by Richard Pevear and Larissa Volokhonsky.

Borges says (in *Conversations with Richard Burgin*) that had Browning written *The Ring and the Book* in prose, he would be regarded (i.e. read) as the forerunner of Henry James and Kafka, perhaps as the forerunner of all modern literature. In his short monograph *Pound*, Davie found a polite way of saying that nobody (I would qualify this by saying 'apart from Borges') need read *The Ring and the Book*. After explaining that both Hardy and Pound owe much to Browning and reminding us that Browning's 'Sordello' helped instigate the *Cantos*, he writes of Pound: 'In *Lustra* there had appeared "Near Perigord", a poem of capital importance which boiled down into fewer than 200 lines the central concern of *The Ring and the Book*—that is to say, the seeking for historical truth through the conflicting testimonies of interested witnesses.'

I am struck by something Davie wrote on the final page of *Poet as Sculptor*, his longer book on the American poet, Pound: 'There was a face behind the mask, and a person within the vortex. It is an elusive person, certainly. But is it any more elusive than other persons who are equally given up to, and dispersed in, the energies of their language?' Shakespeare, Dryden and Keats are, says Davie, 'the appropriate fellows for this poet of our time who magnanimously lent his energies to the language that we share, rather than bending that language to his own egotistical purposes.' I have two comments to make on this: it is a proud and generous homage to a poet whose shameful errors Davie does not skirt or ignore elsewhere in the book, and yet it has to be true of all who write. Pound himself writes in a letter (8

July 1922): 'I'm no more Mauberley than Eliot is Prufrock. Mais passons. Mauberley is a mere surface. Again a study in form, an attempt to condense the James novel. Meliora speramus.'

Davie's book on syntax in English poetry, *Articulate Energy*, and his *Purity of Diction in English Verse* are on my desk. I fell upon his two path-finding works with the full force of revelation. At Cambridge, in the final undergraduate year, Barrell was supervised by Davie, who also supervised his thesis at Essex. Eagleton's thesis was supervised by Raymond Williams. Their relationship with the two senior figures could serve as case studies in a book about influence, a successor to George Steiner's *Lessons of the Masters* and possibly entitled *Creative Misprisions*. Barrell's powerfully focused intelligence (like Eagleton's) mesmerized me at Cambridge and, for some years after, is shown to good effect in *Poetry, Language and Politics* where, in the best essay, on Dorothy Wordsworth and 'Tintern Abbey', one of my favourite poems in the language, he argues with *Articulate Energy*. As it happens, 'the two languages [of the poem], the language of natural description and the language of the meditations which seem to be produced by the contemplation of nature, of landscape' are what the essay is about. The acknowledgements at the beginning of the book contain the following sentence: 'I do not imagine that Donald Davie will like these essays, but I hope he will acknowledge a number of them as bastard offspring of his own teaching.' Here, we are light or maybe heavy years away from their personal conflict at the University of Essex. I know something about the conflict from Davie himself, but even in Barrell's first book, *The Idea of Landscape and the Sense of Place 1730–1830* (a study of John Clare), he writes in the acknowledgements: 'This book is dedicated to Donald Davie, because while writing it I discovered how much my approach to poetry owes to his own.' Davie, in the penultimate paragraph of his autobiography *These the Companions*, writes that he is 'conscious of so much left out . . . [including] variously frenzied people known in Essex in the 1960s'. Was Barrell one of the frenzied?

Charles Tomlinson

. . . Reason's song / Riding an ungovernable wave'
—From *The Necklace*

There is no more undeviatingly serious British poet than Charles Tomlinson. The syntax of *Seeing Is Believing* and later books, imbricated with the poet's impeccable versification and diction, demands close attention; it projects an intellectuality so subtle that it is a perfect counter to the visual imagination of a man who is also a graphic artist (*Words and Images* and *In Black and White*, a book of his frottages, collages, decalcomania, etc.). The pictorial aspects of the poems are, paradoxically, more like a sustained pedal note or subtext, grounding the sounds and obviating simple ekphrasis. His friend Paz introduces *In Black and White*: 'His poems are neither a painting nor a description of an object or its more or less constant properties: what interests him is the process which leads it to be the object that it is.' Paz quotes Tomlinson, who is quoting Kafka: 'To catch a glimpse of things as they may have been before they show themselves to me'. Paz also names Hercules Seghers as Tomlinson's 'intercessor' at a time when the poet was obsessed by black to the detriment of his graphics: 'each of us has the intercessors he deserves', a characteristically brilliant remark on the part of the Mexican poet.

Incidentally, Jacques Dupin and other French poets crossed the Channel to study the etchings of Seghers in the British Museum print room; David Gascoyne went to Amsterdam to see them.

'A Meditation on John Constable' in *Seeing Is Believing* is revealing of Tomlinson himself:

> A descriptive painter? If delight
> Describes, which wrings from the brush
> The errors of a mind, so tempered,
> It can forgo all pathos; for what he saw
> Discovered what he was, and the hand—unswayed
> By the dictation of a single sense—
> Bodied the accurate and total knowledge
> In a calligraphy of human pleasure . . .

In Black and White is revealing, too: 'When words seem too abstract, then I find myself painting the sea with the very thing it is composed of—water.' And: 'Visual art: not an unleasher of "the sub-conscious" but a cure for blindness'. Despite the remark about the subconscious, Tomlinson (now sadly blind) looked to the surrealists in painting, whereas, with his poet's hat on, he, like his immediate senior and mentor Donald Davie, looked to William Carlos Williams and the Objectivists. Ted Hughes, at the time, was looking to Eastern and Central Europe. One could say that in Tomlinson's work (verse and graphics taken together), surrealism meets objectivism. *Seeing Is Believing* was praised by William Carlos Williams, about whom Tomlinson wrote so well in the Penguin selection of Williams that Tomlinson edited, quietly suggesting his own influence: 'He has divided his line according to a new measure learned, perhaps, from a new world.'

Charles came to our flat in Belsize Park in April 1970 for a cup of tea and to sign his books: he was one of the few poets whose every book I bought in the days when poetry was at the heart of my reading. With him were his wife and one of their two daughters. Here is his first publication, the Hand and Flower pamphlet *Relations and Contraries*. On the back there is a list of the first eight pamphleteers, seven well or vaguely known to me, but 'Arthur Constance'? What became of him? On my desk are all the individual volumes by the 'chaste' (Davie's word) Tomlinson, reprinted later in *Collected Poems*. The reprint of Tomlinson's second and most Stevens-influenced publication, *The Necklace*, is introduced by Davie. If a young poet were to ask me for examples of great mastery of phrasing, where Davie's 'articulate energy' is incarnate in the syntax, I would point him/her in the direction of Charles Tomlinson.

Among the books Tomlinson signed was his *Versions from Fyodor Tyutchev*, introduced by Henry Gifford (by inference, the co-translator). The whimsical message reads: 'April 1970, Brenda and Tony, with the kind regards of Fyodor Tyutchev'. I underlined one sentence in the Tyutchev introduction: 'the aim of these translations has been to preserve not the metre, but the movement of each poem: its flight, or track through the mind.' The rest of the paragraph sums up my own attitude and, with luck, practice, in words I cannot better and I add them here as the best statement I know of what poetry translation should aim to incarnate:

> Every real poem starts from a given ground and carries the reader to an unforeseen vantage point, whence he views differently the landscape over which he has passed. What the translator must do is recognize these two terminal points, and to connect them by a

180

coherent flight. This will not be [I would say 'this cannot be'] exactly the flight of his original, but no essential reach of the journey will have been left out. Features are thus transposed, or suppressed only to come out elsewhere in a disguised form. These are liberties of the translator, but liberties assumed for the sake of a new order. Sometimes the original thought would be compromised by appearing in a poem for the twentieth century. It must therefore be diffused in the atmosphere of a new poem. For a new poem the version must be: otherwise it cannot live. Translation is resurrection, but not of the body.

Michael Hamburger

I received a letter from Michael Hamburger saying that his next visit to London, for the launch party not only of the third edition of his *Poems of Paul Celan* but also of his new book of poems *Circling the Square*, would be his last. Old age and ill health were taking their toll on this fit and active man who could no longer cultivate his apple orchard and large garden with its sundial, seen in a doctored photograph in Sebald's *Rings of Saturn*. At the event, Gloomberger as Christopher Middleton used to call him, was smiling and relaxed. Later, when I learnt from Dinah Livingstone that Michael, a friend of mine for forty years, had died, I phoned his wife Anne Beresford. Anne, a fine lyric poet, reminded me that I had agreed to her private request, some years earlier, to recite Kaddish at Michael's eventual funeral in the village church, because she wanted to honour his origins. What would Paul Celan have made of Kaddish in a church?

Michael Hamburger was born in 1924 on 22 March (the day of Goethe's death) and died in 2007 on 7 June (the day of Hölderlin's death). For years, this distinguished poet and translator of the two greatest German-language poets prior to Rilke and Celan was my German expert. The professional aspect of the loss of this friend hit me one morning when I wanted to talk through the meaning of *dichten*: I had been rereading the pages on Basil Bunting in Pound's *ABC of Reading*, where Bunting is quoted as having discovered the equation 'dichten = condensare . . . while fumbling about in a German-Italian dictionary'. This was, wrote Pound, Bunting's 'prime contribution to contemporary criticism'. *Dichten* involves one word where in English we need three: 'to compose poetry'; the poetics underlying the equation—'condensare' obviously meaning to condense or to compress—has been hugely influential. I have by heart a sentence Isaac Rosenberg wrote to Lawrence Binyon: 'I am determined that this war, with all its powers for devastation, shall not master my poeting; that is, if I am lucky enough to come through all right.' He uses the verb form '. . . my poeting . . .', which derives from a non-existent verb 'to poet'. Is it possible that, knowing Yiddish, which uses the same word *dichten*, Rosenberg invented the verb in English, 'to poet' being the one-word literal translation of *dichten*? I think I have made a discovery. One final gloss: Wittgenstein wrote somewhere that 'Philosophie durfte man eigentlich nur dichten': 'Philosophy ought to be composed like poetry' or 'philosophy ought to be like poeting.' I decided to run this past Christopher Middleton who has succeeded Michael Hamburger as my German expert, with Bill (W. D.) and Christine Jackson as first assistants. Middleton came up with 'philosophising should be like writing poems', something Coleridge agreed with, albeit the other way round. He also confirmed that the Italian lexicographer, very conveniently for Bunting and with great knock-on effects, was perpetrating a false etymology, whether deliberately or not.

After reading Geoffrey Hill's 'Pindarics (after Cesare Pavese)' in *Without Title*, I yearned to chat with Michael about Hölderlin and Pindar. Instead, I opened the translator's *An Unofficial Rilke* at the poem 'To Hölderlin': 'Oh, what the best aspire to, you, undesiring, laid / brick upon brick: it stood up. But its very collapse / left you composed,' and thought about his several versions of the complete poems of Hölderlin over the years, untiringly revised, for only the provisional endures, as they say in France. Rest in peace, Michael, exemplary poet translator, role model nonpareil: what's more, you remained a socialist and a radical to the end, and were one of the few people I could speak frankly to about my fears of nuclear or climate apocalypse arriving sooner rather than later, for you shared them one hundred per cent.

Christopher Middleton (with Gael Turnbull and small presses)
The work of certain writers discovered when I was young is secure in my permanent affections and receives my periodic attentions. I am profoundly

grateful for those rafts which emerged from the storms when I was all at sea, and in need of lighthouse beacons, *phares*. To know that these writers lived or still live is a consolation, and a sighting or recollection of their work brings back the old days. All the books of Christopher Middleton, one of my favourite modernists, are on my desk. In *Two Horse Wagon Going By*, he has a powerful poem in memory of the literary critic Peter Szondi who died in the same way as his friend Paul Celan, and not long after him.

> Something else
> has him by the throat,
> something else calling the shots, his
> discipline a terror, his protective
> passion sapped by the microbe,
> intolerable ache
> of millions driven living
> into the gas

Middleton's enormous and awesome *Collected Poems* begins with *Torse 3*, his first official book after he renounced two Fortune Press books published during the war before he was twenty—presumably Rimbaldian or New Apocalypse juvenilia. John Barrell owned *Torse 3* in Cambridge: lines like 'What did it mean (I ask myself), to climb a pebble' aroused our curiosity. Drawing the reader into a super-rational surrealistic meditation on this question, the poem ends: 'I struck the pebble, digging, as the sun went up'. Characteristically, *Collected Poems* concludes with '. . . Work in Progress'. There are many more poems to come from this formidable intelligence, now eighty-six. Still climbing, still digging, Middleton presses the button. 'Effervescence and distillation are the poles between which one plays one's peculiar games,' he says in his book *Palavers and a Nocturnal Journal*, where we find his thoughts on Mallarmé: the best short introduction to this poet in English.

I used to tie myself in knots trying to figure out if I and/or Menard Press was part of the avant-garde but, much as I wanted to be (as so often in my life, I willed the end, not the means), I wasn't, at least not entirely. Nor, however, was Menard in the establishment mainstream. But in the early 1970s, when the press was a recipient of funding from the Arts Council, one could not take the Council's shilling and fairly pretend to be entirely outside the establishment. In those days, the structures of distribution were different: we sold at book fairs, to private customers by mail, and in about twenty bookshops up and down the country, mainly London—the ICA, Compendium, Better Books and so on. I know now that boundaries and definitions only matter if one is writing sociology or history. The overlaps were considerable everywhere. Thus, Goliard Press had an arrangement with Cape, and later on avant-garde poetry was published by Picador. My poetry, such as it was, was influenced by the American Objectivists and East European models. What then were the avant-gardes? There were the beat poets round Michael Horovitz overlapping with the pop and Liverpool poets, and enjoying a Bohemian lifestyle—if that means anything after the Larkinian year of 1963. But in terms of radical syntax, prosody and metrics, we have to be talking about J. H. Prynne and the 'Cambridge' poets associated with him, as well as, institutionally, small presses such as Goliard, Andrew Crozier's Ferry Press, Tim Longville and John Riley's Grosseteste, Anthony Barnett's Allardyce Barnett and Asa Benveniste's Trigram.

In the days when I fantasized about whom I would publish at Menard, I regularly thought about Gael Turnbull, but this remained a fantasy. I have dated my copy of *A Very Particular Hill*. This was shortly before the arrival on the scene of Indica and Compendium. Only one London shop would have stocked it, Better Books on Charing Cross Road, where I would repair during the lunch hour of my first day job in 1964: a graduate traineeship with the British Travel Association on St James' Street, about ten minutes walk from the bookshop. Bill Butler or Anthony Barnett would have sold it to me, since Paul Buck and Bob Cobbing were not employed there till later. This is one of my talismanic books, although in a letter the poet expressed amazement that someone remembered it. Turnbull, yet another writer/doctor (*There Are Words* is his collected poems), wrote more for the 'common man' than do Middleton and, say, Roy Fisher (*Collected Poems*). Turnbull is Rakosi to their Zukofsky and Oppen. If Middleton has his homologues in modern avant-garde classical music, and Fisher in jazz, then Turnbull's opposite numbers are folk singers. In 2010, I published a fortieth-anniversary-keepsake catalogue, which tells the beginnings of Menard in the vortex of the late 1960s. In 2007, I published Menard's final book: *If from the Distance*, two essays by Middleton. And so the press came full circle, our first title having been a special issue of the *Journals of Pierre Menard*, on Michael Hamburger, back in 1968.

Ted Hughes and Thom Gunn (with Sylvia Plath)

Ted Hughes was one of 'the seven best living British poets' on a list John Barrell, with my help, drew up in 1964 after browsing together at a bookstall in Cambridge Market Square. John spotted *The Hawk in the Rain*, priced sixpence (two and a half new pence), a first printing, and said I could have it provided his own copy was also a first printing. It was, so I got lucky. I met Hughes at the first Poetry International in 1967. Thanks to Alberto de Lacerda, Nathaniel Tarn had shown my translations of an invited poet, Yves Bonnefoy, to Hughes, who was to recite them, but he had hurt his back and so, contrary to the custom of the times, the translator read his own translations. At some point in the early 1970s, my chartered accountant father became Ted's financial advisor. At the time, the firm was already auditing the books of the Poetry Society (auditing the poets was what the audience did). Here are almost all of Ted's books including *Crow* (a signed Baskin screenprint of a 'Crow' poem is on the wall outside my front door) and *Tales from Ovid*. I gave Paula a copy of the latter, hoping it would inspire her but, paradoxically or not, she has not drawn on it perhaps because, metamorphosis being her job,this would involve a meta-metamorphosis. Here too is *The Iron Man*, which I well remember reading to my children. *A Choice of Shakespeare's Verse* is inscribed: 'For Tony, The new boat finds the old rocks, love from Ted, August 1992'. The book is dedicated to Roy Davids, who ran the rare-books department at Sotheby's and was often a fellow visitor at the Hughes household in North Tawton when my parents went down there for weekends. The concept underlying the book is simple, audacious and deeply unfashionable, so unfashionable that A. C. Bradley made the same point in *Shakespearean Tragedy* at the beginning of the twentieth century: theatre performances, however great, can get in the way of an appreciation of the greatest poetry in the language. The extracts are numbered, but not identified till the end of the book, followed by a forty-page 'note'—one of Hughes' best essays—which he later expanded into a over-long book that unsurprisingly had a mixed reception, *Shakespeare and the Goddess of Complete Being*. Towards the end of his 'note', referring to Shakespeare's sonnets, Hughes says something that is germane to his own best work: 'The control and order of art are there, but none of the defences. None of the distancings and obliquities.' I marked two other passages of great insight: 'Poetry has a warrant for the office of truth-teller only in so far as its music becomes a form of action. And the music of a voice is action, and persuades us . . . only . . . on the level of intuitive empathy.' And, again, on the sonnets: '. . . he was, to a degree, obsessed with the knowledge that the heart's truth is inexpressible without some guarantee and down-payment or indemnity on the physical plane.' The later book deals with the 'complexities of Shakespeare's great evolving mythos' which Hughes' earlier essay says he will steer clear of, in favour of discussing 'the historical forces that gave shape and "reality" to the mythos itself'.

It took a monumental effort on my part to finish this book, just as I have never been able to finish *The White Goddess*, a forerunner of Hughes' *Goddess*. Graves too was obsessing about material that had been generated by the mental sustenance which fertilized his poems. Lorca was doing the same thing in his seminal Duende essay but he kept it short. I like to read about Hughes (see Elaine Feinstein's *Life of a Poet* and Daniel Weissbort's *Ted Hughes and Translation*), for he was a stupendous presence and intelligence, second to none in my long life as a go-between. Christopher Reid did not include two letters I sent him for his finely edited volume, *Letters of Ted Hughes*, one to me and one to my mother after my father died. Never mind. The book is structured as a narrative and this has involved a particular kind of selectivity, with individual letters of quality and fascination omitted in the interests of a greater good.

Until the early 1980s (and to a lesser extent later), I bought new books by a small number of poets, as and when they came out. The latest slim volume, on the day of publication—that was a moment to be savoured. Ted Hughes and Thom Gunn were like Edrich and Compton or Morecambe and Wise or Hillel and Shammai. The two poets found themselves paired, partly because they had the same publisher (who marketed them together), partly because of the Cambridge connection, partly because of their ongoing friendship. I have no inscribed copies of Gunn books, only a postcard from him. Ted and Thom were chalk and cheese, the Romantic driven figure of Hughes, a cross between Heathcliff and Shelley, and the cool gay classically quatrained figure of Gunn who admired Yvor Winters and J. V. Cunningham and took himself off to San Francisco, partly for reasons of the private life. It is hard to know which of the two was more influential among younger poets in the early 1960s. Hughes was (Shakespearean/Hugolean) Nature, Gunn (Donnean/Baudelairian) Culture. Both men were incredibly well read, and both were free spirits, so my capitalized binary opposition is a touch glib, and yet it says something about them. I remain unsure whether the famous Gunn attitudes and self-projections in his first three books *Fighting Terms*, *The Sense of Movement* and *My Sad Captains* are entirely free of irony, the classic English first line of defence and comfort zone. For Gunn is never on the defensive, to put it mildly. Let us say that any irony encompasses or spotlights his own poses: he is the first to charge himself with existential inauthenticity: 'I know of no emotion we can share. / Your intellectual protests are a bore, / And even now I pose, so now go, for / I know you know.'

If the personal is political, we doubtless prefer Gunn's eponymous sad captains to his overdogs in *The Sense of Movement* (the latter including the rough boys in the playground 'who would not play with Stephen Spender' as well as Spender's own band of the 'truly great') but we register his confidence in generalization, his certainty that impersonal statement does not preclude self-revelation, which is to say revelations to the self via the other, rather than of the self to the other. Nonetheless, some readers want more of other people in all their particularity and quiddity than Gunn allows us in his first three volumes. There is a tantalizing glimpse of alternative paths on the flowchart in the Empsonian final line of 'On the Move' in *The Sense of Movement*: 'One is always nearer by not keeping still.' The young poet is announcing possibility on the other side of the seemingly frozen tableaux that make up the early work.

Positives has photos of 1960s London taken by Gunn's brother Ander. Thom Gunn must have selected from a much larger bunch of photos and he clearly enjoyed writing his basically seven-syllable-lined (with considerable variations) sophisticated ekphrastic illustrations of mainly working-class London at work or relaxing, with no hint of swinging London. *Positives* was first published in 1966: you would not know that the film *Blow-Up* came out the same year. *Touch* and *Moly* are his next books. At the heart of *Touch* is the remarkable sequence 'Misanthropos'. It shows Gunn moving into specifics where a 'thou' has finally entered the stage, even if an I/Thou modality awaits the final three books. The last and marvellous poem in the book, 'Back to Life', reveals the poet walking through park and street, full of curiosity and interest in the boys and girls round him, 'As if the light revealed us all / Sustained in delicate difference / Yet firmly growing from a single branch.' But, the next stanza begins, 'If that were all of it! / The branch that we grow on / Is not remembered easily in the dark.' Sympathy is one thing, empathy another. Maybe he remains a poet of statement and ideas after all. In *Moly*, he writes, 'I deal a grown man's fate.'

And now, irrespective of his ability to individuate the feelings of others, the poet is indeed a grown man and a lord of language, apparently effortless in his ability to sew and reap verses in understated song. His final three volumes are more explicitly gay, more personal by his standards: *The Passages of Joy* ('In their fathers' gardens / children are hiding / up in orchard trees, seeking / to be lost and found'), *The Man with Night Sweats*, a book composed at the time of the AIDS epidemic ('How like you to be kind, / Seeking to reassure. / And, yes, how like my mind / To make itself secure'), and the marvellously titled and moving last book *Boss Cupid* where he remembers his dead. Gunn's elegy for Robert Duncan conjures up the poet composing on the San Francisco ferry, and ends with Duncan 'in sight of a conclusion, whose great dread / was closure, / his life soon to be enclosed / like the sparrow's flight above the feasting friends . . .'—an allusion to Bede. The elegy for Donald Davie is less successful, perhaps because Donald was already in heaven while Duncan was still on earth, albeit no longer composing poems because of major kidney problems. The brilliant poem 'Shit', subtitled 'essay on Rimbaud', ends: 'he was as cool as a vivisectionist,' a line Jeremy Reed, true son of the Gunn, could have written. Harry Guest in his fine book *Some Times* ends his memorial poem for Gunn with praise for the poems couched in an allusion to one of his most famous lines: 'I know you know we know how good they are.'

Along with single poems by Charles Tomlinson and Robert Creeley (discussed elsewhere in this book), among the very first contemporary poems

I read were the *Ariel* poems by Sylvia Plath which Al Alvarez published in the *Observer* in 1963 shortly after Plath's death. I bought Plath's *Ariel* on publication in 1965 and her novel *The Bell Jar* in 1966, when it was reissued under her own name. Earlier in 1966, I found *The Colossus* in Ann Arbor at Peter Wyman's bookshop Centicore, the Compendium Bookshop of the Middle West. Of these three books it was *Ariel* that had the most impact, although there are marvellous poems in *The Colossus* such as 'Watercolour of Grantchester Meadows'. After Primo Levi died, a foolish writer in the *New Yorker* queried whether Levi's suicide invalidated his work. This is as ridiculous as making (which some did) the opposite point about Plath, namely that the manner of her death somehow cast a retrospective imprimatur on her work. Like Levi's masterpieces, *Ariel* contains the light and shadow of its truth and beauty irrespective of its generative matrix in the life, the body and mind, of its author. The comments made about Levi and Plath imply that suicide is inevitable whereas on the flowchart of a life there are almost always choices; a reading of the evidence (e.g. Ted Hughes' letter to Anne Stevenson and various books on Primo Levi, including my own) makes it clear that in both cases things could have been different.

Geoffrey Hill

In the autumn of 1966, I met Geoffrey Hill for the first time (thanks to our mutual friend, Hill's student Jon Silkin) while I was on attachment to the Leeds branch of the Automobile Association, early in the second of several disastrous day jobs. I was a trainee in the 'organization and methods' department of the organization. Not me at all, but in those days I applied for many jobs that were not my 'cup tea or piece cake', as my grandfather used to say in his Polish/Yiddish English. Being good at interviews and nothing else, I would be taken on and then last about three months. Hill bought me lunch at the university and thus began a sporadic epistolary relationship, with the occasional hello at a reading. For over forty years I pressed his claims on Yves Bonnefoy and others in France. Hill, who eventually lectured at the Collège de France and was translated into French, has a reputation for being distant and severe. He certainly could never be accused of pandering to popular taste and some would say he sometimes keeps the reader at mind's length via an armature of scholarly prose and elevated poetry. Yet, when giving a public reading, he delivered entertaining patter between poems that would have impressed Ronny Scott or Humphrey Lyttelton.

While I have all his books and note that his productivity has increased many fold (thanks, they say, in part to lithium)—there have been many books since the *Collected Poems* of 1990—it is to his earlier books I return, as I do with Jon Silkin, Charles Tomlinson, Thom Gunn and Ken Smith. This reflects recent demands of autobiography in my own work, not necessarily a belief that the earlier work of these poets is better than their later work. *King Log*, *Mercian Hymns* and *Tenebrae* remain among my favourite and, indeed, talismanic poetry books, along with Silkin's *A Peaceable Kingdom* and Tomlinson's *Seeing Is Believing*. Hill's first book, *For the Unfallen*, imposed itself immediately on readers, like another famous first book, Bonnefoy's *Du Mouvement et de l'immobilité de Douve*. It seems as though the poems were always there, parthogenetic despite the real influences. The voice imposed itself, right from the start.

Earlier I mentioned Tomlinson's phrasing. Hill's early music works on a broader span than Tomlinson's; the prime unit in any given poem is longer than in a Tomlinson poem. Hill seduces the reader with his line, thereby leaving the dazed and honour-bound recipient with little choice but to seek an understanding of the thought, which is often difficult. As he said in an interview, 'difficult poetry is the most democratic, because you are doing your audience the honour of supposing that they are intelligent human beings.' Amen to that.

In 1968, I must have been impatiently waiting for *King Log* to come out because my copy was inscribed to me—'At last! Brenda'—by my then girlfriend, whose [ex-] husband I later became. This book contains the marvellous 'Song-book', a sequence by the apocryphal Spanish poet, Sebastian Arrurruz (1868–1922). Removed from Hill in time and language, he speaks in a slower, softer, more languorous voice than his ventriloquist. Hill wrote this poem in the late 1960s, when the great modern flowering of poetry translation was just getting under way. That may have been one of the influences generating the conceit of translation deployed in 'Song-book'. Hill, in those days, was close to *Stand* magazine under Jon Silkin's editorship. *Stand*, like another magazine he contributed to—William Cookson's *Agenda*—was a major player in the translation renaissance.

'Funeral Music' is another wondrous sequence from the same book. The eight sonnets are, in the words of Hill's note, 'a commination and an alleluia for the period . . . known as the Wars of the Roses'. This is 'history as poetry', the title of another poem in the same book, a poem with affinities to the earlier poems of Paul Celan, although I don't know if Hill was yet reading Celan. The later *Tenebrae* (1978), however, contains 'Two Chorale-Preludes' on melodies of Paul Celan. 'History as poetry', needless to say, does not mean that the 'florid grim' (Hill's own words) 'Funeral Music' is a narrative. It commemorates a dreadful and bloody time. In the words of the final sonnet: 'So it is required; so we bear witness, / Despite ourselves, to what is beyond us, / Each distant sphere of harmony forever / Poised, unanswerable.'

This is a poet who, like Charles Péguy (subject of a great and long poem by Hill), is a Christian and, I would say, a communitarian. Not only does Hill think redemption, think atonement, think 'the tongue's atrocities' ('History as Poetry'), he thinks them in poetry (which, in the words of Rosanna Warren in her distinguished book *Fables of the Self*, is 'language suffering the condition of its utterance'), and this is a blessing for us, whatever the cost to the poet. In the *PNR* essay I commissioned from Hill (see the section on F. T. Prince above), he speculates about where Eliot would have gone as a poet had he extended or completed the Coriolan sequence: this would have 'taken Eliot forward in a direction from which "Burnt Norton" deflected him: into a synthesis . . . of Dryden's two forms of satire, the heroic and the burlesque'. Hill's own high modernist multivoiced rhetorical synthesis in his later books, unabated into his eighties, shows that the concept of a late style, whether serene or turbulent, has little to teach us about the work of a grand poet fired up with things to say, and nowhere else to go.

Jon Silkin

Jon Silkin is one of the good friends who flit in and out of *Silent Conversations*. I have everything he published, including his pre-first book, *The Portrait*, which he paid a printer, Mr Stockwell of Ilfracombe, to bring out. He is one of a group of writers from the generation that had produced its first and second volumes about ten years before I became interested in poetry, a group whose work means so much to me; the interest was fostered and nurtured by John Barrell, my contemporary and, in some ways, role model at Cambridge. I owed my long (and sometimes difficult) friendship with Silkin to Barrell, who introduced me to him in Cambridge in 1963, at the gate of Kings College, where this tough-minded, touchy and radical figure was selling *Stand*. I bought it and remain to this day a regular reader of the magazine, to which I have contributed over the years as reviewer, essayist, poetry translator, fiction writer and, eventually, poet. Silkin and I had our differences—his confrontational approach was not to my taste—but this was a real friendship for over thirty years. I learnt about editing from him as well as from Miron Grindea of *Adam* magazine and was inspired by the poet's political commitment, not a primary concern of Miron's.

Here is Silkin's luminous, indeed numinous, inaugural volume of 1954, *The Peaceable Kingdom*, with the heart-rending poem 'Death of a Son' and his strong Jewish/fox poem 'No Land Like This', published a few years before the latterly more famous fox poem by Ted Hughes and even more years before Ken Smith's. The tone of this book originates in the diction of the 1940s poets: Silkin was never influenced by the 1950s' 'Movement' reaction against the romanticism and colour of the 1940s. He had already found his voice in that masterwork of a first volume so deadly serious, so light in touch, although later he would fight to make the finest distinctions in poetic argumentation and force the reader to make the effort to inhabit his knotty and gritty poems. He did not always live up to his own comment in *Contemporary Poets*: 'The syntax must have an onwardness, and even when it's motionless, a moment, it must not be repetitious or anxious to produce an effect.' The final poem in *The Psalms and Their Spoils*, 'Wildness Makes a Form', contains two lines—'this is the very kingdom, artifice / of survival among strength in disorder'—which get to the heart of Silkin's project. The critic Merle Brown wrote an afterword for a revised edition of *The Peaceable Kingdom*, in which he rightly says that this wondrous book is uniquely integrated among the poet's works, is indeed itself a unified and peaceable kingdom. Jon was a major presence in English poetry and, simply, one of the best poets. Here on my desk are a pile of his books including *The Re-Ordering of the Stones, Nature with Man, Amana Grass, The Principle of Water* and *The Ship's Pasture*, to name only the ones with natural phenomena in the titles. A collected poems is long overdue. Jon Glover and Rodney Pybus are on the case, and I'm on standby in case I'm needed.

I have already intimated that readers sometimes struggled with his syntax. However, when he dealt with his Jewishness in verse, I used to think he was, paradoxically, less tangled up in the very roots of language: his struggle with the angel was gentler, the thought was clearer, the tone less aggressive. I would put it differently now, but he certainly wrote the strongest Jewish poems (poems, that is, which wrestle with theological and existential dilemmas of Jewishness, not at all poems which merely happen to be written by a Jew) by any Anglo-Jewish poet since Isaac Rosenberg. These poems culminate in the key sequence 'Footsteps on the Downcast Path' (in *The Ship's Pasture*), a lengthy meditation on martyrdom.

As a critic, Silkin wrote with commitment, empathy and high intelligence about the war poets, in particular Rosenberg. *Out of Battle* is a major critical study of the war poets. Rosenberg's syntax and diction, influenced by the Yiddish he heard all round him in the East End before heading for the trenches, plainly (i.e. colourfully) influenced the younger poet. When the time came, in 1997, it fell to me to arrange Silkin's funeral at Bushey Jewish cemetery, and the tombstone setting some months later. I recited, too, the Kaddish at his memorial meeting in Conway Hall. I recall visits to his house in Newcastle. On one occasion he showed me a review of my pre-first book pamphlet: he would not print it, he said, it was so harsh. The reviewer was right to lambast the pamphlet, but all the same he had misread a persona poem—written between quotation marks in the voice of 'The Dance'—as the poet's own voice. Jon used to stay at our flat in Belsize Park on his quarterly visits to London, when we would sell *Stand* in cinema queues and pubs, colleges and poetry societies. I remember one or two regular purchasers of the quarterly in the gay pub in Hampstead, The William, where they joked about the name of the magazine. Every copy sold meant a percentage for the seller and usually we earned enough to have dinner at our local curry house in England's Lane. I learnt from Silkin that it was not enough to produce handsome and professional-looking books and magazines, you had to dirty your hands, sell the magazine directly to the customer and also—a dress rehearsal for Menard books—persuade booksellers to stock the product. Not for nothing was his anthology from *Stand* called *Poetry of the Committed Individual*. Those were the days of retail-price maintenance and long before the arrival of the big chains, centralized buying and huge discounts. It was never my favourite part of the process of being a small press publisher, but it had to be done, or what was the point?

It was a source of regret to me that Silkin never published one of my poems. However, this was something Jon Glover as editor later 'put right' and I have to believe my poems have improved, not that Glover's standards are lower than Silkin's! I spoke to Silkin on the phone several times in his last few months, partly to discuss the possibility of a Menard book: his translations from the Hebrew of Uri Zvi Greenberg. Tenacious and argumentative, Silkin will be wrestling with the angel until the Messiah, whose coming was part of Silkin's project, finally shows up and we all find ourselves at home in Edward Hicks' 'Peaceable Kingdom', a favourite picture of Jon's. A month before he died, he sent me an affectionately inscribed pamphlet, *Watersmeet*, a work which is of considerable interest to his close readers since it contains different versions of different sections of the poem as well as comments by friends. The last time we spoke on the phone—within a week he was dead—he said: 'Tony, we are old troupers.'

Jon Silkin and Jon Glover

In a week when the three hundred executed World War I British soldiers were pardoned for desertion and 'cowardice'—compared to twenty-five Germans and no Australians—it is salutary to pick up a book about a war that never goes away for long, a war whose modes of killing led directly, on the technological and moral flowcharts, to Hiroshima and Auschwitz: *The Penguin Book of First World War Prose*, edited by Jon Silkin and Jon Glover. This important anthology sits on the shelf next to *Out of Battle* and Silkin's anthology *The Penguin Book of First World War Poetry* (along with a few necessary books such as Nicholas Murray's *The Sweet Red Wine of Youth*). Glover, a fine poet in his own right (*Magnetic Resonance Imaging*) is a fellow survivor of the Silkin inner circle, along with two other fine poets, Jeffrey Wainwright (*Clarity or Death*) and Rodney Pybus (*Darkness Inside Out*), and we remain in close touch. Amidst the usual suspects in the two Jons' anthology are discoveries and a surprise: Uri Zvi Greenberg. It's not clear from the note to Greenberg's poem—the only poem in the whole book and a kind of prologue—whether he wrote it in Hebrew after he changed to that language on moving to the Yishuv (pre-Israel Palestine in 1923) or whether he translated it from his first language, Yiddish. I asked an expert, Glenda Abramson, who replied that the poem was indeed written in Hebrew, which was rare for Greenberg since most of his war poetry was written in Yiddish. He published his first book of Yiddish poems in 1915 when he was drafted into the Austrian army, around the same time as his exact contemporary and *landsman*, my relative Zygfryd Rudolf. Surprisingly or not, this powerful poem, 'Naming Souls', has distinct affinities with works by another contemporary of Greenberg's, Isaac Rosenberg. In this early poem, Greenberg, later a ferocious right-wing revisionist Zionist, is not in the least particularistic in voice or intended audience.

Another jewel in the anthology is Herbert Read's description of a stealth raid on the enemy's trenches, with instructions to kill as many men as possible and bring back one prisoner. He reports the conversation in broken French he had with this man, and their common enthusiasm for Beethoven and Chopin: 'He even admired Nietzsche and thenceforth we were sworn friends.' Finally, he quotes *Old Soldiers Never Die* by Frank Richards: 'The clergy on both sides were a funny crowd: they prayed for victory and thundered from the pulpits for the enemy to be smitten hip and thigh, but did not believe in doing any of the smiting themselves. They were all non-combatants with the exception of the Catholic priests who were forced to serve in the French army the same as anybody else.'

Ken Smith

Ken Smith, whom I met through Silkin, signed and dated ('20/5/67') my copy of *The Pity* at his house in Exeter. *The Pity* signalled the arrival of a distinctive voice even though the matrix or agon is evident to the reader and acknowledged in the posthumous *You Again*, where he says that he 'learned, in part, from two poets who were at Leeds, Jon Silkin and Geoffrey Hill, that being a poet is a matter of growth, a way of living, integral'. Here are four later poetry books by my old mate, self-styled 'anarchist-in-waiting to the republic of survival': *Terra* (he dated his inscription '*7/5/86, The Sun*', a pub we frequented in Covent Garden), *Wormwood*, *Wild Root* and *Fox Running* as well as *Inside Time*, a remarkable prose account of his work with prisoners in Wormwood Scrubs. In prison, writes Smith, 'there's disinformation, the fox weaving in and out of his home trail'. That is a clue about his private concerns—unnoticed by all the reviewers save one . . .—if you know Smith's poetry and his 'fox' persona. 'Fox Running' is a wonderful poem, a riff of personal desolation amidst the riff-raff of a great city, and a necessary centrepiece of any anthology of London poems. *Anus Mundi*, his 'black sonnets in prose', is cheerfully signed: 'As promised: world's asshole. Best, Tony, Ken Smith'. The punctuation suggests that the phrase is a translation of the book's title, and not an invocation of the recipient, *nicht wahr*, Kenny? Here are his anthology of poems for Bosnia, *Klaonica*, edited with his wife Judi Benson, and *Beyond Bedlam*, poems of mentally ill people, edited with Matthew Sweeney; finally, his vivid eyewitness prose account, *Berlin: Coming in from the Cold*, after the wall came down.

'I'm on the blink and fading fast': at Ken's green funeral in an East London park, a fox, as if in homage, ran by while one of several friends was reading a Smith poem. To die of legionnaire's disease from contaminated water in a foreign hotel, that is wormwood and gall, and now the running fox has returned to his wild roots. What survives beyond memory is the poetry, collected in *The Poet Reclining* and *Shed*. *You Again* contains his final poems and other texts, as well as pieces by poet friends, including Jon Glover, who rightly calls him a great poet, and an extraordinary poem to Ken by his wife Judi, reprinted in her own book, *The Thin Places*. One New Year's Eve, Judi and Ken phoned me from a call box saying they could not find my block of flats to come to a small party. Trouble was they were in a road of the same name about four miles away. Ken and I often spoke on the phone in likelier circumstances, about poetry, and especially about politics, not least about Israel. For Ken, as for several other friends, I was the only Jewish person to whom they felt they could express reservations about Israeli government policy without being accused of antisemitism. It goes without saying that I claim no credit for this, but what an appalling indictment of some brethren. Whenever I pass the French Pub in Soho I think of Ken, and remember too Chicago, the retired boxer always in the same place, extreme left as you came in, at the bar.

Richard Berengarten (with sightings of Tom Lowenstein, Peter Russell, W. S. Graham and John Burnside)

Of the notable student poets at Cambridge, John Barrell and Terry Eagleton seem to have abandoned the practice of poetry or been abandoned by it over the years, while becoming distinguished scholars and academics. Tom Lowenstein and the late Andrew Crozier continued, as did Alexis Lykiard and Tom Clark and the late Angus Calder. I want to salute Tom Lowenstein, a poet and ethno-translator of distinction (whose *Eskimo Poems from Canada and Greenland* is a significant book), to whom I remember showing my miserable earliest efforts in the cafe on the roof of the Arts Theatre. Nor have I ever forgotten lines from a poem of his in *Granta*, then a student magazine edited by John Barrell: 'Even the heart's exhausted thunder / timed to be extinguished/unexpectedly / thuds on', with that syntactic ambiguity in the third quoted line, an enjambement to break the heart of Nicholson Baker's hero in *The Anthologist*. I wonder what became of Jim Philip and Caroline West (Rebecca West's granddaughter), who were big names in undergraduate magazines at the time. It's just as well I cannot lay my hands on those magazines, I would only wallow in nostalgia: better to make a virtue out of necessity and to trust my relatively fine-meshed colander of a memory.

I don't need to make an effort to remember Richard Berengarten (then Richard Burns: he has adopted the ancestral surname his father abandoned on arrival in England from Poland), whom I met in the final weeks of our final year: it was enough to trigger a lifelong friendship and we remain in regular touch. He has been a productive and distinctive poet, European rather than English in spiritual provenance. He was also inspired by Octavio Paz, whom I introduced him to when the great Mexican poet spent 1970 in Cambridge. Paz countered the Peter Russell side of Berengarten, which to my mind was not going anywhere although it did bring him to the kind of

197

crossroads described by Yves Bonnefoy in *L'Arrière-pays*. Russell, like Jeremy Reed later on, was a poet with a capital P, but Russell, unlike Reed, was too obsessive and repetitive to be taken as seriously as the nature of his high-flown poetry demands. Time and again, there are reams of verse surrounding a golden nugget of poetry. It is no accident that his best poems are, as Kathleen Raine also thought, *The Elegies of Quintilius*, Quintilius being a Latin poet he invented, inspired by Pound's Propertius. Berengarten sees Quintilius as a Pessoan heteronym, but I am not so sure. Nonetheless, the classical figure seems to have supplied Russell with the necessary distance to invent a live world in words radiating energy that are projected far from the poesy and flights rampant in the main body of his work. He was a mentor for Berengarten, who ironically enough has ended up writing some of the best Peter Russell poems himself. The problem may have been that Russell wanted to devote his entire life not merely to poetry but to writing poetry. That is not a good idea, unless you are the author of *Malcolm Mooney's Land*, now in *Collected Poems*. For W. S. Graham, what's more, language as such is central to his project. Peter Russell was admired by Ezra Pound and Hugh MacDiarmid, but surely not his entire *oeuvre*.

I have a pile of Richard's books, all inscribed, by my desk, beginning with *Keys to Transformation*, on Ceri Richards and Dylan Thomas, beautifully designed and printed by Skelton's Press, my all-time favourite printer. Berengarten's long poem *Avebury* is dedicated to Octavio Paz. It says something about Richard's European rather than English provenance that his books have been translated into several European languages while at the same time he has found himself marginalized in his own country for years, unreviewed and unappreciated. Five volumes, published simultaneously in beautiful hardback editions, including *The Manager*, do not appear to have changed this situation. Like Paul Auster's *The Invention of Solitude* and Elaine Feinstein's *Russian Jerusalem*, *The Manager* is the author's least classifiable book. Written in *versets*, the theme of *The Manager*, like that of W. D. Jackson's remarkable Menard book, *Then and Now*, is the eponymous figure so central to the workings of our world. All these books draw on their authors' skills as poets, fiction writers, critics, translators and so on. But my particular devotion to those texts may say something about my own taste for crossover, in music and art as well as in literature. Another of Berengarten's books, *The Blue Butterfly*, is a high peak in his mountain range of a poetic *oeuvre*. Here his facility and fluency in verse work to poetry's advantage, under pressure as they *are* from the dark subject matter—the Kragujevac massacre of 1941.

[Coda: Richard Berengarten introduced me to John-Paul Dick, whose Trakl-haunted pamphlet *Homing* we jointly published at Los and Menard. Later John-Paul Dick emerged as John Burnside, now a famous and lauded poet (*Feast Days*), novelist and autobiographer. To bring out the first book by a young poet who moves on to wider exposure through commercial publishers is one of the *raisons d'être* of small presses.]

Anthony Howell (with Susan Hiller/David Coxhead and others)

Let me open a bunch of books inscribed by Anthony Howell, including *Why I May Never See the Walls of China*. One inscription reads: 'for Anthony, "thinking of a foreign tongue", love Anthony'. Michael Schmidt recalls, as I do, a party in my old Belsize Park flat on the top floor of 1 Primrose Gardens when Howell undressed down to his string vest, certainly because he felt that this gathering for two Donalds, Rayfield (translator of Nadezhda Yakovlevna Mandelstam's Menard book *Chapter Forty-Two and the Goldfinch*) and Davie, was too formal. Howell is a brilliant dandy poet—expert tango dancer and performance artist too; through him, I met David Coxhead and his wife Susan Hiller. Hiller, somewhere between Christian Boltanski and Joseph Cornell, pursues an extraordinary enterprise of recovery and commemoration that moves me, and then educates me. Her major installations are both lyrical and documentary, and the whole characterized by a luminous intelligence, equalled only by Sophie Calle. As a cultural phenomenologist, an endotic anthropologist, she is more self-conscious than Cornell (although he was no naive, no outsider) yet succeeds in holding the two poles of her work in balance, creating visual art of great beauty in the process. Coxhead, whose fine novel *Run Come See Jerusalem* is on my desk, will forgive me for re-telling the story of his visit to the Paris-based publisher of erotica and pornography, Maurice Girodias, in the hope of a pseudonymous commission. 'Coxhead is not a bad name, if a little obvious. What is your real name, David?'

199

Anthony presented me with his first book, *Inside the Castle*, in 1969 at a well-lubricated launch party in his attic room with its skylight, on 18 Caledonian Road. The only other person I 'clearly' remember being there was the late, learned and brilliant poet Peter Porter (*The Cost of Seriousness*). The drunkenly scrawled inscription in Howell's book reads: 'For Anthony bon [sic] chance!! Anthony (onanist commendation this!) and of course Brenda, xxx reserved for Brenda xxxxxxx'. Inserted in the book is a letter from my old American mentor, Andrew Glaze, slating Howell's poems in some detail, a copy of which I had evidently sent him as a present, a sign of my regard for both of them. Glaze's own distinguished and distinctive work includes a selected poems, *Someone Will Go on Owing*. Andy and I became friends in New York in 1966 as fellow employees of the British Travel Association; I later sent him my first poems in manuscript: his reply, which I still have, is a masterpiece of tact. In 2012, aged ninety-two, he was appointed poet laureate of Alabama. The back cover photo on *Inside the Castle* shows the young Anthony Howell, a hint of androgyny about the lips. As always, I am fascinated by the names of other writers listed on the jackets of books, in this case 'from our poetry list': D. M. Black, Tom Buchan, Frances Cornford, Jaquetta Hawkes, John Knight, Gil Orlovitz, Ruth Pitter, an eclectic bunch, for sure. I recall Ruth Pitter from the Sunday afternoon television 'Brains Trust' on the mono-channel BBC when I was a child. She was a blousy traditionalist with a plummy accent. So bloody what? It serves me right that, unexpectedly (during a Google search), one of my favourite poets Thom Gunn turns out to have admired her work. It therefore feels like a moral imperative to check her out in the Poetry Library on the South Bank.

Menard co-published with Medames Press—a new press set up by Howell and myself over a plate of foul medames at Gabi's bar on Charing Cross Road—Anthony Howell's book *Spending*, with subtly traced graphics by Dilys Bidewell. The only review received by this book of apparently rude poems and apparently rude drawings—which in fact deploy the conventions of rudeness, another matter entirely—was in *Forum*, amidst the sex articles and advertisements. *Spending* remains the first and last book from Menard/Medames. Howell also edited *Near Calvary*, the selected poems of Nicholas Lafitte. Lafitte, who suffered from acute schizophrenia, died by his own hand in 1970. I well remember the name of his father, Professor François Lafitte, from my childhood. He was the son-in-law of Havelock Ellis and a public figure in his own right, specializing in social policy at LSE, a world my father and, even more, my father's cousin Reggie Forrester were close to, intellectually and personally. I wrote Lafitte a letter after receiving the book and mentioned that my mother Esther Rosenberg had known him when young. In his reply, he stated that he could not remember her name and could I supply more details. I answered that she said she met him at a writing class in the Marx Memorial Library around 1931 or 1932 and at The Forum on Charing Cross Road, and that they went out together a few times. For whatever reason, he did not reply.

Veronica Forrest-Thomson

Veronica Forrest-Thomson was a force of nature, perhaps an odd image for a woman whose first book was called *Language-Games*. I wrote about Veronica in *Poems for Shakespeare IV*, which I edited for Sam Wanamaker at the Globe Theatre. I have already mentioned Henry Reed in this context. Unlike Reed, Forrest-Thomson did manage to fulfil the commission but she did not turn up for the reading in Southwark Cathedral in April 1975. Her parents were in the audience. She had died the previous evening, accidental rather than suicide, it is now believed. Her book *On the Periphery* contains a postscript by Jeremy Prynne: 'Her commitment to the writing of poetry was absolute and intrepid, and this commitment was in a vehemently dialectical and changing relation to her writing of poems.' The apparent paradox is the key to her power and ferocity in discussion and debate, as is clear from the surviving tape of a meeting about poetics held at my flat in Belsize Park in about 1970, when she dominated the assembled men, none of whom were slouches. The interweaving of poetics and poetry was a rare phenomenon in the UK, although familiar enough to someone like Michel Deguy in France. Empson, *Tel Quel*, Lacan, Wittgenstein: all were grist to her poetic mill. We had discussed the possibility of Menard publishing her translations of Marcelin Pleynet and Denis Roche, but nothing came of it. In his text, Prynne goes on to draw attention to her pamphlet *Cordelia or 'A Poem Should Not Mean, but Be'*. She had changed direction: now 'irony and abandon compete for the final control, which eludes both and comes to uncertain rest in the fullest (i.e. formal) acceptance of passion . . . Swinburne and Tennyson supplant the *Tel Quel* theorists, but the strongest presence is Sappho. Venus attached to her prey.' Her French translations were finally published in a handsome hardback, *Collected Poems and Translations*, meticulously edited by the publisher himself, Anthony Barnett. According to one of his notes, I supplied Barnett with the (possibly unique) typescript of the French translations. Veronica Forrest-Thomson's early death is on a par in terms of lost consequences with that of Gillian Rose, greater indeed, because Rose lived longer and produced more.

Andrew Crozier and other poets

I have written about Andrew Crozier elsewhere in this book. He was one of the key figures in the world of non-establishment poetry for more than thirty years. *All Where Which Is* collects his work from 1967 till 1982. On the day of our final results in 1964, as I stood at Senate House, not daring to read the notice board while guessing the worst, and stared at with pity—so I, projecting my self-pity, imagined—by fellow-students in my own faculty of anthropology, only Crozier had the courage to tell me the truth: I had obtained a non-honours degree, a so-called ordinary or pass degree. At some point, we fell out for reasons I forget, but almost certainly because of my low self-esteem as a writer and a projection onto him of my *ressentiment*. Later, we fell in again and remained in fairly regular contact. I always respected and admired him, though it took a while before I appreciated what a treasure he was. His widow Jean sent me *Star Ground*, a finely produced posthumous pamphlet containing three unpublished poems, one of which is the poignant and beautiful title poem dedicated to her and ending: 'Frost heaves all night / To rise like waves / spent on the margin / On the enduring / Particular resistance of our love.' These are plainly the last words of a man who knows that his brain tumour is going to kill him, perhaps soon, as it did.

It is not an exaggeration to say that John Barrell, then a poet now a senior scholar, was a benign foundational influence throughout my student years. Heaven knows what he made of his sidekick. I would have found me a pain had I been him, but I wasn't him, so that wasn't my problem; except it was.

However, I was not one hundred per cent *tabula rasa* or *virgo intacta* when it came to literature, thanks mainly to Miron Grindea of *Adam* magazine, whom I met when I was a sixth former. But poetry, like politics (except the Dreyfus case), was not Grindea's thing. His things were fiction and memoir, music and Jewish culture. One of the people in his circle was Anthony Barnett who turned out to have been at school with John Barrell. Barnett is a poet and translator, musician and musicologist. We fell out for a few years, officially concerning translations of Edmond Jabès but more likely because of my hang-ups. Barnett edited the magazines *Nothing Doing in London* and *The Literary Supplement*. In recent years he has run a publishing house, Allardyce Barnett, from his home in Lewes: recently his collected poems and translations have appeared. Like Paul Auster, he looked to Paul Celan and French poetry for an undercover story of foundation, well interpreted by Peter Riley.

William Cowper

The person of William Cowper, in Brian Lynch's fine novel *The Winner of Sorrow*, serves as a manifold trope for Lynch's exploration of madness, desire, poetry and religion, all constructed as modalities of language and embodied in one suffering genius. I have not read widely this poet of 'credit and renown', and it is time for me to explore my copy of his collected poems and take another look at Donald Davie's anthology *The Late Augustans* which reveals what Wordsworth ('as much the last poet of the eighteenth century as the first of the nineteenth') would have been reading, and ends with Cowper, whose death early in 1800 announced the end of the eighteenth century in more ways than one. That Cowper influenced Wordsworth and Coleridge is well known: in 'My First Acquaintance with Poets', William Hazlitt reports Coleridge as saying that Cowper is the best modern poet. I am intrigued by the Coleridgean sound of 'The Castaway', Cowper's last poem, written in 1799, one year after the publication of *Lyrical Ballads*. This contained 'The Ancient Mariner' which Cowper could in theory have read, although Lynch has his doubts.

> No voice divine the storm allay'd,
> No light propitious shone;
> When, snatched from all effectual aid,

We perish'd, each alone:
But I beneath a rougher sea,
and whelm'd in deeper gulphs than he.

Samuel Taylor Coleridge

Dear Mr Coleridge,

'Was not writing poetry a secret transaction, a voice answering a voice?': Virginia Woolf in her novel, *Orlando*, a book my friend the poet Deryn-Rees Jones recommends to both of us. If you agree to come to dinner in Finchley, my friends (including Deryn, who will bring another poet, Michael Murphy) and I will listen closely to the music of your thought and attempt to engage with you.

I would not have the cheek to ask you about your 'delegated man' (hired in Bristol), your 'external conscience' as De Quincey [*Recollections of the Lakes and the Lake Poets*] describes the fellow responsible for preventing you from entering the apothecary's to buy opium, or about the person from Porlock, who may have been the local pharmacist.

Commissioned by the *Daily Telegraph*, my friend Victor Osborne invited me to join him in a walk following in your and Wordsworth's footsteps. We stayed at Alfoxton Park Hotel, once William's house, and visited your cottage at Nether Stowey, where you wrote one of your most beautiful poems, 'This Lime-Tree Bower My Prison'. We wandered through the garden of the cottage and imagined the route your friends Charles and Mary Lamb took that day while you stayed behind, having hurt your foot, and composed the poem.

Your biographer, my Cambridge contemporary Richard Holmes, includes the poem in his brilliant and original anthology of your work [*Selected Poems*] under the rubric of 'Conversation Poems'. These come immediately after 'Sonnets', and are followed by: 'Ballads', 'Hill Walking Poems', 'Asra Poems', 'Confessional Poems', 'Visionary Fragments' and 'Topical Poems'. Holmes's ambitious project 'is to transform Coleridge's reputation'. And, indeed, how many people know your work beyond three or four anthology mainstays?

Holmes has done you proud, having made the necessary intellectual effort to honour your range, power and depth, your insatiable curiosity concerning philosophy, psychology and perception, concerning religion and mythology, and to present, in an enlightening framework of categories, the hard won rewards in more than a hundred poems, poems which now belongs to the ages, that is, to your grateful readers in the 21st century. Your most famous poems find themselves in different groups where they take on new meaning in unexpected contexts and receive new gifts of understanding from the surprised and grateful reader.

Yours sincerely, Anthony Rudolf

PS I will invite H. J. Jackson if she is in England. You may want to discuss her fascinating book *Marginalia* in which you are one of the key figures. She writes that your 'marginalia in their desultory way dramatize the process of reflective reading'.

The attendant lord's trope of directly addressing the prince should be kept short. It is the kind of self-promotion (notwithstanding implied protestations of humility) intended to amuse the lord in question himself and even the reader, though for no longer than a paragraph-minute, if I may coin a unit. As if to warn me proleptically, De Quincey describes the sad reality of dinner parties at which Coleridge 'knew he was expected to talk, and exerted himself to meet the expectation'. The trouble was he was gloomy, withered and blighted (De Quincey's words) 'and passively resigned himself to the repeated misrepresentations of several of his hearers'. This 'regal mind' was 'threatened with overthrow . . . by the treachery of his own will and the conspiracy as it were of himself against himself', a sentence I heavily underlined thirty years ago and which still speaks volumes to all who in their own small way have experienced this treachery. 'The restless activity of Coleridge's mind in chasing abstract truths, and burying himself in the dark places of human speculation, seemed to me, in a great measure, an attempt to escape out of his own personal wretchedness.'

Let me open Richard Holmes' 'Asra Poems' section, Asra being the anagram for his muse, Sara Hutchinson, 'that woman beyond utterance dear': 'Hence, viper thoughts, that coil around my mind, / Reality's dark dream!'.

205

I have reread 'Dejection: An Ode' for the nth time against its matrix poem nearly three times as long, namely 'A letter to Sara Hutchinson'. Holmes tells us that Coleridge showed this magnificent confessional poem to Wordsworth within two weeks of writing it. This is recorded in Dorothy's journal and, assuming she read the poem, one does wonder what she made of this record of another man with two women. It is a tribute to Coleridge's fundamental emotional honesty that section twelve, which can be read as self-deceiving existential 'bad faith', was written down at all: 'Be happy, and I need thee not in sight' and 'To all things I prefer the Permanent', etc. In his note to the later poem, Holmes asks rhetorically which is the more moving work of art, 'the spontaneous outpouring to Asra or the profound meditation on imaginative renewal?' We have to answer the former, but sometimes we will want to read the more impersonal of the two works. 'Dejection' is a great poem: 'O Lady! we receive but what we give, / And in our life alone does nature live / ours is her wedding garment, ours her shroud.' The matrix poem has 'Sara' instead of 'Lady' and *our* in italics, thus reinforcing the personal element. The gift of renewed understanding is ours to offer the shade of Coleridge. Poetry of this quality teaches us how to give and receive simultaneously, and its roots were nourished in the poet's 'shaping spirit of imagination' (the phrase survived from the earlier poem), that most profound of mental—intellectual and emotional—transactions, which sometimes emerges from the artist's inner battle to become the very embodiment of gift exchange between two special people: writer and reader.

American Poets

Wallace Stevens (with William Carlos Williams)

> I am what is around me
>   —Wallace Stevens, 'Theory'

> Where my spirit is, I am
>   —Wallace Stevens, 'Sailing after Lunch'

Wallace Stevens once found himself in a fistfight with Ernest Hemingway. I find this difficult to square with the image of Stevens composing poems while walking to his day job in Hartford, Connecticut, dictating them to his secretary, and then settling down to work in his collar and tie, the very model of a top insurance executive, which is what he was. The example of Stevens validated the uncomfortable realization that whatever my dreams and ambitions I had to have a conventional day job immediately, however lowly and unglamorous, unlike my clever friends with their firsts and PhDs, embarking on the road to professorships. I have already mentioned that my day jobbing began in 1964, as a graduate trainee with the British Travel Association. After about a year, I was posted for six months to the Chicago office as assistant manager. A top executive I could never become and never wanted to become, but the example of Stevens was still pertinent.

Wallace Stevens and William Carlos Williams complement each other: I go to Williams when I need to be grounded ('no ideas but in things'), what with my tendency to float off into an empyrean of abstraction, an 'academy of fine ideas', to quote a Stevens title. If, however, I am feeling not grounded, instead ground down by what Stevens calls 'the malady of the quotidian' and require validation for 'supreme fictions', then I turn to the poet who knew that 'things as they are / are changed upon the blue guitar' and that 'we shall forget by day, except / the moments when we choose to play / the imagined pine, the imagined jay'. Williams persuades us that the pine is not imagined, Stevens that it is imagined, and they are both right. 'The bread of faithful speech' (Stevens) nourished these two magnificent poets, who knew Europe and its literature but stayed home—about a hundred and twenty miles from each other and both living close to members of my family—whereas Eliot and Pound came over for good, discounting the latter's years in a Washington psychiatric hospital.

'An Ordinary Evening in New Haven' by Stevens is a meta-poem if ever there was one, with affirmations avowed and disavowed simultaneously: '. . . We seek / The poem of pure reality, untouched / By trope or deviation, straight to the word, / Straight to the transfixing object . . .' Segue to the last stanza of 'Esthétique du Mal': 'And out of what one sees and hears and out / Of what one feels, who could have thought to make / So many selves, so many sensuous worlds . . .' One poem by Stevens deeply germane to a live thread running through this book is 'The House was Quiet and the World was Calm'. Given that this beautiful poem about reading tells us that 'the words were spoken as if there was no book', can we infer that the book being read is a book of poetry, just as the words we are reading, perhaps aloud, in the book of Stevens are those of a poem written by this man who, by imagining and incarnating in words a reader's evening harmony of mind and world, succeeds in equating, for the time of the poem and even beyond, the poet and the reader? The reader of the poem becomes the reader in the poem, indeed 'the reader became the book'. This is akin to those paintings containing a reader, which always intrigue me and which I discuss elsewhere in this book. Stevens conveys through high example the redemptive nature of poetry, figured as the act of reading.

In his excellent book *Wallace Stevens: A Mythology of Self*, Milton Bates discusses Stevens' view of Williams, a poet Stevens admired for his conjunction of the 'unreal and the real, the sentimental and the anti-poetic', (preface to Williams' first *Collected Poems 1921–1931*, which was published in 1934), although the words, intended as praise, offended Williams. Bates goes on to tell how Stevens approached Marianne Moore's work with more enthusiasm and tact; in his eyes she was a more modern poet. Later, Bates quotes 'The Bed of Old John Zeller', and points out that it is a critique of Stevens' own 'projection of a supreme fiction or central poem'. While the Zeller poem amounts to a seemingly unexpected agreement with Williams' famous injunction: 'No ideas but in things', Williams' red wheelbarrow is more *thingy* than Stevens' jar in Tennessee. This jar could be anywhere. Tennessee is not even needed for a rhyme. Is it, however, needed for the metre? In that case, is Tennessee a dactyl or an anapaest? Williams' wheelbarrow is doubtless in New Jersey but he doesn't say so.

There is a confused discussion of the Stevens preface to Williams in the latter's *I Wanted to Write a Poem* (our source for his taking offence), but we learn that he was deeply moved by 'the lovely gesture from my own gang' (the Objectivists), that is to publish the *Collected Poems*, even though, he tells us, 'it didn't sell at all.' Mrs Williams is quoted: 'I've never understood what upset you about [the preface].' Stevens' first book *Harmonium* contains a poem entitled 'Nuances of a Theme by Williams' and his very last poem is called 'Not Ideas about the Thing but the Thing Itself', ending with words about a bird's cry, which '. . . was like / A new knowledge of reality'. Susan Weston, in her *Wallace Stevens* is one of many critics to touch on the poetic interaction of these two great poets. 1923 saw the publication of Stevens' *Harmonium* and of Williams' *Spring and All*, the year after *The Waste Land*, the early *Cantos* and *Ulysses*. Stevens was four years older than Williams but had published far less. His first royalty cheque was six dollars seventy. Weston ends her third chapter with the kind of biographical comment which always fascinates me in the writers I most admire: 'It was not the lack of royalties that hurt, but the lack of acceptance. For whatever combination of reasons— the indifferent reception of *Harmonium*, his growing responsibilities at the insurance company, the birth of his daughter in 1924, or the aesthetic impasse he arrived at by the end of "The Comedian as the Letter C"—Stevens apparently stopped writing for six or seven years.' I doubt that this ever happened to Williams.

While sadly you cannot insure against such a silence, it is certain that it should not be described as writer's block, often a vulgar psychologism pulling down an iron curtain between art and life. Consider the words of the composer and violinist George Enescu that Stevens used as an epigraph to a late poem, 'The World as Meditation'. Stevens left it in French, I have translated it: 'I have spent too much time performing on my violin, too much time travelling. But nothing has ever halted the essential exercise of the composer in me—meditation—. . . I live a permanent dream, which never ceases night or day.' A good poem negotiates a form of words, a peace treaty, between ideas and things. Stevens worried more about ideas, Williams about things, but we need them both and they can both rest in peace, armed with their treaties. I shall never open books *on* Stevens again; his poems, though, will find themselves revisited soon enough, as will the poems of Williams.

In *Secretaries of the Moon*, the correspondence between Stevens and his Cuban translator José Rodriguez Feo, Feo asks him if he has read *Paterson* 1: 'Williams is an old friend of mine. I have not read *Paterson*. I have the greatest respect for him, although there is the constant difficulty that he is more interested in the way of saying things than in what he has to say. The fact is that we are always fundamentally interested in what a writer has to say. When we are sure of that, we pay attention to the way in which he says it, not often before.' That is strong stuff, although some may think it also applies to Stevens himself. In his reply, Feo agrees: 'What you say of Williams is quite true. I find his *Paterson* the best example of that constant preoccupation with how to say things in a new manner. He told me that himself one day I visited him in New Jersey. He was obsessed with finding an American rhythm, and thus to describe the American scene in a new language.' One of the most interesting aspects of this correspondence is the progression towards ultimate mutual disillusion, summed up by Feo's comment: 'You say I am deeply set in literature. But I find no difference between what I read and what I live . . . I think a man from your latitude has other intentions when he picks up a book.'

William Carlos Williams and the Objectivists (with Wallace Stevens)

William Carlos Williams had a serious day job, but right from the start I knew he wrote poems on the back of prescription pads, and did not guard the boundary jealously between the professional and the personal, although Michael Heller tells me Williams' women were mostly not his patients. Now that Williams and the young housewife of his famous poem, after whom he lusted, are long dead, we can concentrate on what the poem is saying. After all, do we hold it against Carlo Gesualdo, a musical genius, that he murdered his wife? It was WCW's 'The Young Housewife' which John Barrell showed me one afternoon in early 1963, along with Charles Tomlinson's 'Paring the Apple' (from *Seeing Is Believing*), and 'Sunday Morning' by Wallace Stevens. These reinforced the change in my life which began a few months earlier with the fateful discovery of Yves Bonnefoy's poems in a bookshop. When I first read 'The Young Housewife', I am sure it was the rhythm and diction that bowled me over; ditto the other two poems. Today, I note that 'The Young Housewife' is a poem about lust, and a cruel poem, if you look closely at the two mentions of leaves. But, apart from *The Waste Land*, the three poems just mentioned were my first sightings of modernist poetry in English, and they changed things (and things' words) forever. Here too are WCW's *Collected Earlier Poems* and *Collected Later Poems*, as well as his early *Kora in Hell*, a

210

key signpost on the path to Rimbaud later taken by some younger American poets. The one book by Williams that arouses no enthusiasm in me is *In the American Grain*. D. H. Lawrence's praise is quoted on the cover, but I am not persuaded that I cannot live without 'The Discovery of Kentucky'.

In a letter, George Oppen refers to himself as 'unaudenized and dzielioted'. In a letter to Williams, however, he remarks that he has 'a new respect for Auden', because Auden too 'thinks "Asphodel" one of the beautiful poems of the language'. This remark has immediately triggered a rereading of the glorious late poem of Williams. Auden and WCW each wrote a poem about Pieter Brueghel's *Icarus*, and I feel good about being a link in a chain of lovers of 'Asphodel', including two such special ones; Williams' long, ravishing and heart-warming poem addressed to his wife in the form of an *apologia pro vita sua*, firstly as a poet and secondly as a husband, is irresistible. Auden's immediate destiny is to spend this paragraph basking in the shade of Oppen's approval, if only as an admirer of 'Asphodel, that greeny flower'.

Oppen: I cannot think of a non-living twentieth-century writer, apart from Primo Levi, who means more to me. Nor am I alone. Quite a few of my contemporaries and friends—John Taggart, Mike Heller, Paul Auster, Anita Barrows—are among those who adopted him as a mentor. William Bronk, Jonathan Griffin, Denise Levertov, Harvey Shapiro, Charles Tomlinson, Michael Hamburger and others closer to him in age have had the profoundest respect for this poet who remains on the margins, notwithstanding a Pulitzer Prize and at last, in 2006, an appearance, however attenuated, in a mainstream anthology, the *Oxford Book of American Poetry*. I have severe doubts, however, about a poem in Donald Davie's final *Collected Poems*, 'Recollections of George Oppen in a Letter to an English Friend', the friend from explicit internal evidence being Charles Tomlinson, Davie's former student. In this ferocious long poem, which intertextualizes Coleridge's 'This Lime-Tree Bower My Prison', and makes Tomlinson complicit with the points of view expressed, Davie argues that Oppen's dealings with language ('in verse, in prose, in conversation') had anticipated his Alzheimer's: 'A hideous justice'. Having said that, my dear Donald, it is too late to continue: 'I've not the energy nor the confidence / for playing God like this with George's shade, / his fragrant shade my prison.'

211

Here are the old New Directions *Collected Poems*, the Fulcrum Press *Collected Poems*, and the late Michael Thorp's Cloudform edition, *Poems of George Oppen*, selected and introduced by Tomlinson, which I reviewed: '. . . one of the truly important poets of the century, whose every line presses on our minds and, by changing our perceptions, changes our lives.' Here too are *George Oppen: Man and Poet*, edited by Burten Hatlen, and *The Objectivist Nexus*, edited by Rachel Blau Duplessis and Peter Quartermain. Michael Davidson's edition of Oppen's *New Collected Poems* is a valuable book, textually and critically essential, although Davidson's introduction takes a somewhat eccentric 'language poetry' line in respect of Oppen and could do with an overhaul. I received an email from Professor Peter Nicholls, then of Sussex University, now at NYU, who was in the final stages of his fine book, *George Oppen and the Fate of Modernism*, and wanted help in clarifying certain problems. He reminded me that I wrote to Oppen that Donald Davie was 'moved by the Jabès (and the two pieces on him)'. He speculated that this referred to something by Jabès I published in the magazine *European Judaism* in the 1970s. He was right, for the Jabès text had moved Davie to the point of writing a poem, 'His Themes', subtitled 'After Reading Edmond Jabès'. I still get a kick out of being needed by professors, I with my non-honours degree. My whole life has been an attempt to redeem myself after that failure. It is pathetic to draw attention to that time, pathetic to indulge in a meditation on the process whereby some decades later, amidst a lifetime of editing and translating, I ended up having written seven poems, six stories, five essays, four meditative fragments, three short memoirs, you get the drift. Am I a songbird or an ornithologist? Answering Barnett Newman's question is strictly for the birds.

As students of American poetry are aware, 'Objectivists' was a label of convenience for a group of six poets who had little in common apart from the fact that four of them were left-wing urban Jews; all six, inspired by Williams and Pound, were looking for a way to make their mark. The chosen vehicle *Poetry Chicago*, which hosted an Objectivist issue in 1931, midwifed by Ezra Pound and edited by Louis Zukofsky. The inner group consisted of Carl Rakosi and Charles Reznikoff, George Oppen and Louis Zukofsky, Lorine Niedecker and Basil Bunting, as well as the older William Carlos

Williams. The issue was soon reprinted as the *Objectivists' Anthology*. Zukofsky, the adopted father of the so-called Language Poets, signed my copies of his collected short poems *All* and of '*A*' (1–12) after a reading at the American embassy in Grosvenor Square—not a fortress in those days—on 21 May 1969. Zukofsky's *A Test of Poetry* is a lineal descendent of Pound's *ABC of Reading*. Both books surely influenced Hugh Kenner's little known and brilliant textbook *The Art of Poetry* and Louis Simpson's *An Introduction to Poetry*. Zukofsky juxtaposes specimens of verse and makes characteristically spare and direct comments to guide the reader. Dipping into this book almost inclines me to have another go at '*A*'. In Oppen's case, the significant interaction of his life and work (he was deeply involved in radical politics as an activist and, like André Malraux and Sorley Maclean, survived service in World War II) engaged me so strongly that I had an incentive to attempt to understand the inherent difficulties of his work: 'We would have to know the force which causes a thing to be'—Oppen cited on the back of an envelope containing a press cutting about Paula which Claude Royet-Journoud, the poet's first French translator, sent me. The other major Objectivists were more straightforward. Niedecker and Reznikoff have much in common as poets, as Eliot Weinberger points out. It was Zukofsky, needless to say, not Reznikoff, who was Niedecker's lover.

It has been one of the privileges of my life to have been a friend of Oppen and Rakosi and to have corresponded with Reznikoff. They had a huge influence on my way of thinking about poetry, and about what a life informed by poetry might amount to. Here on my desk are the individual volumes by Oppen, revisited with a sense of homecoming. After George died, Paul Auster phoned me with his memory of a remark Oppen had made to him about old age: 'What a strange thing to happen to a little boy.' This I published in my MenCard series.

It somehow seems in keeping with the *patience* we associate with Charles Reznikoff that William Carlos Williams wrote to him as follows: 'I never read the book you gave me twenty-five years ago. I want you to know that I have it now and that it is remarkable.' (There is a different version in a letter of 30 March 1948.) On my first visit to New York, in 1964, I picked up, at the late lamented Gotham Book Mart, West 47th Street, mint copies of two of

Reznikoff's self-published and self-printed books from his own Objectivist Press, 10 West 36th Street: *In Memoriam: 1933*, published in 1934 and *Separate Way* (1936). Among the books Reznikoff had already published were the first *Collected Poems* of William Carlos Williams and Oppen's *Discrete Series*. This was a major small press, no doubt about it, and yet thirty years later there were all those mint copies on the shelves of Gotham. It would be another twenty years before Black Sparrow would arrive on the scene, with its unprecedented ability to distribute and sell poetry books, another twenty years before a generation of Reznikoff admirers would show up: that fine poet and autobiographer Michael Heller, an Oppen pioneer (*Conviction's Net of Branches* and, later, *Speaking the Estranged*), would draw the attention of readers to the wondrous work of this modest and self-effacing poet. Menard played a small part in the process: my late friend Milton Hindus, earliest champion of Reznikoff, wrote, partly at my behest, the first book on Reznikoff; he also edited the poet's letters. I did a deal with Black Sparrow, whose generosity, encouraged by Hindus, enabled Menard to buy at cost price five hundred copies of their edition of *Charles Reznikoff*, with a Menard title page and spine: I sought to raise his non-existent profile in the UK—non-existent, that is, outside the circle of the late Andrew Crozier. Crozier had put me in touch with Reznikoff in 1967 and presented me with a copy of the UK edition of *Family Chronicle*, the poet's prose book of 1963, self-published when he was nearly seventy, in which he gives voice to his two parents, an auto-fiction or auto-narrative that has influenced my writings on my grandfather. On the flyleaf, Crozier wrote in pencil Reznikoff's address: 180 West End Avenue, New York, New York 10023. The third section is in Reznikoff's own name. For anyone unfamiliar with his style, which embodies a morality, the narrator's restraint when confronted by pain has something of Anton Chekhov, Ernest Hemingway or Raymond Carver. His descriptions of his mother and the woman in the bed next to her in the cancer ward where she dies contain no outward emotion. He describes what he sees. Such restraint honours the dying. He trusts us to bring the emotion to our reading, emotion we might flinch from if its import were transcendental rather than immanent. The restraint implies that we have no absolute right to be there, but once there, we shall be silent, in public at least. This little-known book is fifth commandment payback time, honouring the parents whose immigrant way of life and mode of labour were not for him; and yet they were 'for him', for he would recycle their lives and that of their Jewish ancestors throughout his long life below the salt.

Here are various editions of *Testimony*, his 'recitative'. It is one of the most remarkable documentary poems ever written. He covers many aspects of the social history of the USA from 1885 to 1915, the years of the great immigration of Jews, Poles, Irish and others into New York (and London, Montreal, Buenos Aires, Paris and other cities), although he does not only write about immigrants. His concern is to document, via the law reports he edits as poems, the way industry impacts, and for the worse, on poor and helpless citizens (especially immigrants) without the protection of the welfare state, not least in terms of health and safety regulations, welfare whose beginnings would have to await the New Deal. Reznikoff trained as a journalist and a lawyer and wrote entries for a legal encyclopaedia. Here, as in his later *Holocaust* based on the Nuremburg trial records, the objective court reporter or stenographer obviates the need for a prosecutor. *Testimony* (almost as much as *Holocaust*) deals with episodes of violence: terrible industrial 'accidents', lynchings and mock lynchings. This gentle mild-mannered poet did not flinch from the worst of his country. He was part of the patriotic opposition I associate with John Steinbeck and Upton Sinclair, James Agee and Walker Evans, Woody Guthrie and Studs Terkel. This opposition created radical pressure on the Democratic Party, leading to Lyndon Johnson's progressive legislation in the mid-1960s. Here are Reznikoff's *Collected Poems*, edited by Seamus Cooney. Reznikoff's poetry kept Oppen going while he lay wounded in a foxhole in Alsace in World War II. In the preface to volume two of his friend's poems, Oppen writes: 'If we had no other poetry I think we could live by virtue of these poems, these lives, these small precise these overwhelming gentle iron lines and images of all that is and our love and pride and our small life . . .' Or, as his in memoriam poem on the back cover concludes: 'heroic this is / the poem // to write // in the great / world small'.

Reznikoff wrote three other prose books, *By the Waters of Manhattan*, *The Manner Music* and *The Lion-Hearted*, a historical novel about the Jews of mediaeval England. The title of *By the Waters of Manhattan*, first published in 1930, could not be more explicit about the idea of Jewish emigration being, in some sense, an exile. Reznikoff, however, unlike his Zionist wife Marie Syrkin (biographer of Golda Meir), never visited Israel, indeed, he never left the United States. What is more, apart from a few years in Hollywood (the background to *The Manner Music*) during the Depression, he never left New York City, perhaps not even Manhattan. The title is therefore an intimation of inwardness to a religious tradition that he no longer abides by. He rewrote parts of the prose as verse (or the other way round), something that would be unthinkable in the poetics of Zukofsky. Scandalously, he appears to be in only one mainstream anthology, Geoffrey O'Brien's *Bartlett's Poems for Occasions*, a fine book I often buy for young friends as a present.

Carl Rakosi, who lived till he was over a hundred, was the sweetest and dearest man. Had he, the only American Objectivist born in Europe, been Reznikoff's age (i.e. ten years older) or Isaac Rosenberg's (thirteen years older), he would have been old enough to be my grandfather. He was the wittiest and most provocative of the Objectivists, allowing himself short sharp sallies foreign to the others, although Oppen could be harsh in letters, when necessary. Rakosi stopped writing from 1941 till 1965. It took Andrew Crozier to get him going again. Crozier kindly sent me *Poems 1923–1941*, which he edited with Rakosi's help and which brings together for the first time all his earlier work in the form and order they were written. *Collected Poems* presents later revisions and gathers the work thematically. Carl replied to a letter I wrote him about an early poem: 'As for "Sitting Room by Patinka", I was so taken by Wallace Stevens at the time that I simply <u>had</u> to write something in that vein to express myself, but since I am not Stevens (can you imagine <u>Miss Levi</u> being the protagonist in a poem by Stevens, who was no friend of Jews or blacks?) in the process of doing that and in changing it as I went along, what I found I had written was something that could be read both ways, both straight and as a parody.' I could not resist sending this to Crozier for his comments: 'I don't agree that "Sitting Room" can be read both ways; I think it flips in and out of both as one reads, and at the level of intention is massively [word illegible], but balances through the freely wrought artifice of diction and stanza. Again, although the poetic intention may have been focused on Stevens, the scenario and the devious presentation of erotic intrusion remind me more forcibly of Eliot.' Crozier was always interested in Jewish matters and consulted me several times in that territory. In his introduction, he writes that Rakosi's Jewishness was 'not a trope for poetic selfhood but, as it were, something recuperated and, on occasion, expressed in it. Throughout his life poetry appears to have been for Rakosi a desire and a commitment potentially at odds with the needs of work and economic security.' Rakosi was a social worker and family therapist. As early as 1924, he translated Aragon while participating in a radical literary and socialist group of students at the University of Wisconsin. Remembering that he wrote blurbs for books by Jonathan Griffin and others, including myself, as well as a poem for my son's wedding, let me end with a poem Howard Schwartz and I used as an epigraph for our anthology *Voices in the Ark*:

'Israel'
I hear the voice
            of David and Bathsheba
and the judgment
            on the continual
backslidings
            of the Kings of Israel.
I have stumbled
            on the ancient voice
of honesty
            and tremble
at the voice
of my people.

Although not American, Basil Bunting belongs here, with the Objectivists. I have a letter from him in reply to my request for suggestions about what poetry translations to include in *The Journals of Pierre Menard*, the forerunner of Menard Press back in the late 1960s. A few years later I met him and, literally, sat at his feet at a poetry conference, at the Polytechnic of Central London. Bunting was the mentor of a brilliant young Geordie poet, Tom Pickard, who had sought him out in the early 1960s just as Andrew Crozier sought out Rakosi, except that Pickard and Bunting lived in the same neck of the woods. Barry MacSweeney too admired him greatly, but MacSweeney's mentor was J. H. Prynne. It was a blessing that, thanks to Pickard, Bunting emerged from years of obscurity, this surviving high modernist, a great poet who, like William Carlos Williams, had not been taken on by Eliot at Faber and Faber, although they did publish Pound's *Active Anthology* in 1932, a promo for Zukofsky and Bunting. It was left to Tom Pickard's Mordern Tower and Stuart Montgomery's Fulcrum Press to honour themselves and do us all a favour by publishing Bunting. Here are a proof copy of the Fulcrum edition of Bunting's *Collected Poems*; his later and exemplarily edited (by the late Richard Caddell) *Collected Poems*; *Uncollected Poems*; a pamphlet—*The Spoils*; his masterpiece *Briggflats*, as well as *Loquitur*, whose final section 'Overdrafts' contains translations from a number of languages. There is a splendid footnote to 'Overdrafts'; I know it by heart: 'It would be gratuitous to assume that a mistranslation was unintentional.' Bunting's English verse is a thing of wonder, pitch-perfect. His masters are Wordsworth and Pound; Zukofsky too in terms of maximizing the musicality of the line, but there is a human depth to Bunting (see also Pickard's short memoir *More Pricks than Prizes*), a personal warmth, which draws one in (*Briggflats* is his *Prelude*), whereas Zukofsky keeps the reader at bay.

Ezra Pound and T. S. Eliot (with F. R. Leavis)

The mutual respect of Ezra Pound and T. S. Eliot is touching: Eliot's 'il miglio fabbro' and Pound's homage: '. . . later, on his own hearth, a flame tended, a presence felt'. Up there in the captain's tower, these two great poets, fighting or not, cast long shadows over contemporary reading (and therefore writing) even at this late date. Yet, where there is shadow there is light, even on desolation row. Pound was a wondrous poet at his best. His *Cantos* (in different editions amounting to a complete edition) are on my desk together with Valerie Eliot's facsimile transcript of *The Waste Land* and other Eliot books, including Christopher Ricks' edition of the early poems: *Inventions of the March Hare* and my battered copy of *Selected Poems* bought in 1962. I read and reread *The Waste Land* and 'Prufrock' and Pound's 'Mauberley' as we all did, and found my way to *Four Quartets*, indeed I later published Claude Vigée's French translation after complicated negotiations with third parties. Cyril Connolly was right to say in his review of Mrs Eliot's edition of the transcript that nearly all Pound's suggestions were improvements. Nonetheless, Pound wrote to Eliot with characteristic generosity and honesty (and perhaps a touch of justifiable self-regard): '*Complimenti*, you bitch, I am wracked by the seven jealousies.' Here too are Pound's letters, essays and translations and other books, as well as Ernest Fenollosa's ars poetica, 'The Chinese Written Character as a Medium for Poetry', which became so influential thanks to Pound's editing.

I am glad to have J. P. Sullivan's *Ezra Pound and Sextus Propertius*. In the new and more relaxed world of post-1965 translation studies (when Sullivan's book was published and Ted Hughes and Daniel Weissbort founded *Modern Poetry in Translation*), Pound's approach, which had so scandalized conventional Latinists since the poem first appeared in 1919, gives us no grief. We are free to read this remarkable version of the Roman love poet as a great poem in its own right (up there with another major exercise in irony, 'Mauberley'), bringing to it the idea of 'homage' as persona, the title of one of Sullivan's chapters. Propertius, or Pound's critique (Michael Alexander's word) of Propertius, serves as a template for Pound himself: Propertius, as it were, translates Pound. Sullivan has an appendix quoting poets who used Pound's translation as a model, including Robert Lowell whose 'The Ghost (After Sextus Propertius)' first appeared in his second book *Lord Weary's Castle* in 1946: 'You cannot turn your back upon a dream, / For phantoms have their reasons when they come: / We wander midnights: then the numb / Ghost wades from the Lethaean stream.' We learn from Michael Alexander's *Poetic Achievement of Ezra Pound* that, according to a letter Pound wrote Hardy, the use of the word 'homage' derived from works like Debussy's 'Homage to Rameau'. Alexander suggests that if the poem is successful, it doesn't matter what Pound did to or with the original Latin. Well, we certainly don't want uncreative translation. But you do have to ask yourself what the original poet might think of your efforts: over to you, Rilke—what do you think of Robert Lowell's versions of your poems in *Imitations*?

F. R. Leavis argues, in *New Bearings in English Poetry*, for the greatness of 'Mauberley', whose author has 'the completest integrity and the surest touch'; the poem is 'a weightier achievement than any single thing to be found in

Yeats', implying perhaps that the complete *oeuvre* of Yeats is greater than that of Pound, although in a later book, *Lectures in America*, Leavis asserts that 'the great poems are a very small proportion of the whole'. As for Pound, 'only in Mauberley has he achieved the impersonality, substance, and depth of great poetry'. Leavis is wrong to reject the *Pisan Cantos*. While accepting that the critic's hatred of fascism and antisemitism is not the reason he disallows even the best *Cantos*, I cannot agree that Pound's versification is boring and that he has no creative theme. What about memory and language, loss and disgrace?

Gertrude Stein

I want to salute this magnificent writer whose teasing prose rhythms and syntax bewitch readers, and still influence writers. No one, if I may gloss William Gass' introduction to *The Geographical History of America* by Gertrude Stein, has ever played with variations on sentences as Stein did, using repetition within and between sentences, deploying her verbal music— ut musica poesis??—to make a simulacrum of the process of perception, whether direct when looking at something or, at one remove, when reading a book. I, for one, can read more pages of Stein at one go, than of Joyce's *Finnegans Wake*. Her sheer intelligence and wit are bracing. It would not be a bad idea to read a page or two of Stein everyday before beginning to write. That she, an American Jewish lesbian, lived through the Nazi occupation of France in the open, does not negate her literary gifts: she is up there with Ezra Pound and Louis-Ferdinand Céline.

What makes you do something is your motive, she writes, but this is not the reason you do it. (Compare Dag Hammarskjold in *Markings*: 'It is more important to be aware of the grounds for your own behaviour than to understand the motives of another.') Her seeminglessly endless reflections are generated by the process of writing—probably the opposite of the way Wittgenstein worked—and this is her subject to the extent that an abstract painting is about painting. Did she and Wittgenstein read each other? Certainly not. Had they even heard of each other? Possibly. She reminds Guy Davenport not only of Wittgenstein but also of Philip Glass and Picasso the Cubist. *The Autobiography of Alice B. Toklas*, published in 1933, three years before *Geographical History*, ends with the statement that she is going to write the autobiography of Alice 'as simply as Defoe did the autobiography of Robinson Crusoe'. I wonder if this is an ironic allusion to the fact that Alice was Gertrude's Man Friday. One thing is for sure, long marriages involve a mysterious alchemy which is experienced as a double helix of bonding by the couple concerned, invisible to them and, a fortiori, to outsiders. Or so I, after a short marriage, imagine.

Still inserted in the excellent Stein selection, *Look at Me Now and Here I Am*, are my reading notes, including a message to myself: 'Write to Barthes with my poem when I have read *Plaisir*.' (*Le Plaisir du texte* was published in 1973, around the time I read the Stein book on holiday in Lionel Blue's flat in West Mersea.) In the margin of one page, against a paragraph-long sentence (a fact of significance given Stein's writings on sentences and paragraphs), I wrote: 'beautiful'. It still is, thirty-five years on: 'There is then also the English people's history of their English literature but then after all that is their affair as far as I am concerned, as I am deeply concerned, it is none of my business.' Stein's long poem, 'Before the Flowers of Friendship Faded Friendship Faded', is one of the most amazing translations of all time, translation in the sense that Pound's 'Homage to Sextus Propertius' is a translation and Baudelaire's 'Je n'ai pas oublié, voisine de la ville' is, as Bonnefoy says somewhere, a translation of Pushkin. Debussy's *Prélude* is, in its own way, a translation of Mallarmé. Stein composed the poem after reading a poem by Georges Hugnet she had agreed to translate. He was not happy about the result.

Marianne Moore, Elizabeth Bishop and Emily Dickinson (and others)

> It [the sea] is like what we imagine knowledge to be:
> dark, salt, clear, moving, utterly free,
> drawn from the cold hard mouth
> of the world, derived from the rocky breasts
> forever, flowing and drawn, and since
> our knowledge is historical, flowing, and flown.
> —From *Complete Poems*

The conclusion to 'At the Fishhouses' by Elizabeth Bishop is as inevitable as, say, that of Philip Larkin's 'The Whitsun Weddings'. It feels redemptive, but redemption is subverted by her insistence on the 'historical': there can be no

221

definitive awareness or understanding. 'Questions of Travel' ends: 'Is it lack of imagination that makes us come / to imagined places, not just stay at home? . . . Should we have stayed at home / wherever that may be?'. (Compare Jean Améry: 'One must have a home in order not to need it.') Elaine Feinstein, in a poem on Bishop in *Badlands*, is right to apostrophize 'the friendly toughness of your spirit'. Rachel Blau du Plessis, in her notes to Oppen's letters, refers to a 1925 essay by Williams praising Marianne Moore, and one can see why he and the other Objectivists would give Moore the time of day. Robert Lowell in his *Paris Review* interview has this to say of her work: 'Conservative and Jamesian as she is, it was a terrible, private, and strange revolutionary poetry.' Yes, Moore's is a radical poetics that even after all these years makes demands on us and it is instructive to read her 'against' Bishop. The latter's book of uncollected poems and drafts, *Edgar Alan Poe and the Jukebox*, has recently been published. If I find such texts irresistible, is it because the visible processes of trial, error, rejection, revision, damage limitation and weakness, humanize genius?

I also have a soft spot for thoughtful and subtle books on the creative process, especially when they deal with influence and friendship. One such book is David Kalstone's *Becoming a Poet*, on Elizabeth Bishop's (mainly epistolary) relationships with Marianne Moore and Robert Lowell. As she lived in Brazil, airmail made this possible. Fax, text messaging and email would post-date the two poets. I read somewhere that Western Union sent its last telegram in February 2006, after more than a century of saving the day, or several days. Feedback has become so fast that unconsciously we have speeded up our guilt trips for not replying to messages sooner. Our neediness has increased, our attention span has shortened. Episodes within television programmes are shorter than they used to be, too. On the question of the kind of documentation Kalstone draws on for his critique—poetry drafts and letters with their integral role as mediation in the making of poems—these days such material resides in email folders and Word files. Wendy Cope has apparently sold her emails to a library. I discuss Mike Heller's archive later.

Marianne Moore's *Selected Fables of La Fontaine*, edited by the Ledéserts of *Harraps Dictionary* fame, is a book to treasure, although it has been out of print for years. Moore's *La Fontaine*, perhaps selected from an earlier complete translation, ought to suit Paula. She made a one-off 'La Fontaine' for her Jane Eyre series, 'La Ligue des rats', which Adèle recites by heart in the original French to Mr Rochester. Ah, how many times have I thought: 'such-and-such a text would be perfect for Paula'. Except it can only ever be perfect if, by whatever process of mediation, Paula enters the idea into her ongoing meditation on her life—the endless retelling of significant events and thoughts, memories and things—in order for it to emerge *as her own*. Rare indeed are the occasions when the match is immediate, for example 'The Nicotine Cat', a poem Augustus Young wrote with the explicit intention of catching Paula's studio attention and it did, albeit in a more intimate way than his intentions may have foreseen.

In his essay in Herbert Read's *Surrealism*, 'Limits not Frontiers of Surrealism', André Breton, who had studied medicine and psychiatry, writes that in *Les Vases Communiquants* and *Nadja* he has attempted to 'maintain the brevity and exactitude which prevail in medical observations'. The remark bears a distinct affinity both to Marianne Moore's requirement in 'Poetry', her most famous poem, that poets should be 'literalists of the imagination' and to her remark to Wallace Stevens about the 'enchantment of accuracy', although her accompanying note, which sources Yeats as the author of the phrase, quotes the Irish poet—I paraphrase—as saying that it explains why Blake's very intensity was the cause of his limitations as a visual artist. Moore's 'Picking and Choosing' has a quote from Eliot containing a famous dig at Henry James, which is followed by a less well-known passage: 'In England ideas run wild and pasture on the emotions; instead of thinking with our feelings (a very different thing), we corrupt our feelings with ideas; we produce the political, the emotional idea, evading sensation and thought.'

Recently, an American friend, the poet Lisa Russ Spaar, quoted Emily Dickinson's poem 'Compensation'. A point was made. It spoke volumes:

> For each ecstatic instant
> We must an anguish pay
> In keen and quivering ratio
> To the ecstasy.
>
> For each beloved hour
> Sharp pittances of Years—

Bitter contested farthings—
And Coffers heaped with tears!

Or as Dickinson wrote in a letter quoted by Natalia Ginzburg in *Never Must You Ask Me*: 'The supper of the heart is when the guest has gone.' Spaar has just sent me her new book *Satin Cash* (good Dickinson phrase): very strong stuff, with evident auto-narrative between the lines and a powerful erotic undercurrent, which disturbs and enchants. She tells me that Camille Paglia called Dickinson the Marquise de Sade of Amherst. Adrienne Rich, I read recently in *A Human Eye*, quotes the young Denise Levertov as calling Dickinson 'a bitchy little spinster'. In Lisa's view, Emily Dickinson is 'a site of projection for everyone'. I should quote these remarks to Spaar's contemporary Rosanna Warren and see what the author of another strong and marvellous book, *Ghost in a Red Hat*, has to say about them.

Laura Riding (with Marianne Moore and Edith Sitwell)

I touched on Laura Riding in my introduction to *Silent Conversations*. Her abandonment of poetry is as significant as Marcel Duchamp's magnificent challenge to visual artists. It came with all the authority of her mighty accomplishment, namely the *Collected Poems* of 1938. Her introduction to that book still raises issues we need to think about, just as our attempt to understand twentieth-century art has to juxtapose Picasso and Duchamp: 'So read, so exist: with your very best reasons. Any other reasons are not reasons, or no longer reasons—mere compulsions from without, or mere glosses upon nightmares long ago ridden off the map of experience. It is less difficult to read or exist well, than to read or exist ill.' I wonder if her comments on difficulty in poetry are in some kind of dialogue with the unnamed Marianne Moore, whose thoughts on the matter are better known. Moore was a tough-minded and devious lady, but she was a less rebarbative personality than the radiantly intelligent and bloody minded Riding (Robert Graves refers to Laura's 'bladed mind') and certainly made fewer enemies, which is not to be held against her. Here too are Riding's early poems, *First Awakenings*. Apart from the final sequence, the poems collected in this book were not published until 1992, so the poem 'Jazz Jubilate' could not have been read by Edith Sitwell, whose 'Façade' of 1923 must have influenced Laura Riding. Riding, however, would mature into a great poet which Sitwell never did, although (Louis Simpson tells us) the American poet respected Sitwell: 'Trot-trot-trot / See a lady Hottentot / Hobnobbing with an ambassador / Along the slippery floor'. Sitwell, however (see Deborah Baker's life of Laura *In Extremis*), described Riding as 'an American loon or screech owl'. As for Marianne Moore, Ed Field, in the 'Poetry File' which concludes *A Frieze for a Temple of Love*, reckons that Bette Davis 'with her verbal mannerisms and quirky rhythm' would have been the perfect person to record Marianne Moore. Who, by that token, should have recorded Elizabeth Bishop or Laura Riding?

Robert Duncan

One of the major figures to emerge from the celebrated arts college at Black Mountain in North Carolina is Robert Duncan. Along with poet Kenneth Rexroth—author of an eccentric survey, *American Poetry in the Twentieth Century*: tendentious, its value lies in the passing mention of completely forgotten names some of whom should be checked out—Duncan was central to what became known as the San Francisco Renaissance. There is a famous supposed binary opposition between raw or Redskin beat poets like Allen Ginsberg and cooked or paleface poets like Robert Lowell, but Duncan's work could not be more cooked and yet at the same time the self emanates from his poems as dramatically as in the highest Beats. Black Mountain had a huge influence in the 1950s and its poetics in some ways leapfrogged the Beats and poets who wore ties. It made its way to the UK via American poets like Ed Dorn, Tom Clark (visiting the University of Essex) and Donald Davie (already at Essex). About ten years earlier, Elaine Feinstein, who wrote to Charles Olson under the name of E. B. Feinstein (in case he might not reply to a woman), received a reply from the rector of Black Mountain, in which the big man explained his ideas of projective verse and field composition, later published in Donald Allen's influential anthology *The New American Poetry 1945–1960*.

Duncan's *The Truth and Life of Myth* is a key example of 'mythopoeic weavings', to quote his own phrase about Pound's *Cantos*. Duncan is a poet I respect rather than love, just as Guy Davenport, in a letter to his and Duncan's publisher James Laughlin, finds him 'far too mystical and cerebral,

225

but . . . a poet of the highest order'. Laughlin says he only understands about fifteen per cent of Duncan but gets a great feeling of 'mind music' from him. This doubtless reflects a limitation in my own taste, since friends of mine such as Heller and Berengarten have a high regard for him. But now and then flashes of lightning strike me in his storms. His implacable oceanic emanations of the self can be overwhelming, yet their containment and objectification in mythic frameworks, while not grounding them in Stevens' 'malady of the quotidian' or Rimbaud's 'rough reality' and not risking exposure to Browning's 'dangerous edge of things', still work, at least on occasion, because his ear operates auto-ekphrastically to limn the visions of the inner eye. Duncan is speaking of himself when he writes: 'And facts, what men actually do, are, in the lives of . . . poets like Dante or Blake, not true in themselves but true in a Poetics whose Poetry is the real world.' This apparent tautology is Duncan's invitation to himself to ground a vision that would otherwise take off and vanish in the blink of a pineal eye.

On my desk are the poet's three major collections, all from the 1960s: *Bending the Bow, Roots and Branches,* and *The Opening of the Field,* an explosive transcendence of his plainly evident and openly admitted influences such as Olson. Another influence was Ezra Pound and, indeed, in a reprint collection of Duncan's early work *The Years as Catches* we find 'Homage and Lament for Ezra Pound in Captivity May 12, 1944'. Duncan writes in the introduction to this reprint: 'From the beginning I had sought not the poem as a discipline or paradigm of my thought and feeling but as a source of feeling and thought.' Early influences, he tells us, were John Milton and Gerard Manley Hopkins, and two poets a few years older than himself, George Barker and Dylan Thomas. He also namechecks Saint-John Perse and Federico García Lorca. I am surprised he does not mention Rilke. *Duino Elegies* and *Sonnets to Orpheus* are surely around, somewhere. A recent letter from John Taggart discusses Duncan in the context of Denise Levertov: the published correspondence between the two poets awaits my attention.

John Berryman (with Dylan Thomas)

John Montague, in *The Figure in the Cave*, has written that John Berryman is 'the only writer I have ever seen for whom drink seemed to be a positive stimulus'. Without the drink, not only would that work of genius, *Dream Songs*, not exist, without it the work would not have taken the form it did. But the drink caught up with him, as it would. Despite recovery programmes, he died an alcoholic, leaving a young wife and children. He had been attending both the Catholic church and the synagogue, a novel form of Pascal's wager, suggests Montague, and had earlier published his one and only story, 'The Imaginary Jew', as a postscript to his autobiographical novel *Recovery*, with an affectionate preface by Saul Bellow: 'At last there was no more. Reinforcements failed to arrive. Forces were not joined. The cycle of resolution, reform and relapse had become a bad joke which could not continue.'

'. . . Imaginary Jews, / like bitter Henry, full of the death of love' turn up in one of the early dream songs, and it was with the two volumes of dream songs—*77 Dream Songs* and *His Toy, His Dream, His Rest*—that Berryman became a great poet. These constitute one of the grand literary deployments of the double, like the long poem which made his early name, 'Homage to Mistress Bradstreet'. Henry is a white American, sometimes in black face, sometimes addressed as Mr Bones. He is a dialectical or dialogical incarnation of a self in the process of exploring itself. Easy to suggest that Henry in some sense replaced the father who, like Berryman himself, committed suicide, but Berryman pours into these three-stanza poems (each stanza of six lines) his heart, his soul, his mind, his body, with the protean prodigality one is more accustomed to associate with prose fiction: Ralph Ellison's *Invisible Man* or Henry Roth's *Call it Sleep*, or Saul Bellow's third novel, *The Adventures of Augie March*; the first one Berryman liked. On my desk are *Berryman's Sonnets* and *Short Poems* as well as his last two books, *Love and Fame* and *Delusions Etc.* Berryman's exciting, feverish, often wild excursi, marinaded in the booze, are his way of shoring up his self against the claims of ruin. Fragments they are not.

John Montague was probably right not to mention Dylan Thomas as a drinker alongside Berryman. Thomas was born two days after Berryman in 1914, although predeceasing him by nearly twenty years. Perhaps a comparison can be made between John Berryman and Francis Bacon, like Berryman a great artist, and one whose grand *oeuvre* cannot be imagined outside the context of his lifestyle, which is not to say he did not work every day. Bacon lasted a lot longer than Berryman. Maybe the dream songs freed the poet to write unadorned in his own persona. In *Delusions Etc.* there is a poem entitled 'In Memoriam (1914–1953)'—referring to Dylan Thomas, whom he visited in hospital shortly before the Welsh poet died. It ends:

> Scribbled me once, it's around somewhere or other,
> word of their 'Edna Millay' cottage at Laugharne
> saying come down to and disarm a while
> and down a many few.
>
> O down a many few, old friend,
> and down a many few.

'The Heroes'—Pound, Eliot, Joyce and Yeats—in *Love and Fame* is a marvellous tough-minded exploration of hero worship, and one which surely hits home hard to those of us who manifest this tendency. I pencil-marked the following in 1972:

> I had, from my beginning, to adore heroes
> & I elected that they witness to,
> show forth, transfigure: life-suffering & pure heart
> & hardly definable but central weaknesses
>
> for which they were to be enthroned and forgiven by me.

In another poem, 'Monkhood', Berryman writes of self-doubt, and even if the question he poses below suggests a certain false modesty, inviting the response, 'yes, dear sir, you already have,' nonetheless we may suspect that by implication he is measuring himself against the highest masters, Shakespeare, Racine, Baudelaire, Hölderlin, Kleist, Kafka (the last three named as such in another poem), and is therefore entitled to a smidgen of anxiety:

> Will I ever write properly, with passion & exactness,
> of the damned strange demeanours of my flagrant heart?
> & be by anyone anywhere undertaken?
> One *more* unanswerable question.

I would not argue that it is essential for poetry to be read aloud, but hearing John Berryman recite live his *Dream Songs* (especially the first volume) gave me pause for thought, if pause is what you do when you go into mental overdrive: the *Dream Songs* involve a dramatic juxtaposition of the main voices that the poet's aural projection teaches you how to differentiate. Henceforth, I could read and reread the *Dream Songs* on the page with that singular and brilliant poet's voice echoing in my inner ear.

John Berryman/Eileen Simpson/Anne Sexton/Poetry International

Poets in Their Youth, the title of the memoir by John Berryman's first wife Eileen Simpson, is taken from her epigraph, two ironically chosen lines from that proof text of Romanticism, Wordsworth's 'Resolution and Independence': 'We poets in our youth begin in gladness; / But thereof come in the end despondency and madness'. The book evokes brilliantly Berryman and his friends, including Robert Lowell (and his first wife Jean Stafford), Randall Jarrell and Delmore Schwartz, the last named the subject of a Lowell poem. Traditionally, the first wife is well placed to cast an educated and, with any luck, affectionate rather than vengeful eye on clever boys and their dangerous toys. I read this book at a time when I could not read enough by and about Lowell. Mrs Berryman lifts the frontline curtain on the short but intensely lived lives of this remarkable group of writers; psychoanalysis, alcohol, relationships, poetry, genius, death: her book ranks with Ruth Brandon's fabulous and entertaining collective biography, *Surreal Lives*, although Brandon, luckily for her, was too young and too far away to marry any of her geniuses. Simpson is an acute and non-judging judge of character, which would later serve her well in a post-Berrymanian life as a novelist and psychoanalyst. One cannot emphasize too strongly that books like this derive their charge from our admiration for the genius of the driven subjects on the stage revealed by the raised curtain, but Eileen Simpson knew that. Berryman's *Dream Songs* were ventriloquially astonishing projections of voices from his head, while Lowell too was a great and, after *Life Studies*, widely read poet, far more influential than Berryman. Delmore Schwartz (immortalized by Bellow in *Humboldt's Gift*) is a key figure in Eileen Simpson's book. I can live without Schwartz's poems but long ago I read and liked his short stories, *In Dreams Begin Responsibilities*. I love the photo of Berryman's wife—she was three years younger than my mother—taken in the early 1940s when Simpson became engaged to Berryman. I recall a family photo where my mother's hat and hairstyle could pass for Eileen Simpson's.

With this difference: ours was not a bohemian set-up. We admired the artistic products of Bohemia, but did not cross the frontier into that fertile land.

I met Berryman in 1967, at the famous Hotel Sixty Nine in Cadogan Gardens: I have sometimes wondered if the Arts Council intended a sexual joke by lodging the poets of the first Poetry International at this small hotel and doubtless the foreign poets did too. I went to the bedroom of Anne Sexton for the sole purpose of getting her to sign her book *Live or Die*. The sheets were singed with cigarette burns. Al Alvarez tells me that it would not have been wise to have an affair with Anne Sexton. I should have been so lucky, but what did (or do) I know from wisdom? According to Diane Middlebrook's biography of Sexton, George Macbeth did enter Sexton's bed in that very room. Pause now for reflection while I reread a few of Sexton's *Love Poems* and recall a poem from an earlier book which begins with the unforgettable 'You Doctor Martin, walk / from breakfast to madness'. Seven years after that festival she killed herself. It is impossible for me to imagine her as she would be now, aged over eighty. She belongs forever to my hero-worshipping days. After Sexton died, her daughter edited the manuscript of *Mercy Street* where in the section called 'The Divorce Papers' she, like her younger friend Sylvia Plath in 'Daddy' (Plath, as a poet, had one more skin than Sexton and therefore the influence was in that direction, i.e. from Plath to Sexton) risks appropriating a readymade and therefore too easy metaphor, and what's more, twice over. It fails through disproportion: 'the courtroom . . . / a gas-chamber for the infectious Jew in me / and a perhaps land, a possibly promised land / for the Jew in me'. This was a pioneer trope, and an example of what Michel Deguy calls metaphoricity.

On the stairs of the hotel, I witnessed Octavio Paz shake hands with Pablo Neruda, marking the end of a quarrel that went back many years, to the heyday of Stalinism if not the Spanish civil war. In this hotel, Yves Bonnefoy, Guiseppe Ungaretti, Allen Ginsberg and others stayed during what was for me, if for no one else, a dreamtime of experience, a song line of devotion. During one of the festival's evening events at the Queen Elizabeth Hall (Ted Hughes' role in my participation is explained earlier in this book), I read my translations of and with Bonnefoy. Alvarez introduced the readers to the full hall. Behind us on stage were Auden and Ungaretti and Ginsberg.

'I wish that young man would hurry up,' said Auden, 'I need a drink.' It was probably my first public reading and I was in no hurry.

Robert Lowell (*with Norman Mailer and Ted Hughes*)

Robert Lowell is an iconic figure, the very figure, the very type of the poet, an artist who spoke truth to power, as Norman Mailer well understood in *Armies of the Night* although, in his third-person narrator persona, he has problems if not issues with the Boston Brahmin and judges the poet 'to possess an undue unchristian talent for literary log-rolling'. In a postcard, Lowell tells Mailer he is the finest journalist in America; in a second card, he praises Mailer's book of poems, *Death for the Ladies*, but Mailer notes that he never praised it in public. Lowell repeated the remark about journalism on the steps of the Pentagon, occasioning the reply: 'Well, Cal, there are days when I think of myself as being the best writer in America.' Lowell is one of the poets in Walter Lowenthal's anthology *Where Is Vietnam?*, but he never resorted to agitprop, nor did he embrace silence the way Oppen did, precisely because at the time and in the radically different and differently radical circumstances of the 1930s, Oppen (nearly ten years older than Lowell) could not conceive of a political poetry that was not agitprop. 'Mailer' then addresses himself and Lowell: 'The only subject we share, you and I, is that species of perception which shows that if we are not very loyal to our unendurable and most exigent inner light, then some day we may burn.' More experienced in protest than Lowell, he explains to the poet, who hopes to get away in time for an important dinner, that he must be prepared to stay on longer to ensure that if there are any arrests the two senior and well-known figures will be among them, to prevent the authorities from claiming that the demonstration (in the persons of those arrested) exclusively involved bohemians, radicals and nutters. Louis Simpson's essay on Lowell in *A Revolution in Taste* is unfair to Mailer, taking the 'best writer' quote out of context and seeing the author's 'preoccupation with himself' as 'confessional' (i.e. bad) rather than 'personal' (i.e. good).

Lowell's *For the Union Dead* to some extent returns to the strict metrics he deployed before *Life Studies*. I'm ashamed to say that not since school days have I memorized whole poems, but more recently Keith Bosley and I enjoyed reciting in unison two ferocious lines from 'Beyond the Alps', a poem which originally appeared in *Life Studies* minus one stanza, later restored in *For the Union Dead* 'at the suggestion of John Berryman': 'Now Paris, our black classic, breaking up / like killer kings on an Etruscan cup'. I do know by heart parts of a wondrous poem from *Near the Ocean*, 'Waking Early Sunday Morning', whose last stanza begins: 'Pity the planet, all joy gone / from this sweet volcanic cone'. Starting out under the aegis of John Crowe Ransom and Allen Tate, Lowell lightened up under the influence of poets unlike himself—the younger Ginsberg, the older Williams—and generated a freer poetry, so-called raw poetry. *Life Studies* was the turning point; deservedly, it is one of the most influential poetry books since the war.

My favourite books by Lowell are from his mid-life: *Life Studies*, *Imitations*, *For the Union Dead* and *Near the Ocean*. *For the Union Dead* contains a powerful poem 'Fall, 1961', written during the Cuban missile crisis, and prompting comparison with Oppen's 'Time of the Missile' written around the same time (and which I discuss later). There are poems to admire in the later books but my sense is that they are more for dipping in than reading through. All Lowell's books are now gathered in *Collected Poems*, an essential book despite egregious editorial flaws noted in a review by James Fenton. In a letter to his sister Olwyn, Ted Hughes praises Lowell's second book (which contains revised versions of many poems from his first book) and then, from a great height, rubbishes his third book. Not having reread Lowell's earliest works for many years, I take a short dip and conclude that Ted is right about the second book and may be right about the third book. More interesting to my mind and ear is that *Life Studies* is not such a definitive rupture with the diction and tone and rhythm of the earlier works as it is supposed to be or as I supposed it to be. The pathfinding and radical volume of 1959 leapfrogs over his third book, *The Mill of the Kavanaughs*, and picks up from some of the poems in *Lord Weary's Castle*, the second book, modifying the sometimes grandiose rhetoric with forays into the demotic. It must be because *The Mill of the Kavanaughs* immediately preceded *Life Studies* that the latter book is thought to be even more of a revolution in his work than it is. *Lord Weary's Castle* contains some of Lowell's best poems (and therefore anybody's best poems) and all written before he was thirty. If you think I am exaggerating, take another look at 'The Quaker Graveyard in Nantucket' and 'Mr Edwards and the Spider'. As a student in the early 1960s, on the margins of the action, I recall that the undergraduate magazines were full of Gunn poems and Hughes poems. Lowell's influence, coming from across the pond, would make itself felt later, in part mediated via Plath, Alvarez and Ian Hamilton.

Robert Creeley (with Charles Olson and Cid Corman)

Robert Creeley was a poet to whose '. . . hands come / many things. In time of trouble / a wild exultation' ('For WCW'). I would guess that he influenced younger poets far more than Duncan did, or maybe the American poetry I paid attention to had Creeley's stamp on it. His snappy short lines and dramatic enjambments were a kind of educated and subtle precursor of text messaging. They bespoke urgency, intensity, pressure, cool, even a version of hip. In a 1962 *Village Voice* review of *For Love*, Olson draws attention to the way 'Creeley lands syntax down the alley, and his vocabulary—pure English—to hit a meter and rhymes all of which are spares and strikes.' Where Duncan looked to Pound, Creeley looked to Williams, and both looked to Olson, who created a kind of dialectical synthesis between Pound and Williams. Where Duncan suggests classical music and old English poetry, Creeley's affinities are with Miles Davis, John Cage and R. B. Kitaj, who painted him. The first two volumes of *The Complete Correspondence* of Olson and Creeley cover a mere five months. How many volumes will there be for the full twenty years? This amazing exchange is so lacking in small talk (unlike, for example, Davenport and Laughlin's), so generously mutual in exploration, so plainly a dialogue on poetics between equals (with all due respect to the senior figure), that on some level they must have wanted it to be published. Olson had the highest regard for 'The Figure of Outward', as he calls Creeley in his dedication to *The Maximus Poems*, here on my desk together with *Mayan Letters*, *Call Me Ishmael* and *Archaeologist of Morning* (Olson's self-description), which is his non-Maximus collected poems. Olson's *Letters for Origin*, that is to say his letters to its editor Cid Corman, contains an unexpected sighting of Claude Vigée, whom Corman had translated. Olson writes: 'I cannot recommend to you & to Vigée too strongly, the idea

of getting a piece for #11 [i.e. *Origin* 11] from Pierre Boulez, the composer
. . . For Boulez is one of the singular men alive.'

The first of my five Creeley books, *For Love*, was brought to me by a
visitor to Cambridge in February 1964, my final year as an undergraduate.
She was a friend of an American cousin of mine, to whom I wrote asking for
the book. All I remember of the visitor is that she told me her mother said
she should marry a dentist, which she duly did. What we learn from this is
that wisdom is not only in the tooth and that jokes about pulling power are
in poor taste. More to the point was his 'I know a man', which reinforced the
initiation represented by Tomlinson's 'Paring the Apple' (which I explained
earlier). Here are Creeley's other collections of poetry and his prose, which
works less well for me: a novel *The Island* and stories, *The Gold Diggers*. Cid
Corman, whose day job was running an ice-cream parlour in Kyoto, spent
his time editing *Origin* and writing poems. Apart from Michael Hamburger,
Corman was the speediest answerer of letters in the whole history of the
world, as I know to my cost. These days he would have answered your email
even before you sent it.

Denise Levertov (with Adrienne Rich)

William Carlos Williams greatly admired and encouraged Denise Levertov,
half Russian Jew, half Welsh, who immigrated to the USA from the UK when
she was young. She loved and cherished the older man and writes in
'Williams; an Essay': 'nerves / muscles, rivers / of urgent blood, a mind /
secret, disciplined, generous and / unfathomable . . . He loved / persistence—
but it must / be linked to invention'. She, like her near-contemporary
Adrienne Rich, was, thanks to the Vietnam War, one of the most politically
engaged poets of her generation (and a precursor of poets like Carolyne
Forché, whose *The Angel of History* I loved), which does not mean that every
poem is political, only that the public sphere is not placed in a separate box
but segues in and out of the private as the situation in life, and therefore in
art, demands. Public themes make their first appearance in *Relearning the
Alphabet* yet, for all its sorrows and disgraces, the world is a place of infinite
possibility for all who pay attention, as a poet does: *Oh Taste and See* is the
characteristic title of one book. She speaks of 'all that lives// to the

imagination's tongue, / grief, mercy, language / tangerine . . .' Levertov was a prolific poet, always keeping her antennae open in order not to lose any potential sensation that might generate the language of a poem. Equally characteristic of her phenomenology and indicative of her vision are titles like *With Eyes at the Back of Our Heads*, *Footprints*, *To Stay Alive*, *The Freeing of the Dust* and *The Sorrow Dance*. It is instructive to compare Levertov's long (for her) poem 'During the Eichmann Trial' in *Jacob's Ladder* with Michael Hamburger's 'In a Cold Climate', written about the same time. There is no way that her more free and less solemn (but not less serious) poem on this theme would have been written in this way had she stayed in England. A more meditative mood pervades two later books, *Oblique Prayers* and *This Great Unknowing*.

Adrienne Rich was a more assertive poet, partly because her Judaism contains less Buddhism than Levertov's. I have three books: *The School among the Ruins*, *Snapshots of a Daughter-in-Law* and *Your Native Land, Your Life*. 'Poetry never stood a chance / of standing outside history', writes Rich, sounding like Oppen: 'It doesn't matter what you think. / Words are found responsible / all you can do is choose them / or choose / to remain silent.' Equally assertive is her uneven book of essays, *A Human Eye*: the best one is on Muriel Rukeyser.

John Wieners

I had purchased three of John Wieners' books by 1970, when I was twenty-eight. I can't remember who recommended him to me. Lee Harwood? Paul Buck? Another possibility is that I found them in the Eighth Street Bookshop or Gotham Book Mart. My hands are slightly trembling as I dip into *The Hotel Wentley Poems*, *Ace of Pentacles* and *Nerves*. Like Lepke in the Lowell poem, I feel as though I 'am hanging . . . in [my] air of lost connections', but I shall now make an effort to recover the connections. Noting Wieners' words in 'A Poem for Vipers' in *The Hotel Wentley Poems* ('. . . The poem / does not lie to us. We lie under / its law, alive in the glamour of this hour / able to enter into the sacred places / of his [Jimmy the pusher's] dark people . . .'), I suspect and even dimly recall that what grabbed me long ago in that book were—seemingly belying the dramas—the understatement, the modesty, yet the authority, of his impeccable phrasing within and across the line, the low-key composition by breath and quantity, although accent and stress are everywhere in the often achingly lyrical *Ace of Pentacles*, for example this complete poem, 'Two Years Later':

The hollow eyes of shock remain
Electric sockets burnt out in the skull.

The beauty of men never disappears
But drives a blue car through the stars.

The poet's subject matter regularly involves strong stuff about gay and straight lovers, the drug scene, physical and mental illness, violence, stuff which is sometimes mediated via art, visual art. It is not all darkness: there is illumination from dream, from dance—'The time is gone. / The dance goes on.' The poet, who died in 2002, was a hyper-romantic (a Knight on Black Mountain, like his friend and older colleague, Duncan), and had evidently experienced that tradition from Keats through Baudelaire to *The Great Gatsby* (Morgana La Fay in *Nerves* bumps into F. Scott Fitzgerald and Lester Young) and Tennessee Williams, while remaining utterly in his time and milieu, a poet of Boston and New York (and briefly San Francisco) at home in the jazz scene, with all its connotations and associations. The poet Fanny Howe, in her introduction to the *The Journal of John Wieners: 707 Scott Street* (written in 1958–1959 at the time of *Hotel Wentley* but only published in 1996), writes that the poet is a witness of the dispossessed: 'John's poetry . . . narrows the gap between longing and calling.' On 17 July 1958, Wieners writes in verse lines: 'I can count on countless years before me with no food in my stomach / writing out history in some dark room, doing my bit towards creating / a new structure / from love.' On 6 August: 'And if I cannot speak in poetry, it is because poetry is reality to me, and not the poetry we read, but find revealed in the estates of being around us.' On 13 August: 'I will use the distractions of this world, and erect a structure of them that will be of the poem.'

The distractions of this world, the estates of being round him, these were not my own distractions or estates. Yet, but reading him long ago in my late twenties, in the glory days of discovery of a version of one's own self that one could live with and by, mediated through a reading of the self of others (in this instance, that of Wieners and of those he witnessed), I know that this was one of the routes—during a crucial phase for me, what with the Prague Spring, the Paris May events and, a year earlier, the Six Day War—that would, dare I say, lead me into a serious adulthood, where I would acknowledge fully the long process of self-transcendence involved in facing the aspects of darkness and horror in personal and political worlds that it was one's duty as a human being and citizen and writer to combat. Perhaps I glamorized Wieners' estates of being, perhaps I obtained a vicarious thrill, but really it was amazement that this was what real life was like elsewhere. By the time I read *Nerves*, I knew he had no illusions, as 'Supplication' makes clear: 'Return me to the men who teach / and above all, cure the / hurts of wanting the impossible / through this suspended vacuum.'

[Coda: Patricia Scanlan's Artery Press has published a handsome book: *Strictly Illegal*, uncollected poems of Wieners, selected by his passionate devotee, Jeremy Reed.]

Joel Oppenheimer, Ed Dorn, Gilbert Sorrentino

Three other poets I read in the mid and late 1960s were Joel Oppenheimer and Ed Dorn—both of whom had studied at Black Mountain—and Gilbert Sorrentino. I have four treasured books published by Totem (the imprint of Leroi Jones, now Amiri Baraka) or Totem/Corinth from 32 West 8th Street, the bookshop run by a maestro bookseller Ted Wilentz, which I remember well from my first two trips to New York in 1964 and 1966: Oppenheimer's *The Love Bit*, Dorn's *Hands Up* and *The Newly Fallen*, and Sorrentino's *Black and White*. Corinth was Wilentz's own imprint. Dorn, already very ill, signed my copy of *The Newly Fallen* at a reading he gave in 1995 in London that I attended with Augustus Young, a friend and reader of his. Here too are Dorn's *Gunslinger* 1&2 and *Geography* but it is the four Totem or Totem/Corinth books which move me today, because their appearance has dated the most, although not their contents. The young man who avidly read these cleanly printed books, which are slim enough to be stapled, has gone for good (he too was slim enough to be stapled), but when his successor opens the pages and rereads Oppenheimer and Sorrentino (less so, Dorn), the clock is rewound and he . . . I remember a permission granted by myself and to myself, a permission to listen and then find my own way of giving voice, a way validated by Plath, Creeley and Tomlinson, author of my first modern poem by a living poet. This permission came after another permission—to put pen to paper at all—which had been granted by the French poet I translated over the years, continuing long after I came out as a writer (and, on a good day, an occasional poet), in my own right.

Jack Spicer and Gary Snyder

And there was Jack Spicer. Here are UK editions of *Lament for the Maker* and *After Lorca*. The former contains the priceless note: 'In early draft of Dover Beach, "lips" was "cock" and "Robert Browning" was "Robert Duncan".' The later line: 'Damn it all, Robert Browning, there is only one bordello', is a witty allusion to a famous line in Ezra Pound. Here too are the original White Rabbit Press edition of *Language* and the magnificent *Collected Books of Jack Spicer* edited and introduced by Robin Blaser who, along with Duncan, Rexroth and Snyder, was at the heart of West Coast poetics. Blaser, in his essay, quotes Octavio Paz's book on Marcel Duchamp approvingly as shedding light on Spicer: 'Vision is not only what we see; it is a stance taken, an idea, a geometry . . .' and 'a beauty free at last from the notion of beauty' and, finally, 'the conception of language as a structure in movement'. This last can also be applied to W. S. Graham's use or experience of language as a thematic in his otherwise very different poetry.

I have two books by Gary Snyder, *Regarding Wave* and *Earth House Hold*, the latter a precursor of what we would call today green attitudes and green writing, and an argument for a synthesis of the wisdom of both East and West in order to arrive at a 'totally integrated world culture'. Nearly forty years on, globalization has arrived, integrating us all in a terrifying vicious circle at the heart of which climate change is worsening and all the models of capitalism on offer increasing the gap between the haves and have nots, a bermuda triangle into which the finite resources of a battered and plundered planet are pouring—uncontrolled, wasted, contaminated. He saw it coming.

Raymond Carver

Raymond Carver is a better short-story writer than he is poet. His stories in the Gordon Lish-edited *What We Talk about When We Talk about Love* affect my perception of life, his characters project their lived lives onto the screen of my own little but real world, whereas the crow in a poem 'that sat there on the branch for a few minutes' and then 'picked up and flew beautifully / out of my life', flies, precisely, out of his life, not out of mine. His found poems from Chekhov add little to the original. Nonetheless, many poems in *All of Us: The Collected Poems* are more moving, sometimes epiphanically so, than the chips off the prose block usually are in writers who attempt both mediums, but are primarily prose workers. I read one of his poems at the memorial meeting for the radio playwright John Casson, which I chaired some years ago. It was big John who had originally introduced me to Carver's work via his book *Fires*, which I have here along with his uncollected writings, *No Heroics, Please*. The last time I spoke to John at his flat in Waterloo, he was off to the hospice for a break. The next day he was dead. Within two years, his diminutive partner Lesley Howling was diagnosed with a brain tumour. You couldn't make it up. And now my dear friend the Canadian poet Dee September, whose book *Making Waves* is here, has been struck down by an aggressive cancer. This is one lottery ticket you don't buy at the newsagent's. There is no escape. Like books, we have our fate.

[Coda: Dee and Lesley have since died, both in their fifties, poet and photographer, reaped by the grim one before they had sown to the full.]

Beatrice Hawley (with Mark Strand)

The side of me that reads Georges Perec and Jacques Roubaud, and is interested in the formal structures of memory, wonders forlornly who introduced me to the poet Beatrice Hawley. Here are two of her books, *Making the House Fall Down* and *Nothing Lost*, the former with a message: 'on the happy occasion of the exchange of several pieces of paper', 14 February 1984. I am not surprised Mark Strand supplied a quote for the cover of this early book, her best work has something of the elemental lyricism of his best poems (such as 'Moon' in the recent *Man and Camel*; Strand's true Penelope is Stevens). Two years younger than me, Hawley died the year after we met, aged forty-one. Levertov's introduction to the collected poems reminds me that the poet was also a political activist, although possibly in some moods she would reverse the two descriptions. I note with pleasure that Denise too finds affinities with Mark Strand and there is much food for thought in the following sentence: 'A person who regularly, and of necessity, does physical work [and Bea continued to have to cook and clean and sow, both at home and for a living, throughout the years when she was in graduate school and teaching] has less time for creative work than is desirable, yet has the advantage of a grounding, a mine of objective correlatives, often missing in those who seem luckier in their privileged leisure or more intellectual labour.'

Anthologies

Introduction

My anthologies are sorted into piles on the floor. Let me pick out a few that have particularly interested me. Then, like Henry in Berryman's 'Dream Song 77', head full and heart full, I'll be 'making ready to move on'. I shall give a miss to annuals, to ephemera, to unwanted or unappreciated gifts, to minority language semi-official anthologies of translations published to project soft power. Before I take unwanted books to the charity shop, I salute the anthologies where, maybe, I found a poem I would not otherwise have discovered.

Herbert Read and Caroline Forché

I was browsing with Paula in a lovely second-hand bookshop in Edinburgh, she at the folklore shelves and I at the poetry shelves, when a book called *The Knapsack* caught my eye. Edited by Herbert Read and published in 1939, it was, as its title suggests, for the use of soldiers with little space for books in their kit. The painter Merlin James tells me that David Jones reviewed the anthology in *The Tablet* on 13 January 1940. (Cue to visit the British Library periodicals reading room in Colindale.) Jones writes that he trusts Read because he served bravely in World War I. Jones himself took two books when he went to war: Palgrave's *Golden Treasury* and an unknown title (wouldn't we love to know what it was!). We learn from Read's preface that his own constant companion was Robert Bridges' anthology, *The Spirit of Man*. Read now finds fault with this book for its lofty tone, its serious moral and its abstract idealism. He tells us he wants an anthology with more action, more contradictions, more experience. On the other hand, he says he has been guided by the conviction that 'the love of glory, even in our materialistic age, is still the main source of virtue.' The book, in short, is as high-minded as *The Spirit of Man*, despite the disclaimers. The last section contains credos by Sir Walter Raleigh, Socrates and others, and a letter from Nicola Sacco addressed to his son Dante and dated 18 August 1927, nine days after sentence of death, five days before he and Bartolomeo Vanzetti died in the electric chair. (Cue to listen to Woodie Guthrie on the theme.) Robert Graves went off to the war with Blake, Leavis with Milton; Edgell Rickword took Grierson's recently published edition of Donne, Ernst Junger took *Tristram Shandy*. In World War II, the poet Bernard Spencer took little books of paintings by Masaccio, Fra Angelico and Giotto. Eisenhower's bedside book, unexpectedly, was Thomas Carlyle's *Sartor Resartus*.

Caroline Forché's *Against Forgetting*, subtitled 'Twentieth Century Poetry of Witness', usefully places André Breton among World War I poets and Auden in the Spanish civil war section. Pound, Oppen and Pavese are in the World War II section. There is a section called 'The Holocaust, the Shoah', her refusal to choose between the two words indicative of an unusual sensitivity evident throughout this exceptional anthology. Here she has rightly included the Italian Edith Bruck and the Israeli Dan Pagis, alongside poets who choose themselves, such as Paul Celan and Primo Levi. With sections like Latin America, India and Pakistan, civil rights in the USA, her book incarnates an international answer to Celan: 'Who shall bear witness for the witness?'

Stoddard (Chip) Martin

My friend Stoddard (Chip) Martin selected choice extracts from Nietzsche, Lawrence and Byron for a series called *The Sayings of . . .* However, I shall quote from the Pound volume, edited by G. Singh: 'The perception of the intellect is given in the word, that of the emotions in the cadence.' This is a valuable insight into the way the best literary writing works, prose no less

241

than poetry. Singh quotes from *ABC of Reading*, which I remember studying on a train to Paris in the early 1960s, and having the feeling, both sinking and uplifting, that I had better create a programme of reading for myself if I was to do more than pay lip service to writing: 'Most writers fail from lack of character rather than lack of intelligence.' This could not be truer, and reminds me of a collateral remark by the fine poet Louis Simpson (*Collected Poems*), possibly in his autobiography *Air with Armed Men*, to the effect that he could no longer write better poems by improving his technique; now he had to improve his character. Modesty and vanity, once again, prove to be conjoined twins.

When it comes to Lawrence, it is perhaps not surprising that his non-fiction generates better quotations than his fiction. 'The secret, shameful things are most terribly beautiful': this, from *The Rainbow*, has deep resonance in the novel, but out of context it carries no weight or the wrong kind of weight; it suggests a highbrow fortune cookie; whereas 'Never trust the artist. Trust the tale. The proper function of a critic is to save the tale from the artist who created it,' prompts recognition and cogitation, if not immediate assent on the part of the reader. It is a proper 'saying'.

Nathaniel Tarn

Con Cuba is a classic Cape Goliard book from the late 1960s and early 1970s. I doubt that it could be published today—the economics of culture have changed in terms of scale, attitude and technology. Barry Hall's Goliard was a classic small press that did its own letterpress printing, like Asa Benveniste's Trigram. It was taken under the wing of Jonathan Cape during the glory days of Tom Maschler (and Nathaniel Tarn's Cape Editions) and, although it lasted only a few years, a number of essential books were produced. Among the poets in Nathaniel Tarn's *Con Cuba* are two talismanic friends of mine, Pablo Armando Fernandez, now the senior poet in Havana, and Isel Rivero, ex Havana, New York and Vienna, who lives in Madrid; on my desk are two fine books, Fernandez's *Parables* and Rivero's *Relato del Horizonte* with a cover by Paula. At Arnold Wesker's house during Pablo's farewell party we all sang 'Guantanamera', a song as redolent of the 1960s as 'We shall overcome' and 'The girl from Ipanema'. If I were to ask myself: where have all the flowers (snows of yesteryear, etc.) gone?, I would be indulging in rhetoric triggered by the Greek root of the word anthology, but this anthology has plunged me into a foolish nostalgia for the time when I was young and full of hope, the time when 'a promise of happiness' (in the phrase Stendhal used of art) was possible, and received or made in the intuitive knowledge of youth that wrong paths taken at crossroads could be remedied or redeemed later.

Jerome Rothenberg

Some anthologists have designs upon the reader. Sometimes their ego and didacticism turn the reader off. Sometimes the author, by virtue of visionary purpose, commanding intelligence and lateral focus, can change our perception of poetry and life not only by increasing our knowledge but, more profoundly, by rearranging our existing knowledge. Many readers are indebted to Jerome Rothenberg for *Technicians of the Sacred*, which gathers poetry from ancient and so-called primitive sources. Creation myths and namings and events set the scene for poetry from Africa, America, Asia and Oceania. The final third of the book is taken up with detailed commentaries: here the poet/anthropologist is in relation to the word as the best visual artist/anthropologists such as Susan Hiller and Sophie Calle are in relation to the image. *Technicians of the Sacred* works synchronically, evoking a space, in which, as the title suggests, all the poetry interacts as events and happenings. Its companion volume *America a Prophecy* works, as the title suggests, diachronically and, although not teleological, operates as a Borgesian revisioning of the past in the light of the present. The matrix or matrices of the book are Native American poetry and images. 'Map One' begins with Mayan texts and moves via Jeffers, Olson, Duncan and Ginsberg via Sioux and other texts to Pound, Melville, Simic, Dickinson and Poe and so on. Never was the old pun on routes and roots better incarnated than in this valuable introduction to American poetry, although you won't find Lowell, Wilbur or Hecht. Rothenberg's *Revolution of the Word* is a postscript to *America a Prophecy*, focusing on avant-garde poetry from 1914 to 1945. Here too the distant past and the latest word (in its time)—Riding, Oppen, Duchamp, Stevens, Stein—interact vertiginously.

Small Presses

Phyroid Press, Burning Deck and others

Among the memorable and singular small presses of the early 1980s was Phyroid Press, set up by poet–painter–musician Billy Childish to publish himself, Sexton Ming and Johnny Moped of a circle which also included Bill Lewis, Charles Thompson (future Stuckist) and Alan Denman. It was centred on Chatham art school, where Paul Buck taught, and Victoria Centre for the Arts at Gravesend, where Richard Berengarten taught. Some of their names recall nothing so much as the punk comic *Viz*, with its characters like Johnny Fartpants and Buster Gonad. On the back of *7*, a pamphlet by the famously dyslexic Billy Childish, is a photograph of him with his girlfriend Tracey Emin (or Traci Emin as she was then known), aged about eighteen. The other Phyroid Press publication on my desk, apart from a stapled Ming/Childish pamphlet *The Wild Breed Is Here*, is *Big Cunt* (title on the inside front cover only). Deciphered, a letter from Childish reads: 'Dear Mr Rudolph hear are some ming's The ming says he gonna puke . . . if you don't show some gratitude regards billy'. After many such pamphlets, Childish, who was also a member of a garage group called the Milkshakes, went more upmarket with, on the whole, better produced books from Hangman Press, such as *Ten No Good Poems of Slavery Buggery Boredom and Disrespect*. Hangman also produced (and still produces?) records. Bill Lewis was different and his leanings towards folk song, William Blake, Latin American radicalism and a new-age syncretic Christian Judaism with Gnostic tendencies continue unabated, and can be found in his collected poems, *Blackberry Ghosts*. I have not seen the Kent or Medway people for many years, apart from Tracey Emin, whom I met in a lift during the opening party for Tate Modern. I offered to reintroduce her to Paula, who had given her a tuition session, edgy in both directions, long ago at the Royal College of Art, and she said yes.

At different times, I have been in dialogue with or at least kept a close eye on other small presses and magazines: immediate predecessors like Enitharmon (first under Alan Clodd, now Stephen Stuart Smith), Trigram, Writers Forum and Cape Goliard; my exact contemporaries, Carcanet, Anvil, *MPT*, *Aquarius* and *Curtains*, then Bloodaxe and John Welch's Many Press a little later, followed by a successor generation including Tony Frazer's Shearsman, Ken Edwards' Reality Street Editions, Chris Emery's Salt, John Lucas' Shoestring—all the editors poets/translators in their own right. Let me add a brief word about poetry readings such as the Blue Bus series at the Lamb in Lambs Conduit Street run by David Miller, a fine poet (*Collected Poems*) and musician. Another, now defunct, group was Sub-Voicive, run by Lawrence Upton, a close associate in word and deed of the late Bob Cobbing and whose book *Wire Sculptures* is here. These readings are not primarily about promoting or launching a new book, although this does happen from time to time. They are the expression of a group or community ethos, where the like-minded (although not necessarily like-worded) gather to hear new work, sometimes in draft. I recited my longest poem 'Zigzag' at Blue Bus (then in the Plough in Museum Street), having recently completed it. I stumbled over a particular stanza, apologized and stumbled again. Now I knew it was not a slip of the tongue, it was a clumsy phrase revealed to me by the ear. I should have picked it up earlier. I revised the stanza on the tube going home.

In the USA the small press scene has been graced by, for example, Cloud Marauder and Panjandrum on the East Coast, Talisman, Sun and Totem/Corinth in New York and, in particular, Keith and Rosmarie Waldrop at Burning Deck in Rhode Island. This brilliant couple are poets, publishers, scholars—and translators of, among others, Edmond Jabès. I should note too that Rosmarie and Keith, whose immensely knowing and subtle Perecian double act *Ceci n'est pas Keith Ceci n'est pas Rosmarie* is well worth reading, still do their own letterpress printing: here is *Words Worth Less*, their co-written poetry pamphlet and several more texts by themselves—in the classic tradition of small presses—and other distinguished poets, including Middleton. Burning Deck and, in the UK, Gabberbocchus Press, run by an equally brilliant couple, the late Stefan and Francesca Themerson, are among the great and exemplary small presses of the modern era.

In France, too, there are small presses, such as William Blake and Co. in Bordeaux under its genial and brilliant director Jean-Paul Michel, himself a fine poet. Black Sparrow Press in San Francisco, thanks to one or two authors like Bukowski, became a commercial publisher. It was eventually taken over by Godine in Boston. The small press scene, like Indy record labels and the artists' studio movement, deserves a full and careful account. Even from my perspective, a detailed exploration of these themes must await my eventual history of Menard Press, if that is ever written. There were times when it felt good to be part of a movement which published people outside or rejected by the mainstream, and reached people untouched by the establishment.

Poets

The career of a fine poet like John Welch reveals that people who only ever read books by commercial publishers miss out on some of the best work around. His two biggest publishers are Shearsman and Anvil and here are *Blood and Dreams* published by Reality Studios and books from other small presses, including his own imprint, Many Press. Another classic small press is Dinah Livingstone's Katabasis, set up to publish her own poetry and translations of left-wing Latin American poets, as well as work by English poets such as Christopher Hampton and Anne Beresford. Anvil and Shearsman are giants next to Katabasis. A stalwart of the humanist, pacificist and radical worlds, Livingstone is a trouper. Her books and pamphlets include *Second Sight* and a translation of Ernesto Cardenal's *Nicaraguan New Time*. A long poem in *Second Sight*, 'Say Not the Struggle', brings together her political, spiritual, artistic and emotional concerns, ending 'But the struggle continues', and so it does, especially to ensure a viable world for her grandchildren, for my grandchildren Charlie and Leah, and for all their contemporaries. Here is Livingstone's *Poetry of Earth* published in the same year as a book on similar themes, Jonathan Bate's *Song of the Earth*, followed by John Felstiner's powerful study *Can Poetry Save the Earth*?

Ireland and Scotland

Introduction

It was in the early 1970s that I encountered my first Irish poets, including senior figures like George Buchanan ('a table for one in the long dining room', not the same kind of table as Aharon Appelfeld's) and Brian Coffey. John

Montague was one of several interesting people I met at the Struga/Ohrid Poetry Festival in Macedonia in 1972. Later, in London, he introduced me to a poet who became a close friend, Augustus Young. It was Augustus who introduced me to Brian Coffey, the work and the man. Montague had strong links with Paris—translating Frénaud, Deguy and other mutual friends—and that brought us together for the few years we kept in touch. I admired his book *The Rough Field*, which I reviewed in *Tribune*. His memoir *Company* is entertaining, revealing and characteristically sly. In the hilarious and affectionate chapter about Samuel Beckett, Olivia Manning is put in her place for not knowing it, after she had let rip a flow of insults at Sam, a writer she despised, which tells you all you need to know about her.

Thomas MacGreevy

Thomas MacGreevy was a gay Catholic republican from Kerry, half a generation older than, and friend of, that trio of important post-Yeats Irish modernists, Dennis Devlin, Brian Coffey and Samuel Beckett whom he introduced to Joyce. In Paris, according to Young, 'Beckett and MacGreevy were close, and Brian was something of a breakwater between them.' Beckett would always support an old friend and his cover quote for Thomas Dillon Redshaw's pioneering 1971 edition of the *Collected Poems*, which perhaps oddly is not found in Beckett's foreword, states: 'he is an existentialist in verse, the Titchener of the modern lyric. It is in virtue of this quality of inevitable unveiling that his poems may be called elucidations, the vision without the dip, and probably the most important contribution to post-War Irish poetry.' MacGreevy is a fine low-key post-Imagist poet, one who hopes his poetry 'doesn't make a noise'. Beckett's singular and mannered foreword, dating from 1934, begins with a wondrous remark (elaborating a remark by Nicolas Malebranche later quoted by Paul Celan): 'All poetry, as discriminated from the various paradigms of prosody, is prayer.' He continues, perhaps influenced by Edward B. Titchener, a well-known psychologist: 'It is from the nucleus of endopsychic clarity, uttering itself in the prayer that is a spasm of awareness, and from no more casual source, that Mr MacGreevy evolves his poems.' The later *Collected Poems* (1991) was edited by Susan Schreibman, an American then living in Ireland with whom I was in contact at the time. The book is fatter than the earlier collected poems, but apart from two previously uncollected poems and a number of beautiful translations from the Spanish of Rafael Alberti, Jorge Guillen, Juan Ramón Jimenez, Federico García Lorca and Antonio Machado, the size is accounted for by lengthy and generally valuable annotations. As befits such a translator, MacGreevy's own poems sound like those of a modernist who has read Spanish and other modern European poets: Guiseppe Ungaretti, George Seferis and so on. 'The Six who were Hanged' (i.e. by the British), a poem from 1930, reads like Miłosz fifteen or twenty years later. This painterly—an attribute unsurprising in a man who was director of the National Gallery of Ireland for thirteen years—religious and political poet leaves one wishing he had written more. The reasons for the returned exile, the prodigal son, not having done so are discussed at some length by the editor: Ireland is found wanting, but Schreibman still sees the poet as a precursor of many of the poets young enough to be cosmopolitan without having to leave for Paris or London. Let me end this personal rediscovery of a fine poet with the comment that both Wallace Stevens and W. B. Yeats admired him.

Other Irish poets I have here (see bibliography) include Paul Muldoon, Thomas Kinsella, Tom Paulin, Paul Durcan, Michael Longley, Dennis O'Driscoll, Geoffrey Squires and Seamus Heaney, among whose books is his libretto for Leoš Janáček's song cycle *Diary of One Who Vanished*. Here too is Cherry Smyth's *When the Lights Go Up*. I met this sexy bisexual on the Northern Line (as you do), who told me about her forthcoming book (and sexy it is too). My recollection is that we were both reading a poetry poster and identified each other as like-minded.

Augustus Young

Menard Press has published six books by Augustus Young, including the 'Credit' series, *Danta Gradha* (love poems from the Irish), *Lampion and His Bandits* and, by adoption, a volume of prose memoirs, *Light Years*. He is one of three or four readers to whom I entrust occasional drafts, with a licence to speak his mind robustly. Since he quit his day job as a high-level epidemiologist, Young has produced a multi-vocal body of neglected poetry and prose non-fiction in different modes, complex and compelling. As prodigally inventive as Paul Muldoon, with a laser intellect and an acute ear to match, I am fortunate to have Augustus as a friend and critical reader. I have all his books from other publishers (see bibliography) including the genre-busting *The Nicotine Cat*—the follow-up memoir to *Light Years* and *Story Time*—which is a witty and learned meditation on people and ideas, on language and languages. Young, emailer nonpareil, is touchier than I am, and more honest. He rightly puts up with less nonsense from other people than I do, meaning he wastes less time albeit at the cost of occasional unfairness. When misunderstandings happened, his late wife Margaret, dear friend and reader extraordinaire, or our father time, would step in, and all would be well again.

Hugh MacDiarmid and Sorley MacLean

I am only too aware that Hugh MacDiarmid is a poet who deserves more attention than I have given him over the years and I remain ashamed that I let myself down by neglecting this grand and extraordinary figure. Here is his *Selected Poems*: he was to Scots what Sorley MacLean was to Gaelic. He was 'masculine' while MacLean represented the feminine principle, according to Ian Crichton Smith, as relayed to me by Stan Smith. On the other hand, I did not fail to read Sorley MacLean, a great Gaelic poet who translated himself into English. I recall a particularly memorable event in Harrogate when MacLean was supposed to read with MacDiarmid. For his own reasons, the latter did not turn up (thus forfeiting twenty pounds and a bottle of whisky, said to be his standard fee), so MacLean read both MacDiarmid and himself. Notwithstanding his intellectual powers and immersion into the dark realities of his era, MacLean was a traditional bard and held forth appropriately. I have marked various stanzas and passages in his collected poems, *From Wood to Ridge*: 'There is no knowledge of the course / Of the crooked veering of the heart, / And there is no knowledge of the damage / to which its aim unwittingly comes.' And: 'And the brain has no foothold / To lower a rope to my heart.' Finally, the strange ending to his poem on Yeats: '. . . there is an excuse on your lips, / the excuse that did not spoil your poetry, / for every man has his excuse.' I link this to his comment in the introduction to his collected poems: 'I think two of my reasons for my long silences and burning of unpublished poems have been my long years of grinding school-teaching and my addiction to an impossible lyric ideal.' Surely by reason, he means excuse . . . MacLean, who ended up as a headmaster, translated himself but was also translated by Iain Crichton Smith in *Poems to Eimhir*. Crichton Smith has rightly written that MacLean was a great love poet, a great political poet and a great poet of war. He served and was wounded in Africa, although he berated himself for not going to Spain, for 'family reasons' and because 'in my heart of hearts I knew then that I "preferred a woman to crescent history".' Unique in MacLean's bilingual collected poems is his translation into Gaelic of John Cornford's poem 'Heart of the Heartless World'. It can be inferred from the index to George Oppen's letters that he did not know MacLean's poetry: he would have been fascinated and would have passed some remark.

Poetry Translation

INTRODUCTION

Poetry translation, as I wrote earlier, was my cover story when I was young, a cover story aimed as much at myself as at others. Translation was also an apprenticeship. In both senses of the word, it was my practice. It all started when I picked up Yves Bonnefoy's *Hier régnant désert* in Bowes and Bowes bookshop in Cambridge. That was in 1963, exactly half a century before the publication of the present work. At that moment I *knew* my life would be changed, and therefore it *was* changed. I set to work and sent him my first translations of poems. He replied warmly and asked to see my own poems—I had to confess I had not yet written any—and invited me to visit him in Paris. In 1963, nineteen years older than me, he was forty, nearly thirty years younger than I am at the time of writing, but he always will be nineteen years older and, in the future perfect (which is the human version of the unrealizable perfect future), when both of us are dead and gone, he always will have been nineteen years older: 'Trading in future perfects I'll come through / liminal transit,' I wrote in my poem 'Mandorla' (reprinted in *Zigzag* from Julia Farrer's glorious *livre d'artiste, Mandorla*).

I have in another room all the many books by and many of the many books on Bonnefoy. My friends John Naughton and Stephen Romer have translated books by him, as has, into Russian, Mark Grinberg. Other translator friends and colleagues have their poets; 'alter ego' would exaggerate the intimacy between the pairs, but still conveys something of the elective affinity such work calls for: Michel Couturier and John Ashbery; Ted Hughes and Yehuda Amichai; Elaine Feinstein and Marina Tsvetayeva; Daniel Weissbort and Nikolai Zabolotsky; Robert Hass and Czesław Miłosz; Ruth Feldman and Primo Levi; Keith Bosley and André Frénaud; Jonathan Griffin and Fernando Pessoa; Stephen Romer, Paul Auster and John Taylor, Jacques Dupin. I wrote affectionately in an essay for Bonnefoy's eightieth birthday book that we translators are attendant lords at the court of our poetry princes or princesses, an allusion that requires no translation.

Here is one of the hundred copies of a selection of Dupin, *Fits and Starts*, translated by Auster and published at his own imprint Living Hand; a rare book, affectionately inscribed by the translator, it contains an original lithograph by Alexander Calder. Given that there is no particular organic or artistic link between Calder and Dupin, I would guess that Calder was a Maeght artist and that Dupin, who directed Maeght at the time, was helping Paul cover the cost of the unlimited edition of a thousand copies, by organizing a limited edition that would sell to collectors. Young poets and editors often depend upon generous gestures to kick-start this kind of small press.

There can be no doubt that since around the mid-1960s ours has been a golden age of translation, a harbinger of the globalized interactivity that in certain respects we don't approve of. These days, poets and scholars and translators email each other with drafts, just as the Slovene writer Ifigenija Simonovic and I used fax machines when working on translations of her poems. Ted Hughes and Daniel Weissbort were deeply involved from the mid-1960s in opening up Eastern and Central Europe, partly out of curiosity, partly out of a sense that English poetry needed an inflow of foreign poetic currency. This was why they founded *Modern Poetry in Translation* in 1965, which inspired my own *Journals of Pierre Menard* and Menard Press a few years later. I am no longer interested in actively discussing theory of translation with fellow practitioners (nor are most of them, I suspect), since many of the problems fall away or become strictly academic (possibly in the best sense of the word) if you are transparent concerning your procedures. Like writing poetry itself, poetry translation is an art whose very practice supplies the answers to the questions it poses. It is, in the phrase of Pierre Leyris, *un travail d'écoute*, listening work. I, for one, proceed by repeating variations aloud until I find the best one, relatively speaking.

Nothing annoys a certain class of reader more than works which would not exist without the inspiration or example of a foreign original and which take off as a new work in the poet's own language beyond the attempt to make a poem in the new language that chooses to summon the original as a witness to its own execution, in the positive sense of the word. Even then, susceptibilities can be assuaged if the book makes clear what is going on: thus, Rothenberg's *Lorca Variations*, Lowell's *Imitations* and Pound's *Homage to Sextus Propertius* are *loci classici* of the poem as free translation by a powerful poetic intelligence intent not only on possessing the original text beyond the aura of elective affinity but also claiming equal standing with the original poet. But, as I wrote earlier, you do wonder what the translated poet might have to say on the subject.

I cherish the Penguin Classics, Penguin Modern European Poets and Oxford World Classics I bought over the years. Penguin Classics published the remarkable versions of Horace and Propertius by a Menard author, W. G. Shepherd. His highly entertaining and instructive account of collaborating with Betty Radice, the series editor, can be found in *The Translator's Art*. I also particularly liked the chapters by the late Rabbi David Goldstein, on translating the name of God, and Michael Alexander, the marvellous translator of *Beowulf* and *The Earliest English Poems*, who contributed an Old English riddle to my MenCard series. Menard was to have published his complete *Old English Riddles*, but not for the first or last time had to abandon a project for lack of resources; Peter Jay's Anvil Press stepped in and took over. I remember, when Keith Bosley and I were working in Bush House, we had a drink with yet another contributor to *The Translator's Art*, the old Foreign Office man, Arthur Cooper of *Li Po and Tu Fu* fame. This book and Angus Graham's *Poems of the Late T'ang*, a masterpiece of the art of poetry translation, were required reading for everybody hungry to go beyond the parameters set by Arthur Waley's *Translations from the Chinese* of 1918 (originally published under a different title, a definitive edition came out as *Chinese Poems* in 1946) and Ezra Pound's *Cathay* of 1915 (which includes his wondrous poem 'The River Merchant's Wife'). These two books inaugurated the modern fascination with Far Eastern literature in the English-speaking world. 'As for *Cathay*,' wrote T. S. Eliot, quoted in Marianne Moore's tribute to Pound, 'it must be pointed out that Mr Pound is the inventor of Chinese poetry for our time.'

Sometimes a prose translation of poetry meets the occasion (Georges Conne's French version of Browning's *The Ring and the Book*, Mallarmé's French Poe), but contrary to myth a prose translation is never literal, provided it is good. Perhaps the myth is associated with the oft-expressed liking of artists and writers—Kitaj, Paula, Bonnefoy and others—for the old black-and-white Phaidon editions of the greatest painters of the past, two of which I have here and which I used to look at when I was a child and indeed still look at. Nobody has a bad word for most of the Penguin volumes with prose cribs at the foot of the page of the original but, nonetheless, they raise mirror-image questions to those raised by Omar Pound's versions, which I discuss later. One technique in the territory between the two apparent extremes is for a scholar (e.g. the late Geoffrey Bownas) to hand over the draft translations to a poet (e.g. Anthony Thwaite) and proceed thus to a book (e.g. *The Penguin Book of Japanese Verse*). An excellent short volume translated by Anthony Howell and W. G. Shepherd—*Silvae* by the Neapolitan court poet Statius—contains both approaches. Howell, according to Shepherd's introduction, does 'creative translation', J. P. Sullivan's term about Pound's *Propertius* and 'tries to see for himself, in his own *persona* and style, what Statius sees, adopting a diction and style which are the results of imagining that English was the language of Rome'. Shepherd himself, however, tries (in his own words) 'to translate line for line, imitating Statius' counterpoint of syntactic layout against lineation, *and to arrive at an outcome which is a poem*' (emphasis mine).

[Coda: RIP Bill Shepherd.]

I have here a classic production from the 1970s, John Porter's translation of *Beowulf*—if you can find it, compare and contrast it to Seamus Heaney's and Michael Alexander's versions. It is published by Bill Griffiths' Pirate Press and printed by him and Porter at the Poetry Society on a duplicator. Sixty-two copies out of an edition of five hundred were printed for 'subscibers' (*sic*) of which this is number thirty-one, signed to me personally by the translator. I have kept the letter from Griffiths detailing the credit and debit of the edition: there were thirty-one contributions of five pounds, making a kitty of one hundred and fifty-five pounds. The debit items include forty-two reams of paper, an IBM Icelandic golfball typehead, ten tubes of brown ink, envelopes and postage on subscription copies, adding up to one hundred and fifty-five pounds. Ian Robinson's later description of this publication as a 'printing masterpiece' is hyperbole, but never mind.

FRANCE

T. S. Eliot: *Pierre Leyris/Claude Vigée*

According to his *Independent* obituarist, 'Pierre Leyris was generous in encouraging and giving scope to younger translators and writers in collaborative projects.' The poet Yves Bonnefoy, recalling the Shakespeare project of almost half a century before on which, as a young man, he had been invited to collaborate, describes the way in which Leyris would discuss the translated version, 'word by word, with the patience which springs from the heart allied to the intelligence'. I keep Leyris' remarkable translations of T. S. Eliot's *Poésie* next to the master's collected poems. As a friend and translator of Claude Vigée, I had long known about his version of *Four Quartets*, which lay untouched in a drawer for half a century because Eliot, who read (and admired) Vigée's translation, had, three weeks earlier, agreed to exclusive rights in Leyris' version. I told Vigée that the time had finally come to find a publisher. Faber and Faber raised no objections; Valerie Eliot and Kathleen Raine wrote supporting letters. Yet the French publisher of Leyris was adamant that there could be no rival version in France. I proposed Menard Press, based outside France. To this suggestion, they eventually said yes, but only if Leyris agreed. Naturally, I wrote to the master in appropriate and respectful terms. He replied politely, saying that it was impossible for him to say no, only that I should make sure Vigée had respected the difference

254

between 'durée' and 'temps' when translating the word 'time'. I wondered about this: was it naive on the part of Leyris? If Vigée needed to be told, then he was not the man to translate Eliot, and this was a reason to refuse permission. Or was it a broad and unsubtle hint that, although he still had doubts, he could not stand in Claude's way? Still and all, *Quatre Quatuors* was published, with an essay I commissioned from Gabriel Josipovici, which was translated into French for the occasion. The Menard book also contains a previously unpublished letter by Eliot himself, which enabled me to (sort of) claim him as a Menard author and indeed as one of its Nobel Prize winners (along with full-on Menard Nobels: Octavio Paz, Ivo Andric and Sir Martin Ryle). Stephen Spender (in his *Eliot*) wrote that the quartets were influenced by Rilke's *Duino Elegies*. The Spender/Leishman versions came out in 1939, in time for Eliot to have read them. I assume Eliot read the elegies in the original and also in translation.

SPAIN AND SPANISH AMERICA

Robert Bly; César Vallejo, Miguel Hernandez, Blas de Otero

Many of the best books of poetry in translation were and still are published by small presses. In the mid to late 1960s, when I was starting out, I came across the Sixties Press (which had been the Fifties Press and would morph into the Seventies Press), run by Robert Bly, a poet later to become famous for his prose book *Iron John*. Mike Heller prefers Bly's translations to his poems and also prefers Clayton Eshelman's Vallejo to Robert Bly's. Bly, he says, once performed an amazing feat, reciting Lorca's *Poet in New York* from memory in both the original Spanish and his own translation, which I assume was better than the standard one by Ben Belitt. Heller may not have seen Barry Fogden's excellent translation of César Vallejo's first book *The Black Heralds* (the original published, to one's amazement, as early as 1919), though he must know Dorn and Gordon Brotherston's *Selected Poems*: 'I shall die in Paris in heavy rain / the day is entered in my brain / I shall die in Paris—and that's a promise / maybe some Thursday, like this one, in autumn.' Vallejo (1892–1938) is a poet not only of the same lifespan as Mandelstam (1891–1938), but also the same stature.

The Sixties Press published an opinionated and occasionally satirical magazine ('when we can stand it no longer') called *The Sixties*, which I loved reading when I was young, just as I thrilled to Ian Hamilton's *The Review*. Bly was politically more radical than Hamilton. His poetics too were different. Where Hamilton drew on W. D. Snodgrass and Robert Lowell and the territory covered by Al Alvarez's influential anthology, *The New Poetry*, Bly derived mainly from Spain and Spanish America, from the non-French surrealism and personal politics of poets like Hernandez, Neruda, Vallejo, Cernuda, de Otero and Machado, the last named also published by Hamilton, it is fair to say. As we would expect, Bly loved Trakl, who died in World War I. His love affair with Rilke came later. There was a time when I would have told my young friend Will Stone, whose Nerval I published, to send Bly his new translation of Georg Trakl's *To the Silenced*, but my energies as a go-between are declining by the month. Bly's focus was on what he called deep image, a poetics strenuously opposed to pictorial poems *à la* Williams. Deep image incarnated a dream-like interiority that moved the poems more slowly along than was the case with Black Mountain or Beat. Ted Hughes has a letter on Sylvia Plath and deep image. In the same letter, to Plath's biographer Anne Stevenson, he writes that one reason they moved to Devon was to be upwind of a possible nuclear accident. Ted and I once had a long talk about Lord Zuckerman and two subjects on which Solly was an expert, nuclear weapons and badgers. Ted took aim with a pretend airgun and said 'they [Russians and Americans] won't use them,' which was Solly's view too, subject to his concerns expressed in his Menard pamphlet and the famous speech he wrote for Lord Mountbatten to deliver to NATO. About badgers, Solly and Ted disagreed strongly, with Solly in favour of culls.

What a thrill it was to buy a Sixties Press book, for example, Blas de Otero's *Twenty Poems*, translated by Hardie St Martin: this sends signals from my eyes to my heart via the parts of my brain that recall to my mind how I felt as a young man, in the mid-1960s, on the road to myself via Paris and New York. This was a long journey. The route was scenic and did not always justify the detours. But I found [*out*] things, and eventually I was found out— by myself, in both senses. Tony or Anthony was a detective, a stalker, on the trail of Anthony or Tony, hero-worshipper and wannabe poet, dressed in his verbal motley. Someone, himself, had processed the black-and-white film into other peoples' colours, the wrong colours. Only now, half a century later, has the motley come off. Got up in black and white, perhaps I am ready to put on my own coat of many colours. It has taken a painter to encourage me to write fiction where I can project onto completely invented characters some of the dilemmas and complexities that a certain minimalism deriving from my old admiration for poets like Creeley and Williams encouraged me to avoid: the two Americans were so prodigally various and productive that 'minimal' refers only to the unit of composition and not to the kind of repression and laziness I masked as a poetics learnt from others. Even with fiction, I leant for years towards such solo voice-centred texts or *récits* as those masterpieces, des Forêts's *Le Bavard* and Camus's *La Chute*, rather than novels teeming with characters. Now, perhaps I have begun to go native—through posing for Paula, who admires the pre-Raphaelites and Hogarth and other storytellers—and am learning to incorporate more traditional narratives into my *imaginaire*.

The *Selected Poems* of Miguel Hernandez, edited by Ted Genoways and translated by old Sixties Press hands, is an impressive collection of work by this great poet. It ends with a beautiful short memoir by Octavio Paz dating from 1942, the year Hernandez died of tuberculosis, in prison; the two men had met in 1937: 'Let me forget you, so that in this forgetting your voice can continue to grow, stolen now from your body and in the memory of those of us who knew you, free and tall on the wind, unchained from time and from your misery.' Hernandez had three phases: early work from 1923 to 1936; the civil war poems from 1936 to 1939—the work on which his reputation rests; and the prison poems from 1939 to 1942. According to Thomas Jones in his selection *Songbook of Absences*, it was thanks to the efforts of Neruda that the poet's death sentence was commuted to life imprisonment by the fascist authorities. 'Absence in all I feel. / Absence. Absence. Absence'. I published some of Bly's translations of tiny poems by Issa on an early Menard Press leaflet.

Federico García Lorca

The Poet's Work, edited by Reginald Gibbons, contains a selection of prose by twentieth-century masters, including Lorca's 'Duende', which I must have read almost as many times as Walter Benjamin's 'Theses on the Philosophy of

History'. Lorca's text, which fascinated Paula's husband Victor Willing, who doubtless arrived at it via his interest in Nietzsche and the cult of Dionysus, is a dazzling and classic example of a poet generating or inducing theory from practice. The reverse does not work: you cannot instruct yourself or even inspire yourself to write poems out of such a matrix. Its considerable power comes from its association with the primary work of a wondrous poet. Lorca, who was inspired by and himself inspired flamenco music, needed to find out about the duende, to write about the duende, perhaps because like his friend Picasso he was from Andalusia, though the Picasso family left Malaga for good when he was ten, whereas Lorca, for all his wanderings would always return to Granada, ultimately to his death. Outside Andalusia, the word merely means hobgoblin, but in that region it symbolizes daemonic inspiration: 'an obscure power which can speak through every form of human art, including the art of personality'. As Seferis, quoted by Gibbons, writes in his diary: '*In essence*, the poet has one theme: his live body.' And yet, a few years later, the great Greek poet would write: 'Day by day we live our life; we don't write it— writing, no matter what you do, is only part of life.' Folded into J. L. Gili's bilingual *Lorca*, which contains 'Duende', is a letter from Gili thanking me, already a busybody, for pointing out a (careless) mistake in his translation of 'Malaguena', a poem which inspired one of mine, drafted on a holiday in Spain while chaperoning my thirteen-year-old daughter and niece. Pray for me, that I may tidy this flat and find my missing papers, among them this poem that only Merlin James has read. As I recall, it imagined a tavern with a basement, a ground floor and a first floor. I cannot remember if I had Freud's tripartite image of the psyche in mind. Edward Hirsch's study of duende, *The Demon and the Angel*, quotes from Ralph Ellison's *Invisible Man* where, writes Hirsch, an old woman sings 'a spiritual as full of weltschmerz as flamenco'. But surely we associate weltschmerz more with fado than with flamenco?

PORTUGAL

Fernando Pessoa

Jonathan Griffin's *Selected Poems of Pessoa* is a significant book for me, partly because I own Griffin's copyrights, not in my capacity as his literary executor, rather because his generous heiress Julia Farrer donated them to Menard Press. The money will go towards the costs of printing a collection of the miscellaneous translations of this fine and neglected poet whose *In Earthlight* is out there for those who wish to check him out. Griffin's translation of Fernando Pessoa's *Message* has been reprinted in association with Tony Frazer's Shearsman Press, one of a number of co-publications which, with any luck, will help keep the name of Menard, now dormant, alive. Frazer has embarked on a large Pessoa library, including the collected poems of the main heteronyms and *Lisbon*, the strange guidebook Pessoa wrote in English: 'Over seven hills, which are as many points of observation where the most magnificent panoramas may be enjoyed, the vast irregular and many-coloured mass of houses that constitute is scattered'. Here are two versions, by Iain Watson and Richard Zenith, of Pessoa's most personal work, *The Book of Disquiet*. In the section Watson entitles 'Our Lady of Silence', the narrator's disgust for women in the flesh is made plain. Ironic that he should write years before Dior: 'You occupy the gaps in my thoughts and the interstices of my feelings. How I long to create the New Look with which I could see you, the New Thoughts and Feelings thanks to which I could think and feel you . . . If I was certain of your existence, I would construct a religion on the dream of loving you.' This book, the matrix of Pessoa's heteronymous poetry, is written by a persona: in the poet's own words, 'I was another', an obvious allusion to Rimbaud. Watson, quoting the late Italian novelist Antonio Tabucchi (who was a friend of Paula's, lived in Portugal and was Pessoa's Italian translator), writes that this is the 'I' found in Rilke's *Notebooks of Malte Laurids Brigge* and Valéry's *Monsieur Teste*. Augustus Young, currently working on a book about Rilke, disagrees, seeing Malte as Rilke's alter ego: 'Malte, c'est moi'.

Here too is *A Centenary Pessoa*, whose poetry section is translated by Keith Bosley. The book opens with a famous essay by Octavio Paz which contains a riff on Pessoa's name (person in Portuguese), itself derived from the Roman word for mask, persona. Richard Zenith has edited *Poesia Inglesa*, a collection of Pessoa's English poems. Here the attitude to women's bodies suggests a troubled and repressed but basically heterosexual man rather than the homosexual Pessoa is sometimes perceived to be. *The Surprise of Being*, translated by James Greene and Clara de Azevedo Mafra, contains poems Pessoa wrote under his own name: these, say the translators, are where 'he is most "at home", that is to say, estranged'. However, Z. Kotowicz, in his book on Pessoa, *Voices of a Nomadic Soul*, reminds us that Pessoa said 'Pessoa' was a disciple of Alberto Caeiro. *Fernando Pessoa* by Maria José de Lancastre, introduced by Tabucchi (whose novel *Requiem* incarnates Pessoa just as *Pereira Declares* is one of the great Lisbon novels), is an evocative iconography of the poet. There are photos of Ophelia, his only known love, a relationship which lasted several months, with two phases separated by a nine-year interval. Paula phoned me one morning in high dudgeon to say that a Portuguese television poll, to discover the greatest Portuguese person, was won by Antonio Salazar, with forty per cent of the votes. The old fascist who, according to Henry Kissinger and Stephen Spender, was not a proper dictator compared to Franco, casts a long shadow. Tell that to the tortured in the Pide jails. Fernando Pessoa and Luís de Camoens were among the ten finalists in the poll.

ITALY

Giacomo Leopardi, Primo Levi, Lucio Piccolo and Eugenio Montale

Apart from Dante, Italian literature, on my shelves, begins with Giacomo Leopardi, a recent passion. Primo Levi once translated a few lines for me and enclosed them with a letter. This led me led me to write an essay on the links between Levi, Byron and Leopardi. Here are the *Canti* in versions by Jonathan Galassi and J. G. Nicholls, and translations of his *Operette Morali* and *Pensieri*. Bonnefoy too has translated him. The *Zibaldone*, his major prose work, is shortly to be published in English. Sometimes sounding like Coleridge, sometimes like Hölderlin, Leopardi's work ('A sad and angry consolation', writes Geoffrey Hill in *The Triumph of Love*) bears traces of Dante and Rousseau. This is a giant figure, quite evidently an influence on later generations of Italian poets, and I wish I were a better linguist, able to hear his music at least to the extent that I hear the music of French poetry and, to a lesser extent, Russian and Hebrew poetry. Italy, after all, has been a serious component of my *imaginaire* (I know that 'imaginary' exists as a noun but it sounds wrong) thanks to opera (second only to Russian opera) and

Renaissance painting. There is, however, only so much time in the life of a disorganized go-between, over-extended attendant lord, serial sidetracker and master digressionary.

Back in 1975, the poet Ruth Feldman of Cambridge, Massachusetts, sent me out of the blue her translations (some made with Brian Swann) of Primo Levi's earlier collected poems *Shema*. Levi was already a hero of mine. Many years before, Feldman, a young and childless widow, had embarked on a lifelong love affair with Italy and I have a bundle of old-fashioned air letters sent from the Hôtel de la Ville in Rome each summer. She would snort at Umberto Eco's possibly facetious remark: 'Italy is not an intellectual country. On the subway in Tokyo everybody reads. In Italy, they don't. Don't evaluate Italy from the fact that it produced Raphael and Michelangelo.' The Levi translations constitute her most important legacy, though she also translated books by Marguerita Guidacci and co-translated with Brian Swann books by Vittorio Bodoni, Andrea Zanzotto, Rocco Scotellaro and Lucio Piccolo—Sicilian aristocrat and cousin of Guiseppe di Lampedusa.

In 1954, the unknown Piccolo sent his poems to Eugenio Montale. Feldman told me that Montale, to whom every wannabe poet sent work, was about to throw the package—on which, according to John Pilling's account in his very readable book on modern European poets, Montale had had to pay excess postage—into the wastepaper basket, but was sufficiently intrigued by the old-fashioned handwriting on the envelope to open it. The rest is history or rather poetry. The world-famous Italian poet arranged for the 'young' and unknown poet to be invited to a literary conference. According to another account, he and the world were expecting an 'ephebe in blue jeans' (do we think this squares with the handwriting on the envelope? The jeans would have had to be imported from the USA at that date, according to my expert, Peter Golding), and were astonished to find a man of courteous disposition, the great man's contemporary, and so knowledgeable about poetry that Montale found it almost ridiculous to be chairing the reading. Piccolo was accompanied by a manservant and by someone introduced as the Prince of Lampedusa, who had written the accompanying letter to Montale. (No connection with *The King of Lampedusa*, a famous Yiddish play based on the real-life exploits during World War II of Sergeant Syd Cohen.)

Apparently this bizarre and wonderful occasion triggered Lampedusa's own creativity, for he went home and, aged nearly sixty, snapped out of a long depression and wrote *The Leopard*; this wonderful novel was published posthumously, in 1957. One thing is certain: Piccolo, who had corresponded with Yeats when he was twelve years old, knew what he was doing when he took his chances with Montale. He is a strange, cool, intellectual, existential and 'neo-baroque' (Pilling's word) lyric poet. According to the critic Guido Cambon, Piccolo's 'non-historical stance matches Lampedusa's entropic sense of time'. In Piccolo's own words, 'If the fleeting is dismay / eternity is terror' and '. . . all around outside / night is still as a memory / of forever . . .' As for Montale himself, I have four volumes as listed in the bibliography.

A brief word about other Italian poets on my shelves: readers of Ruth Feldman and Brian Swann's translation of Zanzotto will be intrigued by the similarities and differences to be found in Anthony Barnett's translations of the same poet. Montale's peers were Ungaretti and Quasimodo. Ungaretti was the only one not to get the Nobel Prize. Everyone can list the geniuses who didn't get it: James Joyce, etc., and the minor figures who did: Sully Prudhomme, etc. Everyone knows that these days it helps to have appropriate politics. Everyone knows that it is essential to have been translated into English or French and not to have slept with the wife of an influential member of the committee. Like Montale, if not Quasimodo, Ungaretti ticks all the boxes of a winner, save that he had a passing flirtation with fascism. This undoubtedly did for Céline and Pound. 'Enough of the Prize!' say I hypocritically, having earlier boasted of Menard's winners.

GREECE

Constantine Cavafy and Homer

I bought my first Constantine Cavafy translation in Paris in 1964: Marguerite Yourcenar's prose versions, *Presentation critique de Constantin Cavafy*, published in 1958. Her long introduction suggests, between the lines, an empathic solidarity with the gay poet. Homosexuality would be legalized in the UK in 1967, as part of Harold Wilson's enduring social liberalization in several areas. The liberalization, discussed later, was perhaps his major legacy along with the Open University. In France, legalization of homosexuality would have to wait until Mitterrand in 1982, hence Yourcenar's indirection. Cavafy was a favourite poet of mine for years but latterly I have been reading him less. Early passions are not always easy to reconstruct. I wrote one or two poems in the manner of the Alexandrian poet and if they were the apples, then the tree was planted in the soil of my reading. Here are *Poems by Cavafy* translated by John Mavrogodorto, *Complete Poems of Cavafy* translated by Rae Dalven with an introduction by Auden ('Cavafy has three principal concerns: love, art, and politics in the original Greek sense', i.e. the city rather than the entire country), and Edmund Keeley and Philip Sherrard's versions, *Collected Poems*, which are the best. Keeley joined forces with George Savidis to translate the book-length *Axion Esti* by the Cretan poet Odysseus Elytis, born in Herakleia, where I met the self-proclaimed 'last Jew on Crete', owner of a jewellery shop near the airport. Yannis Ritsos' *Selected Poems* was translated by the late editor of the Penguin series it appeared in, Nikos Stangos, a beautiful gay poet, his looks immortalized in Kitaj's 'Smyrna Greek (Nikos)' where Nikos poses, appropriately enough, as Cavafy. I have everything available in English, verse and prose, by George Seferis, one of my favourite poets in any language and discussed elsewhere in this book.

Two of my oldest and most battered books are the *Iliad* and *Odyssey* in E. V. Rieu's old Penguin Classics versions. On the flyleaf of *The Iliad*, my father in his distinctive hand has written my name, which I tried to copy. In my hand is information about another book: 'Going to the Headmaster's Study' by 'O. Crikey', evidence that I read Billy Bunter as well as Greek classics. Although a swift comparison of Rieu with Martin Hammond's later translations gives Hammond the edge, I shan't forget the thrill of reading Rieu when I was nine or ten: Ajax, Diomedes, Hephaestus, Poseidon, Menelaus and other names still trip off the tongue. Naturally I supported the Greeks against the Trojans, just as I supported the redskins against the cowboys. Here are Nikos Kazantzakis' *Odyssey*, his modern verse sequel to Homer, translated by Kimon Friar, and Josephine Balmer's translations of Sappho, *Poems and Fragments*, as well as those by Mary Barnard, who was described to me by George Steiner as a 'modish imagist'. Nonetheless, her version of 'Lament for a Maidenhead' is beautiful. *The Poems of Meleager* is an instructive, intelligent and, indeed, exemplary book: it contains verse translations by Peter Whigham and literal translations, notes and an introduction by the book's publisher Peter Jay. Enter this book, and you step into an authentic workshop of poetry translation.

AUSTRIA, GERMANY AND HOLLAND

Erich Fried, Hans Magnus Enzensberger, Johannes Bobrowski, Horst Bienek, Judith Herzberg

Herbert Kuhner, the Viennese remigré (a word he may have coined), has been an indefatigable interpreter of the literature of the country he returned to with his mother after the war, despite profound misgivings. In his bilingual anthology of Jewish Austrian poetry (*If the Walls between Us Were Made of Glass*), we find his own poem 'Remigration', where he compares the unpleasantnesses he experienced in Vienna as an adult to his mother's ordeal when ordered to scrub pro-Austria slogans from the pavement in 1938. Understandably, he squeezes Celan into the anthology even though the poet was born in 1920 and his Austro-Hungarian birthplace in the Bukovina region, now part of Ukraine, no longer existed as such after 1918. One of the Celan poems features, in apposition to 'despair', the phrase 'black earth', a key image in Mandelstam and Tsvetayeva (see later in this book). Kuhner has made many translations in a long life as a go-between, despite official and unofficial opposition in unreconstructed Viennese circles. An unusual book is his *Hawks and Nightingales*, poems by Burgenland Croat émigrés, a large number of whom live in Austria, and also in Slovakia and Hungary. And so the patchwork quilt of Europe has continued, interwoven and overlapping, for centuries, told in word and image by poets and painters, translated by devoted and talented intermediaries like Harry Kuhner.

German-language literatures have always interested me, in part because of the Jewish nexus, which has meant that with my poor Yiddish I have also acquired a poor knowledge of German, in part because so much of the best work has been translated by poets equal to the task, not least Michael Hamburger and Christopher Middleton, two of the tutelars of this book. Above all, German is, by a bitter and appropriate irony, the language of the greatest European poet since World War II, Paul Celan. I have here the anthologies which educated me in those early years: Hamburger and Middleton's *Modern German Poetry*, Hamburger's *East German Poetry* and Middleton's *German Writing Today*. Other books on my shelves include *Eve Blossom Has Wheels*, an anthology of German love poems translated by Keith Bosley, better known as a master of Finnish translation, and individual poets: Heinz Winfried Sabais translated by Ruth and Matthew Mead, Sarah Kirsch translated by Wendy Mulford and Anthony Vivis, and Hans-Jurgen Heise translated by Ewald Osers. On my shelves and hence in this book, the same names turn up for each language: thus, in German, Hamburger, Rothenberg, Middleton, Kuhner, Waldrop, Vivis, Mead, Osers, Constantine—I salute the go-betweens. Another is Joachim Neugroschel, whose translations include *Mausoleum* by that powerhouse of poetic intelligence, Hans Magnus Enzensberger: the 'Thirty Seven Ballads from the History of Progress' in this book tell the lives of influential figures like Frederick Chopin, Charles Babbage, Charles Fourrier and Alexander von Humboldt. I need to pay more attention to these poems, what with my interest in collage and documentary techniques. Here too is Enzensberger's *Selected Poems*, translated by Hamburger, Rothenberg and the poet himself.

The Viennese-born Londoner Erich Fried was a harsh, powerful and astute poetic commentator on the daily insults and injuries to common decency and historical truth that regularly turn up in the press and from the mouths of government spokesmen. His poems are laser-tipped (or taser lipped) attacks on the enemy, like those of a younger man influenced by him, Herbert Kuhner. Fried, translated by Georg Rapp, is often formulaic, reminding me of Guillevic and other prolific and fluent poets with acute powers of condensed observation:

'Answer'
Someone
came to the stones
and said:
Be human
The stones
replied:

We are not
hard enough
yet

A wondrous poet, out of the German lyric tradition from Hölderlin to Trakl, was the East German Johannes Bobrowski, born on what were the borders of Lithuania and Germany. After action on the Eastern front in World War II, he became a prisoner of war in Russia. Bobrowski has affinities with two poets I published at Menard Press, Rudolf Langer and Walter Helmut Fritz, but sets his poems more deeply in a particular landscape, in its history and mythology: the old Roman province of Sarmatia reconfigured by a poetic imagination, 'stretching from the Vistula and the Danube to the Volga and the Caucasus' (Matthew Mead in *Shadow Lands*, an expanded version of *Shadow Land*, see below). This was no reactionary project. Bobrowski was a communist and a Christian who had fought unwillingly. Jews appear here and there in his work; he witnessed round-ups in Lithuania and Poland; he knew very well what Hitler's final solution was about. Russia too is a presence, Christianity a lodestar. Rivers, villages and churches people his work. Horst Bienek, another fine poet who was in a post-war forced-labour camp, shares a *Selected Poems* with Bobrowski, both poets beautifully translated by Ruth and Matthew Mead. Among the writers Bobrowski addresses are Else Lasker-Schuler and Gertrude Kolmar: in the eponymous poem about the latter in *Shadow Land*, he writes:

But the dark time
is not dead, my speech
wanders and is
rusty with blood.

In 'Always to be Named', he writes:

Signs, colours, it is
a game, I am thinking
it may not end
well

'The Word *Man*', the last poem in *Shadow Lands*, perhaps Bobrowski's final poem, chimes with Fried's 'Answer'. It ends:

I hear the word, I hear
the word often here, I can
name those who use it, I can
begin to.

Where there is no love
do not utter the word.

Horst Bienek's prison poems would certainly receive a quiet assent from
Andrei Sakharov:

Only night keeps you
Waiting for her.
She is choosing
Her darkest dress—
You will die soon.

There is an echo of Primo Levi in the short poem 'Afterwards':

The grey summer is behind us
The hour of shootings
        farewell
        forgetting
Now we can say the simplest things
Simply again

Five years younger than Anne Frank, Judith Herzberg too was hidden in
Amsterdam during the war but, unlike Anne, survived. Here are her *Zeepost*
and *Beemdgras*. Dutch is easier than German to sight-read, and when there is
an English translation one has the pleasurable sensation of reading a poem
in the original with more understanding than is in fact the case. I was in touch
with Herzberg while working on my anthology of Jewish poets, *Voices in the
Ark*. Jewish poet was easier to define than Jewish poem: for our purposes a
Jewish poet was not defined in strict religious terms but someone who said
they were Jewish or, if one could still ask them, would say they were.
Pasternak, we decided, would not have wanted to be in the anthology, whereas
Mandelstam would. Joseph Brodsky agreed to be in, so did Bob Dylan, except
his agent asked for too much money.

What is a Jewish poem? The question is discussed at greater length in the Jewish section of the present book. On 13 December 1976, Judith Herzberg wrote to me in English: 'Now that I have a free moment, I am looking through my books to see which poems could qualify as Jewish. And am shocked. All of them in a way. Because, knowing my own background (as I do), none of them is completely without undertones that point at peace (and so at war), at having a blonde daughter . . .' Unfortunately, the rest of the letter is missing. In a second letter (22 March 1977), she told me that she was enclosing some rough translations: 'Can you please return these to me some time, as I have no copies? I'm not entirely unpleased with the way they look now. Maybe you can touch them up a little where they're really terrible English. Do you think they're Jewish? I wish I could say yes.' It turned out that my friend Shirley Kaufman was translating Herzberg, which suited me as Howard Schwartz and I already had plenty on our plate putting together what became a fourteen-hundred-page book. Eventually Kaufman published a selection of Herzberg's work under the title *But What*, with beautiful poems like 'Yiddish', whose sixteen lines begin:

My father sang the songs
his mother used to sing,
to me who half understood

I sing the words again
nostalgia flutters in my throat
nostalgia for what is mine.

Strictly speaking, this is a Dutch poem made over into English. However, while the fifth line quoted contains a universal statement, the sixth line is a strong assertion of personal identity, and gives it a Jewish tinge. [Later: while giving me permission to quote the letter, Judith Herzberg writes that she no longer agrees with her old views and refers me to a letter by Richard Feynman to Tina Levitan (February 1967) which you can find online. It may be that my prior instinct to include Herzberg outside the Jewish section was correct. Sadly, it is too late to discuss Feynman here. Suffice it to say, I do not think his (and Herzberg Two's) views are incompatible with Herzberg One. It was generous of Judith to agree to publication and perhaps inevitable that I would give myself the last word.]

CENTRAL AND EASTERN EUROPE

Hungary: János Pilinszky and others

I bought Willis Barnstone's *Modern European Poetry* in 1965, in fact modern West European poetry. This was three or four years before my exposure to Central and Eastern Europe, which became a major concern in the late 1960s and early 1970s, under the influence of Hughes, Silkin, Weissbort and Alvarez.

Hungary has a particular redolence and resonance for me, because Budapest was a staging post in my grandfather's travels from East Galicia to London in the early years of the twentieth century. Whenever she visits her native Budapest from Geneva, my friend Judit Kiss emails me that she has spotted Joseph Rudolf in a side street or on the river: one of his jobs was as a steward on a boat plying between Vienna and Budapest. Hungary's great poets include János Pilinszky, whose tone and demeanour left a lasting effect on all who met him, a way of being that is evident in his work: see *Selected Poems* (translated by Ted Hughes and Janos Csokits), *Crater*, differently translated by the poet and publisher Peter Jay, who '[brings] the English closely towards the poet's Hungarian' and the recent *Passio* translated by Clive Wilmer and George Gömöri. Pilinszky, a Christian existentialist like Dostoevsky and Van Gogh according to Wilmer, sometimes reminds me of Hans Werner Cohn, a Menard author. Style does not come plainer than Pilinszky's or Cohn's. Here is a complete poem of Pilinszky's from *Crater*, and not the shortest:

'Relationship'
What a silence, when you are here. What
a hellish silence.
You sit and I sit.
You lose and I lose.

Miklos Radnoti wrote poetry in an extreme situation, a forced march culminating in his murder. The poems were found in his pocket. Another major figure, Attila Jozsef, committed suicide in 1937. Here are *Selected Poems and Texts* translated by John Batki, and *Poems* translated by various hands, including Michael Hamburger. Hungarian is a language co-translators have to take entirely on trust, so opaque is it to the English ear, whereas with

Romance, Germanic and Slavonic languages, one has a sense, rightly or wrongly, of access to the music of the poet's voice and the verbally incarnated *pathétique* of his or her inner life (I am trying to avoid the word soul).

Czechoslovakia: Vladimir Holan and Miroslav Holub

The poetry of Czechoslovakia was another of the worlds that came to our attention in the flowering of poetry translation that took place from the mid-1960s. One of the most important and prolific go-betweens was my old friend the late Ewald Osers. He translated from several languages, mainly Czech, including three volumes of Jaroslav Seiffert, as well as Antonin Bartusek's *The Aztec Calendar and Other Poems*. Bartusek's title sequence is a powerful parable reflecting the helplessness of individuals in our own time. Ondra Lysohorsky wrote in Lachian, a dialect halfway between Czech and Polish, and in German; his *Selected Poems* are translated by Osers and others, including W. H. Auden no less. Osers also translated Miroslav Holub's *On the Contrary*, while George Theiner and Ian Milner shared the responsibility of translating his *Selected Poems*. Holub, an immunologist by profession, wrote wise and playful poems which made a huge impact on a generation of British readers and writers of poetry. His presence was as vital as that of Vasko Popa and Zbigniew Herbert. Reflecting glory, I once introduced myself to him as 'Yves Bonnefoy's translator' and he smiled, as Tàpies did not when, many years later, I played the same card at the opening of his museum in Barcelona. Finally, Jarmila and Ian Milner translated *Selected Poems* of Vladimir Holan, some of which are bleak indeed, written in the darkest years of Stalinist governance, if that is the right word. Thus, 'Ubi nullus ordo, sed perpetuus horror':

> To live is terrible since you have to stay
> with the appalling reality of these years.
> Only the suicide thinks he can leave by the door
> that is merely painted on the wall.
> There is not the slightest sign that the Comforter will come.
>
> In me the heart of poetry bleeds.

The provenance of the title is not explained. Bruce Ross Smith thinks the phrase has its origins in Job.x.21 (in the Vulgate), which crops up in both

Chaucer and Langland, and in Dante (*Purgatorio* ix). Did Milton have Job in mind when he evoked 'darkness visible'? From the 1946 Soncino translation:

> Before I go whence I shall not return,
> Even to the land of darkness and of the shadow of death;
> A land of darkness, as a darkness itself;
> A land of the shadow of death, without any order,
> And where the light is as darkness.

Poland: *Zbigniew Herbert and Tadeusz Rozewicz*

I first met Zbigniew Herbert at the Struga Poetry Festival in 1972. He presented my (then) wife with a small plastic witch on a string. I asked him if he was related to George Herbert. Whether in jest or mythologizing or possessing a smidgen of evidence, he said he was. We kept in touch through the 1970s when he lived in France and Germany. In 1980, encouraged by my friend Felek Scharf, I published *A Reading of Ashes*, Keith Bosley's translations of Jerzy Ficowski, a Polish Catholic poet obsessed with Jews and Gypsies, who later became the biographer of Bruno Schulz. I knew Ficowski was much admired by Herbert and I pestered the latter for a preface. Who, after all, had heard of Jerzy Ficowski? Zbigniew Herbert, on the other hand, was already a famous poet of European stature, at least in the relatively small circle of persons who bought poetry books. I remember phoning him in Paris, when his wife Katarzyna sympathized with me concerning his procrastination, and some time later in Berlin. Time was running out if a schedule was to be maintained. 'Hi Zbigniew, where's my Ficowski preface?' Silence as he registered who I was, and then: 'Anthony, I'm going home tomorrow morning?' Silence, as I registered the significance of this statement. 'I understand,' I replied, disappointed and reconciled to defeat. Within a few days, the preface arrived in an envelope postmarked Berlin. He must have written it there and then. That's what I call grace under pressure. What I had forgotten until I discussed the episode today with our mutual friend Marius Kociejowski was that I had phoned Zbigniew on New Year's Eve, 31.12.1980. We know this because he wrote a letter to Marius dated New Year's Eve, stating: 'in a few minutes I go home—direction Poland, Solidarnosc.' So he

271

posted or asked someone else to post letters to two of his friends in London and then returned home from exile to participate in the politics of revolt. Trust him to choose a symbolic date for a real return.

Here are Herbert's *Selected Poems* and *Report from the Besieged City*, both translated by John and Bogdana Carpenter. Elsewhere in this book, I have touched on his essays collected in *The Barbarian in the Garden*. He is a classic exemplar of that splendid synergistic tradition, the European poet/essayist (Osip Mandelstam, Yves Bonnefoy and Czesław Miłosz are other examples), a highly educated and intellectual writer, and in his case an offensive ironist, as it were, rather than a deployer of the defensive irony beloved of our own dear literary tradition. While not adopting a mythography of the eternal return, he nonetheless draws on political history and past literature to read the runes of our own time, its absurdity and squalor as well as, now and again, its dignity and nobility. It is not for nothing that one of his great poems is 'The Elegy of Fortinbras', a soliloquy addressed to Hamlet. Nor is it a coincidence that the poem is dedicated to C. M., that is, to Czesław Miłosz. The poem can be found in *The Penguin Book of Post-War Polish Poetry*, a vital anthology edited and translated by Miłosz, and also in *Polish Writing Today* edited by Celina Wieniewska, the late first wife of my friend Peter Janson Smith.

I write about Miłosz on other pages. On my desk now are this remarkable and prolific poet's translations of his friend Aleksander Wat's *Mediterranean Poems* (see too Wat's marvellous autobiography *My Century*, based on interviews with Miłosz) and Anna Swir's *Happy as a Dog's Tail*, with powerful lyric poems in the personae of three women: Felicia, Antonia and Stephanie. Aleksander Wat was born, like Herbert and my friend Piotr Rawicz, in L'wow, West Ukraine, a region strongly Polish in culture and language. 'A rental shop of dreamy happenings /or a second history of the world': this possibly deliberate echo of Bruno Schulz is from Miron Bialoszewski's *The Revolution of Things*, translated by Andrzej Busza and Bogdan Czaykowski, a small book I photocopied in its entirety for Lee Harwood.

Gone AWOL from my shelves is the work of that ultra-minimalist Polish poet, Tadeusz Rozewicz ('they forget / that modern poetry / is a struggle for breath'), but he's in the two anthologies mentioned earlier. He has affinities too with Hans Werner Cohn, Celan and Pilinszky. Rozewicz pared his poetry down to the bone because, as Miłosz writes in his anthology note on the poet: 'he hated art as an offence to human suffering' and therefore 'invented his own type of anti-poem stripped of "devices" such as meter, rhyme and even, most often, of metaphors, and limited to the simplest words'. Stephen Spender, in his introduction to the *Selected Poems* of Abba Kovner and Nelly Sachs, quotes Rozewicz: 'I cannot understand that poetry should survive when the men who created that poetry are dead. One of the premises and incentives for my poetry is a disgust with poetry. What I had revolted against was that it had survived the end of the world, as though nothing had happened.'

The Balkans: Vasko Popa, Miodrag Pavlovic, Ivan Lalic
How easy it is to forget, in the light of events in the Balkans over the last twenty years, that the part of Europe once known as Yugoslavia meant so much to Western socialists: 'Neither Washington nor Moscow', we used to say. Tito held the country together as a member of the non-aligned movement with great skill and toughness. I forget now if I met Vasko Popa for the first time at the Struga Poetry Festival in 1972 or a year or two later in London. His magnificent *Collected Poems* is prefaced by a poem, dated 5 June 1981, which he wrote overnight at the Cambridge Poetry Festival on learning of the death of his main translator, that modest yet scholarly and authoritative Oxford philologist, Anne Pennington, who had an ear for his music. The next day his publisher Peter Jay, Daniel Weissbort and I sat at a cafe table and produced the following version together, first published as a *MenCard* and then in *TLS* before coming to rest in *Collected Poems*:

'Anne Pennington'
Until her last breath she enlarges
Her Oxford house
Built in Slavonic
Vowels and consonants

She polishes the corner-stones
Until their Anglo-Saxon shine
Begins to sing

273

Her death is like a short breath-stop
Under the distant lime trees of her friends

My fondness for this poem, my nostalgia for the circumstances of its creation, my pleasure in the translation by three friends, probably with help from Popa in French, all feed an unrequited dream of fellowship in or through poetry. Vasko Popa told me later that he had stolen or borrowed Menard's idea of poetry postcards for his own series edited in Belgrade. Daniel, he said to our mutual friend, 'qu'as-tu fait de tes lions?' What have you done with your lions? The answer, I suspect, is: 'translated them'. Anne Pennington also translated (with Andrew Harvey) Popa's colourful anthology of 'stories, songs, spells, proverbs and riddles', *The Golden Apple*. ('He who listens to everyone does wrong, he who listens to no-one does worse.') I particularly cherish Popa's first book in English, *Selected Poems*. Later I wrote a poem for the emperor priest, which is the translation of his name. A major aspect of my literary and human formation has been my education by the works of those poets I was privileged to meet: Herbert, Popa, Pilinszky, Holub, Stanescu and others of that remarkable generation of East European poets who were teenagers or very young adults during World War II.

Two other major poets of former Yugoslavia are Ivan Lalic and Miodrag Pavlovic. Pavlovic was one of the significant figures I met in the glory days of the 1960s and 1970s, or so they seemed to a youngster wanting to know what was going on and, better still, wanting to be part of the scene. Pavlovic's *The Slavs beneath Parnassus* was translated by the late Bernard Johnson (editor of *New Writing in Yugoslavia*), another of the go-betweens performing on that stage. While Pavlovic and Popa were both deeply consonant with the history and mythology of their land, Popa was the more playful poet, with the lightest of touches. His poems work best in sequences, while individual poems of Pavlovic have a weight which ballasts a single poem. The work of Lalic too, whom I discovered later through the remarkable translations of Francis Jones (thus, *The Works of Love*), was instinct with the myths and history of his region and, in the words of Richard Berengarten, 'epitomises the Balkan way of being, perceiving and experiencing', and this even after the breakup of Yugoslavia. In the case of Lalic, it is clear from a reading of his work that the concept of region covers more ground than that of the regions of Popa and Pavlovic. In a poem like 'Mnemosyne', Lalic sounds like Seferis, although the Serbian works in a fuller throttle than the Greek poet. Lalic embraces the Mediterranean in a way that Popa and Pavlovic, broad and deep as they are, do not.

HEBREW POETRY (INCLUDING YIDDISH)

'The Jewish Time Bomb'

On my desk is a piece of stone engraved *amen*,
one survivor of the thousands and thousands of fragments from
    graves
in Jewish cemeteries. And I know that all the shards
are filling up the biggest Jewish time bomb
together with other splinters, fragments from the Tables of the Law,
filling it with broken altars and crosses, rusty crucifix nails,
and broken bones, broken holy vessels, broken houseware,
and shoes, glasses, artificial limbs, dentures,
and empty canisters of lethal poison: all these
are filling up the Jewish time bomb until the end of days.
And even though I know about these things and about the end of
    days,
this stone on my desk gives me tranquility.
It is a stone of truth left to its own devices,
wiser than any philosopher's stone, a stone from a fractured grave
and this stone is absolutely perfect,
this stone testifies to all the things that have ever existed
and all the things that will exist for ever, an Amen stone and love.
Amen, amen and may this be His will.

Yehuda Amichai

> (his final poem, translated by Miriam Neiger-Fleischmann and
> Anthony Rudolf)

Yehuda Amichai (and translators)

It is a peculiarity of Hebrew that only poetry and modern prayer books are printed with the vowels, that is, the dots and dashes underneath the letters.

275

Without these I am lost. So no Hebrew prose for me, although I can take a stab at Yiddish prose, always written in Hebrew letters, because I recognize the Germanic substratum. But I can read Hebrew poetry with the help of a dictionary. It is interesting to compare *A Poet's Bible* and *Job Speaks* by David Rosenberg with the translation of *Song of Songs* by Chana Bloch and Ariel Bloch. Rosenberg's are audacious and radical workings of this great love poem. The translator, as befits a former student of Robert Lowell, has produced imitations, whereas the Blochs, it seems to me, have brought a marriage of true minds—he the Hebrew scholar and she the poet of *The Secrets of the Tribe*—to the special work of co-translation, and produced a superb version, in a handsome book with impeccable notes. Combining the roles of poet and Hebrew scholar, Marcia Falk, a correspondent and long-distance colleague in the far-off days when I was editing *Voices in the Ark*, is closer to David Rosenberg, treating the *Song* as a collection of lyrics, and arguing the case in a lengthy and authoritative essay. My inscribed copy of Stephen Mitchell's fine version of Job, *Into the Whirlwind*, has his handwritten corrections. It is impossible to disagree with or improve on the wording of the conclusion to his Afterword: 'Literal translations of *Job* may convey its sense more or less accurately, but no literal translation can hope to embody the grandeur and pulsating urgency of its style. In trying to make *Job* into a living poem, my primary obligation has been to the rhythms and images in English. I have translated closely when possible, freely when necessary; and have not hesitated to improvise, on those few occasions when less drastic methods seemed inadequate.'

There are many volumes of Yehuda Amichai in English, a man who secreted poetry endlessly, like Pablo Neruda and Allen Ginsberg. *Amen* was translated by the author with Ted Hughes; *Selected Poems* is edited by Hughes and Weissbort, *Selected Poetry* by Chana Bloch and Stephen Mitchell; Menard's contribution, *Travels of a Latter-Day Benjamin of Tudela*, is translated by Ruth Nevo. Hughes tells us in his introduction to *Selected Poems* that Amichai 'is the poet whose books I still open most often, most often take on a journey, most often return to when the whole business of writing anything natural, real and satisfying seems impossible'. Other volumes include the *Selected Poems* translated by Assia Gutmann and Harold Schimmel, with an introduction by Michael Hamburger. Amichai and Hamburger were both born in Germany in 1924, with Amichai among the minority of German Jews who went to Palestine, and indeed a member of the minority of the minority who were religious. He was a melancholy and funny man whom I met for the first time at an early Poetry International in London. We got on well and became friends. Years later, when I interviewed him for Radio Three, I was struck by his comment that Israeli/Hebrew poetry should be thought of as a Mediterranean sibling to Greek and Italian poetry. This was his educated and hopeful alternative to the dialectical readings of Israel's literary culture in relation to Judaism or to the Jewish diaspora or to Arabic/Muslim poetry. He was sensitive to the issues involved in the conflict with the Palestinians, and proved it in poems. He understood the Palestinian hurt and empathized with them in their dispossession.

The attitude to translation embodied in *Amen* and in Hughes' introduction, could be described as minimal: 'what I wanted to preserve above all was the tone and cadence of Amichai's voice speaking in English, which seems to me marvellously true to the poetry, in these renderings.' This possibility, even this reality, has to be linked to an earlier comment in the same introduction: 'What he has in common with Herbert, Holub and Popa, is a language beyond verbal language, a language of images which operates with the complexity and richness of hieroglyphs.' The bringing together of these four poets reminds me of that halcyon period—the late 1960s through the early 1970s—when *MPT*, Penguin Modern European Poets, Anvil, Carcanet and, in a small way, Menard began acting as conduits and triggers for poets seeking asylum in the English language, without the translations serving as straitjackets.

Yehuda Amichai, Leah Goldberg and Robert Friend

Leah Goldberg's *Selected Poems* is one of my favourite Menard books: lyrics by a major Hebrew poet of the twentieth century commensurately rendered by Robert Friend, a gay poet whose best translations were of women—Leah Goldberg, and also from Menard, Ra'hel's *Flowers of Perhaps*. Both books have specially written introductions by Yehuda Amichai, better known in the UK than the two women poets and their translator. The Goldberg book contains

Gershom Scholem's funeral eulogy to her, published against his wishes, although he raised no objections afterwards: I like to think he understood that his presence added lustre to an already lustrous book. Indeed, my action may have intuited his (non-)reaction; intuition is a valuable weapon in a publisher's armoury, but one to be deployed sparingly, for it is no defence against illegality. Robert Friend also translated Gabriel Preil, a great Hebrew poet of the Diaspora, and Natan Alterman, one of the most popular of all Hebrew poets, whose work, like Ra'hel's, was often set to music.

The Poetry of Survival, Daniel Weissbort's important anthology of the poetry of post-war Central and Eastern Europe contains, along with Vasko Popa, Zbigniew Herbert, Czesław Miłosz, Paul Celan and other expected figures, three Israeli poets: Yehuda Amichai and Natan Zach (both born in Berlin) and Dan Pagis, born, like Celan, in the Bukovina. On a visit to Israel long ago, I bumped into Zach (whom I'd known in London) at the entrance to the grand Bahai temple in Haifa, close to where he lives. *The Countries We Live In* is a new edition of Peter Everwhine's fine translations of Zach. I recall the last night of my most recent visit to Israel, back in 1995: Friend gave a goodbye party for me, to which Amichai came. Down the road, in Mishkenot Sheananim, there was a memorial meeting for the poet, Carmi. We had been friends years earlier, but we didn't see eye to eye on various matters, although we had made up. Nor did he and Amichai get on. Not being bilocatory, I could not attend the memorial meeting. Here, however, are books by this true poet of love and loss, *The Brass Serpent* translated by Dom Moraes, *Somebody like You* translated by Stephen Mitchell, and *At the Stone of Losses* translated by Grace Schulman. *Voices of Israel*, edited by one of Isaac Rosenberg's three biographers, Joseph Cohen, contains useful interviews with Amichai and Carmi, as well as three major Hebrew novelists, Oz, Yehoshua and Appelfeld.

Yiddish

It is odd that my two friends with the best knowledge of Yiddish, apart from Claude Vigée and since the death of A. C. Jacobs, are both Canadian poets of distinction: Sharon Nelson and Seymour Mayne (see Mayne's anthology of Jewish Canadian poetry *Jerusalem*). More significant is the fact that Nelson and Mayne are children of immigrants rather than grandchildren. Vigée's

Yiddish is Rhenish, perhaps the ur-Yiddish, whereas the two Canadians' Yiddish, like mine, is the eastern mutation of this wonderful lingua franca, and it contains Slavic words, unlike the Rhenish variety. *All My Young Years*, edited by Heather Valencia and introduced by Bill Fishman, the Grand Duke of the East End, contains the Yiddish poetry written in Weimar Germany of Avram Nochum Stencl, the Polish-born poet who ended up in the Englisher shtetl Whitechapel. There Stencl edited his magazine *Loshn un Lebn* (Language and Life) and there he sold me a copy outside the public library where Isaac Rosenberg had studied and my uncle Jack, now nearly a hundred and one, met my aunt Fan, my mother's sister, at the beginning of their eighty-four-year relationship. The library is now part of the redesigned Whitechapel Gallery. Fishman writes that Stencl was 'the last of the dreamers of the ghetto'. The translations by Haike Beruria Wiegand and Stephen Watts are, fortunately, a great improvement on earlier efforts by others.

ARABIC AND PERSIAN POETRY
Abdullah al-Udhari

Among the earliest Menard publications were three poorly printed pamphlets by Abdullah al-Udhari, a much-loved denizen of the Poetry Society in the early 1970s and now resident in Italy, one of which may have been the first anthology of modern Arab poetry, *A Mirror for Autumn* (later expanded into *Modern Poetry of the Arab World*). The others were his anthology of classical Arabic poetry, *Fireflies in the Dark*, and his own poems, *Voice without Passport*. *Fireflies in the Dark* has a confident introduction, which ends: 'The fact that both Arabic and English belong to different language groups is of no significance, since translations deal with concepts and not with grammar. Moreover, the range of experiences and responses of poets, whatever their language might be, is the same.' Publishing the Arab anthology was to make a serious point at a time when I was embarking on a series of Hebrew books in translation. Many years later, al-Udhari's remarkable study, *The Arab Creation Myth*, was written and published in English. Isomorphic with Genesis and Gilgamesh, the text is the author's remarkable reconstruction from fragments of the pre-Islamic Arab Jahili Genesis story.

Omar Shakespear Pound

Omar Shakespear Pound, whom I knew a little in the old days, translated *Arabic and Persian Poems*, a fine collection introduced by Basil Bunting. He explains in his preface that he 'uses a few lines from one poem, a restatement of a point of view in another, a synthesis of two poems by an author elsewhere'. He even translates allusions 'to avoid the distraction of footnotes'. Thus, in a poem by the twelfth-century poet Anvari we find references to Claridges and Crufts. The epigraph to the book is from the Qur'an: 'Lo! Man was created anxious', which I can testify to, although not as a consequence of reading Omar's book. Bunting, in his preface, writes: 'Omar Pound has detected something that Moslem poetry has in common with some of ours. He makes it credible. He makes it a pleasure. By such steps, though they may be short and few, we can at least begin our Hajj.' Although some people won't approve of Omar Pound's versions, it should be noted that the introductions and notes reveal a scholar. You are allowed to break rules, provided you know them. Indeed, it is impossible to break rules if you don't.

Russian Literature

To the memory of R. A. D. and Theresa Ford

Introduction

When I was young, I loved playing 'the Volga Boatmen' on one of our 78 rpms, sung by Paul Robeson. Later, as a teenager, I read Fyodor Dostoevsky in my father's copies of Constance Garnett's translations, with their distinctive orange and yellow colours, among them *Crime and Punishment*, *The Idiot*, *The Possessed* and *The Brothers Karamazov*, one of two books Leo Tolstoy had with him when he died, according to George Steiner's *Tolstoy or Dostoevsky*, the other being the essays of Michel de Montaigne. I learnt too about the Russia of a promise—to liberate men and women from their chains—a promise that failed. I later interpreted this promise as a secularized version of Jewish messianism. I knew from quite early on that we, the capitalist West, tried to strangle the revolution at its birth, just as years later the insane rush to impose free markets on Russia in the early years of globalization showed that, in the minds of some, capitalism and democracy were one and the same thing. Today, without a radical social democratic reconstruction of the global economy and a successful fight against the depredations of climate change, the social and physical world will be damaged beyond repair.

This interest in Russia did not influence why I learnt the language. My first French lesson was at prep school; I took up Russian in the sixth form solely because the school told my father and mother at a parents' meeting that I had more chance of getting into Oxbridge with modern languages than with classics. Thus, destiny's sortilege sets its stamp on the future of a young person. Some of my Russian books date back to the single year I studied modern languages at Cambridge, after which I changed to social anthropology. Writing this book has enabled me to make my peace with social anthropology, in which I failed so dismally. I now study and learn from that fascinating literature without a parrot of self-destruction squawking into a receptive ear.

Lately, I have made a renewed attempt to read Russian literature in the original, which for some years I was able to do. Unlike my French, my Russian never became fluent enough to survive completely unscathed when unused, although on two trips to Ukraine in the early 1990s I was grateful for what I was able to summon up and deploy, without which I would have been in trouble. Of my books on the language, the most battered is Anna H. Semeonoff's *A New Russian Grammar*, which was what the cohort of seven— the first boys to study Russian at my school—used under the skilled aegis of our young teacher, John Davidson. Semeonoff's *Russian Syntax* I bought at Cambridge in 1962. My copy of *Die Russischen Verben*, by Edmund Daum and Werner Schenk, is inscribed July 1963, that is during the summer-vacation course I attended following my first year of anthropology studies: I was keeping up my Russian as well as French after officially abandoning modern languages. Here too is Lucien Tesnière's *Petit vocabulaire russe*, the title found by removing the protective wraparound cover supplied by Joseph Gibert's famous bookshop on the Boul' Mich.

Nineteenth-Century Classics

Alexander Pushkin

Studying Alexander Pushkin in the sixth form and in first-year university studies is tough. The rewards are fugitive and hard won to the point of failure. His genius calls for experience and sophistication whereas the major fiction writers (Anton Chekhov, Ivan Turgenev, etc.) speak to our lives in a way that even when young we can project onto and thrill to—perceptually, existentially, psychologically, historically and, sometimes, politically. It took performances, when I was older, of Pyotr Ilyich Tchaikovsky's *Eugene Onegin*,

Modest Moussorgsky's *Boris Godounov* and Thorold Dickinson's film *The Queen of Spades* before I could warm to and read with any enjoyment the great verse novel and other works of Pushkin, and even then I would dip into the original and read it against English translations, including Vladimir Nabokov's and Sir Charles Johnson's. My copy of Nabokov's four-volume edition of *Eugene Onegin* is somewhat battered because I lent it to Elaine Feinstein, who evidently put it to good use while writing her valuable biography of *Pushkin*. The Nabokov is, as she agrees, a wonderful and mad work by a magus. Almost two-thirds of it is the exhaustive, sometimes exhausting, commentary, the rest being the introduction, the original Russian, the supposedly literal translation and the ultra-detailed index: how appropriate for a study of a novel in which everybody *reads*. I open the commentary at random and light upon the word *toska* (chapter one, stanza thirty-four, line eight): 'Opyat toska, opyat liubov´', which he translates as 'Again the ache, again the love', a line Douglas Hofstadter in his *Eugene Onegin* translates miserably as 'Once more she's mare, once more I'm stud' . . . Referring to the different levels of meaning, Nabokov tells us that 'toska' conveys '. . . a sensation of great spiritual anguish . . . a dull ache of the soul . . . a vague restlessness, yearning . . . nostalgia, lovesickness . . . ennui, boredom'. Somewhere in there is the Portuguese word *saudade*, which is the predominant mood of fado. The Russian word cannot help but remind one of the opera heroine, but the name in Italian means a woman from Tuscany, not grief, although Puccini did set some of Pushkin's poems to music.

I picked up my second-hand Russian *Selected Prose* of Pushkin on a school trip to Moscow and Leningrad in 1959, the first such trip apparently, but Russian had only recently entered school curriculums. Translated, the inscription reads: 'To our dear son from papa and mama, 7/VIII-1948'. Somewhere in Moscow, perhaps, lives a boy, now doubtless in his late seventies, who once looked at these atmospheric illustrations, probably reproductions of old prints. Here too are Semeonoff's Russian edition of *The Captain's Daughter*, a Russian edition of *Boris Godounov*, and the Bradda Books school edition of *Eugene Onegin*. Apart from what I could find in anthologies, the first English-language volumes of Pushkin I have here are *Poems of Pushkin*, translated and self-published by Henry Jones, and *Poems*,

Prose and Plays of Alexander Pushkin, edited by A. Yarmolinsky, which I found in a second-hand bookshop in Paris long ago. Those were early days, before the modern revolution in poetry translation, and the translations are unacceptably poetic. A little better are versions by Walter Morison and Walter Arndt. Better still is Nancy Anderson's *The Little Tragedies*, and best of all is *Mozart and Salieri*, Antony Wood's versions of the little tragedies. John Fennell's Penguin *Pushkin*, with its prose translations, is invaluable. The title poem of D. M. Thomas' translations, *The Bronze Horseman and Other Poems*, is one I would once have liked to translate, but this version in blank verse, a change Thomas defends in his introduction (compare his ear to Arndt's), serves my purposes. I am no longer up for it, nor up to it. So at least I won't be up against it, unlike my friend Weissbort, who, now sadly ill, was working on his translation for some time and still recites parts of it off by heart.

Mikhail Lermontov (with Boris Pasternak)

Mikhail Lermontov was born on 2 October 1814, one hundred years to the day before my father's birth, such coincidences or rhymes being momentary stays against the nothingness of contingency and accident which constitute daily existence—so, trivial they are not, say I defensively. Here are Lermontov's eastern poem *The Demon*, and that strange novel, *A Hero of Our Time*. Boris Pasternak's great sequence, *My Sister, Life*, is dedicated to Lermontov, which must have confused Nabokov who admired Pasternak strictly as a poet and despised Lermontov, according to a letter he wrote Edmund Wilson. The first poem is written to the memory of Lermontov's demon. In the second poem, 'About these Verses', Pasternak asks the 'kiddies' what century it is outside and then speaks of smoking with Lord Byron and drinking with Edgar Alan Poe; this, I suspect, is a mediated image, a Baudelaire-inspired absinth fantasy. The poem concludes: 'I soaked my life in vermouth, / like my lips, like Lermontov's shudder', this final image surely bizarre yet indicative of the long journey Pasternak was about to take. His invocations are payments of an eternal due to romanticism but, with these extraordinary poems, contemporaneous with Apollinaire and cubism and other manifestations of the modernist spirit, Pasternak's journey would become one of the great adventures of the twentieth century. The syntax of the poems is complex, imbricated and difficult to untangle, a far cry or perhaps far whisper from the hard-won simplicity—following the years of Stalin and of working on translations—of the Zhivago poems. I tried to discuss the book with Valentina Polukhina, who fobbed me off with an unrepeatable fantasy of herself as a Roman empress and informed me that Elaine Feinstein borrowed *My Sister, Life* only the other day. Talk about synchronicity.

Ivan Turgenev

Turgenev, Dostoevsky, Chekhov, Gogol, Tolstoy: one could nourish one's sister, life, with a diet drawn from these writers. I read as much of the first three as I could over the years, and was much taken with Ivan Turgenev's exploration of politics and ideology, an exploration that did not go far enough for the Dostoevsky of *The Possessed*. If it would take a Dostoevsky to portray the depths of modern fundamentalism, it would take a Turgenev to characterize the contortions of so-called liberal hawks, the fig leaves of reaction. On my desk are editions of his fiction, Russian, English and bilingual.

The Diary of a Superfluous Man is the link in the chain between Turgenev's predecessors, namely Pushkin's Onegin, Lermontov's Pechorin and Dostoevsky's later underground or basement man. In *Politics and the Novel*, Irving Howe suggests that Julius Martov, called by Trotsky 'the Hamlet of democratic socialism' and taken seriously by Lenin as, in effect, the leader of the opposition, was 'the last of Turgenev's heroes, the last of the superfluous men'. Over the years a pattern in my Russian reading emerged: long novels were read in English or French; short prose, plays and poems in Russian, usually with a dictionary to hand. While I was researching my pamphlet *Byron's 'Darkness'*, a poetic masterpiece which predicts or appears to predict the effects of nuclear winter, I discovered that Turgenev himself had translated it. According to the notes to the collected works of Turgenev in Russian, which I consulted at the London School of Slavonic Studies, the Tsarist censors cut two passages on grounds of blasphemy. Turgenev had, as we would expect, studied Byron at school and was well read in English literature. According to Edmund Wilson, Nabokov was wrong in assuming Prosper

Mérimée (*Carmen*, etc.) knew no Russian and in effect ghosted his translations of Turgenev. He was coached by Turgenev himself.

In his introduction to Anatoly Nayman's *Remembering Akhmatova*, Joseph Brodsky wrote: 'A poet is always the product of his—that is, his nation's—language, to which living experiences are what logs are to fire. Of course, when both experience and language are Russian, the fire burns you even in translation.' Turgenev, one of whose *Poems in Prose* is 'The Russian Tongue', would have loved that:

> In days of doubt, in days of painful reflections on the various fates of my homeland, you alone are my support and mainstay, oh great, strong, true and free Russian tongue! How can one not fall into despair, seeing everything that is being done at home? But it is impossible to believe that such a language was not given to a great people!

It feels good to translate Russian again after several years. At the same time, I am cross with myself for having spent so much time not wandering down this pathway to a particular world of signs and wonders. The Russian grape is a heady experience and I call on myself, in the words of the prophet, to continue drinking from the fruit of this particular vine.

Fyodor Dostoevsky/Leo Tolstoy/Nikolai Gogol

Among the writers I read when young and have not (yet) reread, Dostoevsky remains a presence in my life, not only for his great novels but also for works like *Notes from Underground*, *The Double* and *The Dream of a Queer Fellow*, all three so resonant today. Dostoevsky spoke to and for the future. He knew us like no other nineteenth-century writer apart from the Melville of *Bartleby* and the Flaubert of *Bouvard and Pécuchet*. I read him with a great passion when I was still in high school and was moved years later to see the house where he lived in Florence, close to Browning's apartment, not far from the Pitti Palace. Even so, to reread him now would involve a decision not to read major English novels such as *Middlemarch* or *Our Mutual Friend* for the first time. I contributed a poem to *A Mutual Friend*, Peter Robinson's anthology for Charles Dickens' two-hundredth anniversary. My 'research' revealed that Dostoevsky interviewed Dickens: such nodes give pleasure.

[Later: I discovered that major modern biographers, Michael Slater and Claire Tomalin, say this interview never took place. Ah well, *se non é vero, é molto ben trovato*.]

There is no point in beating my breast about the masterpieces I may never read or reread. The important thing is to read as much as possible consonant with writing as well as one can, and with having a life off the page. The problem of rereading also arises with Tolstoy: I devoured *Anna Karenina* in Chicago in 1966, *War and Peace* a few years later. My copy of the latter contains the following dedication: 'To Ian Anthony Rudolf, in the hope that by the time you can understand this book War and Peace will only be a hypothetical discussion. From Uncle Leon, Dec. 1942. Henry and Esther, I don't think Ian will mind if you borrow this book.' I was three months old. Oddly enough, I have never been known as Ian, despite 'Ian Anthony' being on my birth certificate. Meanwhile, I have been indulging in a reverie about my parents: was one of them reading *War and Peace* on 2 February 1943, when the Germans were finally defeated at Stalingrad? That would be timely and appropriate. It was the moment when my cousins in hiding in West Ukraine knew that the allies would win the war. Had the other parent begun the book when the Germans began destroying the Warsaw Ghetto on 19 April, and finished it by the time Jewish resistance ended on 16 May? Were they in London or out of London at the farm near High Wycombe to which we were briefly evacuated, returning because it was too quiet? As for Gogol: *Dead Souls*, yes, and *The Government Inspector*, yes yes, but Molly Bloom's triple affirmative I reserve for his two stories, *The Greatcoat*, from which Dostoevsky said 'we all sprang', and *The Nose*, a proto-surrealist tale which only gets two pages in Nabokov's *Nikolai Gogol*.

Anton Chekhov

Chekhov's fiction and plays are centrally important to my *imaginaire*, and yet the present book gives far more space to writers who mean less to me. It will be clear by now that *Silent Conversations* is not exclusively concerned with the great masters (unlike, say, Harold Bloom's *Anatomy of Influence*) or the greatest works, among which that profound and beautiful play *Uncle Vanya* takes its place. My brush is broad, as befits a reverie, a network of association. Still, who would disagree that Anton Chekhov is up there with Jean Racine, William Shakespeare, Henrik Ibsen, Georg Büchner, Samuel Beckett and Tennessee Williams, among the great dramatists of the world? He is one of those writers whose very presence on this earth I rejoice in; his short life, centred on medicine, politics and literature, is a beacon in the dark and stormy sea of our existence. I have already touched on his work in my drama section and elsewhere: Among the elements I love is the apparent inconsequentiality of remarks which turn out to be choruses, comments on some change in a life, in a human destiny. 'By indirections find directions out' is truer of Chekhov than of any other great playwright since Shakespeare. Structure is function here, and the structural–functional gestalt, which is the play, is born from the matrix, distilled from the crucible, of artistic intelligence at full stretch: beauty always at the service of truth. Here in English are *Seven Short Novels*, including *My Life*, *Ward No. 6* and *In the Ravine*. And here is G. A. Birkett and G. C. Struve's edition of *Chekhov Stories* in Russian, some of which we studied with our sixth-form Russian teacher, John Davidson. In it, there survive in my handwriting several pages torn from a notebook, containing a long list of Russian words and their English translations, whose purpose was to be learnt off by heart on the tube to and from school. W. H. Bruford in *Chekhov* and David Magarshack in *Chekhov the Dramatist* disagree about the ending of *Uncle Vanya*, Bruford, with whom I agree, finding it less optimistic than Magarshack does. *Uncle Vanya* is first among equals in Chekhov's *oeuvre*. Matthew Arnold ('The Buried Life', quoted earlier in my Baudelaire section) would have loved it and Chekhov would have found that Arnold's poem spoke to the condition of his characters.

Twentieth-Century Writing

Sergei Yesenin and Vladimir Mayakovsky

Sergei Yesenin, who killed himself in St Petersburg in late 1925 at the age of thirty, had five wives, six if you include another woman who was the mother of his child, the poet and philosopher Alexander Yesenin-Volpin, whose *A Leaf of Spring* contains an absurdity in the blurb concerning poems privately circulated in the USSR: 'Many young intellectuals even consider his poetry superior to that of his famous father.' The famous father had children with his first two wives. Wife number five was the granddaughter of Tolstoy. Who knows if his third marriage, to Isadora Duncan, might not have lasted longer if either of them had spoken the other's language? I bought a second-hand Soviet edition of Yesenin in the late lamented Collets Russian Bookshop on Charing Cross Road up from Dobells Jazz record shop. His last poem was written in his own blood, performance art with a vengeance. I discussed the published translations of this poem with the ace translator of Vasily Grossman, Robert Chandler, who is editing a new Penguin anthology of Russian poetry. We found ourselves agreeing that none of them was satisfactory. So we both prepared new drafts and eventually decided to merge them into one version:

> Farewell, my dear friend, farewell—
> > you're present in my heart.
> We'll meet again, the stars foretell,
> > though now we have to part.
> Goodbye for now, goodbye, dear friend—
> > no handshake, words or grief.
> To die is nothing new—but then,
> > what new is left in life?

In his translation of Vladimir Mayakovsky's *How Are Verses Made?*, G. M. Hyde prints the Yesenin poem as a prelude to Mayakovsky's 1926 farewell poem to Yesenin. Mayakovsky's own suicide note, four years later, can be found in *Electron*, a book of versions by Jack Hirschman and Victor Erlich. It has never crossed my mind before that a suicide note in the form of a poem, even if the poets are as significant as the two Russians, is an extraordinary way to sign off: it is as if dying by your own hand is an art and requires an art form to commemorate its imminent or, even, immanent completion: 'Dying is an art,' wrote Sylvia Plath, 'like everything else I do it exceptionally well.'

Osip Mandelstam

The Prose of Osip Mandelstam, edited by Clarence Brown, contains three major texts, including *The Noise of Time*. This volume complements Osip

Mandelstam's collected critical prose and letters. These two books, along with Nadezhda Yakovlevna Mandelstam's *Hope against Hope* and *Hope Abandoned* (the first is one of the great biographies/autobiographies of the age, the second essential reading too, not least for its portrait of Anna Akhmatova), are key accompaniments to the poems. It is evident from the autobiographies and also from her *Mozart and Salieri* that Nadezhda Yakovlevna was a brilliant literary critic. The latter, 'an essay on Osip Mandelstam and Poetic Creativity', is valuable too for its casual asides: 'Pasternak once said to me about Mandelstam: "He got into a conversation which was started before him."' I published Donald Rayfield's translation of *Chapter Forty Two and the Goldfinch*, omitted from *Hope against Hope* by its English translators because, allegedly, it makes no sense to readers without Russian: in it, Nadezhda Yakovlevna brilliantly analyses a few related poems, opening 'the doors into the recesses of the poetic imagination', to quote the book's editor and translator, Donald Rayfield.

That wondrous surrealistic novella, *The Egyptian Stamp*, found in *The Prose*, is discussed in Marshall Berman's *All That Is Solid Melts into Air*, whose title, taken from the *Eighteenth Brumaire*, is one of Karl Marx's great instinctive literary sentences. This book attempts, in the words of its subtitle, to explore 'the experience of modernity'. Let me briefly engage in a virtual dialogue with Clarence Brown and Marshall Berman. Berman sees Mandelstam and Petersburg (which the poet, in poems, also calls Petropolis and Leningrad, but not Petrograd) as having the same sort of synergy (my word, not his) as Dostoevsky and the same city, Dickens and London, Baudelaire and Paris, Whitman and New York (we can continue this list, if we wish: Pessoa and Lisbon, John Fante and Los Angeles, Joyce and Dublin, Kafka and Prague). The use of a classical neologism such as Petropolis hints at Mandelstam's deep involvement with Greco-Roman culture and history, although Brown tells us that there is still no evidence that Mandelstam visited Italy; nor does it matter, as with Shakespeare and his non-travels or, at least, travels unknown.

Parnok, the hero of *The Egyptian Stamp*, a classic *raznochinets* or bourgeois intellectual who is also a 'little man' or 'loser'—with strong ancestral roots in the city of Pushkin's bronze horseman, of Gogol's overcoat and Dostoevsky's *The Double*, and with affinities or routes to Blok, Mayakovsky and Eisenstein—is trying to write a novel but, like Mandelstam himself, is, let's face it, a poet and autobiographer rather than fiction writer. In *Jews in Russia after the October Revolution*, Efraim Sicher writes with sensitivity and moderation about the Jewish Mandelstam and his Russia (symbolized in *The Noise of Time* by the opposition between the grandparents' wooden house and the stone buildings of St Petersburg), taking issue with those who see him as a 'self-hating Jew' and connecting his Jewish memories with those of Isaac Babel in 'Gedali'. *The Egyptian Stamp* is set during a single day in 1917 and bears the same relationship to reality, fiction and life as André Breton's *Nadja*, a book (coincidentally or synchronistically?, happily, for sure) published in the same year as Mandelstam's—1928. The hero of the story is as much the city itself—city of music, city of dreamers, city where the worst of the past and the worst of the future are themselves held in a kind of synergy—as it is Parnok. Parnok, based on a real person, Valentin Parnakh, poet, translator of Nerval and jazz musician. Parnakh, who introduced jazz to Russia (see the four minutes of him on Youtube playing with Louis Armstrong), finds his third-person singular (*sic*) adventures interrupted by his alter ego, the author with his pen and his manuscript: 'Destroy your manuscript, but save whatever you have inscribed in the margin out of boredom, out of helplessness and, as it were, in a dream.' It is no accident that both Breton and Mandelstam, two of the greatest writers of the twentieth century, wrote quasi-fiction, though neither wrote a novel. 'The measure of a novel is human biography or a system of biographies,' says Mandelstam somewhat simplistically in a short essay called 'The End of the Novel', which depends on a restrictive reading of fictional invention and in which he claims, quite wrongly of course, that the multi-volume *Jean-Christophe* by Romain Rolland (a middlebrow fictionalization of Beethoven which I read as a child while ill in bed) closes the circle of the novel. Parnok is a Jew, in a story saturated with Jewish names, jobs and places from the Petersburg of the day, but he is also a Hellene and, to quote Berman's paraphrase, 'his fondest dream is to obtain a minor diplomatic post at the Russian embassy in Greece . . . where he can serve as a translator and interpreter between two worlds.' (Mandelstam writes that Parnok would like to 'persuade Greece to undertake some risky adventure, and write a memorandum'.) Berman's is a wondrous fantasy built on Mandelstam's passing remarks and proposes an equally wondrous synthesis—the Jew interpreting Greece to Russia and Russia to Greece—that brings to mind the historical Jews in mediaeval Spain (as translators) 'going between' Christians and Muslims. Brown characterizes Mandelstam's autobiographical nostalgia as 'onomastic and toponymic'. We find this nostalgia in *The Noise of Time* (it was Nabokov himself who persuaded Brown after much hesitation to stay with 'noise' and not go with 'sound') and also in *The Egyptian Stamp*. A late mutation of this literary world is the recent memoir by Zinovy Zinik, *History Thieves*, with its strikingly measured and typically subtle and funny account of Soviet Jewry mediated through Berlin and London.

In *Hope Abandoned*, Mandelstam's widow tells how he fantasized that one of his ancestors was a Jewish poet chained up in a dungeon of the Spanish inquisition, who wrote and memorized sonnets (like Jean Cassou, see *Thirty-Three Sonnets* [*of the Resistance*], so beautifully translated by Timothy Ades). Whenever they went to the Hermitage, the first painting they looked at was Rembrandt's marvellous 'Return of the Prodigal Son' and that Mandelstam said of the father: 'he had kind hands.' Nadezhda Yakovlevna speculates that an old Dutch Jew would have been the model for the father. The most resonant phrase in *The Noise of Time* is one I underlined about thirty years ago, 'the chaos of Judaism', which he would flee, and yet he writes in the next chapter, 'The Bookcase': 'As a little bit of musk fills an entire house, so the least influence of Judaism overflows all of one's life.' The following chapter, now called 'The Judaic Chaos', is an affectionate yet clear-eyed account of his childhood, including a visit to grandparents in Riga, when his grandmother kept asking 'Have you eaten? Have you eaten?' and his grandfather put a prayer shawl round his shoulders and tried to get him to say a prayer. The particular chaos first mentioned in *The Noise of Time* is embodied uniquely, as Brown points out, in *The Egyptian Stamp*. Post-revolutionary Petersburg is more broadly chaotic, too, and made strange (in the technical sense) by Mandelstam's extraordinary imploding kaleidoscope of imagery. Brown's description of Mandelstam as a 'a miniaturist and digressionary' is spot on. Throughout this book, I have referred to myself as a sidetracker (digressionary is perhaps a better word) and the 'world history of my soul' (Kafka) as a writer has always involved miniaturism. Thus, once again, this go-between, this attendant lord, finds a court where he can pay homage to a master.

Alexander Tvardovsky

Alexander Tvardovsky, editor of *Novi Mir*, operated as an insider. He published Alexander Solzhenitsyn's *One Day in the Life of Ivan Denisovich* in 1962. He did all he could to widen the realm of the possible, while pressure from outside the system was applied by bad boys, whether dissidents or awkward squad: Solzhenitsyn, Sinyavsky, my hero Sakharov, the Medvedev brothers and so on. Theirs is a roll of honour, but the good boys and girls working from within in order to reform the system interest me greatly. Perhaps I identify with them. The story of the publication of Solzhenitsyn's novella is told in Zhores Medvedev's fascinating *Ten Years after Ivan Denisovich*. Nikita Krushchov approved publication, six years after his famous speech to the Party Congress and two years before he was deposed: the window was slammed shut, with dire consequences for Solzhenitsyn and, differently, for Tvardovsky. In 1976, Solzhenitsyn, two years after his deportation, came to Bush House on a visit to the UK for an interview in the Russian Service of the BBC. He refused even to meet let alone be interviewed by the suave dapper charming liberal Jew, Anatole Goldberg, born in St Petersburg, former head of the Russian Service and at the time of this episode its chief commentator. Probably Solzhenitsyn was informed or believed, quite wrongly, that Goldberg was pro-Soviet. Anatole was the most popular broadcaster to the Soviet Union from anywhere in the world, just as another friend of mine Pierre Rouve (aka Petr Ouvaliev ex Sofia) down the corridor was the most popular broadcaster to Bulgaria. The Russian novelist was firmly told that the World Service chooses the interviewer, not the interviewee, whoever he may be. There was no interview. Anatole Goldberg, whom I enjoyed learning from in the Bush House canteen, died in 1982 and Rabbi Hugo Gryn officiated at his funeral in Golders Green Crematorium.

I bought Evgeny Pasternak's biography of his father *Boris Pasternak: The Tragic Years 1930–1960* from the catalogue of David Gascoyne's library issued by my former *patron* at the obituaries page of *The Independent*, Jamie Fergusson. We learn from the book that Pasternak greatly admired Tvardovsky's *Vasily Tyorkin*. In the early 1970s, Carcanet asked me to translate Tvardovsky. C. P. Snow, who wrote the introduction, liked my translations; his wife, Pamela Hansford Johnson, hated them. I translated extracts from *Vasily Tyorkin* and *Tyorkin in the Other World*, the second originally printed in an edition of a hundred and fifty thousand copies. Tyorkin was the Russian common soldier, Tommy Atkins if you like, with a hint of the good soldier Schweik. We also included a wonderful story, 'The Stovemakers'.

Boris Pasternak and Anna Akhmatova (*with Nikolai Zabolotsky*)

Donald Davie translated Anna Akhmatova's 1936 poem 'Pasternak' (less successful than his translation of the Zhivago poems), presumably written after the dark summer of that year. Lines three and four—'For plenishing the world with a new accord / In the new spaces of respondent stanzas'—could refer to poetry translations by this genius of the art, given that this was what he was writing during those years. Elaine Feinstein, who agrees with this speculation, adds that Akhmatova did not altogether approve of Pasternak's Shakespeare. I was close enough to touch the hem of Akhmatova when she gave a reading in London in 1965, having come to the UK to receive an Oxford honorary degree. Here are *Poems of Akhmatova* translated by Stanley Kunitz and Max Hayward, *White Flock* translated by Geoffrey Thurley and *Selected Poems* translated by Richard McKane with an introduction by Sinyavsky. McKane too translates Akhmatova's 'Pasternak' but with 'mirrored stanzas' rather than 'respondent stanzas' and reminds us in a note that Pasternak wrote a poem to Akhmatova eight years earlier. Ronald Hingley's *Nightingale Fever*, a study of the four great poets who suffered from the disease of being a poet (Mandelstam's image supplies the book's title), ends with Akhmatova's poem 'Four of Us', which invokes the others more explicitly than, say, Eliot invokes Yeats in *Four Quartets*, both in the body of the poem and with three epigraphs from the work of her colleagues, including Mandelstam: 'Lithe gypsy—can she too be destined / To suffer all the agonies in Dante?' Hingley adopts the questionable strategy of translating second person singulars as 'thou' or 'thee' throughout the book. Finally, Daniel

Weissbort's versions of Nikolai Zabolotsky's *Scrolls* and *Selected Poems*, the latter dedicated to the memory of the translator's close friends Hughes and Brodsky, may be his supreme achievement as a translator. Zabolotsky was arrested in 1938, a few weeks before Mandelstam but, unlike him, survived the Gulag, returning home and continuing as a poet. The book contains a painful account of his deportation and imprisonment.

Andrei Sinyavsky (with Boris Pasternak and Varlam Shalamov)

The most sophisticated and brilliant writers who survived the Gulag were Varlam Shalamov and Andrei Sinyavsky. Two of Shalamov's stories of Kolyma can be found in *Russia's Other Writers*, edited by Michael Scammell. For Shalamov, like Robert Antelme, 'poetry is one of the fundamental human desires', and he describes how he organized poetry readings in the Gulag hospital. These were known as Athenian Nights. I cannot remember where I was when I read *Fantastic Stories* and *The Trial Begins* by Abram Tertz (the pseudonym of Aleksander Sinyavsky), but I certainly recall where I was reading *A Voice from the Chorus*. For four years running, I took the children to 'activities holidays' run by an organization called CHA, The Countrywide Holidays Association, originally a late Victorian temperance organization. The first year, 1983, when Than was nine and Nao seven, we went to the CHA Devon centre in Westward Ho, where in obedience to the attitude of the founders, my nightcap bottle of Scotch appeared to have vanished from the bedroom by the time we returned from the first walk: the maid, perhaps untrue to her standing orders, had hidden rather than confiscated it, a suitable compromise I thought. During these holidays, when not engaged in collective activities, I read books, as you would expect. At the CHA centre in Hope, Derbyshire, I read *A Voice from the Chorus*, even managing a few pages while everyone else was abseiling, as well as reading it in bed after boycotting square dancing and other evening events. I deliberately chose a book made up of short fragments, to allow for interruptions during a holiday with two young children. (Another year, on one of these holidays, my reading matter was *The Letters of Van Gogh*, for the same reason.) Sinyavsky, born in 1925, was a major dissident. As his dedication to his wife tells us, the book is drawn from letters he wrote her during his six years of forced labour. *A Voice from the*

Chorus—the title taken from an Aleksander Blok poem you can find in *Selected Poems*—is a great classic of prison literature, a book by a believing Orthodox Christian about life and death, language and spirit, religion and art, art above all, a book Robert Antelme and Primo Levi would have been proud of.

Sinyavsky writes: '. . . a man's private parts are more visible. A man may also bear the additional badge of shame of being a Jew. Every man is a Jew.' Valentina Polukhina agrees with me that this may be an allusion to Tsvetayeva's 'All poets are Jews' (or 'All poets are Yids'); of course, there is no way of knowing for sure. Today, with Israel in the doghouse, to some extent as a result of its own lamentable failure to engage with the Palestinians, the Jew as symbol of victim or survivor may have run its course. Sinyavsky's own words are cross-cut with the words of other prisoners, the chorus he refers to, almost all its members lacking his own cultural and intellectual range yet still speaking from the depths in a range of demotic idioms. Having found his faith before captivity, there is a sense in which Sinyavsky was free, in the camp, to be himself.

'If they are to have a soul, things must be ancient. This is the beginning of all stylization. And the justification of anything new—which only dares to be new because centuries and centuries hence, if it still exists, it will be old.' I still find that striking. Other passages I have marked in the margin include one about brackets, unsurprisingly given my addiction to them: '. . . A verbal construct moving on parallel and intersecting ways or levels, which can be shown graphically by means of brackets, brings writing close to certain forms of geometric art, where the eye jumps from object to object, from one point to another, setting off the verbal field in a kind of relief, bringing to it unevenness, a layered depth—something in which brackets can, in principle, play a major part by forming the dams, caves and canyons whence the main all-pervading sense flows and percolates throughout the text as a whole.' This is a beautifully balanced sentence (all honour to the translators, Max Hayward and Kyril Fitzlyon), and the author's judgement or intuition was surely right: no brackets . . .

My 1965 Soviet edition of Pasternak's poetry contains a long and important introduction by Sinyavsky, who had been a pallbearer at

Pasternak's funeral, and would remain for the rest of his life a memory-bearer, a treasure-guardian, of the great poet. This essay is in Donald Davie and Angela Livingstone's *Pasternak*, along with essays on the poet by Osip Mandelstam and Marina Tsvetayeva.

Andrei Sinyavsky told Elaine Feinstein that Abram Tertz was a real-life Jewish gangster, a tough one (no Benya Krik he) and that he chose the name as it was like a knife in the ribs of Russians. Yevtoushenko told the Canadian poet Robert Ford, who had been wondering why Sinyavsky chose a Jewish name, that the writer thought it was an effective disguise. Dostoevsky's biographer, Joseph Frank, emails: 'It seems the name was taken from a popular ballad about thieves that was widely sung and very well known. Whether anyone by that name actually existed is not clear.' Max Hayward, in his introduction to *A Voice from the Chorus*, states that the censors passed the Pasternak essay for publication three months before Sinyavsky/Tertz was arrested.

The other book I have by 'Abram Tertz' is *Misli Vrasploh* [*Thoughts Unaware*], a collection of aphorisms and other short prose texts. The lengthy and useful survey of 'Tertz' in Andrew Field's introduction, places the Russian in the line of Gogol. I translate one or two aphorisms: 'When you are running late, it is good to slow down the pace a little.' 'But, all the same, more than anything in the world, I love snow.' 'What is the body? An outer shell, a diving suit. And I, sitting in my diving suit, am all apologies.' 'My whole life consists of cowardice and supplication.' And his final one: 'Thoughts end and no longer arrive, as soon as you begin to collect them and think about them.'

Yevgeni Vinokurov

Yevgeni Vinokurov too worked within the system, as Tvardovsky's poetry editor at *Novi Mir*. On one occasion he published Weissbort and myself in the magazine. Despite suspicions among hard-line émigrés, Vinokurov was no timeserver; indeed, he had the friendship of Akhmatova, no less, whom he used to visit as a young poet after the war, and the respect of dissidents, whom he quietly supported. I know this, not only because he told me, but because two of them confirmed it when I asked them: Vladimir Bukovsky and Joseph Brodsky, who probably knew about the Akhmatova connection.

Long ago, Weissbort and I discovered we were translating this poet independently of each other; we offered our separate translations to Michael Schmidt at Carcanet, who duly published a short volume, *The War Is Over*. When making the final selection, we further discovered, to our astonishment and relief, that we had not overlapped at all, which meant we did not have make difficult decisions about whose version of any particular poem was better. One of my translations was reprinted in several anthologies, including Daniel Weissbort's *Post-War Russian Poetry* and Al Alvarez's *The Faber Book of Modern European Poetry*. The poem describes a scene that is reminiscent of World War I experiences of Isaac Rosenberg or Wilfred Owen, rather than those of World War II poets like Keith Douglas or Alun Lewis. Douglas was born five years before Zhenya Vinokurov, who was already a platoon commander on the Ukrainian front at the age of eighteen. All the men under his command, he told me, were illiterate.

> 'Eyes'
>
> Exploded. To the ground. On his back. Arms apart. He
> Raised himself to his knees, and bit his lips.
>
> Across his face were smeared not tears
> But eyes shot out.
>
> Awful awful. Bent double, I heaved
> Him to one side. He was all
>
> Covered with clay. I could hardly
> Drag him across to the village.
>
> In the field-hospital he cried
> To the nurse: 'Oh it hurts! When you change
>
> The bandage it's hell!' And I gave him, as one does,
> Something to smoke as he lay dying.
>
> And when (taking him away) the wheels began
> To whimper sharply, over all the voices
>
> I suddenly remembered, for the first time:
> My friend had pale blue eyes.

I have here the warmly inscribed books that Vinokurov sent me from Moscow over many years. I first met him at the Biennale de Poésie in

Knokke-le-Zoute in 1963, having been taken there (Southend/Ostend flight) by Miron Grindea. Zhenya was a one-off in Russia, a quiet voice, a reserved man who did not go in for the large-scale public readings associated with Voznesensky and Yevtoushenko, both of whom I met on several occasions in London and some of whose books I have in the original Russian. I cannot pretend I read them with the same attention I gave to Vinokurov, but then I was not translating them. Zhenya and I read together in London and other cities, including Oxford and Cambridge. His Russian editions, all of which I have here, were typically of fifty thousand copies and, once, in 1967, one hundred and twelve thousand copies—*Golos* (*Voice*). One of the unfinished projects I shall make time to complete is a revised and expanded version of my Vinokurov translations. I know I have it in me to do this fine poet and good friend justice. In another room, a box full of drafts and revisions and material relating to him sits quietly awaiting my attention. *Half-Way to the Moon*, new writing from Russia edited by Patricia Blake and Max Hayward, contains a Vinokurov poem translated by Auden himself, doubtless after a trot supplied by the editors.

Dimitri Prigov

Dimitri Prigov, one of whose books is signed for me in Russian, was the world's most prolific poet. At the last count [20 August 2005], he had written thirty-five thousand three hundred and fifty poems. He and I were the witnesses and only people present at the wedding of Dan Weissbort and Valentina Polukhina, one of his editors, in Marylebone Town Hall; he read a sound poem at their reception in Kings College later that week. Dan, whose own fine books are here, including *What Was All the Fuss About?*, reckons that one in a hundred of Dimitri Prigov's poems is really good, which amounts to three hundred and fifty poems, a good-sized volume, and he is still only sixty-five.

[Coda in 2007: I emailed Weissbort for Prigov's address so that I could update the grand total. Dimitri had just died.]

Elaine Feinstein's Russia

Elaine Feinstein's highly original and most personal work *The Russian Jerusalem* is a deeply sad book. The author imagines herself back into the company of 'familiar compound ghosts', four great poets and a short-story writer of genius: Marina Tsvetayeva, Anna Akhmatova, Osip Mandelstam, Boris Pasternak and Isaac Babel, perhaps the most tragic, enigmatic and fascinating of all these writers. She speaks of being 'ensnared by the dangerous glamour of these ghosts'. The three men were Jewish Russians, the two women non-Jewish with important Jewish associations, such as Tsvetayeva's half-Jewish husband, Sergei Efron. The narrator also meets the Yiddish poet Der Nister and that complex figure, Ilya Ehrenberg. She is at once a barfly on the wall of the famous Petersburg tavern The Stray Dog and proactive, participating in the lives of writers she has ordinarily or professionally met on the page.

'The barfly ought to sing,' wrote Anne Sexton in her poem, 'Sylvia's Death'. Each chapter of *The Russian Jerusalem* begins with a plangently evocative poem in the classic Feinstein voice, and indeed the book as a whole works like a long poem, perhaps because the prose reads like the story of a dream, with flashes of nightmare, and draws the reader in. Our task is to keep her company and perhaps make her safe in the dangerous time and place of Stalin, although, and this is a subtext, she is well aware that her fantasy presence demonstrates, through a glass darkly, the safety of Jewish life in Britain despite what some see as increasing levels of anti-Semitism disguised as anti-Zionism. This is sometimes exaggerated by my brethren, especially those whose relatives who perished or suffered terribly during the dark years of Hitler and Stalin, in the towns and surviving shtetls of Eastern Europe. Feinstein's primary injunction is to remember and commemorate, a classic Jewish obligation.

On visits to the Soviet Union while researching her biographies of Akhmatova and Tsvetayeva, she meets, in real time and real life, later Jewish poets such as Margaret Aliger, Yunna Moritz and Joseph Brodsky. Traces of Yiddishkeit and Jewish experience enter the spirit of the book as she finds familial and other parallels with her own life, including cuisine: she notes, for example, the difference in sweetness between Russian and Polish pickles. Back in Cambridge, England, she has a major public disagreement with Brodsky about translation—he takes a typically Russian hard line on the obligation to reproduce the metre and rhymes of the original. I well remember that meeting at Churchill College back in the 1980s. The disagreement goes to the heart of literary translation and matters greatly. Similar discussions went on in the camps, as we know from the testimonies of Jorge Semprún, Robert Antelme and others.

Distinguished and distinctive as a biographer (Ted Hughes, Alexander Pushkin and Bessie Smith), poet, literary critic, translator of Tsvetayeva and novelist, Feinstein, in *Russian Jerusalem*, obliterates traditional boundaries and genres—Sebald's *The Rings of Saturn* and Bonnefoy's *L'Arrière-pays* come to mind—and enters a new and fertile land where, I trust, she will labour for years to come as the Grand Duchess of Anglo-Jewish letters, a woman who, if the cards had fallen differently, might have been Babel's lover or, closer to home, might have been drinking lemon tea in Odessa with her beloved Zeida (grandfather), rather than in the safe haven of her childhood Leicester.

R. A. D. Ford

Robert Ford, Canadian poet, translator and diplomat, who died in 1998, had muscular atrophy from the age of nineteen; he was not expected to live long. Ford was the most extraordinary person I have known in my lifelong role as a go-between. I made contact with him in 1982, during the days of my involvement in the struggle to educate myself and, by extension, the constituency of concerned and frightened people who had been reading the Menard Press pamphlets about the nuclear threat, which I published between 1980 and 1985. Back then, I wrote about my three political gurus or mentors, Sir Martin Ryle, Lord (Solly) Zuckerman and E. P. Thompson. The twenty pamphlets included three by Ryle and two by Zuckerman. Thompson went out of his way to publicize Ryle's first pamphlet *Towards the Nuclear Holocaust* as the best account of our fearful dilemma. Thanks, in part, to his intervention, it sold fourteen or fifteen thousand copies, easily Menard's top selling book.

In my political publishing heyday, all kinds of 'moderate' and mainstream people were, along with radicals, in touch with Menard, because as a poetry publisher the press was understood to be independent of supposedly dangerous extremists like CND—the Campaign for Nuclear Disarmament. At one point, I was asked to attend a meeting at MI5 after a Soviet diplomat visited me to buy pamphlets. Not long after, in a separate incident, I found myself on the line to or from the Ministry of Defence security police, when I had not phoned them or been phoned by them. I reported this to a privy councillor friend, the former Housing Minister Reg Freeson, who made enquiries. The ensuing meeting with MI5, near the British Council offices in Trafalgar Square, was so interesting that I asked if I could come back. I made my usual speech about loyal opposition blah-blah. I was struck how young and pretty the intelligence officer was: a deliberate choice to disarm me?

By the time I met him, Robert Ford was special adviser on East–West relations to the Canadian Prime Minister, Pierre Trudeau, having retired as ambassador to the Soviet Union. One of Canada's, indeed the West's, most important and influential diplomats since the war, Ford had sub-ambassadorial postings in London, Sao Paulo and Moscow followed by ambassadorial stints in Colombia, Yugoslavia and Egypt, before returning to Moscow for sixteen years (1964–1980). He ended up as *doyen* of the diplomatic corps. Such a long stint was rare, if not unique, because of fears that ambassadors left abroad for too long may go native in the bad sense. There was no danger that Robert the diplomat would succumb, precisely because going native was the province of Robert the poet. He told me that, because of his disability, he was the only foreigner or maybe even non-member of the politburo allowed to use the lift in the Kremlin. He was, too, the only Western diplomat to have met all Soviet leaders from Stalin to Gorbachev, although the meeting with Stalin was more like observation at close quarters. Robert was already in a wheelchair when I first met him. He never complained, never admitted to pain, always behaved as if nothing was wrong.

Ford and his wife Thereza, a brilliant and charming Brazilian heiress, retired to a small castle near Vichy, where I stayed with them. They had met in London in 1946 at the first General Assembly of the United Nations: 'At the opening reception in the House of Lords given by Clement Attlee . . . I heard an attractive member of the Brazilian delegation making amusing remarks about the Canadians. I could not resist the temptation of saying in Portuguese that the latter was not a secret language. This led inevitably to marriage.' (I like his deployment of the word 'inevitably', with the erotics of the interaction left entirely unspoken and buried between the words of the short sentence.) The castle, La Poivrière, which had been the residence of the German ambassador to Petain's regime, was beautifully decorated with Russian folk art, including butter dishes, gifts from their close friend Lili Brik, the elegant and talented Jewish mistress of Mayakovsky and sister-in-law of Louis Aragon. The Fords owned wonderful works of art, including a Kandinsky painting on glass. Over dinner, out of the blue, Thereza said: 'Anthony, everybody thinks Robert depends on me and will be helpless if he outlives me, but the opposite is true. I need him more than he needs me. I want to die first.' I looked at him in expectation of some kind of reaction, but he sat there impassive, like the Buddha or a rocky mountain (goat) or a figure in a Poussin painting. Like Pope's Gainsborough, he was 'a man who had a rare capacity / to snatch a grace beyond the reach of art'. After a short illness, Thereza's ambition was fulfilled in 1983: Robert outlived her, producing sad true lyrics to her memory and, as such, to his own memory.

I went up to my bedroom and opened my suitcase. It was empty. I was perplexed until it dawned on me that one of the two servants must have put my stuff away—and there the gear was, in the en suite bathroom and in the wardrobe. The next morning, after breakfast, we faced each other in the sitting room and Robert, notebook and pen at the ready, asked me about the peace movement and whether it was infiltrated by the Russians (yes, I said, and infiltrated by the Americans and the British too) and the politics of disarmament. I spoke honestly and carefully, perhaps for fifteen minutes. Thank you, he said, I shall be writing a memo to Pierre Trudeau. That felt good: for almost the only time in my life I had a direct if minuscule input into politics at the highest level, although a few indirect inputs—for example, Martin Ryle's pamphlet was the subject of a widely circulated unofficial refutation by the Ministry of Defence—suggested that Menard must have been doing something right. One other direct and verifiable input: I sent a phrase I coined ('unilateral nuclear rearmament') to Neil Kinnock, then leader of the opposition, enabling him to use it in a speech and briefly turn the table on the Tories, since 'unilateral disarmers' was their term of abuse for CND and its supporters. Although the great campaign was a coalition of nuclear disarmers, unilateral and multilateral, the unilateral aspect was always and mistakenly to the forefront. When Kinnock went to Moscow he already knew about Byron's poem 'Darkness' which was quoted at him by Russians, because he had a copy of my Menard pamphlet about the circumstances of the poem's writing.

Over the years, in correspondence and on the phone, Ford and I continued discussing security issues, Israel (which fascinated him and generated many questions), poetry (he gave me his books as listed in the bibliography) and translation. Although not a reactionary and not a professional cold warrior, he was conservative, but on the nuclear issue he, like Zuckerman, had no doubt that a new approach was needed. Thompson and Ryle were more radical than Ford and Zuckerman. I was privately torn, settling eventually on the 'freeze' as common ground between unilateralists and multilateralists (the freeze was a position which many members of both camps, wrongly, rejected), which belongs in a political book I shan't be writing. Zuckerman, Ryle, Thompson and Ford were highly cultivated men, influential in their fields, and immensely powerful personalities of a kind I have been drawn to, if not actually sought out. They were all married to remarkable women, who matched them in depth and range. Long marriages between equals interest me, but this too is a topic for another occasion and, perhaps, a different genre, namely fiction. Robert Ford was the only one of the four with whom I had a literary as well as a political dialogue, and that brought me close to him, although Martin Ryle too was a good friend. On the other hand, Solly Zuckerman and Edward Thompson were my colleagues in a common cause and friendly acquaintances, much as I would like to claim them as friends.

In 1983, I arranged three events for Ford in London: the first was a lecture at the now-defunct GB–USSR Association, then run by my old friend John Roberts. The meeting was chaired by the former foreign secretary, David Owen, Ford's colleague on the Olaf Palme Commission. Ford's UK buddies, retired top diplomats, showed up. Earlier that day, the Canadian ambassador had made a lunch for him. All I remember, thanks perhaps to good wine, was the presence of Carmen Callil and John Mortimer. The other events were a poetry reading at Canada House and a Russian translation reading at the old Poetry Society in Earls Court. Robert Ford was a meditative poet, hibernal rather than aestival; Norwegian rather than Italian, if you like. Perhaps this is a roundabout way of saying the matrix of his poetry is Canada, which, after all, is situated in North North America, the Arctic and Russia not that far away. Ford himself said that the 'Russian landscape, so much like that of the Ottawa Valley, has been an important factor in shaping my verse.' The firs, the pines, the birches, the snow reminded him of Canada, of home. Naturally, he translated some of the Zhivago poems. Autumn, however, is different, greyer and more melancholy in Russia than in Canada. Two Canadian poets, friends of mine, Sharon Nelson and Seymour Mayne, tell me Ford is no longer on the literary radar in their country, though Mayne himself is personally an admirer, and his wife Sharon Katz drew portraits of Russian poets for Ford's personal and beautifully translated selection, *Russian Poetry*.

In 1989, Ford sent me his book *Dostoevsky and Other Poems*. My thank you letter, preserved in a carbon copy, speaks rather formally of his 'austerity of diction, the edgy and disturbed rhythms, the way the syntax plays against the lexicon: all the registers serving a vision where intelligence of the heart doubles the heart of intelligence'. After a conference in Arles in 1997, which brought together the translators of Yves Bonnefoy from across the globe, I returned to Paris via Robert's house for what we both knew would be our last meeting. Now virtually paralysed by his lifelong condition, worsened by a stroke, he greeted me from bed with a movement of his little finger. By then the childless widower had moved with his household, a long service and devoted Portuguese couple, and possessions, from his small chateau, to a lovely house in the castle's village, Saint-Sylvestre Pragoulin. With hindsight, I now read the scene at the bedside, especially when the manservant brought tea, as a gloss on Paula Rego's painting 'The Family'. How I wanted to free him from his affliction!, just as the children in her painting are trying to raise the male figure from near death—the original title of the painting was, indeed, 'Lazarus'. I looked again at the Kandinsky painting on the wall facing his bed. Ford told me that the painter's estate had recently written to him, withdrawing its certificate of authenticity. This, he said, was rubbish, and all the experts said it was rubbish, but he was in no position to fight the estate. I wonder what has happened to that picture, indeed to all his pictures and his library.

Robert Ford's literary friendships and activities while in the Soviet Union were in a creatively dialectical relationship with his professional work, which is not surprising since he was a poet and translator of distinction and a profoundly thoughtful man of the highest intelligence. His diplomatic reports became famous, like those of Isaiah Berlin from Washington during World War II. The personal and political fed into each other, perhaps uniquely. Given Canada's significant position within the broad western coalition and the importance of the country of his final posting, he is certainly the most influential poet diplomat from any country since Saint-John Perse and George Seferis. Nonetheless, he had no illusions concerning where main power lay, namely with Canada's North American neighbour, and that Canada's scope for independent initiatives was limited. According to one obituary, when George Schulz became Ronald Reagan's Secretary of State in the USA, he sought a briefing from Ford.

I do not claim that Ford is a poet in the league of those other professional diplomat poets, Perse, Paz, Neruda and Seferis—how many poets are?—but his elegiac *oeuvre*, though small and narrowly focused, is distinctive and, to my ear, beautiful. However, his understanding of the psyches and mentalities of individuals in the elites, political and artistic, of the country where he was posted, influenced his diplomacy more than it influenced his literary works, unlike Paz, one of whose most important books is *Le Singe grammarien*, *The Monkey Grammarian*, which could not have been written without his profound experience of India.

Here on my desk is the first of Ford's two memoirs: *Our Man in Moscow* (1989, with a cover photo of him and Leonid Brezhnev) and the French edition *Diplomate et Poète à Moscou* (1990, sporting a photo of him with Andrei Voznesensky). These photographs of Ford as a young and middle-aged man reveal a handsome, elegant, self-confident and self-possessed personality, reminding me of Clark Gable or Anthony Eden, when he was Foreign Secretary during the war. Although Robert came across as a reserved and highly cerebral man, classically opposite to his passionate and extravert Latin wife, the passion was there beneath the armour of the intense discipline of a man schooled in illness and diplomacy. In private, he always spoke his mind, and from the heart. He held strong views, and could be aroused to sharpness when one was naive or stupid, but he also wanted to learn from those, including myself, with areas of knowledge beyond his specialities. Reading these two memoirs, we realize that the diplomat was accredited to the Soviet Union, a country with many nationalities and literatures, whereas the poet was accredited to Russia, her literature, her poetry, her soul, as becomes clear in *A Moscow Literary Memoir* (1995), which tells of his life 'among the great artists of Russia from 1946 to 1980'. Here he is off-duty, and not constrained by the responsibilities of the day job, although in that city, and in a country, as Mandelstam said, where poetry is so important the poet is sometimes killed, you could never entirely divorce art and politics, which is one of the major themes of this valuable record of a passion and a time. It is not, however, an ambitious literary work, in part because it had to be written and edited in the difficult circumstances of his final years.

Although Ford lived on until late in the presidency of Boris Yeltsin (whose commitment to democracy he doubted), *Our Man in Moscow* was written during the high optimism of Gorbachev's rule: for my money Mikhail Gorbachev, even more than Nelson Mandela, is the man of the (twentieth) century, since he managed the change, *perestroika* and *glasnost*, in such a way that war, nuclear war, was avoided. Despite the optimism of the times, and despite Ford's admiration and respect for Gorbachev, whom he saw as a Kerensky figure, Robert Ford appears to agree with Vasily Grossman: 'When will Russia ever be free? Perhaps never.' As I said, he had gone native, not in the negative sense that requires ambassadors to move on before they succumb but in the Keatsian sense of negative capability. He had become the poets he loved, *echt Russisch*, one who knows that the Russian soul is something unique unto itself, like the Russian language praised by Ivan Turgenev in the prose poem I translated earlier. Although Ford writes that the proposition was and is debatable, part of him agreed with the poet Fyodor Tyutchev whom he quotes, in his own translation, at the end of the memoir:

Russian cannot be understood
Only with the mind—no normal
Standard can judge her
Greatness. She stands alone, unique.
In Russia one must only believe.

Ford died before George Bush and the neoconservatives came to power, and before we could have a conversation about my considered view that the project called democracy was in fact a project to promote capitalism, and deregulated capitalism at that. In his early days as Foreign Secretary, David Miliband, in a speech timed to second-guess or echo President Obama, struck me as naive in his unreconstructed promotion, if necessary by military means, of the admirable and essential concept called democracy, naive about its relationship to economics and climate change. What does Great Britain look like to normal Europeans like the Spanish, the Portuguese, the Italians, the Germans, the French, who managed to dispose of their imperial pretensions along with their dictatorships? NATO and the USA (pre-Obama at any rate) have not been straight in their dealings with Russia. When will we (and Putin's Russia too) learn that security in the modern world is not a zero-sum game? Ford predicted in the mid-1990s that Greater Russian nationalism would re-emerge, and that is surely correct.

Ford's literary recollections, as he says, put the flesh on the skeleton of the country portrayed in the political memoir. *A Moscow Literary Memoir* tells of Ford's friendships with the poets of the 'thaw': his closest friend Andrei Voznesensky, Yevgeny Yevtushenko, Bella Akhmadulina, the prose writers Yuri Nagibin and Konstantin Simonov, the ballerina Maya Plisetskaya ('Plisetskaya is the Tsvetaeva of ballet,' wrote Voznesensky), Nina Kandinsky, the widow of the painter, and of course Robert and Thereza's dearest friend, Lili Brik. 'The inner tug of war between the eastern Slavophile and the western liberal is the eternal conflict in Russia . . . The whole of Russia today is an epic drama by Dostoevsky, being played out before our very eyes'.

There is a wonderful photograph of Brik with Mayakovsky, Pasternak and, am I imagining it, a haunted-looking Eisenstein, taken in St Petersburg in 1924. Lili looks very elegant in her cloche hat, reminding one that Lenin had only just died and Stalin was not yet fully in control. She explains to the Fords that her marriage to Osip Brik became platonic as the *ménage à trois* with Mayakovsky gathered apace. At a dinner party with the Fords and Voznesensky, she says: 'I have no objection to falsehoods, but there is a big distance between honest lying and dishonest lying.' As for Pasternak, she much preferred his poetry and *The Childhood of Lyuvers* to *Doctor Zhivago*, and Ford agreed with her. On Pasternak and Akhmatova, Ford writes that they [like Robert Lowell] appear to put his own art above other people's lives, namely Olga (the model for Lara in *Doctor Zhivago*) and Akhmatova's son, Lev. 'It is an anguished question,' writes Ford. He and Thereza visited Pasternak's grave in Peredelkino, prompting a poem, 'The Grave of Pasternak':

> The wind withers
> At the windows of the voices,
> Tapping gently, then lost
> In the infinite space.
> The snow is convent pure.
> In the first light
> Of Peredelkino
> He lies alone with one
> Paper flower, faded, wet,
> Staining the snow.
> The voices can be heard again.
> And the windows reopen.

I take my farewell of Robert with the memory that I wanted to hug him when it was time to go, but didn't, knowing it would embarrass him. I held his finger for a moment and left with tears in my eyes. He knew what he meant to me. Here is his translation of the final stanza of Yesenin's poem on death:

> I know in that other country
> There are no fields golden in the haze.
> That is why I cherish those who have
> Spent on earth with me their days.

(Auto)biographies, Letters, Journals and Memoirs

Introductory Note

The categories of (auto)biographies, letters, journals and memoirs overlap to a considerable degree but separating them out makes for easier reading, and doubtless writing too. As with (poetry) translation, although I respect the participants in the theoretical debate about the subject and acknowledge the importance of the debate, I no longer keep up with the scholarly literature.

Autobiographies

INTRODUCTION

A few years after my memoir of childhood, *The Arithmetic of Memory*, was published, I was invited by Michelene Wandor to teach the autobiography module in the creative writing degree at London Metropolitan University. I had to create a course from scratch, which included field trips, first to the National Portrait Gallery and then the National Gallery, where the impassioned and entertaining lecturer Colin Wiggins spoke on autobiography in painting: Rubens, Velázquez and Caravaggio. After three years at LMU, I spent five more years as a part-time teacher, working one or two days a week as Royal Literary Fund fellow, at the University of Hertfordshire and then at the University of Westminster, helping students improve their essay-writing techniques. I preferred this to teaching creative writing, but the preparation for my course in autobiography (the word itself was coined by Robert Southey) aroused my interest in the history of the genre, with its roots in Romanticism. The two great foundational texts are Wordsworth's *Prelude* and Stendhal's *La Vie de Henry Brulard*, both clearly influenced by Rousseau's

Confessions. I see from my student handout that I coined a word, hetero-biography, to replace biography. Hetero-biography: biography of the other; and auto-biography: the two modalities of biography. I mentioned this to Alan Wall, whose reaction was that students would understand 'hetero' to mean heterosexual, and that I should drop the idea. Although my classes were supposed to be seminars or workshops, my inexperience and nerves meant I found myself giving lectures. On my first appearance, I squeezed three hours of material into one hour. A few years later, I distilled my notes into a three-hundred-line poem called 'Zigzag', on, but not of, autobiography. Rereading the original notes, I realize that my methodology was crazy. Either you write out the notes in full or you have bullet points. My notes were neither one thing nor the other. No wonder the course was something of a roller coaster.

AMERICAN

Ernest Hemingway

A Moveable Feast (now published in a fascinating revised edition about which I reserve judgement, says he lazily) is a beautiful book and one of my talismanic texts. I have not underlined a single word in my much-thumbed copy, as if to say the prose works on me like a poem. I know the last two sentences by heart: 'Paris was always worth it and you received return for whatever you brought to it. But this is how Paris was in the early days when we were very poor and very happy.' On several visits to Paris in my twenties and thirties, I would follow a route Hemingway took to Place Saint-Michel, via the Pantheon, starting out from his flat on rue Cardinal Lemoine. Ostensibly pursuing a trail like a pilgrim, I was without doubt engaged, unconsciously, in magical thinking: maybe something of the genius of a supreme short story writer would rub off onto me. I had read the stories while living in Chicago in 1966. The reverse route was a good way to reach one of my regular ports of call in the 1970s and 1980s, the flat of my friends Edmond and Arlette Jabès at 7 rue de l'Epée de bois off rue Mouffetard, whether I was coming from Claude Royet-Journoud's studio on rue de la Harpe or from the Quartier Latin bookshops or the small and atmospheric and counter-intuitively named cheap hotel where I stayed in those days, l'Hotel des Grands Balcons, rue Casimir Delavigne, off rue Monsieur-le-Prince; before it was ruined (and doubtless saved) by modernization in the mid-1990s, it had been a base for Sorbonne lecturers and poets and literary visitors to Paris from 1945, perhaps earlier.

Edward Dahlberg

If, like those two masterpieces, Edmund Gosse's fictionalized autobiography *Father and Son* and Samuel Butler's autobiographical novel *The Way of All Flesh*, David Daiches' *Two Worlds/Promised Lands* is one of the great father books, then Edward Dahlberg's *Because I Was Flesh*, whose title strangely echoes Butler's, is one of the great mother books, a rhapsodically beautiful and compelling portrait of a loved person. Dahlberg was not a loveable man and was, I am told on good authority, cruel to his students. Great writers are human. Not all of them are loveable, not all of them are kind. All the same, reports or sightings of an autobiographer's life are possibly more germane to the present proceedings than those of a novelist. *Because I Was Flesh* is something of a test case if you want it to be, for it uses some of the same material as his novel *Bottom Dogs*, published in 1929 when he was twenty-nine, with an introduction by D. H. Lawrence or David Herbert Lawrence as he is described on the dust jackets of French translations. Are initials a peculiarly British phenomenon, extending to India, New Zealand and other Commonwealth countries? Lawrence's introduction ends: 'I don't want to read any more books like this. But I am glad to have read this one, just to know what is the last word in repulsive consciousness, consciousness in a state of repulsion. It helps one to understand the world, and saves one the necessity of having to follow out the phenomenon of physical repulsion, for the time being.' Within a few months, Lawrence was dead.

William Carlos Williams (with Max Apple and Dan Jacobson)

William Carlos Williams' *Autobiography* is a 'conventionally' constructed work in terms of chronology and approach. It is, however, a classic not only because it is so patently truthful and well written but also because it succeeds in its primary object: to show how the making of art is compatible with a demanding and serious professional day job. In his case, the two fed into each other so that his understanding of the human clay was that of a great sculptor. From Rabelais and Paracelsus via Keats and Beddoes to Dannie Abse and Iain Bamforth (editor of a terrific literary anthology of modern medicine, *The Body in the Library*), there have been many distinguished doctor-writers, although it can't have been much fun being a patient of Rabelais, and doubtless his job satisfaction was not in the Williams league: 'From complete occupation with either a poem or the delivery of a child, I come away, not fatigued, but rested.' I read the Williams autobiography in the 1970s and underlined a number of things, including the immensely revealing remark: 'Men have given the direction to my life and women have always supplied the energy.' He tells us he instinctively avoided a New York City practice, always working in Rutherford and Paterson, New Jersey, and that *The Waste Land*, although a work of genius, was a catastrophe because it gave poetry 'back to the academics'. He takes a pointless swipe at Shakespeare for allegedly claiming that art is all about holding a mirror up to nature. But Shakespeare was talking about acting not writing, and mirrors then were not up to the standards we expect.

In his introduction to Harold Norse's vivid translation of *The Roman Sonnets of G. G. Belli*, Williams writes: 'These translations are made not into English but into the American idiom in which they appear in the same relationship facing English as the original Roman dialect does to classic Italian. The idiom spoken in America is not taught in our schools, but is the property of men and women who, though they do not know it, use one of the greatest modern languages, waiting only for a genius of its intrinsic poetry to appear.' This appears to refer to Norse, actually it applies to Williams himself, consciously or not. The father book by Daiches and the mother book by Dahlberg are, needless to say, biographical *and* autobiographical. WCW's *Yes, Mrs Williams* is an attempt at an objective record of his Latino mother's voice, of her very being. He has used her actual voice, and also recreated her voice. This is a rare, almost unique model for my eventual grandfather book, along with Charles Reznikoff's books in his parents' voices. Dan Jacobson's *Heshel's Kingdom* is a haunting and exemplary grandfather book but he never knew his grandfather: in fact, 'if he had not died prematurely, I would never have been born.' Compare Max Apple's *Roommates: My Grandfather's Story*, which deals with the years the young Max lived with the old man; this enchanting book, however, leaves one entirely—how could it not?—with the image of the grandfather, not of the boy who grows up to be the narrator. Although the Williams book and, to a lesser extent, the Jacobson one, remind me of the formal problems I shall be facing when I return to my own project, it is Apple's fine book that moves me most, for a simple and obvious reason: he is my exact contemporary, and our grandfathers were typical poor Jewish immigrants from *der heim*.

Alfred Kazin and Michael Heller

In *New York Jew*, the sequel to Alfred Kazin's *A Walker in the City* and prequel to *Writing Was Everything*, the author writes perceptively that, unlike Scott Fitzgerald, Norman Mailer was 'so insatiably mental about everything that he became his ideas, his heroes. Oddly, he was too reflective to be content with fiction.' (Kazin died before he could read Mailer's last book, his autobiography, *On God*, a bad book which proves Kazin's point.) At the time of the student revolution in 1968, Kazin (my father's exact age), faced with the anger of his son (my own contemporary), sees himself as one of Blake's horses of instruction and his offspring as one of the tigers of wrath. Reciting the Kaddish prayer at his father's grave, he suddenly remembers as a boy being introduced to people by his father as 'my kaddish', a metonymy for the person who will say the words of praise to God and life when the end of his own time comes. Another autobiographer who, unlike Kazin, puts the very genre under the spotlight and has made a beautiful narrative partly out of this awareness and partly despite it is the American poet Michael Heller. *Living Root*, his memoir of growing up Jewish in Brooklyn and Florida—with its poems, its photos, its documents, its journal entries, its letters, its footnotes, all subtly meshed in an intense meditative prose segue—constructs a poetics of the self which makes serious sense to those who experience the reading of their own life as an 'active voice'. As a poet (*This Constellation Is a Name*) and essayist (*Speaking the Estranged* and *Uncertain Poetries*), Heller is on the cusp of experimental modernism, while remaining firmly in a resonant humanist tradition of concern, often anguished, with last things and first causes. Art and language could not mean more to him, but the pulse of life—individual, social and political, and their interface (I and Thou)—is what he takes and what grabs him.

William Hazlitt

William Hazlitt's *Liber Amoris*, which spoke to my own state of mind during a phase of my life more conducive to fiction than to memoir, deals with, and in a literary sense idealizes, obsession in the form of infatuation. It was written more than a hundred years before Breton's convulsive idea of love as elaborated first in *Nadja* and then in *L'Amour fou*. More recently, Barthes has explored the modalities of unrequited love in *A Lover's Discourse*. Poor Hazlitt lived too early to enjoy or endure the experiences of dream and love and desire available to two great French writers in the light (and shadow) of Freud and other researches. Hazlitt's painful memoir about obsessional love (and between the lines, sexual frustration) is excruciatingly embarrassing and, far more than Rousseau's *Confessions*, the first confessional book in the modern sense: Ginsberg, Sexton, Mailer, Burroughs, yes: four times yes, but their post-Freudian self-awareness inevitably and fortunately escapes this great literary critic and supreme essayist, friend of Keats, who died two years before the book was published. As Christopher Ricks has shown in *Keats and Embarrassment*—a book I abandoned and picked up again many years later when I was ready to read it, having in the meanwhile embarrassed and been embarrassed sufficiently to get the point—Keats in his letters and poems negotiated embarrassment more subtly than any other writer; it was one of his great themes, and one would love to have read a letter from Keats on the subject of Hazlitt's strange and haunting book, this classic example of a 'temperamental journey', to use a phrase Herman Hesse borrowed about an episode from his grandfather's youth. The poet would surely have hated it. He died two years before his friend's book came out.

Edmund Gosse and Samuel Butler

I marked many passages in Edmund Gosse's *Father and Son*. By the sentence 'It was the Sea, always the sea, nothing but the sea', I have noted 'PV', meaning Paul Valéry. In best Borgesian style, let me point out that the sentence translates rather well the fourth line of 'Le Cimitière marin': 'La mer, la mer, toujours recommencée.' The wonky metre is excusable since Valéry's poem wasn't published until 1920, whereas *Father and Son* was published in 1907. Gosse wrote disparagingly about Mallarmé and positively about Gide, and, since he lived till 1928, it is possible he read Valéry's poem. I like to think he noticed that the line involved a Borgesian retro-influence. You will have spotted my subtext: what a shame Valéry had most likely not read *Father and Son* . . . On a hunch, I google 'Valéry/Gosse' and find that the French poet gave a talk at the house of Lady Colefax, and Gosse was in the audience, so Gosse probably did read the Frenchman, but the other way round? Samuel Butler in *The Way of All Flesh*: 'Sensible people get the greater part of their dying done during their own lifetime.' And this, which moves me to tears: 'We are as days and have had our parents for our yesterdays.' Paula and I found a statue of Butler in the hills near Lake Orta where we were checking out the hillside Sacro Montes (see my discussion of Lou Andreas Salomé), marvellous examples of mediaeval and baroque frescos and wooden sculptures on which Butler, a local hero with his own statue, turned out to have written a book.

Rosamund Lehmann and others

I told my students that it is very rare in autobiography for people to write about their children. Children and parents understand each other better than we think. In memoirs, it is normal, even correct, for children to have a go at parents who stuck too closely to the straight and narrow. However, having a go at your children is not on. This is said to be why Doris Lessing did not write a follow-up to her autobiography: she could not bring herself to write about the young people, her 'children', such as Jenny Diski, a stellar intelligence and wit who lived with her at different times, and whose *Rainforest* and *Nothing Natural* are on my desk. I clipped an interview with Diski and inserted it in *Nothing Natural*. It shows her handling with great tact an interviewer, who is either prurient or literal-minded, on the subject of the woman's sexual masochism in *Nothing Natural*. Diski explains that she recognizes the subject matter of the book as part of her mindset, as a component of her *imaginaire*, while firmly rejecting the simplistic implication that she herself has participated in such activities, and even if she has, it is no business of the interviewer, because it is—she implies and rightly so—irrelevant to a deep reading of the book. Yes, invention in art draws on life, but the artist's life includes fantasy, projection, empathy, literary precedent and so on. In Paula's case, too, interviewers, including sympathetic ones, sometimes make simplistic extrapolations from stories which have generated what are complex pictorial statements that deal with a content deeper than the subject matter. Indeed, it is the structural dialectic between subject matter and formal concerns that generates the deep content of a work. The girls in the abortion pictures are not merely crying out 'it is high time to legalize abortion in Portugal', they incarnate, in the workings and reworkings of the some of the best pastel paintings since Degas (the workings and reworkings of Paula's mind, eye and hand), *survival* in a troubled and dangerous world. The same goes for her Jane Eyre images, as well as the rabbits inspired by a photograph of the Iraq war. Even these deal with fear rather than 'merely' war.

Rosamund Lehmann's wondrous and moving daughter book, *The Swan in the Evening*, is the only book by her that I went out and bought rather than inherited from my father. I did that not because it was by Lehmann, but because it was written after the death of her daughter Sally (the wife of P. J. Kavanagh, author of his own fascinating autobiography *A Perfect Stranger*) at the age of twenty-four. I confess to an abiding interest in [books about] people who die young, whether from natural causes (against nature, as we know) or suicide or execution or murder. Lehmann's *Swan* belongs with Mallarmé's *Pour un Tombeau d'Anatole*, a heartrending book of fragments for his little boy I discuss on other pages. These books segue appropriately to Hattie Gordon's *The Café after the Pub after the Funeral*, an account of her suicide brother Gareth by the daughter of Margaret and Giles Gordon. Margaret, a children's artist ('The Wombles') died several years ago and was buried on the day their divorce was due, which meant that Giles (*About a Marriage* and other novels) attended the funeral as a widower. He himself died after a fall not long after Hattie's book came out, a book which is strong stuff to come from the hand of a thirty-year-old.

Kathleen Raine

Kathleen Raine, poet indeed Poet, was a *monstre sacré* and a super-elitist (as Herbert von Karajan said of himself), one of nature's conservatives, if not the extreme right-winger à la Yeats her daughter once described to me. Even so, I was fond of her and we were good friends. I knew her well in her last twenty years, when she became a grande dame, and indeed revelled in it, which I'm not sure you're supposed to. She became a guru of Prince Charles, whose handwritten letters (with the hallmark flourishes of a large Mont Blanc pen) she used to show visitors. Once upon a time Kathleen was a wild and crazy and sexual woman, one who identified with her near namesake, the heroine of *Wuthering Heights* and, indeed, saw herself as Emily Bronte. Three of the most beautiful and revealing prose pages Raine wrote can be found in *India Seen from Afar*, volume four of the autobiographies which I now have on my desk, the others being *Farewell Happy Fields*, *The Land Unknown* and *The Lion's Mouth*. In the India volume (overall, the least interesting of the four) she discusses two predecessors, foremothers, of genius, and the gradual process by which becoming a public person has affected her relationship to her own poetry. And this, from a page whose number I wrote on the flyleaf twenty years ago: 'I was in a dream of poetic love—and love seems always to absolve. No, all that is over, I know that nothing is ever cancelled or absolved or wiped away in the pure dew of the solitary places of the hills.'

Margaret Gardiner

My old friend Margaret Gardiner, in *A Scatter of Memories*, honourably owned up to being rich, a chronic condition that enabled her to live the life she wanted, although sadly her fiancé, Bernard Deacon, anthropologist and subject of her memoir *Footprints on Malekula*, died while doing fieldwork before they could marry. Fortunately for us, modern art and progressive (although often lost) causes were her passions. She lived in a Hampstead house (where Auden used to stay), near the Freemason Arms. It was full of Hepworths (Barbara was a close friend and the subject of another Gardiner memoir, *Barbara Hepworth*) and Nicholsons (Gardiner's collection now resides in the Piers Art Centre in the Orkneys, which she donated to the nation) and I sometimes acted as her chaperone, all the time encouraging her to tell me stories. We met through Solly Zuckerman—I suspect she had been his first lover in the 1930s after he arrived from South Africa—whose 1980 pamphlet was Menard's first foray into political publishing. She had a one-night stand with Louis MacNeice. I went with her to a press conference for the launch of one of Zuckerman's books. She was dressed to the nines and all a-flutter, saying she hoped she would not put him off his stride. His reaction proved that this was a sweet and harmless projection. Hers demonstrated that she was (still) as much in love with him as I was in awe of him. Desmond Bernal too—his first book *The World, the Flesh and the Devil* is on my desk—met Gardiner through Zuckerman. Bernal was a great lover of women, *and* Gardiner was one of the three most important, according to his biographer Maurice Goldsmith in *Sage*. The others were his only wife Eileen, and Margot Heinemann who, although Goldsmith does not point this out (why?), was the lover to whom John Cornford's beautiful farewell poem from Spain beginning 'Heart of the heartless world' was dedicated, the phrase taken from a famous and eloquent passage in Marx that contains the sentence: 'Religion is the sigh of the oppressed creature, the heart of the heartless world, just as it is the spirit of a spiritless situation.' (Karl Marx is more generous to religion than Richard Dawkins and Christopher Hitchens, though Terry Eagleton, given his mellow *The Meaning of Life*, would assent to Marx's view, as would Ronald Aronson, whose *Living without God* I discuss elsewhere.) Gardiner would have been wryly amused to learn that Vanuatu (Malekula is one of its islands) is supposedly the happiest country in the world, or at least the best place to live according to the *Guardian's* value-added table. Was the paper flooded with enquiries?

Gabriel Josipovici

Gabriel Josipovici and I are near contemporaries. This novelist, playwright and literary critic has been a key figure for me in that, instinctively and intellectually, I too am hooked on the high modernists. He is a master reader of Kafka, Proust and Beckett. Long ago, when I edited the magazine *European Judaism*, I asked Josipovici to review a volume of Kafka's letters. He turned in a long essay of such magisterial authority, quiet eloquence and probing empathy that, after more than forty years, I measure my own and everybody else's criticism by this standard. Mention of the Williams and Dahlberg mother books earlier, brings me to Josipovici's contribution to the genre, *A Life*—that of his mother Sacha. I knew Sacha, who was from that Egyptian Jewish world which brought forth Edmond and Arlette Jabès, the poet Joyce Mansour and the kabbalist Carlo Suarès, author of an early Menard book, *Genesis Rejuvenated*. In a sense, Edward Said belonged to the same world, having attended the same Cairo school as Josipovici. All honour to him for his collaboration with someone who deserves the Nobel peace prize, that exemplary musician and humanist Daniel Barenboim, in founding the magnificent West Eastern Divan Orchestra, which brings together young Israeli and Palestinian musicians, and which all people who seek a peaceful solution to the political conflict should support.

Sacha Rabinovitch was tough, having been schooled during World War II while hiding in France with her toddler son. Not an ounce of flab on her body—her fitness was evident on long walks across the Sussex downs—nor indeed on her mind, her mind being something she always knew. She fought you all the way, down the line, to the wire, concerning your preferences. Something there was that depended on this perpetual agonistic engagement. The something was her sense of self which generated the kind of integral truth that emerges from dialogical encounters, such as those we find pre-eminently in the Talmud. Thus, God himself acknowledges after three years of argument between Hillel and Shammai: 'Enough already. Both these and these are the words of the living God.' The approach of Shammai is held to be legitimate, even though the precedent almost always defers to Hillel. In other words, the process of dialogue is the winner. It is not recorded how Shammai felt about this. Within our own parameters, Sacha, who published a book of poems—*Heroes and Others*—as well as many translations from the French and Italian, had no time for two of my favourites, Balzac and Jabès, and no amount of friendly persuasion made an impact. I know that Gabriel thinks my writing works, if it works at all, by association and collage rather than by rational argument, and he's right; I should try harder, certainly as a literary critic. And yet, as the lower case author of *Six Non-Lectures* wrote in a poem: 'I'd rather learn from one bird how to sing / than teach ten thousand clouds how not to dance.' All the same, perhaps

[C]ummings would agree with John Fowles that 'the true sister of poetry is dancing [dance would be a better word—AR], which preceded music in the history of man.'

FRAGMENTARIANS

Walter Benjamin

Fragments, quotations, commentaries: *The Arcades Project* is one way of entering the manifold world of Walter Benjamin. Another would be a short text I reread recently, perhaps for the fiftieth time, the 'Theses on the Philosophy of History' (in *Illuminations*), possibly modelled on Marx's 'Theses on Feuerbach'. Benjamin's eighteen theses are endlessly reverberating, a dizzying sequence that works like a long poem. Benjamin's *Berlin Childhood around 1900* was revised and completed in 1938, when he was forty-four, and remained unpublished in his lifetime. In this text and the earlier *Berlin Chronicle* (published in *One-Way Street* and also in *Reflections*), Benjamin demonstrates affinities with a slightly young writer, Michel Leiris: 'Remembrance must not proceed in the manner of a narrative . . . I am talking of a space, of moments and discontinuities' (*A Berlin Chronicle*.) In *Berlin Childhood*, we find this beautiful sentence: 'When my mother—although she was staying at home this evening—came in haste to say good night to me, I felt more keenly than ever the gift she laid on my bedspread every evening at this time: the knowledge of those hours which the day still held in store for her, and which I, consoled, took with me into sleep, like the rag doll of old.' Natalie Sarraute and other great autobiographers, anti-*Funes the Memorious* to a man and woman, dig among the ruins of remembrance, coming up with shards of sound and colour that are then composed, as if music or painting, in hyper-organized juxtapositions that mirror our own loved fragments, our own broken origins. Memories are retrieved in the space of time. The rag doll episode is as much about memory as it is about a specific memory, for Benjamin refers to 'every evening' not to a unique event. It is, in one definition of the phrase, a screen memory.

Hannah Arendt's book of essays *Men in Dark Times* contains a major critique of Walter Benjamin, which also serves as the introduction to

Illuminations. Benjamin's mind is a *flâneur's* mind, for he entrusts 'himself to chance as a guide on his intellectual journeys of exploration'. And Arendt says something important about this mind—one of the most distinguished imaginable—in its relationship to his passion for collecting: 'The figure of the collector, as old-fashioned as that of the *flâneur*, could assume such eminently modern features in Benjamin because history itself—that is, the break in tradition which took place at the beginning of [the twentieth] century—had already relieved him of the task of destruction and he only needed to bend down, as it were, to select his precious fragments from the pile of debris.' As she reminds us, not only did he collect books, he also collected quotations, which he scribbled into small notebooks and read out to his friends, for example, a report from Vienna dated Summer 1939 saying that the local gas company had 'stopped supplying gas to Jews. The gas consumption of the Jewish population involved a loss for the gas company, since the biggest consumers were the ones who did not pay their bills. The Jews used the gas especially for committing suicide.' Benjamin himself, dead by 1940, could not have known about the sinister association, and Arendt was more subtle than I am in not drawing attention to the irony. Later, Piotr Rawicz would write in *Blood from the Sky* about the German occupiers making it easier for Jews to buy cyanide on the black market. What guided Benjamin's thinking, she concludes, 'is the conviction that although living is subject to the ruin of time, the process of decay is at the same time a process of crystallisation'. Benjamin was the pearl diver engaged in rescue work. In *Moscow Diary* (16 December 1926), Benjamin describes his meeting with Joseph Roth in a luxury hotel, having gone there on a sleigh towards midnight. He reports Roth as saying that he had come to Russia as a (nearly) confirmed Bolshevik and was leaving it as a royalist. Roth died of despair in his and Benjamin's favourite city, Paris, after a slow-burning alcohol-fuelled suicide, aged forty-four, sixteen months to the day before Benjamin too died of despair after a swift self-slaughter, aged forty-eight.

The time has come, wrote Octavio Paz in the days when I still had hope for the future and enthusiastically adopted such thinking, 'to build an ethics and a politics on the poetics of the now'. Stanley Mitchell's introduction to Benjamin's *Understanding Brecht* draws attention to 'the two ideas or predispositions that dominated Benjamin's thinking during his last years: *Jetztzeit* ('the presence of the now') and *Ermattungstaktik* ('tactics of attrition'), the explosive intervention and the long slow grind. Compare the endlessly repeated time associated with commodities or the heroic time of the tragic hero, as Eagleton points out in his book, *Walter Benjamin: Or Towards a Revolutionary Criticism*. Glossing Mitchell and Eagleton, I would say that the presence of the now is a projection, in terms of ancestral prophetic hope, of the Jewish messianic redemption that shall come at the end of days. There is a sense in which, for Benjamin, politics and religion are reconciled in what is dialectical thinking at its best. No wonder Scholem saw Benjamin as the Janus-figure between Brecht and Scholem himself.

The pathos of Benjamin's death strikes me yet again. My mind's eye focuses on the powerful monument by Dani Karavan to Benjamin, near the cemetery in Port Bou that I visited with Augustus Young (described in his book *Storytime*) and Margaret Hogan after crossing the border from France, where they live in Port Vendres, only a few miles from those dark days. Michael Taussig's book-length meditation, *Walter Benjamin's Grave*, quotes Hannah Arendt as informing a sceptical Gershom Scholem 'that it is by far one of the most fantastic and beautiful places I have seen in my life'. Taussig reads allegory into the sense of place and space 'as a mix of beauty and death and namelessness'. Under a spell of death and terror, all understanding is frozen and naturalized and we end up with the state of emergency asserted in Benjamin's 'Theses'. Taussig then refers to the culture of terror produced by our leaders in their War against Terror. Mitchell quotes the pessimistic poem Brecht wrote after his close friend died: 'The enemy who drove you from your books / Will not be worn down by the likes of us', which remains true.

Michel Leiris

Michel Leiris' *Manhood* begins with a famous figure, 'The Autobiographer as Torero'. The torero is compared to the ballet dancer, even though the latter does not have the shadow of a bull's horn hovering over the performance, especially at the moment of maximum danger, namely the *coup de grâce*. Only when threatened by danger (admitting to shameful thoughts or behaviour, for example), can the autobiographer justify the pirouettes and entrechats of literary style, and risk being accused of terrorism, to deploy the terminology of Jean Paulhan's *Les Fleurs de Tarbes*. 'Every confession contains a desire to be absolved,' says Leiris, hoping at the same time that the reader 'is less a judge than an accomplice', which recapitulates Baudelaire's 'hypocrite lecteur, mon semblable, mon frère.' Leiris refers to Baudelaire's 'my heart laid bare' as being what his project is about, but the rule of his autobiographical game is derived from, where else, Breton's *Nadja*, despite his having broken with surrealism—no invention but in facts. For Leiris, this requires a collage or rather a montage technique. But although, he says, the danger to the writer is not potentially mortal, nonetheless psychically the rules he imposed on himself involve a technique of combat and ritual. This is no soft option. After talking about self-illumination and self-liberation through writing that succeeds in communicating itself to others, he concludes his introduction to one of my favourite books by rightly insisting that the writer must 'contribute evidence to the trial of our present system of values and tip the scales, with all the weight by which he is so often valued, towards the liberation of all *men*, without which none can achieve his own'. Leiris, as a surrealist and ethnologist, can be situated at the interface of Lévi-Strauss and Breton. Benjamin in his 1940 survey of French literature discusses both aspects of Leiris, and how they relate to Freud. Commenting on Leiris' readings of Lucretia and Judith, Benjamin is, not surprisingly, struck by two successive and contrasting sentences: 'I have always loved purity, folklore, all that is childish, primitive, innocent. I aspire to evil because a certain evil is necessary to entertain me,' evil being a topic Benjamin explores in his work on allegory and elsewhere. In the end it did for him.

Nathalie Sarraute, Denise Levertov and others

Nathalie Sarraute, like Michel Leiris, is a fragmentarian. Her marvellous late book *Enfance* is shot through with her characteristic listening in to undertones and overtones; she orchestrates the fluidity of experience, refusing Joycean and Proustian epiphany (I am assuming these exist in the first place), generating instead what she calls tropisms, as found in her eponymous first book, with its proses gathered like poems, of which there are fascinating echoes and after-images in the even later book *Ici*. After *Tropismes* and before *Enfance* come her novels, plays and criticism. Unsentimentally installed amidst the deep structures of felt experience, she is gentler and more introspective than the younger Duras. I love them both. Leila Berg's *Flickerbook*, William Cooper's *From Early Life* and Paul Bailey's *An Immaculate Mistake*—engaging fragmentary books—are to the day what Sarraute's books are to the moment. Another book with affinities to these, which also reminds me of the haiku poet Issa's 1819 autobiography in prose and verse, *The Year of My Life*, is Denise Levertov's *Tesserae: Memories and Suppositions*. The conscious or unconscious implication of a work in fragments is that a joined up book is not how memory works, or that such a book is appropriate for a sportsman or politician but not for someone whose life is in the written word and for whom the workings of memory are part of the very plot of the play rather than of the production. Whenever I am being sentimental about connections, which is often enough, I console myself with Levertov's comment that her father seeing Kropotkin in the British Museum Reading Room 'gives me such a sense of linkage, however flimsy'. Once she was visiting John Hayward in the flat he shared with T. S. Eliot and saw 'Mr Eliot's hat and rolled umbrella on the hall stand'. Hayward was one of those 'shadow figures who (themselves unaware) hover at the edges of one's life'.

Perhaps I should examine the word 'sentimental'. I appear to be saying that if a poet as fine and subtle as Levertov is moved by a remote or vicarious connection, then I too am allowed to be. What I really think is that it is people unmoved by such connections who have the explaining to do. So much of existence is undifferentiated and inexplicable ('the whole world was a mass of hidden words and sealed things' says the Midrash as quoted by André Neher in *The Exile of the Word*) that a link such as Levertov's to Eliot is surely full of beautiful possibility, of virtual meaning, of matrixial poetics. This is a far cry from celebrity sightings. Once I found myself alone with Madonna in a room at a Tate Gallery reception. I hesitated too long to say hello (not an intrusion if one is a fellow guest) and a bodyguard came up and that was that. I always regretted not going to a champagne breakfast in Paris at Prince Yusupov's apartment in 1961, which would have meant I was at one remove from Rasputin. Among my own friends, the marvellous sculptor

325

Raymond Mason (author of a learned and entertaining memoir, *At Work in Paris*), knew well Giacometti and Picasso; the poets Avraham Shlonsky and Octavio Paz knew Trotsky; the critic Pierre Missac (who, under the name Pierre Bonasse, was with the Free French in London and met my parents), was a friend of Walter Benjamin and Georges Bataille. It doesn't make me more important. To accuse me or to accuse myself of name-dropping or vicarious glory may be accurate but is not the main point, which is that the phenomenon adds branches and lines to the ontological flowchart. It is all part of the tesserae that make the mosaic more fascinating. And it is talismanic. In that case, superstitious is a better word than sentimental. But I am not superstitious. If that were the case, I would have to take Hemingway's route *every* time I am in that part of Paris. I don't. It's just that when I do, I am priming myself as if I were a canvas or a *tabula rasa* and indeed, for the purposes of writing, that is what I am. I understand very well why Levertov kept on looking for a lost leather luggage strap which had a long history in her family: 'Something more than my suitcase is insecure without it.' I pray that my long-vanished autograph album will turn up in a cupboard. [Later: it has, after thirty years and, guess what, I dropped everything to write a short book about it.]

F. Scott Fitzgerald

I used to read and reread regularly F. Scott Fitzgerald's *The Crack-Up*, edited by Edmund Wilson from uncollected or unpublished texts. I would quote Fitzgerald's gloss on St John of the Cross: 'In the real dark night of the soul, it is always three o'clock in the morning.' This morning, after many a summer, I revisited the book. I had forgotten that those words serve as the epigraph for John Peale Bishop's 'The Hours', a beautiful elegy to Fitzgerald included in the book and that (see Fitzgerald's essay 'Handle with Care') the exact words are: 'In a real dark night of the soul it is always three o'clock in the morning, day after day.' I don't think violence is done to Fitzgerald's painful observation if one drops the last three words, since they are implied in the rest, though 'a' is better than 'the': less tendentious. Picking up on the idea, Bishop (his *Selected Poems* is on my desk), a poet much admired by Anthony Howell and the late Nicholas Moore, glosses his friend: 'The hour of death is always four o'clock /

It is always four o'clock in the grave.' Today, the poet Elizabeth Cook emailed me a quote about memory from the poet-gardener Wendel Berry; I replied with the following paradox from *The Crack-Up*, which I underlined all those years ago and whose truth is hitting me throughout my research into the reader I used to be: 'It is sadder to find the past again and find it inadequate to the present than it is to have it elude you and remain forever a harmonious conception of memory.' Memory, as Victor Hugo wrote, is the neighbour of remorse. Ralph Waldo Emerson had plenty to say on this theme.

Letters

Introductory Note

I love letters, mainly those of writers: John Keats, Robert Lowell, Charles Reznikoff, Thomas Mann (asking Theodor W. Adorno for advice about his fictional composer's music), Rainer Maria Rilke's correspondence with Lou Andreas-Salomé; Paul Celan's correspondence with his wife (two magnificent volumes), with Nelly Sachs, with Ilana Shmueli, with Ingeborg Bachmann; Anton Chekhov, Marianne Moore, George Oppen (among whose correspondents are twelve friends of mine plus myself), Ezra Pound, Elizabeth Bishop, Vladimir Nabokov/Edmund Wilson, Charles Olson/Robert Creeley, Walter Benjamin/Gershom Scholem—and the complete, classic and instructive short epistolary exchange between two poets with an even wider age gap, Denise Levertov and William Carlos Williams. Mozart's letters are irresistible while Van Gogh's have some claim to being the best epistolary account of creativity. It is, indeed, fascination with the inner workings of creativity that leads readers to books of letters.

Elizabeth Bishop/Robert Lowell, Graham Greene

Unlike journals and diaries, letters are for the most part not written to be published, even unconsciously; Elizabeth Bishop's to her mentor (Marianne Moore) and her peer (Robert Lowell) are the most important and enthralling in her collection: for example, the deservedly famous one of 21 March 1972 where she ticks off her friend for using—changed or verbatim—his wife's

327

letters in *The Dolphin*, to Lizzie's great eventual distress: 'art just isn't worth that much.'

There is an intriguing synchronicity in the fact that on 21 March 1972 Bishop was writing to Lowell and Lowell was writing to Ricks, seeking his advice about the revision of *Notebook* as *History* and *For Lizzie and Harriet*. (Christopher Ricks also gets an acknowledgement from the editor of Lowell's letters, Saskia Hamilton, for reading the manuscript.) A week later, Lowell replies to Bishop's letter: 'I did not see them [Lizzie's letters] as slander, but as sympathetic, tho [*sic*] necessarily awful for her to read. She is the poignance of the book, though that hardly makes it kinder to her . . . The trouble is the letters make the book, I think, at least they make Lizzie real beyond my invention. I took out the worst things written against me, so as not to give myself a case and seem self-pitying . . . It's oddly enough a technical problem as well as a gentleman's problem. How can the story be told at all without the letters? I'll put my heart to it. I can't bear not to publish *Dolphin* in good form.' Lowell attempts a reckoning—letting himself off the hook a little too easily—in the last poem of *Dolphin*, which ends: 'My eyes have seen what my hand did . . .'

I doubt if anybody can bear to read an entire book of letters over an unbroken period. It feels wrong to read such a book in this way, uninterrupted by other books. It would perpetrate a violence against the nature of epistolary life. All the same, letters, like poems, are perfect reading matter for those with a short attention span and interrupted reading times. I have a hunch I shall read more writers' letters as I get older, in order to test their dialectical strategies concerning life and work against my own strategies. In this respect, Graham Greene's letters to his wife (in *A Life in Letters*) are of particular interest. His devotion to Evelyn Waugh does him credit, for Waugh spoke his mind about those books of Greene that he didn't like. Greene wrote in his Africa journal *In Search of a Character*: 'I would claim not to be a writer of Catholic novels, but a writer who took . . . characters with Catholic ideas for his material.' Did his adopted Catholicism enable him to mine material that could not have been accessed in other ways? It seems to have offered this singular intelligence a resistance that triggered narrative reaction. I read his *The End of the Affair*, *The Power and the Glory* and *The Heart of the Matter* with great intensity on buses and tubes while commuting to my first day job nearly fifty years ago. Many years later, I borrowed Paula's father's copy of *Brighton Rock* to read on a return flight from Lisbon to London, and bought *The Quiet American* for a flight to New Zealand. Paula's father and mine had similar taste in fiction and non-fiction, and often owned the same edition of the same book. Little by little I shall end up having read all of Greene's novels.

As for my own letters, I only write a handful now, mostly replies to the hardcore letter writers who do not have, or do not admit to having, word processors: Harry Guest and Christopher Middleton, Claude Vigée and Terry Eagleton, for example. Elaine Feinstein tells me that she has fifteen thousand email letters filed away in her computer. Earlier in this book, I mentioned Wendy Cope sold her emails to a library. In New York, Mike Heller showed me his archive [now sold to Stanford University] in a rented storeroom on Eighth Avenue. I was his top sender of faxes when he had email and I still didn't: yellowing my old faxes are, and folding at the edges, the ink fading. They remain copyright of course . . .

Emails and faxes are not letters. One of my mature students wrote her essays in prose that laboured under the combined and fatal influence of emails, text messaging and bullet point presentations—staple diet in her day job in the fashion industry. Back to the Graham Greene letters: it is a well-edited book and, like the Ted Hughes letters, thanks to careful selection it presents a narrative shape to that side of the writer's life. It would be interesting to compare letters written in the days before telephones (Van Gogh) with those written in the days of telephones and pre-email (Hughes and Greene), then fax, and so on. Considered or unconsidered, such letters are on the way out. And this is a great loss to reader and writer. I have been rereading for a conference paper on F. T. Prince my intense correspondence with him in the 1970s, his handwritten and single-spaced, typed air letters. The stuff of history now, apparently.

Vincent and Theo Van Gogh; *Wolfgang Amadeus Mozart*

Is there a more revealing or more moving self-portrait, epistolary or not, of a human being, in this case a painter—indeed one of the greatest painters who ever lived—than the letters of Vincent Van Gogh? They should be explored when courage fails, when self-pity encroaches, when example is called for. The immensely long letter to Theo of July 1880 reveals the quality of the man's mind, spirit, intelligence and self-understanding. The whole book is instinct with Vincent's sense of duty to his calling. As usual, I made marks in the margins where I particularly approved of something during readings over the years, especially when I first read it. In July 1882, he writes to Theo: 'I cannot keep from working any longer. Art is jealous. She does not want us to choose illness in preference to her, so I do as she wishes.' And in August 1883: 'The world only concerns me insofar as I feel a certain debt and duty towards it because I have walked that earth for thirty years, and, out of gratitude, want to leave some souvenir in the shape of drawings or pictures—not made to please a certain cult in art, but to express a sincere human feeling.' Arles, September 1888: 'I can very well do without God both in my life and in my painting, but I cannot, ill as I am, do without something which is greater than I, which is life—the power to create. And if, defrauded of the power to create physically, a man tried to create thoughts in place of children, he is still very much part of humanity.' My last quote is from November 1889: 'It is the experience and the meagre work of every day which alone ripens in the long run and allows one to do things that are more complete and more true. Thus slow long work is the only way, and all ambition and resolve to make a good thing of it, false. For you must spoil quite as many canvases when you return to the onslaught every morning, as you succeed with.'

Mozart's [selected] letters, less introspective and less thoughtful than those of Van Gogh, still yield insights into the eternal disjunction between a sublime *oeuvre* and the human situation of a genius who often had to be away from home and could not pick up a phone: 'see that Karl behaves himself. Give him kisses from me. Take an electuary if you are constipated—not otherwise.' On 19 May 1789, Mozart writes from Berlin a letter that Rousseau (whose *Confessions* was published seven years earlier) would have cherished: 'Oh how glad I shall be to be with you again, my darling! But the first thing I shall do is to take you by your front curls; for how on earth could you think, or even imagine, that I had forgotten you? How could I possibly do so? For even supposing such a thing, you will get on the very first night a thorough spanking . . . and this you may count upon.' The tone suggests that this activity was a traditional part of their foreplay repertoire, a drumroll overture before the full opera. Perhaps Mozart had read *The Confessions* and was aware of the philosopher's predilections, although I am not suggesting an erotic influence, rather an affinity. David Cairns, a distinguished musicologist whom we meet every year at Tom and Ann Rosenthal's New Year's Eve party, might know about Mozart's taste in reading. Ah, New Year's Eve in Gloucester Avenue for well over a decade: the annual gathering of an ageing cohort. Bless the hosts. I phone Cairns who says he will check out the complete edition of Mozart's letters and other sources. He calls back to say that although Mozart's *Bastien and Bastienne* was a parody of Rousseau's *Le Devin du village*, there is no evidence that Mozart, despite being a voracious reader, had read *The Confessions*. The work was commissioned by Dr Anton Mesmer no less, who himself would later be parodied in *Cosi Fan Tutti*. Wolfgang Amadeus Mozart was twelve years old. Still curious, I went to my public library and, after consulting the librarian's computer, ordered Robert W. Gutman's *Mozart: A Cultural Biography*. It arrived within a few days. I checked out the Rousseau references. These confirm Cairns' view but they also demonstrate that Rousseau loomed large in Mozart's intellectual world (or culture, as Gutman has it) and since, as Cairns says, the composer was a voracious reader, I think it is a virtual certainty that he read *The Confessions*.

Stendhal

In the high street shop that sells second-hand goods to support the local hospice, I found *To the Happy Few*, Stendhal's selected letters, translated by the poet Norman Cameron. The novelist talks about the composition of *The Charterhouse of Palma* in a long and fascinating letter written the year before he died (three drafts of the letter are presented; it is not known what the final version contained) to the man he flatteringly but truthfully calls 'the King of Novelists', Honoré de Balzac. This was in response to the latter's long (seventy two pages!), intelligent and highly favourable review (with inevitable reservations about style), where we infer from Stendhal's third draft that Balzac owned to reading the novel three times. These drafts present a remarkable example of the dialectical relationship between life and work, so wrongly perceived by Yeats to require a choice.

From the first draft: 'I compose twenty or thirty pages, then I feel a need for distraction—a little love-making, if I can, or a little dissipation. Next morning I have forgotten everything, and when I read the three or four final pages of yesterday's chapter, today's chapter comes to me. The book you have taken into your protection was dictated in from sixty to seventy days. I was under a pressure of ideas . . . I agree with all you say except about style. I know of only one rule: style cannot be too clear, too simple . . . Often I ponder for a quarter of an hour whether to place an adjective before or after its noun. I seek to be 1) truthful, 2) clear in my accounts of what happens in a human heart.'

From the second draft: 'While writing the *Chartreuse*, in order to acquire the correct tone I occasionally read a few pages of the *Code civil* . . . I could never read twenty pages of M. de Chateaubriand . . . In short, monsieur, while putting down much of your excessive praise to pity for a forsaken child, I am in agreement with you on all matters of principle . . .' Robert Alter, in his biography of Stendhal, *A Lion for Love*, thinks this is a 'polemic fabrication for Balzac's benefit, to illustrate Stendhal's stylistic ideal, which was not Balzac's own'.

From the third draft: 'Permit me to employ an obscenity. I do not wish to f . . . g the reader's soul ["Permettez-moi un mot sale. Je ne veux pas branler l'âme du lecteur." As late as 1952, Cameron felt obliged to take "evasive action", as James Campbell likes to say, when using the word "frig" in a book.] The poor reader lets pass such ambitious expressions as "the wind uprooting the waves", but they come back to him when the moment of emotion has gone by . . . As half-fools become more and more numerous, the part played by form diminishes. If the *Chartreuse* had been translated into French by Mme Sand, it would have had some success. But to express what is told in the present two volumes she would have needed three or four . . . Think of [David] Hume: imagine a history of France, from 1780 to 1840, written with Hume's good sense. People would read it even in patois. In fact, it would be written like the *Code civil* . . . I take a character well known to me, I leave him with the habits he has contracted in the art of going off every morning in pursuit of pleasure, and next I give him more wit . . .'

Osip Mandelstam and Rainer Maria Rilke

Two of the irresistible remarks in Osip Mandelstam's *Collected Critical Prose and Letters*—and signalled as such by my marginalia from 1991, the year before Menard published the late Masha Enzensberger's Mandelstam translations—I take from his 1921 essay 'Word and Culture'. First: 'Poetry is the plough that turns up time in such a way that time's abyssal strata, its black earth, appear on the surface.' Compare his poem 'Black Earth': 'A thousand mounds of furrowed language / And something unbounded within these bounds', as translated by James Greene. On my desk are Marina Tsvetayeva's *Selected Poems* and *Black Earth*, where Elaine Feinstein's elective affinities triumph. The two Russian poets both lived, at different times, in Voronezh, the centre of the black earth region. How could such a resonant phrase not find its way into their poems? The second quote from 'Word and Culture': 'Is the thing really master of the word? The word is a Psyche. The living word does not designate an object, but freely chooses for its dwelling place, as it were, some objective significance, material thing or beloved body. And the word wanders freely around the thing, like the soul around an abandoned, but not forgotten body.' As it happens, thirty-five of the letters in the book were written to his wife during 1926, the year which saw a unique three way correspondence between Pasternak, Tsvetayeva and Rilke, later published as *Letters Summer 1926*.

I have put asterisks against a profound remark, which became the epigraph for my unpublished novel, in the margin of a letter Tsvetayeva wrote to Rilke on 22 August 1926, four months before his death: 'Love lives on words and dies of deeds.' Then, in a letter to a friend that is included in the book because it deals with the German poet's death, Tsvetayeva writes of Rilke: 'Every line [of poetry] is a collaboration with "higher forces" and a poet is doing *very well* if he acts as a good secretary. Have you ever considered the beauty of that word secretary (from "secret")?' I *have* considered it: in the context of Balzac's *Unknown Masterpiece*, a story Rilke loved and I translated. Rilke himself wrote about the story in a key letter to his wife dated 9 October 1907, where he tells her the story of Cézanne's identification with Balzac's hero Frenhofer. One can make a further play on the word secret, namely 'secrete'. Nothing, it would seem, is impermeable.

333

I resist the temptation to riff on Walter Benjamin's wonderful meditations on porosity—a project for another night. However, I cannot resist a final Tsvetayeva quotation, from her letter to Pasternak of 9 February 1927, in which she tells him that the last book Rilke read was by Valéry (unlike Jabès, whose last book, his wife told me on the day of the funeral, was by Leiris; also unlike Greene, whose last book was, perhaps unexpectedly, *The Letters of Ezra Pound*). In the same letter to Pasternak, Tsvetayeva writes of Rilke: 'for you, his death is not in the natural order of things. For me his life is not in the natural order of things.'

In a letter to his wife written a few days before the 9th October letter, Rilke writes at some length about memory and work. This letter was written in the hotel at 29 rue Cassette where thirty years later Joseph Roth would stay, as we know from the magnificent pictorial biographies written and compiled by Heinz and Victoria Lunzer:

> I succeed only in my best moments, whereas it is precisely in the worst that it is most necessary. Van Gogh could . . . paint the most direful objects on his direst days. How else could he have survived? . . . Oh that we had no memories of not having worked, memories that are still pleasurable! Memories of lying quiet and letting pleasure come. Memories of hours idled away over the fingering of old illustrations, over the reading of casual novels: multitudes of such memories right back into childhood. Whole tracts of life lost, lost even for the re-telling by reason of the seductive quality that still proceeds from their languorousness. Why? If we had nothing but work-memories from our earliest days—how firm the ground would be beneath us: we could stand . . .

This recalls Proust's essay on reading and the letter continues in the same vein. There is, however, such relish in the account that it succeeds in disavowing the proclaimed wish: 'Oh that we had no memories of not having worked'—one for the anthology I shall never edit of simultaneous avowals and disavowals in literature.

Rilke and Proust were exact contemporaries: Rilke lived for fifty-one years and four months, Proust for fifty-one years and one month. They have influenced more writers and readers than most. They interested Benjamin, who translated Proust and wrote a brilliant essay on him. In a letter written about a month after Proust's death, Rilke reminds a friend that he was one of the first to read and admire the French novelist. Perhaps the last letter he ever wrote, indeed perhaps his last written words (apart from an anti-climactic parenthesis) was to Supervielle. Written in French, it ends: 'I think of you poet, friend, and in doing that I still think of the world, that poor debris of a vase which remembers that it once was clay.'

Nadezhda Yakovlevna Mandelstam and Paul Celan

Larissa Naiditch's *Paul Celan* contains the facsimile reproduction of a letter of 12 July 1962 from Nadezhda Yakovlevna Mandelstam. In her exceptionally clear hand, she writes that, thanks to Ilya Ehrenberg, she has already read Celan's translations of her husband, and found them close to the original. The book will be a test of my Russian, but I am highly motivated, for Celan, like Rimbaud, is one of my 'phares'. Later on, we learn from John Felstiner's book on Celan, Mandelstam's widow changed her mind about Celan and associated his versions with Lowell's imitations. Others strongly disagree with her and find Celan's Mandelstam to be among the supreme achievements in translation, identifying everything, including himself, with the original and the creator, and producing a miracle of work. Celan even said: 'I consider translating Mandelshtam into German to be as important a task as my own verses.' Felstiner quotes a love poem of 1948: 'Only faithless am I true. / I am you, when I am I.' ('Ich bin du, wenn ich ich bin.') Translation and poem are simultaneously one and not one, like lovers. Indeed, long ago, I wrote that the activity involves one language making love to another. Keith Bosley rebuked me: 'In public, they are just good friends.' When I clicked on Celan in 'find and replace', his name came up as itself in all but one case: 'Iceland'. You could construct a cryptic crossword puzzle clue: 'Cold country buries poet in Freudian concept'. This particular computer function leads to weird and wonderful discoveries. Thus, since we are with Freud, Paula's surname is found in 'superego', just as 'ego' is already found in 'Rego'. What a resource that would have been for that remarkable sound poet, Bob Cobbing! Kurt Schwitters would have loved it—pure *merz*.

Paul Celan

Here is *Correspondance*, the handsomely produced, boxed, two-volume set, exemplarily edited by Bertrand Badiou, of Paul Celan's letters to and from his wife, sent by the publisher at Le Seuil courtesy of Yves Bonnefoy, who organized the gift when I reminded him that Gisèle Celan-Lestrange had been a friend of mine. That it begs to be read goes without question, especially if one considers Celan to be the greatest poet of his time. I am moved by these traces of the poet's travelling life, including the Stork Inn (Zurich), associated too with Friedrich Hölderlin and others, where Celan met Nelly Sachs and wrote the famous poem dedicated to her and where Paula and I stayed in the room with the best view, 323; I am further moved by the way certain poems can be glossed and shadowed in the light of letters.

At the funeral of Edmond Jabès at Père Lachaise in 1991 I saw a woman I only half recognized, until with a pang I realized it was the widow of Celan, now mortally ill and a shadow of the beautiful and elegant woman I had known: 'Gisèle?' She looked at me, and there was a pause, as if to complete my half-recognition and make it whole: 'Anthony?' We hugged each other. Less than a year later, she died. Gisèle, herself a distinguished print-maker and artist, exasperated by the amount of time she had to spend dealing with copyright questions, anthology requests, etc., asked me in Cambridge after dinner at George Steiner's if I thought Michael Hamburger would agree to be the exclusive translator of her late husband; it would simplify her life no end, she said. I told her that Michael had always insisted he was, on principle, against exclusivity when it came to poetry translation, although it was clear that other considerations had to enter the frame with a long prose book; therefore, what she proposed was not the solution. Anyone who wants to write an account of the relationship between a [male] poet and a [female] artist could do worse than study closely this intense and enthralling exchange of letters, the most significant of its kind since that of Rilke and Lou Andreas-Salomé.

[Coda: A few years after reading the French edition of Celan's correspondence with Shmueli (see the account of my 2006 Paris trip), I was sent the American edition by its publisher Stanley Moss. Rereading the poems Celan enclosed with his letters, I am struck by the way syntax and rhythm, always dialectically charged in the best poetry, in his poetry seem to be one and the same thing: 'The content draws its reality from the structure' (Claude Lévi-Strauss quoted by Pierre Boulez). I am also struck by the way Shmueli sometimes sounds like Celan in her replies: similar in that to some of Kafka's correspondents].

Kathy Acker and Paul Buck

A book of letters like no other is *Spread Wide*, Paul Buck's extraordinary collage work based in part on communications from that powerful writer of 'textual and narrative pulsations', his close friend Kathy Acker, who died in 1997. From Buck's persona text: 'Writing is the making of pleasure, as is living, as is death. They want me to take all the violence out of my writing. They want me to take all the sex out. They want me to take all meaning out. They want me to remove the language. And then they send in the anaesthetist to make a TV show on me. No wonder nobody ever kept a video of it. Oh so pretty. Pretty in pink. Each of us must use writing to do exactly what we want.' And Acker does just that: 'My cunt used to be a men's toilet. Or should I say my cunt used to be a gent's toilet? Cos I had every intention of setting Daphne du Maurier as my stylist. And you know, style rules. Like George, you gotta have style.' I had my suspicions and Buck confirmed that Georges Bataille was being referred to. The book is replete with facsimile letters, illustrations, varied typographies and lists of resources. As the blurb says, the book's title does not only refer to thighs, but to writing itself: 'To examine the mapping of the book is to yield to memory, to escape, to delirium; to accept utopia, fiction, fable; to visit the monuments, the abominations, the horrors of the texts, one's own monuments, abominations, and horrors, without ever having to rise from the sofa.' Buck, rightly pleased, told me that Susan Hiller called the book, among various superlatives, 'loving'. This would not be the word she would use to describe *A Cunt Not Fit for a Queen*, an earlier hand-typed book by Buck published in Amsterdam: we find these words on the title page, but they were dropped from the cover, presumably on the assumption that Inspector Luff of the Yard would not look inside. Had he done so, he might have thought Wimbledon rather than Amsterdam, since in its pages Georges Bataille meets Gertrude Stein in the mixed singles: not a gone world, rather agon world. *Pimot*, Paul's sharply articulated first book, fizzes with intent, even though the extent of his talent had to await later developments, such as *No Lettuces for Miss Lush*, a book dating from 1981 but with a photo of him on the cover labelled 'author as hitman 1965'. His new and enthralling book *A Public Intimacy*, based on his lifelong practice and discipline of scrapbooks, has arrived in time for me to read it: how I envy his ordered mind and tidy files! What nostalgia to see a clipping from *Le Monde* sent by Claude Royet-Journoud with the same inscription as several he sent me: 'In case you missed it'.

Roland Barthes, in *Sade, Fourier, Loyola* writes something germane to my (and perhaps your) reaction to Acker's remark about toilets, my own reaction being that I have to make a concerted effort to visualize her metaphor, and the effort neutralizes any shock, which is not to say that she, given the matricial narrative in which such phrases are embedded, *intended* to shock in a way that would have been the case had the phrase been written by virtually any other woman writer I can think of. Compare the cunt in Gustave Courbet's 'L'Origine du monde', once on the wall in Lacan's dining room and now at Orsay; in this painting, the woman's pubic hair serves as clothing, yet there is an erotic charge, precisely because of the 'clothing' and a directness of gaze that bypasses delay since, by definition, no effort has to be made to visualize what is not a metaphor but an image unmediated by concept and figure of speech. Barthes: 'Everything is restored to the power of the discourse. This power, which one hardly ever thinks about, is not only one of evocation, but also of negation. Language has this faculty to deny, to forget, to dissociate the real: written, shit does not smell; Sade can inundate his partners with it, we receive no effluvium, only the abstract sign of an unpleasant occurrence.' Oddly enough, in *Essais critiques*, Barthes writes of Robbe-Grillet (unexpectedly Nabokov's favourite French novelist) that his 'major project . . . is to insert the object into a spatial dialectic'—almost a definition of what happens in painting.

Diaries/Journals

Clifford Odets (with David Ignatow and David Hare)
Clifford Odets' 1940 journal, *The Time Is Ripe*, has been resting on a shelf I

cleared today after opening the French windows in an attempt to cool the flat by allowing what little breeze there is to percolate through to the open kitchen window across the hall. The very fact Odets kept a journal for only one year of his adult life gives it a particular cachet, and it is clear he intended to publish it at some point. In general, the nature of entries in journals, which are spontaneous or, at any rate, immediate even if, as with Odets, intended for publication, makes them different from memoirs or autobiographies written years after the events described, although sometimes authors draw on private diaries. 'Its pages cover almost a full year in the personal life of a "successful" writer living in a very "successful" country,' writes Odets. Odets wanted young people to understand the nature of success as hinted at by his quotation marks. Arthur Miller and Tennessee Williams rose to prominence after the war: they were ten and five years younger than Odets; doubtless this is why there is no reference to them. Mind you, there is almost nothing about Eugene O'Neill who, Clifford Odets reckons, was influenced by August Strindberg. Meanwhile, elsewhere in the city, the poet David Ignatow, a very different writer, has begun early entries in what would later be published as his *Notebooks*. This was a poet with a proper day job as office manager in a bookbindery: 'I hate the whole fucking shop, its noise, its arguments, its problems, its jealousies and intrigues.' Ignatow's poems in *Say Pardon* speak the mind's I of a man who would transcend his quotidian reality. It's not that he's a poet, therefore he goes beyond the daily bread, it's that he has to go beyond the daily bread, and the only way to do that is make poems.

Odets was married to both Luise Rainer and Bette Grayson. Famous and successful playwrights and screenwriters meet and marry film stars. *C'est normal*. Odets lived at 1, Fifth Avenue, north of Washington Square, during some of this period. On Wednesday 21 August 1940, he writes that Trotsky had died of his wounds the previous day: 'This depressed me and yet was the right way for him to die, for surely he lived by the sword. He was one of the few characters living who could be said to be on a tragic plane of life and suffering. In his life there is an epic play.' The use of the word 'character' is slightly odd and is doubtless linked to the idea of Trotsky's life as a play. Odets quotes Waldo Frank as saying: 'The artist, like an advancing army, should stick close to his source of supplies.' One source for Odets is Rilke, of whom he is a fervent admirer (in translation), and it tells you something about Rilke that he turns up in the journals and autobiographies of so many writers and artists. It tells you something about Odets too, and I find it surprising that there is no mention of Eliot, Pound, Stevens or Auden, to name the four major living Anglophone poets a man like Odets would have been aware of in 1940.

I asked David Hare what he thought about this semi-forgotten figure, remembered by old lefties like my mother. Hare explained that, along with O'Neill, Odets is a historically significant figure as the father of socially serious drama in the USA. Before these two, there was nothing. Naturally I mentioned Miller as a younger near-contemporary of Odets, and was interested to learn that Miller told Hare that O'Neill had read and admired *Death of a Salesman* while in hospital during his last illness, but David had doubts about this. Who can blame Miller for wanting O'Neill, perhaps more than any other living person, to admire his great play? Here, not so by the way, is *Acting Up*, the diary of Hare in his role as tyro actor, starring in London and on Broadway in his own monologue, *Via Dolorosa*. I did not see the stage production, catching it on Radio Three during a long car drive. There are worse ways of passing time on a motorway than listening to a man acting in his own monologue, one which requires no stage props and whose subject matter is close to my heart, namely Israel and Palestine. When I reviewed Antony Sher's *Primo*, a vain and poorly judged account of Richard Wilson's production of Sher's monologue (adapted from Levi's *If This a Man*, a book I have written about extensively), I held up Hare's book as the sort of book Sher should have written.

Mihail Sebastian (*with Max Blecher*)

Clifford Odets' journal spanned a mere eleven months, while Mihail Sebastian's fascinating *Journal* lasted from 1935 till 1944. A playwright and novelist, he survived the war and the Holocaust, only to be killed in a road crash in 1945. He was a close friend of the renowned scholar and supporter of the antisemitic Iron Guard, Mircia Eliade. Another friend, the writer Emile Cioran, was also a member. Fortunately, a third friend, Eugene Ionesco, was neither a fascist nor an antisemite. Sebastian was not in the ghetto, nor was he deported, so he could reveal through his journal what 'normal' life was like round him, albeit not in the detail found in Victor Klemperer's remarkable Berlin diaries—on which Tom Paulin based a poem in *The Invasion Handbook*—and his *Language of the Third Reich*. On Monday 11 October 1943, Sebastian writes: 'Saturday was Yom Kippur. I do not try to put any order into my "Judaism". I fasted, and I went to the synagogue in the evening to hear the sound of the *shofar*, the ram's horn. I tried to intone the "Avinu Malkenu". Why? Do I believe? Do I want to believe? No, not even that. But it is as if, in all these unthinking gestures, there is a need for warmth and peace.' On 16 April 1938, he quotes Nietzsche's *Daybreak* as referring to 'the Jewish ballast' in Christianity. This remark comes after he has been listening to the Saint Matthew Passion; the previous autumn, he continues, he stopped at Chartres Cathedral to look at the Circumcision of Jesus: 'It was just like an ordinary *bris*: an old man, holding the ritual knife in the one hand and the child's "willy" in the other, looked like the Moishe Shoikhet in Braila.' One wishes Sebastian had survived, for his own life's sake, but also because he would without doubt have entered into dialogue with the younger figure of Celan. Max Blecher was a close friend of Mihail Sebastian. Blecher died aged twenty-nine from tuberculosis of the spine, having written a book of poems and two novels, the first of which is the marvellous *Scarred Hearts*. The young poet, immobilized in his sanatorium in Berck-Page, would like to die, reports Sebastian. 'There is no hope, it is given up', the last line of Sylvia Plath's poem 'Berck-Plage', serves us, appropriately enough, as an epitaph. The whole poem is live with the medicalized atmosphere of the seaside resort, so brilliantly evoked by Blecher.

Isaac Babel

Isaac Babel kept his *1920 Diary* for four months. He was far more disciplined than Odets, which is not what you would expect of a Cossack although it was a useful attribute in an urban Jew assigned as a journalist on the Soviet army newspaper, *The Red Cavalryman*, to Semyon Budyonny's rebellious Cossack cavalry during the Polish–Soviet War. The Cossacks were famously antisemitic and Babel's ethno-religious background was concealed from them, including using a false name as a precaution, for he was certainly not in rebellion again his Jewishness, as many beautiful stories bear witness. Babel: what kind of name is that? As an East End Jewish boy, my uncle Isidore used to play table tennis against a neighbour and future champion called Ernie Bubley. The Babylonian Talmud is known as the Talmud Babli, so that is probably the source, or could it be the tower of Babel? Isaac Babel also kept the records for the division and did all kinds of other jobs including interrogating prisoners. Odets writes about society and politics and personal relationships but Babel is training his eye and his ear, and he regularly reminds himself to go into certain things in more detail. The diary is a template for future stories. Folklore research conducted by another Jewish visitor to Volhynia and elsewhere in the Pale of Settlement, S. Ansky, some years earlier led to another literary masterpiece *The Dybbuk*. Babel certainly saw this play, which was produced by his friend Solomon Mikhoels, who was later murdered by Stalin.

Carol Avins, in her excellent introduction to Babel's diary, rightly states that some entries read like anthropological field notes. They remind me of Ansky, who died in 1920. Perhaps Babel read the playwright's diary, which would have enthralled him. Avins reminds us that this was the period of Chagall's glorious stage sets for the Yiddish State Theatre in Moscow. On 23 July 1920, Babel finds himself in Demidovka: it is the Sabbath and the eve of the ninth day of the month of Av, a fast day second only to Yom Kippur in the Jewish calendar, a day when terrible destruction either took place or was said to have taken place, a day when history and myth intertwine like a double helix. He, supposedly a Russian, is billeted on a religious Jewish family. He tells them fairy stories about Bolshevism (with the implication of consolation and perhaps optimism rather than barefaced lying for, like Mandelstam, he welcomed and supported the Revolution) and listens while the son of the house tells the story of the destruction of the Temple (both Temples were said to have been destroyed on the ninth of Av). 'Outside— Demidovka, night, Cossacks, all just as it was when the temple was destroyed'. A couple of days later, he feels 'anguished, I need to think about it all, Galicia, the world war, my own destiny'.

In Brody on 31 July 1920, this Jew pretending to be a Russian and riding with the Cossacks finds a German bookshop, with magnificent uncut books about the west and chivalrous Poland, and we recall that Joseph Roth had left the town a few years earlier for Berlin and Vienna and that the language of Roth's education and early upbringing, in this important centre of Haskala (the Jewish enlightenment), was German. 'I tear myself away from the bookshop in despair.' As well he might, for what is he doing there, or rather, who is he being there? And what there is there? (Compare Gertrude Stein on Oakland, California.) Well, not far away are the ancestral towns of Sigmund Freud, Henry Roth, Bruno Schulz, Aharon Appelfeld, Piotr Rawicz and Shmuel Yosef Agnon, as well as Paul Auster and yours truly. It was a good idea to leave if you were Jewish. If Ukrainians or Russians or Poles didn't make your life a misery—and his description of Polish cruelty is incomparable in its horror—the German occupiers would oblige twenty years later, but Babel was dead by then, murdered because he was a free spirit. 6 August 1920, Khotin: 'Why can't I get over my sadness? Because I'm far from home, because we are destroyers [he himself is no exception on a low yet real level, and he admits it], because we move like a whirlwind, like a stream of lava, hated by everyone, life shatters, I am at a huge, never-ending service for the dead.' Not far away, too, are the years when he will write many of his stories; and then, after his death at forty-six (Mandelstam at forty-seven), the years of his unwritten stories (and Mandelstam's unwritten poems).

George Seferis and Stendhal

> Wherever I travel, Greece wounds me.
>
> —George Seferis, 'In the Manner of G. S.'

George Seferis' *A Levant Journal* and *A Poet's Journal* command my attention again, after a number of years. Here are his *Collected Poems* translated by Edmund Keeley and Philip Sherrard—always to hand, and versions—and other translations. When you know and love the work of a great poet, you will be moved by his or her journal, especially those entries that amount to a critique of, or warning to, yourself, which was why I put a mark in the margin against certain thoughts. Thus, 16 August 1946: 'Poros, enclosed as it is, nonetheless reminds me how few things I need, that I should dispense with things that prevent me from seeing'; 25 January 1947: 'My weakness (and occasionally strength) of never being able to concentrate on one thing alone. This too, as

I go along, grows steadily'; 5 June 1949: 'In my youth I had a tendency to jot down moments of distress. Perhaps it's progress: I now feel sorry when I note that the expansion of joy didn't impel me as easily towards paper.'

On 15 March 1950, Seferis writes that he had received some books from Z in Paris, including Stendhal's *Journal intime*. He quotes in French the beginning: 'Milan, le 28 Germinal an IX: J'entreprends d'écrire l'histoire de ma vie jour par jour. Je ne sais si j'aurai la force de remplir ce projet, déjà commencé à Paris. Voilà déjà une faute de français; il y en aura beaucoup, parce que je prends pour principe *de ne pas me gêner et de n'effacer jamais.*'; 'I undertake to write the story of my life day by day. I don't know if I'll have the strength to fulfil this project, already begun in Paris. I have already made one mistake in my French; there will be many more, because it is a principle of mine *not to restrain myself and not to correct anything.*' Seferis explains that the italicized emphasis is his and that he has been thinking about that passage in recent days. After discussing his old journals, he continues: 'I also wrote, much more irregularly, "without restraint and without correcting anything". But I didn't plan "to write the story of my life day by day". Day by day we live our life; we don't write it—writing, no matter what you do, is only a part of life.' This is a fascinating gloss on a deeply intriguing passage by Stendhal. In his lowlier day jobs, the French novelist didn't work as hard as ambassador Seferis would over a century later; all the same, he doesn't need to be told by Seferis that writing is only a part of life—in any case, writing [dictating] *The Charterhouse of Palma* in nine weeks must certainly feel like the whole of your life! Although Seferis' poem 'Stratis the Mariner among the Agapanthi', quoted in my introduction to this book, was written in one day, this, even pro rata, was not an equal achievement in terms of quantity. But to compare the apple of a great poet to the pear of a great novelist is pointless, even though Seferis gave me the idea in the first place!

Examining those opening sentences in their own right, rather than through the prism of Seferis' journal, one is struck by Stendhal's programme, its extraordinarily modern self-reflexive nature: What principle is involved here? It is not that he wants his prose to flow more freely; that would only be true if he was talking about the first draft. On the contrary, he wants to problematize it as part of a strangely modern strategy, deployed in a more complex way (with mistakes, false starts, diagrams, contradictions, etc.) in *The Life of Henry Brulard*, and this is one of the reasons why, as I suggested earlier, *Henry Brulard* (together with *Memoirs of an Egoist*) is a work a century ahead of its time, a forerunner of Italo Calvino and Max Sebald; it is, as I have also suggested, the first modern autobiography, along with Wordsworth's *Prelude*. As for the mistake in the French, I thought it should perhaps read 'accomplir ce projet' and emailed Bonnefoy, whose reply here I part translate and part leave in French, for obvious reasons: 'Yes, probably Stendhal is incriminating "remplir", and rightly so. On ne remplit pas un projet, on le réalise. Ce que l'on remplit, ce sont ses obligations. But employing the future after "si" is fairly doubtful too, in correct usage the present tense is required. "je ne sais pas si je suis capable de mener à bien ce projet".' So, two mistakes in two sentences: not bad going. Stendhal has designs on his readers and he stated as a fact (and also 'without self-pity', as Canetti writes in *Crowds and Power*) that it would be many years before he found readers beyond the original 'happy few'. Italo Calvino's *The Uses of Literacy* and Ilya Ehrenberg's *Chekhov, Stendhal and Other Essays* discuss Stendhal with love and insight. Ehrenberg ends his essay on Stendhal by quoting Chekhov: ' "You can lie in love, in politics and in medicine, you can deceive people and God himself—there have been cases of that, too—but you cannot deceive in art." Thus Henri Beyle lived, wrote and loved. Can any writer ask for more?'

David Gascoyne

> *Multiplicity is my daemonia* . . . what is important is above all continuity (secret unity of selfhood) . . . Suspended as it were between *analytical* and *lyrical* utterance, one ends in silence.
> —David Gascoyne, *Collected Journals 1936–1942*

Keith Bosley's translations of Pierre Jean Jouve (*An Idiom of Night*) were eventually followed by David Gascoyne's translations of the French master (*Despair Has Wings*); Roger Scott's introduction to the Gascoyne volume ends with a quote from Balthus about Jouve, his close friend, a few months before the fall of France: 'a voice that is the last refuge of light in this dark night, a glimmer of the dawn to come'. Scott has also edited Gascoyne's *Selected Prose*

1934–1996, which includes major essays such as the introduction to his early book *Hölderlin's Madness*. In this essay, Gascoyne discusses the affinities between Hölderlin and Blake; Hölderlin also reminds him of Beddoes, Coleridge and, above all, Rimbaud. He quotes the carpenter Zimmer in whose charge the poet was during the thirty years he spent in the tower room (room = zimmer in German) in Tübingen: 'if he went mad it was not because he hadn't enough mind but because he had too much'. According to John Felstiner, Paul Celan, the day before he killed himself, was reading a biography of Hölderlin. The poet underlined these words: 'Sometimes this genius goes dark and sinks down into the bitter well of his heart.' He did not underline the rest of the sentence: 'but mostly his apocalyptic star glitters wondrously'. Stephen Spender, in his ventriloqual poem, 'Hölderlin's Old Age': '. . . How strange it is that . . . / . . . / In my mad age, I rejoice, and my spirit sings / Burning intensely in the centre of a cold sky'.

Gascoyne's *Collected Journals 1936–1942* cover his Paris years. Here too are his *Journal 1936–1937* and *Journal 1937–1939*, both gifts to me from Jeremy Reed, and published in reverse order. A few days after the poet's twenty-first birthday in 1937, he quotes the critic Jacques Thibaudet on Stendhal: 'The presence, degree or absence of energy, that is what makes [for] a destiny.' And a quote which hurts because I know all about such deadlock: 'The chief cause of my laziness: a sort of *deadlock*. If only the energy always simmering in me *au fond* could find a direct, unhindered outlook, what a mass of work I should achieve.' Later in the journal he writes: 'One must learn never to be discouraged by muddles or disappointments, but always to preserve enough energy to begin again.' This is from the long entry of 14 November 1938. The nobility and depth of his thought, even at the age of twenty-two, is inspirational. What a remarkable journal Gascoyne's is, a rare exploration of the inner life of a poet who for a few years produced marvellous work. To think the journals were done by the time he was twenty-six, and that they were written in cafes on the same streets in the Quartier Latin and Montparnasse where I have dreamt and lazed and sometimes worked during many visits to Paris over the last fifty years.

Jean Clair

Jean Clair, former director of the Picasso Museum and one of the grandest mandarins in Paris, curated the great Melancholy exhibition, from Cranach and Duhrer to Ron Mueck's 'Big Man'. *Journal atrabilaire*, with 'Big Man' on the cover, is a selection from Clair's journal of thirteen months, organized taxonomically into topics, which gives me pause for thought, since the first draft of the book you are reading is the only time I have ever written in an immediate unedited way, generating a large block of words, and culminating in a work that was carved out in later drafts rather than moulded right from the start. Clair ends his journal with a quote from Julien Green: 'The secret is to write anything, because when you write anything, you begin to say important things.' However, you still have to discern what is important and what is dross, and Clair's implication is that his journal of moods contains the important things. Naturally, the section about throwing out books caught my attention. Such a process, he says, makes you reread what you are about to sacrifice, renew your knowledge in the light of the last judgement. Needless to say, you don't reread whole books. A sample is sufficient to reassure. 'The book itself has become stale, like a hunk of bread.'

He does not spare ministers and civil servants, especially in the cultural sector, with their acronyms embedded in dead prose, their fashionable pandering to fashion. He speaks movingly of his peasant and working class origins and publishes what may be his first poems. He finds it significant that pornography and abortion became legal around the same time and we learn that Hitler read Madame Blavatsky. He tells us that the first reference in literature to Auschwitz, the place itself not the camp, is in Stefan Zweig's journal dated 15 July 1915. Zweig was fascinated by the multiple networks of railways found in this corner of the planet. Not only, as Clair says, could Zweig not have imagined at the time what use these railways would be put to a generation later (a major theme in Lanzmann's *Shoah*), he and his wife committed suicide in Brazil in February 1942. This was before they could have known for sure, even at the time, of the shame and disgrace of the railways, although by the end of that year it was common knowledge both in the Diaspora and the Yishuv in Palestine. My grandfather, describing to me in 1975 his route to London from East Galicia in 1903, said that the journey from Lvov (near his town of Stanislawow) to Hamburg (docks) involved changing trains at Oswiecim, Auschwitz, 'an important railway junction'. If 1915 saw the first literary mention of Auschwitz, 1923 saw the first and highly prescient mention of Hitler in a book, Joseph Roth's novel, *The Spider's Web*.

'Women love mirrors and men love death': Clair's Picassoan statement requires defence in the form of an argument, but here it stands alone, an aphorism as self-admiring as the sentiments expressed. However, I like his defiant love of familiar haunts, a cafe in Amsterdam, a market in Vienna, the statue of Cagalibri, the melancholic book shitter in Venice: an iconography, he says, oscillating between 'concoction and sublimation'. Finally, we are assured, or reassured, that, thanks to mobile phones, Ariadne and Theseus will have cordless contact: labyrinths are not what they were.

Memoirs

Jean Echenoz, Jérôme Lindon

Jérôme Lindon is a characteristically short and brilliant book by Jean Echenoz about his legendary publisher and mentor. Memoir is, taxonomically speaking, a subcategory of biography, biography with a focus, sometimes an intense focus as here, a close-up on a person, or an aspect of the person, a one-on-one take on a person. Jérôme Lindon, the legendary publisher of Beckett, was, until he died (and even afterwards as the ghost of his eponymous company), Echenoz's only publisher. In nine thousand words, as carefully constructed and paced as any of his novels, we learn what it is like to be an author in the context of dealings with a publisher; above all we learn by inference how a single-minded person operates and makes something as special as a house of that quality. Echenoz never says this explicitly, but after a while he clearly understands that if Lindon has time of a certain kind for him, regard of a certain kind, time and regard where he matters greatly to the publisher (close and loving attention) and also where he does not matter (why is he ignored so much or on occasion treated improperly?), it is that there are other authors all of whom Lindon has to nourish, and there is also editorial work, finance and administration and whatever else the head of a small firm has to confront. Certainly Lindon is a 'difficult man', but there is no point in resenting this since, if he were not a difficult man, he could never have married energy to intelligence and will power on this level and created a house of such distinction. Who has been his English or American equivalent? John Calder? Peter Owen? Barney Rosset of Grove Press?

John Cheever

At one time, I became interested in the prose of John Cheever, doubtless through personal recommendation. I remember reading *Falconer* with pleasure during a holiday in 1983 or 1984 with my young children at Lancaster University summer school, where we enrolled on different courses and met at meal times and during evening entertainment. However, it was the collected *Stories* which grabbed me. Cheever is up there with Alice Munro, Mavis Gallant and Raymond Carver, even with Ernest Hemingway and F. Scott Fitzgerald, in the North America short haul stakes. Cheever believed that Fitzgerald (a major influence on him) had his finger on the pulse of America. Susan Cheever, in *Home before Dark*, has a finger on the pulse of her father and provides the matrix for his life and art and death, telling the story of alcoholism, depression and cancer, of anger, charm and gossip, of ambition, pride and self-doubt, of family, marriage and a secret gay life, of friends, family and animals (cats and dogs, with the dogs reigning; he hated the cats, especially the one called Delmore Schwartz), in the distinctive prose of a true writer. It is a beautiful book and, by indirection, as revealing about the loving unsentimental author-daughter as it is, by direction, about the classically difficult man who was her father. I discussed books by daughters about fathers earlier. Cheever's book and Musa Mayer's *Night Studio* about Philip Guston were written within a year of each other. Their fathers were exact contemporaries, born within a year and dying within two years of each other. A comparison of the two lives—Guston was involved in the Federal Art Project, Cheever in the Federal Writers Project—and the books (with their echoing titles) by the two daughters would make a very nice topic for a smart post-graduate student. Both men, as they prop up the artists' bar in Valhalla, can consider themselves fortunate that future biographers will have these remarkable exercises in filial devotion and non-piety to draw on.

The Journals of John Cheever has an introduction by Susan's brother Benjamin. Cheever must have done something right as a father, to have produced two children possessed by such lucid and intelligent loyalty. These journals were the workbooks for his fiction, secondary matrices. Benjamin quotes John in the introduction as saying that publication might be difficult for the rest of the family. 'I said that I thought we could take it.' Then, after reading through all of the workbooks: 'I was surprised at how little any of us appeared, except perhaps my mother, who was not getting the sort of treatment that leads one to crave the limelight.' Finally: 'A simpleton might think bisexuality was the essence of his problem, but of course it was not. Nor was alcoholism. He came to terms with his bisexuality. He quit drinking. But life was still a problem. The way he dealt with that problem was to articulate it. He made it into a story, and then he published the story. When he discovered that he had written the story of his life, he wanted that published too. I think the prospects of publication [i.e. of the journals] somehow lessened the fear of death. Suddenly death was an opportunity.' This last sentence brings to mind Gore Vidal's attested comment on hearing about the death of Truman Capote: 'A good career move'. On the other hand, one suspects our old friend Ben Trovato had a hand in the reply given to an interviewer who asked whether Vidal's first sexual experience was with a man or with a woman: 'I was too polite to ask.' There are only two annotated lines of approval in the margin of my copy of *The Journals*, which comes as a surprise, until an effort of memory brings back the thought I had that there was no point in underlining half the book. Here is Cheever's definition of a melancholic, which carried a particular resonance for me: 'full of ambitions that he does not have vitality to requite' and then: 'we perform our passions in the large scene of what we have done and left undone in the past'. Or as Yeats wrote in lines that surely haunt us as we get older:

> Things said or done long years ago,
> Or things I did not do or say
> But thought that I might say or do,
> Weigh me down, and not a day
> But something is recalled,
> My conscience or my vanity appalled.

Susan Kennaway

Susan Kennaway, the widow of the novelist James Kennaway, constructed after his death the sort of collage book I particularly like: *The Kennaway Papers*, with both their names as authors. There was a third person in this marriage (as Diana said of Camilla), James' close friend, another novelist whose name is given only as David: David Cornwell, better known as John Le Carré. David and Susan fell in love. She quotes from Kennaway's letters, diaries and notebooks to build up a picture of difficult freedom and pain before his premature death at forty. Sometimes you get the feeling that James' equation of sexual and psychic energy is a good excuse to screw around while defending the space he needed to write, and sometimes there is a sense that this is not much more than a 1960s case study (of those people for whom sexual intercourse began well before 1963 and who would have been puzzled by Ian McEwan's *On Chesil Beach* and Julian Barnes' *The Sense of an Ending*), but it is more than that, largely because of the excoriating self-knowledge, as in this letter to Susan: 'My impulse at the moment is Gauguinesque. In every cruel action to wound you, especially when there has been no compensating bed, I have demonstrated a clear desire to exchange the responsibilities of art. No man is born an artist. Various strains—and aspirations—make him one. Fantastic concentration and selfishness—I have watched it in every living artist I know—bring him to his goal.'

Biographies

Peter Paul Rubens

Biography as an art form—leaving out of contention popular biographies and academic tomes (the two modes you tend to find in France)—is an Anglo-Saxon genre. Compared to the number of autobiographies in this room, I own few biographies, but I do possess several of Rimbaud and Kafka in English and French, as well as more specialist studies. Here, however, is my friend Paul Oppenheimer's scholarly but non-academic biography, *Rubens: A Portrait*. Oppenheimer, historian of science, professor of mediaeval literature and Germanist (editor and translator of *Til Eulenspiegel*), strong poet (*Before a Battle*) and novelist (see the sophisticated, possibly confessional, fiction *Blood Memoir*), is what we sometimes call a Renaissance man, appropriately enough when your subject is Rubens. In our day, it is more difficult to warm to Rubens than to Rembrandt. And yet, at last, for me, there can be no doubt of his importance, thanks to Paul, and also to Paula, with her insistence that I put my prejudices to one side and *look*; thanks, too, to Colin Wiggins of the National Gallery who instructed my students about autobiography in painting, including Rubens' elegiac and valedictory 'Autumn Landscape'. Paul, in his conclusion, sees Rubens as being up there with Shakespeare and Galileo at what he calls 'the division point', a crucial moment in western thought, embodying, reflecting and contributing to the radical changes associated with the division, which is 'one between those consumed with reality as energy, motion, process and change and those interested in it as stasis'. While Breughel and Caravaggio seize the moment and fix it forever—their influence leads to still photography—Rubens foreshadowed cinematography: 'He perfected a manner of painting that, without his knowing it, corresponded to Einstein's unveiling of the fact that all mass has energy, as all energy carries mass.' This book received far less attention than it deserved, precisely because Rubens is not a flavour of our time. For all Paul's persuasive advocacy, one cannot fail to relate more closely to the preoccupations of Rembrandt, whose inwardness has affinities with that of Hamlet: when we look into their mirrors, we see ourselves. *A Life beyond Ideology*, his biography of Machiavelli has just arrived from New York. Time only to read his epilogue with its unexpected comparison—favouring both men—between the subject of the book and Tom Paine.

R. W. Dixon

Jonathan Griffin introduced me to the work of the minor poet, Canon R. W. Dixon, whose moral support and critical perception were so important for Gerard Manley Hopkins. I have been looking at his *Christ's Company* and dipping into Jeremy Sambrook's biography *A Poet Hidden*. I like learning about attendant lords, sympathetic and, sometimes, influential ordinary figures in the circles of the great. It would appear that Dixon's influence was decisive in persuading Hopkins that his two vocations could finally be reconciled: 'Surely one vocation cannot destroy another: and such a Society as yours will not remain ignorant that you have such gifts as have seldom been given by God to man.' I learn too from Sambrook that Ezekiel's image 'terrible crystal' was not Hopkins' own phrase about poetry or creativity (which I had always assumed), but used by Dixon of his friend's work. No mention in Sambrook's index of Oscar Wilde. Did Hopkins and Wilde ever meet at St Aloysius in Oxford, where Hopkins was unhappily attached for part of 1879, as a curate administering communion, during a period when, according to Bruce Ross-Smith, Wilde was known to have come up from London to attend Mass and have breakfast with Hopkins' superior, Father Parkinson? These near misses or unrecorded meetings that *could* have taken place send the shivers through me. I admit that it is a shiver of greed on the part of a hero worshipper, but it also feels like a loss to our collective wisdom (?) that two such different geniuses did not leave an exchange, a recorded exchange, perhaps over the breakfast table. On the other hand, the *charge*, the *frisson*, I get from the non-meeting or the unrecorded meeting, begotten by hope on possibility (as Andrew Marvell didn't write) is full of energy, compacted like George Herbert's box containing sweets, and it triggers Yeats' 'excited reverie'. Yet, as Marvell did write, what is 'truly parallel, / Though infinite can never meet'. Conjunction of the mind is mine, theirs the opposition of the stars. Rest in peace, Hopkins and Wilde.

Léon Blum

The writing of biography involves something foreign to my temperament and attention span (which on a bad day is somewhere between that of George Bush and a goldfish), namely the long haul. Still, if I were going to write a biography, whose would it be? To generate the buzz and inwardness required to fuel the work, the ideal candidate would probably need to be French and Jewish, and a man or a woman with literary and political dimensions, with published evidence of an inner life and attitude to the inner life, which could be deployed in order to test their character and destiny as a public person. Step forward Léon Blum, who has the additional 'attraction' of having survived the Holocaust. It was by no means certain that the conventions surrounding a political prisoner of his stature would be respected by the bosses of Buchenwald, where he was housed outside the main camp for two years, and indeed at the end of the war there were orders to execute him after he had been moved elsewhere, but these were ignored by those in charge of him. If, as a prisoner, the former associate of Proust, Gide and Mallarmé, the youthful author of books on Stendhal and on Goethe's associate Eckerman, visited Goethe's oak tree, which famously was within the perimeter of Buchenwald and survived until an allied bombing raid in 1944, this would have been the mother of all ironies.

Born in 1872, Léon Blum was an anglophile, a member of the legal team defending Alfred Dreyfus and a disciple of Jean Jaurès. In 1929, the acclaimed lawyer, writer and man about town became deputy for Narbonne (where there had been a Jewish kingdom in the eleventh century) and proceeded to build a political career that culminated in his election as France's first socialist prime minister—Jean Lacouture, in his breathless and excitable *Léon Blum*, insists Blum was a socialist democrat not a social democrat—and first Jewish prime minister, and leader of the Popular Front. During World War II, he was, along with de Gaulle, the embodiment of real France, deep France, to the point that at the end of the war he was elected virtually unanimously by parliament to serve as prime minister for a few months, in order to usher in the Fourth Republic. De Gaulle was already in internal exile: it would be more than thirteen years before he would establish the Fifth Republic. Yes, it would be an enthralling task to write a biography of Blum, another case study of the intellectual in politics, one of the topics that have most interested me during my adult life. Naturally there are passing references to him in all kinds of books, including Soma Morgenstern's *Fuite et fin de Joseph Roth*, where Roth alludes to French intellectuals and generals 'who prefer Hitler to Blum', and I have read, in addition to Lacouture, *Léon Blum: The Formative Years 1872–1914* by William Logue. Tipped into this book is Roy Jenkins' 1973 three-part *Times* essay on Blum. Shortly before Blum died in 1950, he wrote a tribute to Israel's first president, Chaim Weizmann:

> A French Jew, born in France from a long line of French ancestors, speaking only the language of my country, nourished chiefly by its culture, having refused to leave it at the very moment when I was in the greatest danger, I nevertheless participate with all my heart in

the admirable effort—miraculously transported from the world of dreams to that of historical reality—which henceforth guarantees a dignified, equal and free nation for all Jews who have not had, as I did, the good fortune to find it in their native country. I have followed this effort since President Weizmann explained it to me. I have always felt, and I feel so more than ever, in solidarity with it.

I reprint this in order to remind myself and others of the mood of the time. The Palestinian issue was not yet on the minds or in the hearts even of the progressive world, and would not arrive on the agenda until the Six Day War and the occupation of the West Bank and Gaza. Blum's last written words, according to Lacouture, were 'I believe it because I hope for it.' This is not naive optimism, how could it be after his experiences of the dark night of Nazism? This is a version of Benjamin's 'Only for the sake of the hopeless ones have we been given hope.' Today I know that we have no choice other than to live our lives as if there are grounds for hope. Armed with that philosophy, I can look my grandchildren in the eye and promise them that for their sakes I shall not abandon hope. From a late and beautiful poem by Coleridge: 'Work without hope draws nectar in a sieve, / And hope without an object cannot live'. Compare Bossuet: 'We drag behind us to the grave the long chain of our disappointed hopes.'

Lou Andreas-Salomé

'We were rather like primal siblings, before incest had become sacrilege,' wrote Lou Andreas-Salomé several years after she wrote her memoir of Rilke, *You Alone Are Real to Me*. This short book is required reading for those seeking insight into the mind and psyche of the stellar poet that is Rilke. Even his bullshit is stellar ('Nothing would be more counterfeit and inaccurate than to reconstruct an image of Rilke primarily from his lamentations and from his self-loathing'), though the title of the book is something he said to her and he meant it. An ex-lover of an artist who remains a faithful friend has a map of the terrain unavailable to others, not least if that lover has the intelligence of Andreas-Salomé. 'Productive hours depended not only on undisturbed immersion in thought but rather on nothing less than the correct impressions that afforded the opportunity for such immersion. One could say . . . that the creator finally reveals only that which his hours are inclined to conjure up and thereby places himself in an incomprehensible rapport with the most repressed and primal part of himself . . . He focussed on the hour of productivity that is impossible to command but necessary to obey.'

We learn from the introduction to *Rilke and Andreas-Salomé: Love Story in Letters* that the day before Lou Andreas-Salomé's official betrothal to Paul Andreas (her prior condition having been that they abstain from sex forever), 'he plunged a knife into his chest during an argument with her, barely missing an artery but collapsing unconscious'. They were married a year later. The marriage survived placidly for five years before turbulence once again entered the equation, followed by polite coexistence. He seems to have had an affair with the housekeeper and produced a child. Ten years after the marriage, she met Rilke, fifteen years her junior, in Munich. They became lovers and saw each other nearly every day for three years. Circumstances were strained and several times they were close to an irreconcilable break but—how reassuringly normal this sounds—'to help them through such periods of stress there was the discipline of shared studies, most doggedly of Russian literature and culture, the routine of daily chores and the enjoyment of nature, and, not least, their need for complementary emotional support'.

The book's introduction continues with a threefold description of Rilke's self-image as it emerges in the letters: (1) 'the presence of an exemplary artist', such as Pushkin, Tolstoy, Rodin, Cézanne and Valéry, 'existing in the imagination and implicit in all his epistolary monologues as a powerful, often overwhelming challenge'; (2) his inner Enemy-Doppelganger, 'what he and Lou called the "Other" in him—that is, the unknown, stubbornly defiant side of his personality'; and (3) 'an understander, pre-eminently, but not exclusively, Lou, as the embodiment of a superior mode of being, who will explain to him the anxieties and phobias that block his creativity, and whose empathic affirmations encourage him in his struggle to break through to new aesthetic beginnings'. Such demands, plus the arrival of his future wife Clara on the scene in 1900, were too much even for this hyper-intelligent and self-aware muse, and she abdicated as 'mother-protector'. The friendship recovered when, in 1903, after finding himself as a writer via his monograph on Rodin, he made overtures and was not rejected. However, the *folie à deux*, if that is the right phrase, was over forever. Fortunately, we might think, or they would have destroyed each other. But they both had work to do, so mutual destruction was, in reality, only a theoretical possibility. Within a few years, having found the right lover and friend (the neurologist Friedrich Pineles), 'she could be there' for Rilke, a psychic safety net, irrespective of whether she was able to make sense of all the poems he wrote in and around the great year of 1907. Her epistolary presence was crucial after he wrote *The Notebooks of Malte Laurids Brigge*, for early in 1912 it helped generate or trigger the first of the *Duino Elegies*. That she no longer insisted he be psychoanalysed was because it would have involved someone other than her, yet they were never closer than in the few years before World War I. In 1913 she became a member of Freud's inner circle. Rilke and Lou did not meet again after 1919, nonetheless their intense correspondence continued through the completion of the *Elegies* in the great year of 1922, when *Ulysses*, *The Waste Land* and the first *Cantos* were published. She told Rilke that after the uplift he felt on completion of his *Duino Elegies*, he was likely to experience a rebound: 'Don't be frightened by it when it comes, it is how the Marys feel too, after the birth that is incomprehensible to their carpenters.'

According to Jesse Browner's introduction to Rilke's *Letters to Merline* [the mother of Balthus], Andreas-Salomé was 'the only *true* love of Rilke's life' and, one should add, his best friend. One of the most important letters Rilke wrote is the lengthy one to Clara on 17 December 1910. It is about the unusual nature of his maturation: 'I began my work (and Lou was the first person to help me towards it) not transported beyond life's heaviness but only beyond its difficulties.' Andreas-Salomé, an immeasurable influence for the good on his work, was way ahead of her time, but the time she was ahead of could never have happened without feminist precursors such as herself— albeit one who had reactionary views on female achievements that sometimes read like biological determinism—whose lived lives are as important as, or more important than, the words they left behind. A confidante of Nietzsche and Freud (see *Freud's Women* by Lisa Appignanesi and John Forrester), as well as Rilke, this author of an early book on Ibsen was one wild duck that was never tamed, except by herself, given her remark that she would like to be on a long lead held by Freud—a line from an Ibsen play or what? (Ibsen and Freud read each other's work in the original.) Andreas-Salomé, the *ur-jolie laide*, has been described as a serial polyandrist but this does not make her a femme fatale, which would certainly not have impressed the three geniuses of her life.

Andreas-Salomé was a woman of action, a psychoanalyst and psychologist who also wrote books, not very good ones, by some accounts. In *The Riddle of Freud*, Estelle Roith—and I agree with her—finds Freud's judgement of Andreas-Salomé's writings 'highly ambiguous', considering she wrote seventeen books and a hundred and nineteen articles: 'She never spoke of her own poetical and literary works. She clearly knew where the true values in life are to be looked for.' However, on rereading the remark, I now incline to the view that it does not have to imply doubt on his part concerning the quality of her written work. What a woman she was, what a life she led!

Lou Andreas-Salomé was, as they say, well ahead of her time. Angela Livingstone, in her biography of Lou, describes what she meant by 'infidelity': a woman can, as paraphrased by Livingstone, 'expose herself to the lightning and then repeatedly re-plant the tree, starting afresh from the seed, and this will be called "infidelity", even though she has not abandoned one man for another but has left the man in order to go temporarily back "home" into herself.' Tell that to Franz Wedekind, who was so cross with her that he took revenge by creating Lulu. The remarks also shed light on my own major mid-life relationship (which lasted a decade) and are close to the bone. Rilke's wondrous definition of mature adult love, which I underlined when, aged twenty-three, I first read, in French, *Letters to a Young Poet* ('two solitudes that protect, complete, border and salute each other'), may well have emerged from his relationship with Andreas-Salomé. Her insightful nature went awry when she sought to understand why her husband, with whom she had no intention of consummating the marriage, left her after two years: she told herself that his departure was due to self-hatred. We have all known psychotherapists and psychoanalysts whose wisdom does not stretch to all their own dilemmas. Nor is this a job requirement. Are all doctors healthy? Are all piano teachers virtuosos? Are all football fans soccer geniuses? Her optimism and hyperbole are sometimes intolerable and I know she would have been impossible as a lover. But she matters.

[Coda: Intrigued by the fact that Andreas-Salomé wrote a book on Ibsen's women and also by the suggestion that she was a model for Hedda Gabler, I emailed Vigdis Ystad, a friend of my friend Anniken Thue in Oslo, who pointed me to this world expert on Ibsen. Some years ago, Vigdis was kind enough to answer my similar flight of speculation about a possible connection between *The Wild Duck* and Mrs Mallard in Kate Chopin's 'Story of an Hour' (in *The Awakening*). 'Lou Andreas Salome's book on Ibsen's women is still of great importance. She has seen more in these characters than many more recent scholars have been able to . . . I appreciate her book very much. I doubt however that she was a model for Hedda. The Swedish novelist Victoria Benedictsson (alias Ernst Ahlgren) is a more obvious candidate, together with Emilie Bardach, whom Ibsen met in Gossensass in 1889.']

Stephen Crane

In one of his notes to *A Prose Miscellany* by Keith Douglas, Desmond Graham, editor of the definitive *Collected Poems*, points out that Douglas later omitted from *Alamein to Zem Zem* a reference to Stephen Crane that we find in a draft fragment, the reference being a pointer to a literary ancestor of Douglas' prose masterpiece, Crane's remarkable short novel *The Red Badge of Courage*: 'Stephen Crane speaks of a dead man on the battlefield who had the air of knowing the answer to life. It is the silence of the dead that gives them this air; their triumphant silence, proof against any questioner in the world.' In his critical study, *The Poetry of Stephen Crane*, Daniel Hoffman quotes a letter from Crane (minimalist poet par excellence, see almost every poem he wrote) to Cora Stewart-Taylor: 'Brevity is an element that enters importantly into all pleasures of life, and that is what makes pleasure sad; and so there is no pleasure but only sadness.

Stewart-Taylor was Crane's girlfriend or common-law wife. From a wealthy Boston family, she was one of the first women war correspondents and went to Greece with him in 1897 to cover the Greco-Turkish war. Cora was the madame of a Jacksonville Florida brothel or bordello called, ironically or jokily, Hotel de Dream or Hotel de Dreme (various sources and a name worthy of Tennessee Williams) or 'hostess' in a nightclub ditto (according to

Nicholas Delbanco in *Group Portrait*). While nightclub sounds more respectable than brothel, Delbanco's quotation marks round the word hostess suggests she was a prostitute, whereas a madame is often but not always a working girl retired from the fray. After the war they moved to England and lived in some style until Crane died from tuberculosis in 1900. Aged twenty-eight, he was only four years older than Keith Douglas was when he died in action in 1944. Cora returned to Florida and opened what she called a 'palatial brothel'.

She died in 1910; her tombstone, touchingly, is inscribed Cora Crane, although they never married: her English baronet husband had refused her a divorce. Delbanco comments: 'The image of the poète maudit, half in love with easeful death, is clearly one that compelled John Berryman in his biography of Crane,' and it was how the young writer was widely perceived, by Willa Cather among others. We learn from Delbanco that Crane 'talked style' with Henry James when they were neighbours on the Kent–Sussex borders, members of the 'group' whose portrait Delbanco paints. Delbanco speculates that *The Sacred Fount*, which James wrote during Crane's final illness, 'may have derived some of its poignancy from the vision the novelist had of the way in which Crane was visibly dying while Cora thrived, seemingly unaware of the tragedy being lived out under her roof'.

Boris Pasternak

Tonight I was dipping into *Boris Pasternak*, the biography of a great poet by a good poet, the late Peter Levi, also a translator of the psalms and a fine critic. Levi could read Russian and rated Pasternak more highly than any other European poet of the twentieth century, above Rilke, for example, whose subject, in Levi's opinion, 'is beauty rather than reality'. Rilke, however, was of central importance to the young Pasternak and without the Prague-born poet 'one does not know what might have become of Pasternak in the whirlpools of futurism', a negative speculation of the sort we are all tempted by on occasion, and not one of Levi's most profound insights. All the same, the poet Levi's admiration for the poet Pasternak is an advantage, perhaps a virtue, when writing the biography of his hero. *Boris Pasternak* is a crisply written, mercifully short book about a fascinating and complex figure, in whose wondrous novel *Doctor Zhivago* (pulp fiction according to Nabokov), the eponymous main character is not only a doctor but also one of the great fictional poets, perhaps the great fictional great poet, whose interiority no film, not even one by David Lean, can convey. Furthermore and essentially, the texture of the poems is grounded in the prose which builds up to the concluding and conclusive poems. This prose demands and obtains the culminating poems; the culminating poems require and complete the prose of the novel. Boris Pasternak himself told Olga Carlisle that the plan of the novel is outlined by the poems accompanying it. Donald Davie has discussed this at some length in his neglected and brilliant book *The Poems of Doctor Zhivago*, containing his translations of the poems and also criticism, although Levi is less taken with Davie's criticism than I am, while admiring the translations.

The Zhivago poems are comparable to Pessoa's heteronymous or heteronymic poems in that like Zhivago's diary in chapter nine they were written by an invented character, offering a rare case of a framed work of art that is as literary as the frame—compare Balzac's *The Unknown Masterpiece*, where what is framed (as it were) is a painting, which Balzac is not required to paint. It is a shame that the translators of the first English-language edition of the novel, Max Hayward and Manya Harari, made literal translations and felt that the only alternative was a 'version by an accomplished English poet who knows Russian'. In those days, co-translation by scholar and poet was less common than it is today. In addition to Davie, we have Lowell's versions of a few poems as well as a few by other translators in anthologies. The question of Pasternak's Jewishness (Levi's own paternal Jewish ancestry seems to have been unproblematic; the former Jesuit priest saw himself as a Christian Jewish poet, ontologically if not in Jewish religious law) is touched on when Levi says that Pasternak's insistence he was Russian and not Jewish led to *Doctor Zhivago* never being translated into Hebrew. I found this difficult to believe, especially as Levi also tells us of a biography in Hebrew, and I dispatched two emails to Israel—one to a poet and the other to a scholar—in order to find out. As I suspected, the novel was translated into Hebrew soon after it first appeared in Russian (in the USA) in 1958. I cannot resist quoting Alfred Kazin's journals where he quotes his lunch host Dag

Hammarskjöld as quoting David Ben-Gurion on *Doctor Zhivago*: 'the most disgraceful book ever written by a man of Jewish origin'. The novel was not published in the Soviet Union until perestroika in 1988. As for Zhivago, being a fictional doctor he does not appear on that fascinating website, the Roster of Physician Writers, which the late Cecil Helman, himself a physician-writer, alerted me to when I asked him if he knew that Thomas Lovell Beddoes was a doctor. There are hundreds listed, and some notable omissions, for example the Portuguese poet and fiction-writer, Miguel Torga. It is, though, intriguing if not entirely surprising that this day job, sorry, profession, better yet, vocation, may well coexist more comfortably than any other with being a writer.

'By its inborn faculty of hearing, poetry seeks out the melody of nature amid the tumult of the dictionary, and then, picking it up as one picks up a tune, abandons itself to improvisation upon that theme. By scent, and according to its level of inspiration, prose seeks and finds the human being in the category of speech,' wrote Pasternak. Half a generation younger than the grand symbolists Blok and Bely (on my desk are Bely's *Reminiscences of Alexander Blok* in Russian and *The Dramatic Symphony* in English) and their contemporary Rilke, Pasternak was one of the great quartet of Russian poets of his generation, the others being Mandelstam, Tsvetayeva and Akhmatova, septet if one includes Mayakovsky, Yesenin and Khlebnikov. The son of a painter and a concert pianist, Pasternak wrote short, evocative and fascinating autobiographical texts, such as *Safe Conduct*), which was dedicated to the memory of Rilke and published in 1931, and the post-Zhivago *I Remember*, also called *An Essay in Autobiography*. I emailed the following comment from *I Remember* to Christopher Ricks, who was preparing a lecture on onomatopoeia: 'I did not go to his [Bely's] lectures because I have been, and am now too, of the opinion that the music of the word is not an acoustic phenomenon and does not consist of the euphony of vowels and consonants, taken by themselves, but of the relationship between the meaning and the sound of the words.' There is a chapter on the composer Alexander Scriabin, and a marvellous portrait of Mayakovsky, where Pasternak rejects the self-destructive Romantic conception of the poet, as found in Yesenin and Mayakovsky himself: 'Romanticism always needs philistinism and with the disappearance of the petty bourgeoisie always loses half its poetical content.'

Boris Pasternak: The Voice of Prose, edited by Christopher Barnes, a Cambridge contemporary of mine, is dedicated to the memory of Nikolai Andreyev, who was doubtless his supervisor, as he was mine. Andreyev lived on the main road that led to Girton and I remember cycling there to discuss my latest attempt at a 'prose' (i.e. a translation into Russian) during my short and inglorious career as a modern linguist. My fellow tutee was Edward Braun, who later wrote books on Vsevolod Meyerhold. Barnes includes his own and superior translation of *Safe Conduct* and the highly personal short stories like 'Zhenya Luvers' Childhood', which are also included in Stefan Schimanski's volume. Here too are the poet's *Letters to Georgian Friends* and autobiographical novella *The Last Summer*, which is introduced by Pasternak's sister Lydia, Craig Raine's late mother-in-law, whom I met in Oxford when reading there with Yevgeni Vinokurov. I have inscribed my copy: 'Anton Kirilovitch Rudolf [my father's first names were Henry Cyril, the second lending itself perfectly to transcription into Russian as my patronym], December 1963' and written above it: 'full of extraordinary images'.

Edgell Rickword/Hart Crane

(Letter to Hugo Williams, 17 August 2006)

Hi Hugo,

Re your recent *TLS* column, I spotted an Islington reference you may have missed: Charles Hobday, in his study of Edgell Rickword, *A Poet at War*, quotes an essay by the poet in which he describes taking tea laced with rum with Hart Crane at a pull-up for car men in Upper Street near the Agricultural Hall. Was the pull-up still there in your early days as an Islington denizen?

I love Rickword's handful of war poems. The First World War is never far away from us. Only yesterday I read in the papers that the men shot as 'cowards' have finally been pardoned. Rickword was an officer before he was twenty and won the Military Cross. Hart Crane: I read his *Collected Poems* on my first visit to New York.

Crane told Rickword he'd read Moby Dick 'at least three times'. I like the 'at least'.

Working on a long memoir here.

First grandchild due next week.

Regards, as ever, Tony

Williams' reply is suitably impressed by the fact that Rickword and Crane were friends and that 'Crane came to Islington!!' He continues: 'the pull-up has miraculously materialised out of my slightly over-excited imagination but I am not quite clear as to what I should be remembering. You mean a tea stall—like the ancient one in Shoreditch?' He ends: 'Grandchildren are good, especially if they don't live four-hundred miles away in Cornwall. My heart is broken for my darling Silver (aged three), a wood nymph of silent humour and intense (for me) charisma, whom I never see. With love, Hugo'.

Yes, I wanted him to tell me the pull-up was still there even though I know that part of Upper Street well enough to be certain it isn't, but more important than the relationship between two elderly London ambulatory writers and places associated with dead masters (and the prestige and glamour and *mana* generated by a visit to such places) is the relationship with grandchildren: his Silver, my Charlie. Charlie now lives in New Zealand and I am envious of Hugo's southwesterly situation, a mere four hundred miles away. [Later: I now have a second grandchild, Leah, living round the corner.] Rereading some of his poems, I would say he has in common with Ginsberg that he moves, or seems to move, straight from lived experience, *erlebnis*, to the verbals without apparently needing to enjoy or endure a ride on the roundabout of ratiocination or the swing of irony. The endless parade of I in the poems manages to avoid narcissism, although not always in his articles where the self-deprecation sometimes does not work, but the journalist's I describes and sometimes incarnates the matrixial compost of his life, and always with good humour, so his readers forgive him because he is genuinely interested in minute particulars of feeling and observation. He is a conduit for the generation of these elements.

Lives of the poets

Echoing Samuel Johnson, Michael Schmidt's extraordinary and enormous *Lives of the Poets* (to be followed by *Lives of the Novelists*) is my first port of call for a brief account of a poet, and this will usually satisfy my curiosity. Thus, after reading *The Winner of Sorrow*, Brian Lynch's novel about William Cowper, *The Winner of Sorrow*, I wanted to find out more about this tragic figure, in broad brush at any rate, before deciding whether to proceed with reading a full biography or critical work. I have known Schmidt boy and man for over forty years, ever since he invited me to read my Bonnefoy translations at the Oxford Poetry Society in 1968. His house has many rooms, starting with poetry, which includes *The Love of Strangers*—containing portraits of persons unnamed, although I recognize George Buchanan, to whom he is unkind—and recently the sadly neglected *Collected Poems*, which needs the one person to promote it who cannot do it. The manuscript of an early book dedicated to 'Miss Elizabeth Bishop', *Bedlam and the Oakwood*, is here, a gift from our house guest in Belsize Park before he began rooming at the Savile Club). Other rooms in this house: criticism, translation, fiction, anthologies, magazine, publishing house, networking, fundraising. Cooking is not his thing, as an episode involving Robert Lowell and a burnt omelette at Pin Farm, South Hinksey testifies, but nobody is perfect. Schmidt was born in Mexico, his father a younger member of the same generation of immigrants as Frieda Kahlo's father. He is a prodigious worker: his two enormous bio-critical books must have involved vast quantities of primary and secondary reading, and yet the one already published is in no way bland or dull, indeed it is written with his characteristic sharpness and dialectical understanding of the elements and dimensions that make a poem. Recently, he sent me a new poem and said he couldn't decide between two versions of the last line. I was chuffed that he accepted my suggestion, a combination of his two. Over thirty years ago he published my poetry, both a pamphlet I later disowned and a book that I still believe in. (This book, *The Same River Twice*, was read in manuscript by our mutual friend Val Warner, a fine poet, who regretted the way I always cut poems when I revised them. She was not to know that I was trying to disappear.) Recently Michael co-published with Northern House my book *Zigzag*, a quarter of a century after the earlier book. I plucked up courage to ask him whether he would consider a small collected poems: he said he would be glad to consider a manuscript, but that friendship and previous publication were no guarantee that he would like the work enough to publish it. I have consulted *Lives of the Poets* several times while writing this book, for example to see what he has to say about Laura Riding. There are errors of judgement: for example, not nearly enough attention paid to Oppen or Niedecker. Overall, however, Schmidt is a force of nature, that is a force of culture, to be reckoned with, and I wish I was three-quarters as clever as him, and worked three-quarters as hard.

Literary Criticism, Reading and Translation, Essays, etc.

I should like the window to open onto the Lake of Geneva—and
there I'd sit and read all day like the picture of somebody reading.
—John Keats, Letter dated 13 March 1819

Introductory Note

Perhaps not surprisingly, the sections on reading and translation are quite
short: the former is, after all, the *raison d'être* of the entire book and the latter
is a major theme on other pages. Also, it will be clear by now that theories of
reading and translation are not primary concerns of this book or this writer.

Literary Criticism

Tillie Olsen

'Yonnondio! Yonnondio!—unlimn'd they disappear' (Walt Whitman). And
they do, they do, unless faithful readers spread the word. One of my favourite
writers is Tillie Olsen, whose short stories *Tell Me a Riddle* and supposedly
unfinished novel *Yonnondio: From the Thirties* always move me. Despite
criticism on the part of certain post-feminists, there is no better insight into
authentically incarnated feminist intelligence and educated feeling than her
classic work about women's creativity, *Silences*. Moving straight to one of the
passages I marked many years ago, I find her words on Rebecca Harding. I
wondered then and I wonder now why she puts the valuable concept of
'trespass vision' in inverted commas without a footnote as to the provenance.

Perhaps it is her own invention and this is the first time she has used it? In 2007 I tried to find out if she was still alive, but there was no reply to a letter, and John Felstiner in Stanford who, like me, knew her in the old days no longer had any idea how to reach her. I clicked onto an Internet directory service and obtained an address and phone number in Berkeley. However, she had moved and the new resident had no idea how to reach her. Finally, I tracked down another address, thanks to the Menard Press USA distributor SPD Inc., Berkeley, in the person of Laura Moriarty. Then sadly, I received an email from Jerome Chanes in New York to tell me that Tillie had recently died (aged ninety-three), which proves that one should always act on impulse, especially when it comes to the very old.

Here is the full passage: 'She [Rebecca Harding] must have had to use "trespass vision", eavesdrop, ponder everything, dwell within it with all the resources of intellect *and imagination*; literally make of herself (in Henry James' famous phrase) "one on whom nothing is lost". Each walk, each encounter, had to be freighted with significance, each opportunity for knowing seized. More, with demeaning, painful, excited, stratagem, she must have had to *create* opportunities for knowledge, and for a knowing relationship with those outside the bounds of her class.' This is a good account of the way the imagination works. Maybe, like T. S. Eliot's use of Washington Allston's phrase 'objective correlative' (which Eliot put in quotes but did not source), 'trespass vision' was borrowed, and for some reason she did not make acknowledgement beyond the quotation marks.

I had to reread Claire Harman's *TLS* review of Myles Weber's *Consuming Silences* ('a study of famously stalled or one-hit writers') to make sure my eyes had not skipped a few sentences. No, I was right first time. There was no reference to *Yonnondio*. Olsen's confused manuscripts turned up in the early 1970s and she reworked them nearly forty years after writing the book. Nor did Harman make any reference to Ralph Ellison's second novel *Juneteenth*, also unfinished (he lost whole years because part of the manuscript was consumed in a fire), which I have not read. It received a mixed critical reception. (More on Ellison later.) For me, *Yonnondio* is no more unfinished than Schubert's symphony or Paula's 'Deposition', a beautiful picture, which finally left the studio when Paula decided she could do no more with it. There are two possibilities concerning the omissions: either Weber did not mention the two books or Harman herself failed to mention them. If Weber did not mention them, Harman should have rebuked him severely, assuming she knew of their existence. If he did mention them, perhaps she was unconsciously seeking to improve the story of silence on the part of two prose fiction writers who, on the strength of *Tell Me a Riddle* and *Invisible Man*, count as major figures in American literature.

Ralph Ellison, whose *Invisible Man* is one of Barack Obama's favourite books, wrote many extraordinary essays in addition to a second novel. To judge by Harman's account of Ellison (or her account of Weber), you would think Ellison did nothing for decades but worry about *Invisible Man*. The review vilifies and ridicules Olsen's *Silences* and is simplistic (or Weber is simplistic) when it comes to Olsen's class politics, which have to be read and understood alongside the legendary long silence of a great poet, her near contemporary and fellow San Franciscan George Oppen. Franz Kafka's Dora Diamant, as described in the biography by Kathi Diamant, would have admired Tillie Olsen.

Jean Starobinski

Visiting Fontaine-de-Vaucluse while on holiday in Provence, I bought a copy of Jean Starobinski's *La Poésie et la guerre* in the Museum of the Resistance (the Vaucluse is the territory of René Char, a senior maquis figure). The book collects this great Swiss critic's early texts on poetry and poets written during the war. 'In a time of catastrophe', the twenty-two-year-old writer proclaimed on 1 January 1943, what is needed can be summarized by Jouve's words on Rimbaud: 'the contraction of historical time into personal time'. The poet is not only 'the witness of history before eternity . . . he is also the witness of eternity faced with the world in which he lives, and as such the role of the witness can take on the sacred meaning of martyrdom'. Already at the beginning of 1943, the young critic's words makes us think of Miłosz, and of Celan, the latter by then in a forced labour camp, writing his early poems that will culminate in 'Death Fugue' nearly two years later. Starobinski tells me in an email that he was born within a few days of Celan. That year Starobinski published his first book: a translation of Kafka stories. Later there would be many critical works of the highest distinction, to name only two: *La Mélancholie au miroir*, a study of Baudelaire and the wondrous *Le Poème d'invitation*, which also includes a text by his friend Bonnefoy.

A. Alvarez

Although Al Alvarez is best known as a literary critic and anthologist, he is also a poet, novelist, autobiographer (discussed later under 'Samuel Menashe') and writer of books on an interesting combination of themes: mountain climbing, poker playing, suicide and divorce. His paternal ancestors did the Jewish equivalent of coming over on the *Mayflower*: they were Spanish marranos who arrived in London not long after Cromwell, in 1656, encouraged the return of Jews to England following their official expulsion in 1290. Cromwell probably had two motives: to fulfil the biblical prophecy and to encourage mercantilism. Alvarez's two books on poker made a good birthday present for my son one year. Alvarez and my son Nathaniel are members of the group who play occasionally in Martin Feinstein's house. *Life after Marriage* begins with Al's divorce from his first wife, the granddaughter of D. H. Lawrence's widow. Published in 1982, the year after my own marriage ended, the book's account of attitudes towards divorce in the USA, Sweden and elsewhere spoke vividly to my personal condition of man. It sits on the shelf next to his famous study of suicide, *The Savage God*. Alvarez's first book, *The School of Donne*, was a searching study of the metaphysical poets; it deals with the consequences of intelligence (of the heart and of the mind), whether good or bad. This is one of the big themes running throughout his work. *Under Pressure* is a study of the *intelligent* (in the Russian sense), writers and intellectuals in communist Eastern Europe and the USA during the 1960s. In 1962, Alvarez brought out his influential anthology *The New Poetry*, with its once controversial introduction.

I first met him in 1967 at the inaugural Poetry International when he introduced several sessions, seemingly in seventh gear, speeding like a maniac. Rock climbing and poker, his two main activities off the page, propose a mindset antithetical to speeding but not incompatible with his prose style after *The School of Donne*. His early book of essays on English and American poets, *The Shaping Spirit*, certainly helped shape mine as a young reader. One need not agree with certain judgements (e.g. that Roethke's talent is more slender than Eberhart's) to learn from his readings of poets. He has much less time for Wallace Stevens than I have, allowing only two poems as masterpieces, which is to say, in his own terminology, poems where poetic intelligence as opposed to poetic intellect is at its highest level: 'Sunday Morning' and 'Notes towards a Supreme Fiction'. The most important chapter is the one on Lawrence as a poet. It is good to find this poet in the company of Eliot, Pound, Crane and Stevens, and to be reminded how he moved not from the iambic pentameter to free verse, but from prose: it shows and it is shown. So much depends on a red geranium.

Christopher Ricks

I had an interesting correspondence with Christopher Ricks in the wake of his first Oxford lecture as a professor of poetry (later published in *TLS*), on the hierarchy of poetry/prose from Coleridge to Bonnefoy. Alan Wall, never deferential though more cautious than I am, didn't speak to me for a week when he discovered I had mentioned in an email to Ricks the rumour that he, Ricks, was the 'man whose head was exploding' in the Bob Dylan song, *Day of the Locusts*. He thought Ricks would mind, but the man whose head was not in fact exploding didn't mind, and indeed couldn't see why he should. Here is part of a letter I wrote him after reading his lecture.

> One point you did not touch on was the tradition of prose poetry in France, and the important role of such poems in a literature where the rules concerning poetry in the strict sense have been so, well, strict . . . .
>
> Charles Reznikoff in a letter talks about poetry as vertical, prose horizontal. I thought well of that non-judgmental distinction until I came across Ed Dorn's explanation why a particular poem was a poem and not: poetry, he said, is centripetal, prose centrifugal. This is an improvement on Reznikoff.
>
> There is surely the matricial ghost of metrics behind parts of Shylock's speech. As for the supreme prose of S. Beckett: if we only had his official poetry, he would be a footnote by now or published only by small presses, like his friend Brian Coffey.

371

Ezra Pound's lines serve as a nice gloss on your words about the effect of 'return' in prose and poetry: 'See, they return; ah, see the tentative / Movements, and the slow feet, / The trouble in the pace and the uncertain / Wavering!'

By the time I got to know Ricks personally, he must have realized that I was trying to impress him. To his great and enduring credit, he won't allow hero worship. Mentor yes, guru no. If you try to impress him, he will compete, raise the stakes, do unto you what you do unto him. Your move. It is a compliment, and a landmark in my lifelong education as an attendant lord and instinctive disciple.

On my desk are the master's *Beckett's Dying Words* (a brilliant book until, some of us think, the final chapter) and his exemplary edition of Eliot's early poems, *Inventions of the March Hare.* This kind of textual labour is difficult but rewarding, as I found out when working with John Rety on the *Collected Poems and Selected Translations* of A. C. Jacobs, which we co-published. Ted Hughes loved the Jacobs book and recommended it to people; it was widely reviewed and sold well, a rare occurrence in the small press world. Here too is Ricks' enthralling *Decisions and Revisions in T. S. Eliot*: 'Of course one can "go too far" and except in directions in which we can go too far there is no interest in going at all; and only those who will risk going too far can possibly find out just how far one can go.' This quote by Ricks from Eliot's preface to a book by Harry Crosby means a lot to me. Specifically, it puts into words my awareness of what happened once in a painting by Paula that I was in, and how she went too far, and lost something I pleaded with her to retain. Not 'leave well alone' so much as leave 'best' alone: that is the point, she is only able to make nine 'bests' because she is prepared to suffer the loss of the tenth. On this occasion, it was my face, and the best likeness she had ever got. Paula now claims that I preferred the earlier one because it was more flattering, but I don't buy this (quite). I would also add that worrying about 'best likeness' begs a lot of questions. The model in her paintings is not sitting for a portrait.

Gabriel Josipovici

One of Gabriel Josipovici's several best books is *Touch*, which argues the case for a sense that has been neglected in favour of sight and hearing in discussions of our negotiations between self and world. He touches briefly on Rembrandt's 'Jewish Bride', a reproduction of which is on my bedroom door, and concludes: 'Touch establishes the boundaries of each and their dependence on each other, neither perpetual solitude nor perpetual merging but an acceptance of difference in their free decision to make their lives together.' This is a beautiful gloss not only on a tender and masterful painting which speaks to all of us but also on Rilke's definition of love, which I quote elsewhere. Stephen Nadler, in *Rembrandt's Jews*, is sceptical about there being any Jewish association with 'The Jewish Bride', whether contemporary with Rembrandt or biblical (e.g. Jacob and Rachel or Isaac and Rebecca). As far as I am concerned, and doubtless Gabriel too, a Jewish association would be a bonus, but would not deepen the profound feeling expressed. As Harold Bloom suggests in *The Anatomy of Influence*, even if it could be proved Whitman was heterosexual, there would be no cognitive or aesthetic added value. Josipovici illuminates familiar geniuses, often with a supremely well-chosen quote from an early work or a letter. *The Singer on the Shore* and *The Lessons of Modernism* are essential texts and his edited book, *The Modern English Novel*, contains one of his loveliest and most insightful essays, 'But Time will not Relent: Modern Literature and the Experience of Time'. His radio plays are as good as any of the novels he has written, which are quietly high modern, some almost entirely in dialogue, with Nathalie Sarraute, Henry Green, Ivy Compton-Burnett (Thomas Love Peacock? Denis Diderot?) as precursors. Book-length dialogue at its best, and it is only readable at its best, is as demanding as poetry. Almost all his fiction books are here, including *Four Stories*, which I published at Menard Press. My two favourites among the novels are *Contre-Jour* (think Pierre Bonnard) and *Moo Pak* (think Jonathan Swift).

Metrics

I have two books on metrics, Seymour Chatman's *A Theory of Meter* and Reuven Tsur's *A Perception-Oriented Theory of Meter*. Tsur was an Israeli prosodist living in London in the 1970s. After one or two personal seminars with him, I felt I understood his theory, derived from Morris Halle and Jay Keyser, involving 'stress maxima', enabling one to distinguish metrical from unmetrical lines. In the epilogue, Tsur quotes Donne's line 'Batter my heart, three person'd God; for you' and says that it can be performed as iambic or trochaic. Tsur, however, prefers an iambic reading because only thus are stress pattern and meter 'established as perceptual units'. He has a long discussion of metric deviation or apparent negligence (as Pope saw it) in Donne (as opposed to the 'metapoetic certainty of divergence' in Milton), and I only wish I could stay with this subject, but I have to move on. Time and again (space and again) in this book, I come up against the imperative of priority. Apologies to Seymour Chatman, whose unread book, like many others, reproaches me in silence on its shelf.

Reading and Translation

Hallucinatory power of reading which raises a voice, page after page. Like the voice of the spirits, it cannot not be registered, and yet it is real and singular enough for us to retain its elusive echo, long after we have closed the book. Provided we are able to hear this imperceptible whisper, we will continue reading.

—Jean Clair, *Journal atrabilaire*

All of creation is given to us as a book, a picture, and a mirror.

—Alain of Lille, twelfth century, in Ivan Illich's *In the Vineyard of the Text*

READING

Introduction

Reverie is solitary. Reading, however, even alone and in silence, is communal, for the object of our intimate attentions is a work (fashioned alone and in silence) of language, which belongs to all its speakers. How much have I learnt from master readers like Christopher Ricks, Victor Brombert and Alfred Kazin! Another is Michael Sheringham, author of two major studies: *Everyday Life* and *French Autobiography*. A *TLS* review by Sheringham led me to

Marielle Macé's *Façons de lire, manières d'être*, a remarkable and very demanding book-length essay on reading. As a serious reader of Yves Bonnefoy, Sheringham will recall Bonnefoy's insistence that interruption is built into the process of reading, and rightly so. 'Why do we like reading in trains?,' asks Macé, master or mistress reader extraordinary. Because the view from the window is different each time we look up, miming the changes in the book. 'The past is cities from a train,' writes Lowell. 'I like travelling by train,' writes Ilana Shmueli to Celan from Zurich, 'it is so out of time and then also no man's land and I can dream.'

Robert Southey

According to Seamus Perry in the *TLS*, Robert Southey's 'My Days among the Dead', a poem Casaubon alludes to in *Middlemarch*, is 'a love song to his library, and a bleak masterpiece to the repressed life'. Although Geoffrey Grigson tries to make a case for Southey in the introduction to his selection from the poet's work, one finds oneself agreeing with Coleridge, as quoted by Grigson, that the poems are founded on books and fancy and—damning with faint praise—that Southey was a prose master of English without fault. Grigson tells us that in his dotage Southey 'could only sit and pat his books affectionately with both hands'. *Pace* Perry, the poem is too inert to be a poetic masterpiece, though 'tinged with agreeable . . . bookish morbidity'. It is a salutary text for persons who spend much of their life reading, and equally so for those who write, and in particular someone writing about his books. I understand Southey a bit too well for my own comfort.

Bernard Berenson

One Year's Reading for Fun is Bernard Berenson's account of life in 1942 during his enforced seclusion in Italy with his wife and secretary. On 6 September that year, the very day I was born, he began reading Albert Béguin's *L'Âme romantique et le rêve*. He complains that Béguin seems unaware of Wordsworth's existence, or indeed that of 'any of the English Romantics, Platonists or mystics'. On 26 September, somewhat to my surprise, we find him reading Henri Michaux's *Ecuador* which 'begins too whimsically, too Dada, but of a sudden is filled with genuine observation and reflection, too trivial to have been jotted down by others, yet striking if only because someone had the courage to take note of them'. This is a lucid account of the naive view held by some that if they had time they could do it too. They forget that making time for creation has little or nothing to do with temporality, as the late J. G. Ballard, the widower with the pram in the hall, could have told them. On 30 September, Berenson finished, for the first time, a Dickens novel, *Our Mutual Friend*, and surmised that it was written under the influence of Eugène Sue and Victor Hugo, given the plot, the chopped-up narrative and the characters. For example: 'the intriguing, reciprocally hating married people' strike him as 'far more French than English'. Let me, as an unconditional admirer of *Bartleby the Scrivener*, end with an unintended recommendation on Berenson's part (remember Tolstoy: 'Chekhov, your plays are even worse than Shakespeare's.' The compliment Tolstoy paid Mallarmé is equally disparaging) concerning Dino Buzzati's *Tartar Steppe*: this book about a young lieutenant at a distant frontier post 'was suggested no doubt by Kafka, and is as dreary almost as *Bartleby* . . . . He passes thirty years there and nothing happens.'

Frederic Raphael, Francine Prose and Anne Fadiman

Bookmarks, edited by Frederic Raphael, whose outspoken and entertaining journals, *Personal Terms* and *Rough Copy* and *Cuts and Bruises*, I have enjoyed along with some of his novels, is an anthology of 'writers on their reading': 'All men may be what they eat, writers alone are what they read' is an understandable exaggeration, penned with the left hand, unless Raphael is left-handed. Madame Bovary was destroyed by her reading, and Gustave Flaubert had other inputs than his reading. Alan Sillitoe's account of his autodidact reading is of great interest. A man who lived by his pen, he, like Mike Moorcock, was a true pro. When I was a boy my father told me about a neurosurgeon called Russell Brain and a philosopher called John Wisdom. Recently, my son the barrister received a letter from the Lord Chief Justice, Judge [Igor] Judge. So my father would have enjoyed—my son and I have been enjoying—the detail that the author of *Reading like a Writer* is Francine Prose. Prose, whose textbook incarnates pleasure in text and the joy of reading, was one of the writers invited by Peder Zane to participate in *The*

Top Ten: Writers Pick Their Favourite Books: no surprises there, and why should there be? Chekhov, Cheever, Proust. Of *The Charterhouse of Palma*, Prose comments that Stendhal is 'in love with his characters for all the right reasons. One can only imagine how Tolstoy would have punished Gina.' *Ex Libris* is an enchanting book by Anne Fadiman: when affairs of state lay heavy on William Gladstone's shoulders, he 'felled larger trees with an axe; walked around London talking to prostitutes; or arranged books'. The last named was said to be the safest and most satisfying. Fadiman believes that 'books—buying them, reading them, annotating them, indexing them, housing them, and writing about them—saved Gladstone from paralyzing stress'.

Bruce Chatwin

Bruce Chatwin's *The Songlines* and James Cowan's *Mysteries of the Dream-Time* (the latter a gift from Kathleen Raine) are valuable readings of a remote and fascinating world. The final text in Chatwin's collection of previously uncollected writings, *Anatomy of Restlessness*, 'theorises' his short and last novel *Utz*. With glances at Sigmund Freud, Donald Winnicott and John Bowlby, he explores possession and fetish: 'The true collector houses a corps of inanimate lovers to shore up the wreckage of life.' Chatwin is mainly talking about art collectors and, strictly speaking, persons like myself with thousands of books are hoarders rather than collectors. All the same, the essay makes for uncomfortable reading. However, there is a positive side: 'I suspect that all the time and effort we spend in making or wanting new things . . . merely compensates for the ideal territory from which we have estranged ourselves. Only at our roots can we hope for a renewal. The Australian aborigines would wander afield throughout the year but return at seasonal intervals to their sacred places to make contact with their ancestral roots, established in the "dream time".' Sometimes we can construct what Chatwin calls an ideal territory where we are safe to explore danger. This is the space/time of the library, where the mind of a western reader or writer can push the 'dream time' into unexpected reconfigurations. *A la recherche* indeed . . .

Daniel Halpern

Daniel Halpern's *Literature as Pleasure*, begins badly with a selection of 'Notes on Pleasure' that read as though they have been selected from Google or rather, given its date (1990), from dictionaries of quotations. The selection is, however, redeemed by the episode from *To the Lighthouse*, where Mrs Ramsay picks up an anthology and reads aloud quotes, including only one that I recognize, a Shakespeare sonnet. Another chapter, 'On Reading', is by a favourite of mine, Guy Davenport. In the spirit of Proust's eponymous essay, Davenport describes when and where he read certain books, including *A la recherche* . . . : 'These settings are not merely sentimental; they are real interrelations. The moment of reading is integral to the process.' Davenport read Yeats' *A Vision* in a small hotel, 59 rue Monsieur-le-Prince, a street I know well. Not all readings are nostalgic, he tells us: his own marriage was disintegrating in 'violence and paralyzing misery' while he was making his way through the *Iliad* in Greek. Ah or oh, that sentence is constructed the wrong way round: a good example of the rhetorical device hysteron proteron. Bizarrely, two friends emailed me about the device on the same day: Paul Buck reckoning a French writer he was translating had confused it with metanoia and Aharon Komem wrongly proposing a mea culpa concerning his essay on Shakespeare's phrase 'exits and entrances'. Were Davenport still alive, I would have teased him by asking whether I have a point about the construction of the sentence.

Davenport discusses the enormous pleasure of dining alone in a restaurant while reading a book, in this instance Spinoza's *Ethics*: 'Soul and mind were fed together.' Not a million miles and about a hundred and sixty years away, Keats asks to be given 'books, fruit, French wine and fine weather and a little music out of doors, played by somebody I do not know'. We would *expect* the music to be played by somebody we do not know, and so for Keats to spell it out emphasizes with characteristic delicacy the pleasure of reading alone in a public place. A writer previously unknown to me, David Long, reflects on rereading, as I have done in this book: 'What we read again is . . . an intimate expression, a distillate, of who we are: single lines, fragments marked off with a highlighter . . . .' Donald Hall, in an illuminating essay, 'The Way to Say Pleasure', almost out-writes Guy Davenport, which is quite an achievement.

Hall can be aggressive and sarcastic, not sparing the likes of Helen Vendler and Joseph Brodsky; still, an educated and subtle mind that goes over the top in the name of its true love (in this case, poetry) shall be forgiven, for you do not have to take the high road to bring back treasure and truth.

Philip Davis

'Memory,' concludes Philip Davis rather unfashionably, in his distinguished first book *Memory and Writing: From Wordsworth to Lawrence*, 'is the very ground of imagination.' And: 'As well as being the reservoir of our experience, it is also in its visitations a revelation of the heart-shaking seriousness of a person's life, preserved within.' The dialectic between memory and imagination is relevant to an appreciation of, for example, Paula's paintings, which often mediate the two by copying from life or from sculptures she herself has made, such as 'The Pillowman'. As with all the best artists, her work is wiser than she is, wiser than she is on the subject of painting that is, for she sometimes forgets or does not need to remember that autobiographical memory and fictive imagination need not be at odds with each other. 'Memory needs invention, needs imagination and the arts of writing, for purposes of support, revitalisation, freedom and justice.' Here Davis' argument meets Elaine Scarry's in *On Beauty and Being Just*, which I discuss elsewhere. His later books *The Experience of Reading* and *Real Voices: On Reading* are close to my heart, as you would expect. I thought that he and I had lost touch, but I renewed contact after discovering he had written a biography of Malamud, a follow-up to *Malamud's People*, a remarkable experimental book as neglected as Malamud himself. Davis edits an indispensable magazine, *The Reader*, at Liverpool University where he is a professorial colleague of another friend who is also one of the email interlocutors in the present book, the poet and critic Deryn Rees-Jones, whose *Burying the Wren* is a beautiful book and not only because it contains a poem inspired by Paula.

Postscript

On a trip to Paris during a late redaction of the present work, I picked up a book of essays—*Emmanuel Levinas: La question du livre*—at the Museum of

Judaism, where I had seen a moving and instructive exhibition of Walter Benjamin's archive. Returning home on the Eurostar, I decided to read one of the essays: I chose the one on Levinas and Blanchot. What particularly struck me was the word 'intropathie', a Husserlian term which Levinas used to describe the practice of reading and writing. Intropathy connotes cognitive/affective empathy and introspection and I like it.

TRANSLATION

> Translation is rendered possible only through the mediation of an inner place which unifies the separated languages and allies them, reconciled in the heart of our silence. We have to survive, like them in *perhaps*, in *despite everything*.
> —Claude Vigée, *Les Portes eclairées de la nuit*

William Gass and others

Let me begin with fiction, a book recommended to me by a librarian friend, Stephanie Lafferty: Anita Desai's three limpid, wondrous novellas collected as *The Artist of Disappearance*, of which the second, *Translator Translated*, conveys perfectly the mind of a translator, an attendant lord. After an early flurry, I could never bring myself to study the theory of translation, although its practice has been so central to my work. True, I wrote a handful of articles, but they always amounted to a rationalization of my intuitions about a literary activity which combines hubris and humility to an exceptional degree. I did not manage to write something for Daniel Weissbort's *Translating Poetry: The Double Labyrinth*, an excellent collection of essays, many of which originally appeared in his magazine *MPT*, by the usual suspects: Felstiner on Celan, Hamburger on Hölderlin, Peter Jay, Auster, Bosley, Hughes and Silkin. Hamburger's dispersed essays on Hölderlin should be collected. By any reckoning, his editions of the poet amount to one of the great achievements in twentieth-century translation into English and only a distinguished Anglophone poet with a native command of the original could have done it that way. *Reading Rilke: Reflections on the Problems of Translation*, by that oddball lateralist William Gass, is a fascinating meditation on perhaps the most widely translated of all twentieth-century poets—'Rilke's strategy for the defeat of time was to turn it into space'—and on translation, culminating in his version of *The Duino Elegies*. 'Rilke's life is the life of a great writer,' says Gass, 'a poet who trained on prose, who made his weaknesses into warriors. It is therefore a life which is built of those great moments when, at white heat, he creates whole populations of poems and stories.' Perhaps this is one way into the conundrum of why Rilke, who often annoys us, is a touchstone writer for so many. He was the most single-minded of poets, and enchanted all the women who came his way, never betraying them because he never even pretended to commit affectively or sexually in the first place. In other respects, he gave as well as took, as his letters—an education in self-discipline for budding poets and writers—show. The only person who had his measure was, as you know, Lou Andreas-Salomé.

Other useful collections of essays are listed in this section of the bibliography. They include *On Translation* edited by Reuben Brower. He reprints Roman Jakobson's essay 'On Linguistic Aspects of Translation' and W. V. Quine's 'Meaning and Translation'. The book ends with a deeply eccentric bibliography by Bayard Quincy Morgan, containing a large number of quotes from the items listed, beginning with Cicero. Nabokov's absurd polarization reveals the Russian attitude in all its glory: 'the clumsiest literal translation is a thousand times more useful than the prettiest paraphrase', as those are the only two options. Weissbort, whom I saw hauled over the coals by Brodsky in public, can testify to this radically exaggerated approach. Alfred Orage, best known as the editor of *The New Age*, is quoted as writing in 1922 that 'the period for perfect translation has not yet come'. He expected it around 1970. This was a good intuition, for a translation renaissance was already under way, videlicet Anvil, Carcanet, *MPT*, Menard, Poetry International, Penguin Modern European Poets, as well as more radical enterprises such as Paul Buck's *Curtains*. Robert Bly wrote two books on translation, *Leaping Poetry* and *The Eight Stages of Translation*, and was busy with his magazine *The Sixties*. Menard's fortieth-anniversary-keepsake catalogue discusses the history of this moment.

George Steiner

At Cambridge, my late friend Roger Poole introduced me to George Steiner who, to this day, arouses contradictory feelings in many of us. Steiner can be inspirational. Certainly his Friday morning lectures on Marx, Freud and Lévi-Strauss were attended by more people, and from all faculties, than any other teacher's. He famously paints with a broad brush and did not take on board, when the paperback was due for publication, mistakes in *After Babel* pointed out by that redoubtable scholar the late Professor Edward Ullendorf, in a magisterial review of the hardback. Nonetheless, I remain grateful for this tour de force: it is a pioneering book which changed attitudes towards translation, as did Steiner's *Penguin Book of Modern Verse Translation*. He was a central figure in the translation renaissance of the 1970s. We need most of his books but his autobiography, *Errata*, falls tantalizingly short of the best: we are frustrated by cryptic silences, by a loss of nerve, for example when he writes on his mother, or rather not on his mother. Some of this otherwise fine book, unchanged, could have gone into his critical books. The personal stuff, sporadically revelatory, might have been better off re-imagined as fiction, see for example his *Anno Domini*.

To a lesser extent, the same critique can be made of what may be Steiner's final work, *My Unwritten Books*. 'The Tongues of Eros' is a new take on translation, although there is a glaring and disingenuous contradiction between his sexual revelations in this chapter and his inveighing against invasions of privacy elsewhere in the book. The most powerful, perhaps the most personal, chapters are 'Zion' (his latest attempt to define diaspora Jewish responsibilities and achievements) and 'Invidia', which is about Cecco d'Ascoli's (read Salieri's and Steiner's) envy of Dante (read Mozart and Celan). Historically, belles-lettres became distinct from cultural criticism when a specialized terminology in various critical discourses began to be deployed. Some of the tension in Steiner's books springs from his work at the interface of those disciplines and a broad humanistic investigation of our destiny as thinking reeds, in the phrase of Blaise Pascal. The summum of his writing is the magnificent uncollected essay published in *Poetry Nation Review*, 'Ten (Possible) Reasons for the Sadness of Thought', doubtless read by no more than a few hundred people.

Steiner is an eloquent non-Zionist, a position Israelis tend to see as anti-Zionist, just as my own post-Zionism is often misunderstood. My old grandfather was a pre-Zionist, but that is another story. Once Steiner made a very strong critical comment about Israel in public—the next morning he phoned me to ask for the address of a charity where he could send a cheque to help wounded Israeli soldiers. On a good day (ambiguous that), I think of him as 'Uncle George Steiner', on a bad day as 'Professor F. George Steiner (Geneva)'. As I get older and kinder and maybe wiser, he is uncle and I look back with some embarrassment to the days when he and others put up with my youthful self-importance, vanity and insecurity, not to mention the frenetic busyness of an overgrown boy scout. In 1974, he gave a lecture on Kafka at the National Book League in Albemarle Street, which I had organized for the magazine I edited, *European Judaism*, on the fiftieth anniversary of K's death. He spoke quite brilliantly and without referring to a few scribbled notes. On another occasion we were sitting together at the ICA before his colloquium speech on poetry translation; he had earlier asked me to brief him about recent trends. At one point, he whispered in my ear that the subtext of translating poetry is that the translator wishes to make homosexual love to the poet being translated. This did not explain why I had translated male and female poets. Only years later did it occur to me that the remark was a *jeu d'esprit*, though I would not be in the least surprised if the words, 'would you like me to translate your poem?', spoken at a literary conference or festival, were not an effective chat-up line.

Anvil Press Reading

I went to an Anvil Press launch at the *London Review of Books* bookshop. This was for *Treading Lightly*, the fine translation of Jacques Réda by my friend Jennie Feldman, whose first and fine book of poems, *The Lost Notebook*, was published simultaneously. Feldman is in her mid-fifties and cannot be accused of rushing into publication; her book reveals a mature lyrical gift that was well worth waiting for. Peter Jay, who runs Anvil, and I, have known each other since the first Poetry International in 1967, just before we (and indeed Michael Schmidt of Carcanet) founded our presses. Anvil and Menard co-published the first *Collected Poems* of F. T. Prince because Menard did not have the resources to publish it solo, following the two Prince pamphlets I had brought out earlier. When Feldman and Réda were about to begin their reading, the question arose as to whether the translation or the original should be read first. I suggested from the floor that the translation be read first and they did this with the first poem; at this point, a German woman said in excellent French that the original should be read first: 'for the music'—I suspect she believed there was a protocol, with the translator bringing up the train. My reason, perhaps counter-intuitive, for beginning with the translation is that you get a sense of the poem, which you retain while immersed in the original-language reading, especially if you don't know the new language. There is more to foreign poetry than exotic sonority, as Goethe understood when he said that the poetry is what survives translation, a more intelligent remark than Frost's famous, possibly apocryphal, one, and indeed a pre-emptive rejection of it.

Essays, etc.

INTERVIEWS AND CONVERSATIONS

Bialik

In *Bialik Speaks*, an admirer and camp-follower presents the thoughts and *obiter dicta* of the first great modern Hebrew poet: 'Your eyes are beautiful, young lady, and our sages said: "if a bride's eyes are beautiful her entire body need not be examined."' It is difficult to believe that such a sophisticated and intelligent poet actually said this, as with some of Kafka's remarks reported by Gustav Janouch in *Conversations with Kafka*. The matrix of the tactless remark is that of a culture where an incredible amount of energy went into ensuring that every woman was found a husband. Thus, Bialik is also quoted as saying: 'When I see a proper daughter of Israel who has reached a marriageable age and is left to her virginity with no one to relieve her from it, I turn into a corner and I weep.' One should bear in mind that Bialik, like Agnon, was on the cusp of two Jewish worlds, and the face he presented to women was an interface. His remarks about eyes are echoed in *Uncle Vanya*: Sonia is told she has beautiful hair—'No! No! When a woman is plain people tell her: "You have beautiful eyes, you have beautiful hair." ' A Turgenev character, possibly in *Rudin*, expresses a similar thought. How can I not reread this short novel after discovering recently that it 'loomed over' Roberto Bolano for years, 'like a serial killer or a question mark'?

Djuna Barnes

Long ago, I read *Nightwood* by Djuna Barnes. I remember that I did not understand what was going on. Was this my 'fault' or the book's? Mine, I suspect, in that I was too young to 'get it'. Although I did not annotate the book itself, I kept a scrap of paper noting certain phrases: 'His memory was confused and hazy, and he found himself repeating what he had read, for it was what he knew best.' Checking other noted phrases, I realize that I would love this book now, but I have reached the age when severe choices have to be made, and this is one of the reasons for writing the book you are reading. The choice, as all ageing readers know, boils down to this: if I reread *Nightwood*, indeed even if I don't reread *Nightwood*, I will have to decide between authors I never read in the first place, Anthony Trollope or Benito Pérez Galdós, for example. (I have belatedly read Anthony Powell's *Dance to the Music of Time*, in the twelve hardbacks my father bought seriatim on publication, and am very pleased I did.) Sadly, I *am* participating in a zero-sum game. Still, at the end of the night, I am lucky to be a reader, and that's an end to it.

Back to Djuna Barnes, whose *Interviews* I have on my desk. I bought this book thinking she was the interviewee, when in fact she turned out to be the interviewer, work done, she claims, to pay the rent. One realizes from the introduction that she faked some of the answers while interacting with her interviewees in a way you are not supposed to. Consciously or not, she was practising techniques of dialogue and characterization she would later deploy in her fiction. She outlived all the interviewees, which is not the same as outliving all the people whose obituaries one has written, except that many of her interviewees too were mentors, and therefore older than her. At least one of my interviews (with Felek Scharf) was a rehearsal for the eventual obituary, as he well knew. I had no excuse for getting any facts wrong, nor did I, so far as I know. One of Barnes' interviews is with her future friend

James Joyce, dated 1922, the year he published *Ulysses*. Again, according to the note, *Ulysses* influenced *Nightwood* (she was an author Eliot praised as highly as he praised another of his Faber authors, David Jones) and, apparently, *Nightwood* influenced *Finnegans Wake*. The interview with Joyce was conducted in Les Deux Magots: '*Hamlet* is a great play, written from the point of view of the ghost' (which reminds one of Artaud's opinion that the Ancient Mariner's crime was Coleridge's crime, and the Albatross was Coleridge himself). Like Paula Rego, Joyce loved reading the book of saints (presumably Voragine's *Golden Legend*). 'He is never without it.'

[Coda: I have now reread *Nightwood*. It was well worth the detour, as Michelin says.]

Paris Review

The *Paris Review* interviews always gave me a buzz when I was reading the magazine in the 1960s and 1970s. The interview as a form lends itself to magazine publication, surrounded by poems and short stories and illustrations, and also lends itself to value-added lustre in your list of contributors, which is what I did at one time by getting big names to offer a single translation to Menard's postcard series, with a fee of a hundred copies. I have here the second series of *Paris Review* interviews, *Writers at Work*. It is, quite frankly, a disappointment. I should reconsider my idea of gathering together my own published interviews, lest the words of Elvis Costello return to haunt me: 'It was a fine idea at the time, now it's a brilliant mistake.' Many of the questions and answers are predictable and tedious, even though the authors could not be grander: T. S. Eliot, Marianne Moore, Ezra Pound, Robert Lowell, etc., and the interviewers are distinguished writers in their own right: Donald Hall, Richard Poirier, etc. Maybe I am in a sour mood today but I feel that the interviewers have not worked the interviewees hard enough; they are only too relieved to take it easy after a long life at the coal face: it beats writing a lecture, any day. Paula is interviewed in public from time to time and the best ones happen when she is pushed hard.

ESSAYS

William Hazlitt

I discussed William Hazlitt's *Liber Amoris* in the autobiography section of this book. Here is my father's Nonesuch edition of Hazlitt's *Selected Essays*. I'm glad we didn't read Hazlitt at school, for I have a lingering prejudice against Charles Lamb, whom we did read. It follows that Lamb deserves another chance. But today we have naming of Hazlitt, the greatest English essay writer and one of our greatest critics. I see that this copy of the essays is a 1946 reprint of the 1930 edition. I imagine my father reading it in our lounge, perhaps during the harsh winter of 1947. In a house without central heating, the log fire is blazing. Before dinner, doubtless, my father has tried to complete the *Times* crossword, having read the paper on the tube from Moorgate to Golders Green. After dinner, he and my mother have listened to the nine o'clock news on the Home Service, now Radio Four—there was no television in the house until we rented one for the coronation in 1953. I, aged five, and my sister Ruth, aged two, have been asleep for a long time. If there were no visitors, or no Labour Party meeting, or no office work brought home that day, what did my parents do before going to bed? They listened to the radio or they read books. Anthony Powell had not yet begun publishing his sequence; Graham Greene and Ernest Hemingway, J. B. Priestley and André Gide were on the shelves. But the book my father was reading that evening was this very copy of Hazlitt. Let the essay he was reading, for this is a book you pick up from time to time, not one you read through until it is finished, be 'On Depth and Superficiality'. He surely noted the wisdom, the wit, the understated passion and the sublimation.

Charles Lamb

I picked up in the local hospice shop Charles Lamb's *Essays of Elia*, a serendipitous discovery that gives me an excuse to return to this writer whose 'Dissertation upon Roast Pig' so put me off at school. Pressed for time, let me, for obvious reasons, turn to the essay entitled 'Detached Thoughts on Books and Reading': 'When I am not walking, I am reading; I cannot sit and think. Books think for me.' Charles Lamb, *hypocrite lecteur, mon semblable, mon frère*. With the exception of 'all those volumes which "no gentleman's library ought to be without" . . . I can read almost anything'. Yes. And then: 'Much depends upon *when* and *where* you read a book. In the five or six impatient minutes, before the dinner is quite ready, who would think of taking up "The Faerie Queen" for a stopgap, or a volume of Bishop Andrewes' sermons?' Quite so, but we infer that Lamb read these two authors at other times. Most of the essay leaves me cold. In Hazlitt, the prose is instinct with the quality of thought, with the pressure of thinking: Hazlitt's prose is literature, Lamb's the higher journalism. Lamb deserves that I read a few more essays but, so far, it is a no-brainer to choose between him and Hazlitt, despite the view of Virginia Woolf.

Virginia Woolf

Here are *Moments of Being*, which contains marvellous autobiographical pieces, and *The Common Reader* from which I have reread two or three essays, including the classic 'How should one read a Book?' The essay ends with Judgement Day and the Almighty saying to Peter, 'not without a certain envy when He sees us coming with our books under our arms, "Look, these need no reward. We have nothing to give them here. They have loved reading." ' I can say, with absolute certainty, of myself and of any readers this book finds, that the one and only thing we unquestionably have in common is that we love reading and that the survival of literary culture depends on us. On rereading Virginia Woolf's Hazlitt essay, I am struck that she rates him below not only Montaigne but also Lamb, a perfect example of how one common reader makes a discovery about a lifelong preference and is influenced to reconsider this *idée fixe* by reading another common reader, in reality an uncommon common reader, one of the best in the business. Yes, I have spent my life preferring Hazlitt—whom I revere—to Lamb. Nonetheless, if Virginia Woolf, no less, rates Lamb more highly, who am I not to doubt my thoughts about this writer? There is pathos in the fact that Lamb, the most loyal of friends, was one of the six people who followed Hazlitt's cortege from his Frith Street lodging house (now a posh hotel) in Soho, where the writer died penniless, to Saint Anne's churchyard: a route I followed one night with Octavio Paz, himself an essayist of the highest order. I am in a win–win situation. Were I, on further reading, to change my mind about Lamb, then the pleasure is all mine and I would be enriched. If, however, Lamb were to remain a lesser writer than she says, then another pleasure is all mine: that of disagreeing with a reader of the quality of Woolf.

One evening, driving home from the University of Westminster's Harrow campus after my day of remedial teaching on the Royal Literary Fund scheme, I was listening to Sean Rafferty's programme and heard him quote the words by Charles Lamb from 'Dream Children' which are the epigraph to Edward Elgar's chamber work of the same name: 'We are nothing; less than nothing, and dreams. We are only what might have been . . .' This is the kind of statement that particularly moves me after a couple of glasses of evening wine, but even at an earlier hour it was enough to send to me to the Internet and download Lamb's short essay, described by him as a reverie.

Israel Zangwill

One of Paula's occasional Sunday afternoon visitors and closest friends is John Mills, former senior scientist at the National Gallery, world expert on carpets, and voracious reader, whether at his house in Ventnor or his flat in London. He frequents second-hand bookshops as other men frequent pubs or Internet cafes and is one of the great rereaders of all time, mainly nineteenth-century fiction and essays. George Gissing is a big favourite, Israel Zangwill too. Perhaps because I had been talking about Verlaine and Rimbaud's London house, Mills gave me a copy of Zangwill's essays *Without Prejudice*, which I was curious to dip into, having long ago pigeonholed the author as the early chronicler of the late Victorian East End—not long before my grandparents arrived there—in *Children of the Ghetto* and *The King of the Schnorrers*. The English writer describes his visit to the sick and frail Verlaine, 'whose later verse is as obscure as Mallarmé', a curious judgement. Zangwill's *Dreamers of the Ghetto* is a useful source, even now, for information about characters like Uriel Acosta, an immediate precursor of Spinoza—Spinoza as Jewish outsider rather than great philosopher. Acosta continues to fascinate people interested in or participating in what I once called 'liminal Judaism', or indeed liminal religion. The 'philosophic excursions' of Zangwill, a late-Victorian man of letters, take him from Paris to Slapton Sands, from Venice to Ventnor. If you, like me, have read little of Zangwill, try these names: Robert Buchanan, Mrs

Alexander, Louis Becke, Humphrey James, S. R. Crockett, J. R. Watson, J. T. Bealby, John Oliver Holmes. They are listed along with Mark Rutherford and Joseph Conrad in a list of Fisher Unwin's 'Six Shilling Novels' at the front of Zangwill's book. Well, as so often, I am generalizing from my own ignorance. There are nineteen thousand Google hits for Louis Becke.

Essays by poets: W. H. Auden and others

Essays by poets on poets and poetry have a special place in my library. For example, Eugenio Montale's *The Second Life of Art* ('Sweeney Agonistes' reminds him of Gilbert and Sullivan) and the crucial *Poet in Our Time*, Joseph Brodsky's *Less Than One* and *On Grief and Reason*, Seamus Heaney's *Finders Keepers*, Robert Pinsky's *Poetry and the World*, Michael Heller's *Uncertain Poetries* and Louise Gluck's *Proofs and Theories*. Gluck's lovely essay on George Oppen contains an allusion to what she calls Wallace Stevens' 'autoerotic sensuousness', a phrase straight out of a Lucy Ellmann heroine's mouth, which I would like Gluck to clarify. Pinsky too champions Oppen. A comparison he makes between a Williams and an Oppen poem generates insight: 'it is the difference between the mystery of experience, evoked in Williams' poem, and the mystery of meaning, in Oppen's.' Pinsky suggests that this distinction explains why Williams is the greater artist, but he still sees Oppen's work as having 'a vital importance of its own, as well as an immense sweetness'. Even though I would prefer 'tenderness' to 'sweetness', I am grateful to find the chapter on Oppen between chapters on Bishop and Heaney. I have folded into Pinsky's book a letter from him defending the account of his bar mitzvah, which, I infer, I told him he had got wrong in one or two details.

As for W. H. Auden, there have been few poets more learned than the old curmudgeon and yet possessing the common touch. In *The Dyer's Hand* and *Forewords and Afterwords*, he is always hugely entertaining and regularly instructive. The essay on Goethe ends with a quote from the poet which Auden approves of, as it casts retrospective validity on his own practice when translating the great German: 'If the translator has really understood his author, he will be able to evoke in his own mind not only what the author has done, but also what he wanted and ought to have done. That at least is the line I have always taken in translation, though I make no claim that it is justifiable.' Auden's commonplace book, *A Certain World*, is not all treasure: what could be more tediously uninformative than William Feather's remark that 'With all her experience, every woman expects to do better when she marries a second time, and some do'? Not knowing who Feather was, I googled him and found a whole bunch of tedious quotations.

Essays by prose writers

Prose writers too collect their essays and interviews: here is *Homo Poeticus* by Danilo Kiš edited by Susan Sontag, herself an essayist of distinction, especially when the essays are the length of a novella, such as *Illness as Metaphor*, *On Photography* and *Regarding the Pain of Others*. In the last named book, she sometimes generalizes falsely: thus, 'to catch a death actually happening and embalm it for all time' is *not*, as she claims, 'something only cameras can do'. She forgets death masks, and the humble sketch, for example John Berger's of his dead or dying father or Paula's of her aged mother. Curiously, Sontag refers to 'one of the most poignant images from World War I: a line of English soldiers blinded by poison gas', which could be an image 'from one of the searing movies about the war'. She implies it is a photograph, but the image imprinted on her mind's eye is of a famous painting by John Singer Sargent in the Imperial War Museum. And does Robert Capa's iconic photograph of the dying Republican soldier lose *all* value if it was, like Robert Doisneau's lovers kissing, staged? I am quibbling. Why? Competing with Sontag is fine provided that my comments are accurate and interesting. More directly, I am interpreting my marginalia and underlinings, which here turn out to be disagreements. As always with this author, I learnt a lot from *Regarding the Pain of Others*, but it is nothing like her best book.

Essays on more general themes, such as Adam Phillips' *Promises, Promises* or Robertson Davies' *A Voice from the Attic*, would once have come under the rubric of belles-lettres, a term I am politically correct enough to eschew. (It is politically correct of me even to use the phrase 'politically correct', when I mean conventional or, more flatteringly, up-to-date.) Guy Davenport (*The Geography of the Imagination*) writes about a walk in Italy and France 'with two books only, a Donne and a *Cantos* . . . My first response [to Pound] was to learn Italian and Provençal, and to paint in the quattrocento manner. All real education is such unconscious seduction.' Is 'unconscious' the right word? Never mind, we know what he means. Here are William Bronk's collected essays *Vectors and Smoothable Curves*, with a particularly brilliant one on Herman Melville, as well as his essential poetry.

Davenport, Bronk (on whom that fine poet Henry Weinfield has written so well in *The Music of Thought in the Poetry of George Oppen and William Bronk*), Duncan, Olson and others of their ilk, unlike Auden, all wrote for an elite readership, some of who in turn disseminate to a wider audience what the masters have to say. I wish I could find the generous and wise phrase Auden used about Patience Strong which Ian Hamilton quoted to me in his Soho office local, The Pillars of Hercules, behind Foyles, on the occasion when he wrote an affectionate dedication in my copy of his poems *The Visit*. He said he was going to use the Auden phrase in an article in the now defunct (like him, sadly) *New Society*. We met from time to time in the 1960s and 1970s and then lost touch until later. He was responsible for what may have been my first published work, a Bonnefoy translation (*TLS*, March 1966), and proposed a Bonnefoy supplement to his magazine, *The Review*, although sadly it never happened. How thrilling it was for this young man when William Cookson's *Agenda*, Jon Silkin's *Stand* and Ian Hamilton's *The Review* arrived through the letterbox. Here are Ian's sixtieth birthday book of memories and reflections, *Another Round at the Pillars*, and his posthumous *Collected Poems*, edited by Alan Jenkins, whose painstaking work is exemplary.

Cambridge

My Cambridge has sentimental value for me, as does another, more specialized book of essays, *Gown and Tallith*, published on the fiftieth anniversary of the founding of the Cambridge University Jewish Society, of which I was a member and, so help me, the social secretary during one term. The essays that interest me most in *My Cambridge* are by Donald Davie, Thom Gunn and Raymond Williams, because all of them already interest me as writers. Gunn's essay is hugely entertaining and full of self-knowledge. He cheerfully quotes one of his early failed poems, 'A Village Edmund': 'When it was over he pulled his trousers on. / "Demon lovers must go," he coldly said. / And she stared at the pale intolerable moon.' Davie's essay is a dry (yes, dry) run for the longer account of Cambridge in his memoir *These the Companions*. Williams begins his essay: 'It was not my Cambridge.' Nor was it Wittgenstein's, and yet its silent continuities always evoke a sense of virtual fellowship when I visit this place (in mind or on the ground), a place which contributed, for better or for worse, to the formation of my magpie mind and where I was often miserable and, in my final year, depressed. Wittgenstein is included in *Gown and Tallith* in a bizarre list of deceased Jewish graduates of the university.

The book contains a beautiful poem by my friend Elaine Feinstein, 'New Year': 'How are we Jewish, and what brings us together / in this most puritan of protestant centres?' Oxford has been said to be cavalier, Cambridge roundhead, indeed Oliver Cromwell's skull is buried somewhere in Sidney Sussex College. Davie asks: 'is [the Cambridge ethos] Cromwellian? . . . [it] leaves no margin for *caprice*, for that free-running, freely-associating, arbitrary and gratuitous play of mind out of which, not exclusively but necessarily, art-works arise'. This dovetails very well with the conclusion of Williams' essay: 'so many things have been done here, and so often they have been done quite against the grain.'

Peter Vansittart and Humphrey Jennings

Peter Vansittart's house in Hampstead (where that neglected and now almost invisible writer Fred Grubb had a room) had no number on the door, apparently to confuse the German invader. There is more logic in his brilliant polyphonic anthology, *Voices from the Great War*, which includes Britons, Germans and Russians, poets and journalists, soldiers and monarchs, Hitler, Trotsky and Churchill. He deploys unexpected and cunning juxtapositions: thus, for example, the Balfour Declaration is surrounded by two passages from Isaac Rosenberg. Another Rosenberg extract—'What is happening to me now is more tragic than the "passion play". Christ never endured what I endure. It is breaking me completely' (from a letter to Edward Marsh)—is immediately followed by Kipling's 'Gethsemane' (1914–1918). We learn from a letter Freud wrote on 23 February 1918 that he supposed 'we have to wish for a German victory, and this is 1) a displeasing idea, and 2) still improbable.' Vansittart uses the polyphonic technique in *Voices 1870–1914*. This book works less well, because the period covered is too long and verbal energy, in the form of collage and polyphony, is not generated by the mere fact that wars begin and end the years under observation, even by such an intelligent and humane anthologist. Still, Vansittart, in the voice of Clemenceau, is right: 'Beware! The dead are powerful persuaders. One must pay attention to the dead.'

Vansittart's *London: A Literary Companion* is a narrative consisting entirely of enjoyable and sometimes penetrating asides: 'Naomi Mitchison . . . remembered a homosexual friend being given a guardsman for his birthday.' Vansittart quotes *Oliver Twist*, Bill Sikes' trial after the murder of Nancy, which thrilled me as a child because I knew the terrain: Caen Wood (Kenwood), the Vale of Health, Dick Whittington's stone on Highgate Hill. Another remarkable polyphonic book is the posthumously published *Pandaemonium* by one of the luminaries of the Crown Film Unit, the surrealist poet and painter, Humphrey Jennings. It is about the coming of the machine age, that is, as it built up during the two centuries before the starting date of Vansittart's second book. The book begins with Milton, whose *Paradise Lost* gave Jennings his title, the word *pandaemonium* ('all the devils') being a coinage by Milton. It is, in Milton's words, 'the high Capital of Satan and his Peers'. Jennings is quoted as saying that the book can be read in several ways, including thematically, which requires the index compiled by Charles Madge. Madge tells us that the illustrations included are contemporaneous with the texts. This explains why the John Martin image is not from his marvellous *Paradise Lost* series. Did Blake know the images of his much younger contemporary John Martin, which plainly suggest 'satanic mills'? Yes, says Bruce Ross-Smith, citing his friend Ruthven Todd's book *Tracks in the Snow*.

HOMAGES AND FESTSCHRIFTS

Eric Mottram

Alive in Parts of This Century is a celebration of Eric Mottram on his seventieth birthday. Mottram was professor at Kings College London, poet, literary critic and a serious member of the awkward squad. Like his close friend and collaborator Bob Cobbing, he never made concessions, nor could you accuse him of being charming. I knew him for many years, although not well enough to be asked to contribute to this book; yet, as someone on the margins of his social, professional and aesthetic life, I am someone to whom the book speaks. Of the eighty-one contributors, I know personally about a third; a few are friends of mine, such as Elaine Feinstein and Nathaniel Tarn. But what would you expect from an inside job in a small world such as the poetry subculture? One learns from Feinstein's text that J. G. Ballard wrote a pamphlet called *Why I Want to Fuck Ronald Reagan*. This was in the context of the prosecution of Bill Butler for the sale of pornographic books. As she reminds us, part of Mottram was part of the mimeograph revolution which enabled radical poets and others to bypass commercial publishers.

During the mid-1970s, I contributed a couple of times to *Poetry Review* when Mottram was editor, though I had already been voted off the General Council of the Poetry Society, which published the magazine. There was the mother of all pitched battles between rival camps over a number of years, and I suppose I was considered a wimpish centrist, midway between the radical and conservative positions. Peter Barry has written about this period in *The Poetry Wars*, as has Robert Sheppard in *When Bad Times Made for Good Poetry*. A few years later, I was fighting another war, this time with the Arts Council of Great Britain in the person of Charles Osborne, involving Menard Press' grant. I had my say in a document I called 'Open Letter to Sir John Witt', who was probably chairman of the ACGB.

William Golding

In *The Man and His Books*, a tribute to William Golding on his seventy-fifth birthday, edited by John Carey, Golding states: 'I don't think there is any language but metaphor. If you start to try and find the language that is not metaphor, then what you're stuck with is mathematics. Mathematics is one huge metaphor, or no metaphor at all. And if there starts being metaphor in mathematics, it goes haywire, or that's how I conceive it. I'm not a mathematician.' I'm not sure I find this helpful, although whoever thinks up the names for hairdressers' shops would probably agree with it, puns being condensed metaphor. 'In the beginning was the pun,' wrote Beckett. We who love verbal and visual puns in literature and art can be snobbish when it comes to shop signs and advertising, where the chickens of literature and art, in particular surrealism, come home, well downmarket, to roost. If all language is metaphor, then this tells us nothing about language (or mathematics), still less about the literarity of serious and beautiful novels such as *Pincher Martin*, *Lord of the Flies* and *The Spire*, where sound and rhythm and narrative are as important as metaphor, but Golding knew that.

Fiction

Stories of the Stories or 'Where do my writing duties begin?'

Introduction

As I explained in the introduction to this book, many writers or books could be included in a different section. Some French fiction writers are under 'France and French Literature', some here, and the same goes for Jewish writers. This is a given of my approach.

Having completed only one book of short stories or, better yet, fables, I am taking something of a liberty when I call myself a fiction writer. There is a hint of vanity about the description. Still, three or four of the shortest have appeared in magazines and I hope a publisher will bring out the book. As for my poems, some of them have been published in book form and I hope that a short collected poems will eventually appear. These days, I suppose I am an autobiographer and literary critic. Poetry, sadly or not, is no longer at the ontological centre of my *imaginaire*. It hardly needs pointing out that these labels only matter if they matter. If not, not.

I have written essays about fiction, and tell students that there is no better way of accessing the inner life of other people, and therefore of oneself. Yet when push comes to shove, I don't read many novels. Just as I prefer historiography to history, I prefer books at the interface of fiction and autobiography ('auto-fiction') to fiction proper: books like John Berger's *Here Is Where We Meet* or any of Max Sebald's major prose books, such as *Vertigo, The Emigrants, Rings of Saturn* and *Austerlitz*. Jean Echenoz, too, writes fiction/biography in an original and rewarding way: thus, his *Ravel*. My favourite French novels include auto-fictions by Sarraute and Duras. And there is the fiction of poets: Nerval, Rilke and others. Nonetheless, I intend to make more time for the 'fiction fiction' on my shelves, mainly English-language, French and Russian.

At seventy, I no longer possess the need or desire, time or energy, to read at random or to explore neglected areas: virtually all Eastern literature, most Latin American literature, Arabic and Persian. Also, as will be evident from the contents of the present work, I am not about to read many history books, or economics, or philosophy or—the shame and disgrace—science, except for neuropsychiatry, which feeds into my stories. This is the point. I know what books I want to write, and they require a certain amount of reading as matrix, call it professional reading if you like, save that it's fun, and almost all of it is the best of its kind. The reason my fables occasionally require research involves a principle: mistakes should be on purpose, especially when one introduces historical figures amidst invented ones. 'In fact', the historical figures are sometimes more invented than the invented ones, in that I colonize the latter with characteristics of friends and enemies: this woman may have X's luminous mind, Y's polymorphous creativity, Z's long arms, A's short legs, B's dress sense, C's morality, whereas the historical figures, especially the dead, require a far greater effort of the imagination to enter into their psychic structures, hence my excitement at *Ravel*.

Certain fiction writers of the front rank I have not read at all or, at least, not read enough: it's time I woke up at the back and paid deserved attention. I could subdivide their books into those I tell myself I should buy and read, and books other people tell me I should buy and read. This reduces the seemingly infinite number of unread books in the universe to a number that, all the same, nine lives of uninterrupted reading would not yield enough quality (let alone quantity) time to read properly, that is introject and digest. Barthes writes: 'not to have read Hegel would be an exorbitant defect for a philosophy teacher, for a Marxist intellectual, for a Bataille specialist. But for me? Where do my reading duties begin?' Well, where do mine begin, specifically with respect to fiction? Let me take a look at writers I have neglected.

Writers I Have Neglected

Theodor Fontane

I still have not read *Effi Briest*, Theodor Fontane's classic of 1895, which I bought more than ten years ago, according to the date on the note from the publisher, Antony Wood of Angel Classics. Angel specializes almost exclusively in translation classics, mainly from the Russian. The existence of a note suggests I wrote to the publisher, whom I know personally, perhaps asking for a discount or offering a Menard book in barter. I know why I wanted this particular work: I had read somewhere that it was Beckett's favourite novel, if not his favourite book. There are passing references to Effi in *Krapp's Last Tape* and *All That Fall*. Paul Buck has copied the video of R. W. Fassbinder's film version for me, which will doubtless postpone a reading of the book. There are a considerable number of books here that I bought years before I read them or indeed did not read them. It's like this: I get a feeling in my bones, call it a frisson, I *know* I shall eventually want to read this or that book. With *Effi Briest*, there is a frisson at the (magical) thought that one will get closer to Beckett by reading a book he loved, therefore I shall read it, unlike an embarrassingly large number of the books that congregate in the great unread, whether or not they were bought as a result of frisson.

Joseph Conrad

Heart of Darkness—which, according to Thomas Mann, inaugurated the twentieth century—is the only book by Joseph Conrad I have read, despite urgings from two mavens who revere him, Mike Heller and Alan Wall. In fact, I need no urging, only an executive decision as to whether he should take precedence over other novelists of the extended great tradition I have neglected to the same extent: George Eliot, Benito Pérez Galdós, Eça de Queirós, Thomas Hardy, Jane Austen, Henry James (although I have read his wondrous long stories and novellas), and, to a lesser extent, Charles Dickens, D. H. Lawrence and William Faulkner. In the case of Hardy and Lawrence, I have not neglected their poetry. They are among the handful of major novelists who are also great poets. Victor Hugo was both, and also a visual artist of distinction. These days, Conrad's name is sometimes mentioned in the context of 9/11. Is it my duty (certainly it is my self-interest) to read

Conrad? Do I have time? Am I, like Nabokov, 'too old to change Conradically? What are my priorities?' 'Une nuit d'amour, un livre de moins': 'One night of love, one less book' translates this grandly absurd idea of Balzac's, although the pedant in me wonders if it shouldn't be 'fewer', save that it sounds funny when the noun is singular. Balzac, by the way, was talking about writing, not reading. He didn't mess about. This is my cue to phone Wall and ask him: what should I read if I intend to donate precious time to a second Conrad book, *The Secret Agent*? No, he says, read *Under Western Eyes*. An email from Heller arrives, disagreeing with Wall: *Victory* is the one to read, and he adds, for good measure, that James' *Princess Casamassima* is a great Dickensian novel about anarchism. Ah, whoever is reading this, you are witness to one of the digressionary techniques I employ or deploy to avoid uninterrupted work on my own writing, in this instance contacting friends who have never met and eliciting their reactions to each others' thoughts, ostensibly as part of my research.

Virginia and Leonard Woolf

My only Virginia Woolf novel, *To the Lighthouse*, I read with respect rather than love when I was too young. Time now to take a dip in deep waters. Here is my old Everyman edition. 'Who shall blame Mr Ramsay,' says his wife in her free indirect speech, 'if he requires sympathy, and whisky, and someone to tell the story of his suffering to at once?' His wife and son are 'lovely and unfamiliar from the intensity of his isolation and the waste of ages and the perishing of the stars'. The paragraph, plucked at random where those two quotes appear, alone suffices to tell my belated ear that this is a fiction writer I should make time for: a self-evident discovery better made late than never, not forgetting the two novels of her husband, a man I sometimes find myself identifying with: like Leonard Woolf, albeit on a more modest level, I am a London Jewish publisher who has written books and am involved in politics and went to the same college as him. Doubtless I shall find out more: Paula bought me Victoria Glendinning's biography, which has a broader canvas than Duncan Wilson's political biography. The *Jewish Quarterly* reviewer of Glendinning argued that she has failed to convey the complexity of Woolf's Jewishness and indeed only three pages are devoted to his perceptions of this aspect of his identity. At the time of writing I haven't read the book and so I reserve judgement, since the pages will read differently within the context of the entire book, the entire life. I have enormous sympathy and respect for Leonard, a role model of a caring partner. Virginia's own essay on William Cowper and Lady Austen can be read against what is known about her intimate life with Leonard, with her in the role of Cowper. One trivial matter in Glendinning's work caught my eye: Leonard lived for two years in a room at the top of a staircase in New Court, Trinity College Cambridge. In my first year, I too had a top-floor room there. I wonder if it was the same room. I thought that Nabokov's Trinity room as described in the complete edition of *Speak Memory* was the room I had in my third year (the Great Court staircase reassigned to Angel Court) but a swift dip into Brian Boyd's biography disabuses me.

Cesare Pavese, *paradoxically*

I remember well the root cause, the generative source of my quondam profligate enthusiasm for Cesare Pavese. I had been overwhelmed by the intelligence, mood and pathos of his diaries of 1935–1950, *This Business of Living*, which I read in the Isle of Man in 1965 while enduring a week attached to the island's Tourist Board as part of a graduate traineeship in the early months of my very first day job, with the now defunct British Travel Association. My salary was seven hundred and fifty pounds a year, but younger readers should bear in mind that the rent of my bedsitter in Powis Square, Notting Hill, was only one quarter of that, which was the percentile rule of thumb at the time.

The diaries led to my buying a large number of novels and volumes of short stories by Pavese, many of which I have not read, for example *The Moon and the Bonfire*. They are in classic 1960s small paperback format with cinema-poster-style covers. Here are two hardback collections of stories, *Festival Night* and *Summer Storm*: we learn from the introduction to *Summer Storm* that, aged twenty-four, Pavese translated *Moby Dick*, a book Primo Levi much admired.

My battered copy of Pavese's diary (in the undistinguished translation by A. E. Murch), which he began in prison—incarcerated for anti-fascist journalism—and which was published in 1952, two years after his suicide, bears much pencilled evidence of attentive and passionate reading. Many of these markings I would repeat today, if I were reading the book for the first time: 'Giving is a passion. Almost a vice. We must have someone to whom we can give' or 'Oh! The power of indifference! That is what has enabled stones to endure, unchanged, for millions of years.' Pavese quotes Louis Lavelle's *L'Erreur de Narcisse*: '. . . the only thing that counts is what we are, not what we do' and, a few days later, writes his own version: 'A person counts for what he *is*, not for what he does. Actions are not moral life.' How Baudelaire and Malraux would disagree with this! Then: 'Only rarely does one suffer a real out-and-out injustice. Our own actions are so tortuous. In general, it always turns out that we are a little at fault ourselves, and then—goodbye to the feeling of a winter morning.' This was worth emphasizing, but he goes too far with the two sentences that immediately follow the painful insight: 'A little at fault? It's all our fault and there's no getting away from it. Always.' Such insights followed by an exaggeration amount almost to a trope in the diary.

Dare one say that this is linked, in some way, to his suicide, the ultimate expression of his depression? I no longer find his thought that 'water is more *all-pervading* than any lover' interesting or worth saying in the first place, assuming it means anything. And why did I underline 'The only reason why we are always thinking of our own ego is that we have to live with it more continuously than with anyone else's'? I must have thought the comment was profound or at least relevant to my own experience and understanding of the world. Today, if anything, I would say it is not true. Other people's egos impinge on me more than my own, whereas my ego may be a problem for others . . . Finally, my 1965 question mark against 'The richness of life lies in memories we have forgotten' was, as it had to be, that of a twenty-three-year-old. Today, after nearly half a century of remembered memories and forgotten memories, and with my own *Arithmetic of Memory* exploring this very question, experience confirms that Pavese was right. I don't know if he had been reading Bergson when he made that entry on 13 February 1944. I am reminded too that I read somewhere that Alzheimer's is caused by or accompanied by the inability to forget. That is, the inability to select. Like the character in one of the finest stories by Borges, 'Funes the Memorious', the afflicted person remembers everything, but then, in order not to go crazy, finds that the system shuts down entirely. In a letter, George Oppen, whose Alzheimer's led to his death, quotes his mother's suicide note: 'I cannot face the business of living.'

This Business of Living, a work of literature in its own right (and which runs parallel with Canetti's journals, as he points out in *Notes from Hampstead*), led me to Margaret Crosland's selection and translation of Pavese's poetry *A Mania for Solitude* (later reprinted as *Selected Poems*) which, again, profoundly moved me: 'death shall drink to me with your eyes' (I chance my own free translation of the famous line), and this in turn led to the buying spree of his fiction. It may well be too late for me to read the Pavese novels that await my attention but I shall read something from *Summer Storm* on the very field of my writing 'at this moment of time'. Five minutes later: I have completed the beautiful six page story 'Freewill', an exploration of the nature of children, whose tone reminds me of Natalia Ginzberg, Pavese's former colleague at the publishing house of Einaudi.

Here are *Dialogues with Leuco* and *Selected Letters 1924–1950*: there is no mention of Primo Levi in the index of the latter book, nor in *An Absurd Vice*, the biography of Pavese by Davide Lajolo. Yet it is impossible that Pavese did not read Levi's *If This Is a Man*, whose first edition came out in Italy in 1946. I am sure Levi told me, when I met him in 1986, that he was taught by Pavese, and yet Ian Thomson in his *Primo Levi* is adamant that Pavese was a supply teacher who only taught girls at the Lyceo in Turin during Levi's first year, 1934–1935. Was my wish father to the thought? In May that year, Pavese was arrested on suspicion of subversive activities. Around this time, the first stage of Mussolini's war against the Jews, which would culminate in the racial laws of 1938, was beginning. Perhaps it is not surprising that Pavese did not associate the younger writer with the famous Lyceo, and he had other things on his mind in the final years of his life. Levi, however, must have read his fellow Turin writer's first collection of poems published in 1936 or the revised and expanded version published in 1943. These may even have influenced the younger man's poems: something in the tone calls across the waves in both directions. In the second of Pavese's two essays which accompany the poems in the 1943 edition, there is a fascinating paragraph:

It is certain that once again the problem of the image will dominate the situation. But it will not be a question of narrating images, an empty formula, as we have seen, because nothing can distinguish the words which evoke an image from those which evoke an object. It will be a question of describing—whether directly or by means of images is immaterial—a reality which is not naturalistic but symbolic. In these poems the facts will speak—if they speak—not because reality wishes it but because intelligence decides it will be so. Individual poems and the whole body of poems will not be an autobiography but a judgment. As happens in *La divina Commedia* (we had to reach this point)—a warning that my symbol will want to correspond not to Dante's allegory but to his images.

Thus, when we listen to Bach, for example the late and wondrous Lorraine Hunt Lieberson singing 'Ich Habe Genug', we need not share the theology or the religious belief powering the music in order to be moved and instructed, just as Dante's allegorical subscendence need not bother us either. Reflecting on Pavese has got me thinking about other nineteenth- and twentieth-century Italian poetry and fiction, and how fine and wondrous this blessed country's literature is. Here, for example, are Dino Buzzatti's *A Love Affair* and Giorgio Bassani's *The Garden of the Finzi-Continis* and *The Heron* and books by Giacomo Leopardi whom I wrote about earlier, in the poetry section. Back to the Pavese novels I have not yet read: you see the problem. At my age, I am caught up in a zero-sum game: a victory on one front, reading more Cesare Pavese, involves a defeat on another front, missing out on Joseph Conrad or Stanisław Witkewicz. Not even the greatest and most disciplined reader in the world can read everything. What a blessing it is to read the best literature. Read as much as you can, as well as you can, without skimping on your writing or your loved ones or your responsibility towards the planet. It's as 'simple' as that.

[Coda: the Pavese diaries have just been reissued in a facsimile edition, in other words the publisher did not commission a new translation. Still, the edition is graced by a new introduction from the pen of that peerless guide to European literature, John Taylor. Taylor is particularly insightful on the quality or nature of the relationship between that old married couple, literature and life, so painfully explored in the diaries. Truly, for Pavese, the dialectical relationship between life on the page and life off the page was so all-consuming that we can risk saying he had a problem with boundaries, unlike, say, Stendhal, who never confused the two, or the recently deceased Jorge Semprun. What would one give for Pavese's reaction to the latter's *Literature or Life*, but then, had Pavese lived long enough to read it, he would not have been the man who wrote these diaries.]

Adolf Rudnicki, Witold Gombrowicz and Czesław Miłosz

Adolf Rudnicki wrote in one of his weekly Warsaw feuilletons, collected in *Les Feuillets bleus*: 'Reading is always an adventure filled with caprices and mysteries . . . in which the main character is the reader himself . . . In solitude, in solitary reading, one is to a great extent a tributary of one's own nostalgias, one's own hungers, and their range is frequently narrower.' My friend Z. Kotowicz has urged on me for years the books of Polish prose writers. I say prose writers advisedly because I was already a reader of the great poets: Herbert, Rozewicz, Miłosz. Certainly, I had read short stories by Schulz and Rudnicki, the latter in French and at the urging of Rawicz, who persuaded Gallimard to publish him in bulk. Thanks to Rawicz, the publisher sent me several of Rudnicki's books, including *Les Fenêtres d'or*. However, the novels of Stanisław Witkewicz, Witold Gombrowicz and others in what Z. Kotowicz sees as a neglected alternative modernism to the taught canon, those have been off my radar. Here, then, is Gombrowicz's *Ferdydurke* (as well as his *Diary* with its polemic 'Against Poets'), and when am I going to read it? I've resisted reading Miłosz's fiction, such as *The Seizure of Power*. He is one of my main men, a central figure in my reading and understanding of our life and times, and I think my resistance to his fiction comes from a fear that it may not live up to the poetry and to criticism such as *The Witness of Poetry*. Can this be right? Is this a reason or a rationalization?

James Baldwin and Eldridge Cleaver

Shall I get round to books by James Baldwin I did not get round to? I did read *Giovanni's Room*, *Go Tell It on the Mountain* and other novels, as well as several non-fiction books including *The Fire Next Time* and *A Rap on Race*, this last a fascinating dialogue between Baldwin and Margaret Mead. They both regret that what she wrote twenty-five years earlier seems to have failed as a worldview: 'appreciate cultural differences, respect political and religious differences and ignore race'. In *The Fire Next Time*, which I read forty years ago, I marked the following thought: 'Love takes off the masks that we fear we cannot live without and know we cannot live within.' This still speaks to me. Browsing, I am briefly restored to these 'other voices, other rooms', the title of Truman Capote's beautiful first novel written in his early twenties, on my desk now with *Breakfast at Tiffany's* and *In Cold Blood*.

For no apparent reason, I stopped reading Baldwin, but not before I sent him a letter—I had his address in Saint-Paul de Vence from Miron Grindea—containing a neutral structuralist analysis, complete with tables of pluses and minuses, about the four different ways he treated the word 'Jew' throughout his work. He did not reply. (Fess up, perhaps I took offence and stopped reading him for that reason. If so, pathetic and whose loss?) *Soul on Ice* by Eldridge Cleaver contains a ferocious attack on Baldwin, expressed in terms that only a fellow black writer could use, at that time anyway. There is more torment in Baldwin than in Cleaver, and this is connected to sexuality, a subject on which Cleaver does not mince his words. The Baldwin and Cleaver books have evocative titles: 'Some say the world will end in fire / Some say in ice . . . .' (Robert Frost). Either way, 'the Western world will live by what it professes to believe in or it will cease to exist,' as Baldwin tells Mead.

Vitomil Zupan

I am writing this paragraph after receiving an email from my friend Ifigenija Simonovic. She is a poet and potter, ex-London, who was widowed in her forties and now lives in the centre of Ljubljana, where she spends much of her time serving literature and writers. Abused by her stepfather when she was young, she has gone the other way, loving and remembering, protecting and promoting writers and artists and the work of all who are neglected. On one of her visits to London, she met me in a bar in Camden Town, having asked me to return a novel she gave me in 1988, *Minuet for Guitar* by Vitomil Zupan, because she wanted to present all his work to the British Library, and that particular book, his only work translated into English and a modern classic, was now unobtainable. Zupan, forty years older than Simonovic, had been in a Slovene prison for seven years, during which time he composed poems in his head, rhyming to make them easier to remember, since he was not allowed paper or pencil. Later, these were smuggled in, and he wrote down the memorized poems. They were smuggled out and Ifigineja published them in seven volumes, after three years of editorial labours in the vineyard of love. I had not read *Minuet for Guitar*, about partisan warfare in Slovenia, and now I shall never read it: this is my loss, though it is also the book's loss, for the aura of a book is constituted by its loving readers. I shall make amends by adding Zupan's prison poetry to my 'Rescue Work' folder, case studies of poems written in extreme situations. As for Ifigenija, she is no longer making pots. Instead, she is hand-painting chairs made by an old craftsman, incorporating her characteristic motifs of faces and lines from her own poems. In the bar, she gave me a copy of her new book of poems, *Hodis Hodiva*, with photographs by her late husband Veseljko, and a poem in draft translation I shall work on.

Shorter Fiction

INTRODUCTION

Novella or novel? These days, Melville's *Billy Budd* (although not the shorter *Bartleby the Scrivener*), Conrad's *Heart of Darkness*, and James' *The Turn of the Screw* and *The Aspern Papers* are considered by many to be novels, although by the standards of their day and the practice of their authors, they could be described as novellas. Today, such fine books as C. K. Stead's *My Name Was Judas*, Cees Nooteboom's *The Following Story*, J. M. Coetzee's *Foe*, Roberto Bolano's *Antwerp*, Hans Keilson's *Comedy in a Minor Key* and Thomas Pynchon's *The Crying of Lot Forty Nine* are all novels. Or are they? And does it matter? Most recently I read Bohumil Hrabal's *Too Loud a Solitude*, a mad, short, wild and disturbing book about reading. Pynchon's tour de force, which he seems to have virtually disowned, is his shortest, by a long chalk. I like novellas or short novels because they can be read in one go. The holistic feedback obtained from a piece of music or a poem or a painting works its alchemical transformation, because reception is completed in one sitting or standing. But the synchronic gestalt of a painting does not involve memory in the way that diachronic art forms do: the mind's eye is busy integrating or inscribing the elements of the picture in the dialectics of space.

I have made faltering attempts over the years to read at least one (short) novel by many of the serious contemporary European writers who have been translated from literatures I have neglected—Nooteboom and Keilson for example—but I am more obsessive when it comes to France, not surprisingly since I am not at the mercy of translation. On a recent trip I bought short books by Pascal Quignard, a prodigiously gifted writer, much of whose work, as with Thomas Bernhard and Max Sebald, is on the borders of fiction and autobiographical telling, where I feel increasingly at home for reasons that may be emerging in the present work: 'The lord whose oracle is in Delphi neither declares nor conceals, but gives a sign' (Heraclitus, *fragment XXXIII*).

Thomas Bernhard

Thomas Bernhard is one of James Hogan's favourite writers and from time to time I read a book by the Austrian I haven't read before. In particular, the short ones grab me, not only because short books take less time to read than long books, but specifically because short books by this demanding author take less time to read than long books by him: thus, *On the Mountain*, *Wittgenstein's Nephew*, *Three Novellas* and *The Voice Imitator*, which is a mordantly funny and disturbing book of fables, drawn from newspaper reports and other sources, with affinities to the work of my Paris friend Marcel Cohen in his *Faits*, although Cohen's vision is not as dark as Bernhard's. 'In Rome' (*The Voice Imitator*) is an angry and beautiful homage to the unnamed Ingeborg Bachmann, a fine poet who came to one of the Poetry Internationals in London and died in Rome in complicated circumstances. Her published correspondence with Celan is often painful to read. Another master of the very short text is Régis Jauffret, whose huge collection of five hundred *Microfictions* is, however, impossible to read from cover to cover. Ever so often I take a dip, as one might down a calvados, tick the newly read microfiction in the contents pages and move on. The same goes for Lydia Davis, mistress of the miniature, in her *Collected Stories*.

Peter Handke and Honoré de Balzac

I have read a number of books by Thomas Bernhard's fellow Austrian Peter Handke, including *The Afternoon of a Writer*: dedicated to Scott Fitzgerald, it is a gloss on the title story in Fitzgerald's *Afternoon of an Author*; Handke's German publisher tells me that the English title was probably the responsibility of the translator, Ralph Manheim, presumably to avoid confusion. The trilogy *Slow Homecoming* segues between autobiography and fiction. The middle section is a characteristic meditation in the voice of Handke himself on Cézanne, on landscape and on creativity. The section begins: 'On my return to Europe, I needed my daily ration of written matter, and I read and reread a great deal.' About twenty pages later, we find the narrator sitting in Cézanne's studio in Aix, reading Balzac's 'Unknown Masterpiece', demonstrably the most discussed story in Western literature, which I myself translated in 1988 and wrote about at length. This was the first complete translation in nearly a hundred years. Since then, there have been several more. Reading the story, Handke discovers that 'French culture had become the home I had always longed for.' He reminds readers that Cézanne identified with the hero of the story, Frenhofer, which tells me that Handke, like me, has read the relevant Rilke letters (no surprise). Picasso too was obsessed by the story, although at the beginning of Françoise Gilot's *Life with Picasso*, Picasso (or Gilot), in the account of her first visit to his studio at 7 rue des Grands-Augustins (where Balzac's character Porbus has his studio), confuses Porbus and Frenhofer.

Kenneth Gangemi

Olt is an extraordinary novella by Kenneth Gangemi. It stood unread on my shelves for many years until my friend, and his, Mike Heller made the crucial recommendation and I remembered I had the book. Gangemi strikes me as a natural, a true original, who probably wrote in this way without Borges on his shoulder or, back in 1969, without Perec, then hardly known. The obsessive-compulsive Robert Olt moves round, observes, makes lists, in a very precise, very lucid way. He also makes things that could not or did not happen in our minds, by generating series of sentences that begin 'He knew he would never . . .', thus implicating us in the rich fantasy life of a prose Joseph Cornell or a prose Susan Hiller. We would like him to 'get a life', except he has a life: generating and generated by a crafty prose master, pulling his strings or pulled by them. Rooted both in the phenomenal world and in an *imaginaire* of pleasure and adventure, the character avoids the up-his-own-bum solipsism that a less disciplined, less ambitious writer would have fallen into, given the mindset.

Gabriel Garcia Marquez and Imre Kertész

Here is Gabriel Garcia Marquez's brief fable of old age, involving the dialectic of eros and agapé and, perhaps, class, if not gender, issues: *Memories of My Melancholy Whores*, perfect for a journey and return journey involving the entire length of the Northern Line. As I wrote earlier, in slightly different terms, the last page of a novella has a sporting chance of being reached within living memory of the first page, the reading of the book thus resembling a sprint rather than a marathon and generating a similar pleasure to that obtained by reading a poem: namely, the uninterrupted tracking of the parabola of the text. Mind you, *Liquidation* by Imre Kertész, which is the same length as Marquez's tale, took me four times as long to read: this, the fourth novel in a remarkable tetralogy by the Hungarian master, involves particular late and postmodernist techniques, albeit in the service of a compelling story.

Stendhal

Stendhal's shorter fictions, *Romans et nouvelles*, include 'Le juif (Filippo Hebreo)', that is, 'The Jew.' It begins: 'Having nothing to read, I write. It yields the same kind of pleasure, but with more intensity. The stove is creating problems. I have cold feet and a headache.' Stendhal wrote the story on 14 and 15 January 1831 in Trieste (a glacial town in both senses, according to the note in this edition), where he had taken up the position of French consul the previous November. It was a difficult time personally and politically, this Central European Italy was not *his* Italy, and he was not happy. And it shows in and through the story. No other writer wrote such modern-sounding sentences as early as the 1830s, except perhaps Georg Büchner.

Americans

F. Scott Fitzgerald

Paula chose F. Scott Fitzgerald's *Tender is the Night* as her book when she was on Desert Island Discs. I have written elsewhere in these pages about *The Crack-Up* and his uncollected stories, *Afternoon of an Author*. I remember buying the latter in Cambridge—the pale blue Bowes and Bowes sticker marks the spot—at the same time as John Barrell did, and because he did. He already owned the collected Bodley Head Fitzgerald volumes, which I didn't; I would have been better off reading the best of the novels than the bits and pieces. Later I would read *Tender Is the Night* and *The Great Gatsby*, but I shall stop now and reread the title story in *Afternoon of an Author*. A few moments later: it was a good idea to reread it after more than forty years; it is so full of subtle observation and writerly insight that you almost don't notice you are reading a story about a writer, a story about writing, and yet it is not a meta-fiction in the manner of, say, Daniel Pennac's *Reads like a Novel*. I can't remember or even imagine what I made of the story back in 1963 or 1964: 'The perfect neurotic', Fitzgerald wrote, the character regarding himself in the mirror. 'By-product of an idea, slag of a dream'— slag as in coal, not as in woman—and then: 'He loved life terribly for a minute, not wanting to give it up at all.' And, after looking in a shop window, 'he wished he were twenty and going to a beach club all dolled up like a Turner sunset.' Then, on the bus, he sees two unselfconscious kids, 'their attention fast upon each other. Their isolation moved him and he knew he would get something out of it professionally, if only in contrast to the growing seclusion of his life and the increasing necessity of picking over an already well-picked past. He needed reforestation and he was well aware of it, and he hoped the soil would stand one more growth. It had never been the very best soil, for he had had an early weakness for showing off instead of listening and observing.' The ending of the story, which I won't quote, is predictable and perfect. On the other hand, 'News of Paris—Fifteen Years Ago', the final story in the volume, is oversold, over-signified in the editor's introduction, yet worth reading to find out why the following perfectly controlled sentence is so marvellous in context: 'The peacocks in the draperies stirred in the April wind.'

Ralph Ellison/Henry Roth

How many times have I read that someone could have *sworn*, he absolutely *knew for certain*, that something happened in a particular place, at a particular time . . . and then irrefutable documentation turns up, revealing that the memory was wrong? It's my turn to confess a classic misremembered memory, with proof positive of my mistake, and a veritable warning of the workings of this trap, this treachery, this black hole, and I shall not make light of it, for shadow is cast, perhaps, on other memories, although not so many that I would have to doubt the validity of the entire enterprise. In the summer of 1964, I made a round tour (New York–California–New York) by Greyhound bus. The days and miles rolled by in the company of two great novels, Ralph Ellison's *Invisible Man* and Henry Roth's *Call It Sleep*, and a book of poems, Yves Bonnefoy's *Hier régnant désert*, of which I was drafting my early translations.

Here, however, is my copy of the first paperback edition of *Call It Sleep*, with the unusual rounded edges to prevent unintentional dog-earing. Two dates leap out: I have inscribed the book 'Anthony Rudolf, New York, 1966'. Now, unless I wrote 1966 by mistake (extremely unlikely), this alone disproves that I read the book in 1964. On the next page, however, things get worse: 'Tenth printing, March, 1965' (good going, Roth, given that the first printing was October 1964, thirty years after original publication). Thus, the two datings confirm each other and humiliate my beautiful story, although it is a minor misdemeanour compared to, say, forgetting that one had not even got round to reading the book: now that's fiction, telling stories. The phrase 'my beautiful story' gives the clue to what must have happened. There is no doubt at all that I read both books in the USA, and I definitely read *Invisible Man* on the Greyhound. I would have read *Call It Sleep* about eighteen months later, in Chicago, where I lived for the first six months of 1966 and did some of my reading while commuting on the Illinois Central line to the downtown Loop from Hyde Park.

Back in London, I well remember buttonholing friends and family and telling them to read these two wondrously intelligent and intense books, which drew on black and immigrant Jewish personal experiences with more educated passion than any or almost any others I have read since. I must have conflated, doubtless for aesthetic effect, the two times of reading because I associated and still associate the two books with each other, and this, I hazard, for four reasons, two of which can be inferred from what I've written above: their innate quality and the symmetry involved in reading them on public transport. The third reason is the pathos induced by another symmetry, or so we all believed until Roth's late spurt in the 1980s and Ellison's unfinished and posthumously edited novel *Juneteenth* more recently (he lost whole years because part of the manuscript was consumed in a fire), namely that both authors wrote only one novel, a great one. This is surely unusual. Great art is not a common phenomenon, but when it happens, its perpetrators tend to produce more than one masterpiece. To write or compose or paint only one work, a great one, or to write or compose or paint a hundred works of which only one is great are equally rare phenomena. A genuine example of an author's only book, a great one indeed, is Robert Antelme's *L'Espèce humaine* (translated as *The Human Race*), that wondrous phenomenology of servitude transcended.

The fourth reason for my trick of memory relates to the fact that I was profoundly moved and affected by the political reality of the early 1960s in the USA, which saw a civil rights coalition in which one of the leading components was a group of deeply committed Jews, religious and secular, members of an ethno-cultural religious minority with profoundly liberal instincts, more so than today. There is a famous, even iconic, photograph of Rabbi Abraham Joshua Heschel marching with Martin Luther King. Three civil rights student activists—one black, James Chaney and two Jewish, Andrew Goodman, who was a friend of my New York girlfriend Linda Goldfine (now Mariano), and Micky Schwerner, who was a cousin of the poet Armand Schwerner—were murdered in the south in June 1964. Despite such setbacks, it was a time of hope after the fears of the Cuban missile crisis; President Johnson and Bobby Kennedy (undeterred, indeed spurred, by President Kennedy's assassination) were embarking on important social and economic reforms; Vietnam had not yet hit the fan; and in September 1964 Harold Wilson would win the election after the famous thirteen Tory 'wasted' years in Britain—whatever else he did or did not do, his government's progressive legislation made the country a more civilized place: legalization of divorce, abortion and homosexuality, abolition of capital punishment and censorship, creation of the Open University, etc.

Yes, for literary, political and aesthetic reasons, I wanted so badly to associate the books by Ellison and Roth that I brought them together, as in a poem, whenever I told the story of my thousands of miles spent reading, writing and translating on Greyhound buses. Let me end with two quotes from Ellison's Epilogue to *Invisible Man* that I underlined at the time: 'I'm not blaming anyone for this state of affairs, mind you; nor merely crying mea culpa. The fact is that you carry part of your sickness within you, at least I do as an invisible man. I carried my sickness and though for a long time I tried to place it in the outside world, the attempt to write it down shows me that least half of it lay within me.' And on the penultimate page of the book: 'In going underground, I whipped it all except the mind, the mind. And the mind that has conceived a plan of living must never lose sight of the chaos against which that pattern was conceived. That goes for societies as well as for individuals. Thus, having tried to give pattern to the chaos which lives within the pattern of your certainties, I must come out, I must emerge.' The invisible man ends by saying that he's shaking off the old skin and leaving it in the hole he's coming out of, no less invisible without it, but coming out nevertheless. The final sentence reminds one of Dostoevsky and Camus: 'Who knows but that, on the lower frequencies, I speak for you?' Dipping into this awesome projection of a voice out of the darkness, out of the depths, I know I want to reread Ellison's book before I die, and that means, ineluctably, that I shall never read this crime novel or that science fiction one: a no-brainer.

[Coda: During final revision of this book, out of the blue I recall that on the boat returning home from the USA in 1966 (aboard I had an adventure reserved for fiction), I read *Le Grand Meaulnes* by Alain-Fournier, a wondrous book when you are twenty-four. Julian Barnes, I recall from a newspaper article, had doubts about rereading the book but took the risk in his sixties and was well pleased. He had the interesting and plausible thought that the title could have influenced Scott Fitzgerald's final choice of title, *The Great Gatsby*. Once again, the problem: if I reread *Le Grand Meaulnes*, that will be one more unread English classic.]

Norman Mailer

In 1968, Norman Mailer, in what may be his best book, *The Armies of the Night*, would write about the anti-war march on Washington. The tableaux include a portrait of Robert Lowell, who famously dealt with public issues in poems and whose appearance in Mailer's book I wrote about in a previous section. The subtitle is *History as a Novel, the Novel as History*. The progressive movement was a house with many rooms, in one of which lived James Baldwin, who spoke of 'the fire next time', the eponymous title of his incandescent book. In different ways we all believed, as I no longer do, that 'deep in my heart, we shall overcome some day'. I used to think that Mailer was an old bruiser, and he liked to give that impression, yet, while he packed a punch, at his best he was a surprisingly graceful and subtle writer, think Cassius Clay rather than Mike Tyson. The only bite Mailer took out of or rather put into your ear was a sound bite, unless you were married to him. His was an educated emotional intelligence projecting into language the evidence of his (im)pulses. Among his non-fiction books are *Cannibals and Christians* (where he tells us that the writer he learnt most from technically was E. M. Forster) and *Advertisements for Myself* (an erotic story, 'The Time of her Time', was omitted from the UK edition). James Baldwin in *Nobody Knows My Name* concludes an essay on his friend: 'He has a real vision of ourselves as we are, and it cannot be too often repeated in this country now, that, where there is no vision, the people perish.' Mailer's novels on my desk include *An American Dream*, with its beguiling opening paragraph: 'I met Jack Kennedy in November 1946. We were both war heroes, and both of us had just been elected to Congress. We went out one night on a double date and it turned out to be a fair evening for me. I seduced a girl who would have been bored by a diamond as big as the Ritz.' A rival candidate for the most striking opening paragraph is Anthony Burgess' *Earthly Powers*: 'It was the afternoon of my eighty-first birthday, and I was in bed with my catamite when Ali announced that the archbishop had come to see me.'

J. D. Salinger (*with Eudora Welty*)

Like many people of my age, I read J. D. Salinger's four books in the 1960s. I devoured *Catcher in the Rye* and *For Esme with Love and Squalor* while I was

415

still in secondary school. The two that followed, *Franny* and *Zooey/Raise High the Roof* and *Beam and Carpenters/Seymour an Introduction*, have unique inscriptions in my library: on the flyleaves I have written the exact date I bought the two hardbacks; they still have their distinctive covers. The first says in my best italic hand: 'Bought day of issue / June 4, 1962 / Cambridge / ex libris Anthony Rudolf'. Nor have I ever used the phrase 'ex libris' on other books, before or since. The second records the information: 'Anthony Rudolf / Cambridge; March 4 / 1963', which may or may not have been the day of issue. They were expensive: sixteen shillings and a guinea, respectively. What I remember is a sense of disappointment. I would not have expressed it this way at the time, but I distinctly recall feeling that the energy had drained away from the writing. I have neither the time nor the inclination to reread Salinger and check out my sense that the two later books do not live up to the standard of the earlier two. Maybe I won't read Ian Hamilton's book on him, although the temptation is there because Ian wrote it and also because it ended up as a book about the attempt to write a biography rather than a biography as such, complicating and deepening the interest. More than thirty years after I read *The Catcher in the Rye*, I bought copies of a new edition to give to young friends, who all loved it. Google enables me to check out early reviews: Eudora Welty no less, whose marvellous stories *A Curtain of Green* I read in my father's copy when I was a teenager, lavished praise. Meanwhile, Alice Munro, again no less, called Welty's 'A Worn Path' 'perhaps the most perfect short story ever written'. We have to read this story, and decide whether the praise tells us more about Munro than about Welty. Either way, it is a win–win situation, for it is *exactly* that kind of recommendation that leads you and me, lovers of books, to places we might otherwise not have visited.

Europeans (Extending to Persia)

Emmanuel Bove and Robert Walser

One of Beckett's favourite writers was the slightly older Emmanuel Bove, recommended to me by Margaret Hogan. His compelling, beautiful and enchanting study of loneliness *Mes Amis* (*My Friends*) inhabits a recognizable world, where we find Godot, Hamm and Clove and Krapp, not to mention Renoir's *Boudu sauvé des eaux*: this is one of the scenarios my *imaginaire* cherishes. I imagine creating a work—a book or a film—in which I walk my favourite fictional worlds in a series of tableaux or volume of photo stills, with a poetic text in dialogue. Did Beckett read Robert Walser? I have here Christopher Middleton's fabulous translation of Walser's *The Walk*, a collection of stories by this strange writer whom, it is well known, Kafka read, as did Sebald. One of the stories, 'The Monkey', begs to be photocopied for Paula, whose Victorian monkey, already starring in her Jane Eyre series as the companion of Bertha, could star in a new studio production, probably a lithograph. A bigger collection of Walser is now available with an introduction by Susan Sontag. The Swiss writer spent the last twenty-three years of his life in an insane asylum: 'I am not here to write,' he said, 'but to be mad.' And that was what he was and did. I would once have said, glibly, that if you can formulate that sentence, you are not mad. In those days I knew even less about madness than I do now, and certainly less about writing.

[Later: Not only did I photocopy the story for Paula, she loved it, so I am going to buy her the Sontag edition. Let's wait and see what happens down the line. Meanwhile, as so often, I find myself agreeing with Wittgenstein: 'If in life we are surrounded by death, so too in the health of our intellect we are surrounded by madness.']

Arnost Lustig

The late Czech writer Arnost Lustig, who died recently, wrote powerful novels about the fate of the Jews in World War II. He deals with cruel elemental themes, as do Kosinski and Rawicz. His characters negotiate deals that risk compromising their minds or bodies or both, in situations most of us have been spared. *A Prayer for Katerina Horovitzova* has been made into one of the few key films in this territory, while *Waiting for Leah* and, especially, *Lovely Green Eyes*, cry out for cinematographic treatment, and indeed he is a major writer of screenplays, his own books and those of others. The last two books mentioned were translated from the Czech by the prolific Prague-born Ewald Osers, whom I have already mentioned. Unusually, he worked in both directions. Osers translated poetry books by Walter Helmut Fritz and Rudolf

Langer from the German for Menard. A MenCard was published on his ninetieth birthday in May 2007, following two previous ones—for his eightieth birthday and his thousandth translated poem—and coinciding with the publication of his memoir, *Snows of Yesteryear*. In it, he reveals that he translated nearly one hundred and sixty books (one hundred and sixty books!) from six languages, over a period of sixty years. More than fifty were done during the first thirty years when he had a full-time day job at the BBC, as a Czech monitor in the world service at Caversham. Certainly his wartime training there contributed to his speed and discipline.

I chaired a discussion between Arnost Lustig and Ivan Klima at Jewish Book Week one year. Participation in such an event provides a case study of what happens to a professional sidetracker: instead of turning down the flattering invitation to introduce two writers, major figures by any reckoning (and give myself more time to proceed with slow long-term projects), I accepted, something I am learning not to do. This involved preparation during the weeks leading up to the discussion, reading recent books by the authors and so on, having previously only read an early book by each of them. I had to become a temporary authority or at least find something to say that would interest the audience and not shame me in the eyes of the two guests. Once the job was done, I did not want to waste my work, nor was it ready for publication. Typically, I have not worked up my notes, which have been filed in a mental box labelled Central European Jewish writers and/or World War II testimony, where they await process, along with more pressing projects. This scenario happened many times over the years, whether it involved book reviews, chairing a meeting or whatever. I was simultaneously insecure and secure enough to agree to commitments that could only be fulfilled at the expense of what I claimed were large-scale books, queuing up to be written. Have I learnt my lesson?

Sadegh Hedayat

The Blind Owl by the Persian writer Sadegh Hedayat was a gift from Alan Thornton, a strange and tormented homosexual friend I had at Cambridge, who worked in the French department of Bowes and Bowes bookshop on Trinity Street and would give me presents of proof copies. He rented a room in a house on Madingley Road, which had, he said, belonged to Kingsley Amis and, before that, to Dorothy Bussy, the translator of André Gide's *The Immoralist* and other books and, for her pains, unrequitedly in love with the French writer. I suspect now that Thornton was at least half in love with me but, entirely aware of boundaries, he suffered in silence. We vanished from each other's lives around ten years after I left Cambridge and something tells me he is dead, even though this breaks my general rule, derived from experience, that absence of news of a death means that the person is alive, until there is proof positive of the opposite. I have written a curious note on the flyleaf, a classic example of something that would have been forgotten had it not been written down: 'Page 62, <u>Elixir of death</u>. I thought this phrase the day before I read it'. Had I been flicking through the book earlier and the phrase caught my eye and I remembered it unconsciously? As for Hedayat, who committed suicide in 1951, the context is wine: 'Deep red wine, an elixir of death which would bestow everlasting peace'. Thornton was a great admirer of Persian and Arabic literature. Perhaps it was he who quoted al-Rumi to me: 'The man of God is drunk without red wine. The man of God is replete without roast lamb.' I raise a glass of red wine to this friend from long ago. We lost touch, it's as simple as that. *We lost touch*: a dead metaphor that resonates the moment one thinks about it, and it would resonate most of all with Alan, for reasons already suggested.

Europe: British Writers

Cyril Connolly

Mention Cyril Connolly to Paula and she will quote the famous or infamous remark from *Enemies of Promise*: 'There is no more sombre enemy of good art than the pram in the hall.' In those days, most of the women who graduated from the Slade, including prizewinners, ended up marrying a painter, bearing his children and generally supporting him. As it happens, this is what Paula did. However, unlike the vast majority, she continued painting. She remains the devoted champion of the work of her late husband Victor Willing. If Connolly's aphorism is a half-truth, another is utterly false, and mischievous to boot: 'The true function of a writer is to produce a masterpiece and no other task is of any consequence.' This is surely nonsense, indeed self-serving nonsense, given his claims (a) that he was a mere critic and editor rather than a true creator and (b) that he was lazy. Still, the belief suited Connolly as it rationalized his failure to write a better novel than *The Rockpool*, which pride ought to have required. The book is on my desk and inscribed April 1963, meaning I bought it when I was a twenty-year-old student. I loved it and I also loved what the author later described as his war journal, *The Unquiet Grave*, which I read in my father's copy of the limited first edition, purchased in 'April 1945', the date written beneath his trademark signature H. C. Rudolf. In that month, the war was approaching its end and my mother was seven months pregnant with my first sister, Ruth. Connolly cites La Bruyère: 'Experience confirms that indolence or self-indulgence and harshness towards others are but one and the same vice.' In our house, on Sunday mornings, Cyril Connolly and Philip Toynbee—whose journals *Part of a Journey* and *End of a Journey* are here, the latter reflecting the nuclear anxieties of the early 1980s—were to books what Harold Hobson and Kenneth Tynan were to theatre. Henry Miller gets closer to the truth: 'The true function of a writer is to keep art alive.' Let's rephrase it more modestly: 'The true function of the writer is to produce the best book in his gift and no other task is of any consequence.' I made marginal marks against things that struck me in Connolly's novel, and I still find the following sentences well said and well true: 'It is part of the happiness of youth that the sense of power, like the mystical apprehension of goodness, can be enjoyed to the full without the necessity of projecting it into the tainted realm of action. As with those public-school men who advertise in the newspapers: "Go anywhere. Do anything", the formula does justice for both will and deed. This conviction of intense *disponibilité* is known as promise and whom the gods wish to destroy they first call promising.'

Julian Barnes (*with the Amises and Alphonse Daudet*)

As Francophile as Connolly, both Barnes and I, in different years, were taught sixth-form French at City of London School by the late Pat Whitmore, a heroic figure who would have enjoyed *Flaubert's Parrot*, the novel which famously won a major non-fiction prize in France. Despite competition from *Arthur and George*, *The History of the World in Ten and a Half Chapters* is Barnes' best book. Recently I reread the Géricault chapter after Paula said the Frenchman was one of the greatest painters who ever lived. She spoke about his portrait of the two little girls (once owned by Yves Saint-Laurent) rather than 'The Raft of Medusa', the subject of Barnes' tour de force (Delacroix was the model for the figure bottom left of the raft), although she admires the history picture too and always heads for it when in the Louvre. I recall Géricault's extraordinary drawings of mad people, which I saw at the Grand Palais some years ago.

Barnes has translated a painful and cruel text never intended for publication, *La Doulou*, *In the Land of Pain*, by Alphonse Daudet, the French writer's response to syphilis, which he contracted at seventeen, dying at fifty-seven. A bigger contrast with the Nîmes-born author's stories of a provençal hero, *Tartarin of Tarascon*, which I read long ago, would be hard to imagine. I remember too reading *Lettres de mon moulin* and visiting Daudet's windmill, in the Alpilles, while in France with a school group led by our third-form French teacher, Taggy Manning.

La Doulou is not exactly a prequel to Barnes' latest book, *Nothing to be Afraid of*, which is a memoir about death; all the same, it goes with the territory. The latter is a rare example of a book I started reading the day I bought it. Among its charms for an oldest child with three younger sisters is a close-up of the perspective obtained from the author as second child, second son in fact, and thus having an older male at close quarters who is not your father. When this older brother is my former classmate Jonathan Barnes, widely regarded at school as the cleverest boy in the history of the world or at least of the school (equalled in one account by John Gross), you need to have your wits about you if you are going to make your mark, something Julian cannot be said not to have done. It is a brave and vulnerable book, honourably frank in its tellings of his fear of death. His love affair with late-nineteenth-century France continues apace in *Nothing to be Afraid* of with a reading of the life and work of Jules Renard, a foxy writer with plenty to say, chorus-like, about death: for Barnes—see his book of essays *Something to Declare*—late-nineteenth-century France starts in 1850 and ends not, as we are often told, in 1914 but in 1925. As might be expected, cheerfulness keeps breaking into Barnes' night thoughts: a brilliant writer in full throttle, riding language like a lover on the crest of a wave, cannot help but entertain us, gaiety transfiguring all that dread, to coin a phrase. He quotes the usual suspects—Montaigne, Stendhal, Flaubert and Stravinsky—and embeds possible allusions to Wittgenstein, Beckett, Browning and Hazlitt, triggering my own silent rattlebag of quotes. Motivated doubtless by a mixture of vanity, altruism, envy, *schadenfreude* and *déformation professionelle*, I emailed him to point out a bad misprint. He replied politely that the misprint was not a misprint. I had to reread the two relevant sentences several times before getting the point. On the other hand, in his reply to a point of mine about a talismanic book, he managed to misspell Henry as Henri in the title of Stendhal's *La Vie de Henry Brulard*; possibly he did this on purpose, to make me feel better. No, that is my sentimentalization of a straightforward situation, my feeble attempt to improve the story.

Another Old Citizen writer is Kingsley Amis, whose *Old Devils* and *Lucky Jim* I have here, as well as his son's *Money* and *Time's Arrow*. The latter book is to Martin Amis what *Henderson the Rain King* is to Saul Bellow or *Bech* to John Updike (and, in reverse, Howard Jacobson's character Treslove in *The Finkler Question*), a book to prove an extra-literary point about Jewishness. We want *Time's Arrow* to be better than it is. Its reverse chronology makes a brave if doomed effort to deal with the problems described by Michael André Bernstein in *Foregone Conclusions*, which I discuss briefly elsewhere. Martin Amis, like Anthony Howell in poetry, is a formidable stylist, a kaleidoscopic powerhouse of literary play, although his best effects are more local than Julian Barnes', which I hasten to add is an observation, not a complaint, on my part.

Lucy Ellmann and William Cooper

Sweetly, Lucy Ellmann sent me her hysterically funny novel *Doctors and Nurses* because I gave her the impression at a Royal Literary Fund Fellows annual party that she had offended me by not answering an email about heaven knows what. I was sure my light-hearted reference to the email and appropriate disavowal of offence had succeeded in disguising my infantile pain, but I had not reckoned with the perceptually honed instincts of this lass from the Chicago suburbs: Broad? Girl? Woman? Lady? Chick? Novelist? Daughter of Richard Ellmann? Sister of Maud? RLF Fellow?: her habit of list-making would be catching if I wasn't already a list-maker myself. Nor had I reckoned with her generosity. Anyway, sometimes a fellow or Fellow needs a break, so I took *Doctors and Nurses*, having enjoyed her earlier novels, *Sweet Desserts* and *Varying Degrees of Hopelessness* long ago, to read on a train. It took millions of years to produce Lucy Ellmann, who has to be one of the triumphs of feminism and therefore of the modern world. There is not an ounce of prurience in her volcanic carnivalesque id-stream of laughter and fury and there is a sense in which she makes you proud to be a man, since it is absolutely clear that she is *not* writing for her sisters alone. We must have done something right. One of the first doctor writers, Rabelais, would have cherished this book. The stellar Angela Carter, whose *Passion of New Eve* and *The Sadeian Woman* are on my desk, would have loved it. Norman O. Brown would have put it on the reading list for his students. James Joyce would have been amused. There is even an affinity with some of Paula's work from the early 1980s, such as her huge painting, 'The Proles Wall' (a take on George Orwell which so offended John Spurling that he ticked her off at the bus stop) and her series of Operas and the Vivian Girls. I bet Lucy Ellmann knows and loves the work of Henry Darger, whose ghost shut the door on Paula's fingers when she visited his room, not fifteen miles from where Ellmann was born. If Ellmann doesn't, she should take the hint when she reads this. And who am I to complain about her use of upper case, given my own predilection for italics, nor if I am ruthlessly honest with myself, her occasional faux-naivety?

I wonder if Lucy Ellmann has read William Cooper. He, another hyper-sophisticated *faux-naif*, would have recognized what is a generationally bent if not a gender-bent mutation of his own sense of humour. Ellmann is Cooper on speed. Cooper's various *Scenes from . . .* and other novels are on my shelves. The novelist Maggie Gee, like me, is a fan of Harry Hoff (his real name); I recall that she and I met him some years ago for a coffee near the Barbican and praised him to his face—it is always good to praise, and sometimes to flatter—and got him to sign our copies of *Scenes from Metropolitan Life*. Except, the inscription says: 'With love to Tony, from the author, Harry, William Cooper, ~~York Minster~~, Oct. 1983, French Pub': but this pub, where I used to drink with Ken Smith is in Soho, not near the Barbican. And yet I *see* us near the Barbican. Did we or I meet Cooper twice in this way? *Scenes from Death and Life*, Hoff's final novel, was published by a small press, perhaps because big publishers were no longer interested in him. I wrote him a letter after buying it: '. . . a beautiful and strong swansong, if indeed it is a swansong. Quite dark too, and rightly so.' I also inserted a letter in the book from my friend John Mills. I had thanked John for the present of a book, and must have mentioned or recommended Cooper. Mills writes that he used to hang out with the novelist in Patisserie Valerie and Legrains, the latter a Gerrard Street cafe that antedated my own Soho years. Patisserie Valerie, still on Old Compton Street, now has branches elsewhere, including the Royal Institute of British Architects, which serves as 'my club'; the RIBA branch is open to the public and a very pleasant place it is, too; this is where I have tea with Edward Field or Kathi Diamant or other friends visiting London, especially on a warm day when you can sit outside on the upstairs terrace. The unhurried atmosphere is opposite to that of the original cafe on Old Compton Street, always bustling and over-crowded.

Friends

Chip Martin and Eva Tucker

In the fiction pile are novellas by Chip Martin, including *South*. Across the room are critical books by Stoddard Martin, 'who writes fiction under the name of Chip Martin'. Chip's fiction is published by Starhaven, the smallest of small presses. Stoddard is not necessarily a better writer than Chip but he is more marketable and finds commercial publishers for his books. Predictably, Chip's first novel, *The Jew-Hater*, created problems for some of the more naive of my brethren: a convincing portrayal of an antisemite is never going to be pretty. He dealt with variations on this theme in later novellas, such as *A Journeyman in Bohemia*. John Adams' opera *Klinghoffer* was received in the same way as *The Jew-Hater*. Alice Goodman's libretto recounts a real incident in which an old Jew was murdered by Palestinian terrorists on a hijacked boat. This too has been attacked by Jewish organizations like the Simon Wiesenthal Centre, which tries to set what it sees as the Jewish agenda by never missing an opportunity to raise Cain—and the old Adam—instantaneously and to cry wolf, either because they unconsciously 'think' that Jewish interests (or would that be the interests of the Israeli government?) are served or because they are under the genuine misapprehension that Jews are always victims or at the very least in the front line of prejudice. Sometimes they get it right, but crying wolf is not a good strategy. Starhaven brought out Eva Tucker's miniature bildungsroman *Berlin Mosaic* and its sequel *Becoming English* in 2005 and 2009. These were Eva's first books since her two brilliant early novels (*Contact* and *Drowning*) published forty years earlier and it has taken a small press, even smaller than Menard, to take her on. This is why we need small presses.

Elaine Feinstein

Elaine Feinstein is four people in one, in the sense that she writes novels, poetry, translations and biographies, and six, if you include radio plays and literary criticism. Here are five of the novels, *The Border* and *Dreamers*: the latter is inscribed 'for Tony, friend and fellow struggler in the literary orchard', which reminds me of a phrase by Edmond Jabès.—'Confidence of the tree in the fruit'. Here too is *Lady Chatterley's Confession*, Elaine's follow-up. The novel is so good that if she changed the names of the characters and gave it a new title it would self-stand without Lawrence, and that is what I have advised her to do when the rights revert to her. The rule with Elaine is that the shorter the novel, the better it is. The one with the strongest affinities to her Tsvetayeva translations—discussed elsewhere as is her unclassifiable *Russian Jerusalem*—is *The Border*: here, the razor-sharp and laser-precise syntax and rhythm of one of our finest poets work and play to best effect. Among her several books of poems is *Gold*, which begins with a narrative spoken in the voice of Lorenzo da Ponte, who could not fail to interest her, given his origins and destiny. A majority of the poems in her latest book, *Talking to the Dead*, are addressed to her husband Arnold who, it is no secret, was a difficult albeit fascinating man. Elaine has cut through the undergrowth of politeness and cant in this territory, to present unadorned and elegiac love poems. In a poem whose penultimate line echoes, for me at any rate, George Seferis as well as Keith Douglas on Stephen Crane, she writes:

. . . most of what we work at disappears.

Little we worry over has importance.

The greedy and the generous have the same end.

The dead know nothing of what we say to them.

Still, in that silence let me write: dear friend.

Michael Moorcock

Michael Moorcock could well be the most productive prose writer since Frank Richards and H. G. Wells. Alan Wall was our go-between. Moorcock sent me the first three volumes of his remarkable *Pyat* quartet: *Byzantium Endures*, *The Laughter of Carthage* and *Jerusalem Commands*, all of which I read, although not back to back. A fan letter I sent him now strikes me as being three parts genuine and one part suspect. My long-standing awe and respect and amazement when faced with a real and professional writer, indeed a writer of large-scale works, emerge: 'Have now finished this thrilling book. It is the product of an intellectual powerhouse, and an organisational master. I can never aspire to such a scale, being a) a miniaturist and b) lazy.' It was an honour to be asked to read in manuscript volume four, *The Vengeance of Rome*, because MM wanted a Jewish consideration of potentially dodgy material, including a sado-masochistic homosexual encounter between Hitler and the hero. My view, as I recall, was that anyone likely to be offended by his treatment (the author's I mean) would be offended by many other incidents in the book, so no problem there. The book came out to excellent reviews, and was immediately reprinted. Most recently he completed his own version of *Doctor Who*.

Anne Serre

Anne Serre, one of my Paris friends, has sent me her books over the years, including *Le Cheval blanc d' Uffington*. Anne is witty, delicate, cunning and hyper-intelligent in her dissection of the forms and substances of love. She would have given a number of eighteenth-century characters, not to mention their authors, a good run for their money. Picture a woman in a Watteau painting as re-imagined by Choderlos de Laclos, and you have Anne. She brings out my best and most fluent French. To exchange playful ideas with this classic Frenchwoman over a bottle of good wine during dinner, at Chez Paule in Place Dauphine or Le Vin sobre, rue des Feuillantines, with mutual friends, typically Raymond Mason (now sadly departed), Mark Hutchinson and Steven Jaron, can be a heady experience. A recent book is *Un Chapeau Léopard*. Even without private knowledge of the real-life tragedy underlying the auto-fiction, so strong is the narrative identity of the author and her masculine alter ego, 'the narrator', that the reader senses the power, and indeed the glory, of this classic *récit* of the tragic destiny with which the book begins. Taking on the persona of the explicit character called the narrator, the author enables a negotiation between invention and factuality. She is at once she and not she, just as Paula's use of the female model in 'The Interrogator's Garden' and the male model in 'Olga' works to naturalize a disjunction in the figurative dialectic. I was honoured to read her next book in manuscript: perfect except for one structural flaw, easily fixed, which Mark and I, independently of each other, identified.

Maggie Gee

My favourite book by Maggie Gee (perhaps for non-literary reasons dating to the time of the great fear, when I and so many friends, including Nick Humphrey and Susannah York, were preoccupied with the Bomb) is her second published novel, *The Burning Book*. It was after reading a newspaper interview with her about the formidable debut novel *Dying in Other Words*, that I wrote to her. Six months later, her name rang a bell when a letter arrived, inaugurating a friendship. *The Burning Book* has a character with a Menard Press pamphlet on his table. I ticked her off for including a postmodern mention of her own earlier book in the later one, which twenty years later she, congenitally resistant to change, finally conceded was justified. But I cannot remember whether it was the first or second book where I spotted, that is, *heard*, not just the pounding prose rhythm, but the metric subliminally working its power on the reader. Indeed, I recall writing out a paragraph in verse lines and sending it to her. I recall too that she was surprised and impressed by this aural observation, though it turned out that she was only referring to my reaction: she did not mean that she herself had not noticed. On the contrary, she explained, the prose rhythm in her books is based on four-beat verse-lines (this would amuse Nicholson Baker: for the reason, you will have to read his charming novel *The Anthologist*), only not laid out as such. Let's test it:

> I met the writer-woman through
> a postcard in the newsagent.
> 'Nice friendly family requires
> trained cleaner.' Trained? What did she mean?
> Not to do *doo-doo* on her floor.
> I was trained to be a teacher . . .

Well, that's from her recent novel, *My Cleaner*, and it is indeed typical, even though the psychic pressure on language was, inevitably, more intense in *The Burning Book*. The great fear abated with Gorbachev, and has now returned, on two fronts, the nuclear again, and climate change: nuclear winter in both scenarios.

Alan Wall

Alan Wall's 'early' works of fiction from 1993 and 1994, a verse/prose *récit* and a novella predating his official corpus of novels, are on my desk; he was over forty when *Jacob* and *Curved Light* came out, a good advertisement for a late start, like the poet Dan Burt. This was the moment when Terry Eagleton introduced us. Wall had already published a few poems and essays, but these two books marked his coming of age as a writer. The next book, *Bless the Thief*, partly because it was published by a bigger house with better publicity, brought him widespread critical attention. His acknowledgements flatter me enormously by association: he writes that the work of Anthony Rudolf 'has many shadows in the text, as does that of Walter Benjamin and Aby Warburg', and I recognize one aspect of myself in the character of Solomon Levine. In this book, as elsewhere, he invents writers and supplies examples of their work, which are so believable that readers, including one famous poet, have been known to go to libraries for more information. In the immediate wake of *Bless the Thief*, he left his day job as a marketing director and embarked on a heroic attempt to live by the pen, writing five novels in as many years. With his wife educating the children at home, he was the sole breadwinner. It could not last, and he now teaches at the University of Chester. It goes without saying that he continues writing in full throttle—poems and essays, as well as fiction. His later works of fiction include *China*, perhaps his best book, even if it is his most 'realistic'. In three books, the acknowledgements include 'Anthony and Nathaniel Rudolf'. At the time, Alan's own children were not old enough to supply feedback, so he asked whether my son would be interested in offering perspective from a younger generation. I was in the privileged position of being a critic with a licence to point out 'deliberate mistakes' at draft stage, just as Alan has been one of a small number of friends with a licence vis-à-vis my work. His latest published novel, *Sylvie's Riddle*, is a lean book, containing multitudes in two hundred and thirty pages. The reader is honoured by being treated as competent to make the transitions and track the imbrications throughout, like reading a score. Licensed critics have different skills and different ways of reacting. Perhaps it is horses for courses, or, in this case, draft-horses for discourses. The primary role of such a critic is to detect bullshit and murder darlings. These days I ring the changes on readers, depending on my morale or the state of intimacy at any given moment.

Clive Sinclair

In this room are Clive Sinclair's books, all but two of them fiction. Here are his collected stories, *For Good or Evil*, and four novels, including *Blood Libels* and *Bibliosexuality*. Here too is a more recent book of stories, *The Lady with the Laptop*. (I deal with his non-fiction elsewhere.) It is a mystery to me that such a seriously funny and entertainingly serious writer as Sinclair sells so few copies, even by the well-known standards of literary fiction in hardback, and that a recent book sold no more copies than my own earlier memoir from a small publisher. Although I did not read it when it first came out, *Bibliosexuality* is a distinguished debut novel, a proud self-reflexive work and yet one that does not vanish up its own arse—the Promethean fire of this book is anything but pale. It is truly a young writer's love poem to sexuality and to literature, to sex and to language, that 'ghostly seducer'.

'Bibliosexuality', we learn at the beginning, is both the act of writing and the intercourse between writer and reader. Narrator and narration go in search of one David Drollkind, who has sent the narrator an outline he has written of 'an extremely refined form of bibliosexuality, hereafter known as "St John's Complaint"', helpfully included as an appendix, together with its notes. While serving as a demonstration of the author/narrator's brilliance as a critical writer/reader of genuine literary texts, the vanished Drollkind's outline and accompanying notes are a hilariously straight-faced parody of academic literary criticism. I have not, however, checked to see if, for example, the reference to an article by Nabokov in *The Listener* is genuine or not—it almost certainly is—but I know my Rimbaud well enough to know that the quote from *Illuminations* is genuine and accurate, apart from one spelling mistake that has to be unintentional. And I know my Chekhov ditto in respect of the perfectly pitched and positioned quote from *The Seagull*, Trigorin's monologue about his destiny as a writer (a monologue rivalling Sonia's at the end of *Uncle Vanya*), where a writer of genius succeeds in conveying the practice and self-image of a successful if minor novelist: 'clever but not as good as Turgenev' is his proposed epitaph for himself. My use of the phrase 'succeeds in conveying' instead of merely 'conveys' connotes a tautology rather than the implied paradox, for given that Chekhov is one of the greatest playwrights who ever lived, why should he not succeed in conveying the essence of a clever writer, albeit one who is not as good as Turgenev? Clive has told me that the appendix in *Bibliosexuality* started life as a piece of academic writing he composed for a seminar. You couldn't make it up, and in one sense he didn't. Nabokov and Borges are serenely present in the elixir of influence, the amniotic fluid floating round him, with the Russian perhaps more expected than the Argentinian in 1973, when the book came out. However, one must remember that everyone, including Clive himself, knows that his short stories are as good as or even better than his novels, and doubtless he discovered Borges in the late 1960s as we all did, and may have even gone to the same lectures given by the master at the ICA in 1970, as we all did. 'We all' is a curious circumlocution for 'I' or, more modestly, 'quite a few friends'.

Clive's new book *True Tales of the Wild West* reads like the special issue of a po-mo fanzine. Celebrating a gone world characterized by Wyatt Earp and his Jewish wife, it is a wonderfully entertaining romanced history of a topic in which I have no interest whatsoever. All honour to him therefore for keeping the show right on till the end of the road. I laughed aloud as I followed the incredible adventures of his alter egos, Peppercorn and Saltzmann, seeking their inner cowboys amidst a larger-than-life crowd of historical and living characters set against real landscapes that are often mediated via remembered movies shot there. The book is a triumph of deadpan inventiveness. The author's riotous and carnivalesque imagination brings to life a history that sometimes seems to have been imagined in the first place. By chance, he has just phoned to say he is going to refer to my pamphlet on Byron's 'Darkness' in a forthcoming review of Cormack McCarthy's new post-nuclear winter novel *No Country for Old Men* and informs me that the author uses the Yiddish word 'toches' for backside, which sticks out like a sore thumb or, I suppose, toches. We both wonder if the word has, like 'chutzpah', entered the American lexicon. Yes, emails Mike Heller. All the same, it could be a clue (in a novel otherwise devoid of clues about origins) that the hero is Jewish.

Fiction I Don't Read

I have read a few crime thrillers: Professor Richard Freeborn's *The Russian Crucifix*, which he sent me after we had corresponded about Turgenev and Byron; Barbara Vine's *A Dark-Adapted Eye*; P. D. James' *An Unsuitable Job for a Woman*; the engaging *Red Mercury Blues* by Reggie Nadelson; James Hadley Chase's *No Orchids for Miss Blandish*. In Gertrude Stein's *Blood on the Dining-Room Floor*, the reader herself is the detective, perhaps the projective detective, Claude Royet-Journoud's 'flic géometrique', as craftily translated by Keith Waldrop. I have not yet read Derek Raymond's *The Crust on Its Uppers*, which I may give a go, if only because the title is a superior example of paronomasia. I read three Geoffrey Household novels and got the worse of a learned exchange with him about Ladino and Hebrew, learned on his part that is. And come to think of it I read a Raymond Chandler novel, which not to its disadvantage reminded me of Hemingway.

431

Historical fiction is another genre that I cannot bring myself to explore, as my former teaching colleague Katharine McMahon intuited when she left me copies of her novels *After Mary* and *Confinement*: 'Don't be burdened with reading these if you can't stand historical fiction.' *After Mary* deals with seventeenth-century recusants, the English Catholic equivalent of Marranos in Spain and Portugal, a subject I have discussed with Alan Wall in the context of Shakespeare's father's putative recusant Catholicism. Paula has encouraged me to read fairy tales, and occasionally I dip into books like Alison Lurie's *Oxford Book of Modern Fairy Tales*, or the stories of Hans Christian Andersen. We saw Renoir's beautiful early work, *The Little Match Seller*, an animated film almost as lyrical as *Partie de Campagne*, and oh so cruel, ending with the hand of her (presumed) father sending her out again to earn money in the cold, thus sentencing her to die ('These violent delights have violent ends') though for me, unlike Paula, fairy stories cannot be a main course in the banquet of creative nourishment. She cuts out the middlemen. Taking herself to the water, she drinks, whereas I await guidance from the horses of instruction . . .

. . . For example friends like Kim Landers and John Brunner and Peter Hoy, all of whom over the years tried to interest me in science fiction. Here too are *A Canticle for Leibowitz* by Walter M. Miller and *Camp Concentration* by Thomas M. Disch—still unread. Why? Not only because of other priorities, but because I have retained a suspicion that science fiction is escapism, like so-called fantasy literature and soap operas and historical novels. Priorities: by the time I reach the end of this book, I hope I will have succeeded in clarifying them. I cannot claim to have a secret fear that I might get hooked and spend the rest of my life reading nothing but science fiction or crime fiction. I know there is no danger. On the other hand, I am well aware that the best books in any genre transcend the genre. A great science fiction or crime fiction book is a great book tout court. It is not too late to broaden my experience and enter a different list. I ought to take advantage of my new friendship with Michael Moorcock and learn more about science fiction, but for heaven's sake, we are talking about reading not writing, I can learn about soccer without being a friend of David Beckham.

School Books, Reference Books, Proof Copies and Such

Introductory Note

Proof copies and reference books in particular lend themselves to lengthy meditations. I have resisted this temptation, mundanely, on grounds of length. I permit myself to dream of a future book in this fertile territory.

Children's Books

Introduction

A few days before I immigrated to south London for a year—to study at Avery Hill teachers training college—from my Notting Hill bedsitter in 1966, my neighbour Michael Horovitz put me in touch with a Portobello Road stallholder called Laura del Rivo. I felt I could not take my books with me and did not want to ask anyone to house them on a temporary basis. How I regret selling most of the books that survived my childhood, and all for the sake of a ten bob note (50p). One of the few survivors from this deeply regretted act is Max Beloff's *History: Mankind and His Story*, an impossible title today. It has a birthday dedication from Kay, who was my mother's help for a few years. I wrote about childhood books in *The Arithmetic of Memory*.

Walter Benjamin and Ernst Gombrich

Jeffrey Mehlman's *Walter Benjamin for Children: An Essay on His Radio Years* is an account of the writer's radio broadcasts for children in Frankfurt and Berlin between 1929 and 1933, composed only a few years after *The Origins of German Tragic Drama*, that 'play of sorrow' (George Steiner in his introduction) which is, writes Benjamin, 'a ruin, a fragment'. Ernst Gombrich's children's book *A Little History of the World* comes later, in 1935, from Vienna. Was he inspired by Benjamin's radio broadcasts? Mark Hutchinson, a great fan of the Gombrich book, wonders whether you could pick up Berlin radio in Vienna at that time. Lucian Freud was ten when he left Berlin in 1933. I sent a postcard to Frank Auerbach, who asked Freud on my behalf: 'Lucian said he had not heard them and would not remember them if he had.' Michael Hamburger informs me that not only did he not hear the broadcasts, his parents did not even have a radio or rather wireless in the house, although one grandparent had a gramophone, the other a crystal set. Perhaps one reason Benjamin and Gombrich made the broadcasts was that they needed the money.

Roland Walker, Frank Richards and Rhoda Power

One of the books I sold in Portobello Road was *Shandy of Ringmere School* by Rowland Walker, which I read countless times, aged eleven or twelve. Curious and nostalgic, I ordered a copy some years ago from a specialist book dealer. Big mistake! Even in the early 1950s it was well out of date in terms of ethos, but that is a neutral rather than negative judgement, unless of course literary quality—not the case here—redeems the setting (boarding school in the Lake District), tone and attitude. Thus, the dedication: 'To my first schoolmaster, Robert Henry Hugill esq, who thrashed me often because he loved me much'. As it happens, unlike many such books, this one contains no floggings. At the end, the senior prefect 'sailed east to join his uncle'. David Bathurst's *Six of the Best*! is a cheerful study of six school story writers, including Charles Hamilton, also known as Frank Richards (of Bunter fame), and Anthony Buckeridge, whose Jennings stories I read and listened to on the wireless. As I type this paragraph, I am half listening to a familiar English folk song, 'Portsmouth', the theme tune from the old TV series of Bunter, the Owl of the Remove. Here is *Redcap Runs Away* by Rhoda Power, which I received as a prize at prep school and read many times: this was the only prize I ever won at an educational establishment, apart from books at Hebrew classes and a sports trophy at college; more on that later.

Eric Thompson

' "Why is everybody being so nice to you, Dougal?," said Florence. "They are frightened about what I might say in my memoirs," said Dougal darkly.' This typical exchange comes from *The Adventures of Brian* by Eric Thompson, a present on my sixtieth birthday from my ex-wife Brenda, in memory of a programme the children loved. Thompson wrote the dubbed script for Serge Danot's brilliant French television series *The Magic Roundabout*, and spoke the voiceover. Later he wrote his own scripts. The sublime characters—Zebedee, Brian, Florence, Ermintrude, Dylan and Dougal (allegedly a joke on the name de Gaulle)—were puppets, so the dubbing created no problems of synchronization. These programmes, like all the best children's works, appealed to adults too (partly for the in-jokes), and how often did we, following Brian, 'laugh like a bucket'?

Maurice Sendak and Norton Juster

There is little doubt that Roald Dahl was *primus inter pares* when my children were young. Nathaniel also particularly loved Norton Juster's *The Phantom Tolbooth*, illustrated by Jules Feiffer, who was popular in the 1960s as a political cartoonist. As for Naomi, she had a special affection for Maurice Sendak's *Where the Wild Things Are*. I once heard her speaking the text of this magical book and dashed into her bedroom—now the room where I work—guiltily proud that my daughter could read at two: she was reciting one page while looking at another, having learnt the book by heart from hearing me read it to her so many times. *In the Night Kitchen*, its sequel, is magical too; too bad that the final book in the trilogy, *Outside over There*, lost the spell if not the plot, although it is Sendak's favourite among his own books. Thirty years later, I have been reading *Where the Wild Things Are* to my grandson Charlie in New Zealand, via Skype. What goes round, comes round. What would a grandfather do without Skype?

[Coda: Maurice Sendak has recently died and now finds himself amidst the wild things of extinction.]

Raymond Briggs and Susannah York

I still own Raymond Briggs' *When the Wind Blows* (the title taken from my favourite nursery rhyme), which begins with the dear couple's best memories of World War II, continues through the nonsense of Britain's nuclear posture, deterrence, civil defence, etc. etc., and ends after the Bomb goes off, with Jim quoting, in the final frame, in total darkness, '. . . rode the six hundred'. Susannah York—a friend of mine and Raymond Briggs from the days of the anti-nuclear movement—was the author of two enchantingly and appropriately old-fashioned children's books *Lark's Castle* and *In Search of Unicorns*. Both are inscribed 'to Nathaniel and Naomi, with love, Susannah'. I have finally handed them over to their owners, to read to their own children.

'A'-Level Set Texts and Other School Books

E. M. Forster and others

Here, tinged by my nostalgia, are five of the set texts we read for English 'A' level: *Antony and Cleopatra*, *A Chaucer Selection*, *Howard's End*, *Vanity Fair* and *Gulliver's Travels*. E. M. Forster's Edwardian liberalism influenced my quondam worldview during pre-university and university years, his main rivals being Albert Camus and George Orwell but not Aldous Huxley. Only much later did I read Yevgeny Zamyatin's *We*, which influenced the Huxley and Orwell dystopias. Quondam worldview is a fancy phrase that translates into the sum of my opinions, which were mainly drawn from my father's *New Statesman* socialism (really a kind of radical liberalism) and indeed from my reading of the paper itself. The old *New Statesman* still floats round my mind, a field of force in the *arrière-pays* of my formation.

Inside my copy of *Gulliver's Travels* is a piece of blotting paper. I suspect that these days it is only ever used for signing ceremonies such as the annual induction of new fellows of the Royal Society of Literature who have to choose between Byron's quill and Dickens' pen. Inserted in my copy of *Howard's End* are revision notes and an essay (headed B+++ in the hand of our teacher Geoffrey Clark), later annotated for revision. I remember sitting in my attic bedroom (ours was, I believe, the second loft conversion in the Suburb after J. M. Cohen's of Penguin classics fame, who lived across the road), memorizing notes in the weeks before English, French and Russian 'A' levels. I went on to read three more Forster novels among the complete set of six on the bookshelves at home: *A Passage to India*, *The Longest Journey* and *A Room with a View*. That was before anybody knew about *Maurice*, which could not be published until years later on account of its homosexual theme. In Cambridge, I was one of many students who knocked on Forster's door at Kings College for a signature. I took a copy of *Abinger Harvest*, which I bought because we already had the novels at home. Some years later I read Forster's celebrated 1939 essay 'What I believe' in *Two Cheers for Democracy*: 'If I had to choose between betraying my country and betraying my friend, I hope I would have the guts to betray my country.' This is Bloomsbury absolutism in personal relationships gone mad, and what Forster goes on to say suggests he has not thought through the question of responsibility in a democracy at war against tyranny, the obvious context of his comments: 'Such a choice may scandalise the modern reader, and he may stretch out his patriotic hand to the telephone at once and ring up the police.' Camus, too, chose his mother over justice when he failed to take a principled stand over French colonial policies in Algeria, thus scoring two out of three, in the words of Susan Sontag's guardedly positive essay on him in *Against Interpretation*: he participated in the Resistance and dissociated himself early from the Communist Party.

There is one reference to Forster in Rayner Heppenstall's journals, *The Master Eccentric*: 'Death of E. M. Forster, aged 91. I admired him in moderation as he would have wished.' This shrewd but unkind remark reminds me of Lionel Trilling's opinion, quoted in an article by Frank Kermode, that the novelist 'refused greatness'. Kermode also quotes what he says may be Forster's most important dictum: 'Art is based on an integrity in man's nature which is deeper than moral integrity.' This is surely true and is one way of articulating our feeling that the best poetry of an Ezra Pound or the best fiction of a Louis-Ferdinand Céline could be produced by persons whose extremist political views shock and outrage us. I once wrote that Pound produced his best work—Canto One for example—from a different part of his mind or a different part of his being than his political writings, but Forster says the same thing better. There is no point in asking how we would feel if Hitler had produced great art. He could not have: the worst villains have no room in their being for the best art. Nobody's perfect.

437

Latin books

Four school textbooks have turned up, Sallust's *Catiline*, Tacitus' *Agricola/Germania*, Michael Pinto-Duschinsky's copy of *Tales from Herodotus* and an Ovid selection. Inside the front cover of the Ovid, the previous owner of the book has written: 'Because the form laughed at me, I am leaving at the end of the term.' In addition to studying for three 'A' levels, I chose to continue with Latin and Greek, which I had officially abandoned after 'O' level. Looking at the Greek of Herodotus now, I find I can still read it. To think one learnt those languages, as well as Hebrew, by rote when young. These days I have the greatest difficulty learning Portuguese, with the same alphabet as ours.

Protest: *the Beat generation and the Angry Young Men*

Strictly speaking, this was not a schoolbook but I remember reading it on a hot summer day in 1960 while I was on my way by tube to watch tennis at Wimbledon, possibly after 'A' levels were over. The scrap of paper with my notes is still in the book. Today it is obvious that the Beats and the Angry Young Men—Allen Ginsberg and Kingsley Amis, Jack Kerouac and John Braine—do not belong in the same book and I cannot bring myself to reread the unsigned introduction, although my marginalia suggest a genuine engagement with the literature. In January 1961, I was off to Paris, where I had the minor part in a private play of ideas directed by Sartre, Malraux, Montherlant and others, as described at the beginning of this book. Sexually latent, my body would not catch up with my mind until after I had arrived at Cambridge the following autumn, but, Bartleby-like, 'I would prefer not to', that is, talk about the process here. Instead, I approach the problem of dualism laterally in my stories.

Education

Introduction

I am able to summon up only memories of a single lesson from my time as a trainee teacher at Avery Hill in 1968, before failing the Post Graduate

Certificate of Education. Influenced by the theories of Ted Hughes in *Poetry in the Making*, I invited the children to imagine that they were fried eggs and write a poem in *propria personae*. The previous year I had been a supply teacher in Paddington. I remember being tickled in the back of my neck by a fifteen-year-old girl while I was writing on the blackboard during Scripture, of all subjects. Or should that read, appropriately enough? It was Friday afternoon and as soon as school ended I took the train to Cambridge where I spent the weekend with Terry and Rosemary Eagleton. I, alone of all my friends, had had to depart academic studies on graduation, to embark on the succession of day jobs which meant nothing to me and which were my lot as a result of self-inflicted academic failure. Years later, Alan Wall (who had been one of Terry's students at Oxford) told me that Eagleton had confided I was in love with the idea of failure. This was a troubling thought, with enough truth in it to cause resentment. 'If I can't be first, I'll be last' was close to being my motto at Cambridge. Talk about attention seeking. My natural level, a lower second, was not good enough for me: if I wasn't cut out for a first, then I would fail, or in Cambridge terms get a non-honours degree.

USA

John Holt's books *How Children Learn* and *How Children Fail* had a strong impact: I had read his essays in *The Nation*, which I bought every week while living in Chicago during the first half of 1966 and which, along with *I. F. Stone's Weekly*, helped radicalize my ideas. That period in Chicago built upon my 1964 trip to the USA and the hopes symbolized by the civil rights movement. However, in the context of the savage prelapsarian restoration of deregulated capitalism by Reagan and Thatcher, defended and extended by later governments, my philosophy of libertarian socialism is not on the agenda. The wealthy beneficiaries of business culture, who pay far too little tax both personally and as corporations, and who are subsidized in all sorts of ways by government, have constructed a nice little earner: socialism for the upper crust, with their losses socialized and their profits privatized.

I read Holt's later book *The Underachieving School*. Its date of publication, 1971, suggests that education remained a matter of concern for me even before my own children arrived (in 1974 and 1976) and even though

I had, to my immense relief and gratitude, been abandoned by the teaching profession. Holt wrote the introduction to *Teaching the 'Unteachable'*, a pamphlet by another radical educationalist, Herbert R. Kohl. Kohl's *Open Classroom* is also here, along with Jonathan Kozol's *Death at an Early Age*. The problems all three writers confronted in Boston and New York were bad enough in those years, how much the more so (as the Talmud likes to say) in our day and age, with the return to the mentality of laissez faire (and its concomitant authoritarianism) associated with the doctrines of Nassau Senior and his contemporary exponents. I also read John Dewey's *Experience and Education* (noting his phrase 'the experiential continuum' for future use) and other educationists such as Jerome S. Bruner.

Comprehensive schools (Michael Duane and others)

Postgraduate education students at Avery Hill College used to take the train from Eltham to Charing Cross and then walk to London University's Institute of Education for lectures by the presiding powers, including Professor Peters, whose *Ethics and Education* and *The Concept of Education* were set texts. Other set texts I did not dispose of after leaving the college are *Risinghill: Death of a Comprehensive School* by Leila Berg, *Growth through English* by John Dixon and *The Secret Places* by David Holbrook. Dixon's book, judging by my annotations, engaged my attention and would have compelled emulation had I dared become a teacher. Berg's book, written in 1965 when Risinghill School was closed down, attracted much discussion at the time and since. It was a brilliant and damning account of a school in dire straits by a real writer, a writer with a passion for education and truth. It tells the story of the headmaster Michael Duane's attempt to rescue the pupils of a neighbourhood comprehensive school in a poor and underprivileged part of inner London. He raised the school from the lower depths but did not have enough talented staff or resources and made too many enemies in County Hall and elsewhere to carry the revolution through.

Some thirteen years after Avery Hill, I invited Duane to participate in what turned out to be Menard's most unusual event, the Conway Hall book launch of John Horder's *Meher Baba and the Nothingness* and re-issue of his first book, *A Sense of Being*. Horder's *idée fixe*, namely that we do not engage in enough non-sexual hugging, was on the agenda and indeed practised by the well-lubricated audience of journalists and poets. The panel also included Margaret Drabble, Michael Duane and James Hemming. Cartoons and leading articles in the national press followed, but made no difference whatsoever to the sales, a salutary lesson. Horder gave me a copy of an unexpectedly good book, Don Stevens' Baba-influenced *Man's Search for Certainty*. Twenty years after Conway Hall, when I had become fascinated by autobiography (its reading and its writing), I discovered Berg's brilliant *Flickerbook*, a lovely account in fragments of her childhood in Manchester; it remained on my reading list for students during the years I taught autobiography.

Reference Books

Introduction

Online research such as fact-checking is an essential part of my life as a writer, but the sheer pleasure obtained by checking out a piece of information in print form and then lingering at random amidst the pages of *Who's Who* or *Debrett's* or a dictionary is hard to beat. Indeed, such *dévergondage* is one of my digressionary techniques.

Two Klossowskis and the Dictionnaire usuel (and others)

Marita Llinares writes in an email: 'On shelves, books are so much closed energy—dead energy, if they're unloved. Reference books have stored energy, ready for use.' Of none of my reference books is this more true than the two-volume *Dictionnaire de Mythologies* edited by Yves Bonnefoy, which sits by my desk in permanence. My much battered *Oxford Dictionary of Quotations* goes back to the days when I was chief assistant to my *Times* crossword-addict father. My job was to check out the quotations that 'we' did not recognize. Here is my long-serving Quillet-Flammarion *Dictionnaire Usuel*, an encyclopaedia/dictionary dating back to 1961. I am a prelims anorak. Glancing at the 'correcteurs-réviseurs' listed among the 'principaux collaborateurs', I recognize a name that would have meant nothing to me in

441

1961: 'Mme Denise Klossowski', the widow of Pierre Klossowski, painter and writer and brother of Balthus. While Denise was correcting and revising the text of this encyclopaedia, her husband was translating Ludwig Wittgenstein's *Tractatus* and *Philosophical Investigations*, two books I keep within reach. Yet the only Wittgenstein in the Quillet-Flammarion is Field-Marshal Prince Louis de Wittgenstein. Such is the delicious serendipity of alphabetical books that we find on the very same page 'Willesden': 'English town in the county of Middlesex'. That's quite a step-up for the nondescript suburb where several friends grew up, and it does make you wonder what principles of proportionality guided the choice of places and philosophers, even if it was early days for Wittgenstein in France. Far less well known than his brother, Klossowski is an interesting and distinctive artist. Denise was her husband's chief model, and a very good one too. Take a look at the erotic drawings of her as Roberte in his self-illustrated novel, *The Revocation of the Edict of Nantes*. At the Whitechapel Gallery exhibition of Bellmer and Klossowski, Paula much preferred Klossowski, with his life-size drawings. Fascinated by his primary objective, which is to tell stories, she was not bothered by his clumsiness, indeed was drawn to it, and brought out her sketchbook. For my part, I stayed in the upstairs gallery with Hans Bellmer, an extraordinary draughtsman as well as the surrealist sculptor of sexual dolls.

[Five years later: It is clear, with hindsight, that the visit to the Whitechapel was a classic turning point for Paula. Her pastel paintings, which used sometimes to be mistaken for oil paintings so *worked* were they, are now better described as pastel drawings. They are never clumsy.]

Dictionaries

Here are my *Harraps* French dictionaries, battered after forty years of service on the front line, and some of my English-language dictionaries, the *OED*, *Chambers* and *BBC English Dictionary*. I was seconded to the BBC dictionary for a few months during my mainly clerical day-job (with the odd nights) years at Bush House, years clocked up when a young family and non-commercial publishing house could not be run on the low income of a freelance translator and writer. The BBC book was aimed at people round the world without English as a first language. It was co-published with

Collins, who supplied the professional lexicographers but needed the BBC's cachet in order to market the dictionary to the faithful millions who would recognize the name. My editorial job was to ensure that controversial entries conformed to newsroom standards of objectivity. I remember making phone calls to BBC correspondents concerning the United Nations, Palestine, refugees and so on. Objectivity is an art rather than a science, although it does have more reality than a mere aspiration. Finally, I salute some old friends: Yiddish, Hebrew, Polish, Italian, Spanish, Portuguese, Latin, German, dictionaries at the ready.

The Bedside Book is a specialized dictionary of quotations. Subtitled 'A Miscellany for the Quiet Hours' and originally published in 1932, it had already reached its twelfth impression by November 1940, when my father bought it, perhaps on 14 November, the day the Luftwaffe bombed Coventry. This was a book to have by your bed in dark times, in every sense. The convention is that of belles-lettres: many of the items are far longer than your typical quotation. The editor, Arthur Stanley, constructed his book symmetrically, with four main sections, each in four subsections. These have titles like 'Lodgings for the Night', 'Romance and Fairies' and 'Small Talk in the Caravanserai'. The third is further subdivided into 'Little Playthings' and 'These from the Land of Nod'. 'Little Playthings' contains an extract from Swift's *Tale of a Tub*, much admired by Gabriel Josipovici, which begins: 'I am now trying an experiment very frequent among modern authors, which is to write upon nothing; when the subject is utterly exhausted, to let the pen still move on: by some called the ghost of wit, delighting to walk after the death of its body.'

Yiddish

Possibly Leo Rosten belongs under 'anthologies', but I deploy the category for poetry and fiction, so his hilarious lexicon *The Joys of Yiddish* shall count as a reference book, which it is. Here is where you go if you want to know the difference between dybbuk and gilgul, and whether ki-bosh is a Yiddish word at all. Rosten's *Treasury of Jewish Quotations* contains, under 'books', the following legend: 'The archangel Metatron, the librarian of heaven, brings new books to the Holy One, who then presents them to the Academy on High, for careful study.' I assume this refers to books written by us and not by angels, though it is not entirely clear. 'All brides are beautiful—and all corpses look pious' strikes me as being an ambiguous compliment to both categories. I wonder how genuine many of the turn of the (twentieth) century *Yiddish Sayings Mama Never Taught You* are. 'Beser fun der ergster ganz der tokhes, eyder fun'm bestn khazn der haldz.' 'Better the behind of the worst goose, than the throat of the best cantor.' Another one: 'Az men pisht klor, kakt men on dem dokter.' 'When you piss clear, you can crap on the doctor.'

Notes and queries

The Guardian's Notes and Queries (volume 2) contains my reply to a question about the origin of Churchill's V for Victory sign: a committee in Bush House on Jonathan Griffin's watch as head of BBC European Intelligence during World War II. Previously Griffin had worked in Prague as a journalist, berating appeasement (David Vaughan's *Battle for the Airwaves: Radio and the 1938 Munich Crisis*). I've had three or four answers published but have not yet posted the following question: 'Many years ago I read an article by Bernard Levin in *The Times* about Lord Goddard, the quondam Lord Chief Justice. In it, Levin quoted someone (the valet in question?) as saying the judge's valet would bring in an extra pair of trousers for his lordship to change into after he had put on the black wig and sentenced a man or woman to death. Apparently, Goddard not only got a charge but also a discharge at the thought that the defendant would be hanged by the neck until he die. Is this an urban myth?'

Yearbook

The Leo Baeck Institute publishes a *Year Book* containing scholarship of the highest order, for example, in 1990, the magisterial essay by Stephen Schwartzschild entitled 'Adorno and Schoenberg between Kant and Hegel'. The yearbook deals with the Jewish intellectual life that was once so vital in Germany and Austria, as well as topics consequential upon exile and uprootedness after 1933. It was edited for many years by Arnold Paucker at the Wiener Library in Devonshire Street (now in Russell Square), which has been a major resource for anyone researching the history of this period, from PhD students to television programme makers.

J. L. Carr

Someone who gives the term 'English eccentric' a good name is the late J. L. Carr, whose book on cricket I write about on another page. For years I bought copies of his sixteen-page letterpress mini-dictionaries, to give as presents. Sixteen pages is a logical length for a logical mind like Carr's, more contained than most. On the inside back cover we find: 'These books fit envelopes 4.5" by 6.3", a common size'. They cost minimum postage. Carr was a schoolteacher by weekday, and Booker shortlisted writer and small press publisher by evening and weekend. The entry on Henry VI in Carr's *Dictionary of English Kings, Consorts, Pretenders, Usurpers, Unnatural Claimants and Royal Athelings* is characteristic: 'd. 1461 aged 50, either of stabbing or melancholia, was so naïve that some unkindly allege imbecility, so chaste that even a hint of a cleavage caused him to exclaim "Fie", so devout that, even aged three, he howled and screamed at suggested Sabbath day travel, so sexually modest that, when his fierce French wife bore an heir, he declared that the father must have been the Holy Ghost. Nevertheless, he is the undisputed progenitor of Eton and King's, Cambridge.' And George, Prince of Denmark: 'Queen Anne's husband, d. 1708, aged 55. This overweight, amiable and virile glutton fathered 18 children, none surviving infancy.' A handwritten letter from Carr inserted in the royal dictionary states that he is suffering from 'cash-flowitis and shall not publish any books for a few months'. I had suggested a mini-selection of Isaac Rosenberg for his poetry series. Coincidentally, he had been reading Rosenberg's biography 'only a few months ago'.

Proof Copies, Review Copies and Rare Books

PROOF COPIES

Yehuda Amichai

> I want once more to be written
> in the book of life, to be written

anew every day
until the writing hand hurts.

This is the final stanza of a poem in Yehuda Amichai's 1979 book, *Time*, of which I have a corrected proof copy. No co-translator is listed and indeed there is no indication that the poems by my old friend were originally written in Hebrew, unless the information was added after proof stage. Whose writing hand is being referred to in this poem? Jewish liturgy and literature are replete with references to the book of life. On the Jewish New Year (Rosh Hashana), which is the beginning of the Ten Days of Penitence or Days of Awe, Jews hope to be 'inscribed in the Book of Life' while on the Day of Atonement (Yom Kippur), the culmination of the Ten Days of Penitence, they hope to be 'sealed in the Book of Life'. It is God who does the writing and sealing, but he also observes closely throughout the year how each individual is writing himself or herself into their own narrative.

On both Rosh Hashana and Yom Kippur, we recite one of the most powerful and shocking prayers in the liturgy, for God decides who is to live and who is to die and, indeed the manner of the dying ('who by strangulation and who by stoning / who shall be at peace and who shall be pursued' and so on). This Jewish *dies irae* is the 'Unetaneh Tokef', a poem or *piyyut* mythically attributed to the eleventh-century martyr Rabbi Amnon of Mainz, but now believed to have been written long before, although Amnon certainly recited it in the synagogue during his death agony, and that powerful theologian Franz Rosenzweig surely had it in mind when he failed to convert to Christianity after entering the last chance saloon on Yom Kippur in 1913. 'But repentance, prayer and charity (*teshuvah, tefillah, tsedakah*) avert the evil decree' runs the best-known translation of one phrase, the word evil meaning the terrifying harshness of the decree concerning life and death; genuine repentance seals you in the Book of Life and buys you another year. 'Who by Fire?', Leonard Cohen's personal version of this prayer ('who by barbiturate', etc.), can be found on YouTube. There is a stupendous saxophone solo by Sonny Rollins; towards the end he could almost be blowing the Shofar. He certainly appears to be echoing the sound.

Unlike Catholicism, Judaism has no one-on-one confessional, unless Freud's secularized psychoanalytic sessions count as such. Yom Kippur is a day of collective, public confession when everyone confesses to everything, thus ensuring that no person and no sin escape the dragnet. I remember too from childhood that those with living parents (i.e. the children and some of the grown-ups) had to leave the synagogue during the recitation known as *duchaning*, when the Cohens present bless the congregation. These putative descendants of the original priestly caste wear white and cover their faces with prayer shawls, creating an atmosphere beautifully conveyed by Jacob Kramer's most famous painting, in Leeds City Art Gallery. How could a child not feel awe on this highest of holidays, the Sabbath of Sabbaths as it is known? Or has my memory been mediated by Kramer's painting and various literary texts? Back to Amichai's writing hand: the poet evidently conflates the Almighty and everyman; he is saying that writing poetry is his salvation but it is a salvation that has to be renewed every day, and it hurts.

By chance, I find myself writing about this poem in the run-up to 5 June 2007, the fortieth anniversary of the Six Day War, a war we all supported at the time but one whose outcome or, at least, aftermath, has turned out be a disaster, an open-ended colonial occupation that, unless resolved, could leave Israel forced to choose between a democratic state with a Jewish majority alongside a Palestinian state on the one hand, and, on the other, a single undemocratic apartheid state where an eventual Jewish minority will seek to enforce its dominion. I take down a book I am proud to have published, A. C. Jacobs' *Collected Poems and Selected Translations*, in order to reread his translation of the poem Amichai composed a few weeks after the Six Day War: 'On the Day of Atonement Jerusalem 1967'. In it, the poet writes about a haberdashery shop in the annexed Old City which reminds him of his father's own haberdashery shop torched in Germany after the family left for the Jewish Yishuv in Palestine in 1936. It is a poignant personal poem, a political poem in that it is about a polis, a polis that concerns us all, Jerusalem. The poem gently but insistently conflates two communities of fate, and whispers of the tragedy that will be, and in many respects is, Palestine/Israel unless a solution is found that honours both peoples.

Geoffrey Bridson

Geoffrey Bridson, professionally known as D. G. Bridson (as in T. S. Eliot

447

and W. H. Auden), gave me a proof copy of *Prospero and Ariel*, his memoir of the BBC and in particular of the Third Programme and its late lamented Features Department. Bridson, as his second wife Joyce Rowe always called him, was a brilliant producer and features writer and ornament of the golden years associated with Louis MacNeice, Dylan Thomas and Charles Parker. A cigar-smoking, burgundy-swilling short priapic man (even his beard had a permanent erection, as Giles Gordon pointed out during Bridson's memorial meeting at Broadcasting House), he was great fun and a generous friend. The memoir's title was inspired by the Eric Gill sculpture outside Broadcasting House. Gill had to reduce the size of Ariel's genitals, after complaints.

At one time Geoffrey lived opposite Highgate School. Joyce enjoyed telling friends that when she moved in with him she hung a pair of knickers out of the window, not to dry, but to send a signal. Sadly, I forget the target of the signal: perhaps the vanquished foe, herself hung out to dry? Or some rival? Although the story is somewhat dated, it touches on the raffish side of Bridson. Bohemia was his world, and he did not get on well with Jonathan Griffin, whose world it was not. Here too are (non-proof) copies of Bridson's collected poems, *Aaron's Field*, *The Christmas Child* (to think that he himself wrote the words of the much recorded 'Johnny Miner'!) and his *Quest of Gilgamesh*, beautifully printed by Rampart Lions Press, with a lithograph by Michael Ayrton, not my favourite artist. All the same, someone should reprint it in a trade edition. I would have liked to discuss with Geoffrey Bridson other versions of Gilgamesh, such as Stephanie Dalley's, Alan Wall's, David Ferry's and the extract by that fine poet the late Bill Griffiths, printed by himself at the old Poetry Society in Earls Court Square. One of many light-hearted stories in *Prospero and Ariel* involves a friend of Bridson's at the theatre: someone farts and then looks round as if trying to discover the culprit. His friend taps the villain on the shoulder and says loudly: 'It's no use, I saw you tilt.' Giles Gordon and I jointly wrote an angry follow-up to the inadequate obit in *The Times*, a disgraceful affair. Although the bottle took to Joyce after Geoffrey died, there is no doubt that together they had a good time. It had been the best of times on the radio.

Samuel Menashe

Back in 1973 Samuel Menashe sent me the galley proofs of his Gollancz collection of poems, *Fringe of Fire*, together with a letter mentioning the firm's publicity director, Liz Calder, whom I had known when she worked at Jonathan Cape. Later she co-founded Bloomsbury. A few years ago, Menashe phoned from New York to dispute Al Alvarez's account of their meeting at my flat in Belsize Park. Alvarez's old Hebrew teacher Sam Dreen, who had been a friend of Golda Meir in Milwaukee, was also present. Someone had drawn Menashe's attention to *I Must Have Got Something Right*, Alvarez's autobiography. Note a classic crux in the flowchart of this book: I could pursue the story and explain what I believe the dispute was about, but I am more interested in the accidental interconnections thrown up by Menashe's old handwritten letter—a sixpenny stamp and 6 September 1973 on the envelope, my thirty-first birthday—than by the dispute itself; yes, I am interested in the structural framework that generates countless memories with no homes, not even a grave: an orphanage of memories. The published book itself was signed and dated 28 September 1973. Samuel Menashe, who left us in 2011, is (along with Lorine Niedecker) the ultimate minimalist lyric poet, highly praised, as he should be, by mavens like Christopher Ricks, Donald Davie and Brian Lynch.

Paul Buck and Clive Sinclair

In addition to a cupboardful of Menard proofs, I have a few proof copies, mainly bound, which were almost always gifts from people in the business. Some of them could equally well be incorporated in my section on rare books. When Paul Buck was the rep for Fulcrum Press he gave me proof copies of the *Collected Poems* of both Basil Bunting and George Oppen. He also gave me a signed copy of his own first novel *The Honeymoon Killers*, which was made into a film and later published in France in the Série Noire. 'The indredible [*sic*] shocking drama you are about to read . . .' With what *schadenfreude* have I phoned Paul to report the misprint, previously unnoticed!

Appropriately enough, Clive Sinclair gave me a proof of Philip Roth's *The Anatomy Lesson*, a Zuckerman novel from the middle period, when I was in hospital nearly thirty years ago for my second hernia operation eighteen months after the first had been botched. Roth's recent *Exit Ghost* is a fine book. It speaks to the physical condition of men of a certain age, but its deeper theme is the place of the imagination in our lived lives.

REVIEW COPIES

I don't know how many books I have reviewed over forty years. Some of the reviews contain, smuggled past the gate manned by my inner censor, unselfconscious writing. Relaxed, I went with the flow. I would like to reprint some of the paragraphs in an eventual collage of occasional work. My first reviews appeared, thanks to the poetry editor Michelene Wandor, in the late 1960s and early 1970s in the quondam small format *Time Out* and in *Tribune*, whose literary editor, the late Liz Thomas, was mother hen of a cohort of young poets and writers. Rudolph Wurlitzer's *Flats* was sent to me by *Time Out*, perhaps after Giles Gordon, the book's publisher at Gollancz, had had a word with me or with the magazine. I remember praising *Flats* highly. Dipping into it now, I still find the rhythms and story compelling. Beckett is lurking there, but the voice is Wurlitzer's own. I was asked by Penguin to write a blurb for their edition of Stevie Smith's *Novel on Yellow Paper*. In the end, they did not use it, so, waste not, and want not, I converted it into a review for *Time Out*. In 1966, on the road, when I was working for the British Travel Association's Chicago office, I spent several nights in motels after visiting Midwest travel agents. I have a newly vivid memory, triggered by Smith's novel—for vivid memories do not always spring up unbidden—of sprawling on a bed somewhere in Iowa, having narrowly avoided a tornado on Route Sixty-Six, reading from her *Selected Poems* over the telephone to my girlfriend Linda, sprawling on her own bed, in the East Village in New York.

The poet Donald Hall was living near the Arboretum in Ann Arbor in the year of my travel-agent visits (memories of chains on office car wheels in the great Chicago winter of 1966) and I visited him courtesy of our mutual friend Ian Hamilton. While in Ann Arbor, I bought J. V. Cunningham's *The Exclusions of a Rhyme* at Centicore bookshop. Before today—I am looking at it for the first time in years—I would have said, if pressed, that Cunningham was merely a formalist of the school of Yvor Winters, but there is a lightness of touch and, sometimes, a ribaldry taking him into territory remote from Winters-land. The Doctor Drink persona poems are moving, sad and comical. This discovery makes me think I should investigate personae poems by Christopher Middleton, Geoffrey Hill and others, and their relationship to the heteronyms of Pessoa: another fantasy project doomed to non-achievement.

If I were to collect my reviews (and separately my obituaries and interviews of friends), I might learn something about the preoccupations—lifelong or changing—of a mind attempting to engage with other minds and imaginations to the best of its ability, for writing a book review is a responsibility. Someone gave much time and effort to the making of a work, and this commands respect.

RARE BOOKS

Allen Ginsberg

I have a number of rare books and a number of valuable books: Most of the rare ones are valuable and many of the valuable ones are rare. As I wrote earlier, I am not a collector, least of all a collector of rare or valuable books, but I have been fortunate enough to be on the receiving end of a few gifts. In 1964, during the three months I spent in the USA before starting a lifetime of day jobs, I phoned Allen Ginsberg in New York and reminded him we had met in Cambridge a few months earlier, when I sat in the front row at a reading he gave in Kings College. Doubtless I went to the reading with John Barrell and/or Terry Eagleton. I nearly died of embarrassed pride when a meditation aid (I recall a musicians' triangle), which he struck while chanting his introductory *oms*, came apart and he asked me to fit the pieces together. It took my trembling fingers what seemed like ages but I succeeded. He must have given me his phone number after the reading.

In New York, Ginsberg, famously hospitable, invited me round to his walk-up apartment in the East Village. There he was, sitting on the double bed, a mattress on the floor; Peter Orlovsky was in the kitchen. Very courteously, the poet invited me to join him (or perhaps them) in bed and, equally courteously, I said no. I remember him saying that what he most enjoyed about Cambridge was checking out the William Blake holdings in the Fitzwilliam Museum. We chatted for about an hour and I left with a gift, William Burroughs' pamphlet, *Roosevelt after Inauguration*, a 'Fuck You/press/ejaculation, printed, published, & zapped at a secret location in the lower east side, new york city, jan 1964'. (The same publisher brought out Auden's 'Gobble Poem', of which I have a copy published by Fuck Books Unlimited in London: I assume this is pirated from the original pirate). The covers of the Burroughs are by 'Allen Ginsberg, L.A.M.F', which probably stands for 'Like a mother fucker' (so Edward Field suggests). On the front, apart from the title and the author's name (Willy Lee alias William S. Burroughs), are a drawing of the US flag with dollar signs instead of stars and another of a Star of David with a skull and flower. The shit-obsessed story tells how Roosevelt gets rid of the Supreme Court judges and replaces them with 'nine purple assed baboons'. The new President also institutes events like 'Turn in your best friend week' and 'Molest a child week'. Candidates for 'All-around Vilest Man of the Year' include a junkie who stole an opium suppository out of his grandmother's ass. This crazy riff is unpleasant but fortunately quite short. It survives, a souvenir of ancient days.

Despite the dark Burroughs-influenced side, Ginsberg himself was a generous and decent man, a radical who practised what he preached, and in *Howl* and *Kaddish* and *Wichita Vortex Sutra* a major poet out of Whitman, the Hebrew prophets and Buddhism. He makes two appearances in Scorsese's fabulous film about Bob Dylan, once horseplaying with the Beatles, and once movingly explaining how Dylan had picked up the torch. Edward Field's *The Man Who Would Marry Susan Sontag* is an entertaining and sophisticated account of Bohemia by an ex-air-force navigator whose devotion and tenderness towards his blind partner Neil Derrick (and vice versa) moves me greatly. As in Sargent's painting of the soldiers poisoned by gas, Neil walks behind Ed with a finger on Ed's shoulder. Ed, more of an intellectual than he lets on, is in his late eighties but has the body of a man twenty years younger and a poet's brain in full throttle. His poems, for example, *A Full Heart*, sometimes remind one of a Jewish Frank O'Hara. He and O'Hara were close friends. And now Diana Athill has published her letters to Field, *Instead of a Book*, in which we get tantalizing glimpses of the poet, whose own letters are not included.

In terms of generational matrix, I am too old to be an ageing hippy, more like a second-generation beatnik, but I never found the energy and time (in other words, I did not have the desire) to read more widely among the beats than a book each by Jack Kerouac, Philip Lamantia, Michael McClure and Robert Kelly, which is my loss. The other day I heard a programme about Kerouac on the radio while on my exercise bike. They played an extract from Ginsberg's live reading of *Howl*. Even now, Ginsberg's way thrills. He had beatitude.

W. H. Auden

Another rare book and, indeed unique—because of its annotations—is a first edition of W. H. Auden's *Look, Stranger!*, from 1936. The annotations were made by the book's owner, the American-born Jerusalem poet Robert Friend. I published his translations of Leah Goldberg and Ra'hel at Menard Press in the 1970s. Auden was Friend's hero, and they met when Robert hosted him in Jerusalem. The book was given to me as a souvenir by Friend's literary executor, the poet Gabriel Levin. I note in passing that a proudly gay man's best translations are of two women poets. Perhaps this is significant in terms of empathy or elective affinities, but gender and sexuality can be exaggerated as components of the imagination, and certainly they are never a *determining* element in the essence of a great book, which is always androgynous or at least non-gendered: *Moby Dick* and *Billy Budd* may contain homoerotic elements yet they are no more gay than *Bartleby the Scrivener*, a resolutely neutral or even neuter character. Reread chapter four of *Moby Dick* and you will see what I mean. I defy anyone sensitive to the tonality and colour of great prose writing to read a [homo]sexual encounter into the shared bed of Ishmael and Queequeg, notwithstanding 'you had almost thought I had been his wife' and 'his bridegroom clasp'. To elaborate a comment by a distinguished poet and scholar Jane Augustine: Ishmael is terrified at finding himself in the arms of *the other*—savage, and/or non-western and/or cetacious and/or man and/or woman—with the heterosexual image appropriately to hand in the context of a bed the two men are sharing for respectable reasons as adumbrated in the chapter.

Friend's annotations include comparisons of poems with their earlier incarnations in magazines such as *New Verse* and later incarnations in *Collected Poems*. His explanatory comments were doubtless for the benefit of his students at the Hebrew University in Jerusalem: three of them would later become famous poets: Natan Zach, Dahlia Ravikovitch and Yehuda Amichai. In the margin of the penultimate stanza of section XV of the Prologue, which begins 'And since our desire cannot take that route which is straightest', and referring also (with an arrow) to the final stanza, Friend writes: 'Homosexuality [an underground love] is like the subterranean love of those who are slowly making their way towards revolution.' And, below this, paraphrasing Auden's conclusion, Friend comments: 'Our love though it is underground today is only shamming dead—it is alive and will dance.' In the other margin, he writes: 'the poem ought to end here', that is at the end of the penultimate stanza. And Friend is surely right. In the poem numbered XX, Friend glosses that 'left-handed' means 'homosexual'; in XXX, 'And it was snow in bedrooms' refers to cocaine. Like Jonathan Griffin and Michael Hamburger, Robert Friend was always better known for his translations than for his own poems. The same remains true of Keith Bosley, a fine and serious poet (see for example *A Chiltern Hundred*: compare its profile to his magnificent translation of the *Kalevala*) who could not be more neglected.

David Jones

David Jones' two masterpieces, *The Anathemata* and *In Parenthesis*, have an epic grandeur rare in his generation. Here is his book of essays, *Epoch and Artist*, a more profound and sophisticated reading of art and religion than we find in Jacques Maritain's *Art and Poetry* and a precursor to the kind of essays Geoffrey Hill and Rowan Williams would write in later years. My copy of the Fulcrum Press edition of *The Tribune's Visitation* is a rare book, thanks to the author's inscription in that immaculate semi-italic handwriting and using three different coloured inks: 'for Tony and Brenda Rudolf from David Jones/Nov. 26th anno ab Incarnatione Xti MCMLXXII', the day John Montague took me to visit the poet in Harrow on the Hill. At the same time, he made two corrections by hand. Here is René Hague's *Commentary on the Anathemata of David Jones*, printed and published by Christopher Skelton. Eric Gill was Skelton's uncle. Before his untimely death Skelton, printer of fifty Menard books, published the magnificent *Engravings of Eric Gill*, which he edited, wrote and printed. He gave me what he called a damaged copy of this very expensive book, but for the life of me I can't see any. I am lucky to have the book and wish he had lived into the productive retirement he so wanted as a hands-on printer working from home: 'treadling myself into the grave' was his cheerful phrase.

Painting and Other Arts

Introductory Note

The painting section is animated by the presence of the dedicatee of *Silent Conversations* with whom I have had countless 'spoken' conversations over many years, except when keeping still and silent during a pose in her studio, my favourite 'absolute place', to use a phrase of Bonnefoy's. It is salutary for an overly verbal person to engage with someone whose primary way of experiencing the world is visual. Paradise, for me, is to accompany her round the Prado or the Uffizi or the National Gallery or the Accademia in Venice: this is an experience rich beyond the dreams of avarice. The metaphorical cataracts on the eyes in my old writer's head are miraculously removed and, encouraged by her educated and passionate gaze, I experience the possibilities inherent in this or that marvellous picture (let's say Titian's final work in the Accademia or Goya's Black Paintings in the Prado) as a kind of redemption, if only from the verbals, to which I must always return.

Music is my other redemption from the verbals, but that is another story.

Painters, Their Work and Their Writers

VISUAL ART

Look what you've gone and done.

—Willem de Kooning, to Philip Guston, after the latter's return to figuration

He has destroyed painting.

—Poussin on Caravaggio, quoted by Louis Marin in *Détruire la peinture*

456

A picture held us captive.

—Ludwig Witttgenstein, *Philosophical Investigations*

Piero di Cosimo

Painters are very strange people, if Piero di Cosimo is typical of the breed.
Giorgio Vasari's *Lives of the Artists* contains a vivid account of the later years
and old age of this great Florentine painter, whose 'Battle between the Lapiths
and Centaurs' in the National Gallery means so much to Paula. That di
Cosimo lived entirely on boiled eggs is well known—an extreme version of
the unvarying lunch menu of Giacometti, Beckett and Mason—so it is no
wonder he spoke of the torments of 'syrups, medicines, clysters and other
martyrdoms' and, for whatever combination of reasons, ended up paralysed.
Di Cosimo praised death by public execution: 'It was splendid to go to one's
end in that manner, seeing so much of the open sky and so many people, and
being comforted with sweets and kind words; having the priest and people
praying for you, and going with the Angels to Paradise.' Was this an ironic
reference to what he would have seen in the days of Savonarola, perhaps
including the death of the bad man himself in the Ducal Square in Florence?
I am reminded of Sandro Botticelli's troubling and troubled painting of the
deposition of Christ which Paula and I saw in Munich and which was done
after he repented, during the height of Savonarola's influence. One of di
Cosimo's disciples was Andrea del Sarto: 'I painting from myself and to
myself, / Know what I do, am unmoved by men's blame / Or their praise
either.' How such a distinguished critic as Harold Rosenberg in *Art on the
Edge* could suggest on the strength of this proud existential projection—put
into del Sarto's mouth by Robert Browning—that the artist was 'by today's
standards a dilettante or a hobbyist' beats me.

Charles Meryon

I lived in Paris for six months in 1961. I visit the city regularly. But my being-
in-Paris is far more conscious and self-conscious than my being-in-London.
Another factor is that London's charms and beauties are more hidden than
those of Paris. To be a *flâneur* in London is less appropriate than in Paris,
native or adopted city of Baudelaire and Balzac, Benjamin and Breton, Mason

and Prévert, Queneau (*Connaissez-vous Paris?*) and Perec, Giacometti and Meryon. Charles Meryon, Baudelaire tells us in his Salon of 1859, 'bade farewell to solemn adventures on the Ocean in order to paint the black majesty of this most troubling of capital cities'. Elsewhere, Baudelaire, Meryon's only champion in his lifetime, says of the artist's wonderful etchings that he has 'rarely seen represented with more poetry the natural solemnity of a great capital city'. One of my most treasured possessions is an original of his 'Tour de l'horloge', which I look at every day. Benjamin in *Charles Baudelaire: A Lyric Poet in the Era of High Capitalism* reminds us that the two men were born in the same year and died within a few months of each other, 'Meryon as a demented person at Charenton, Baudelaire speechless in a private clinic', and he points out that Meryon's verse caption for his etching of the Pont Neuf is closely related to Baudelaire's 'Squelette laboureur'. And, in *The Arcades Project*: 'Meryon turned the tenements of Paris into monuments of modernity'. Concerning visual representations of cities, Paula says that even though she lives in London, it is her magical city (as Paris is mine) and that her relationship to Lisbon is similar to my relationship to London. London has been her haven ever since her father sent her here because he did not want her to be 'educated' under the Salazar dictatorship. The question of how we relate to our place of residence (e.g. the psyche in a megapolis as opposed to a small town or to a village) and also how we relate to the place in terms of inland/coast, high land/low land, flat/house is of considerable interest.

Edvard Munch and Hans Holbein

These days I only love one or two of Edvard Munch's paintings, such as 'Between the Clock and the Bed'. I prefer his prints. Here is a small volume of Munch's graphics, *Lebensfries*, inscribed in Norwegian by Anniken Thue, the friend who gave it to me in 1966. Here too is a little book on trolls inscribed by her in English—'To understand Norwegian women, first you have to understand Norwegian trolls'—as is the copy of Knut Hamsun's *Hunger* she gave me earlier. (*Hunger* was translated by the feminist writer George Egerton: she had had an affair with Hamsun, that 'génie-mâle', for which 'one cannot be sufficiently grateful'.) Facing 'The Scream' in *Lebensfries* is a superb dry point of a powerfully erotic image of a naked maiden embraced by skeletal death, followed immediately by Munch's lithograph of Mallarmé, such as into himself at last the poet is changed, as Mallarmé almost said. Another master printmaker is Hans Holbein the younger, whose *Images from the Old Testament*, cut from woodblocks, contains re-workings of familiar stories such as those of Daniel and Ezekiel. The introduction by Michael Marqusee quotes Erasmus: 'Silent art is rather eloquent.' Marqusee, who also writes on cricket and politics, and thus has a threefold claim on my attention, tries to make this suggestive remark specific to Holbein, but fails. It is there only because he wants to conclude with a modest demurral about the uses of ekphrasis: 'our words are a meagre substitute for the eloquence of silent art', *tacita pictum*, or indeed, the eloquence of Tacita Deane, whose recent film work bears comparison with the wondrous installations of Bill Viola. Viola is a good ekphrastic or kinaesthetic surname for a visual artist.

Paula Rego (with Jonathan Leaman, Ron Mueck and Paul Coldwell)

Another great admirer of di Cosimo is Paula's friend and protégé, Jonathan Leaman. This remarkable and virtuoso painter writes in a letter that he loves the two di Cosimo pictures in the National Gallery, especially the famous 'Battle between the Lapiths and the Centauers' (a Rego favourite too), with its 'wonderful subdued brown tone, a sort of liquid symmetry that is echoed in the design'. But his favourite is 'Forest Fire' in the Ashmolean, 'one of the very few pictures about origins that actually feel like fire might just have come about for the first time'. As always, enclosed with the letter is a photographed detail from a new painting and a vivid account of his current literary and philosophical preoccupations. This is one of those rare painters like the late Kitaj: a great reader who enjoys writing. Jonathan and I had a chat after the opening of Ron Mueck's show in Edinburgh. I watched him hugging the wall closely as he prowled round the room containing the sculptor's giant baby. The educated eye of Leaman, whose hyper-realist paintings have a surrealist dimension absent from that of Ron Mueck's remarkable sculptures—Mueck's recent work, a crucified chicken, is 'beyond belief'—reacts viscerally to visceral art before intellectualizing and rationalizing his gut reactions in letters. Back in the mid-1990s, Ron, who is Paula's son-in-law, made her a Pinocchio while he was still a special effects person in movies: his final 'effects' were made for his brother-in-law Nick Willing's fine film *Photographing Fairies*. Pinocchio led Paula to encourage Ron to become a sculptor, which generated a fundamental ontological change in his attitude to creativity. It also led Charles Saatchi to commission work from him.

One rule had better be invoked: only books shall be in the frame, not exhibition catalogues (except 'reasoned' ones), just as elsewhere I have to draw a line and exclude literary magazines. Tom Rosenthal's 2003 catalogue *raisonné* of Paula's prints was an invaluable account. Nine years later, there is a second edition rather than a reprint, because Paula is so productive. Rosenthal ran the new chapters past me. The book contains a fine essay on her etchings by a distinguished fellow artist, Paul Coldwell, another of whose essays quotes a critic as saying that the Reformation was a defining moment in England, when the word prevailed over the image, although I suspect Henry the Eighth wouldn't have put it like that. Coldwell used to be Paula's printer, working together in what he jokingly called the pizza parlour, a reference to the wheel he turned to generate proofs and editioned etchings in the kitchen of the previous house he shared with Charlotte Hodes, herself a marvellous ceramicist. I shall say little about these editions save that the most useful way I can contribute to the exponentially burgeoning (is there any other kind of burgeoning?) literature on Paula's work will be, one day, to tell my own story (as her *compagne* and principal male model) about this multifaceted *oeuvre*, an *oeuvre* as modern as can be while still remaining inscribed in tradition. Some of the subject matter is revolutionary, for example the abortion series and the later works about female genital mutilation and so-called honour killings (i.e. murder). The way she uses pastels is unprecedented—rarely if ever discussed in the literature—but the fact that one can talk of subject matter already tells us something about points of reference, which are (art) historical: Francisco Goya, Honoré Daumier, William Hogarth, Gustave Doré.

'The Model'

Two of my favourite fictional accounts of the model are stories by Henry James ('The Real Thing') and Guy de Maupassant ('The Model'). I enjoy the rare (leaving aside portraits, how many models are writers?) personal accounts such as Martin Gayford's on sitting for Lucian Freud: *Man with a Blue Scarf*. My presence in Paula's life played a part in her decision to create a number of series involving a male model, including *The Crime of Father Amaro, Jane Eyre* and *Red Riding Hood*. Most recently I have acted in *Dame with a Goat's Foot* and in an original Pierrot costume for a series about Portuguese troubles. However, all who know Paula's work think of Lila, when they think of a Rego model, Lila with whom I have sat countless times in the playground, which is the studio.

I sat and sit for individual pictures too, in drag as 'Olga', as the cockroach in 'Metamorphosis' and as Christ in an additional picture to the Life of the Virgin series commissioned by the then President of Portugal, Jorge Sampaio, for his palace chapel. When the model is the lover of the painter, this must affect the *gaze* of the artist, but everything affects the gaze of the artist. What a flowchart you could, in theory, construct, elaborating choices made: those that leave options open and those that close them down. Visual art is a far cry from writing, especially on computers, where all options remain open. As it happens, keeping the options open was an article of faith when I was young; now it is a version of hell. As for the poor sitter, after collaborating as the artist's junior partner in setting the scene to kick-start the story, he keeps still. Sitting as a model has involved an ongoing collaboration and partnership, and it is *the only way to see the artist in office hours*. Perhaps *Office Hours* would make a good title for my book, rather than my earlier semi-jocular idea, *On the Receiving End*. I make occasional notes when I get home, or even in front of Paula when we have our post-session drink. As a writer fallen among painters, I am enthralled by their freedom to invoke or construct a world within a preordained space, something the writer is spared except in the special case of a fixed form like a sonnet.

On rare occasions it goes wrong; thus, in one picture my legs are too short, but maybe that was Paula's revenge for my harping on about short-legged Portuguese women. She has talked about artists who put figures into space, and those who put space round figures; and she has been asked to design sets and/or costumes for opera. Although I understand the reason for refusing—her priority is to paint and draw and make prints—I cannot but regret the works not made. However, others have used her paintings directly or for inspiration, such as Polly Teale's Shared Experience theatre company, and many works have appeared on book jackets in Portugal and Britain (*The Crime of Father Amaro*) or on UK stamps (*Jane Eyre*), though Paula did only one book jacket as a commission, under the pseudonym of Maria Moreno: for a novel by her late friend Rudi Nassauer. Many poets have done fine work 'after' her: Owen Lowery, Mike Heller and Deryn Rees-Jones, to name but three.

Howard Hodgkin

René Char wrote somewhere: 'the word is very close in time to its application. Painting escorts it, supports it, explains it.' Among the painters he wrote about was his friend Balthus, one of a select band of visual artists whom poets ('magicians of insecurity' in the phrase of Char) and writers love ekphrastically. Paula is another, as are Giorgio Morandi, Joseph Cornell and Howard Hodgkin, whose partner and I were included among the 'wives' asked by an usher to move away when the twenty or so painters in the Encounters exhibition at the National Gallery were about to be photographed by David Bailey before the official dinner. Paula's Encounter was with Hogarth, Hodgkin's with Seurat. A few months later, in Oxford after a miserable traffic-jammed journey taking two and a half hours, I walked from the car park to the Ashmolean in order to chill out before a meeting with my friend Bruce Ross-Smith. I wandered round, checking my favourite pictures, including Nicolas Poussin's 'Baby Moses Saved from the River' and Paolo Uccello's 'The Hunt', then went upstairs to Walter Sickert's works (this artist grows on me more and more), ending in front of a superb early Hodgkin, painted when he was fifteen and, of course, untypical, indeed vanished: 'The Tea Party', with its gratuitous yet inevitable and wholly integrated pair of hands in the foreground. I then stared and stared at 'Like an Open Book', a small figurative picture. The title, ironically intended or not, keeps the viewer, or rather the painter, at an emotional distance. The open book is unmistakeable, and it is clear that Hodgkin is inviting us to think as well as feel: thus, the title is not 'An open book' but 'Like an Open Book'. What we are being asked to read 'like an open book' is the painting itself, which consists

462

of broad-brushed colours that stretch beyond the painting's surface to the frame, liminal terrain where life outside the picture normally begins. There is no secret, no code, no story, nothing but virtually abstracted colour to sustain our attention, care and interest, and our awareness that emotions such as we ourselves feel and autobiography that is being kept secret have fuelled the work.

BOOKS BY ARTISTS

Avigdor Arikha

The late Avigdor Arikha's *On Depiction* is as brilliant and learned as books by scholars who are not themselves artists, such as *Depiction* by Michael Podro. Naturally, given Arikha's status as an artist in his own right, his book carries exceptional authority as does Leon Golub's *Do Paintings Bite?*. Golub sometimes reminds me of Kitaj. Beckett, quoted on the cover of Arikha's book, speaks of his friend's 'incomparable grasp of the past and of the problems that beset continuance'. Arikha writes on favourites of mine—Poussin, Degas, Giacometti and Cartier-Bresson—and also on favourites of Paula's—Mantegna, Ingres and Soutine. He also writes conceptual essays on drawing, on light and on abstraction. One link between Arikha and Kitaj is Arikha's wife the poet Anne Atik, whose book *Offshore* ends with a poem about Drancy and notes on a visit with Kitaj to this place of shame. Over dinner with Arikha after a private view in London, I told him I was reading Aharon Appelfeld's autobiographies. He grimaced, and complained that Appelfeld was too much of a diaspora writer, a complaint that Appelfeld himself tells us has been made by many people in Israel. Now, if a man as intelligent and well read as Arikha can say something so apparently irrelevant to an understanding of the authenticity, power and depth of this great writer's work, then something else is buried deep in the remark, something related to the exchange of letters between Celan and Amichai, which I discuss elsewhere. Arikha and Appelfeld are near contemporaries from Czernowitz and its environs, both survived the Holocaust in different ways and both came to Palestine, Arikha in 1944, Appelfeld in 1946. Arikha was old enough to fight (and be wounded in) the War of Independence in 1948. Later he left

Israel for France. This personal history is what lies buried in his remark about Appelfeld. Even giants fight upon a psychic battleground, a battleground that is the true subject of Appelfeld's autobiography.

Josef Herman

My friend Josef Herman was another of those painters who enjoy writing. In *Related Twilights* he tells his life in Warsaw, Brussels, Glasgow, London and, most famously, Ystradgynlais, where he made his moving and loving images of Welsh miners in pastel, charcoal drawing and oils. I phoned Paula and read out to her his remark that with pastel as well as with pen and ink he got 'nearer to the sculptor's approach to form than at any time before, to such a degree, indeed, that even today I am asked whether I am doing a sculpture'. He explains how Edgar Degas was the first to achieve the full potential of the medium, having primed the paper with watercolour, gouache, 'even with thick but lean oil paint'. However, Herman insists that 'technique must always bend to the subjective needs of feeling and expression, above all to the mood required. In fact, technique and the state of mind are one.' He goes on to say: 'autumn is my season, twilight is my hour', which reflects the mood music of his work. I occasionally visited him in his studio in Edith Grove, where he showed me his wonderful collection of African objets d'art and served up omelettes for lunch. He writes about Constant Permeke, Giorgio Morandi (who, Herman discovered on a visit, owned a Douanier Rousseau) and the revolutionary painters of Mexico. I am struck by a comment in a chapter on Madrid and Andalusia: 'The weight of darkness pulls Spanish painting down to earth and displays the recklessness of human passions with pride and trust.'

Ian McKeever

Ian McKeever's *In Praise of Painting* contains three informal lectures full of interesting and unexpected details I am not ashamed to lift out of context, as well as reminders of valuable insights from the great artists. He quotes Blake: 'nature has no outline', which suggests, in McKeever's words, 'that the line bridged the gap between the nature of things and how we interpret', although the possibly unintended repetition of the word nature in the phrase 'the nature of things' could equally lead one to reverse it to 'the things of nature'.

In a discussion about Vilhelm Hammershoi—a painter I discovered while Paula and I were in Copenhagen—McKeever quotes Wittgenstein: 'Grey is not poorly illuminated white' and also Hammershoi's fellow Scandinavian Gunnar Ekelöff, a weather-wise bard of distinction. I like the dark north European imaginings of these painters and poets more than Paula does: 'all colours a suffusion from that light' as Coleridge wrote in 'Dejection', provided, that is, the light is grey. 'I have always found it . . . surprising', says McKeever, 'that every place on the surface of the earth receives the same amount of daylight hours in a year. It is only that they are distributed differently.' Not a lot of people know that. Nor did I know that a full can of black is far lighter, and a full can of titanium white significantly lighter, than the other colours on the painter's spectrum. White in a painting, he says, yields to the viewer, black does not, but this is a function of the mind's eye, not objective, for both deflect away from certitude when lit. At a dinner in 2003 in a London club for that hardy perennial Patrick George's eightieth birthday, I was seated next to Lucian Freud's picture framer. He pointed to an old painting on the wall with an elaborate gilt frame. 'Do you know why frames were painted gold?' No. The interesting answer was that gold reflected light onto the painting from the nearest candles. I was struck by McKeever's remark that when 'standing in front of a vertical painting, we feel our own pronounced frontality, it affirms what we are; while the spread of the horizontal takes us away from ourselves as individuals, towards a broader sense of place.' He concludes: 'if we are held in place by the vertical, then we are rooted by the horizontal.'

John Digby

John and Joan Digby's *The Collage Handbook* is a fascinating book about a technique once favoured by Paula. The book rightly pays attention to Max Ernst, one of the main twentieth-century influences on Paula. 'Ernst,' says Digby, who is a surrealist poet, 'liberated collage from art, from its concerns with plastic and visual planes, and turned it into a theatre of the irrational.' Max Ernst invented frottage, although not in the literal sense envisaged by Georges Bataille in Orleans. It is no coincidence that the young Yves Bonnefoy, fresh from his short but deep involvement with André Breton and

465

surrealism, took the title of his little magazine *La Révolution la nuit* from a painting by Ernst, that connoisseur of oneiric chaos. I have framed and hung on my wall a text written by Bonnefoy and revised by Breton, and which was published and signed by twenty surrealists, protesting the war in Indo-China: 'Liberty is a Vietnamese word.' Thinking outside the box, I am reminded of Joseph Cornell who combined found objects with collage: this 'puritan constructivist' (in the phrase of Robert Hughes, RIP this very week of my final revision) took his own possessions and, combining them with objects from the flea market, made haunting reliquaries that enabled him to go on living.

WRITERS

If a question can be framed at all, it is also possible to answer it.
—Ludwig Wittgenstein, *Tractatus Logico-Philosophicus*

The concept is the original sin of knowledge.
—Yves Bonnefoy, *Le Sommeil de personne*

Yves Bonnefoy

When Yves Bonnefoy's collection of essays and tributes with its resonant and beautiful title, *Dans un débris de miroir*, in which he speaks of friends and encounters with key figures, arrived, I dropped everything to read the four or five pages on his friend (and my acquaintance) Alexander Aspel and the Poussin painting in Cedar Rapids, which the two men did not see together because Bonnefoy's planned flight there was diverted by the weather to Quad Cities Airport. In a short space, Yves touches on friendship and art, on exile and loss of faith, on American geography and names. Thinking about Nicolas Poussin reminds me that I have not yet read Tim Clark's experiment in art writing, *The Sight of Death*. This study of two great Poussin landscapes, which are among my favourite paintings in the world, 'Landscape with a man killed by a Snake' and 'Landscape with a Calm', looks as though it will rival a book I touch on later, *Remaining in Light*, John Taggart's study of a Hopper painting (and Ernest Farrés' book of poems *Edward Hopper*, so brilliantly and meta-ekphrastically translated from the Catalan by Lawrence Venuti), as an exploration of image and perception, with this difference, Clark is an art historian, Taggart a poet and Venuti a translator-poet or poetry translator. But we all have two eyes and one brain with left and right sides, whatever our inclinations.

Bonnefoy's *Le Sommeil de personne* was inspired by Rilke's self-epitaph, found on his tomb: graced by Farhad Ostovani's atmospheric pastel landscapes, this essay is non-fiction prose writing at its densest and most implosive by a writer worrying away at his themes syntactico-rhythmically, like Charles Péguy in *Clio*, Maurice Blanchot in *The Writing of the Disaster* or François-René de Chateaubriand in *Mémoires d'Outre-tombes* and, like them, pursuing a profound meditation on life and death, art and thought. The writing demands the closest attention, yet it is not gratuitously difficult. Bonnefoy's fine-bladed axe, in Kafka's image, cracks the frozen sea within us, forcing our slower minds to work harder than we are accustomed. The matrix of Bonnefoy's text is two hundred years of French prose written by poets, prose that was essential to the life of literature because French poetry was 'a very calculated, self-conscious form, and thus at a far remove from everyday speech—from which it followed that a number of experiences that might have become poetry were left behind by verse and had to seek other means of expression, most notably in prose. And indeed they did. For example, the eminently poetic feeling for nature, which in England is active in the poetry of Wordsworth and Keats, has found its home in French in . . . the prose of Rousseau, Joseph Joubert, de Guérin or Chateaubriand.' That quote is from another and more 'popular' essay, translated by John Naughton, published in *TLS* and written as a reply to an Oxford lecture, mainly about Yves Bonnefoy, by Christopher Ricks in an earlier issue of the journal.

Wordsworth was Chateaubriand's exact contemporary, born two years after him and dying two years after him. I sometimes forget that the English poet was already in his twenties when Keats and Shelley were born, and had left Cambridge by 1791. Did he meet Chateaubriand while the latter was ambassador in London? Did Paul Gaugin and Robert Louis Stevenson meet in Tahiti? Did Rimbaud meet Doré in London in 1873? If so, did he see the artist's image of the Metropolitan Line (the mainly overground underground, the first in the world) at the Doré Gallery on Old Bond Street before he wrote his prose poem of the same name? Or did he perhaps see it in Doré's *London*, which came out in 1872—a work Vincent Van Gogh admired and which has affinities with James Thomson's once widely read 'City of Dreadful Night'?

The extraordinary energy and potency of Bonnefoy's prose, 'sa gravité enflammée' in the fine phrase of Philippe Jaccottet, are the result of a tension. This tension is, to simplify, between presence and concept: concepts, like number, are arrogant excarnations born of gnostic duality, denying presence, finitude, mortality and death. In one of Bonnefoy's prose masterpieces, *L'Arrière-pays* this tension is brought to its most extreme, in that it impinges on the poet's own spiritual journey. Italy and its art generate a way of thinking about concept and presence: compare Francesco Borromini and Gian Lorenzo Bernini, concludes Bonnefoy, and find a kind of synthesis in Poussin and his search for the key to a 'musique savante'. (The splendid English translation by Stephen Romer, a fine poet in his own right, is at last available together with new texts by the French poet.)

Conceptual thought always runs the risk of reductiveness to a single aspect (as in science and law), runs the risk of abstraction or idealization of what Rimbaud calls 'rough reality', the risk of alienating the gaze, in a word, the risk of dogma and fetishization. Poetry guards against this by mirroring these dangers in a perpetual agon, for only thus can presence make itself felt in plenitude. 'Poetry is an unceasing battle between representation and presence,' Bonnefoy writes in a remarkable essay 'Georges Poulet et la poésie' (in *La Communauté des critiques*), where he confronts these issues and admits to having polemicized in earlier writings which had been misunderstood by some readers, including me. He also confronts the issues in an essay 'Poetry and Truth', originally written in English, which I lightly edited for publication in *MPT*. In this essay, Bonnefoy tells us that poetry which, unlike prose, 'knows its own mendacity', is 'the memory of truth', a place where hope is reawakened. Like Rilke in the *Duino Elegies*, he names and celebrates the fundamental things, the simple things, of our world. Like that of Wordsworth, 'a man speaking to other men', his poetry incarnates what it means to be a human being—one who thinks life, who thinks death, who thinks art, who thinks thought. 'Contradiction is the fatality of the real,'

Bonnefoy writes in *Rimbaud par lui-même*. I no longer think there is a contradiction between poetry and concept in Bonnefoy's thought. I conclude by saying that his work is a two-track adventure in poetry and prose that has few equals since Baudelaire and Leopardi.

Guy Davenport and Rainer Maria Rilke

Here are two books by my occasional correspondent the late Guy Davenport: *Objects on a Table: Harmonious Disarray in Art and Literature* and *A Balthus Notebook*. The first is on still life, while the Balthus book is an engaging, learned and witty meditation on this painter beloved of many writers and poets, including myself. Davenport throws off a thousand *amuse-geules* for thought: 'Roland Barthes might have been one of Gide's sensitive adolescents.' The book is a template for the kind of book I would like to write on this writer or that painter, but to talk about future texts is in some way to contaminate the ludic and oneiric modalities of desire, whose free-flowing interplay is the *sine qua non* of creative beginnings, and so hush little baby, don't say a word, lest the diamond ring turn into brass. One unfortunate misprint would have amused its victim: *Molloy* is trans-sexualized into *Molly*. I particularly like Davenport's insistence, drawn from Montherlant, that influence is an integration of forces. Balthus could not be influenced by Vermeer if he was not also influenced by Colette and Emily Bronte. Davenport would have liked Jean Clair's crucial meta-meditation, *Les Métamorphoses d'Eros*, on Balthus' profound and wondrous translations of great predecessors into an idiom belonging to himself and his own times: Masaccio, Piero, Veneziano, Cranach, Sassetta, Lorenzetti, Bellini, Courbet.

I have underlined several passages in *Objects on a Table*, including a quotation from Walter Benjamin deeply germane to the room of books where I work: 'The interior [i.e. furnishings of a room] is not only the universe, but the case of the private individual. To inhabit means to leave traces.' I was pleased that Davenport, a singular and learned scholar poet, wrote me a letter praising a public lecture I gave, published as *Wine from Two Glasses*: I had sent it to him thinking or suspecting it would be of interest to him and hoping he would like it. It was and he did. Perhaps I was already a little on the old side to be making contact with a writer unknown to me personally. Never mind.

Davenport was a distinguished poet and fabulist and, above all, an essayist of great depth and range; it meant a lot to me to please him, and that's not a sin, or even a mistake. Guy Davenport, in some ways a cult writer *à la* Edward Dahlberg, was little known outside certain subcultures within the minority that reads serious literature, those overlapping circles in which we dance the light or not so light fantastic on the sidewalks of our mind, sometimes alone, sometimes with a real partner, sometimes with an imaginary one.

More on Balthus, aged fourteen, in Rilke's *Letters to Frau Gudi Nölke*: 'My little friend . . . with his . . . uncommonly adaptable capacities, especially as he has long been used to testing them in life-size emergencies. His considerable artistic talent, which, like his mother's, though of a different nature, is always essentially and uninterruptedly productive, might contribute something too, if not by teaching in the literal sense, at least by stimulating activity and observation among the young people.'

William Carlos Williams and Wallace Stevens

Here is the Loeb edition containing the *Ars Poetica* of Horace. *Ut pictura poesis*: I dread to think how many bad poems have been perpetrated by those followers of William Carlos Williams who, sometimes or regularly, make paintings in words without the supreme word painter's deep reading of modernist visual art allied to his pitch-perfect ear for apparently unmediated ekphrastic writing. (R. S. Thomas got it right in *Ingrowing Thoughts*.) According to Bram Dijkstra in *Cubism, Stieglitz and the Early Poetry of William Carlos Williams*, Marianne Moore and Wallace Stevens 'expressed an initial desire to become painters, and painting obviously had an important influence on their work', but they are far more literary as poets than Williams, and none the worse for that, it has to be said. How I wish I could have attended an exhibition at Stieglitz's gallery 291 (291, 5th Avenue) and not only because I might have met the owner's wife, Georgia O'Keefe. Stevens in *Opus Posthumous* makes the Horatian assertion that 'to a large extent, the problems of poets are the problems of painters, and poets must often turn to the literature of painting for a discussion of their own problems.' There is some truth in this, all the more so because you cannot confidently reverse the proposition, not a bad test of that kind of comment. What Stevens does not say is that much of this literature is written by poets, sometimes to the amusement, sometimes to the irritation of painters, some of whom cannot be doing with literary readings of their work.

The remark takes on a different gloss when one looks at his essay on 'The Relations between Poetry and Painting' in *The Necessary Angel*, a book on 'reality and the imagination' which I first read forty years ago. Near the beginning of the essay, Stevens broadens or narrows his point to refer to what painters themselves have said. Thus: 'Does not the saying of Picasso that a painting is a horde of destructions also say that the poem is a horde of destructions?' And 'When Braque says "The senses deform, the mind forms", he is speaking to poet, painter, musician and sculptor.' I spoke too soon about the testing of a comment by reversing the proposition, for Stevens goes on to write the following sentence which today dismays me: 'Just as poets can be affected by the sayings of painters, so can painters be affected by the sayings of poets and so can both be affected by sayings addressed to neither.' Oh dear, this from one of the three or four greatest English-language poets of the twentieth century. He famously wrote that 'the poem must resist the intelligence / almost successfully'. The problem with the sentence quoted is that it resists his undoubted intelligence entirely successfully. He is playing at being a plain man, a businessman poet fallen among scholars. But he is not a plain man. When I discussed this issue with Alan Wall, he commented that it wasn't fair to argue against the worst essay Stevens ever wrote. He had a point when he went on to hint that I was aggrandizing myself vis-à-vis Stevens. But that's what comes of reading one's own past via vistas observed on the byways of a writer like Stevens. Mine is a classic professional deformation of the attendant lord at the court of the great, but not a hanging offence.

John Taggart

John Taggart, epistolary friend and ace poet (see, for example, *Pastorelles*), has written what he calls 'ant meditations on a painting by Edward Hopper', that iconic late work (1961) 'A Woman in the Sun'. The meditations form an entire book, *Remaining in Light*. It strikes one like a double dream of summer. The book is a reading of this wondrous painting about an exposed and tragic woman in what Taggart calls 'afflicting light', afflicting light in what he calls her 'recurrent circle', which is almost Claude Royet-Journoud's 'Cercle nombreux', my own 'manifold circle'. At the same time, the book is a reading of the process of reading, which summons into the witness box Deleuze and Derrida, Jabès and Emerson. If, as Taggart says, the figure is a prostitute, then a question I used to ask myself (has she just got out of bed or is she about to get into it?) does not apply. We can say that there is a story in the picture, unusual in paintings where there is only one figure. As Paula says, Bacon almost always has only one figure in order to avoid a psycho-narrative.

Anthony Rudolf

The Poetry of Solitude: A Tribute to Edward Hopper is an anthology of poems collected by a senior Hopper scholar Gail Levin. Hopper (see Levin's *Hopper's Places* and Lloyd Goodrich's enormous book, *Edward Hopper*) is one of the painters most generative of poems and other writings by poets, along with Balthus and Morandi. Why should these particular painters trigger the adrenalin or whatever it is that flows from the retina via the pineal eye to the inner eye, which is the bliss of composition, but for eye read also ear? It must have to do with the element of time in their work, as translated into space: we sense a before and an after, a temporal elsewhere that tempts interpretation. There is also a quality of dream, which demands reactivity in the onlooker or inlooker whose time-space is translated into the space-time of the poet's *imaginaire*, which the meditations of his heart convey via the words of his mouth. The last line of John Hollander's poem on Hopper's 'Seven a.m.' is a gloss on the high-flown riff just played: 'Meaning is up for grabs, but not for sale.' My own poem in the book faces the 1932 picture 'Dauphinée House': I no longer remember if I suggested it to Levin or if she chose it, with or without consultation. I seem to recall that I had more than one painting in mind.

> Objectivists are metaphysical.
> Over against the stillness of the house
> what is not still need not be on the move.
> And yet, upon my word, the absence moves
> to the presence, by the railroad, of the house.

Reality, no way into this house
that is nothing but a structure of his mind
painted alone because it was not there.

Paul Durcan

Paul Durcan's *Give Me Your Hand* contains poems inspired by paintings in the National Gallery, including Paula's 'Crivelli's Garden' (on permanent display in the Sainsbury Wing Brasserie), which has triggered the worst poem in the book because the persona narrator illustrating the only painting on the premises by a living painter does not benefit from the temporal slippage, the differential calculation, found in other poems. The story he tells already seems dated and trivial, a risk not taken by his strategy elsewhere in the book. The poems are introduced by Bryan Robertson, who begins with a quote from Jules Renard: 'I have a passion for the truth and for the fictions it authorises', a sentiment Jorge Semprun would applaud. I'm not sure what the sophisticated urban writers Robertson names would make of his sentence: '[Durcan] speaks with the autobiographical, circumstantial assurance of the sophisticated provincial, as in Joyce or in Beckett or in Svevo'. Robertson unintentionally comes across as an imperialist Londoner, a metropolitan snob. Dublin and Trieste for Joyce, Dublin, Paris and London for Beckett, Trieste and travels to other major European cities for Svevo: provincial? Even so, what's wrong with provincial if it produces a novel as beautiful and subtle as *As a Man Grows Older* or as sophisticated as *Confessions of Zeno*? Maybe Robertson, on a better day, would agree that the problem is not provincial but parochial: narrow-mindedness is found as much in London as anywhere else. Maybe, indeed, that is what he is trying to say.

LIVRES D'ARTISTES AND ILLUSTRATED BOOKS, ETC.

Stéphane Mallarmé/Édouard Manet

The association between poetry and painting has led to many beautiful books, inaugurated by Stéphane Mallarmé and Édouard Manet's remarkable prose and visual translation of Edgar Allan Poe's 'Raven' (originally a parrot!) in 1875, although, strictly speaking, it was preceded by a Manet/Charles Cros collaboration in 1874, reference Jean Khalfa: *The Dialogue between Painting and Poetry*. It was followed, a year later, by the collaboration on 'L'Après-midi d'un faune', which I discussed in the French section.

If you are Poe and your translators include Mallarmé and Baudelaire, you are likely to be taken seriously not only as a prose writer (which is right and proper) but also as a poet, and this accounts for your high reputation in France as a poet, even though this sometimes bemuses the Anglo-Saxon world. On my desk are Poe's *Poetical Works* and *Edgar Alan Poe* by Georges Walter, whom I met at a dinner in Anne Serre's tiny flat on rue Cardinal-Lemoine. 'King Oedipus has an eye too many perhaps': Walter quotes this troubling thought from Hölderlin's 'In Lovely Blueness', that extraordinary prose poem which, according to Michael Hamburger, might be by someone else. When I visited Kitaj in his Los Angeles house, I saw his complete collection of Manet's prints, including a signed original folio of 'The Raven'. Some years later, I went to the British Museum to study the catalogue *raisonné* of the prints in order to check out the etching 'states' of the two Baudelaire heads I own, one a wedding present from Jonathan Griffin. This was a good opportunity to take a look at the folio of 'Raven' lithographs. The Print Room's copy is signed by Sir Sidney Colvin, once Keeper of Prints and Drawings, and who therefore must have donated his copy, numbered 64, to the museum. I note that Mallarmé has signed it Stèphane Mallarmé, misspelling his own forename by using a grave instead of an acute accent. 'Ce n'est pas grave', I wrote in an email informing Bonnefoy about the misspelling: common enough, he replied, when one is writing quickly and automatically. In *Poésie et photographie*, Bonnefoy alludes to Poe's 'great poem' whose 'resonance can be explained in part, I'm convinced of this, by the transcription into words of the effect of photographic imagery'. If so, this may be the first example in literature. A final word on Poe's raven: the word echoes 'never' in the refrain 'Nevermore'. A sonority to relish.

After his day job teaching English at the Lycée Condorcet, Mallarmé would regularly visit Manet in his studio. If modern art, as Gaëtan Picon says, was inaugurated by Manet rather than by Cézanne ('the first modern painter' is the predictable subtitle of Michel Hoog's *Cézanne*) or Van Gogh (Simon Sciama's view in his disappointing TV series on artists), then it is no accident that Manet was in on the beginning of the *livre d'artiste*. This most remarkable of the 'painters of modern life' (the Goncourts awarded the Palm to Degas) was a friend of Gautier and Zola (whose fictional work was more complex and inward than the theoretical naturalism he promulgated), but it was the close links with Baudelaire and Mallarmé that helped set the scene for the radical formalism of a very great painter, whose canvases are more 'self-expressive', in my view, than any previous painter's.

Alexander Blok

Les Douze is a facsimile reproduction (plus added French translation) of the original edition of Alexander Blok's great poem in the orthography and typography of the era; the poem was accompanied by the drawings of Georges Annenkov, artist and court photographer to the czars and, briefly, of the Bolsheviks. This was an illustrated book rather than a *livre d'artiste*. However, according to Blok, Annenkov's drawings were 'a parallel graphic text, a drawn twin brother'. The book was launched in 1919 with a recital by an actor from Stanislavsky's troupe and a magic lantern projection of the drawings, specially coloured by the artist for the occasion. Annenkov, whom I met thanks to an introduction from Miron Grindea, gave me a copy of the book when I visited him in his Montparnasse apartment, 31 bis rue Campagne-Première, in 1970, a few doors from Chez Rosalie, the restaurant where Modigliani offered drawings in exchange for lunches. On the same street, according to a plaque, Breton, Duchamp, Rilke, Picabia, Kisling, Man Ray, Satie, Tzara, Mayakovsky, Aragon, Elsa Triolet and Kiki of Montparnasse lived in the Hotel Istria, now a shell of the original building. Close by was a building, now demolished, where Rimbaud lived with Verlaine, who evoked this phase of their life in 'Le Poète et sa muse' and 'Vers pour être calomnié'. Annenkov showed me a famous photograph of the Bolsheviks he himself had taken. It was later airbrushed by Stalin to remove all traces of Trotsky.

I stared at the title page of *Les Douze*—nearly a century on still an explosive poem—for ten minutes, wondering why there was Hebrew written on it and the credit line to the translator crossed out, and indeed why there were marks by the same hand throughout the book. At last I remembered: I had shown it to my dear friend the poet Avraham Shlonsky on one of his visits from Tel Aviv, around 1972. He was excited and asked to borrow it in order to produce a new facsimile edition, replacing the French with his own Hebrew translation. Shlonsky, the great poet-translator of his generation, even translated *Hamlet* from the German of Schlegel and Tieck *and*, at the same time, the Russian of Pasternak. According to T. Carmi (himself a poet and master translator), Shlonsky intuited what the English must have been. I have many memories of Shlonsky, but this particular one would not have come to mind without *Les Douze* pulling the trigger. He later sent me his edition. I recall the first evening of my first visit to Israel, in 1969. I attended his family Passover *seder* in Gordon Street, Tel Aviv. He conducted the readings from the secular, indeed atheist, Haggadah he himself had edited for the left-wing Kibbutz Artzi movement. On the wall above the armchair I sat in (where Sartre had sat) was a Fernand Léger painting.

Skira

The theme of Skira's beautifully printed series, Les Sentiers de la Création, as its name suggests, was the process of creation. When Gaëtan Picon took over as editor he commissioned a number of critically important books on literature and art, including Paz's *Le Singe grammarien* and Bonnefoy's *L'Arrière-pays*. Books by Picon himself are among the titles: the admirable *Admirable tremblement du temps*, *Paris 1863* and *La Chute d'Icare*, a short book on Picasso's gouaches and drawings for his UNESCO mural in Paris. When I first read the Picasso book more than thirty years ago, I underlined something and I translate it now: 'Before the work [travail] on the work [*oeuvre*], there is a way of being—of which moreover the work is not necessarily the confirmation: those who dream of a work, but who—whether through impotence, inhibition or renunciation—do not end up making one are, in their relationship with existence, closer to creators than those who have never dreamed of a work.' This is a strange, moving, elliptical and seemingly autobiographical comment on the part of this pre-eminent literary and art critic. It led me to wonder whether Picon, for some years the senior civil servant at the Ministry of Culture set up by its first head, André Malraux, had ever published what he would have seen as primal work: fiction or poetry.

I asked Bonnefoy, an intimate of Picon, about this. He replied that I was not wrong about the autobiographical import of the quote. However, he pointed out that Picon had written two 'primal texts', fiction-meditations, *L'Oeuil double* and *Un Champ de solitude*. As it happens, these are the only two books by him that I have not read, and this shall be remedied. Yves also suggested that 'réalisateur' might be a better word than 'créateur', which is a problem for the shade of Picon, not for me. Bonnefoy's introduction to the English-language edition of *Paris 1863, The Birth of Modern Painting*, discusses Picon's transition from art and literary criticism to personal creation (or realization) as well as his reasons for focusing on Manet as the true begetter of modern art. In an interview, Picon hints at mixed feelings about certain later developments: 'Time is for me the very space of art. All that I think, all that I feel, all that I love is dominated by the theme of time, not the juxtaposed structures of space.' Plenty of time in (and worth spending on) his first-rate literary criticism: *Lecture de Proust* and the two volumes of *L'Usage de la lecture*. Picon signed my copies at a hotel in South Kensington during our only meeting, when he visited London with his wife Genevieve.

Patrick Caulfield

I wish I could afford to buy the superb screen prints of Jules Larforgue poems by Patrick Caulfield, a wondrous artist whose funeral in Highgate cemetery we attended a few years ago: a traditional jazz band and five speakers by the graveside did the honours. Caulfield's first wife is a devout Catholic, his second wife, the painter Janet Nathan, a secular Jewess. He himself was a deeply lapsed Catholic, and his funeral wishes were respected. His final painting on show in Waddingtons was a powerful and affecting image of doors (to the other side, surely) within a classic Caulfield setting. On the wall in his flat, where everyone repaired after the funeral, was the tender and heartrending goodbye painting he made for Janet. According to one obituary, Caulfield suggested that his epitaph should read 'dead, of course'. What do I want when my time comes? As a non-believer but one for whom the God I do not believe in is Celan's 'Niemand' ('Praised be your name. No one'), that is, the God of Judaism, I should start thinking about these matters. Paula wants Amalia Rodrigues played at her funeral, which will be a Catholic religious service.

ART CRITICISM

Edgar Degas/Gustave Courbet

Max J. Friedländer's *Reminiscences and Reflections* is a collection of the kind of fragments I enjoy reading. He includes a quote by top fragmentarian Paul Valéry although it is 'probably' by Edgar Degas himself: 'There is a great difference between seeing a thing without a pencil in one's hand, and seeing it while drawing.' Compare Porbus in *The Unknown Masterpiece*—'Painters should only meditate brush in hand'—and Wittgenstein's remark about the eye and the hand, both discussed on other pages in the present work. Figurative art done from life is truly a strange and wondrous process. There is a sense in which it is like translation. The translated poem only exists 'courtesy' of an original poem and is generally considered to be a lesser thing, unless it is a free translation done by a major poet, whereas a portrait is expected to be a good likeness. A painting, however, is not a photograph or, rather, a painting is not a mirror. Also, what is meant by a likeness when it comes to poetry translation is a matter of great complexity: we enter the territory of representations, recreations of the original. Note the word 'recreations'. Recreation is another word for play. The translation must play even as it works for us. It must *re*-present rather than represent. A figurative painting (e.g. Gustave Courbet's 'Origin of the World') only exists courtesy of the model's agreement to pose for a great painter (one of the themes of Henry James' story 'The Real Thing'), and yet it transfigures the original (probably Whistler's lover, Jo). No longer three-dimensional, it moves from our eye into our brain, where our mind processes an image of an image amidst cultural, biological and personal assumptions about nakedness and possession.

Marc Chagall

My well-thumbed *Chagall* by Jean Cassou contains a postcard of a Song of Songs painting which the artist signed for me when Brenda and I, on holiday in Saint-Paul de Vence in 1973, visited the painter and his wife, thanks to an introduction from Miron Grindea. After tea, Marc Chagall stood up. I stared at a small Bonnard by the front door until, smiling, the painter put his hand on my arm and ushered us out. When Jonathan Wilson told me he was writing a book on Chagall, I mentioned the incident to him and he became excited: he had heard that Chagall hung his own paintings on his walls, and nobody else's. An advance flyer for the book is not wrong to claim that Chagall is the emblematic Jewish artist of the twentieth century, although one immediately tries to think of rivals: Jacob Epstein, Chaim Soutine, Amedeo Modigliani, Mark Rothko, Ben Shahn, Philip Guston, Adolph Gottlieb. More recently, Kitaj. No, even if Chagall is not greater than any or all of these, 'emblematic' belongs to him.

Jonathan Wilson's *Marc Chagall* has arrived. Even at my age, it is nice to see one's name in print. There I am, described as lingering by the door until I was 'gently moved on'. Chagall is ripe for reassessment now that the charge of sentimentalism associated with *Fiddler on the Roof* is old hat. Or rather, it is I who am ready to reassess Chagall, having too easily gone along with the prevailing winds. This excellent book enables the beginnings of a reassessment, though there is one egregious mistake which should be corrected in the next printing: Primo Levi's use of Dante has nothing to do with being 'chrétianisant' and everything to do with being Italian. On the subject of Jews and Christianity, Wilson makes a good case that the painter wanted to Judaize Christianity rather than, as some Jewish critics aver, Christianize Judaism. Wilson tells the story of the painter's time as a commissar in revolutionary Russia and how Kazimir Malevich betrayed him, and his complicated relationship with Israel. Discussing what we mean by Jewish painting, Wilson, in the context of Chagall's fellow Jewish artists like Soutine, Guston and Rothko, makes a simple and serious point: 'A Jewish hand at work with a Jewish consciousness guiding it may indeed produce Jewish painting but when Jewish subject matter is absent, it cannot promote anything other than highly speculative discussion.' Like Mike Heller, Jonathan Wilson regrets he did not make contact with Kitaj in good time, and now it is too late. I have the same regrets vis-à-vis Balthus, whom I was too timid to contact when in Rome despite having his phone number thanks to Bonnefoy.

Arshile Gorky/Joan Miro

The seven Penguin monographs I kept from my father's library include *Graham Sutherland* by Edward Sackville-West and *Edward Burra* by John

Rothenstein. All were published between 1943 and 1945. Edward Burra is a great favourite of Paula's and I have therefore paid him some attention in recent years but the revelation is Graham Sutherland, who was clearly an influence on Bacon and who deserves more attention than he has been getting in recent years. There is an astonishing power of expression and expression of power in the landscapes done during the war, even when not ostensibly on a war subject. Another favourite of Paula's is Arshile Gorky, who committed suicide in 1948 aged forty-three, after a studio fire, throat cancer, divorce and an automobile accident in which he broke his neck and his painting arm was paralysed. Harold Rosenberg's *Arshile Gorky* ends with André Breton's 'Farewell to Arshile Gorky', which contains the lines: 'You had nothing left / But to take for yourself the magical death of Gerard de Nerval'. Much as I admire Breton, that 'connoisseur of freedom' (Susan Sontag), I object to his use of the word 'magical' in the context of both suicides.

'A scholar of the invisible' is what Robert Bringhurst, in a remarkable book *Everywhere Being Is Dancing*, which Rowan Williams recommends to those who will listen, calls Miro. Gorky and Miro were undoubted influences on Paula at one stage. Here is James Johnson Sweeney's *Joan Miro*, where I learn that in 1926 Joan Miro and Max Ernst did the scenery for *Romeo and Juliette*, a ballet by Constant Lambert and Bronia Nijinska. The surrealist exhibition at the Victoria and Albert Museum revealed that Breton ('I seek the gold of time') and Picasso (later a millionaire) opposed this involvement by the two surrealists, on the grounds that they were selling out to commercialism, what would later be described by someone as 'the time of gold', when Breton's possessions were sold at auction, a crime which prompted a rare, possibly unique, public intervention (in *Le Monde*) by Bonnefoy.

Mark Gertler/David Bomberg

Mark Gertler was the exact contemporary of David Bomberg. They came from the same impoverished Polish Jewish background. Gertler grew up in Spitalfields, Bomberg in Whitechapel, both very close to where my maternal grandparents were living at the time. Mark Gertler, John Rodker and Isaac Rosenberg used to meet at David Bomberg's studio in Tenter Buildings. Bomberg's lost pencil drawing 'Head of a Poet' is reproduced in William

Lipke's monograph *David Bomberg*. Rosenberg appears softer and slightly fleshier than in his self-portraits. A great poet, he was not the equal (nor did he live long enough to approach the level) of Gertler and Bomberg as a visual artist, but how many other significant poets (or fiction writers) produced visual art, and vice versa? Cue for a game to be played with an appropriate interlocutor, Paul Buck, shortly.

Mark Gertler followed William Rothenstein in drawing congregants of the Machzike Hadas synagogue on the corner of Brick Lane and Fournier Street (formerly a Huguenot chapel, now a mosque) and, who knows, maybe my pious maternal grandfather, a member of this *shul*, was drawn by one of them. In 1954, Bomberg and his wife moved to one of my talismanic places, Ronda in Andalusia, talismanic for its association with Rilke, whose room at the Hotel Reina Victoria is now a small museum. The Bombergs attempted to set up a school of painting. It failed and David returned to England where he died, partly for want of recognition. Gertler eventually moved to a studio in Hampstead, which is now the workplace of David Hare, who brings the painter into his TV play, *Page Eight*. Gertler committed suicide in June 1939, demoralized because he could not sell his pictures. I first saw his most famous and magnificent painting, 'The Merry-Go-Round', in the curator's office or hall of the old Ben-Uri Gallery above the Dean Street synagogue in Soho, where it was impossible to stand at an appropriate distance to appreciate the picture properly. Later, in order to survive, the Ben-Uri had to sell it to the Tate Gallery. Jonathan Wilson has written a thrilling novel, *A Palestine Affair*, inspired by Bomberg's time in Jerusalem. As in his earlier novel *The Hiding Room*, Wilson's themes are secrecy, betrayal and love, and the way political responsibility impacts on private life. The main character of *The Hiding Room*, Archie Rawlins, is based on the poet Keith Douglas, who had an affair with a Jewish woman in Cairo during World War II and later died in Normandy. Wilson has drawn on Douglas' memoir of the Western Desert, *Alamein to Zem Zem*, as well as his poems.

Self-Education

I continued my self-education in the visual arts when I was a student at Cambridge—after kick-starting it in Paris—by visiting the Fitzwilliam and

Kettle's Yard, where I talked on more than one occasion to its legendary founding creator, Jim Ede. I read four books. These (predictably enough?) were E. H. Gombrich's *The Story of Art*, Kenneth Clark's *Landscape into Art*, Herbert Read's *The Meaning of Art* and Ernst Fischer's Marxist analysis, *The Necessity of Art*. After nearly half a century, I still see myself in my Trinity garret room, K staircase New Court, lying on my narrow bed, reading Herbert Read. There is annotational evidence that, after Gombrich, I read one of the other three books in each of my three undergraduate years, although I must have been reading the Clark book during a summer vacation since on page 146—where he is discussing the use made by Picasso and Braque of Cézanne's remark about 'sphere, cone and cylinder'—I have written: 'Braque died today. 1.9.63', Braque, of whose flower paintings Giacometti wrote: 'It is not the flowers, it is we and the paintings that are the most fragile. The flowers, they continue to grow impassively and their darkness is not our darkness.' Later that month I celebrated my twenty-first birthday by taking some friends, doubtless at my father's expense, to a Chinese restaurant, probably the China Garden on Brewer Street. The past, as Stendhal says, is a faded fresco. However, I remember two presents: Nicky Strauss, now a barrister and part-time judge, gave me Sir Richard Burton's *Kama Sutra* and a condom. Patricia Hammerson gave me a silver propelling pencil engraved with my name, which survived until it dropped out of my pocket on the campus of Warwick University more than thirty years later, on the day when I was delivering my son, about to embark on his law studies.

Another book for the self-educator was Kenneth Clark's *Civilisation*, based on the TV series and perhaps the first book of its kind. It contains a paeon of praise to Urbino, described as one of the high points of civilization: 'One may not like courts, but at a certain stage it is only in a court that a man may do something extravagant for its own sake, because he wants to, because it seems to him worth doing.' This overstates the point. Think of the Marquis de Sade in gaol, or of Abelard or Jesus. Perhaps they created their own courts. The atmosphere in Urbino, generated by architecture and paintings, gave us much to reflect on when Paula and I drove there, some years after Euan Uglow and Natalie Dower made the same journey on a motorbike: we were on the Piero della Francesca trail (Piero was Euan's great hero), with me as lead enthusiast.

Paula was well pleased when our host in Arezzo Howard Caygill took us to a painting by the great mannerist, Rocco Fiorentino.

VISUAL AND VERBAL

Picasso

Walter Sorell's *Three Women*, comprising studies of Alma Mahler-Werfel, Gertrude Stein and Lou Andreas-Salomé, quotes Gertrude Stein as saying after reading Picasso's poems, 'Pablo, go home and paint' and quotes a passage from *Everybody's Autobiography*, which targets Jean Cocteau too: 'You see I said continuing to Pablo you can't stand looking at Cocteau's drawings, it does something to you, they are more offensive than drawings that are just bad drawings now that's the way it is with your poetry it is more offensive than just bad poetry . . . Words annoy you more than they do anything else so how can you write you know better.'

Paul Buck/Anthony Rudolf list

The first list comprises writers who were also visual artists: Victor Hugo, Henri Michaux, Hans Christian Andersen, Gunter Grass, Mario Cesarini, Antonin Artaud, Jean Cocteau, Bruno Schultz, August Strindberg, William Blake, Isaac Rosenberg, Wyndham Lewis.

The second list comprises visual artists who were also writers: Michelangelo, Picasso, Giacometti, Magritte, Bellmer, Masson, Klossowski, Kitaj, Klee, Arp, Schwitters.

Henri Michaux

Here is Malcolm Bowie's study *Henri Michaux*, the first of a truly distinguished series of books by a writer who was also a scholar of French literature and of psychoanalysis, and who was cut short by an early death. I miss him keenly and always enjoyed our rare meetings in London, Oxford or Cambridge. Bowie sets up a polar opposition between Valéry, who trusted language, and Artaud, who didn't (*mutatis mutandis* Levi and Celan), whereas Michaux moves restlessly between the two poles: 'the poem is possible, but only just possible.' Henri Michaux is on Paula's radar as he too was a visual artist, a gestural artist, to whom Victor Willing had paid attention in the old days. Painting, to Michaux's relief, meant the disappearance of 'the word factory, the speech appetite'. His drawings turn their back on the verbal. They liberate. From my own humble point of view, this is why I like to write about painting; literary criticism, on the other hand, is, in Paz's phrase, a net made of words with which we fish for words.

William Blake

The writer/artist 'opposition' does not work when it comes to conceptual art: from Duchamp to the most brilliant modern practitioners, Susan Hiller and Sophie Calle, the distinction between verbal and visual loses its meaning in the sense implied by the list above. When I first told Paula about the game, she mentioned Wyndham Lewis. Good idea, I said, I'll add his name to the first list. But he belongs in the second list, was her reply. The difference between us may reflect her lack of knowledge of his books or my lack of knowledge of his paintings. As for William Blake, who did not come up in our conversation, Paula (a) has a higher regard (in the literal sense, deeper regard?) for his visual work than I do, and (b) also knows his writings. As elsewhere in this book, just when I am getting ready to move on, a new book arrives on the topic I am about to quit, in this instance a present from Paula, Donald Friedman's handsome book *The Writer's Brush*, which is supposed to be about my first list, that is, writers who are also visual artists. Most of my writers are in his book, including Wyndham Lewis . . . I shall have to leave for another time, if ever, a consideration of the relative quality of the visual art of the writers he includes and its relationship, if any, to their writing. Some, visually speaking, are major figures like Hugo and Schulz, others minor figures such as Rimbaud and Dostoevsky. The book could have been subtitled *Second String on Ingres' Violin*.

Art Spiegelman

Art Spiegelman's *Maus* was a fiftieth-birthday present from my former chief babysitter Amber Jacobs, now a lecturer at Birkbeck College and author of a learned and difficult book *On Matricide: Myth, Psychoanalysis, and the Law of the Mother*. *Maus* is an amazing work of art, in the tradition of Will Eisner, whose early works must have influenced Spiegelman. A phone call to Clive Sinclair confirms this view, although he does not recall Spiegelman ever saying so. However, Sinclair does recall that Jules Feiffer and Robert Crumb have expressed indebtedness to Will Eisner, whose final comic strip I have here, *The Plot*, which is his account of that infamous forgery, *The Protocols of the Elders of Zion*. Suddenly I am reminded of Raymond Briggs, a favourite of ours when the children were young, and of Posy Simmonds, who is strictly for the grown-ups. Paula and I went to the ICA for a mutual interview between Phillip Pullman and Art Spiegelman, she rooting for PP and I for Art, and both of us were right, and both of us were wrong. Paula loves those old troupers Tintin and Bécassine, the latter a strong presence in her childhood.

Thomas A. Clark and Richard Long

Thomas A. Clark and Richard Long too belong round, if not in, this territory. In *Poets Poems*, Clark—a poet inhabiting a parallel universe but with intriguing affinities to that brilliant and singular artist, the sculptor and photographer Richard Long—includes work by, among others, Gary Snyder, Ian Hamilton Finlay and Lorine Niedecker. The names of Long and these particular poets give some sense of Clark's environment as found in small and beautiful books from his own Moschatel Press, with poems by him and drawings by Laurie Clark: *A Meadow Voyage* and *Pauses and Digressions*. Here too is a bigger and more easily obtainable book, *The Path to the Sea*. Clark's work is quieter than that of Long, a more forceful character: as types, Long is a sailor, Clark a farmer. Clark too walks, but in his case the walk generates art that is predominantly verbal, whereas Long's art is predominantly visual, almost abstract. Samuel Palmer rather than William Blake is an inspiration underlying Clark's Romantic work. The notation is exquisite without being precious, and also suggests a slower rhythm than that of Long, whose 'blessed rage for order' (Stevens) springs eternal. 'Solvitur ambulando': it is solved by walking. Long, as he once said, measures the world when he walks and, I would add, takes the measure of himself as an extraordinary everyman whose interventions in nature end up untraceable, save for the traces he keeps in photographs and diagrams. Unlike Paul Klee, he does not take the line for a walk; rather he takes the walk for a line.

485

Neither Clark nor Long engages in conversation while walking: such conversations always move me—Paz and Breton strolling through Les Halles one night, for example. 'Surrealism [is] the sacred malady of the world,' said the Mexican poet to his mentor. I finally tracked down this quote to the beautiful and moving essay on Breton in Paz's *Alternating Current* (a book I remember reading at University College Hospital during a hot August night in 1976 while waiting for my daughter Naomi to be born, she still is a night bird), after asking Eliot Weinberger, who in turn asked Breton's former secretary, Monique Wong Furst, who found a French version on the Internet.

Dada and surrealism

Dada, like any manifestation of radical subversion outside its historical context, can be tiresome; nonetheless, some of the short sharp digs in a book like Henri Béhar's *Dada en verve* survive the decades and the changed world, a world changed partly by surrealism, of which Dada, influenced by Lautréamont, Rimbaud, Russian nihilism and so on, was a forerunner, left behind when Dali, Duchamp, Breton and others moved on—onwards and inwards. There is much punning by Marcel Duchamp and Robert Desnos, some efforts by Tristan Tzara (although he is at his best not in short fragments but in that amazing long poem 'L'Homme approximatif', translated by Lee Harwood, a fine poet, in *Chansons Dada*) and several entertaining pieces by the painter Francis Picabia, obsessed by the third, or perhaps the fourth, eye, depending on whether you include *l'anus solaire* among the eyes and/or whether you are as scatologically inclined as he is: 'Don't hide your secrets in your arse, everyone will get to know about them' and 'those who speak behind my back, my arsehole is watching them' and 'knowledge and morality are nothing but flypaper, I advise the flies to live in the confessionals, sins being a more pleasant form of nourishment than shit.'

I have fond memories of a playful, crazy and difficult epic novel with an exotic title, each long chapter consisting of one paragraph. I bought *Grabinoulor* by Pierre Albert-Birot in 1964, when its abridged version was published. On its first appearance, in 1919, it was championed by Guillaume Apollinaire, Max Jacob and Louis-Ferdinand Céline. According

486

to Jacob's blurb, Albert-Birot was chatting with the poet about his concept, 'surnaturalism': 'it's the wrong word.' All right, said Apollinaire, let's change it to 'surrealism'. (He may also have known that Nerval uses the word 'supernaturalism' with respect to dreams.) According to James Williams' *Cocteau*, however, Apollinaire coined the word for *Parade*, which Cocteau created for Diaghilev and the Ballets Russes in 1917, with sets by Picasso and music by Satie. On the other hand, Jonathan Wilson, in *Marc Chagall*, tells us that Apollinaire coined the word (again in 1917) after seeing the painter's 'Hommage to Apollinaire'. Peter Cook has a wonderful surrealist sketch (which I found on YouTube) about the stone-age man who invented the bandambladastiddle: he had much less success than his neighbour, whose identical invention was called the wheel. What fun, therefore, to find in Mark Ford's essay on Breton in *A Driftwood Altar* that, one month later, Apollinaire subtitled his own play, *Les Mamelles de Tirésias*, 'a surrealist drama' and offered this explanation of the term: 'when man tried to imitate walking he created the wheel, which does not resemble a leg. He then performed an act of surrealism without realising it.'

How shaming it is to pick up French books with uncut pages, proof positive that, along one flowchart, enough unfulfilled good intentions amount to an afterlife destiny: residence in a windowless pied-à-terre on a cul-de-sac in the circle of hell reserved for lazy readers. All the same, one recalls gloriously happy moments when intention, desire, will, energy, time, hope and performance were lined up in a row and, paper knife at the ready, one embarked on the journey along the cutting edge of that unbroken hymen: the beginning of a new French book. My unreading of Alain Jouffroy's oneiric surrealist novel *Un Rêve plus long que la nuit* lives up to its haunting epigraph, apparently a Jewish saying, from which he took his title: 'You can make your dream last longer than the night.' Ah, a reader's conscience is an addict, requiring ever increasing doses of willpower; *ultima ratio regum*: it would require an entire army projecting such power to enforce my reading, like Coleridge's companion, a superego incarnate, paid to use force (if necessary) to prevent the poet from entering the pharmacy for his opium.

Erotica/Eroticism

As Jorge Luis Borges might have said, the Marquis de Sade takes George Bataille to the extreme. Bataille's was the *other* surrealism; its world is darker and more disturbing than Breton's. Here are some books by Bataille including *Le Petit* and *Blue of Noon*, this last in Harry Matthews' translation. Open *Blue of Noon*, on this page Pierre Klossowski, on that page Alain Jouffroy's 'technician of the impossible', Hans Bellmer. I also have a few rude books, mainly French erotica. I met Dominique Aury and Jean Paulhan at the offices of the Nouvelle Revue française in the early 1970s. You could have knocked me down with a feather when I later discovered that *Histoire d'O* by Pauline Réage, prefaced by Paulhan, was written by Aury herself. I suppose I thought that only men wrote that kind of book (Paulhan had been rumoured to be the author), also she was in her early sixties when we met, and it didn't seem likely to someone half her age that this conventional looking 'old' woman could have experienced or even imagined the goings-on in *Histoire d'O*. That shows how little I knew about the human heart (and body) and/or the imagination. Forty years on, I like to think I know a thing or two—when you know something, as James Hogan likes to say, you know something else—and what goes on is nobody's business, at least not outside fiction. Here is a paperback containing both *The Exploits of a Young Don Juan* by Apollinaire and Aragon's *Irène*, originally *Le Con d'Irène*) translated and inscribed to me by Alexis Lykiard, who was a star at Cambridge when I was a speck of solar dust. Long ago Olwyn Hughes thought I should translate Aragon but nothing came of it.

Architecture

Daniel Libeskind and Julia Farrer

I have come late to an appreciation of architecture's thrilling intellectual possibilities as an applied art; this was partly thanks to dipping into the work of Charles Jencks after visiting the house I described earlier, but mainly to Daniel Libeskind, who has made the discipline sexy for me and who, in public at any rate, talks about it in a language I relish and understand. He is a cross-disciplinary artist, musician and intellectual, whose centre is architecture. I knew one of his buildings well, the graduate centre in London Metropolitan University, Holloway Road, where I taught undergraduates for three years in an ugly part of the non-campus. To point out that it is the most beautiful and impressive building in the four miles of Holloway Road is to say nothing, let me say only that it works as music in space and cries out to be implicated by future new buildings in the vicinity. It reminds me of Cubist and Constructivist shapes and projections, and has the nobility of Concorde or an old sailing ship. I sent the foregoing to the painter Julia Farrer, who lives close to Libeskind's building and who replied to my email with the learned advice that I read Deleuze's book *The Fold: Leibniz and the Baroque*, a constructivist approach to mathematics, art, architecture and music. I phoned her immediately, since I realized the implications of this concept for our or, more modestly, her *livre d'artiste Mandorla*: 'Pli selon pli', I said brightly. Libeskind would surely admire Paula's museum in Cascais, designed by another great architect, Eduardo Souto de Moura.

[Coda at proof stage: Kitaj had a major exhibition at the Libeskind-designed Jewish Museum in Berlin in 2013. It has arrived in the UK, divided between the Jewish Museum in London and Pallant House in Chichester. We attended the private view in London. The museum is in the same Camden Town street on which Paula lived for many years. Two other architects associated with Kitaj are Colin St John Wilson and his wife M. J. Long: they kept a diary (published as *Kitaj: The Architects*) of their experience of sitting for a portrait by Kitaj, a subject of particular interest to this fellow sitter.]

Photography

Death speaks to us in photographs of the dead, looks at us with their eyes.

—Roger Munier, *Requiem*

Introduction

Photography was on the agenda when Paula and I went to Edinburgh for

Ron Mueck's big show, since the show overlapped with a centenary exhibition of Cartier-Bresson. Earlier, I had translated Yves Bonnefoy's catalogue essay on the close relationship between Henri Cartier-Bresson and Alberto Giacometti for the Kunsthaus exhibition in Zurich. In this essay, and in his difficult book *Remarques sur le regard*, Bonnefoy draws a distinction between painters of the eye (Picasso) and painters of the gaze (Giacometti); I have discussed with Paula, Mark Hutchinson, Paul Coldwell and others what he means by this potent thought. Raymond Mason, for one, had trouble understanding it. Paula's interpretation is that some artists are consciously concerned about the act of looking, the gaze: Giacometti, Uglow and Morandi. Others are not: Picasso? Paula herself? I translated Jean Clair's essay on Cartier-Bresson for the Thames and Hudson catalogue of the Hayward Gallery exhibition, *Europeans*, though you have to take your curiosity and a microscope to the colophon page in order to learn that the essay was not written in English; translators are accustomed to this treatment.

The '[h]auteur' photographers such as Bill Brandt and Robert Doisneau, Robert Frank and Jacques-Henri Lartigue, as well as Henri Cartier-Bresson, are somewhere between performance artists and what used to be known as fine artists. When Cartier-Bresson retired from photography and returned to his first love, drawing, his friends Avigdor Arikha and Raymond Mason made clear to him that his drawings did not cut the mustard; perhaps only artists of their distinction had the right (as well as the chutzpah) to say this to such a distinguished figure (see Raymond's memoirs referred to earlier). Apparently Cartier-Bresson took it in good part. Paula has a higher opinion of his drawings than Arikha and Mason did. At the exhibition in Edinburgh, where we met Cartier-Bresson's widow, the photographer Martine Frank, Paula was, perhaps for the first time, moved by 'art' photography, and I could tell she was storing certain images up to draw (on) later, but she never uses photographs as a substitute for painting from life. There is at least one artist she admires who, she says, would make better pictures if they were painted from life rather than from photographs.

'There is no other place of which one can say with so much certainty that one has already been there': Freud on the mother's womb, quoted by Barthes, who knew better than most what this means. Carol Mavor's book

Reading Boyishly is a remarkable study of the links between mothers and sons as witnessed by Roland Barthes, J. M. Barrie, J.-H. Lartigue, Marcel Proust and Donald Winnicott. Even the acknowledgements pages, ending with an unexpected androgynous eroticism, attest to a singular writer, and one whose work is a far cry from your usual academic studies of literary memory. The marvellous photographer Lartigue, non-writer among writers, is only apparently the odd one out. Reading this book has involved a vertiginous journey. Thanking Mavor for the book—sent at the suggestion of a mutual friend, Marina Warner—and already feeling a kind of sibling affinity, I was minded to quote famous phrases from two Baudelaire poems: 'mon enfant ma soeur' and 'mon semblable mon frère'. Marina herself writes about photographs (Lewis Carroll's and Conan Doyle's and others) in her fascinating study of the contents and forms of fantasy and the imagination, *Phantasmagoria: Spirit Visions, Metaphor and Media into the Twenty-First Century*, with the authority and lucidity that characterize all her deservedly applauded cultural explorations.

Walker Evans and James Agee; André Kertész

One of the great 'photography' books, one of the great books period, is *Let Us Now Praise Famous Men* by James Agee and Walker Evans. Of all the books I read when I was young it must be in the top ten when it comes to my under-appreciating the literary quality of what, in this instance, I knew mainly as an exercise in compassionate and progressive documentary witness testimony from the worlds of John Steinbeck and Charles Reznikoff, of Mass Observation and the GPO/Crown Film Unit. Checking out the contents pages, looking at Evans' photographs, rereading several sections of the book and the later introduction by Evans to a masterpiece that sold only six hundred copies in the first edition, make me realize just how 'constructed' it is and how much more I would get out of it were I to reread the magnificent prose work in its entirety. It is no surprise that *Fortune* magazine, which originally commissioned Agee and Evans, turned them down: content and style were too much for them. It was, he says somewhere, 'a *book* only by necessity'. Its documentary impulse is powered and complicated by personal, existential need and desire. Yes, *Let Us Now Praise Famous Men*, with its implied vision of a world where people shall not be oppressed, goes into a short list of books to reread in toto before I die. *Unclassified* is a fascinating collection of Evans' unpublished photographs and writings, including postcards and newspaper clippings which anticipate the combination of visual and verbal that entered the mainstream as conceptual art well after he died in 1975.

I went to the Photographers' Gallery near Covent Garden to see a small exhibition, *Bound for Glory*, which included Walker Evans and Dorothea Lange. I then went on to the Barbican to see what I knew would be a wonderful exhibition of European photographers, *Guide in the Face of History*, including my French favourites: Eugène Atget, Robert Doisneau, George Brassai and André Kertész, the last two Hungarian-born. The exhibition contained two remarkable and brave Jewish photographers, working under the Nazi occupation: Henryk Ross in the Lodz ghetto and, new to me, Emmy Andriesse in Amsterdam. They gave a visual face to the verbal world of Anne Frank and Etty Hillesum. Kertész's book of highly evocative photographs, *On Reading*, reminds one that there is nothing, but nothing, so absorbing as the activity of reading, except perhaps sex; the self is at once fully engaged and fully taken over by the text, *nicht wahr* Ralph Waldo Emerson and Rosanna Warren, whose imagery is suggestive: 'To read is to take possession. But it is also to give oneself completely, if temporarily, to the keeping of another mind', thus Warren in *Fables of the Self*, a remarkable self-writing in the meta-guise rather than dis-guise of literary criticism. No film or painting or person works on one in this way.

Roland Barthes

Roland Barthes hated public photographs of himself, according to Alain Robbe-Grillet in *Why I Love Roland Barthes*, for 'photography belongs to the domain of death', which is fine if the photograph represents the child one was but not the adult one is. All the same, Barthes has written with deep insight and outsight on photography. His use and discussion of photographs in *Barthes par lui-même* and his concepts of *studium* and *punctum* in *La Chambre claire* have influenced the way many of us interpret these images written in light. Who can forget the photograph of a man on the eve of his execution? Forever alive (like the people in the photos taken by the Khmer

Rouge of their victims), he accuses reception, as the French say in another context. As W. J. T. Mitchell writes in an important book, *What Do Pictures Want?*: 'The *punctum* or wound left by a photograph always trumps its *studium*, the message or semiotic content that it discloses.' Italo Calvino, in *The Uses of Literature*, in an essay about his friend and the day of his funeral, discusses the two Barthes: 'the one who subordinated everything to the rigour of a method and the one whose only sure criterion was pleasure' and says each Barthes has his supporters. But this opposition has little mileage and Calvino only sets it up in order to tell us what we already know, namely that 'these two Barthes are really one,' as Robbe-Grillet clearly understands. What Calvino does not say is that the early death of this great writer (like that of the Italian writer himself, who did not live to complete the already essential *Six Memos for the Next Millennium*, with its reading of Balzac's *Unknown Masterpiece*) deprived us of wonderful works. But Barthes, who was hit by a car after lunch with President Mitterand at the Collège de France, was moving towards literature rather than meta-literature (if Robbe-Grillet would allow that description), whereas Calvino may have been moving in the other direction.

John Deakin

The first photography book to hand is by John Deakin. I found it in a charity shop a few months ago, along with some books on printing and etching I gave Paula. I know very little about Deakin save that he drank with Freud and Bacon in the Colony Room, where Paula met him on a couple of occasions, and belonged to a Soho set that included Henrietta Moraes and Paula's late husband Vic Willing. *Henrietta*, a Soho autobiography from a later period than Chaim Lewis' classic *A Soho Address*, contains Deakin's photograph of her posing in the nude and a photograph of a Bacon portrait done after a Deakin photograph, possibly the same one. The book also has a photograph of a Bacon triptych for which Henrietta posed, as well as a Freud nude of her on the cover. A brave book about the booze, it has bottle. Deakin was the mother of all drinkers. His *London Today*, published in 1949, is intriguing. Deakin loaded the dice when he loaded the camera. The photos seem to have been taken in mid-afternoon on a gloomy November day, with a mild London fog or smog in evidence. Big Ben, framed by some railings, is at twenty to three, and that could be the time in most if not all the pictures. The pictures play to the gallery. Very moody, very atmospheric, they have designs on us. The Albert Memorial is, unusually, captured from behind, with the Albert Hall a blob of grisaille. The man looking closely at the books in a Charing Cross Road shop window is wearing his trilby at a rakish angle and holding a cigarette. He has a ring on the little finger of his left hand and a bracelet watchstrap. Nowadays, a photography book called *London Today* would not show us Canada House, South Africa House, Australia House or the Roosevelt memorial in Grosvenor Square, all fully frontal. All Souls Langham Place, photographed from behind and framed by the entrance railings to the Langham Hotel, has not yet had its bombed steeple restored: this is still the immediate post-war period. Two photos, of barges on the river at Battersea and at Albert Bridge, are redolent of Jean Vigo's *L'Atalante*. The Prospect of Whitby, again, recalls French films of the 1940s. The view from the empty bar to the river is highly stylized, almost insistent that we adopt a melancholy mood. Despite the serious proximity of the photographs to my own way of envisaging cityscapes, something in me resists this book, partly because almost all the photos are of the West End, the City and Chelsea.

In general, I do not pore over books of London photographs. *Kafka's Prague*, where I have never been, yes: for me, Jiri Gruzha's book of photographs is an electrocardiogram of the history of the breaking heart, to use Adorno's wonderful phrase about Mahler's music. Austria–Hungary, here I come again. Deakin's best London photographs are his portraits. Had he done a book of Paris views, I would be more in tune with the mood music. For all my love of that city, I am not an insider there. My love of Paris sights and sites is mediated far more by art and cinema and literature and song and indeed photography than is my love of London. You can take me out of London, I can take myself out of London, but you cannot take London out of me. From the day I started at my school on Victoria Embankment at the age of eleven, I saw and knew and loved London with my own eyes—the spectacle was refracted through my spectacles—before I explored its complex beauty through the arts. The beauty of the world is deepened by the beauty of its representations.

The East End

Bill Fishman's *The Streets of East London*, with photographs by Nicholas Breach, has enormous resonance. A photograph of the Brune Street building, with the words 'Soup Kitchen for the Jewish Poor' and 5661–1902 (lunar and solar calendar dates) visible, is a reminder of the days when the community consisted mainly of poor immigrants. Some were economic migrants, like my grandfather Joseph Rudolf, others like my maternal grandmother Rebecca Winnick Rosenberg were mindful of recent pogroms in Bialystock. Little remains of 'my' East End today, but the house where my mother was born, 3 Wilkes Street, in the shadow of Christ Church Spitalfields, survives, as does, fifty yards away, the former Princelet Street synagogue, above which her older sister my aunt Fanny was born in what would later become known as Rodinsky's Room (see the postscript in the paperback edition of Iain Sinclair and Rachel Lichtenstein's marvellous counterpointed book, *Rodinsky's Room*). Paul Lindsay's *The Synagogues of London*, and *Memories of the Jewish East End*, edited by Aumie and Michael Shapiro, complement Bill Fishman's book. I could spend hours looking at these photos of the East End of my parents' childhood. Why?

> Quand tout renait à l'espérance,
> Et que l'hiver fuit loin de nous,
> Sous le beau ciel de notre France,
> Quand le soleil revient plus doux,
> Quand la nature est reverdie,
> Quand l'hirondelle est de retour,
> J'aime à revoir ma Normandie,
> C'est le pays qui m'a donné le jour.

> When everything's reborn in hope
> And winter flees so far away,
> Beneath the lovely sky of France,
> When the gentler sun returns
> And nature reverts to green,
> When the swallow's back again,
> Oh how I miss my Normandy,
> Where I first saw the light of day.

I still have the first stanza of this intensely patriotic song off by heart. We used to sing it during the annual Modern Languages Singsong at my school, led by one of the French teachers, Rocky Cornish, and I was always strangely moved by the last two lines, which I have deliberately over-translated. One can well imagine a resistance fighter from Normandy humming it during the night before his dawn execution or, after the last cigarette, singing it before being cut off in mid-sentence by a guillotine blade or bullet. East London was where I first saw the light of day, for my mother went back to the western borders of Hackney to have me, but it wasn't the East End proper and, what's more, I am far more sentimental about Bill Fishman's streets than my mother and father were. But I'm on Bill's side (although three of my four grandparents arrived here in the early 1900s during the years covered by his wonderful *East End Jewish Radicals 1875–1914* and *East End 1888*) and I enjoyed serving as amateur literary agent for his final book, *Into the Abyss*, a short study of George 'It was Christmas Day in the workhouse' Sims. One of the pleasures was 'persuading' Beryl Bainbridge to write a preface. Now that Fishman's first book *The Insurrectionists* has been reissued, everything by my old friend ('BA Wapping, failed') is in print.

John Berger and Bill Brandt

John Berger has written profound essays which embed photographs in the argument. They do not serve as illustrations; rather they enable the construction and conceptualization of an argument that is essentially an education of and appeal to our common humanity. One such is *The Seventh Man* with Jean Mohr's photographs: this book, distinctively designed by a master, Richard Hollis, explores the world of the migrant worker, the guest worker. Berger writes 'all photographs are a form of transport and an expression of absence' but, as he reminds us elsewhere, this depends partly on who is looking at it. In *Selected Essays and Articles* Berger writes that, unlike a movie or a painting, '*what [a photograph] shows invokes what is not shown*' (emphasis in the original). If I look at a photo of a loved one, for example my grandfather Joseph Rudolf, it is indeed an expression of absence. If I show it to you, who do not know him, it is an expression of presence. Absence, says Emily Dickinson, is condensed presence, so I shall gloss Berger by saying

496

that presence and absence are dialectically related, and that their synthesis can be an incarnation of memory in the form of a poem, or indeed photograph. However, Berger's narrative of photography does not apply to the kind of work in Peter Lacey's *The History of the Nude in Photography* where, for example, Bill Brandt's section contains highly stylized, virtually abstract images mediated by sculpture and painting as they hit the retina. Practically the only visual image not by Victor Burgin in his cool and subtle exploration, *Some Cities*, is Brandt's wondrous photo of chimneystacks and railway lines in Halifax. Burgin maintains a distance between himself and his material, unlike Berger. His cultural theory baggage is worn lightly but then he is a professor in the History of Consciousness, and this position surely enables the sharp focus that we might associate with both an acute visual sense and a post-Benjaminian dialectical praxis.

Berger's *Here Is Where We Meet*, a wondrous auto-fiction summoning up the ghosts of his dead, has a fine passage on the pathos involved in close relationships with older or old people, family and friends. The time comes when we too are older and then we are old and, as we pick our path through the vale of soul-making, we learn to recapitulate what the old taught us in the way we ourselves relate to the young (am I imagining that Rilke has a poem on this theme? If not, he should have). Most of us for most of our lives are older or younger than somebody we know. On the brink of seventy, I am at an age when one still has a fair number of elderly friends while simultaneously learning to be friends with younger people. Of course, one's oldest (in the other sense) friends are one's contemporaries, a cohort that ages together and shares its sorrows and joys and neurones, as Mary Rowan Robinson said to me. This is the phase when, if you are lucky, grandchildren enter the scene. It is a phase in the slow process of learning how to die, or at least how to accept death, owning your death in the Rilkean sense. The deaths of dear friends are so many practice runs for one's own, down the line. Being killed in your fifties by an aggressive cancer, like my dear friend the Canadian poet Dee September, which I mentioned earlier, is another matter.

Here is another beautiful book by Berger: *And Our Faces, My Heart, Brief as Photos*. It has a meditation on Caravaggio and moves from poetry to prose and back again in the manner of certain books by Claude Vigée. I have just bought Berger's new book, *Hold Everything Dear: Dispatches on Survival and Resistance*. Reader, whose books do you read the moment they arrive in the bookshops, that is in the remaining bookshops which stock the books we want to read? Berger is one of the few writers whom I honour in that way, by which I mean whose books honour me by demanding immediate involvement. His dispatch from Israel and its West Bank colony makes painful reading, although, with his political and emotional intelligence and aware he is in a minefield, he chooses his words so carefully that no Jewish defence organization could accuse him of anything untoward, except perhaps being wrong in his analysis and descriptions, so he will be ignored.

Cinema

All Mickey Mouse films are founded on the motif of leaving home
in order to learn what fear is.

—Walter Benjamin, fragment from *Mickey Mouse*

Introduction

I reviewed Robert Bresson's *Notes on the Cinematographer* (translated by Jonathan Griffin) for an early issue of *Time Out* about forty years ago. Bresson's self-command, 'Your imagination will aim less at events than at feelings, while wanting these latter to be as *documentary* as possible', maps the royal road, or a royal road, of artistic endeavour. I regret not having devoted more time to movies, and would still like, one day, to write an essay on the supreme masters who feed my *imaginaire*: Ingmar Bergman, Michael Powell and Emeric Pressburger, and the directors touched on below.

Paris: Jean Vigo, Jean Renoir, Jacques Tati, Louis Malle

1961: When I went to Paris for my gap year, as it wasn't known in those days, I was determined to educate myself in all the arts. My own master at last, I was able to attend the Cinemathèque in rue d'Ulm more regularly than I had attended the National Film Theatre in London when still at school. I bought, in Joseph Gibert's bookshop, two Que Sais-je books, the French equivalent of our Teach Yourself books: Henri Agel's *Esthétique du cinéma* and Lo Duca's *Technique du cinéma*. I also read a book about one of my early enthusiasms, Jean Mitry's *Eisenstein*. On a later visit to Paris, I bought Jean Collet's *Godard* and Edgar Morin's *Le Cinéma*, as well as the latter's study of mass culture, *L'Esprit du temps*. Morin (consulted about society, probably to his surprise, by Nicholas Sarkozy) famously christened Hollywood—either in this book or in *The Stars* (flipping through both, I can't find the phrase)—'the factory of dreams', a phrase that impresses me less today than it did at the time: do we not think, rather, that 'wish fulfilment' or 'fantasy' is the product of the factory? However, he is right to say in a sentence I underlined: 'The dialectic of actor and role can account for the star only if the concept of myth is applied.'

I bought a book in Paris in 1961 on Jean Vigo, whose *L'Atalante* is one of my all-time favourite films. There is no better comedy actor than Michel Simon, whether in *L'Atalante* or in Jean Renoir's *Boudu sauvé des eaux* or in the latter's completely crazy silent movie *Tire-au-flanc* (its mood is a conflation or synthesis of *Brief Encounter* and *Dad's Army*, only possible in French cinema), which Paula and I caught at the National Film Theatre during the Renoir season. We also went to Renoir's second talkie *La Nuit du carrefour*, praised by Jean-Luc Godard in extravagant terms: Godard being Paula's least favourite director, I did not intend to reveal this till after the film lest she cry off, but finally I confessed and was rewarded with a version of the expressive face that tells me I have pulled a fast one. As for the film, it is a curiosity, overpraised by Godard in the sense that *Tire-au-flanc* is the film that leads more organically to the director's masterpieces. Paul Buck tells me that Godard greatly admires Jacques Tati, this after I told him we had watched *Mon oncle* for the first time in forty years and how struck I was by the beauty and sophistication of the film, its hyper-choreographed, hyper-constructed shots and takes throughout. The same goes for *Les Vacances de Monsieur Hulot*, although it is not as good as *Mon oncle*. I haven't yet read a monograph on the great director of *Lacombe Lucien* and *Au revoir, les enfants*, but Louis Malle is one of the few directors, along with Robert Bresson and Claude Lanzmann, I would have entrusted with filming my cousin Jerzyk's diary, *I'm Not Even a Grown-Up*. Andrzej Wajda too, but he has retired from filmmaking.

Luis Buñuel

Here is *My Last Sigh*, the ghostwritten autobiography of Luis Buñuel, who has a central place in my university contemporary Ruth Brandon's *Surreal Lives*, to which I contributed one or two minor research leads. It is just as well Ruth included a chapter on Buñuel, since Paula said that the book would be worthless if it ignored her favourite director, the greatest surrealist of them all. The book is a joy to read because the characters form a constellation as brilliant as the cast of Linda Kelly's *The Young Romantics*. On my desk I also have Gwynne Edwards' *The Discreet Art of Luis Buñuel* as well as the director's selected writings, *An Unspeakable Betrayal*. Surely we are not surprised that the director's film reviews are more interesting than his strictly literary pieces: here he is, talking about Carl Dreyer's *Joan of Arc*, one of my desert island films and one that I saw long ago in my teenage autodidact days of movies and plays and saw again with Susannah York, at the Mermaid, around 1985: 'and the humanity of the Maid of Orleans spills forth from this work . . . we all wanted to give her a little thrashing just to be able to hand her a sweet right after . . . We have kept one of her tears . . . a drop from the purest spring.' It comes as no surprise to find him quoted somewhere as saying: 'sex without sin is like an egg without salt.'

Gérard Philipe

Anne Philipe wrote a beautiful book about her husband Gérard Philipe. *Le Temps d'un soupir* is a memoir of their love and his death at the age of thirty-seven from liver cancer. As soon as I picked it up, I remembered I had translated a passage which began: 'Now all I have are ashes and a dream', but the translation is nowhere to be found. Here is the passage, the only one in the whole book with a pencil mark beside it, retranslated after nearly fifty years: 'Now all I have are ashes and a dream. Whatever was steals away and I discover how that famous idealisation is born, that complaisant memory which little by little schematises truth and takes its place, that treason all the more natural given that presence is no longer there to contradict the pleasant image which forms in the mind.' I begin a list of Gérard's films: *Le Diable au corps*, *Les Liaisons dangereuses* . . . a memory list which, like a London underground escalator, leads me to the green paradise, if not of childhood loves, then of my early twenties. 'The pleasures of our youth reproduced by our memory resemble ruins seen by the light of a flame,' wrote Chateaubriand in his *Pensées*. Anne Philipe died in 1990, the author of several books, including, unexpectedly, a lengthy interview with Seferis, published in Greek.

Susannah York

Susannah York has died. I introduced her to another dear friend, the poet Inge Elsa Laird, at a private view of Paula's work in the Marlborough some years ago. Susannah and Inge were born within a fortnight of each other in 1939 and died within a fortnight of each other in January 2011. David Shipman's *The Great Movie Stars* ends with York. I never gave up hope of seeing her again on the big screen, perhaps in something by one of her and my great favourites, Tennessee Williams. During her post-movie era, I, like other friends, travelled the country to see her in plays (sometimes directed by herself), a rare intelligence disguised as enchantment. One of her favourite roles was the telephone monologue in Jean Cocteau's one-act play, *La Voix humaine*. I don't think an actress has ever played it accompanied by Francis Poulenc's music, originally written for a singer. I plotted with myself to encourage David Hare to direct it—too late.

Joe Queenan and Nick Willing

Joe Queenan, writing on Melanie Griffith in *If You're Talking to Me Your Career Must Be in Trouble*, is full of insight into the way people conflate the kind of parts a star plays with the inner reality of their life, guilt by association in either direction. 'Because she has been married twice to Don Johnson, who has never been mistaken for Soren Kierkegaard, there is a natural propensity on the part of the press to mistake her for a dim bulb.' His ferocious and funny essay on accents takes a swipe at many truly awful attempts to speak broken English in movies, with Cher's Italian accent in *Moonstruck* 'every bit as odious as Olivier's Jewish accent in [the remake of the remake of] *The Jazz Singer*'. Among Olivier's accent rivals is 'the widow Olivier. Oh to have been a fly on the wall when these two meatballs were in the shower at home practising their bad accents together.'

Paula's brilliant film director son Nick Willing (whose new Jackanory was a great hit on television and whose *Tin Man*, a version of *The Wizard of Oz*, has broken all records on the Sci Fi channels) gave me the anthology *Hollywood Wit* one Christmas. Its editor Rosemarie Jarski rightly praises 'kickass journalists' like Queenan as opposed to the 'kissass lickspittles' more typical of this particular playing field. This is the inevitable curate's egg, in the current meaning of the phrase rather than the insult its author intended. It does not contain Sam Goldwyn's comment about a film: 'I laughed so much I almost pissed in my girlfriend's hand', nor his comment to Warren Beattie, who wanted Goldwyn to produce what turned out to be Beattie's overlong first film as a director: 'Sorry Warren, that was a three-piss movie.' When I was sorting my father's books, I gave Nick a bunch of Penguin film annuals. I am finally learning to let go. There is no better gift than the one that results in its ending up in a better, that is more appropriate, home than one's own. One book I didn't give him at the time was Paul Rotha's *The Film Till Now*, because it was inscribed by my mother in her familiar spidery writing, 'H from E, Oct 2nd, 1950', my father's thirty-sixth birthday. But I changed my mind later and it is now his. This is a book I used to consult after or before seeing the classics I attended at the National Film Theatre when I was young.

Dinner parties

The film *Lemming* contains the mother of all disastrous dinner parties, with Charlotte Rampling at her best, behaving atrociously. Over dinner, after seeing the film, Paula and I recalled two other dinner party movies, *Babette's Feast*, and the wondrous last film of John Huston, *The Dead*, based on James Joyce's story in *Dubliners*. It is impossible not to read the conclusion of the dying Huston's film as a self-epitaph and I turn to the story in order to quote accurately the utterly magical final sentence, which I promise myself I shall memorize: 'His soul swooned slowly as he heard the snow falling faintly through the universe and faintly falling, like the descent of their last end, upon all the living and the dead.'

Drama

Introduction

I love going to the theatre; at the same time, I confess I do not like reading plays, and never have. Arnold Wesker's *Roots* is on my desk but I have not read it, although I was bowled over when I saw the original Royal Court production as a schoolboy. After some years, it was good to see him again in that very theatre, where I had taken my son to a Sam Sheppard play. I make exceptions of course: Racine and Shakespeare, great poets both. But my old three-volume Shakespeare, which was a bar mitzvah present, is awkward to read and the red gilt is coming off the covers. However, I have Jonathan Griffin's cheap but serviceable reading set, and various Penguin and Arden editions.

Peter Brook (and Jorge Luis Borges)

'Without a doubt Hamlet is more complex now than when Shakespeare originated him; [Hamlet] has been enriched by Coleridge, by Bradley, by Goethe, by so many people.' If anyone but Borges had made that remark would I have been so impressed by it? Is it perhaps a little obvious? Or is it only obvious because after Borges everyone reads literature in a different way than they did before him? Performance in theatre builds on or reacts against previous performances as well as on critical assessments. Peter Brook ends his short study of theatre *The Empty Space* by saying that it is already out of date, for it is 'an exercise, now frozen on the page'. Nonetheless, it is an education. I have never forgotten the production of *Carmen* at his Bouffles du Nord theatre in Paris Xe in the 1980s (close to where I lived as a student in 1961), in which he bypassed Bizet's libretto and returned to Merimée's story. More recently, Paula and I saw his production of Michel Piccoli's one-man Chekhov at the Barbican. For Brook, 'truth in the theatre is always on the move', and so is he, a restless and radical spirit, a genius who would never run a National Theatre, unlike Peter Hall. This is not a criticism of Hall, who is the other genius of their generation of directors, merely a statement that there is room for both ways of being in the theatre, in the world.

Georg Büchner; David Hare

One of my two editions of Georg Büchner's *Collected Plays* includes this great writer's extraordinary short fiction *Lenz*, exactly contemporaneous with Balzac's *The Unknown Masterpiece*. Both of these stories prefigure modernism. *Lenz*, much admired by the poet Iain Bamforth, author of an essential volume of essays *The Good European* (Bamforth lives in the historical Lenz's Strasbourg, near the village where the story is set), reaches forward well over a century to Celan's 'Meridian' and 'Conversation in the Mountains' (see the critically important *Collected Prose* and *The Meridian*). The ultimate motto for those who believe in non-violence as a creed or ideal but who balk at pacifism is found in Büchner's masterpiece *Danton's Death*: 'Where self-defence ends, murder begins.' This is one of the greatest of all political plays and is of the utmost relevance for our own time. Büchner's *Wozzeck* too fascinates me. We saw a production at the Barbican with lyrics by Tom Waits and sets by Robert Wilson, which reminded me of Patrick Caulfield's paintings. I mentioned this to Caulfield when I next saw him, thinking he'd be pleased. He replied gruffly that they hadn't asked his permission.

Paula has painted a portrait of David Hare as a man who writes from the heart. In many respects, this fascinating and complex painting is even finer than her Germaine Greer, which, like the Hare, was commissioned by the National Portrait Gallery. It was to Hare's credit that, when shown the list of artists to choose from, he said Paula Rego or nobody. Whatever he wanted or expected, it certainly could not have been bland flattery. The pose suggests a biblical prophet, appropriate enough for such an eloquent and outspoken man, with a hint of the saint as represented in old art, which may have been how Paula mediated the prophetic element. People have misinterpreted a *Guardian* article or possibly a headline as saying that Hare hated the portrait. In fact, despite the mutual banter between him and Paula, which was accurately reported, there was no suggestion whatsoever that he had negative feelings. Indeed, I have an email from him in which he says that although the picture terrifies him (serves him right for insisting on Paula), he loves it. He must know that it reveals how emotional he is, as Nick Serota commented to Paula before she started. David Hare was listening to Burt

Bacharach and Maurice Ravel during his sittings, unlike Greer, who sat through *The Ring* six times.

Arthur Adamov and the Absurd

I have very few drama books and very few books on drama, two being Martin Esslin's *Brecht* and his influential *The Theatre of the Absurd*, in which the four main chapters are devoted to Samuel Beckett, Jean Genet, Eugene Ionesco and Arthur Adamov. A swift phone call to Paul Buck confirms that Adamov has rarely been performed here. We both vow to explore one more of those neglected figures who abound in the worlds we inhabit. At the Rosenthals' New Year's Eve party, I met, as usual, John Peter the theatre critic, who believes that Adamov is far less significant than the other three. He volunteered the information that Beckett hated Esslin's book and its conceptual framework. Such a framework reminds me of the Objectivist poets or the Young British Artists, in terms of editorial or promotional construction. I asked Susannah York what she thought, given that she knew a lot about French theatre and famously performed in *The Maids*, but Adamov was off her radar too, which leaves David Hare. He writes that Pinter as well as Beckett objected to being pigeonholed in this way and refers me to his friend Tony Bicât, who directed Adamov's *Ping Pong* as a student. For Bicât, Adamov is a formerly fashionable figure now somewhat passé, like the so-called Theatre of the Absurd in general. His worldview was bleak and he killed himself. I recall now that Adamov and another suicide Piotr Rawicz knew each other. In a long chapter devoted to other playwrights, Esslin has, already in 1961, nothing but the highest praise for Pinter. George Welwarth's *The Theater of Protest and Paradox* makes more of Jarry as a precursor than Esslin does, who rightly summons up Büchner. Esslin tells us that Yeats and Mallarmé were present at the first night of *Ubu Roi* (with sets by Bonnard) and argues that the immediate precursor of the great Absurdists was the 1947 adaptation of Kafka's novel *The Trial* by André Gide and Jean-Louis Barrault.

Kenneth Tynan in *Tynan on Theatre* buys into Esslin's historiography of the Absurd back to Dada and the surrealists, while objecting to the incorporation of Shakespeare and Goethe as distant precursors. He notes that Adamov ('pure Dostoevsky' he calls him in *Letters*) is neglected in Britain and that Esslin makes a good case for him. Tynan concludes by objecting 'to the disillusioned Western individualism' and 'the pervasive tone of privileged despair', which he finds in the four main figures, a perspective we might expect from the foremost British champion of Brecht. I well recall as a teenager reading Kenneth Tynan in *The Observer* and Harold Hobson in *The Sunday Times* after my parents had finished with the papers, which in those days were not divided into several sections. The two critics were brilliant entertainers and instructors. My father pointed out Hobson at the Aldwych Theatre one evening, and, indicating by a discreet glance that he had recognized him, Hobson bowed his head in acknowledgement. It occurs to me now that this was not a first night or press performance, for who would have invited us? Perhaps it was a charity performance. The only marginal annotation—'Borges'—in my copy of Richard Coe's monograph *Ionesco* is alongside a quote illustrating the point that long-term relationships depend not so much upon memory as upon 'the memory of a memory, like a thought grown foreign to me, like a tale told by another'. The inscribed date under my name and the nature of the annotations in Toby Cole's *Playwrights on Playwrighting* tell me that this was one of my autodidact books in Paris in 1961, along with books on music and the visual arts. I seem to have been particularly interested in Strindberg, not least his links to Zola, whose *La Bête humaine* and other books are sitting here. Nowadays I am more interested in Strindberg's links to Munch. Here, as it happens, are the Swedish playwright's *Days of Loneliness* and *Inferno/From an Occult Diary*. Munch's 1896 lithograph of the playwright, which Tom Rosenthal has on his wall, misprints his name as Stindberg.

Jonathan Griffin: Heinrich von Kleist, Henry de Montherlant and Paul Claudel

Jonathan Griffin's translation of *The Prince of Homburg* by Heinrich von Kleist was published in *Plays of the Year 36*. Menard Press took over the copies after the publisher remaindered it. One customer for this book was Ted Hughes, who sent me a fiver along with an affectionately inscribed copy of his and Seamus Heaney's anthology *The Rattle Bag* and a letter: 'my heart leaped when I beheld a clue to a translation of Kleist's *Prince of Homburg*.'

Beckett hugely admired Kleist's essay on marionette theatre, while Kafka had the highest regard for the stories: 'They are the root of modern Germany's art of language' (Gustav Janouch: *Conversations with Kafka*.) Here too is one of Griffin's Montherlant translations, *Port-Royal*, in an anthology of French plays, as well as the originals of *La Reine morte* and our sixth-form edition of *Le Maître de Santiago*, for which Montherlant wrote a special preface: 'Throughout its history, the British nation has been fertile enough in men of character and men who take things seriously, for this play to risk interesting it to some degree, provided the essence of the work has been sufficiently elucidated.' Griffin also translated Claudel's *Partage de Midi*, which he graciously allowed Susannah York to revise when she wanted to appear in it.

Tennessee Williams

Pace the publisher's blurb in Tennessee Williams' *Collected Poems*, it is not true that 'if Williams had never written a single play he would still be known as a distinguished poet.' Distinctive yes, distinguished no. Unsurprisingly, his most admired poet was Hart Crane, but Williams did not engage in sufficient cranial therapy to energize his verse in the way that he energized his marvellous prose plays—here is a volume including *The Glass Menagerie*—and thus transcend the conventional poetic influences of his younger years. Never mind. In Paula's and my eyes and ears he is one of the great playwrights of the twentieth century and we go to every production; what's more, his poetry is better than Pinter's and Beckett's, and much better than that of novelists with a second string like John Updike, Ernest Hemingway and William Faulkner.

George Bernard Shaw and Harold Pinter

When I chose which books to take from my father's library, I could not resist the huge *Complete Plays* of George Bernard Shaw, even though I knew that the likelihood of my consulting it was close to zero, and this despite Shaw's recent comeback in London theatre. The Shaw plays was a book that I have always remembered being *there*, and therefore talismanic. About twenty years ago, when Susannah York appeared in *The Applecart* at that beautiful Regency theatre, The Haymarket, she had the second-best dressing room because Peter O'Toole, whose rarely given autograph she obtained for the young Nathaniel, was entitled to the best one. In recent years, O'Toole has been a bigger star than York, but what if two stars are equal in prestige? Do they toss a coin? Alternate? Paula and I saw a miscellany of early Pinter sketches at the same theatre. Nathaniel and Helen videoed for me the 2006 Royal Court production of *Krapp's Last Tape*, played by Pinter himself. At a charity dinner, perhaps for Writers in Prison (one of three or four good causes I support with pound notes), I asked Pinter when he would next write a full-length play: 'All my plays are full-length,' he replied a trifle wearily, albeit with a twinkle in his eye. More on Pinter under cricket, where else?

Performance art: Anthony Howell

I choose to include performance art under 'Theatre'—with its links to mime and dance and ballet—rather than under 'Art' or 'Conceptual Art', even though Gilbert and George and other artists undoubtedly merit the association. I possess one book in this field of force, Anthony Howell's learned and enthralling *The Analysis of Performance Art*, which deploys colour theory, Freud, Bakhtin and French theoreticians (such as Lacan and Deleuze) to explore his chosen themes—Orlan, Bobby Baker and Gilbert and George. He too quotes from *Danton's Death*. Like *Serbian Sturgeon*, the journal of his visit to Belgrade and his only other non-fiction prose text, this is a *work*, exceptionally well written and constructed, unlike many or even most handbooks of this kind. Howell is a former ballet dancer, whose recent dance involvement has been entirely with tango. He is a mental star, instinct with creative energy, powerhousing ideas across the board, indeed across the boards, in his performances. He has performed with pigs. When vegetarians and animal rights people remonstrated/demonstrated, he replied that he saves his porkers from the butcher: the choice is performance art or sausages; porker freedom is not an option. Once, for a performance with horses, he took over the original Manège in Petersburg. I think even a man as hard to please as Nabokov would have been impressed by the sheer chutzpah of the idea.

Paula Rego and theatre

Paula's non-art reading matter is mainly folk material—Portuguese, English, German and so on. Martin McDonagh's play *The Pillowman* affected her so powerfully when we saw it at the Cottesloe that she made a sculpture of a pillowman in her studio and imagined him into paintings via her technique of copying, which is what we want to do when we find something beautiful. Paula and McDonagh have a powerful affinity, no doubt about it. A review came through of the New York production of *The Pillowman*, and lo and behold Paula's work has fed back into its staging. McDonagh sent Paula unpublished stories he wrote when he was young, raw prose and raw material for this and other plays, and these nourished her imagination, as I know from having read the stories and from posing with turtles on my hands, or rather with turtles as my hands. The very first play to which I took Paula, back in 1996, was by McDonagh, *The Beauty Queen of Linane*: she found it attractively cruel and seriously powerful, although she (and I at times) found the stage or cod Irish hard to follow. The stories reveal a cruel and harsh imagination, almost but not quite 'sunk too deep for human tenderness', like the drowning soul in Isaac Rosenberg's 'Dead Man's Dump'.

One August, while Paula was in Portugal, I went to the Yvonne Arnaud Theatre in Guildford to see a play explicitly influenced by her work, Polly Teale's remarkable *Brontë*, which uses Paula's Jane Eyre images as backdrops; these, in turn, affected Teale's choice of costumes. The play integrates the three sisters and their characters in a dialectical counterpoint, as the words segue back and forth, between Bertha and Charlotte, Cathy and Emily. The three men in the famous saga are often neglected, though not by Teale. Branwell Brontë, Patrick Brontë and Arthur Bell Nicholls all come to life on stage, and Teale makes a lot of Branwell as a source not only of pain and grief for the future novelists, but also of psychosexual and indeed sexual information. What, one would dearly like to know, was so shocking in Emily's supposed second novel that Charlotte destroyed it? In the context of Teale's reading of Emily and Charlotte Brontë, it has to have been either religious (her lack of faith, perhaps a prequel to Matthew Arnold's 'Empedocles on Etna' or 'Dover Beach') or sexual (perhaps a prequel to George Sand). Paula suggests a third possibility: Charlotte was jealous. I have just thought of a fourth: it was very bad.

On the way home from Guildford, I telephoned Paula to tell her what I thought about the play and she revealed that a Portuguese newspaper had picked up a *Guardian* feature which I had deliberately kept quiet about before she left London, a ridiculous silly-season piece worthy of a tabloid, announced on the *Guardian* cover as 'the worst ten pictures in Britain': when you opened the paper, they turned out to be ten pictures hated by ten pundits, which is something else entirely. Tristram Hunt, a popular historian and now a Labour MP, chose Paula's 'Germaine Greer'. There was I, trying to protect her feelings before she went to Portugal, and a Portuguese paper reveals Hunt's choice to her a few days before she starts painting the president's portrait in the palace in Beleym! Before we rang off, I mentioned an article in the *Daily Telegraph* about Henry Darger and outsider art, and should I keep it for her. No. The brutal fact is she no longer needs him. Why brutal? That's me being sentimental. Many years ago, Paula went on a pilgrimage to Chicago, to Darger's room, where the door closed on her fingers. The ghost of this extraordinary artist did not like the fact that she was making her own version of his Vivian Girls. The next day, I rang Polly with high praise for her writing and direction and alerted her to one factual mistake in the play, concerning the whereabouts (National Portrait Gallery) of Branwell's portrait of the sisters; he eventually painted himself out of it: as for the Brontës, words did not fail the sisters—and words have not failed Teale, even though Paula is less convinced than I am by the sexual dimension of the play, which she saw in rehearsal.

Music

Music is linked to the circulation of the blood, to the formation of consciousness, to the unconscious even.

—Pierre-Jean Jouve, *En Miroir*

Music: breathing of statues. Perhaps
Stillness of pictures. You language where languages
End. You time
That stands perpendicular on the course of transient hearts.

—Rainer Maria Rilke, 'To Music', from *An Unofficial Rilke*

Percy Scholes, Deryck Cooke and Charles Rosen

Like cinema, music has been one of the areas of special knowledge that I have sporadically attempted to imbibe or introject over the years. Inside my copy of *The Listener's Guide to Music* by Percy Scholes is an invoice from the booksellers A. Soloway Ltd., and addressed to my father at Balfour House, Finsbury Pavement, EC2. It is dated 20 October 1961, the month I started at university. Soloway was a client of my father, and one of the directors was Bernie Leigh, the older brother of R. A. Leigh, who was a childhood friend of my father and became a world authority on Rousseau. The invoice price is in old money: four shillings and two pence, and the phone number is Bishopsgate 5980. I have marked a footnote in the book concerning Beethoven's 'Moonlight Sonata' which I was trying to play on my rented college piano, at which I also accompanied Terry Eagleton on the penny whistle and, once, on the mouth organ. Scholes begins the note: 'Some of the many amateur pianists who play this sonata may like to analyse it in detail, there being a natural human instinct that prompts a child to take its toy engine to pieces to see how it works, and that, similarly, suggests to an intelligent adult the analysis of a work of art.'

According to my inscription on the flyleaf, I bought Deryck Cooke's *The Language of Music* in Cambridge in 1962. I annotated one paragraph in which he compared music to painting and literature, a paragraph that now strikes me as being naive in its assumptions; naive too, as Charles Rosen explains in *Music and Sentiment* (which I read fifty years later along with his *Piano Notes*), about the affective significance of tonal music. If Cooke is right about his examples, then everyone is right about their own examples. I could read music but it took some years before I could follow a score. I enjoyed doing this when Jane Joseph and I went to a performance of *Kinderszenen* by Robert Schumann (the most literary of all composers, according to Charles Rosen) at the Wigmore Hall as part of the soft preparation for our collaboration on a literary and visual equivalent of this cherished work. During the student years I also bought two reference books: *The Concerto* and *The Symphony* edited by Ralph Hill. While still at school, I had bought *Chamber Music* edited by Alec Robertson and must have taken it to Paris with me when I left for my six months of study. I know this because I kept in the book my entrance ticket for the upper balcony of Salle Gaveau in rue la Boétie on Friday, 24 February 1961, when the Hungarian Quartet played the sixth of a series of recitals incorporating all Beethoven's string quartets. My strapontin seat cost four new francs. Also included is an announcement of a concert the previous week under the auspices of the Union of Jewish Students by a trio which included Michael Harisson, an Israeli cellist who, like me, was living at the Jewish students' hostel, 9 rue Guy Patin. In those days I paid far more attention to music than to painting. In recent years, as will be clear from the present book, it is the study of music rather than painting that I have neglected, Paula being a painter. In my fantasy of the deathbed, provided I am not too drugged up with morphine and/or too terror-struck, I shall be listening to Beethoven's piano sonatas, looking at Paula's pictures, and thinking of my loved ones.

[Coda: A public lecture Charles Rosen gave the day before a Chopin recital on the South Bank stretched me to the limit, like hands on a keyboard. When I research my stories, I use my eyes as well as my ears at concerts and recitals. And there is eyeless Radio Three. My character Maria-Ines deploys the same combinations of instruments as Iannis Xenakis and Gyorgy Ligeti.]

[Coda postscript at proof stage: Charles Rosen has since died, Rosen whose hand I shook after the recital, courtesy of his friend Bonnefoy.]

Stewart Macpherson

When I went to Paris, my Uncle Leon Rudolf gave me Leonard Bernstein's *The Joy of Music*, and two primers by Stewart Macpherson: *Form in Music* and *Music and Its Appreciation* (doubtless having asked me what I wanted). It is clear from my annotations that I read both books closely. The latter is a new and revised edition, but no publication date is given either for the original or revised edition—a pity we don't follow the French system and give the date of printing alongside the printer's name. A phone call to the library of the Royal Academy of Music, where Macpherson had been a lecturer, elicits his dates, 1865–1941, and the fact that *Music and Its Appreciation* was first published in 1910 and reprinted in 1941. The date 1910 accounts for the tone of the opening sentence: 'It is hardly too much to say that one of the penalties the Anglo-Saxon race pays for its vaunted and undoubted common sense and hard-headedness is that, speaking generally, it has rarely been included to take art seriously, or to regard it in the light of anything more than a harmless amusement.' One or two pages later, he says: 'In all really great work, be it literary, pictorial, musical or what not, there is undoubtedly an *elemental something* which appeals to most of us with a sense of truth; but this does not necessarily indicate that we grasp its meaning, or appreciate its art.' Despite being deeply grateful for the gift of a phrase I can recycle in a fable—'the elemental something of x or y'—I must not mock this child of his time. Rudolf the autodidact took Macpherson's primers seriously half a century ago.

Morton Feldman (and Philip Guston)

A few years ago I wrote a group of stories in which two characters were composers, Maria-Ines da Costa and Bathsheba Schoenberg, and I would like to return to these two ladies in the not-too-distant future. By the time I come to write the next cycle of stories, I shall have educated myself to a greater extent about a world I do not move in, beyond the occasional concert and opera, Covent Garden as the guests of Yvonne and Dan Burt (Dan is the author of *We Look like This*, a fine volume of poetry/prose), the annual trip to Glyndbourne with the Rosenthals, and the annual invitation to the box of the Proms Director Nick Kenyon. The latter ended in 2007 when he left to run the Barbican. For one year only we were guests of his successor Roger Wright, and met Mark Anthony Turnage, whom I pumped for information about his opera compositional practices. I can use in fiction his revelation that he writes all the vocal parts before turning to the orchestra.

I have already dipped into Morton Feldman's *Essays* (with a Philip Guston image on the cover, as you would expect). He says that what he is after is described by Mondrian: 'I enjoyed painting flowers, not bouquets, but a single flower at a time, in order that I might better express its plastic structure.' I can use that too. There is an essay on how Guston's paintings inform the composer's own thinking about space and time. I was struck by the following: 'In music, the key or pitch centre of a composition is akin to the picture plane of the painter. It determines the degree of audibility (visibility) as well as its timbre (colour). Colour was underscored in both

Guston's earliest and late abstract painting, more to *light* the stage, the way I once observed Beckett light his stage . . . Beckett's voice is also so prevalent on his stage that it is difficult to distinguish *what* is being said from *who* is saying it. As in Guston's paintings, we seem to be hearing *two* voices simultaneously. For a composer, this is a crucial problem: that the means or the instruments you use are only to articulate musical thought and not to interpret it.'

Honoré de Balzac, W. H. Auden and others

Honoré de Balzac, himself a literary genius, writing about artistic geniuses in one group of stories, *The Unknown Masterpiece*, *Gambara* and *Massimilla Doni*, chose a painter and musicians (composer and performer) rather than a writer, since we have no choice but to take music and painting for granted, whereas the writing of an invented writer would have to be written by the writer of the story, and that would never do. How sententious and tendentious W. H. Auden can be, thank goodness, and on any subject under the sun, including music. In *The Table Talk of W. H. Auden*, Alan Ansen reports the poet's view that 'Don Giovanni is a certain type of male homosexual. Neither extreme, Tristan or Don Giovanni, is compatible with homosexual love.' There is more interest in his thought that 'Hofmannsthal is the one librettist you can read apart from the music' (Auden is being modest). I bought one of the volumes of *German Opera Libretti* in order to check out the words of *Der Rosenkavalier*, a work which speaks to my heart for many reasons and which inspired one of my shortest stories. Jonathan Cott's *Conversations with Glenn Gould* is enjoyable, not least when Gould (well portrayed in Brian Dillon's *Tormented Hope*, a study of nine hypochondriacs) has a go at the Beatles, explaining his strong preference for Petula Clark, and claiming that his published article about her has a parallel in the first movement of Webern's *Variations for Piano*. Perhaps *This Man and Music* by Anthony Burgess, composer as well as writer, will help me.

Louis and Annette Kaufman

If ever there was a book to read, and even to write about, while listening to music, it is *A Fiddler's Tale*, the memoir of my dear friend the virtuoso violinist Louis Kaufman, an intimate of Jonathan Griffin. Even as I write this, I am playing the accompanying CD ranging from Vivaldi to Jerome Kern via Korngold and Copeland. Louis was already a very old man, long retired from playing, when I first met him. On his final visit to London, I remember taking him and his pianist wife Annette to dinner in a Greek restaurant in Bayswater, near their hotel. What struck me was that he had become virtually ethereal, down to the bone (in this respect not unlike Sacha Rabinovitch and my Uncle Jack), *essential*, as if he had taken to heart the old Yiddish proverb ('A shroud has no pockets') and would be ready to go when his time came, perhaps very soon. There was a purity and goodness about the man, as sweet and enchanting as his player's tone. This great musician was probably the most recorded violinist in history, partly because, in addition to his classical recordings, he made hundreds of movie sound tracks as concertmaster for Chaplin and many others. When the couple were young and needing to earn a living during the great depression, they went to Hollywood, where Louis found the perfect job for a violinist. He is the solo violin in *Gone with the Wind*, for example, and unseen is heard playing the instrument for the Lesley Howard character in *Intermezzo*. If he is less well known than the famous names of his generation, Heifetz, Elman and others, it is because he rarely played the great platform concertos, preferring early music (including Vivaldi, forgotten until Louis edited him and in 1947 made the very first LP recording of *Four Seasons*) and twentieth-century repertoire, which he personally increased by commissioning work.

Annette Kaufman still lives in Los Angeles, in a house full of paintings by their friend Milton Avery, as well as works by Mark Rothko, who was at elementary school with Louis in Seattle. When I went to Los Angeles a few years ago, I stayed with her, conveniently close to Kitaj's house. It was not long after Louis had died and she was beginning to sort out his papers in order to complete the unfinished autobiography. One evening Kitaj and his son Max came to dinner. Annette remains a friend, one of a bevy (is that the right collective noun?) of widows I love, survivors of couples from a generation that made it together to old age without divorce or murder. Even as I write, I am listening to Louis playing the *Concertino de Printemps* by his friend Darius Milhaud.

Pierre Boulez

The 'unadulterated ecstasy of power' (Wole Soyinka's magnificent phrase) could be sensed in the conversation of Pierre Boulez, one of the grandest figures in the premier division of mandarin Parisian intelligence. Back in the 1970s, I found myself seated at the same dinner table as Bonnefoy and Boulez at the French Institute. Throughout the meal, the entire table was treated to a lengthy soliloquy by this charismatic genius, a 'regal mind', as Thomas De Quincey said of Samuel Taylor Coleridge. Although I have broached and continue to enjoy the work of Berio and Ligeti, I cannot claim to have caught up with Boulez's own music—so far. I do know that when he conducts the music of the past (Mahler for example), your ears are opened to the most unexpected possibilities of colour and timbre, possibilities fully realized in later music, which is his reason for conducting what came before him. We owe him. To my surprise, I have not read a book by him; the time has come to remedy that (purchase of *Boulez on Music Today* accomplished on Abebooks just now), although a more sensible strategy would be to listen to more of his music. During the final revision of this book in 2012, I listened on the radio to the Proms in which Barenboim and his West Eastern Divan Orchestra played Boulez and Beethoven. I paid close attention and was repaid with charged pleasure. I felt I was going somewhere, along with the music.

Eva Hoffman

A wonderful account, which rings so true, of music as experienced by a virtuoso interpreter can be found in Eva Hoffman's second novel *Illuminations*, whose main character is a famous concert pianist, Isabel Merton. Merton gets caught up in a love affair with a Chechyen political exile, who has an agenda she would prefer not to know too much about. On plane trips and in hotel rooms, we also find her reading the journal of her former and charismatic teacher, Wolfe. These three comport the triangle of forces driving the novel as it explores the limits of art and politics and love, an eternal triangle after my own heart. One knows that Hoffman herself might have become a concert pianist and one senses that her inwardness to the character and skills of Isabel, while not autobiographical, are in fact better than that and more propitious to fiction, since they derive from the alter ego or altra ego of the road not taken ('and that has made all the difference'). Her account of what music is and what it means, something at once spiritual and material, caught by the inner and the outer ear, is given in terms of the music of Chopin and Schubert and also the process of playing or interpreting that music. I am sure E. M. Forster would bow his head to the woman who has strongly out-written his description of music in *Howards End*.

Sport

Cricket

Among my father's books is one I read several times when I was a child and still dip into. It is a 'post-mortem on the 1950–1951 Tests' in Australia by Rex Warner and Lyle Blair. The title, *Ashes to Ashes*, is a clever dig at the English team, which lost, and deserved to lose, the Ashes that year, so I am pleased to be writing this during a phase when we have redeemed ourselves. Cricket has the edge (in the gully of my mind) on other sports, not only because of its intrinsic beauty and subtlety but also because it is the only sport where I take sides. Warner and Blair's book takes the form of an exchange of letters, amusing, well informed, and occasionally acerbic. There was a time when I was astonished—how narrow-minded of me!—to discover that this was the same Rex Warner who translated George Seferis. My father owned some of Warner's Kafkaesque novels, which I have never read. Cricket must be the only sport to have been blessed by a correspondent like Neville Cardus of *The Guardian*, who covered the game during the day and classical concerts at night, or Alan Ross of *The Observer*, poet and editor of the *London Magazine*. John Arlott, with his warm Hampshire accent ('Alec Bedser's coming up to bowl from the pavilion end') was my favourite broadcaster, a 1940s' poet whose work one should explore. Yes, the one sport Rex Warner would love and write about is cricket.

What interests me now is the extent to which I remain moved both by statistics and by the names of players. This is the case especially with cricket— I have two *Wisdens*, one of them my much-battered copy of 1951, obviously the year my interest took off, and 1983—but also soccer (my *Playfair Annuals* are lost or sold), tennis and table tennis. How evocative are names and numbers from that gone world! I was not actually present (and mostly I wasn't, even at London venues, Lords and to a lesser extent the Oval), I was following matches, Tests and my county Middlesex, avidly in the newspapers and on radio sports programmes. My son grew up loving cricket, so I must have done something right.

I open the Warner–Blair book at the scorecard for the final test. I note the quondam convention whereby English amateurs are listed with their initials: R. T. Simpson, D. S. Sheppard, F. R. Brown (captain) and T. E. Bailey, whereas the professionals only have their surnames: Hutton, Washbrook, Compton, Evans, Bedser, Wright, Tattersall. The entire Australian team are listed with initials, but in those days they were all amateurs, R. N. Harvey, K. R. Miller, R. R. Lindwall, among them. The England players included J. G. Dewes and J. J. Warr, Gilbert Parkhouse and the very young Brian Close. I was proud that not only Denis Compton but also Warr and Dewes, both Middlesex, played for their country; unfortunately Dewes and Warr failed. Ah the names, the names resonate like Adlestrop, like Uncle Tom Cobley and his mates, a song we used to sing in the car on long journeys in our first family cars during the 1940s and 1950s: Standards then Vauxhalls. Edward Thomas' poem works differently from the cricket score sheets and from the folk song, for what I am remembering in these is my own lived experience, *erlebnis* from the early post-war years, and I have the ache of the psalmist in my heart: *na'ar hayiti vegam zakanti*, I was a youth and now I am old.

Naturally it is the genius of a lyric poet to recreate this pain vicariously, and to educate the heart in the burdens of mortality, the heart a metaphor that neuroscience shall never obliterate or neutralize. The Warner–Blair book concludes with statistics taken from Wisden. These are strictly for the nerds, probably one hundred per cent of the readers. Here too is the original self-published edition of J. L. Carr's *Dictionary of Extraordinary Cricketers*. No one who does not understand what Carr is getting at and where he is coming from as a humourist can claim to understand the cultural landscape of England. The book, newly introduced by the editor of Wisden, has been reissued as a hardback, and I bought it yesterday as a present for my son on his move to new chambers, after some years in the Middle Temple. Under 'George Macaulay Trevelyan, OM, died 1962' we find: 'If the French noblesse had been capable of playing cricket with their peasants their châteaux would never have been burnt.'

The Alternative Wisden on Samuel Barclay Beckett is a laborious joke in the form of an essay by Roy Clements written shortly after the cricketer died in 1989, although it is a useful compendium of the known facts. It is fair to say that even a high appreciation of Beckett as an artist does not require one to appreciate him as a cricketer. A chiasmic reversal of this proposition does not work, given the asymmetry of his achievements in the two fields. It is a moot point whether more people read the first edition of, say, *Murphy*, than saw him play first-class cricket for Dublin University: one of the two occasions was against Northamptonshire in 1926, when he would have noted the name of two Northants batsmen N. Bowell, who was followed by E. F. Towell. Connoisseurs of the author would have recognized him at the test matches he attended when in the UK. American writers (Marianne Moore, Paul Auster and others) have the same relationship to baseball as some of us do to cricket but, as I have written elsewhere, I need persuading about baseball, both as a spectacle and as an objective correlative for life and art. Having lost touch with each other, it is probably too late for Paul Auster and me to resume contact and for each of us to accompany the other to a spectacle that is not mother's milk. There are a number of references to cricket in Beckett's novels, including the man counting out stones in *Molloy* like an umpire remembering how many balls have been bowled, yet this perfectly obvious fact is rejected by Roy Clements, who indeed disputes that there are any references in the work, apart from the explicit 'or on the cricket field' in *Watt*. Clements aims his full tosses at an easy target—naive symbological readers—and then attempts to be funny by inventing unfunny heavy-handed pseudo-explanations of alleged mysteries, thus Hamm is Walter Hammond.

Harold Pinter too includes cricket in his plays, as well as in two of his screenplays for Joseph Losey, *Accident* and *The Go-Between*, the latter adapted from a novel by L. P. Hartley, several of whose books I found on my father's shelves and read as a boy, including the Eustace and Hilda trilogy. The mother of all cultural impossibilities, but dream on, would be to find a cricket story for Paula to paint. And yet, when she was a schoolgirl in Portugal, while the boys were playing cricket, she played rounders at her English school St Julian's before being sent to England by her anglophile father. So, something may have lodged, like a stubborn bail, on the wicket of her brain. On which subject, Pinter had to take legal action against an Italian or German translator, who had understood 'watering the wicket' to mean 'pissing against the gate'. William Baker and Stephen Ely Tabachnick in their monograph *Harold Pinter* argue that his allusions to cricket 'inevitably recreate [an] idyllic—and very fragile—vision of security'. One year, at the Bastille Day bash in the French ambassador's house, Pinter and I talked about cricket and I said that in my autograph album—an account of which I am publishing soon under the title *A Vanished Hand*—I keep an envelope with swaps, and would he like the autograph of the Warwickshire cricketer Jack Flavell? 'Worcestershire', he flashed back instantly, like Sachin Tendulkar playing a late cut to a slightly wide reverse swing from Alan Donald.

One quasi-foreigner who would understand these delicacies is my Anglo-Polish friend Z. Kotowicz, a cricket fanatic because he spent his crucial early years in England, before returning to Poland where he practised fielding by throwing frozen turnips at his stepbrother. Now living in Portugal, Kotowicz reminds me of another Pole, the Canadian of the species, Marius Kociejowski, whose only experience of the game was bewildered participation in the annual poets' cricket match organized by the late and generous poetry groupie (surely she would not object to the word), Audrey Nicholson. I asked Kociejowski if Christopher Middleton was a cricket fan: 'when Christopher comes to stay, and it's cricket season, he sits absolutely motionless, bolt upright, and remains in that position for hours at a time.'

I obtained a copy of the out of print *Billy Wright: A Hero for All Seasons* after tracking down the author Norman Giller, but the title is inaccurate from the vantage point of my teenage years, for Billy was my winter hero, Denis Compton being my summer hero. Here is a King Penguin edited by John Arlott, *The Picture of Cricket*. It contains a print by Rowlandson dated 1811 of a women's cricket match: one of the batsmen or batswomen or, let's say, batters, has her skirt hitched up and tied round her waist, with her bloomers or, rather, petticoats somehow attached to her stockings. Three outfielders are flying round, trying to catch the ball. I want a copy of the original print. Not as much as I want a Rembrandt etching, but I do want one, if it ever turns up and I can afford it. The women remind me of Paula's women, they even look Portuguese. The tent or pavilion or hostelry has a flag raised above it inscribed with the words 'Jolly Cricketer'.

Strangers' Gallery, edited by Allen Synge and a gift from Audrey Nicholson, is signed by one of the contributors, American fabulist and poet, Marvin Cohen, a fanatical cricket lover and regular at Nicholson's annual match. (It was strange, almost counter-intuitive, to meet the Brooklyn-born Cohen by chance in New York recently. A fish in water—whatever next?) When citizens of non-cricket countries express an opinion about the sport, it feels like an intrusion into private joy, but Cohen's essay, which begins 'Life is an elaborate metaphor for cricket', is an entertainingly brilliant text, so I forgive him his chutzpah, a word he incarnates. Cohen would enjoy the song 'Fucking Hell it's Fred Titmus' by a well-known Indie group Half Man Half Biscuit, the late Titmus being a Middlesex star in his day.

Chess

George Steiner, in *The Sporting Scene: White Knights of Reykjavik*, disagrees with Goethe that chess is 'the touchstone of the intellect', a phrase he cites while discussing the relationship between music, mathematics and chess: 'the common bond . . . may, finally, be the absence of language.' Harry Golombek's *The Game of Chess* was given to me by my cousins—the Forrester family—along with my favourite bar mitzvah present, a chess set, practically the only presents to survive the years. One of my regrets is that I have not played more regularly. Still, I taught my son Nathaniel on this very board. Even now, he wonders if his grandfather allowed him to win when they played each other later on.

Table tennis

I have written in other books about my passion for table tennis. I was a good defensive player and only wish my back would allow me to continue playing. Here is Victor Barna's *Table Tennis Today*, with the great Hungarian-born player on the cover making a forehand drive and wearing long trousers, although the book was published as late as 1962. It could have done with some editing in order to lose sentences like the following: 'I learned a lot by playing doubles, and maintain that that is why I did so well in this department in my playing days.' Nonetheless, I annotated it carefully and evidently used it during my playing and training days. Here are Jerome Charyn's entertaining and instructive memoir *Sizzling Chops and Devilish Spins* and Harry Venner's *Instructions in Table Tennis*. Venner was an England international who became a full-time coach. I used to drive to his club down in Putney once a week for training. My exact Cambridge contemporary Howard Jacobson has written a memorable table tennis novel, *The Mighty Walzer*, a much better book than *The Finkler Question*. Jacobson played for the university; I was merely the freshman champion of my college, with a cup to prove it. I thought I wrote a rave review of his *Roots Shmoots* but he didn't take kindly to a cheerful dig at his apparent persona. Maybe the dig was a manifestation of *ressentiment* on my part—sporting, not literary of course.

Human Sciences and Science

Introductory Note

If this book, on one level, is a public record of my self-education, the record reveals severe shortcomings, notably in science and economics. In the coming years, I shall be making more of an effort to understand intellectual worlds I have neglected, but it's too late to reflect that in the present work.

My five-year-old grandson Charlie is influencing me: he's interested in volcanoes, the solar system, the weather. I need to get my act together if I am to have any influence there.

Social Anthropology and Sociology

Claude Lévi-Strauss

My main problem as a social anthropology student at Cambridge, having abandoned modern languages, lay in the unwarranted assumption, soon dashed, that we would be taught French-style theory rather than the deadly dull practice of kinship studies typified by the early fieldwork of our professor, Meyer Fortes. True, a handful of books on the reading list such as Darryl Forde's *African Worlds*, dealing with cosmology, religion and morality, interested me, but the heart of the syllabus involved kinship, politics, economics and law, as manifested in the tribal societies where our teachers had done their fieldwork. Not what I thought I had signed up for.

Privately I read Claude Lévi-Strauss. I was fascinated by *Le Totémisme aujourd'hui* and *La Pensée sauvage*. The title of the latter is an untranslatable pun. The best I can manage, with a nod to Shakespeare, is: *Wild Pansies or That's for Thoughts*. I conveniently managed to forget that this remarkable thinker acknowledged that he could not have done his theorizing without the 'wide-ranging' original research by 'British' fieldworkers, working within an empirical tradition defined by Bronisław Malinowski's ethnographic motto 'from the native's point of view'. Although Claude Lévi-Strauss corresponded with Alfred Radcliffe-Brown on aspects of theory, British functionalism rarely, if ever, examined its theoretical presuppositions in either philosophical or linguistic terms; nor did it think through its practice against the background of the political economy of colonialism. Lévi-Strauss' own fieldwork, written up in *La Vie familiale et sociale des indiens Nambikwara*, is not to be spoken of in the same breath as his other work, and his detractors made much of his limited experience in the field. The complex tensions between politics and the social sciences, between neocolonialism and anthropology, were widely debated after my anthropology days were over. There were those who saw anthropologists as handmaidens of colonialism but Bruce Ross-Smith tells me that fieldworkers were perceived as members of the 'pro-native' awkward squad by district officers and their masters in Whitehall, not least the master fieldworker E. E. Evans-Pritchard himself, whom Max Beloff attempted to have kicked out of All Souls on the grounds that social anthropology wasn't a legitimate academic discipline.

At my first social anthropology supervision, I sought to impress my supervisor, Martin Southwold, by telling him I had read Lévi-Strauss, in French too, since the great man had not yet been translated. Southwold replied: 'We don't teach Lévi-Strauss in this faculty, he's a philosopher.' Although Edmund Leach was already a prominent Lévi-Straussean, at that time he was outside the magic circle. I had made a false start, and never recovered. Maybe the remark merely meant that Southwold saw through me and realized he had better disabuse a potentially lost soul about the nature of the social anthropology tripos. A surviving postcard from my college friend John Barrell to whom I had lent my copy of *La Pensée sauvage* states: 'It's not a system for talking about primitive people, it's primitive people for talking about a system.' A fairer comment might be that it's primitive people for talking about us, who are no different. Ironically enough, in France Lévi-Strauss was seen to have sold out to the Anglo-Saxons both philosophically and anthropologically. Robert Lowie, as Lévi-Strauss said, was more important to him than Émile Durkheim, and the same went for Evans-Pritchard.

I had an older friend at Trinity, Roger Poole, who was doing a PhD on Søren Kierkegaard and indirect communication. He too borrowed *La Pensée sauvage*, with the unexpected consequence that he left for Paris soon after. Later in the sixties, I would occasionally attend Frank Kermode's semiotics seminar at University College London with Roger, and translated two book reviews by Roland Barthes for the sake of the monolinguists present. Poole himself wrote a strange and fascinating book called *Towards Deep Subjectivity* and a lengthy introduction to Rodney Needham's translation of Lévi-Strauss' *Totemism*. According to Ross-Smith, Poole wrote the introduction rather than Needham because the latter and Lévi-Strauss had by this time completely fallen out, whereas Roger, Evans-Pritchard was told by a Julian Pitt-Rivers (a colleague of Lévi-Strauss), was in favour with the great man. So I did Roger a good turn: influence moves in a mysterious way, its wonders to perform. In his introduction, Roger quotes the master: 'It is only forms and not contents that can be common' and 'food prohibitions may therefore be organized into systems which are extra- or para-totemic.' Mary Douglas would later write a long and brilliant structural analysis of *kashrut*, Jewish dietary laws, in the *New York Review of Books*. Structuralism was beginning to take hold of me: 'Is *structuralism* the bridge from Marx to death?' wrote Lowell in *History*. However, it was Barthes rather than Lévi-Strauss whom I elected as maître. He would later mutate into a literary writer, unlike Lévi-Strauss, with the exception of the latter's only literary masterpiece, *Tristes tropiques*: my French and English-language copies are falling apart. In *Against Interpretation*, Susan Sontag calls it an exemplary personal history, like Montaigne's essays and Freud's *Interpretation of Dreams*. It was of course the personal history which scandalized English-speaking empiricists. Sontag argues too that, in respect of sensibility, Butor and Sarraute and Robbe-Grillet are to Lévi-Strauss what Genet is to Sartre, whom Lévi-Strauss argued with at length in *La Pensée sauvage*.

Michel Leiris in *Brisées* describes *Tristes tropiques* as 'super-rationalist'. In 'How I Became an Anthropologist', a key chapter in the book, Lévi-Strauss takes a mighty swipe at two of the rival schools in post-war Paris:

'Phenomenology and existentialism did not abolish metaphysics: they merely introduced new ways of finding alibis for metaphysics.' Georges Perec must have smiled approvingly at the following: 'Anthropology affords me an intellectual satisfaction: it rejoins at one extreme the history of the world, and at the other the history of myself, and it unveils the shared motivation of one and the other at the same moment.'

Tristes tropiques contains a fascinating autobiographical meditation on music: while travelling in areas of Brazil that few outsiders had set eyes on and deploying introspection worthy of his hero Rousseau (the *philosophe* 'who came nearest to being an anthropologist'), Lévi-Strauss asks himself why he entered this particular arena while his friends were busy climbing their professional ladders. Then: 'I found that neither people nor landscape stood in the foreground of my mind. This was occupied by . . . fragments of music or poetry which were the perfectly conventional expression of a civilisation against which I had taken my stand: such, at any rate, was how I must interpret my actions, if my life were to retain any sense of purpose. For weeks on end, . . . I was obsessed not by my surroundings, which I should never see again, but by a hackneyed tune that my memory deformed still further: the third of Chopin's *Etudes*, op. 10, which seemed to me—and I well knew how bitter was the irony of it—to summarize all that I had left behind me . . . At the moment when I left France it was *Pelléas* that gave me the spiritual nourishment so why was it that Chopin, and the most banal of his works, should have had such a hold upon me in the desert? . . . Deeper knowledge of the older composer had led me to recognise beauties destined to remain hidden from those who had not first come to know Debussy.' The idea that, in effect, you come to Chopin via Debussy, is a good example of what Guy Davenport means by influence as an integration of forces and is related to the thoughts of Borges about influence and precursors. Lévi-Strauss continues: 'Was that what travel meant? An exploration of the deserts of memory, rather than of those around me?'

Ultimately, his message is bleak, but not terminally bleak: 'Entropology' not 'anthropology', pronounced identically in French, 'should be the word for the discipline that devotes itself to the study of this process of disintegration in its most highly evolved forms'. Meanwhile we have to think collectively in our attempt, however vain, to save the world: 'Not merely is the first person singular detestable: there is no room for it between 'ourselves' and 'nothing' . . . But no sooner have I chosen than, by that very choice, I take on myself, unreservedly, my condition as a man. Thus liberated from an intellectual pride whose futility is only equalled by that of its object, I also agree to subordinate its claims to the objective will-to-emancipation of that multitude of human beings who are still denied the means of choosing their own destiny.' Lévi-Strauss then builds up to the epiphany which closes his truly great and radical and, yes, literary book, sentences which make one regret that literature (and music) were, for this profound thinker, matrices of thought and feeling rather than children or productions in their own creative right. Barthes, by contrast, already a marvellous and authentic writer (his words generating thought rather than generated by it), died before he could write the unclassifiable books that were his for the answering. Leiris, an anthropologist like Lévi-Strauss, was always a full-fledged literary writer.

I loved reading Lévi-Strauss partly because he wrote in French, and the grass was all the greener after I abandoned modern languages for social anthropology. The old hot-gospeller, as John Barrell jokingly described him in the postcard I mentioned earlier, lost me with the huge near unreadable volumes such as *Le Cru et le cuit*. My copy has a note in it from the late Jean-Marie Benoist, future author of the polemical *Marx est mort*, then a cultural attaché at the French Embassy in London, apologizing for taking so long to give it back. Those books of Claude Lévi-Strauss were the return of the repressed, James Frazer ratcheted up by the master in a rigorous modern theory.

Many years later, Lévi-Strauss published a volume of essays, *Look, Listen, Read*, which deals with aesthetic issues and I briefly returned to the grand master in English translation. Here is his short book, *Myth and Meaning*: 'Only music and mathematics can be said to be really innate, and one must have some genetic apparatus to do either.' On my desk, too, is a volume of radio interviews, *Entretiens*, inscribed London, March 1965. In it is my typical bookmark sheet of paper with notes and page numbers. One note says 'tell Terry [i.e. Eagleton] page 46': here I find I have underlined the following, now translated: 'progress and the realisation of social justice must consist of a transfer of empathy from society to culture' which, says Lévi-Strauss, is his modern reformulation of Saint-Simon's declaration of secular faith that we must move from the government of men to the administration of things. He ends the interviews with a simple restatement of his view that if and when we come to resolve the problem of the origin of language, we will understand how culture can fit into nature and that what differentiates humans from animals is the mind's power to symbolize. Somewhere he employs the word "compossibilities": historically and personally we are not as predetermined as some might think he thinks.

James Frazer, Émile Durkheim, Karl Marx, George Simmel, Max Weber

Thomas Sebeok's symposium, *Myth*, contains a major essay by Lévi-Strauss, 'The Structural Study of Myth', which is also found in the French writer's collection of essays *Structural Anthropology*; other essays in Sebeok include one by the scholar-soldier Lord Raglan, 'Myth and Ritual'. I remember his name as author of a book in the Thinkers Library, a series of small-size books of which my father had several titles, bought when he was a young man, broadening his mind while studying for his accountancy exams and, later, during the war. Despite the earlier remark about Robert Lowie, Lévi-Strauss, in his introduction to Marcel Mauss' *Sociologie et Anthropologie*, makes his debt clear to the fathers of French sociology, Durkheim and Mauss (see also *Marcel Mauss: A Centenary Tribute* edited by Wendy James and N. J. Allen) and their school. Bruce Ross-Smith, on the other hand, tells me that some critics, Louis Dumont among them, argued that in his later work Lévi-Strauss chose to play down his debt to Durkheim and company. Yet one of the specific matrices of his work is *Primitive Classification* by Durkheim and Mauss, who conclude: 'According to him [Frazer], men were divided into clans by a pre-existing classification of things; but, on the contrary, they classified things because they were divided by clans.' It is not recorded whether Wittgenstein met Frazer at Trinity College (I wish!), but in June 1930 a young friend read to the philosopher from *The Golden Bough*, that belated grand narrative of ancient signs and primitive wonders, one thousand pages in its abridged edition, twelve volumes in all. Notes he made on Frazer were found after his death. Maybe Wittgenstein read some of the essayists of

L'Année sociologique; his remark in *Philosophical Investigations* would have given them pause for thought: 'Think of the different points of view from which one can classify tools or chess men.'

I understood that Durkheim and Weber were the grand masters of sociology, fathers of the modern discipline and peers of Marx. I read Weber (see below) and three classics by Durkheim: *The Division of Labour in Society*, *The Elementary Forms of the Religious Life* and *Suicide*. The last subject fascinated me and continues to fascinate me, in part because several writers and artists I knew and admired, including Primo Levi, Piotr Rawicz and R. B. Kitaj, died by their own hand. I shall never get round to reading *Socialism*, Durkheim's study of Saint-Simon's ideas, which he appears to have written under pressure from younger colleagues, including his son, to take a political stand. Marx himself could also be categorized under economics or politics but Thomas B. Bottomore and Maximilian Rubel's *Karl Marx*, a selection of his writings in sociology and social philosophy, belongs here, as do Tom Bottomore's *Classes in Modern Society* and *Elites and Society*, Alfred G. Meyer's *Marxism*, which he defines as 'a historical sociology of knowledge', Terry Eagleton's *Why Marx Was Right*, Francis Wheen's *Karl Marx* and David McLellan's *Marx*. Around forty years ago, I underscored the passages where McLellan says that although Marx believed that force might sometimes be necessary as the midwife of revolution, he thoroughly disapproved of terror and terrorism and that it was the Mensheviks who more closely reflected his view that the revolution could not be hastened.

My copy of George Simmel's *Conflict & the Web of Group-Affiliations* is signed and dated April 1964, meaning I bought it towards the end of my inglorious, indeed lamentable, career as an undergraduate social anthropologist: This title was doubtless on our sociology reading list, and they don't come more theoretical than the German sociologist. In those days, it should be noted, sociology was merely a paper in the social anthropology tripos, not a separate subject. I enjoyed reading this exact contemporary of Max Weber, yet have to confess that Weber himself bored me. I did not return to him until the 1990s when the books of Gillian Rose demanded that I take another look. Here on my desk are Reinhard Bendix's *Max Weber*, H. H. Gerth and C. Wright Mills' *From Max Weber* and my late friend Donald

MacRae's *Weber*. The title of the second of the two long Simmel essays takes on a particular colouring in the age of the Web, the Internet, Facebook and Twitter, thanks to which group affiliation has been broadened (broadbanded), democratized, even universalized, for good and ill.

Arnold van Gennep and Franz Steiner

Henri Hubert and Marcel Mauss' *Sacrifice: Its Nature and Function* and Émile Durkheim's *Sociology and Philosophy* were two more of those theoretical books which took my mind off the prescribed ethnographical studies of kinship we were supposed to be reading: a third was *Death* and *The Right Hand* by Robert Hertz, which is heavily annotated. I must recently have read *Rites of Passage* by Arnold van Gennep, for his name often occurs in my marginalia to other books. His argument is carried forward in a marvellous chapter 'Liminality and Communitas' in Victor Turner's *The Ritual Process*, and in Max Gluckman's essay in *Essays on the Ritual of Social Relations*, where Martin Southwold, no less, is credited in a footnote with a similar observation to Turner's concerning the spatial elements in passage rites.

Here is my copy of *Rites of Passage* and, as we would expect, van Gennep himself had read Hertz's *Death*, which first appeared in 1907, two years before the Franco-German ethnographer's classic. Against the word dexterity in Hertz's second essay I have written 'an adroit left-hander', making an obvious point in the form of a feeble pun. Right-handed, I myself was socially maladroit and clumsy (two left feet my father said on one occasion, a right-angled triangle on another), but I was never sinister. *Taboo* by Franz Steiner is another study of this kind. Steiner, a Prague Jewish poet of distinction (translated by Michael Hamburger), who had left before the war to study under Radcliffe-Brown at Oxford, worked there with Evans-Pritchard until he died of heart failure at the age of forty-three in 1952, leaving behind a distraught Iris Murdoch.

Maurice Halbwachs (and Jorge Semprun)

Jorge Semprun was one of the masters of modern memory, or better, commemoration. He said in an interview that we are approaching the point when the direct memory of the camps will have disappeared, even the Jewish memory. 'Even', because—a point I have not seen made elsewhere—members of the resistance from Poland, France, Italy, etc. were around eighteen or twenty when they were deported, whereas thousands of Jewish children were deported, some of whom survived, and therefore the longest memory of deportation will be Jewish, and that too is beginning to fade, which is why Semprun continued to write. He had already written obsessively about Buchenwald in *The Long Voyage*, *Oh What a Beautiful Sunday* and other books. The eminent French sociologist Professor Maurice Halbwachs died in Buchenwald in circumstances described by Semprun in *Literature or Life?* and *Le Mort qu'il faut* ('The Designated Dead Man'). This is one of the case studies of poetry remembered in extreme situations I collected in my essay 'Rescue Work'. The Spaniard found a way to mark Halbwachs' passage from life to death over a period of weeks. The consolations of religion were neither possible nor desired: at a critical moment, Semprun recited, 'the way one says a prayer for the dying', the penultimate stanza of Baudelaire's great poem 'Le Voyage':

> Oh death, old captain, it's time, let's raise the anchor,
> This country grinds us down. Death, let us set sail!
> So what if sea and sky are black as ink,
> Our hearts—which you know well—are filled with light.

A posthumously published book by Halbwachs (translated as *On Collective Memory*) contains scholarly material (e.g. his comments on Chateaubriand), which I have explored for my own purposes. One need not agree with his 'always' to find the following thought suggestive and useful: 'The succession of our remembrances, even our most personal ones, is always explained by changes occurring in our relationships to various collective milieus.' By chance, a recent *Paris Review* had interviews with Jorge Semprun and Harry Matthews. Probably juxtaposed by accident, the two texts provide an object lesson in the wonderful ways of literature and art, by demonstrating how you can start with the pressure of story and experience (Semprun) and find the language to express it, or you can start with the language (Matthews), maximizing its tricks and trucs, in order to generate what it is you want to say. Semprun is a rare and extreme case: not all writers have been in a concentration camp and then lived a dangerous double life as a secret

Communist agent under Franco, and all the time having to 'forget' in order to live, only after many years allowing himself to remember. He then courted much controversy by blending fiction and autobiography against the conventional wisdom, although the wisdom had its reasons. Claude Lanzmann, if only in this respect, is the conventional wisdom, which gives it weight and integrity. Yet, what constitutes invention is a complex matter, as Semprun himself says of Lanzmann.

Harry Matthews, on the other hand, is a different kind of extreme case: he led a charmed and indeed privileged life (with some of the miseries attendant upon posh origins), then found his life as a writer changed by a recommendation from John Ashbery to read Raymond Roussel. Henceforth, he wanted to abolish psychology and character development: prose becomes a kind of poetry and you generate story or subject matter from language and structure without, for all that, becoming an aesthete; too many Oulipoans have written great books for that accusation to stick. Maybe I am pushing this boat out too far. Semprun is a stylist, Matthews has plenty to say. (See Mark Ford's essay on Matthews in *A Driftwood Altar*.) Most writers, all writers, move back and forth between Paula's poles when it comes to painting, namely the dialectic between the demands of the story and the demands of the picture. In the end, if not in the beginning, it is all one.

Bronisław Malinowski and Edmund Leach

I emailed Bruce Ross-Smith for a gloss on my comments on anthropological empiricism; his reply began with the comment that had I been studying for the Social Anthropology diploma in Oxford in the early sixties (the discipline did not merit an honours school until 'Human Sciences' in the 1970s), I would have been *praised* for reading Lévi Strauss. He continued: 'Malinowski lorded over his students with what Edmund Leach called his 'radical empiricism', which was embodied in the aim of his ethnographic method 'to grasp the native's point of view, his relation to life, to realize his vision of the world'. Bronisław Malinowski's functionalist epistemology was shockingly narrow in its focus on what was practically reasonable in the way cultures 'culture' their lives. Malinowski inverted Boasian relativism, took no interest in Mauss, and saw Radcliffe-Brown as a 'trespasser on the Malinowskian functionalist turf . . .' Malinowski loomed large in anthropology as the teacher of many of the leading anthropologists who taught people of my generation but, like Leach and Lévi-Strauss later on, he also made waves among the educated general public, if not to the extent he would have liked. Despite complete mutual disaffection, Evans-Pritchard towards the end of his life conceded he had learnt more from Malinowski than from anyone else. I remember from childhood the rude pictures in my father's copy of *The Sexual Life of Savages* and I have here another famous monograph, *Argonauts of the Western Pacific*, a set text that I appear exceptionally to have read right through, judging by my marks on many pages. More to my taste were Malinowski's *Sex, Culture and Myth* and *Magic, Science and Religion*.

Here is Edmund Leach's *Rethinking Anthropology*, in which he criticizes Malinowski's approach to classification, the disjunction between his narrow but brilliant fieldwork and universalizing theory, a criticism also directed at Meyer Fortes. I remember Leach from Cambridge, a dishevelled and apparently chaotic figure, reminding me a bit of Edward Thompson. Some years later, after reading 'The Legitimacy of Solomon' in *Genesis as Myth*, one of the Cape Editions edited by Nathaniel Tarn, I wrote Leach a letter, explaining the terms 'mechutan' and 'mechutanista' in Yiddish, which describe the kinship relationship between the two grandfathers and grandmothers of a child: 'opposite number grandfather/grandmother'. I can't remember if he already knew this. I recall only that his friendly reply contained a diagram.

The pseudonymous Tarn turns up under his real name Michael Mendelson as a contributor to Leach's *The Structural Study of Myth and Totemism*. Reflecting on totemism, Mendelson/Tarn accuses Malinowski of operating entirely within the realm of Nature whereas Durkheim, oppositely guilty, operates entirely within the realm of Culture. Now there's a binary opposition for the connoisseur! Few in each of Tarn/Mendelson's two worlds of poetry and anthropology (another binary opposition) knew of his significance in the other, at least not until the publication of *The Embattled Lyric*, a selection of his major essays in poetics and anthropology. Mary Douglas, in the Leach book, argues that Lévi-Strauss' potent image of mythic thinking as bricolage applies only in those areas of the world associated with totemism and that the great bricoleur is Lévi-Strauss himself who, she says, changes the rules as he goes along. Marvin Harris in *Cultural Materialism* takes a strong and similar swipe at Lévi-Strauss and at Leach's own structuralism, using as his example Leach's analysis of traffic lights: 'To propose that this complex process merely expressed the binary propensities in the human mind is to endow mental life with an omnipotence of which only infantile or disturbed minds have hitherto believed.' Structuralism, argues the Marxist Harris, does not teach us how people think, only how structuralists think. They are mythmakers, up their own heads. Still, in fairness, when the head contains the mind of a Lévi-Strauss, perpetrator of a great literary work such as *Tristes tropiques*, I say bring him on!

E. E. Evans-Pritchard and Reo Fortune

Here are *The Nuer* and *Nuer Religion* and *Social Anthropology* by E. E. Evans-Pritchard, the grand duke of Oxford Social Anthropology and one of the official gods I disapproved of during my time as a student anthropologist. Yet it was Evans-Pritchard—at times able, according to Ross-Smith, to present himself as 'a character out of *Boy's Own*'—who lectured annually on Durkheim, Mauss, Hertz, etc. and encouraged his former students to translate books from the great French sociological tradition. Since these were the very books I most enjoyed reading, EP's initiative confutes my ignorant assumption that Malinowskian fieldwork was the be-all and end-all of the British tradition. The translations included the books by Durkheim, Hubert/Mauss and Hertz already mentioned, Mauss' *The Gift* and Steiner's *Taboo*. Mauss, the nephew of Durkheim, was the link between this monumental figure and Lévi-Strauss, who would edit a posthumous volume of Mauss' major essays and who, for once, fully acknowledges his debt to him in his inaugural lecture at the Collège de France translated as *The Scope of Anthropology*, in which he suggests that the Renaissance gave birth to anthropology and colonialism. Evans-Pritchard, in his introduction to *The Gift*, sees Mauss as a son of the philosophical tradition of Enlightenment and also of a world that lost many luminaries (Hertz and Durkheim's son among them) in World War I, just as the generation of Halbwachs would suffer losses in World War II. Exchange, as seen in *potlatch* (Mauss drawing on Franz Boas' fieldwork among the Kwakiutl) and *kula* (Malinowski and Fortune among the Trobrianders and the Dobu, respectively), involves a moral transaction between individual persons, reinforcing community networks, rather than the rational and mechanical transactions the now discredited political economies of capitalism and communism require.

A wonderful page-long footnote in *Sorcerers of Dobu*, that rare and glorious monograph by Reo Fortune, a legendary figure I heard lecture in Cambridge, delineates the difference between the aforementioned potlatch and *kula*, the first based on generous giving, the second on great having. It is true that barter (upmarket) and soup kitchens (downmarket) are making a comeback as the world slowly but surely returns to the dark days. Yet, for the most part, people, especially influential people, are too busy to find the time for social intercourse that manners and civility require. Thus, editors of magazines and radio programmes no longer reply to submissions from writers who are not known figures or personal friends—I speak from personal experience. Fortune also wrote about the morality of the Manus in *Manus Religion*. He tells us that English and Manus are similarly oriented in matters of morality, and words like 'good' and 'bad', 'sin' and 'shame' translate in a straightforward way. 'In this respect, Manus contrasts with Dobu, for the Dobuan language is not oriented in morality as our own and the Manus languages are.' Still, the Dobu are more fun to read about. As summarized by top relativist—Germaine Greer is her successor—Ruth Benedict in a once famous book, *Patterns of Culture*: 'The Dobuan is dour, prudish and passionate, consumed with jealousy and suspicion and resentment. Every moment of prosperity he conceives himself to have wrung from a malicious world by a conflict in which he has worsted his opponent. The good man is one who has many such conflicts to his credit, as anyone can see from the fact that he has survived with a measure of prosperity. It is taken for granted that he has thieved, killed children and his close associates by sorcery, and cheated whenever he dared.' By contrast, a bad Dobu is what we (and the Manus) call a good man. He is esteemed a failure.

Donald Macrae/Erving Goffman/Basil Bernstein

Sociology only became a degree subject in its own right at Cambridge in the 1970s, long after my departure from the university following my non-honours degree in social anthropology. We anthropologists attended lectures for this optional topic by David Lockwood and John Goldthorpe, later senior professors elsewhere. The latter was married to the extraordinarily glamorous Rhiannon, a lecturer in French, whom I praised earlier in the French section of this book. Some years later, one of my neighbours in Upper Holloway was Donald Macrae, a legendary professor of sociology at LSE, legendary both for the large size of his brainpower and the small size of his output. I had written to him c/o LSE, asking if he would review a book for *European Judaism*, the magazine I was then editing and for which I was keen to recruit writers outside the traditional pool of Jewish intellectuals and scholars. He replied that since I lived two doors from him, why not drop in for a drink, which I did, more than once, over the years.

I recall a dinner party at the Macraes: fellow guests were sociologists Daniel Bell (and his wife Pearl Kazin Bell, whose brother Alfred I would later read and correspond with) and Basil Bernstein. I had been much impressed by Bernstein's landmark paper 'A Socio-Linguistic Approach to Social Learning' in the *Penguin Survey of the Social Sciences 1965*. There may be some affinity between his thought and that of Erving Goffman in *The Presentation of Self in Everyday Life* and other books.

Much later I discovered from Maurice Lindsay's *Modern Scottish Poetry* that Donald Macrae was also a poet. During a gathering at the French ambassador's house, John Gross told me that Macrae had written a major work of social theory whose only copy perished in a house fire along with his mother-in-law and that this double tragedy so seared him that he wrote very little afterwards. In his *Weber*, the shortest of the once ubiquitous Fontana Modern Masters, Macrae explains that Weber took his marvellous and evocative phrase 'the disenchantment of the world' from Schiller but that it really means 'driving out the magic from things'. Weber's power as a writer comes from his awareness of the residue of this phenomenon, its survival as a trace in the world of rationality that in principle he welcomed and explicated. Leach concludes his *Lévi-Strauss*, also a Fontana Modern Masters, as follows: 'But if, as Lévi-Strauss seems to be saying, Vico's "poetic cosmography" is a natural attribute of "the human mind", then it should still lie somewhere within the hidden structures of our own collective unconscious. Perhaps even in the age of space rockets and hydrogen bombs Paradise need not be wholly beyond recall.' As it happens, the dialectic between magic and rationality is one way of describing the process at the heart of the literary enterprise.

Marshal McLuhan and others

In New York in July 1964, I bought a book called *Mass Communication* by Charles R. Wright. I read it while living on West 13th Street and underlined a paragraph which argued that too much news results in less direct action on the part of individuals: 'Lazarsfeld and Merton have applied to this dysfunctional aspect of mass communications the colourful label of *narcotization*', with television presumably serving as a substitution for that opium, religion. If what they write was true in 1964, how much the more so today! I also bought a fat paperback edited by A. L. Kroeber and Clyde Kluckhohn, *Culture*, a critical panorama of the title concept. The end of my formal studies in anthropology a few weeks earlier did not mark the end of my interest in the subject; on the contrary, as I embarked on my long march to freedom from examination demons, the interest (surprise surprise) was compounded. The book ends: 'We have tried to honour the philosophical precept of not confusing substance with reality', which I am still working on.

Marshal McLuhan and Quentin Fiore's pioneering book, *War and Peace in the Global Village* (1968), fits under sociology in my grid, even though it equally belongs in history and politics. Their remark that 'every new technology necessitates a new war' has close affinities to the arguments Solly Zuckerman deployed in two Menard pamphlets. The pamphlets were widely read, even in the corridors of power, since Zuckerman was still chief science advisor to the prime minister, and had been an influential policy advisor for decades, ever since working for Eisenhower during the war. Eisenhower's warning against the military–industrial complex in his farewell presidential speech of January 1961 remains deeply pertinent to our situation today. Had John F. Kennedy built upon this insight instead of trying to close a non-existent missile gap, history would have been different and the world a safer place.

Here are McLuhan's *Counterblast, Understanding Media, The Gutenberg Galaxy* and a second book co-authored with Fiore, *The Medium Is the*

Massage. I have always found McLuhan, now sometimes maligned but mostly forgotten (despite a brief appearance as himself: 'if life were only like this', etc. in *Annie Hall*; see YouTube), to be a very interesting writer and thinker. Between and indeed on the lines of these books published in the 1960s, he foresaw the world of the Internet, Google, texting, email and, indeed, YouTube. McLuhan, along with the Situationists, was a precursor of a meta-McLuhan, Jean Baudrillard, the author of *The Spirit of Terrorism.*

Max Gluckman and Eli Devons (and the May Ball)

Closed Systems and Open Minds: The Limits of Naivety in Social Anthropology, edited by Max Gluckman, contains five essays on inter-disciplinary concerns: Victor Turner's 'Symbols in Ndembu Ritual' is the only section of the book I have read till now. The time has come to read the lengthy concluding essay by the editor and his friend, the applied economist and statistician, Professor Ely Devons. Ely Devons was the father of my Cambridge contemporary, David Devons, whose younger sister was my blind date at a May Ball because the person I should have taken I failed to take, for shameful reasons I can only deal with in fiction (thus damning myself in the eyes of Michel Leiris). I could see her looking out from the window of the room of a lecturer friend of hers, a Greek mathematician, as I pretended to enjoy myself downstairs. I wonder what became of her and of Olivia too, tall and pretty in her shirtwaister evening gown, who was on the receiving end of neither my best nor my worst behaviour. At one point in the evening, Olivia vanished, but returned. Later on, we went out a couple of times and that was it. David Devons' and my friend Robin Jacob, now a retired judge and responsible for introducing me to the person I could not bring myself to take, would know about Olivia's destiny; maybe I should renew contact with him.

[Coda at proof stage: Recently Robin and I chewed the cud near his office in University College London, where his main concern is intellectual property on which he is a world expert: I learn that his wife Wendy and Olivia are both artists. From morning till night, *la fête continue . . .*]

That May Ball took place over forty years ago. I was lonely, miserable and, towards the end, depressed in Cambridge. Although I shall never know if social anthropology would have suited me better had I been less miserable in my private life, I do know that *Closed Systems and Open Minds*, which my inscription tells me I bought the year after I left university, has opened up not a can of worms, not a kettle of fish, but a (gold?) mine into whose deepest chamber I have fallen and whence I hope to clamber out with something to show for the experience, perhaps some short stories.

[Coda: I have now read the essay by Gluckman and Devons. With affinities to an excellent book by W. G. Runciman, *Social Science and Political Theory*, it centres on the assumption that all specialists without exception have to make what I would call rules of engagement. If we take social anthropology, the nature of the research (fieldwork) is such that if these rules of engagement did not apply, the anthropologist would be obliged to study and factor in specialized data from economics, biology, genetics, law and so on, as is so often the case in today's inter-disciplinary world. In fact, if he or she does not rely merely on the conclusions of these specialists, does not bracket out and ignore the specialized data, does not take other disciplines for granted, the terrain would be enormous, like the map in 'On Exactitude [or 'Rigor'] in Science', the miniature story by Borges (in *Dreamtigers* and, later, *Collected Fiction*), a map so detailed and so large that it covers the world. 'It is illegitimate for practitioners in another discipline to criticise anthropological compression, unless they can show that this compression invalidates the social-anthropological analysis itself,' write the authors. They elaborate: 'If [the anthropologist] is to carry out any disciplined analysis, he must at appropriate points decide that he has done enough, first in the way of collecting facts, and then in analysing their conclusions. That is, he ceases to follow real connexions, and from them abstracts a set of such connexions as he thinks he can study profitably. He assumes they form a system: he circumscribes them and "closes his system".']

Mary Douglas

Mary Douglas' *Natural Symbols* (translated into Italian by Primo Levi, no less) and *Purity and Danger* were books I studied closely when I was reading more anthropology than I do now and, indeed, more than I read when I was officially studying the subject. I loved her work because she worried about problems that people worried about in France and, more importantly, because

I too worried about them. *Purity and Danger* is a book I recommended to Paula: given that one of her themes at the time was foetuses, she was interested in what I conceptualized as boundaries and ambiguity and fascinated by the Nuer who 'treat monstrous births as baby hippopotamuses, accidentally born to humans and with this labelling, the appropriate action is clear. They gently lay them in the river where they belong' (Evans-Pritchard). *Natural Symbols* contains a reference to Shifra Strizower and Douglas concedes that a criticism of her made by this fellow anthropologist was accurate. I remember a person of these rare names who taught in our Hebrew classes when I was a child. On an impulse, I check her out in Google and find only two references, one to a book she wrote on the Bene Israel community of Indian Jews. What became of her? My guess is that she married a fellow orthodox Jew and settled in Jerusalem or Brooklyn.

Hyam Maccoby

Here is *The Disputation*, my late friend Hyam Maccoby's powerful courtroom drama about the 1263 Barcelona debate between Jews and Christians. I published an extract on one of my MenCards to mark his eightieth birthday, a few days before he died. Douglas and Maccoby exchanged ideas over many years. Three of his books enter our territory: *A Pariah People*, *The Sacred Executioner* and *Antisemitism and Modernity*. Cain committed murder, human sacrifice, and therefore must be punished; this consisted of eternal wandering, eternal exile, but he had to be kept alive as a permanent reminder of his guilt for a necessary crime, the sacred executioner doubling as a sacred scapegoat. Abraham by contrast did not end up committing human sacrifice and the Binding of Isaac (the Akedah) became one of the great foundational myths of Judaism. The early Church Fathers would vilify the Jews who, wrongly seen as the killers of Jesus, became a kind of collective Cain and had to be kept alive because a collective reminder of their evil crime was needed to save mankind. The wandering Jew doubles as the anti-Christ: here, argues Maccoby, is the origin of 'antisemitism'. Hyam's posthumous *Antisemitism and Modernity* was edited by his devoted widow Cynthia. He always insisted on spelling 'antisemitism' without a hyphen, to make clear that the prejudice has nothing to do with

Jews supposedly being Semites. The hyphen involves a racist stereotype, partly derived from nineteenth-century linguistics, long after the singular geo-racial origins of Jews had vanished through intermarriage and other factors, although traces remain in the prevalence of certain illnesses among Ashkenazi Jews and in the DNA of people named Cohen. The chapter on Ezra Pound in particular is required reading and demonstrates what a fine literary critic Maccoby was.

Maccoby would agree with Bruce Lincoln that 'one may perfectly well combine such practices as headhunting, cannibalism, human sacrifice, and the like, with extremely sophisticated and intelligent religio-philosophical systems and rationales.' Lincoln's *Death, War and Sacrifice* is a difficult study of Indo-European religion, myth and language. Lincoln ends with a careful account of George Dumézil's reactionary views, giving a close reading of recent history, that is to say politics, specifically the Turkish massacre of the Armenians, a subject much in the news a few years ago because of French legislation concerning genocide denial. Lincoln's teacher Mircia Eliade was still alive and teaching in Chicago when I was living there in 1966. I bought a number of books by him, including *Aspects du mythe*, *The Sacred and the Profane* and *Cosmos and History*, which my underlinings and marginalia suggest I read carefully. These books, along with Roger Caillois' *L'Homme et le sacré*, really belong under comparative religion rather than anthropology; Eliade is anthropologically naive at times ('Like the mystic, like the religious man in general, the primitive lives in a continual present,' he writes in *Cosmos and History*). Against his comment that 'Existence is established by initiation', I annotated: 'but it is in the very nature of life that one's acts are or are not successful'. Meaning what?

It strikes me that the books Mircia Eliade wrote for the general public are inferior to comparable books by Gaston Bachelard and Octavio Paz: the latter often reads the world through binary opposition and is the author of the brilliant *Claude Lévi-Strauss: An Introduction*. The Eliade books were translated by Willard Trask, editor of *The Unwritten Song*, the hugely important two-volume anthology of the poetry of primitive and traditional peoples. Back in 1968, having recently become a Cape Editions author (in my capacity as translator of Yves Bonnefoy), I asked Tom Maschler if I could have review copies of these expensive books (oddly priced at fifty-five and sixty shillings rather than in pounds). He sent me the books with a letter saying they had been disgracefully neglected and looking forward to my review. My notice, a rave but far too short, appeared in *Tribune*. I badly wanted those beautiful and important books; they will survive any imaginable cull of my library at a later date.

Lewis Hyde

Lewis Hyde signed his *The Gift: Imagination and the Erotic Life of Property* for me in 1993 when I met him at Eva Hoffman's flat. Hyde's remarkable book belongs in this section because when I read it, I was reminded of one of its crucial influences, *The Gift* by Marcel Mauss. I see from my own inscription that I had purchased the book eight years earlier, a good example of the books I have bought knowing I would read them one day, perhaps long in the future. I cannot remember whether the reason for the eventual reading of Hyde was contingent upon accident or design, although some would say we design our accidents, that both are always in dialectical play, with one or other uppermost on any specific occasion.

Hyde's exploration of the artist and the market yields insights as valuable as those of Richard Titmuss in his book on blood donation, *The Gift Relationship*. From Reagan to Bush, from Thatcher to Cameron, the market (with eyebrows mildly raised during the Credit Crunch in 2008, only to be lowered again) has been fetishized to an extent neither Hyde nor I could have predicted even fifteen years ago: all the more reason then to read or reread this book and insert its values into discussions about the arts and the political economy. Few people are prepared to face the fact that the main enemy (climate change and associated modalities) will destroy us unless we fight not only its symptoms but also its causes in untrammelled and deregulated globalized markets, whose crisis is now upon us. Climate change is our equivalent of Nazism or a Martian invasion. The fight will involve concepts of fairness and rationing both nationally and internationally, for promiscuous economic growth is deadly to the species. Only a combination of the best qualities of Churchill, Attlee, Roosevelt and maybe Trotsky could galvanize the people. What have we had? Jack the Ripper in charge of police investigations, in the form of George Bush Junior. Barrack Obama has been a great disappointment. He is not even as radical as Lyndon Johnson, let alone Roosevelt. David Cameron understands nothing. His are the voodoo economics derided by George Bush Senior; his big society is both vacuous and fatuous, except unexpectedly in the form of public sector strikes. I fear for the world in which my grandchildren will be grown-ups. A radical alter-globalism (Derrida's word) is the only way to fight this fear.

Two sonnets and a true story

I did not buy Roland Meighan's textbook, *A Sociology of Educating*; it was sent to me because I gave permission for a catalogue sonnet to be included which Meighan had read in *New Humanist*.

Even though I have some doubts about it, I will reprint here, since it proved useful as a pedagogical aid during the three years I taught the autobiography module at London Metropolitan University. Doubtless one could add, subtract or change 'determinations' in this list. I will comment only on line 12: this is an allusion to the work of Noam Chomsky whom John Lyons taught in the linguistics paper of the social anthropology tripos at Cambridge. The syntactic play in the last line of the poem still pleases me, although it is straightforward enough. Complex and subtle play involving syntax is one of the instructive pleasures in the poetry of, for example, F. T. Prince and George Oppen, two of my lodestars. Indeed, such play is ubiquitous in certain kinds of poetry. I am delighted that Meighan quotes from C. Wright Mills' *The Sociological Imagination* immediately after my text, and I cannot deny that the academic anthropology (and sociology) failure, which is me, achieved consolation, if not redemption, from being quoted in a sociology textbook.

'The Humanist's Sonnet'

I am determined by my class
I am determined by my sex
I am determined by my God
I am determined by my genes
I am determined by my unconscious
I am determined by my childhood

I am determined by my death
I am determined by my climate
I am determined by my homeland
I am determined by my work
I am determined by my newspaper
I am determined by my deep linguistic structures
I am determined by my etcetera
I am determined to be free

I append now a better catalogue sonnet, although its concerns are psychological rather than sociological: I wrote it after reading Antonio Damasio's least substantial book, *Looking for Spinoza*. Following a lecture he gave at the Royal Geographical Society, Paula and I had dinner with him at the most amazing house in London: being in it for two hours was an experience nonpareil. Moving round this completely constructed three-dimensional visual experience, I felt (with hindsight) like Charlie in the Chocolate Factory, except Willy Wonka in this case was Charles Jencks, celebrated landscape architect and begetter of our understanding of postmodernism in architecture, although the word itself is supposed to have been coined by Charles Olson (according to a footnote in Alfred Kazin's *Journals*). I later explained in a letter to Damasio that 'the subtitle of my poem proposes an explanation of the gesture in the painting which you overlooked in your book: they are welcoming Spinoza to the world.' Damasio is not going to like my friend Z. Kotowicz's new book, *Psychosurgery*. It takes great issue with him over mental illness—the case of Phineas Gage—and neurosurgery, but the Portuguese writer raises philosophical questions I enjoy discussing with Kotowicz and my Uncle Jack.

'Damasio Abstracted'

(Sonnet for Dr Tulp and Rembrandt, Announcing the Birth of Spinoza, 1632)

My mind is made up of images.
My mind is made up of sensations.
My mind is made up of desires.
My mind is made up of emotions.
My mind is made up of feelings.

My mind is made up of perceptions.
My mind is made up of representations.
My mind is made up of ideas.
My mind is made up of thoughts.
My mind is made up of relationships.
My mind is made up of essences.
My mind is made up of existences.
My mind is made up.
Please do not confuse me with the facts.

I have it on good authority (the woman concerned told a close friend of hers and mine) that one of the world's most famous social anthropologists, now deceased, blurred the sacred boundary between life and work, supplying connoisseurs of the liminal (all of us) with a sublime example of *déformation professionelle*: while making love to (or with) his novelist partner (*in medias res, in flagrante* even), he got out of bed saying he had to make a note about the extraordinary experience they were sharing. Mother of all participant observers, more detached than a Greek god, he then returned to bed and completed the process he had interrupted. This proves he was not a poet: a poet would have written a sonnet *après coup*. We do not know what the woman thought about her unusual experience. My guess is she recycled it in a novel.

Philosophy

Paris 1961

While I was living in Paris in 1961, I read a once famous and much-reprinted anthology, Walter Kaufmann's *Existentialism from Dostoevsky to Sartre*, before lending it to my old school friend Michael Pinto-Duschinsky, with whom there is documentary evidence I disagreed: 'Mike's idea of freedom is arbitrary and ridiculous because air is in the way as well. He is a *casse-pied*. His argument about music is fallacious. Existence and essence belong to the music not to the paper.' Kaufmann includes part one of Dostoevsky's *Notes from Underground*, a book I was reading in Russian in the lounge of the British

Institute, 7 rue de la Sorbonne, with a friend from the Russian colony in Meudon, Marina Lvoff, in exchange for giving her English lessons. Kaufmann places it stylistically on a continuum between Kierkegaard's earlier reflections and Rilke's later *Notebooks of Malte Laurids Brigge*. I remember finding Karl Jaspers more accessible than Martin Heidegger, and tried to remedy this in the 1980s by reading the latter's *Poetry, Language and Thought* ('Pain gives of its healing power where we least expect it') and George Steiner's remarkable study *Heidegger*, a book haunted by Celan, who wrote in Heidegger's guest book when he visited him in the Black Forest: 'Into the hut-book, looking at the well-star, with a hope for a coming word in the heart', which he later worked into his poem 'Totdnauberg' about this fraught visit: 'Along the paths of German language,' writes John Felstiner, 'Celan could only go half way with Heidegger', a man for whom 'Being speaks German'.

Cambridge 1962

After my single year of French and Russian studies at Cambridge, ashamed of my poor performance in part one of the modern languages tripos, I decided in the summer of 1962 that I must change subjects, a fateful decision indeed, a giant moonstruck step by one who knew not what he was doing. I had three options: English, social anthropology and philosophy, or moral sciences, as it was known. I had read Sartre's *Existentialism and Humanism* and, more promising in respect of Cambridge itself, Russell's *The Problems of Philosophy*. I obtained an appointment with the Trinity philosopher Casimir Lewy, to whom I doubtless mentioned Russell; if I was wise, I kept silent about Sartre. He told me to go away and read *Principia Ethica* by G. E. Moore, Bishop Berkeley's writings and René Descartes's *A Discourse on Method*; I was to read Descartes in English not in French, lest I get sidetracked by literary considerations. If I still wanted to read philosophy, I was to come back and see him again. There are no annotations whatsoever in my copies of Descartes and Moore. Evidently I read Berkeley's *Principles of Human Knowledge* closely: the margins are full of questions, comments and disagreements. I have written ' "Whatever is is right", Pope 1688–1744' against a sentence of the poet's exact contemporary: 'We shall be forced to acknowledge that those particular things, which considered in themselves appear to be *evil*, have the nature of *good*, when considered as *linked with the whole system of things*.' And against section LXXXVII, my comment is as follows: 'This answers the vulgar attacks on his work, but still does not explain for me why the philosophers' matter does not exist, or rather, what is the philosophers' matter, and if everyone agrees it does not exist, wherein lies Berkeley's importance?' I don't know if I was thinking about Samuel Johnson's vulgar refutation of the Bishop's idealism after Boswell had said Berkeley was wrong but impossible to refute, yet this evident engagement with the philosopher surprises me and gives me pleasure forty-five years on. All the same, I remember finding these books too difficult and less compelling than *La Pensée sauvage*, which I also read that summer. As I have written earlier in this book, I ended up changing not to English or moral sciences but to social anthropology.

Denis Diderot

Who can resist Denis Diderot? say I, with a rhetorical flourish. I loved reading *D'Alembert's Dream* and *Rameau's Nephew*. You can find the *Dream* in a well-edited volume by David Adams, *Thoughts on the Interpretation of Nature*. Adams also includes the 'Letter on the Blind for the Use of Those who See', a brilliant and philosophically seditious argument which earned Diderot time in prison, to his great credit, if not comfort. Like David Hume, with whom he has much in common, he quarrelled with Rousseau. Balzac read him, and his influence is discernible in *The Unknown Masterpiece*, which I translated some years ago. Paula phoned as I was completing this paragraph. When I told her what it was about, she recalled that her husband Vic had often suggested she should illustrate Diderot's *La Religieuse*. My English edition of *Rameau's Nephew* (translated by Jacques Barzun) ends with an enchanting essay about possessions, 'Regrets on Parting with my Old Dressing Gown'. Poor Diderot: 'Two engravings that were not without merit—Poussin's "Shower of Manna in the Wilderness" and his "Esther before the Throne of King Ahasuerus"—were shamefully exiled, one (the melancholy Esther) to make room for a Rubens portrait of an old man, the other displaced by Vernet's "After the Storm".' A swift visit to Google reveals that the Vernet is now in the Pushkin Museum in Moscow. Reading Carlos Fuentes' *Myself with Others* during the final revision of this book, I was even more struck by the case he made for Diderot's *Jacques le Fataliste* than for *Don Quixote*. The latter, according to Dostoevsky as quoted by Fuentes, suffers from 'the nostalgia of realism'. Curiously, the worst chapters in this uneven collection (as an essayist he is not a patch on Paz) are on Borges and Marquez.

Søren Kierkegaard

I have opened Søren Kierkegaard's *Journals 1834–1854* and *The Last Years 1853–1855* with a thrill of retrospective anticipation, although I am surprised at the extent of my underlinings in the first volume. Kierkegaard, like the Dostoevsky of *Notes from Underground* and Rimbaud, is one of those nineteenth-century writers who spoke directly to one's own existential concerns when young. Among my friends, he is central only to the *imaginaire* of Augustus Young, who is engaged in a lifelong dialogue with the gloomy Dane (see *The Nicotine Cat* and *The Secret Gloss*), just as Paula remains attracted to Hans Christian Andersen, another solitary Danish genius who, it has finally been proved, did meet Kierkegaard. For Young, Kierkegaard is the equal and equivalent of Marx and Darwin and, without him, there would have been no 'Heidegger, Sartre, Barthes and Kafka' (*The Nicotine Cat*). We learn from *Journals* that on arrival in Berlin in May 1843, everything reminds Kierkegaard of his past. He thinks of his married apothecary's remark: 'one only lives once; one must have someone to whom one can explain oneself.' This recollection was written down less than two years after Kierkegaard broke off his engagement to Regine, and with this act any thought of matrimony or intimate relationship with a human being. It raises two questions: need the 'someone' always be the same person? And is oneself the person this someone explains herself to in return? My answer to the first question is that we divide up our confidences or self explanations between a number of people. A spouse or partner most likely receives the majority or the most important ones (unless there is a dark secret involving betrayal or an honourable white lie or shame, the last possibly involving self-betrayal), but there is often a best friend of the same or opposite sex, not to mention children and parents and professionals of the traditional kind. The person (or persons) receiving one's confidences has her own coalition of persons. Shall we say she is prima inter pares and leave it at that? Meanwhile some things remain untold: we are all marranos, for our inner truths never match the outer ones (to a greater or lesser degree), there is always a 'secret gloss'. This is the territory of fiction, for me at least.

Friedrich Nietzsche and Simone Weil

It was not until the early 1980s that I discovered Friedrich Nietzsche or, more accurately, he discovered me, who at forty was ready to be challenged by the radicality and power of *Ecce Homo* and *Daybreak*. Nietzsche writes in *Ecce Homo* that *Daybreak* is a book whose art makes 'things which easily slip by without a sound, moments which I call divine lizards'. Revisiting his writings on Jews in *Daybreak*, I find it difficult to read him as other than a difficult philosemite (I discuss Jewish philosophers and theologians elsewhere in this book). Simone Weil's *La Pesanteur et la grâce* [*Gravity and Grace*] compels a horrified attention. She did not, or rather could not, understand the attitude to suffering and martyrdom embodied in Auden's 'Musée des Beaux Arts'. Now consider a thought like the following: 'Whence will renewal come to us—to us who have defiled and emptied the whole empty globe? From the past alone, if we love it.' The first sentence is truer than she knew or than anyone knew, when that was written, which was not later than 1942. The second sentence was never true, but the world was safe enough, eternal enough (as Canetti almost said) to contain people with such views. Today, however, it reminds me—not that I need reminding—that we are in the last days and unless we unite to save the planet, we are all finished, and that includes the grandchildren of the directors of oil and other companies doing well out of imperial wars, fought for strategic and commercial imperatives not for democracy and human rights.

Beauty: Elaine Scarry and Jean Paulhan

Blaise Pascal's *Pensées*, number 77: 'What vanity is painting which arouses admiration on account of its resemblance to things that we do not admire when we come across them in life.' This makes me think about Paula's ferocious insistence on copying: her paintings of home-made rough and ready sculptures so alive, so impassioned. Pascal unintentionally praises what he objects to. I wonder what he would have made of Elaine Scarry's beautiful book, *On Beauty and Being Just*, so different from her unreadable *Dreaming by the Book*. Her proof text is Wittgenstein's comment that when the eye sees something beautiful, the hand wants to draw it. This has implications for thinking about many things, including Paula's work as a figurative painter and Giacometti's entire *oeuvre* ('You have to copy exactly what you are looking at'). Beauty is one of the great themes in Jean Paulhan's *Les Fleurs de Tarbes*, in which I have written my name and college address: this means, to my utter astonishment, that I bought the book when I was still a student, back in the early 1960s. I can no longer reconstruct the trajectory of influence or discovery that led me to Paulhan's famous polemic. I read about half of it at the time; the latter half of the book still has the pages uncut. In a short chapter, Paulhan inveighs against those who reject 'mastery' and 'perfection' as mere artifice and useless convention, and, seeking to rule out beauty and virtuosity, privilege thought and feeling. He then quotes an announcement at the entrance to the public gardens in Tarbes: 'It is forbidden to enter the gardens with flowers in your hands.' This symbolizes, for him, the terrorism conducted against rhetoric or, as the terrorists insist, cliché. (Adrian Stokes' essay 'Listening to Clichés' (in *A Game That Must Be Lost*) deals frontally and brilliantly with clichés, including a (psycho)-analysis of the phrase 'he was beside himself with rage' and many slang synonyms for 'psychotic'.) I hope, one day, to cut the remaining pages of *Les Fleurs de Tarbes* and explore Paulhan's nuances. Kevin Hart complicates the issue in *The Dark Gaze* by quoting Yves Bonnefoy as suggesting that rhetoric is in fact 'perfected terror'.

Psychoanalysis, etc.

Bring the real times back.
—Robert Browning, 'Waring'

It is a joy to be hidden, and disaster not to be found.
—D. W. Winnicott, 1963 paper

Introduction

I visit psyche-land from time to time, with fiction and poetry as my Baedeker. Case studies too, like Morton Schatzman's account of the astonishing case of Judge Schreber, *Soul Murder*. The story of Schreber obsessed my late friend Michel Couturier and is discussed by Elias Canetti at the end of *Crowds and Power* and by Brian Dillon in *Tormented Hope*. I have read a certain amount about the history, practice and discourse of psychoanalysis. Now and again these enter—how could they not?—into my ongoing reflection on the Jewish aspects of Austria–Hungary: the Vienna of Gustav Mahler, Ludwig Wittgenstein, Sigmund Freud, Karl Kraus, Jakov Lind; the Prague of Franz Kafka and the golem; the East Galicia of Shmuel Agnon, Henry Roth, Joseph Roth and Piotr Rawicz. Jewish Austria–Hungary is in some ways my homeland, as I explained to Max Sebald in Norwich after giving a talk on Piotr at Max's Holocaust seminar. As for Freud, he understood very well that the poets with their 'defunctive music' (Eliot quoting 'The Phoenix and the Turtle') and novelists had been there before him.

Carl Gustav Jung (anima)

Murray Stein's *In Midlife* is a Jungian exploration of midlife liminality that struck a chord, rang a bell, hit the spot, spoke to my condition as a man playing out, in a post-marital mid-forties relationship, psychic experiences he had neglected in his premarital early twenties. 'At midlife in the encounter with the anima, you are dealing with a goddess!' The account of Circe as the anima of Odysseus and the related links to Hermes and Tiresius offered a narrative that helped make sense of my life. During this phase, I read a number of books on personal development, including Phillida Salmon's *Living in Time*. She quotes the chilling last will and testament of Michael Henchard in *The Mayor of Casterbridge*: 'And that I be not bury'd in consecrated ground. And that no sexton be asked to toll the bell. And that nobody is wished to see my dead body. And that no mourners walk behind me at my funeral. And that no flowers be planted on my grave. And that no man remember me. To this I put my name.'

James Hillman's *Anima* is a fascinating exploration of Carl Gustav Jung's powerful and enabling concept and also serves as an anthology of Jung's writing in that area. Hillman alludes to the association made by Bachelard between anima and reverie, 'in contradiction to animus and the activity of dreaming'. In the margin I have written 'Balthus and Magritte'. Nearly twenty years later, I would say that Balthus fits the idea, but not Magritte. Jung quotes Tristram Shandy as saying a man has two souls, the anima and the animus. I have no doubt that my exploration of what goes on in anima projections has enabled me to understand better the dialectics of my three principal relationships with women, who represent thesis, antithesis and synthesis. But to explore in any detail personal truth of this nature requires the obliquities of fiction, so for now I return to earth with books by authors like David Smail, Daniel J. Levinson, J. A. C. Brown and Andrew Crowcroft. In the Jung anthology, *Psychological Reflections,* I have at last stumbled on a profound thought which moved me for years and which no one, not even Adam Phillips and John Forrester when I asked them, could source to Freud, for the simple reason that Jung wrote it: 'Nothing exerts a stronger psychic effect upon the human environment, and especially upon children, than the life which the parents have not led.' Robert Bly's *A Little Book on the Human Shadow* contains a provocative meditation on Wallace Stevens; Bly's view that Stevens' 'late poems are as weak as is possible for a genius to write' is not persuasive.

Carl Gustav Jung (as echoed by John Welch)

The poet John Welch's *Dreaming Arrival* is a fascinating account of his life and work as a writer in the context of psychoanalysis: the fact that he was keeping a journal led his therapist to comment that it was a way of holding back valuable information from the analysis, a way of maintaining control when he should have been letting go. Welch and I are exact contemporaries and both read modern languages at the same university. We have two or three psychic structures in common. He writes about the 'other' life he had at home: 'writing as the marking off of a "secret" area became a sort of solution to me when I started to write poetry in my mid-teens. Total outer compliance and inner freedom was the trick I tried, with ferocious determination, to pull off but the ferocity exacted its toll and I ended up, aged nineteen, having a breakdown.' For my part, I created a 'little box' in my mind which no one else had access to. Later, Welch talks about 'succeeding at being a failure'. He, however, unlike me, did get an honours degree. Though I didn't officially have a breakdown, I too 'succeeded at being a failure'. Welch asks if we inherit from our parents the weight of their unlived lives, echoing Jung. I believe this to be a widespread condition if not a universal truth, judging by John's self-narrative, my own, and that of several other friends. He surrounds himself with 'unread books, all those potential beginnings'. Like one's many unfinished writing projects. I, like Welch, have looked at excellent single poems in old anthologies by now forgotten poets. They have given us the slip, like Browning's 'Waring', who inspired the title of an early novel by Anthony Powell.

Sigmund Freud

Bruno Bettelheim's *Freud and Man's Soul* fascinated me, not least the way he compares the happy ending of Amor and Psyche to that of Oedipus, and his pointing out that Sigmund Freud used the word 'seele' (soul) for what Freud's first translator James Strachey translated as 'psyche'. Bettelheim quotes HD, the poet Hilda Doolittle, as saying, rather wonderfully in my opinion, that 'Freud was midwife to the soul', this after her analysis with him which, according to the poet and HD scholar Jane Augustine, was conducted in English. HD and Freud agreed that she was not a patient but a student. Paid for by her partner Bryher (who described herself to Freud as HD's cousin), the analysis cost three hundred pounds sterling for three months—a colossal sum. The midwife remark is not in HD's *Tribute to Freud* of 1944 but comes, Augustine tells me, from another text about Freud, *Advent*, written four years later.

Tribute to Freud ends with HD's translation of Goethe's Mignon poem, 'Kennst du das Land' (the title of a painting by Kitaj). Bettina von Arnim, who identified with Mignon, was a muse of Beethoven, Goethe and Marx, and reminds one of Lou Andreas-Salomé. The second stanza of Goethe's lyric tells of a house and contains the lines 'What, poor child, have they done to you there? / Do you know it? There! There, oh / With you, my protector, I long to go.' In the first stanza, the protector is addressed as 'my dearest', at the end of the poem as 'my father' (compare the unprotective father in the poet's 'Erlking', famously set by Schubert). For HD, the father is Freud: 'He raised from dead hearts and stricken minds and maladjusted bodies a host of living children'; Freud, writing to her not long before he died, reciprocates if not her love for him, then her pride and affection in this relationship between equals: 'What you gave me was not praise, it was satisfaction and I need not be ashamed of my satisfaction. Life at my age is not easy, but Spring is beautiful and so is love.' In the first section of the memoir, she quotes the hall porter at the Hotel Regina where she stayed during the months of her analysis: 'You know Berggasse? . . . When the Professor is no longer with us, they will name it Freudgasse.' Seventy-five years after Freud's death, this still has not happened, although there is a Freudgasse in Gerasdorf, on the outskirts of Vienna.

I remember when and where I was reading Estelle Roith's *The Riddle of Freud*: on holiday at Moortown Farm in Devon, which my companion and I had rented from Ted Hughes. Nearby was a village called Inwardley, appropriately enough. Hughes showed us a church sporting a Sheila Nagig and we spent a couple of evenings with him in a pub ('See that fellow, he owns a third of Exmoor') and a morning in Court Green, his house, where I recall pictures by his daughter Frieda on the wall. Freud's relationship to his ancestral religion and community is well documented. His wife Martha, the week after he died, began lighting the Friday night Sabbath candles for the first time since their marriage. The candles had been forbidden by the atheist paterfamilias for whom, in the words of the critic Marthe Robert quoted by Roith, 'the primordial murdered father was Jacob Freud, the Galician Jew, and not a legendary Greek King'. I wrote the word 'Yeats' against Roith's quote from Freud's *Three Essays on Sexuality* in her lengthy discussion of Freud and Andreas-Salomé: 'The genital apparatus remains the neighbour of the cloaca, and [to quote Lou Andreas-Salomé] "in the case of women is only taken from it on lease".' This is Crazy Jane in prose ('love has pitched his mansion', etc.), and we would surely like Yeats to have read Andreas-Salomé's 1916 essay 'Anal and Sexual' (although she is not in the index of Roy Foster's biography of Yeats). Her comment would have raised the eyebrows, if not the manhoods, of Nietzsche and Rilke.

Paula and I went on the trail of Andreas-Salomé and Nietzsche while on a pilgrimage holiday at Lake Orta to see the wondrous Sacro Monte statues on a nearby hillside. We even had dinner at the lakeside hotel where they stayed and where he is supposed to have proposed to her, which put ideas into my head. Andreas-Salomé died on 5 February 1937, a couple of years before Yeats and Freud. The deaths of both men occasioned elegies from Auden; the Freud is a much better poem than the Yeats, perhaps because it is not about another poet. I quoted it in the eulogy I delivered at Jakov Lind's funeral in the Jewish cemetery across the road from Golders Green crematorium where Freud is interred. Stefan Zweig gave Freud's eulogy. Another of my marginal notes in Roith concerns a comparison between 'the Jewish rejection of sexual asceticism' and 'the Christian ethic of chastity'. Roith wants to show that the Jewish position is more complex and less apparently positive than many have said, and draws on a difficult passage from Max Weber. Richard Webster in *Why Freud Was Wrong* has an interesting discussion about Anna Freud's jealousy of the women in Freud's life. Webster quotes appositely from a Rilke poem Anna loved: 'I have no home, no loved one waiting at the door. / There is no place in which I feel I live. / All those things to which I give / Myself grow rich. But I grow poor.' According to Marie Bonaparte, Anna remained a 'vestal' all her life, a deeply appropriate word in every sense, given her unique role in her father's life.

Steven Kellman's biography of Henry Roth, *Redemption*, tells us that the family liked to claim they were (distantly) related to Freud, whose father was born in the same town as Roth, Tyshmenitsa, in what is now Western Ukraine. Marthe Robert's *From Oedipus to Moses* and Yosef Hayim Yerushalmi's *Freud's Mose* are fascinating books, as is the ultimately unconvincing *Sigmund Freud and the Jewish Mystical Tradition* by David Bakan. Yerushalmi's truly pathfinding book is his better-known *Zakhor: Jewish History and Jewish Memory*. Derrida's *Archive Fever* which, among other things—and that qualifier is always true of Derrida—is a reading of Yerushalmi's *Freud's Moses*, belongs here. *Eros and the Jews* by David Biale is a brilliant book, with many of its insights relating to a nuance predicated by Max Weber. The chapter on 'Zionism as an Erotic Revolution' contains a quote from a 1923 polemic by my friend Avraham Shlonsky, the great poet of the Third Aliyah generation of immigrants to Mandate Palestine and translator of Pushkin, Trotsky, etc., against the Hebrew prose he had inherited: 'we demand civil marriage and free love between words

. . . There is too much "family purity" [an area of particular Talmudic concern] in our language. Every combination of words is an act of promiscuity, a one-night-stand.'

I read Freud's non-clinical studies, *Totem and Taboo*, *The Future of an Illusion*, *Civilisation and Its Discontents* (a footnote tells us he heard Mark Twain give a lecture) and *Moses and Monotheism*, during my student anthropology days. Later I studied more strictly psychoanalytic books as listed in the bibliography. I read *Beyond the Pleasure Principle* while 'working' as a doorman or day watchman in a handbag factory on John Street. I bought Adam Phillips' *Freud Reader*, in order to read, late in the day, the essay on screen memories, and to reread the great essay on the uncanny (*unheimlich*). Here is Janet Malcolm's *In the Freud Archives* and two books by the widow of my friend the painter Josef Herman, Nini Herman's *Why Psychotherapy* and *My Kleinian Home*. Two of the many sentences I underlined: 'Are there not children who are pushed to murder their soul each day . . .' and: 'I had no inkling yet that a truly separate life has never been required to serve as an altar for human sacrifice.' I recall not being persuaded by Kleinian theorizing and yet finding Nini's insights and descriptions powerful and true to my own experience. In this sense, theory (see Zola, Marx, Freud, Frazer, Yeats— mythographers all) is scaffolding, a *sine qua non*, that enables the building of a narrative, the narrative of a building. Like scaffolding, theory can be demolished without harm to the (de)construction.

Herbert Marcuse

Herbert Marcuse, a hugely influential figure on the left when I was young, obtained half a million hits as late as 2007 when I googled him. Norman O. Brown had fifty thousand hits, a tenth of that number, Marshal McLuhan a twentieth [2011: McLuhan's stock has risen four years later]. It is salutary to see how far their stock has fallen on the Google bourse, if Google can be said to measure anything important. I believe it does, especially since these are public intellectuals as well as scholars. Once upon a time I would have had to go to the library and see how often their books had been taken out but I doubt I would have bothered. A few more statistics: Derrida has one million one hundred thousand hits, and Baudrillard half a million more than Derrida, but Baudrillard's is certainly swollen by his reported demise. The unexpected figure in 2007 is Marcuse's: very high indeed. His *Eros and Civilisation* discusses Wilhelm Reich, whose *Mass Psychology of Fascism* was given to me by my friend Isel Rivero. Marcuse is right to say that Reich does not differentiate between repressive and non-repressive sublimation. I salute Marcuse while noting Alasdair MacIntyre's harsh critique in *Marcuse* and I also salute Brown, whose thinking engaged me more and who in turn quotes Marcuse in *Life against Death*. Brown too discusses Reich's views on sublimation and repression and, while disagreeing with the older man, takes him more seriously than Marcuse does. George Frankl in *The Failure of the Sexual Revolution* (not a reactionary book) associates Marcuse and Reich more closely than either would wish, I suspect.

Norman O. Brown and Philip Rieff and Z. Kotowicz

I lapped up Norman O. Brown's *Love's Body*, *Life against Death* and *Closing Time* in the 1960s and 1970s, followed by *Apocalypse and/or Metamorphosis* twenty years later. Brown is an exhilarating writer, a trickster figure who deploys collage and fragment and quotation in order to convey the polymorphous perverse nature of men and women as they make their own history, emerging from the shadow of repression into the light of freedom. He quotes a sentence of Rilke I underlined then and would underline now: 'Whoever rightly understands and celebrates death, at the same time magnifies life.' Brown's is a gay science (gay as in merry widow), to use the title of a book by Nietzsche, perhaps his main influence after Joyce and Marx/Freud, the latter twin a towering influence he shares with Marcuse. In many margins, I have noted 'Paz', his exact contemporary, although the fact that Brown was born in Mexico (a year before Paz himself) is pure coincidence relating to his father's employment. Paz certainly read Brown and I would guess that Brown read Paz, and maybe Oppen too. Time and again, Brown comes up with arresting thoughts: 'The intermediate term between psychoanalysis and time, as between psychoanalysis and money, is religion' and he calls on a former hero of mine, Benjamin Lee Whorf, to serve as witness to this poetical syllogism. Talking about money in the chapter 'Filthy Lucre', Brown writes: 'Interest is an increment.' I noted in the margin:

'excrement is increment'. In the last pages of *Life against Death*, he says that what mysticism, poetry and psychoanalysis, political idealism and philosophy have in common 'is a mode of consciousness that can be called . . . the dialectical imagination'. Here he summons up scholars in his own league, Gershom Scholem and Joseph Needham. Dialectical consciousness 'would be a step towards that Dionysian ego which does not negate any more'. Dialectics is 'the metaphysic of Eros', a phrase that Paz could have quoted, and probably did.

In the same way that Ignaz Maybaum reads the Torah, Brown, in his essay in *Apocalypse and/or Metamorphosis* on the apocalypse of Islam, reads the Koran, and once again one berates oneself (a) for neglecting certain similarities between Jewish and Islamic (mainly Sunni) religious fundamentalism and (b) for not paying enough attention to other Islamic traditions, for example Sufism, so similar to Hassidism, and Akhmediya, the Islamic reform movement. Brown's 'Revisioning Historical Identities' is another great essay, deeply learned in philosophy, psychology and literary criticism: 'Perhaps Zukofsky's error was to take Wittgenstein instead of Freud as the representative of modern thought who "appears to have travelled with the flame of the Phoenix and the Turtle".'

My friend Z. Kotowicz phoned this morning and was dismissive when I quoted Brown's 'solution to the problem of identity: get lost'. 'Speaking as a professional', said Z. Kotowicz, reverting to his earlier incarnation as a psychotherapist and untypically pulling rank . . . I rapped him sharply on the knuckles. I need to pay more attention to Philip Rieff's *Fellow Teachers* and *My Life among the Deathworks*. There is much unfinished business arising from my silent conversations, many passing and superficial juxtapositions to explore and flesh out: among them a comparison between Brown and Rieff which would draw on the essay in *Against Interpretation* on Brown by Susan Sontag, once Mrs Rieff and possible co-author of Rieff's first book. My title? Her phrase: 'The eschatology of immanence'.

Alice Miller

Alice Miller, whose books I list in the bibliography, is an edgy writer, occasionally sententious, but she is sometimes troublingly perceptive, especially when she touches on a sore point. In all her books she worries away at the problem of violence done to children and how often this is reflected back in cruelty perpetrated later on, including murder and, indeed, mass murder. She tracks and traces the path of childhood trauma in creativity and destructiveness. In *The Untouched Key*, she dares to worry about the problem of Hitler, and compares the childhood of this wannabe painter to that of a genius, Chaim Soutine who, like Hitler, was beaten for wanting to be an artist. She firmly believes that child abuse leads to wars and she sometimes makes generalizations that raise major issues as well as eyebrows: 'He [Paul Celan, who was ill-treated by his father] had to keep his father's image sacred and displace his feelings onto other people and situations.' She is convinced the cause of suicide always lies in the far distant past, that is, in childhood. Rereading her books, I am less convinced by her approach and conclusions than I was when I first read them (and so, in some respects, judging by her preface to the revised edition of *Breaking down the Wall of Silence*, was she). I wonder if she read Primo Levi on Paul Celan. When I wrote my short book on Levi, it became clear to me that suicide is often, perhaps always, over-determined and multi-causal. 'Those to whom evil is done,' wrote Auden, 'do evil in return': this is Alice Miller's mantra, her article of faith.

Liam Hudson

'All who search (whether for insight, fame, the perfect woman, gold, or what have you) do so, I would argue, from a sense of personal incompleteness similar to that described by Laing. They look for some ideal outside themselves. In a word, they are nympholepts.' If you understand 'insight' to mean, in one modality, insight achieved through writing, one can think about what writers do (and why we do whatever it is we do) in the terms of the final chapter, a speculation on 'original thought', of Liam Hudson's *Contrary Imaginations*, which like much of his writing defies the conventions of his professional world no less than R. D. Laing did. The book is mainly about scientific 'convergers' and artistic 'divergers', although these are polar terms of a spectrum rather than posited as an absolute opposition, as John Dewey understood long ago. Hudson quotes the *Chambers Dictionary* definition of a nympholept: a person affected by a yearning for the unattainable, nympholepsy being 'a species of ecstasy or frenzy said to have seized those who had seen a nymph', and he argues about the dangers of the risk-taking involved in creativity. The integrity of the personality is always at stake, but we come through, and then we start again. Interpreting him in my own terms, I would say that even if we are uptight off the page, we are able to shed our inhibitions on the page. Our shortcomings, dependencies and confusions are the matrices of the need to explain ourselves to ourselves and, by extension and intention, to others. For painters, in other words, inhibitions and exhibitions are dialectically related.

R. D. Laing, Aaron Esterson and David Cooper

R. D. Laing, Aaron Esterson and David Cooper were among the psychiatrists and psychotherapists I read during the 1970s. Cooper ('the guillotine of experience crumbles after the sufficient works of the worms of revolution'), one of the first people in Britain to promote Foucault's ideas on madness, was the most radical of the three, calling at the end of *Grammar of Living* for an end to edadism, which apparently means 'restrictions of sex-love on grounds of age', that is, he is arguing in favour of fucking young children. Laing deals in scapegoats and double binds. Madness has to be understood in the context of the nuclear family. *The Divided Self* made a big impact on me: it helped me find a way to describe in words, and make sense of, a particular state of mind. Thanks to reading Laing, I ended up with a poem, 'The Manifold Circle', which was published in a now disowned pamphlet. When I reprinted the poem in two later books, I dropped the telling epigraph from Laing. I buy up and destroy any copies of the pamphlet that appear in second-hand book catalogues. When I see it on the shelves of friends I steal it and destroy it. All the same, two or three of the poems, including the title poem will survive into any future collected poems, a small book (but my own) that I would like to put together. Let me recycle the epigraph for present purposes, although I'm not sure it added anything to the poem, which is probably why I dropped it in the first place: 'Many so-called disturbances are regarded as pathological in themselves; in fact they can sometimes be a stage in a healing process.' R. D. Laing, like Norman O. Brown, also wrote literary works of which *Knots* falls or jumps into Pinter territory.

Z. Kotowicz wrote an excellent account of the man and his work, *Laing and the Paths of Anti-Psychiatry*. He argues that Laing has been much misrepresented and that his true importance was that he gave the mad a voice. Looking again at Laing's chapters on self-consciousness and the inner self, I am struck by how intelligent, measured and moderate *The Divided Self* is. And the same goes for Esterson's *The Leaves of Spring*. The logic of dialectical reasoning, he argues, is that of social truth in action, an action research. The book was instructive and congenial and I wrote him a long letter, occasioning an instructive and congenial reply.

Laing's other non-literary books such as *The Self and Others* do not awaken my consciousness to the same extent as *The Divided Self*. In the chapter on Sartre's Genet in *Reason and Violence*, a book by Laing and Cooper about Sartre's philosophical thinking in the 1950s, Cooper writes better than he does in *Grammar of Living* and *The Death of the Family*. Once again Bachelard shows up as a resource: Icarus complex to explain Genet's sexuality. In *The Death of the Family*, I have underlined many passages, including 'maturity means a sell-out to the dominant values of bourgeois society' and, after put-downs of leaders like Hitler, Churchill and Kennedy, 'The true leadership principle is embodied by men like Fidel Castro and Mao Tse-Tung.' No, Cooper has worn less well than Laing and Esterson. Still, back in 1971 he does seem to have foreseen the language used to describe the alfresco family structures now so common: 'We don't need mother and family any more. We only need mothering and fathering.'

Jean-Bertrand Pontalis

Jean-Bertrand Pontalis is a distinguished and influential French psychoanalyst. Recently, I read with pleasure his collection of undated fragments, *En marge des jours*, written, as the title suggests, on the margin of his professional work, on the margin of his memory. I noted at once what he wrote about Robert Antelme's *L'Espèce humaine* (translated as *The Human Race*), one of my talismanic books: 'much more than an act of witness: give voice to suffering, abjection, squalor, hunger, your comrades, in brief never leave the "the labour camp" and, without ever betraying the horror of the experience, persist in *thinking the experience*. Utter humility and utter intelligence. Is it because he

561

was able to think these thoughts which saved him (just in time) from death?' (I wonder why Pontalis puts 'the labour camp' in quotation marks, but never mind). Pontalis, a former student of Sartre, owns up to all kinds of thoughts about patients, for example, dreaming of being in bed with one. He discusses a patient who claims he does not suffer from not wanting to pursue various pleasures, from not wanting to indulge his desires: 'I took care not to say that the absence of desire is much worse than renunciation.' In a discussion on perversion, he mediates on the 'polymorphous perverse child. Can the adult who seeks at all costs to prove his normality (the "normopath" according to Joyce McDougall) be described as monomorphous perverse . . . and indeed rather sad? Do we sublimate from the word go? Are we all perverts, more or less held in check, more or less subdued, forcing ourselves to give notice to the wild child, only allowing him to show up in our dreams?'

Pontalis moves on to Leonardo and to Pontormo, that great mannerist painter whom Paula Rego taught me to look at: 'The elegance of the forms, the curves of the languid bodies, the mellowness of the colours: utter delight. The same man confides to his Journal, like a meticulous accountant, what enters his body each day through one orifice—food—and what leaves through another—faeces. Obsession with what is impure. And Michelet, always in a state of excitement, he too confided to his *Journal* the quality of his stools, the frequency of his adored *Madonna*'s periods. Another meaning of fragment: waste product, reject.' Does Pontalis really mean 'impure'? Is there a residual Christian consciousness at work (or at play) here? Perhaps the word his subconscious mind is looking for is 'profane'. Or am I trying to prove I can beat Pontalis at his own game? Later, the writer goes on to discuss his reading, in particular (and this is highly relevant to my own procedures), the question of noting particular phrases or words in books which clarify, as in a dream, thoughts of your own which you had only partly formulated. 'I need the words of someone else, come from somewhere else, to get things going again and thus allow me, with a little bit of luck, to find my own words.' And indeed, a few pages further, when he returns to the subject of Nazism, he quotes the crucial formulation of Laurence Kahn: that during this terrible epoch—when the Night of Long Knives led to The Night of Broken Glass, culminating in Night and Fog—'death changed colour'. He discusses painting: 'A portrait of me is not a mirror. It reveals what I hide from myself' and the nature of dreams: 'A dream is a thought which does not know that it involves thinking.' From which reflection, Pontalis concludes that dreaming and thinking come from the same source while following different tracks: 'More precisely, the dream thinks, but it thinks at high speed, it moves too fast in respect of what vigilant thought demands.' Meditating on representation he quotes Carlo Ginzburg: 'On the one hand representation takes the place of the reality it represents and, consequently, evokes an absence; on the other hand, it makes the reality it represents visible and therefore suggests a presence.' In a discussion on nostalgia, he quotes Antonio Tabucchi: '*Saudade* is a category of the spirit.' Pontalis then segues into a perfect example of his earlier remark about finding his own words thanks to the words of someone else: he wonders whether every language has words which specifically designate categories of the spirit or of sensibility. *Unheimlich* (the uncanny), for example. 'A language does not translate. It can only be shared by those who speak it, live inside it and fail to recognise its strangeness so familiar are they with it, unless, in a dream, a word or an isolated phrase reveals this strangeness to them, revealing at the same time that every language, beginning with the mother tongue, is a foreign language.'

Let me end, because it involves a favourite writer of his and mine, with a riddle he poses: 'Who wrote: "What then within us lies, assassinates and steals?" and "Unknown powers pull our strings. We are nothing, in ourselves we are nothing"? Answer: Georg Büchner. Reread *Lenz*, accompany him in his wandering.' *Lenz*, by the great playwright who wrote *Woyzeck*, is indeed an amazing text (discussed earlier), one of the first studies of madness and mental breakdown. *En marge des jours* has two equally fascinating sequels: *En marge des nuits* and *Avant*.

Language

Introduction

I bought *A First Language* by Roger Brown in 1976, when my son Nathaniel was two and daughter Naomi about to be born or recently arrived. Earlier, I had tape-recorded Nathaniel for a project directed by David Crystal. As I write this, I am transfixed by my three-month-old grandson Charlie, I seat him on my knee and, mindful of Wittgenstein's remark about the limits of language, patiently attempt to teach him to say 'hallo' in English and 'hola' in Portuguese. He does appear to copy me but these are early days and it will be a while before we have a proper verbal conversation. Our primary currency of exchange is less mediated; this is pure presence, he smiles at me, he holds my finger; the language lesson tails off and I am happy to be engaged in the simplest form of human interaction, the loving protection of a new child, at once free spirit and captive audience; his instruction in the arts shall follow when we are both older. I am not taping him, but keeping a diary of my visits and await impatiently the arrival of his cousin, my second grandchild, who is being adopted.

[Coda: Three years on, one grandchild, Charlie, has left for New Zealand and another, Leah, has arrived from China, two shocks to the family system within seven weeks of each other.]

Textbooks (language)

Some of my school textbooks, bought at the school's own second-hand bookshop, survive: here are Benjamin Hall Kennedy's *Revised Latin Primer*, always inked in as *Eating Primer*, and R. Colebourn's *Latin Sentence and Idiom*. Our first Latin textbook was *Paginae Primae*, co-authored by the school's former headmaster, F. R. Dale. I enjoyed Latin and still have some of the texts. Greek too: E. A. Abbott and E. D. Mansfield's *Primer of Greek Grammar* brings back the aorist tense, as well as the race, timed by the master Jack "Boggy" Marsh, to see who could recite the alphabet fastest. These subjects undoubtedly exercised the muscles of our minds, as did maths, but the 'O' levels I obtained—French, Latin, Greek, elementary maths, additional maths, English language, English literature and the 'general paper'—hardly demonstrate a broad education. Horace Brearley, Mike's dad, got me through both maths papers. I failed general science because although I coped with biology (using our teacher R. H. Dyball's *A Biology Course for Schools*) and physics, I could make no sense whatsoever of chemistry. I note that my copy of a sixth-form textbook, J. E. Mansion's *Grammar of Present-Day French*, is the fifth reprint of the 1952 edition; the original 1919 edition was reprinted sixteen times; similar story with the fifth-form *French Grammar* by Margaret Kennedy and the fourth-form grammar, *Simpler French Course* by W. F. H. Whitmarsh. *Progressive French Idioms* by R. D. Blanchard is the twenty-seventh reprint of the original 1909 volume, a book whose very nature you would think demanded the occasional update. 'He is a muff (a milksop)': 'c'est une poule mouillée' did not cry out to be learnt by heart even as long ago as 1960.

Paris

I bought *Dictionnaire de l'argot moderne* on the left bank quais in 1961. Apparently 'afnaf' was French slang for, as the sound tells us, half and half, but Anne Serre, for one, has never heard of it. The phonetics course at the Institut Britannique was taught by the elderly (so she seemed at the time) author of the manual we used, Marguerite Peyrollaz. On one occasion, she invited me for tea at her flat near the elevated metro stop Bir-Hakeim, close to the Eiffel Tower. Why have I never forgotten this trivial detail? To what did I owe the honour of a home visit? Very unusual in France! I still have a mini-tape of me reciting a passage in my best French, recorded in the language laboratory. We repeated and repeated phrases and lines from Racine's *Bérénice* ('Le temps n'est plus, Phénice . . .'), Claudel's *L'Annonce faite à Marie* ('Ne soyez pas triste, mere . . .'), Camus and others. Sometimes we would record our voices and play them back. I recall enjoying the method, ipso facto Marguerite Peyrollaz was a good teacher, for language lessons are inherently less sexy than literature classes.

Linguistics reading list

College textbooks by Zellig Harris, Leonard Bloomfield, C. F. Hockett, A. C. Gimson, Daniel Jones, de Saussure, Otto Jespersen, H. A. Gleason, Joseph H. Greenberg: the virtual lack of annotation and near mint quality of most of these books suggest that I was paying mere lip service (quite a good phrase in the circumstances) to my studies, although later I read *Structuralist Poetics* and *Saussure* by Jonathan Culler, who was married for a while to my late friend the poet Veronica Forrest-Thomson. Long before I read John Lyons'

Chomsky, his lectures had turned me on to the American's powerful intelligence; my annotations suggest that I paid close attention to *Syntactic Structures*. In view of later developments, it is ironic that, according to the great theoretician's acknowledgements, he was supported in his research by the United States army, navy and air force. Here too is his short and magisterial book, *Language and Mind*. The book that gave me a severe headache was *Structural Linguistics* by Zellig Harris: heaven knows what percentage I read, and what percentage of what I read I understood.

Teach-yourself books

Teach Yourself German survives on my shelves but *Spanish* and *Italian* seem to have vanished, along with my ambition to acquire more languages than I have already. Here too are Greek, Bulgarian and Polish phrase books. I must have bought *Serbo-Croat for Foreigners* in preparation for the 1972 Struga Poetry Festival in Macedonia. Atremble with adrenaline rush, doubtless I spent half an hour studying the first lesson, having persuaded myself that I could learn basic structures quickly enough to make myself understood. Let's face it, someone who believes that is an utter fantasist. Yes, I was a fantasist. Still, I use the past tense because cure begins with acknowledgement of a condition. Books, however, remain my chocolate, my alcohol, my nicotine: comfort eating rules okay.

Edward Sapir and Benjamin Lee Whorf, and Roman Jakobson

Here are two books by Edward Sapir, *Language and Culture* and *Language and Personality*, as well as Benjamin Lee Whorf's *Language, Thought and Reality*, which contains the fascinating essay 'Language, Mind and Reality', delivered to a theosophical audience during the war. Outside professional circles, the two writers are remembered, by me at any rate, as the progenitors of the Sapir–Whorf hypothesis. This has been often been exaggerated and simplified, not least by Paul Goodman in *Speaking and Language: Defence of Poetry*, to mean that language determines or conditions thought. Lévi-Strauss demonstrates that language and reality are in a dialectical relationship and puts paid to simplistic versions of the thesis. All the same, its insistence on the centrality of language in any understanding of nature, mind and world is right.

George Steiner discusses the essay in *On Difficulty*: when we study a writer's work, he argues, 'our perceptions of language *in literature* are relativist and, if the term may be allowed, *ultra-Whorfian*' (Steiner's italics). I am moved by the sentimental inscription in Steiner's book: 'To Tony, on his 40th. His birth was like yesterday, love, Mum and Dad'. My father's handwriting moves me too, so distinctive, so few examples of it surviving. Roman Jakobson's *Essais de linguistique générale* and the book he wrote with Morris Halle, *Fundamentals of Language*, bring to mind a lecture he gave at Newnham College, as guest of Professor Lisa Hill, who once said in my hearing 'we don't want students with Thirds in our faculty', a statistically stupid remark that helped drive me out of modern languages, although I was neither vain enough nor indeed modest enough to suppose it was aimed at me personally. Jakobson spoke with such impenetrably poor diction that no one could understand a word. Never mind, I had attended a lecture by one of the intellectual giants of European culture, just as two years earlier I had heard Vladimir Jankélévitch lecture in Paris and ten years later would hear Viktor Shklovsky at the Struga Festival.

The final essay in Jakobson's *Essais*, 'Closing Statements: Linguistics and Poetics' (also found in Thomas Sebeok's *Style in Language*), remains a tour de force if you are interested in the links between morphology, syntax, symbolism, metonymy and other elements of literary language. My copy of Ernst Cassirer's short study, *Language and Myth*, is heavily annotated: it was on a high enough level of abstraction and generality to maintain my interest. I bought Stephen Ullmann's *Language and Style*, according to my signature, in June 1964, *after* the debacle of my final examinations in social anthropology (and linguistics). Ever since those exams, I have been trying to redeem my academic failure, and that book may well be the first one I bought in what has been a lifelong process.

Raymond Williams, Lawrence Fixel, Alan Wall

When Raymond Williams' *Keywords* came out in 1976, I bought two copies and sent one to Lawrence Fixel who, thanks to Edouard Roditi, had put me up the previous year in the basement of his San Francisco house. *Keywords* (expanded edition 1983) was perfect raw material for Larry to 'glimmer' with, glimmering being his personally stamped modality of thought. He would stand at his blackboard and make binary oppositions between words or pairs of words. If you were to cross structuralist analysis with Zen Coans, you could, if you were lucky, end up with a Fixel Glimmer. In social gatherings, friends would wait patiently for him to be struck by a glimmer. Our correspondence over several years generated a core text, later to become his *Book of Glimmers*. Too literary for philosophers, too philosophical for poets, it was Menard's worst selling book (which took some doing); still, I was proud of it, and presented it to all who would accept it. He wrote several books but new readers should begin with his selected writings: *Truth, War and the Dream-Game*. I wish I could find the letter in which he reacted, sympathetically as I recall, to Williams' 'vocabulary of culture and society', whose entry on 'culture' begins: 'Culture is one of the two or three most complicated words in the English language.' A glance through the book suggests that 'class' is another of those words. The entry 'socialist' tells us that Turgenev invented the word 'nihilist' in his novel *Fathers and Sons* in 1862. This felt wrong and, indeed, a swift check shows that Williams has simplified its etymological history. It is uncorrected in the second edition. This serious book explores words that were key to one thoughtful and influential man in mid-twentieth-century Britain. Alan Wall's work-in-progress *Obstupefaction Etc.* has been published in various places, including *The Reader*. He examines the origin of English words and phrases and bids fair to take Williams and Fixel in new and exciting directions. I offer him 'murder your darlings', which we do for each other now and again.

History

Introduction: History and Historiography

I am more interested in historiography and meta-history than in history proper, which is why I don't read historical novels. I read George Vernadsky's *History of Russia* as a student but that was a set book. I still have not read, shame on me, *The Age of Revolution 1789–1848* by Eric Hobsbawm, although I have checked it for references to Lamartine and other writers involved in politics. I prefer books like E. H. Carr's *What Is History?*, which I read along with Edmund Wilson's magnificent *To the Finland Station* back in the early 1960s, although my many marginal pencil marks in the latter did not include one I would make today: approval of his comment that the relations between Sergei Nechaev and Mikhail Bakunin resemble those between Arthur Rimbaud and Paul Verlaine. Thank heavens for indexes: I would surely be sunk and defeated in the present endeavour if I did not have them to check later or current interests against past annotations and marginalia. Memory too plays its part and I vividly remember (as Bertrand Russell used to say) the thrill of Wilson's fast-flowing narrative of the historiographical and intellectual background to the events that culminated in Lenin's return to Russia and arrival in Petrograd on 16 April 1917. Jules Michelet, whose reading of Vico nearly a century before Lenin's arrival at the Finland Station is the starting point of Wilson's great book, fascinates me. I remember too that I loved the feel and look of those old Fontana editions, in which I also have Wilson's major literary study of the symbolists *Axel's Castle* and Mario Praz's *Romantic Agony*.

Jules Michelet

> The historian is a civil magistrate in charge of administering the estate of the dead.
>
> —Jules Michelet, quoted by Roland Barthes in *Michelet*

Alain Robbe-Grillet writes that Barthes and his texts form a kind of torsion coupling: a perfect description of Michelet. Edward Kaplan of Brandeis sent me *Mother Death*, his translation of the journal of Jules Michelet. It is now impossible not to read Michelet's historical works as literature, for history was his defence against death, specifically against the deaths of his nearest and dearest, and the journals track a conscious and unconscious path of psychic survival in order to complete the great works ahead, in which history, like the sea (see his book *La Mer*), would generate the possibility of eternal life, the hereafter reconfigured as the heretofore. *Mother Death* is a chilling book. Michelet would have understood la bouche d'ombre, Rimbaud's mother, who descended into the vault containing the tomb of her son to see how it would feel like to be dead. Barthes's *Michelet* is a key to the *imaginaire*

569

of the historian and, indeed, of Barthes himself. Robbe-Grillet sees the book as a novel. Michelet, a hysteric as Pierre Nora calls him, preferred witnessing the second Madame Michelet's menstruations to having an orgasm. Could his intimate need, or carer role as he saw it, be in some way connected to her falsification of his manuscripts after his death?

Hayden White

Here are three books by Hayden White, a man much possessed by Michelet: *Metahistory*, *Tropics of Discourse* and *The Content of the Form*. I used to quote the following comment by E. H. Carr, underlined firmly in my copy of *What Is History?*: 'Somewhere between . . . the North Pole of valueless facts and the south pole of value judgments still struggling to transform themselves into facts lies the realm of historical truth.' That kept me going until I read White's dictum in *The Content of the Form*: 'A fact is an event under description.' This was a liberation, for it embodied what I wanted to believe and knew intuitively, namely that facts exist objectively (thus seeing off revisionists) and yet there are always several versions of the history of a topic (thus seeing off teleological readings of the Nazi genocide that admit only one interpretation). White's argument with Pierre Vidal-Naquet about Zionism is on the highest level and required reading. In 'The Burden of History'—an important essay in *Tropics of Discourse*—White rightly praises that grand old radical Norman O. Brown for his anti-history *Life Against Death* and even compares the writer to John Cage and other artists for his willingness to exploit literary and other techniques drawn from outside the academy. The fourth book in this field is a collection of essays called *The Writing of History* edited by Robert Canary and Henry Kozicki, with valuable essays by Hayden White, Lionel Gossman and others. White's essay in this collection, 'The Historical Text as Literary Artefact', contains some of his most illuminating writing on what I have called elsewhere 'subjective telling of indisputable factuality'.

Michael André Bernstein

Michael André Bernstein's *Foregone Conclusions: Against Apocalyptic History* belongs here. I shall not seek to summarize his powerful arguments against foreshadowing and what he calls, in a valuable neologism, backshadowing, in favour of Gary Saul Morson's concept of sideshadowing. Claude Lanzmann, when I interviewed him, discussed these issues in terms of a flowchart, the personal experience of the future victim who cannot know what is to come, and the personal freedom of the one who at the next step will or will not become a murderer. Bernstein is particularly illuminating on Aharon Appelfeld and also, in a brief passage, indeed a footnote, on the difference between Robert Musil and Joseph Roth. He implies rather than states a harsh criticism of Roth's foreshadowing of the war in *Radetsky March* and relates it to 'overheated rhetoric'. Ah, Roth and Musil: another essay to be written arising from the present work. Kakania or Not-Roth.

[Note to myself: find time to reread Jonathan Morse's *Word by Word: Language of Memory*. I once elaborated a suggestive passage as follows: history is a syntactical logic inducing meaning from exemplary moments. Myth is a syntactical logic deducing meaning from exemplary moments.]

E. P. Thompson

E. P. Thompson's book about William Blake, *Witness against the Beast*, is now on my desk, along with his unfinished book *The Romantics*, and his *Collected Poems*, which I foolishly declined to publish at Menard Press. Blake, 'the antinomian caught in the enlightenment', and a man less isolated than we hitherto thought, may have been a member of the Muggletonian sect, who were descendants of the Ranters and Levellers, the left wing of the Protestant Reformation; they were radical dissenters, but more mild in their approach than say Thompson himself, one of my trinity of heroes at the time when Menard embarked on its nuclear mission, along with Solly Zuckerman and Martin Ryle. Practically my only marginal mark is alongside the following: 'But a contradiction in thought, which derives from an acute tension of contrasting values, neither of which can be abandoned, can be wholly creative . . . Blake did not achieve any full synthesis of the antinomian and the rationalist. How could he, since the antinomian premised a non-rational affirmative. There was, rather, an incandescence in his art in which the incompatible traditions met—tried to marry—argued as contraries—were held in a polarised tension.' Thompson concludes that, unlike the rationalists, 'Blake, by denying even in *Songs of Experience* a supreme societal value to

571

rationality, did not suffer from the same kind of disenchantment.' The same could be said of Claude Lévi-Strauss as read by two other Blake admirers, Octavio Paz and Nathaniel Tarn, of Walter Benjamin and George Oppen as read by Michael Heller, of Norman O. Brown and of Yves Bonnefoy. And the same could be said of Thompson himself, who seems to be speaking about himself in this strange and compelling book.

H. G. Wells

My father's Thinker's Library copy of H. G. Wells' *A Short History of the World* is an undated reprint, probably from the later 1930s, of a book first published in 1929. Wells explains that the book is a kind of prologue to his *Outline of History*. In the best Leirisian tradition, I own up to shame, shameful ignorance: aged about seventeen, I wrote on a scrap of paper still in the book: 'Where is Malta?'; 'Where is Constantinople?' There are notes to myself: 'Make a list of the main world influences' and: 'Read two or three chapters a day'. The latter remark hints at a neurotic behaviour pattern that has worsened over the years. The penultimate sentence of the book reads: 'Can we doubt that presently our race will more than realise our boldest imaginations, that it will achieve unity and peace, that it will live, the children of our blood will live, in a world made more splendid and lovely than any palace or garden that we know, going on from strength to strength in an ever-widening circle of adventure and achievement?' Thanks to World War II, Wells would change his mind and tune and in 1945 published *Mind at the End of Its Tether*, a deeply pessimistic book which I read along with many other troubled and troubling works during my self-education concerning the nuclear issue in the early 1980s. I was reminded of this phase when I heard [the now late] Oliver Postgate on Desert Island Discs: *The Plain Man's Guide to the Bomb*, by this children's television programme maker of genius, was Menard's bestseller after Martin Ryle's *Towards the Nuclear Holocaust*.

Oral history

I bought *Like It Was* by Cynthia Stokes Brown and other books on writing oral history to help me in the drafting of my eternally unfinished grandfather book. Maybe all I need to inspire me is to read writers who have already worked in the area of what Iain Sinclair, speaking about the poet John Seed, calls 'reverse archaeology': Charles Reznikoff's *Testimony*, for example or the fiction of the Peruvian Jew Isaac Goldemberg, whose *The Fragmented Life of Don Jacobo Lerner* deploys documentary techniques to reconstruct a life. My friend Martha Leigh has written a good oral history: '*Couldn't Afford the Eels*': *Memories of Wapping 1900–1960*. 'No Jews allowed down Wapping' was a well-known song. It took Hitler to change attitudes. John Seed's two books *Pictures from Mayhew* and *That Barrikins* contain poems entirely in the words of the nineteenth-century social reformer Henry Mayhew, that is to say the words of interviewees briefly recorded by his assistants and saved from the ruins of time, the depredations of history and the obliquities of convention by Seed's literary intelligence that cares about the singularity of voice. Reznikoff's *Testimony* uses the same procedure for court records, although he is less concerned about individualizing his voices. The completed section of my grandfather book consists entirely of the old man's words as recorded on tape in 1975 and edited into poems, a kind of recitative or *rezi-tatif* (to coin a word), thirty years later. These were published in Sinclair's anthology *London: City of Disappearances* and my book *Zigzag*.

Travel Books

> ... pure matrix, joining world and mind.
> —Richard Wilbur, 'To the Etruscan Poets'

The Etruscans

In 2011 I saw an exhibition about Giacometti and the Etruscans at the Pinacothèque museum in Paris, demonstrating affinity and influence, this statement occasioning a rare disagreement with Yves Bonnefoy and Alain Madeleine-Perdrillat that very evening. My evidence: 'L'Ombre du soir', the third-century BC votive bronze so romantically named by D'Annunzio. Some years ago at the Grand Palais in Paris, I saw another exhibition about the Etruscans which led me to read Nigel Foxell's *Sardinia without Lawrence* and, belatedly, D. H. Lawrence's *Etruscan Places*. Lawrence's anti-Rome polemic

573

and account of the noble and decent civilization of the Etruscans (although I'm not sure how Macaulay's 'Horatius at the Bridge' fits this image, but by this stage even Lawrence's 'Romanized Etruscans of the decadence' could not avoid martial feats), backed up by (the poet not the playwright) the late Christopher Hampton's study *The Etruscan Survival*, remind one yet again that the conclusion of Auden's 'Spain' is not the last word on the subject of winners and losers: 'History to the defeated / May say Alas but cannot help nor pardon.' In the words of Lawrence, 'Because a fool kills a nightingale with a stone, is he therefore greater than the nightingale? Because the Roman took the life out of the Etruscan, was he therefore greater than the Etruscan? Not he! Rome fell, and the Roman phenomenon with it. Italy today is far more Etruscan in its pulse than Roman; and will always be so. The Etruscan element is like the grass of the field and the sprouting of corn, in Italy: it will always be so.'

Christopher Hampton echoes Jacob Burckhardt: 'The Renaissance was a rebirth not of the spirit of ancient Rome, but of the old Mediterranean spirit reasserting itself out of Christianity . . . In Duccio, in Giotto, in Dante, in Ucello, in Masaccio and Piero and Signorelli and Petrarch, it is not the spirit of Rome . . . that triumphs but the particularising, non-conformist spirit of the Tuscan city states emerging out of the culture of the High Middle Ages . . . The source of it was Italian, Tuscan, Etruscan and Mediterranean . . . Even now the spirit of the Etruscans lingers on in Tuscany.' Hampton, in *An Exile's Italy*, speaks of 'histories changing every moment / with each move we make' and, in his prose book, takes a richly merited swipe at Kenneth Clark for dismissing Etruscan forms in *The Nude*. Hampton continues: 'The irresistibly infectious spirit that is in Etruscan art comes to flower again in . . . the architecture of the cities that had sprung up again out of the roots of Etruscan cities at Orvieto, Perugia, Arezzo, Cortona, Florence, Volterra, Chiusi and Tuscania, these roots lying dormant in the earth and in the blood of the people of Etruria; and perhaps not even yet exhausted.' Yes, look at the urns, vases, votive figures and other art forms of the Etruscans. See how the flowing line of the flute player at the Tarquinian tombs bespeaks non-martial energy, the enchantment of grace. In this society of luxe, calme et volupté—Baudelaire could have been speaking of the Etruscans—women were treated as equals.

Venice

'In the memory of vanished hours so filled with beauty the consciousness of present loss oppresses. Exquisite hours, enveloped in light and silence, to have known them once is to have always a terrible standard of enjoyment' (Henry James, *Italian Hours*). And now the ultimate compliment, from Henry, to my good friend Valentina Polukhina, in Venice in 2006 with her husband Weissbort for the tenth anniversary of the death of Joseph Brodsky, who is buried there: 'an intelligent woman who knows her Venice is doubly intelligent, and it makes no woman's perceptions less keen to be aware that she can't help looking graceful as she is borne over the waves'. Valentina, who has written four books on Brodsky (her husband has written one, and translated his poetry too) is cross that some of us prefer Brodsky's prose to his poetry and his Russian poetry to his English poetry, but he is an amazing literary critic and essayist, and his *Watermark* is a beautiful account of Venice in winter. Here are *Selected Poems* translated by George Klein, a French translation and an original Russian volume, to dip into like a gondolier's oar into the Grand Canal. I would like to 'do' Venice in winter one year, preferably with Paula, but on my own if necessary. We have been to Venice twice during the late summer but the future memory of a winter visit is already lodging itself in my mind.

London

More complex, as you would expect, is the dialectical interaction between my past London and my future London: the presence of this great city in the psyche of a lifelong Londoner has to be plotted on the axis of time as well as space and requires the indirection of multiple mediations; there are so many narratives or readings of the territory now in my sights that they could be represented as stops on a version of Harry Beck's iconic topological tube map. Beck lived locally, at Finchley Central ('two and sixpence from Golders Green' in the words of the 1966 New Vaudeville song), as my grandson Charlie, a Tube fanatic, knows. The London (and environs) of Iain Sinclair, as recounted in many books, all of which are here, including, for example, *Dark Lanthorns* (*Rodinsky's A to Z*), *Slow Chocolate Autopsy* and *King Lud*, has affinities with my own, and doubtless colours it, although less than Perec does. Robert Bond's study *Iain Sinclair* supplies a lateral perspective in literary and cultural terms. Notwithstanding scepticism on the part of persons, Sinclair's psycho-geography has become one of London's compelling palimpsestic myths, along with those of Michael Moorcock (*Mother London*) and Peter Ackroyd, Thomas de Quincey and Charles Dickens, and Ballard and Ken Smith. Sinclair's photographer in several books is Mark Atkins, whom he describes in *Lights Out for the Territory* as 'the direct descendant of John Deakin, the best photographer of the feral Soho *demi-monde*'. If I ever write a book about London and Paris as represented in photography and painting, I would find myself placing a quote from Julien Green's *Paris* alongside an early Hopper interior of the rue de Lille. Paula reckons that Hopper, when living in Paris, looked at and was influenced by the work of Felix Valloton. The Hopper interior dates from the same year that Picasso painted 'Les Demoiselles d'Avignon': 'Paris is a city of staircases that provoke the imagination.'

Portugal

One of my ambitions has been to learn more about Portugal beyond my specialized interest in Marrano culture and history. Had Paula never left Portugal she would still become a painter but her relationship to Portugal would have been different, perhaps to the point of adopting or naturalizing an international modernist style. As it is, living in England since the age of sixteen, her *saudade* for her homeland has generated a matrixial source of subject matter for her pictorial stories. It is true that one of her great gifts ('gift', an interesting word which plays down the work involved) is graphic, illustrational, yet for the writer to concentrate entirely on the story is to neglect the complexity of design, as I saw yet again in a new picture called 'Nada', which Paula thought was finished until she learnt (already unconsciously knew) it wasn't when, on challenge, I could not identify the object in the foreground. Fortunately she was able to fix this without reference to the rest of the picture, which is not always the case. It is for reasons of this complexity of design in the best figurative paintings that a more useful word than abstract is non-figurative. Natalie Dower's non-figurative paintings tell a story. Paula's figurative paintings are complex abstractions. Paula jibs at this, but I have known her turn pictures upside down or look at them in a mirror to get a sense of the design and interaction of the pictorial elements. Paul Buck's *Lisbon*, a conservative book by the standards of this radical experimentalist, takes him off his and my Paris/London beat. Here are Paul Hyland's *Backwards Out of the Big World* and José Saramago's *Journey to Portugal*. Outside books, the only Portuguese places I know are Lisbon, Oporto and Estoril/Cascais. Recently, Saramago disgraced himself by calling on Portugal to merge with Spain, and accept Madrid as the capital and the Spanish royal family as head of state. Paula, who is as much a republican in Portugal as she is a monarchist in her adopted Britain, does not do outrage very often, but on this occasion she did.

Eastern and Central Europe

Eva Hoffman's *Exit into History* is an account of a trip she made to her native Poland and other countries in Eastern Europe. While I was finalizing my long essay on poetry in extreme situations, I received an email from her, telling me about a poem by a nine-year-old girl, Elzunia, which had been discovered recently in the camp archive at Majdanek. Elzunia had hidden the scrap of paper under the sole of her shoe, with a note specifying the tune to which the rhyming verse should be sung, a ballad-like children's song. She also scribbled a few words saying it was important to her that the little poem should be found and remembered. Hoffman commented that this was the most heart-breaking piece of poetry she had ever come across. Elzunia, like Primo Levi's Hurbinek, like the deported children in Serge Klarsfeld's monumental book, stands for all the millions of children who died in similar circumstances. Her hope that the poem would be found has been fulfilled.

> Once there was a girl Elzunia,
> She's dying all alone now
> Her daddy, he's in Majdanek
> Mummy in Auschwitz-Birkenau.

The implication of the word 'in' is hardly touched on in Robert Pogue Harrison's *The Dominion of the Dead*, his poignant and finely written book on burial and what it does to and for the living. 'It seems inevitable that the ancestral dead would have inevitably won out over Rimbaud's adoptive

577

angels': this, from Harrison's brief meditation on the poet, is typical of the fresh insights that his incisive and understated approach generates. And, from his meditation on Rilke, whom we are not surprised to find in this book: 'It is because we are by nature veterans of mourning—veterans of the 'elegy' as it were—that we have it within our power to do for the earth what we have traditionally done for our dead, that is, to transmit its mode of being in us.'

A marvellous and singular work, on one level a travel book, is Claudio Magris' *Danube*, which explores Austria–Hungary in time and space by tracing the great river from its source in Germany to its mouth at the Black Sea. (A precursor of *Danube* is Stefan Zweig's *Journeys*, a book I was led to by its translator, Menard author, Will Stone and whose author Magris must have studied.) In novellas like *A Different Sea* and *Inferences from a Sabre*, Magris deals with neglected or unknown aspects of Central European history. He has some affinities with Sebald, but more with Joseph Roth, although the imperial wire was still live for Roth, who, older by nearly half a century, experienced the collapse of his declared homeland, the dual monarchy, and died in 1939, six weeks before Magris was born in the Italy of Central rather than Southern Europe, in Trieste, one of the few cities I wish to visit for the first time. James Joyce taught English to Italo Svevo, one of several sources for Leopold Bloom, at the city's Berlitz School. Nearby is the castle of Duino, forever associated with Rilke. I emailed my friend Ifigenija, the Slovene poet I translate, in Ljubljana, to ask what she felt about nearby Trieste: 'I love Trieste, bright, long, opened-out docks, sometimes a huge boat there, and an antique market the last Saturday of the month and huge squares, white glistening marble, sleepy sculptures on palaces and beautiful Italian women with their tiny dogs and Italian gentlemen dressed in colourful tweeds and cashmere, soft, sexy and untouchable. More than Trieste itself, I love the journey from Ljubljana, passing villages . . . then suddenly a cliff and urban sea city . . . all in one hour.'

Travel guide

The Guide Julliard de Londres by Henri Gault and Christian Millau, published in 1965, is a period piece. Although it is full of barbs about my hometown, it is a very knowing love poem. The two Frenchmen are denizens of a city with a superiority complex and are addressing another city with a superiority complex, one whose faults or alleged faults sometimes send the authors into understated paroxysms of over-reaction. They are evidently unaware that swinging London was already in full swing, something we promoted at the British Travel Association: Roger Miller's 'England swings [like a pendulum do]' rivals Tab Hunter's 'Young Love' as the worst pop song ever written but we still used it at BTA. At a time of old money, a high price for a meal in the Caprice was three pounds. At the late lamented Shah restaurant on Drummond Street, the authors claim they arrived at 1358 and asked for a beer. Not allowed, snivelled the Hindu waiter, it's 1400. No, it's 1359. I'll check, he said. On his return, they are told 'You were right, it was not yet 1400 but now it is 1401, too late for beer.' The meal, however, was excellent. They award one star to the Etoile on Charlotte Street (well named, they say, quite wittily) and also to the now defunct Wheelers on Old Compton Street, long my parents' favourite restaurant, where as a young teenager I was impressed that the maître d' remembered my father's name. The two authors hate Chez Victor in Soho: 'Le patron mange ici', said a famous notice in the window, and they surmise that the said French patron must have a galvanized stomach. (I remember having a middling dinner there one night with the French poet Anne-Marie Albiach and seeing John Gielgud alone at a nearby table. He smiled. We should have spoken to him or bought him a drink of gratitude.) In the 'London at Night' section, the two authors visit places like my (and Hugo Williams') old haunt, Le Café des Artistes, whose address is given as 266 Fulham Road, although I recall the entrance as being in Redcliffe Gardens. The eyes of the young people are globulous and dead, they say, their clothes ridiculous. But under the red light, in the numerous vaulted rooms of this fabulous cave, they seem to be getting value for money. Ho hum. I pause long enough in the shopping section to note with nostalgia the passing of the record shops, all of which I frequented: Collector's Corner, Discurio, Dobells and Imhofs.

Here is my little red and much read companion, *Paris par arrondissement*, with the maps and streets indexed by neighbourhood, unlike the London A–Z. This is possible because in Paris the districts are in a logical, concentric, order, whereas in London they are all over the place: for example, in what used to be known as Upper Holloway, where I lived hard by the bridge over Archway Road (the only place where you can commit suicide by moving from one postal district to another, said Jonathan Miller), postal districts N6, N19, NW5 are adjacent, meeting at the spot by Saint Joseph's Church and Waterlow Park where Francis Bacon, engaging in experimental science, caught a chill in 1626, resulting in his death a few days later. The French guide has a foldout map, again possible for Paris not for London, because Paris is small enough to fit. I now live in N12: not much of the old Woodside Park, North Finchley and Talley Ho left, judging by the photographs in John Heathfield's *Around Whetstone and North Finchley*, though 1264 High Road Whetstone, opposite the Bull and Butcher (now the I-Bar) where my daughter worked for a time, dates back to 1505.

Politics

RADICAL POLITICS

Exodus

Michael Walzer's book *Exodus and Revolution* spoke loud and clear to me when I first read it many years ago. Ever since early childhood, when I heard the Passover *Haggadah* recited at my maternal grandfather's house in Wessex Gardens, Golders Green, I, like so many others throughout history, have been inspired by the drama of the Exodus, an awesome foundational myth from the kitty of world religions and specifically within Judaism, where it is one of the four cornerstone stories, along with the Binding of Isaac, Jacob and the Angel, and Moses and the Burning Bush. But whereas those three involve an individual faced with God, the Passover tells the story of a people, and its journey to freedom. The post-biblical history of the Jewish people 'from the Maccabean revolt to the Zionist movement' is replete with energies drawn from this collective memory, as recounted annually in the *Haggadah*. More than a thousand years later, Jesus too will go to Egypt and then return to his homeland; in modern dress, I posed as Joseph in Paula's 'The Rest on the Flight into Egypt' for her series inspired by *The Crime of Father Amaro*, the novel of Eca de Queiros about a wicked priest. The Exodus speaks to all slaves and is surely one of the grandest archetypes of liberation in human history. Black spirituals are replete with references to Old Testament stories:

> When Israel was in Egypt's land,
> Let My people go!
> Oppressed so hard they could not stand,
> Let My people go!

And the refrain:

> Go down, Moses,
> Way down in Egypt's land;
> Tell old Pharaoh
> To let My people go!

Moses, the great lawmaker, was succeeded by the man who 'fit de battle of Jericho, Jericho, Jericho / and the walls came a tumblin' down'

> You may talk about the man of Gideon,
> You may talk about the man of Saul,
> There's none like good ole Joshua, and the battle of Jericho.

The Exodus of the Jewish slaves from Egypt is a common reference point, as Walzer points out, for radicals like Cromwell, Calvin, Knox and Savanarola; for Jefferson and Franklin; for the Boers and for black African nationalists. Walzer ends by reminding us that we all live in Egypt, that somewhere there is a promised land, and that 'there is no way to get from here to there except by joining together and marching'. On a few occasions I have been touched by the splendour of this vision of people power (as articulated today by a sophisticated champion, Rebecca Solnit, *Hope in the Dark*) or, more modestly, solidarity (after all, how many defeats have we endured?), notably in 1964 when I was a member of a multinational group from Britain, the USA and the USSR working together at Camp Reinberg near Chicago.

I tremble for my grandchildren faced with the rotten, polluted and unfair world we are passing on to them, and as a consequence one of my dominant modes is anger, of which there is plenty in *The Penguin Book of Socialist Verse* edited by Alan Bold, a book I reviewed forty years ago for *Tribune*, a venerable left-wing journal founded by Nye Bevan. There is plenty of anger too in *You Better Believe It*, Paul Breman's anthology of Black verse from Africa, the USA and the Caribbean, but tenderness too, as in poems by Langston Hughes, whom I would like to spend more time reading. Ever since I can remember, I have worried my head about the relationship between politics and art. Both have animated my life, and the dialectical tension between them has been fruitful, some of the time. I can't always handle the tension: 'I drink wine from two glasses,' wrote Paul Celan. I think of George Oppen and Carl Rakosi, how they went silent under pressure from an angry world in which writing poetry was not open to them.

Liberal socialism

Carlo and Nello Rosselli were Jewish anti-fascist resisters, exiled to France. Benito Mussolini personally ordered their assassination in 1937. Never Marxists, they still honoured Antonio Gramsci. Carlo and his friends founded an anti-fascist movement called Justice and Liberty. Writers like Cesare Pavese and Carlo Levi rallied to it. Two hundred thousand people attended their funeral. Carlo Rosselli's 1930 book *Liberal Socialism* proposed a 'third way' (which at the time had affinities with G. D. H. Cole's 'guild socialism' and can be said to be broadly 'old labour' in its perspective), which is now a historical curiosity; I, however, am an unregenerate old timer. Liberal socialism, a phrase used by Angus Wilson (*The Wild Garden*), Leonard Woolf and others, insists with Benedetto Croce that ethical liberalism is not to be conflated with the free market. Civil rights and social rights are equally important and the challenge for the left is to reconcile them. Presumably, voluntary institutions of fraternity would hold the ring. (*The Neighbour*—essays in political theology by Slavoj Zizek, Eric Santner and Kenneth Reinhard—studies these issues from the matrix of critical theory). Rosselli and his friends remained on the left, unlike certain American Trotskyites who became neoconservatives, allegedly after being 'mugged by reality'. Alfred Kazin had nothing but scorn for the converted Irving Kristol, whose cast of mind remained Trotskyite.

'Liberalism is the ideal force of inspiration, and socialism is the practical force of realisation,' wrote Rosselli. In other words, 'socialism is a philosophy of liberty'. This is precisely why Tony Benn objected to the phrase 'liberal socialism' when I wrote to him about Rosselli. On the same grounds, he objected to 'democratic socialism'. For him, socialism implies democracy and liberalism. The problem remains, however, that socialism and authoritarian communisms have so often been synonyms that sometimes things need to be spelt out. Carlo's last known political action was a broadcast on Radio Barcelona in 1936: 'Today in Spain, tomorrow in Italy'. Rosselli's preface contains a statement that was bound to move me: 'Greek rationalism and the messianism of Israel [i.e. Judaism]. The first contains a love of liberty, a respect for autonomies, a harmonious and detached conception of life. In the second, the sense of justice is entirely down-to-earth; there is a myth of equality, and a spiritual torment that resists all indulgence.' Rosselli's heirs included Norberto Bobbio, a friend of Primo Levi, and indeed, Levi himself. An account of what they understood by civic and social virtues can be found in Robert Gordon's brilliant book, *Primo Levi's Ordinary Virtues*. Levi summarized his views on politics in an interview I made with him in London in 1986: 'I don't see any contradiction between democratic socialism and Judaism. I am basically a socialist, though not a member of the PSI. I believe in mutuality, community and a slow progress towards the messianic age.' A quarter of a century after his death, I miss him.

Noam Chomsky and Paul Goodman

Bitburg in Moral and Political Perspective, edited by Geoffrey Hartman, raises issues. Despite President Reagan's major policy errors and disasters, one of George Bush junior's singular achievements was to have made Reagan look good. For all of us, books such as Hartman's illustrate what the recently deceased Christa Wolf (her *Cassandra* is on my desk and she knows whereof she writes), quoted by Saul Friedländer in his essay in Hartman on *Cassandra*, is getting at: 'What is past is not dead; it is not even past. We cut ourselves off from it; we pretend to be strangers.' That is something Noam Chomsky could never be accused of. On my desk is one of his many books on politics: *The Fateful Triangle: The United States, Israel and the Palestinians*. There is nobody like him. He is a less eloquent and more measured writer than John Pilger, but they are cut from the same radical cloth. Sometimes they are plain wrong and on other occasions I find myself resisting their relentless arguments because these arguments, even when persuasive, mean that things are even worse than I, often accused of exaggeration, say they are. The same goes for Helen Caldicott's *The New Nuclear Danger*, a book I reopened after hearing Gordon Brown's casually articulated yet calculatedly integrated revelation about our future defence posture in terms of nuclear weapons, namely to continue forever in the pocket of the USA, dependent on its technology, policies and permission for our 'independent' deterrent. So-called deterrence claims that nuclear weapons are there to deter, not to be used. However, the USA has been moving for a long time towards a use-posture. The USA and the UK are far more in breach of the Nuclear Non-Proliferation Treaty than Iran. Israel is not even a member. More questions are raised by American attempts at a missile defence system, for well-known reasons.

Paul Goodman, much admired by Chomsky, was an American anarchist on the utopian left (albeit with a practical streak: 'there is no politics but remedial politics'), a poet (*Collected Poems*) and social critic. Goodman's *Little Prayers and Finite Experience* has poems on the left-hand pages, prose on the right. 'How to take on Culture without losing Nature' is the abstract formulation of his programme. I sense the truth of Goethe's 'we commit some folly just to live on a little', which he quotes. But in his journal, *Five Years*, Goodman asserts that 'to work at survival as such is like trying to be happy as such . . . To use survival pragmatically is bound to make it boring and we'll destroy ourselves just for spite. To boast of surviving tempts Nemesis, our deeper impulse.'

Ronald Aronson (*Jean-Paul Sartre and others*)

I have several books by my friend Ronald Aronson, including his *After Marxism*, which enacts, as a chapter in the history of living ideas, and with characteristic lucidity, a process of mourning for a project that for good or ill, for good *and* ill, has influenced as many people as the grand intellectual revolutions of Freud and surrealism. I remember celebrating, in Jimmy's basement tavern in Soho, the publication of Aronson's book *The Dialectics of Disaster: A Preface to Hope* with him and his editor Misha Glenny, later a brilliant correspondent for the BBC. Its title puts me in mind of Gramsci's enabling motto 'Pessimism of the intellect, optimism of the will' (James Joll's typically limpid and lucid book, *Gramsci*, is not at hand to check), said to have been borrowed from Romain Rolland although he in turn, according to Barbara Garvin, may have got it from Jacob Burckhardt. An earlier version of one chapter of Aronson's book appeared in a Menard pamphlet with a harsh subtitle, *Technological Madness: Towards a Theory of the Impending Nuclear Holocaust.* In 1986, I gave a lecture tour in the USA culminating in my literary jury service for the Neustadt International Prize at the University of Oklahoma. One of my stopovers en route to Oklahoma was Detroit where Ron teaches at Wayne State University and where I gave a lecture that almost fell on its nose because of my crazy notes that were neither written out as text nor headlined as bullet points. That's what happens when you want to boast to yourself you can speak from notes rather than read out a prepared speech.

During free time, we saw the Diego Rivero frescoes in the museum and walked round the dilapidated downtown area, where Ron introduced me to his old-timer radical friend, the professional revolutionary and political activist Saul Wellman, one of the 'Detroit Six' in a famous trial. That evening, I was taken out for dinner and noticed we were driving south. 'Where are we going?' 'You'll see.' To my surprise we crossed the border into Canada. I had an *idée fixe* that Canada was north of the USA. The Turkish restaurant owner turned out to be the brother of the owner of a restaurant in Hendon, London, much patronized by Musa Farhi. It's a small world, but not so simple that frontiers run in straight lines like a sober jogger bent on proving a point. Ron's best book is *Camus and Sartre: The Story of a Friendship and the Quarrel That Ended It*, a marvellous study based on original research about the complex relationship between these two grand figures, a friendship personifying the tragic split on the left that has haunted Europe and the world. In 2007, Ron emailed me a Camus text which has, by now, been engraved on a monument, in San Francisco, to veterans of the international brigades, and asked me to tweak his translation. It was an honour to be associated with such a monument, and somehow appropriate for the association to involve a collaborative effort.

> For nine years people of my generation have had Spain engraved on their hearts. For nine years they have carried her round with them like a terrible wound. Spain gave them their first taste of defeat and, thanks to her, they discovered with an enduring shock that you

585

could be in the right and still be defeated, that sheer force could vanquish the human spirit, and that there are times when courage does not receive its due reward. Undoubtedly, this explains why so many people the world over have experienced the Spanish drama as their own personal tragedy.

The title of Aronson's most recent book, *Living without God*, written in the mellow tone of a man who has recovered from cancer and who lives life to the full, speaks for itself. He is not a man who disdains organized religion while still retaining a belief in God or a spiritual homologue of God. Not at all: not only does he live without religion, he lives without God. Ron has always been a resolute Jewish secularist, remaining within the prophetic tradition of the ancestral collectivity, a pneumatic Jew in Celan's phrase, and without the hang-ups of those brought up in families that use religion in the God-sense for communal purposes. The synagogue, like Jewish day schools outside the state system, is a place which enables you to meet and, bottom line, marry other Jews, but because it is a synagogue some commitment to the God of Abraham, Isaac and Jacob is called for. No wonder children are confused. Aronson is a person for whom atheism is a given, not a problem or an enemy. He deals with ideas like hope, gratitude (Margaret Visser wrote a whole book on this: *The Gift of Thanks*) and responsibility and how to live life without illusion or, at least, arrive at an ending whose sense, dare I say, is redemptive (a word he does not use or perhaps avoids), despite all that had been repressed or self-deceptive in the hitherto lived life. One of his proof texts is, of course, *The Death of Ivan Ilyich*. Yet I cannot see that failure to forgive oneself for real wrongs would count as a bad death. On a global scale, our health and wealth depend on the illness and poverty of others. To work, individually as well as collectively, towards a world where resources are devoted to life (that is, health) is essential. Individuals, writes Aronson's teacher, Herbert Marcuse, 'can die without anxiety if they know that what they love is protected from misery and oblivion'. I think of my grandchildren, and the world that lies ahead: risk of nuclear war, climate catastrophe and so on. I shall not die without anxiety, that's for sure. I should have sent Ron a clipping from *Le Monde* which has now gone missing, where Lévi-Strauss, aged ninety-nine, talked about two kinds of project: those that he had a chance of completing and those that he would once have had a chance of completing; he was continuing to plan projects of both kinds. I recall the famous Midrash of the old man planting a tree which he will not live to see, but his grandson will.

The Student Revolt is a useful compendium of texts about the May Events in Paris in 1968, including Sartre's interview of Daniel Cohn-Bendit ('We are all German Jews' was the chant inspired by Cohn-Bendit's origins, as a riposte to hostile elements who brought it up), published in *Le Nouvel Observateur* on 20 May that year. Here Sartre, for once, is learning rather than teaching. Amidst the wishful thinking and adrenalin rushes, Cohn-Bendit, rejecting the distinction between student and worker and replying to Sartre's point about students not being a class, says, echoing Marx, 'we can imagine another system where everyone will work at the tasks of production—reduced to a minimum thanks to technical progress—and everyone will still be able to pursue his studies at the same time.' Aware that this is utopian fantasy, the future Green MEP concedes: 'Obviously, there would be special cases; very advanced mathematics or medicine cannot be taken up while exercising another activity at the same time.'

UK

Raymond Williams

Raymond Williams, whom I met only once but saw several times across a crowded room, was a powerful shaper of my mind and my friends' minds. My instinctive social radicalism was drawn to and reinforced by his *Culture and Society* and *The Long Revolution*, books which interested me more than his literary criticism. On my bookmark, torn from a small notepad, in *Culture and Society* is 'Write Terry' against a page number. This was Terry Eagleton, who was no longer round the corner, since I had left Cambridge by the time I read the book, which is inscribed June 1964. Associated books were Williams' *Communications* and *May Day Manifesto 1968*, Richard Hoggart's *The Uses of Literacy*, Jeff Nuttall's *Bomb Culture*, Richard Neville's *Play Power*, Denys Thompson's *Discrimination and Popular Culture*: all these helped educate me as a political animal whose underlying philosophy was that no one is truly free until all are free. The philosophical underpinnings of this simple, rational and heartfelt worldview came to me from France, the clarion call from the Jewish prophetic tradition. Today, the same applies, only more so. Unless we acknowledge that we are all in the same boat and that in Lorca's phrase, quoted by that senior and significant poet Nathaniel Tarn in a brilliant essay 'Octavio Paz, Anthropology and the Future of Poetry' (collected in *The Embattled Lyric*), 'tambien se muere el mar' (the sea also is dying), we have had it. 'Socialism' or 'barbarism' was Rosa Luxemburg's watchword long ago. We are one species in one world and, as Andrei Sakharov well understood, we shall be fucked if we don't cooperate, which will involve rationing resources, unless we find the will to put in place, before it is too late, solar energy and fusion power to tide us over.

Harold Wilson

The Age of Austerity 1945–1951 edited by Michael Sissons and Philip French has essays on spivs and snoek and the Festival of Britain; and the New Look: 'I thank heaven I lived in Paris in the last years of the *Belle Epoque*,' wrote Dior; in the UK, the New Look's success was sealed by Princess Margaret. There is an essay on the 1946 terror attack at the King David Hotel in Jerusalem by the Irgun under the command of a man with a price on his head, Menachem Begin. *Harold Wilson* by Michael Foot and *Attlee as I Knew Him* are promotional and retirement profiles of two prime ministers who have always fascinated me. Wilson stood up to Lyndon Johnson in a way that Tony Blair never did with George Bush, not that Blair wanted to, which made it worse. Foot's hagiography was published a month before the 1964 General Election, when Wilson, our neighbour in Hampstead Garden Suburb, became prime minister. I played my small part on polling day as open-car chauffeur of Reg Freeson, the successful Labour candidate in Willesden East, later shafted and ousted by Ken Livingstone.

The Wilson book was a fundraiser for the Labour Party and is now a superb period piece. The 1950 Downing Street photograph of cabinet ministers in their waistcoated suits and the one of Harold Wilson playing shove ha'penny at the British Industries Fair in the same year are as redolent of the times as the photographs of footballers with their long knickers (as shorts were called in a 1950s' Arsenal programme I still have) and big-studded boots. Two of the cabinet ministers are smoking pipes, unlike Che Guevara and Fidel Castro with their cigars. Another photo shows Wilson as leader of the opposition in 1963 receiving the future vice president, Nelson Rockefeller, and an unidentified man recognizable as Henry Kissinger, professor at Harvard and doubtless adviser to Rockefeller, then governor of New York. In *Attlee as I Knew Him*, Wilson tells a nice anecdote about his legendarily laconic boss: John Strachey, the food minister, wanted permission to publish a book of poems and, as a cabinet minister, required the permission of the prime minister. 'No, can't publish.' 'Why not?' 'Don't rhyme, don't scan.' Wilson also alludes to a famous occasion when Attlee sought to persuade Harry Truman to rescind what was apparently delegated authority to the military to use nuclear weapons in Korea. According to Wilson, the greatest achievement of Attlee, who during his premiership gave the go-ahead to build nuclear weapons while also nationalizing the utilities and heavy industry, was granting independence to India. What about the creation of the National Health Service?

Robin Butler

Another political category is the prognostication, thus, Sir Richard Acland's *The Next Step* (1974) and James Robertson's *A Choice of Futures*, which went into several printings in the first half of the 1980s, the time of my most political phase, when Menard published its series of educational pamphlets concerning nuclear weapons. The opposite of the prognostication is the post-mortem, such as Lord Butler's report, *Espionage and the Iraq War*. I read this partly out of interest, partly because Paula and I were houseguests of Butler, master of University College, Oxford, when Paula received her honorary degree in 2005, and I wanted to take advantage of privileged access to the man who was Cabinet Secretary at the time of the invasion. Given his position, the (understated) report is 'lethal', as I wrote to him in a letter introducing myself prior to our visit. Thus, in respect of the infamous dodgy dossier, he writes that the Joint Intelligence Committee, which took responsibility for preparing the dossier, 'had strain put on them in seeking to maintain their normal standards of neutral and objective assessment'.

Nowhere does Butler spell out the implications of this, but we take the point that the prime minister, 'influenced by the concerns of the US government' was playing politics, thanks to his a priori decision to go to war, which meant fixing the intelligence, hence the 'sexing up' of the dossier. Again: 'We have not been presented with any evidence that persuades us that there was an insuperable obstacle to allowing expert-level DIS [Defence Intelligence Staff] access to the intelligence.' The report contains many such suggestions of political considerations overriding intelligence.

In my letter, I wrote to Lord Butler: '. . . And so we come to the special relationship, so called. This is the heart of the matter. My sense is that it has corrupted Britain's standing and relevance in a world crying out for good and decent governance. When US administrations were relatively benign and intelligent, things were not much better. Britain's failure to take the lead in Europe after World War II was a grave error of judgment but was directly linked to the history of the war. I suppose it was inevitable. The French idea that we are a US Trojan horse—even if only psychologically but doubtless in other respects too—feels uncomfortably true. So, what is in this relationship for us? Doubtless we are supposed to benefit from military and other intelligence. But what a price we pay. I find the idea that the relationship helps us "punch above our weight" absurd and humiliating. And we are locked into the Star Wars technology. This is scary. But above all we are locked into a mindset that is not in our interest, with our best friend GW and his administration heading for confrontation with Russia and reverting to a pre-New Deal social order at home.' There was little time to discuss this stuff. Lord Butler showed us round his college. We saw Kitaj's portrait of Bill Clinton (not the painter at his best) and Ruskin Spear's fine one of Harold Wilson. This was Paula's day and I was not there to paddle my own canoe.

Capital punishment

As already touched on, the social legislation of Harold Wilson's governments in the 1960s survived time and Margaret Thatcher and remains in place. The abolition of capital punishment was my first political campaign: here are *Hanged in Error* by Leslie Hale and *Hanged by the Neck* by Arthur Koestler and C. H. Rolph. *Turgenev's Literary Reminiscences* contains his 1870 account of the guillotining in Paris of the alleged murderer Tropman: '*absolutely no one present looked like a man who realised that he had been present at the performance of an act of social justice*' (Turgenev's emphasis). He concludes that this is one of the most important issues facing mankind and hopes that his account supplies a few arguments in favour of those opposed to the death penalty. Clive Sinclair tells me that Mark Twain, after witnessing an execution in Nevada in 1868, published an article expressing revulsion at what he saw. And already in 1829 Victor Hugo had published his *Last Day of a Condemned Man*. There is a discussion of Hugo's lifelong political battle against capital punishment in his *Times* obituary of 22 May 1855, reprinted in *Great Victorian Lives*, which John Erle-Drax of the Marlborough Gallery gave me one Christmas. I also read *We Are Your Sons* by Robert and Michael Meeropol, the children of Ethel and Julius Rosenberg, who were sent to the chair as atom spies in 1954. Appropriately enough, their adoptive father Abel Meeropol wrote 'Strange Fruit', that powerful and influential protest song about race (it was inspired by a lynching), which Billie Holiday recorded in 1939.

Radicalism

Strange as it may seem to the generation of my children, communism was on the agenda in my own family circle; friends of my parents were members of the party, although all had left by the time the Hungarian uprising was defeated in 1956. The party, in one sense, was over. They would have read— as contemporary history relating to their personal involvement—George Orwell's *Homage to Catalonia* and *The God That Failed*, edited by Richard Crossman in 1950, which has essays by André Gide, Stephen Spender and others, and tells the story of the religious faith cum love affair which was the relationship between European and American intellectuals and communism. This gave rise to another religion, anti-communism, which has now mutated to anti-Islamic fundamentalism, if not anti-Islam. The alliance between Christian evangelism, neoconservatism, oil interests, far-right Zionism and the military–industrial complex Eisenhower warned against, dressed up in the rhetoric of democracy and freedom, is combustible. On the non-communist left (explored in Anne Fremantle's history of the Fabians, *This*

Little Band of Prophets), a book like R. H. Tawney's *Equality* reveals the kind of thinking which permeated the minds of serious people when I was young and, until Margaret Thatcher, was, in a sense, the default ideology which conservative thinkers had to prove wrong. Books by radicals I read in the 1960s included *The Accidental Century* and *The Other America* by Michael Harrington and *In the Fist of the Revolution*, an account of life in Castro's Cuba by my New York friend Jose Yglesias. Then there were Penguin Specials like Edward Crankshaw's *The New Cold War* and John Mander's *Berlin Hostage for the West* as well as his *Great Britain or Little England*. A quick glance at Mander's conclusion to the latter book reveals that he thought that our nuclear superiority over France's *force de frappe* gave us an advantage in the battle for the political leadership of Europe. I hope this conceptual confusion seemed as absurd then as it does now, not least because we now know that, unlike the UK, the French are operationally independent of the USA. Collections of essays like *Towards Socialism*, edited by Perry Anderson, and *Socialist Humanism*, edited by Erich Fromm in the same year, demonstrate the radical pressures—political, economic and moral—on European Labour governments such as those of Harold Wilson. By the time Tony Benn brought out his 1984 anthology, *Writings on the Wall*, five years after Mrs Thatcher had embarked on a new direction in the political economy of the UK, the tone, in a time of defeat, was already nostalgic: the book contains rousing texts from the radical and socialist traditions which still survive in corners of the foreign field which is forever the England of my childhood, but oddly enough not Colonel Rainsborough's wonderful statement at Putney in 1647: 'The poorest he that is in England hath a life to live as the greatest he.'

Michael Pinto-Duschinsky

The British General Election of 1970 (co-authored with David Butler) and *British Political Finance 1830–1980* by Michael Pinto-Duschinsky are not books I would have opened had my oldest close friend not written them. He is a world expert in three areas: UK political finance, international democratic governance and post-war German historiography. He gives evidence to parliamentary select committees on political finance, among other forums. He has a profound analytic grasp of the specialist terrain which gives his writing a depth charge, and with which I cannot compete, nor would I want to, for my mind operates in a different way, as is self-evident to anyone who has kept me company this far into my book. If someone has radically opposed political views, I suspect one has to know them from an early age if friendship is to survive. The hinterland in which our affection for each other flourishes as we age into the grandparental generation—concern for the future of our children and deep anxiety about the way the world is going—permits each to forgive the other's assumed view of the political economy and human nature in general. We protect each other by leaving much unsaid. I am more viscerally affected by developments: for example, I fear upon my pulses and in my bones an Israeli attack on Iran, a topic often featured in the email 'Bulletins' which I circulated for a few years—and am touched by the way he calms me down, and advises me what to do with my energies in this area, even as I mostly ignore his advice. In recent years, he has been concentrating on his role as expert and consultant. It is time he returned to books. *The Political Thought of Lord Salisbury*, written when he was twenty-three, is a harbinger of the major study of democracy and governance he will write.

Internet

Secret Classrooms by Geoffrey Elliott and Harold Shukman is about the teaching of Russian during the cold war. Like Michael Frayn and Alan Bennett, J. M. C. Davidson, my first-rate sixth-form Russian teacher, was an alumnus of the Joint Services course at Cambridge, where the book is set. That generation, taught by White Russian émigrés, is now retired and its own students are senior teachers of Russian round the country. Considering how much attention I give to politics, it is surprising how few books I have on the subject. And yet, not so surprising: I read *The Guardian* everyday, ditto the electronic *Truthout* and *Reader Supported News* (radical and progressive American views on the USA), watch television documentaries, exchange political mails with friends and family. All this takes time. One day I received notice of E. L. Doctorow's 'Essay on Death and President Bush'. I checked this out at once on the Internet and was so struck by it that I immediately emailed it to a hundred people, some of whom, like Michael Moorcock and Harry Kuhner, forwarded it to their own lists. And so this amazing disseminatory tool serves our end as, no doubt, we serve its. If during an earlier phase you lived in Jerusalem or Carthage or London, you would have wanted to know what they were thinking and planning in Rome. Today, *mutatis mutandis*, we need to know what they are thinking in Washington. Long ago I made certain choices about reading matter, and explicitly political books did not feature, but you can learn a lot about politics from the prose of Norman Mailer, the poems of Robert Lowell, the plays of Arthur Miller, even the songs of Bob Dylan. And I live the ostensible subject everyday. My neglect of history and economics is more serious.

Nuclear

Menard's involvement in nuclear education in the early 1980s brought me into contact with scientists, civil servants, politicians, writers and educators. I renewed contact with an old Cambridge friend Nick Humphrey, published his *Four Minutes to Midnight*, and through him met his then partner, Susannah York. During a dangerous phase of the cold war, I forced myself to read many books about the nuclear dilemma and related topics: among the best were and indeed are Robert Jay Lifton and Eric Markusen's *The Genocidal Mentality*, Jeff Smith's *Unthinking the Unthinkable*, Jonathan Schell's *The Fate of the Earth* and Robert Scheer's *With Enough Shovels: Reagan, Bush and Nuclear War*. I wonder if Freeman Dyson is as optimistic now as he was, in my recollection, when he wrote *Weapons and Hope* and *Disturbing the Universe*. That fine poet Derek Mahon, poetry editor of *The New Statesman* and the journal's acting literary editor while Martin Amis was on holiday, published my review of Schell's remarkable work as a lead. It is a sober and terrifying book about the end of the world. Here too is *Fire and Ice: The Nuclear Winter* by the astronomer poet Michael Rowan Robinson. This could equally well be entered under 'Science' books where I have written about his other books, and this is a temptation if only for the ignoble reason that Science is one of my shortest sections. All the same, I know that this book belongs here, because of the inscription: 'To Tony, whose "Lost Summer and Nuclear Winter" was a major inspiration for this book, with love, Michael'. He is referring to *Byron's Darkness*, my pamphlet about the poem 'Darkness' and Byron's extraordinary intuition of nuclear winter after the famous 'year without a summer' of 1816, following the eruption of the volcano Mount Tambora the previous year.

Michael and I were comrades-in-arms (not the best metaphor under the circumstances) while Menard was producing its educational pamphlets during the early 1980s. *Fire and Ice: The Nuclear Winter*, too long to be a Menard pamphlet, is one of Michael's non-specialist books, science for every man and woman. The book concludes with 'Possible Futures': 'The catastrophe that put an end to the dinosaurs, perhaps very similar to the extreme nuclear winter scenario, only killed off half of the species then alive. Life will go on, but without us . . . the direct consequences of nuclear war are so appalling that humanity must draw back from this abyss. The nuclear winter magnifies the consequences and compels immediate action. We cannot let human existence on this beautiful planet be snuffed out.' Michael was writing in 1985, before the effects of climate change began to be common currency even on the fringes of political discourse. Fortunately there has been a climate change in the metaphorical sense, and people are waking up to the dangers although the pessimist in me thinks it may already be too late. For once, the most urgent voices on this issue are those who know most about it. For eight years, George Bush fiddled while Rome burned; during this period, many citizens engaged in that most ordinary of mental processes, *denial*. In fact, it would be more accurate to say that the emperor was not fiddling at all: he was stoking the fire. And indeed, the atomic scientists in Chicago moved their Doomsday Clock forward from seven minutes to midnight to five minutes to midnight. Since then it moved back to six, but at the time of writing it is five again. They are not scaremongers. We must pay heed. All that is necessary for the triumph of extinction is for good men to remain in denial.

[Memo to self: remember Gramsci's motto and, echoing it, the words of the Greek Orthodox monk Staretz Silouan, as quoted by Gillian Rose in *Love's Work*: 'Keep your mind in hell, and despair not.']

In 1991, Dorothy Rowe, psychotherapist, one of the matriarchs of the nuclear education movement and a wise woman indeed, ended her *Wanting Everything: The Art of Happiness* with these prophetic words: 'Soon our lives will be very different. As the trees disappear, the rains turn acid, the temperature increases and the waters rise, our lives will change but not in the ways we wish . . . We do have a little time . . . Let us use our intelligence.' The world is not being cared for, a perfect storm is brewing and our leaders' heads are in the sand. In 1981, I asked my friends Carl Rakosi and George Oppen to compose messages for a symposium at the Cambridge Poetry Festival, which I had proposed to the founder and organizer of the festival, my old friend and comrade Richard Berengarten. The symposium, clumsily entitled 'After Hölderlin: While Rome Burns—What Use is Poetry in a Time of Jeopardy?', was on the venerable theme of poetry and politics, with nuclear weapons—at the time a huge issue in Europe and centring on the deployment of cruise missiles—as the immediate context. Rakosi's message denounced the concept and was too long to read out. Four speakers were on the panel: George Steiner, Adrian Mitchell, Michael Rowan Robinson and me; the meeting was chaired by the philosopher Bernard Williams. I was told later that there were five hundred people in the Corn Exchange, a venue more accustomed to folk concerts, real ale fests and election rallies.

I asked Jonathan Griffin, senior poet and mutual friend of Oppen and myself, to read out the message, slowly, and twice. Twenty-seven years later, at a centenary conference for Oppen in New York, I recited the message again as well as 'Time of the Missile', a poem George wrote in the wake of, or during, the Cuban Missile crisis of 1961. This crisis, when the world could have ended, hit me during my first weeks as a student, twenty years almost to the month before the conference in the Corn Exchange. The Corn Exchange is only a quarter of a mile from the Cavendish laboratory, home to Rutherford and many other pioneers of atomic physics, including, for a short time, the young Robert Oppenheimer. I am delighted to discover, via the learned Oppen scholar Eric Hoffmann, that George Oppen (*né* Oppenheimer) and Robert Oppenheimer were second cousins, but through George's mother, not, as you would expect, his father. Great humanists, they both had profound and troubled minds. *'I think there is no light in the world but the world. And I think there is light. My happiness is the knowledge of all we do not know.'*

EUROPE

USSR

Mikhail Sergeyevich Gorbachev, an authentic hero of our time, paid the world a peace dividend, inaugurating the possibility of a virtuous circle. Instead of reciprocating, elements in the USA responded with triumphalism, militarism and a headlong rush to impose/install a free market in the USSR. Boris Yeltsin enabled the theft of state assets by robber barons, creating a capitalism that would not disgrace nineteenth-century USA. Later, Dick Cheney, who believed the cold war never ended, had the chutzpah to criticize Vladimir Putin, whose policies were and are the necessary outcome of the post-Gorbachev western failure to continue with the peace dividend. Here is a book which is sadly dated for reasons that are not its fault, *Breakthrough: Emerging New Thinking* and a sub subtitle: *Soviet and Western Scholars Issue a Challenge to Build a World Beyond War*. Among the blurbists on the back cover are, indeed, William Colby, former director of the CIA and Robert Conquest. The book contains a kind inscription to me by one of the editors, Professor Sergei Kapitsa, the Moscow physicist with whom I met in London during the Menard nuclear education phase. His father, the Nobel Prizewinning physicist Piotr Kapitsa, was at Trinity College Cambridge from 1921 to 1934 and returned home when Stalin promised to repatriate his laboratory. Fortunately, the Russian atom bomb was not his only contribution to science. If only Edward Teller had had the same attitude as Andrei Sakharov, that great and heroic man who saw the light after fathering the Soviet H Bomb and whose *Progress, Co-existence and Intellectual Freedom* makes for dispiriting rereading, especially the afterword by his editor Harrison Salisbury, 'The World in the Year 2000'. Some of the predictions and hopes have not come to pass, thanks to the USA's lamentable failure to use its great power and wealth in a way that does not presuppose that international governance is a zero-sum game. In at least one area Sakharov was prescient: climate change and, specifically, carbon emissions. In 1968, he called for 'geohygienic' laws and wrote: 'The salvation of our environment requires that we overcome our divisions and the pressure of temporary, local interests.'

[Checking something online today, 15 August 2012, during my final revision, I learn that Kapitsa died yesterday . . .]

Auschwitz

'The unjustifiable privilege of having survived the death of six million', writes Levinas. Richard Rubenstein's *After Auschwitz*, his political history of genocide *The Age of Triage* and, in particular, his short and intense masterpiece *The Cunning of History: The Holocaust and the American Future* (introduced by William Styron) compelled my attention round the time I was reading Arthur Cohen's *The Tremendum*. 'An extermination centre,' says Rubenstein, 'can only manufacture corpses; a society of total domination creates a world of the living dead.' And: 'We are more likely to understand the Holocaust if we regard it as the expression of some of the most profound tendencies of western civilisation in the twentieth century' (meaning slavery, colonial slaughter and the nature of warfare in World War I). Also: 'Perhaps it was no accident that the most highly urbanised people in the western world, the Jews, were the first to perish in the ultimate city of western civilisation, Necropolis, the new city of the dead that the Germans built and maintained at Auschwitz.' The final chapter of Rubenstein's book written in 1975 contains prophetic words about George Bush/Dick Cheney, which if anything understate their attitude by implying reactive rather than proactive behaviour, such as 'signing statements' as a way round the constitution, and castrating the intelligence services: 'It would be comforting to think that the abuses of power that occurred in the Nixon administration were due solely to his moral and political shortcomings. Unfortunately the problem will not go away with the departure of Richard Nixon. The abuses occurred because *the structure of government* put the capacity to act as Nixon did in the hands of any President willing to employ it and clever enough to get away with such behaviour. The bureaucracy that Nixon sought to use extra-legally might be so used by a future president. Should, for example, the economic crisis continue to deteriorate or should a catastrophic war break out, a future president might be tempted by the readiness of a desperate nation to accept radical measures in order to solve its woes. The overwhelming power of modern government is bound to increase no matter who is president.'

Vaclav Havel

Before and during the velvet revolution, I read everything I could find by or about Vaclav Havel, as well as catching a few of his plays in small theatres. Havel was one of the people whose ideas I sought to address in my Adam Lecture at Kings College, later published as *Wine from Two Glasses*. Here was a literary intellectual with political influence, such as you do not find in Anglo-Saxon countries, and rarely in other countries too: François Mitterand certainly, maybe Joshka Fischer, although their primary face was political. I learnt from Yves Bonnefoy that at an official lunch President Jacques Chirac spoke with knowledge, authority and passion about Japanese poetry, while being the only person drinking beer rather than wine. Here, then, on my desk, are Havel's plays, including *Largo Desolato* translated by Tom Stoppard, and political works: *Summer Meditations, Disturbing the Peace, Open Letters, Letters to Olga* and *Living in Truth*, the last consisting of six texts by him and sixteen homages. Notable among these is something rare in Samuel Beckett's *oeuvre*, namely a text generated for/by a specific political situation (another being the classic 'uptherepublic', his reply to a questionnaire about the Spanish Civil War), his play *Catastrophe*, written during Havel's imprisonment. According to Michael Simmons' biography, *The Reluctant President*, Havel, soon after his release from prison, wrote *Mistake*, a one-act play to honour Beckett.

Vaclav Havel's best prison writings compare well with Wole Soyinka's *The Man Died*. I was particularly struck by one passage in Soyinka's book and marked it in the margin: 'Except as source of strength and vision, keep inner self out of all expectation, let it remain unconscious beneficiary from experience. Suspect all conscious search for the self's authentic being; this is favourite fodder for the enervating Tragic Muse. *I do not seek; I find*' (Picasso's quote, Soyinka's emphasis). However much Havel may have become a prisoner of the establishment (riding round the corridors of the big castle on his roller skates and later buying, perhaps reluctantly, into the liberal hawk position associated with Michael Ignatieff, the late Christopher Hitchens and others), there was a time when he wrote major essays of great power and insight, which had a deserved influence in Europe. (Former) Czechoslovakia has had a special place in my heart ever since the Prague Spring, which along with the May Events and the Six Day War did so much to radicalize persons of my generation. Yes, for a few years Havel 'spoke truth to power', a Quaker phrase that ultimately derives from the Jewish prophets: it is a stance sorely lacking in the Jewish world at the moment. Rest in peace, Vaclav Havel, who died one day after a very different head of state, Kim Jong-Il.

Back in 1973 I asked my late friend and early supporter Elizabeth Thomas if I could review the autobiography of Heda Margolius, *I Do Not Want to Remember*, in *Tribune*. I still remember the understated description of Margolius' last meeting with her husband Rudolf before his execution as one of the fourteen defendants in the Rudolf Slansky show trial in Prague, and even after all these years I am moved profoundly by her account of his final words, which concludes: 'I don't know whether he said anything else, I no longer registered anything except that these were the last moments, the last . . . Rudolf backed towards the door, and as he passed through it, the expression in his eyes changed and what appeared in them for that brief moment was something I shall bear within me as long as I live.' I have read many descriptions of final moments of defeated leaders, of members of resistance movements, of condemned people in the camps, or those with terminal diseases. Perhaps more than committing suicide (which in any case is not always intended to succeed and does not always work even when wholly intended), facing such a death requires the kind of courage that you and I do not know we would possess in those circumstances. I think about the countdown of the previous night, about the fantasy spell of Zeno's paradox to ward off the arrival of the moment or, more likely, 'un long sanglot, tout chargé d'adieux' to borrow a phrase from Baudelaire's 'La Mort des amants'. Perhaps you wonder, as I do, how one would behave oneself? Heroically, with any luck, as in the famous Eluard poem, where political solidarity allows your death to be redeemed and avenged by the eventual triumph of the revolution or at least the defeat of the enemy? Professor Antonio Homem (meaning in Portuguese 'man', appropriately enough) was the leading Catholic theologian at Coimbra University during the Inquisition: he was outed first as a homosexual and then as a Jew. The death of this 'queer Jew' (as John Lennon suggested Brian Epstein should entitle his autobiography) would be the slowest auto-da-fé that could be arranged, even by the standards of the day.

But if I imagine that he was brave in his dying, I am being sentimental. Maybe he was not brave when it came to the crunch, and why should he be? He had been tough, for sure, and indeed brave, while living for years as a Marrano and a closet gay. Recently I returned to the subject when Randy Petillos at Chicago University Press sent me Robert Elder's remarkable documentary account of the death penalty in the USA, *Last Words of the Executed*: not easy reading, and rightly so.

Günter Grass

Günter Grass is a model of the engaged writer. Here are his poetry, *Poems* and *In the Egg*, translated by Michael Hamburger and Christopher Middleton, and his prose including *From the Diary of a Snail*, ending as it does with a chapter on Albrecht Dürer's engraving 'Melancholia 1'. Grass reminds us that the deity of human fate was Saturn, who 'presided over melancholy and utopia'. He continues: 'here I shall speak of . . . how melancholy and utopia . . . fertilise each another . . . [I shall speak] of Freud and Marx, who should have sat for a double portrait by Dürer . . . and of myself, for whom melancholy and utopia are heads and tails of the same coin.' After getting into his stride with *excursi* on tourism, conveyor belts and Marsilio Ficino's anticipation of Arthur Schopenhauer, Günter Grass comes to the serious politics of the day (1969) and his conservative enemy pre-Thatcher and Kohl. This was a decade before triumphalist neoconservative philosophy won the day.

'Melancholia 1' is the best engraving ever, according to Paula, who has a reproduction of it on her mantlepiece: 'My subject,' writes Grass, 'presents not a manic-depressive state but the state of reactive melancholy prevailing in the age of humanism.' This was a dramatic, indeed frenetic, period of transition: Nicolas Copernicus and Christopher Columbus, the Fuggers and Thomas Munzer were active. History was moving from the cyclical to the linear. Dürer's melancholy 'grew from knowledge and understands itself' while the clutter in the engraving 'is a symptom of science's self-doubt, hence of melancholy'. Later, our own melancholy 'sits brooding between ideologies and stunted reforms, impoverished amid inertia. Tired, disgusted by long-drawn-out snail processes [read Fabian gradualism], she too, like Dürer's

"Melancholia", props up her head and clenches her fist.' Grass moves on to the Jews of Europe and his hero Chancellor Willy Brandt's gesture of kneeling at the site of the Warsaw Ghetto. 'Repentance as a social state of mind would then be the corresponding utopia: it presupposes melancholy rooted in insight.' On a trip to Sweden, he asks himself why the hippies—he does not use that word—are cheerful, and supplies his own answer: because 'Saturn has released his children from history . . . Forgetfulness of history is . . . a melancholy expression of utopian flight from reality.'

Grass' *Two States—One Nation*? contains his argument against German reunification, but it is the final essay in the book, 'Writing after Auschwitz', which has helped me formulate my own ideas over the years since it was published in 1990. His comment that Adorno's famous remarks on poetry after Auschwitz 'were not a prohibition but a challenge to be met' served and serves to liberate writers from anxiety about the propriety of writing poetry or fiction (rather than documentary) about the Shoah. In any case, the youngest survivors are now in their seventies and we live in a brave new world. Here is Grass' earlier collection of political essays, *On Writing and Politics*, with its exemplary essay 'The Destruction of the World has Begun': 'In the worst of times, literature has always been sure of one ally: the future . . . Isaac Babel and Osip Mandelstam outlived Stalinism—though it killed them . . . This advance payment, this provision of time, made the poorest writers rich . . . The book I am planning to write can no longer pretend to certainty of the future. It will have to include a farewell to the damaged world, to wounded creatures, to us and our minds, which have thought of everything and of the end as well.'

The revelation in *Peeling the Onion*—the autobiography of this remarkable writer and force for the moral and political good of Europe—that his seventeen-year-old younger self was drafted into an infantry battalion of the Waffen SS, has aroused a storm of protest by people not fit to lick his feet. The only critique of him that says anything valid (all reservations guarded, as they say in French, until one reads the book) is that having made the revelation he appears not have gone into enough detail about its implications for his writings. The idea that he told the newspapers in advance for reasons of publicity is a sick joke. It has always been known he was in the army and not in the minuscule resistance. The fact that he kept quiet about the SS for all these years may not be admirable but it is understandable and does not invalidate his fiction, his non-fiction and his polemical writings. But no wonder he is melancholy. It is difficult now not to read his silence back into the earlier texts. Nonetheless, it must be resisted.

Introduction

I possess a few explicitly feminist books, including *Sex and Other Sacred Games* by Kim Chernin and Renate Stendhal; Andrea Dworkin's *Pornography* and her novel *Mercy*; Kate Millet's *The Prostitution Papers* and *Sexual Politics*; *The Ostrich Position* by Carol Lee; and Sharon Nelson's poems, *Grasping Men's Metaphors*. Feminism has been floating round my mind and body for many years, and some of its arguments, central to our self-understanding as thinking humans, have made their way into my worldview. Janet Radcliffe Richards' *The Sceptical Feminist* argues that many feminist aims can be subsumed under wider social ones and if they can be achieved in non-gender-specific campaigns, then they should be. Only if that fails is a feminist campaign required. I doubt if a philosophical issue is at stake, although the author's philosopher husband Derek Parfit might disagree, but lives are, sometimes in the most literal sense. Paula's abortion paintings and prints were made in order to influence referenda and legislation in her native Portugal. She was and is fighting for human rights as well as women's rights. Her women are seen, that is painted, as survivors not victims, a survivor being a victim who says no, at least in my definition (possibly plagiarized from Primo Levi). By this token, it goes without saying that the genitally mutilated girls she has been painting more recently count as victims. They were and are too young and/or frightened to say no.

Louise Michel

Whisper Louise by the poet Douglas Oliver recounts an autobiographical journey in the open guise of a biographical meditation on Louise Michel, famous for her major role in the Paris Commune. Oliver ends with an appendix entitled 'The Fifty-Eight Potentially Disastrous Pathways', which separately or together will destroy our planet unless we meet the challenge. There is a great pathos to the following words about the violent anarchist for, *mutatis mutandis*, they apply to the author too, who died soon after completing the book, which was published posthumously. Note the poet's sensitivity to etymology in his association of 'kind' and 'kindness': 'Her real story is of this tender heart, of the bedlam of her schoolrooms with their concern for the "developmentally disabled". What kindness! What a sense of kind! What forgiveness! What dignity as a woman! What a light she spreads towards us from those qualities. So often we can glimpse a great goodness in the inadequate performances of her life. In my imagination she returns to her coffin at last and lies there glowing in a light whose colour I can't quite discern.'

Robin Morgan and Kim Chernin

Robin Morgan, then living with my close friend the Cuban-born poet Isel Rivero in Greenwich Village, gave me her own books *The Anatomy of Freedom* and a collection of poems *Depth Perception* when I visited them, just as Susan Griffin, then living with my friend and Menard author, Kim Chernin, gave me her powerful and eloquent *Woman and Nature*. In Morgan's discussion of Psyche as passive and even masochistic, she quotes Rilke as saying that men should 'begin to shoulder *their* part of the burden of love's labours'. Rilke was right, although he never practised what he preached. Still, women almost always forgave this man (including famously Lou Andreas-Salomé), even as they understood him, perhaps because, of all the great male poets, he was the closest in touch with his anima, in the terminology of Jung, who believed the soul was androgynous, albeit with two components: anima and animus. I felt I had to mention to Morgan that I had read (and still have somewhere) a leaflet she handed out at an early Poetry International calling for Ted Hughes' cock to be cut off and stuffed down his throat. She grimaced and said that she later came to regret the campaign, generated by what she saw as the implications of the suicide of Sylvia Plath, and that she owed Hughes an apology. Which was indeed the case. Later, Morgan sent me her book *The Demon Lover: On the Sexuality of Terrorism*, which is dedicated to Isel Rivero. The remark about Hughes was made in the language of terror, and Morgan herself now sees political terror and personal terror as being on the same spectrum: her inner yogi and inner commissar are no longer at war with each other. I cannot remember if I reported the Hughes story back to the then unknown Chernin, whose poetry I published at Menard (*The Hunger Song*, with wood engravings by Willow Winston) and whose *In My Mother's House* I took in manuscript to Virago when Virago was Ursula Owen, Carmen Callil and Lennie Goodings ensconced in one or two rooms on Soho's Old Compton Street. They turned it down at the time. Here too is Chernin's *The Obsession: Reflections on the Tyranny of Slenderness*. Among the people she acknowledges is her fellow San Franciscan, our mutual friend Tillie Olsen, who died recently and who was an inspiration to so many.

Science and Medicine

Symptoms

Here is my much battered replacement copy of Dr Joan Gomez's *Dictionary of Symptoms*. Its indexes and chapter headings are poorly organized but it has come in use from time to time. I had the same local GP for thirty years and arranged to be his final patient on his final day: John Brett, a good doctor and a good man, strongly progressive in his medical and other politics. For second opinions I phone my medical sister Mary or, until age intervened, my Uncle Jack or, when he was alive, my friend and quondam Menard author Cecil Hellman. Cecil had a mantra, spoken in a Yiddish accent from the depths of his self-knowledge: 'oy Tony, you are not a vell boy', whenever he suspected that my problem was mental. So, Cecil, when you broke your ankle and were in agony, did you ask yourself the quasi-Groddeckian question: 'what *mishigas* led me to do this to myself?' Let us not speak of the motor neurone disease which killed him. The Gomez book is a replacement copy because someone stole my first copy on the grounds that I was a hypochondriac; she went on to use it as inspiration for a painting with the same title, which I bought from her later on.

Body

I like delving into *The Phantom Museum and Henry Wellcome's Collection of Medical Curiosities* and Armand Marie Leroi's *Mutants*, although I would prefer not to go into my declared reasons, let alone explore the undeclared, perhaps unconscious ones. Suffice it to say, this is one of the two main areas where my reading explicitly touches on aspects of my short stories, the other being Marrano episodes in Jewish history. The existing stories were written almost exclusively 'from my head', though I am now poking round the literature for additional information concerning ideas I've already had for new stories, and also, why not, for new ideas. My imagination and hence my fictional prose are sometimes triggered, turned on, by thoughts of what the subtitle of Leroi's book summarizes, as Paula, who gave me this book, well knows.

Here are *Alternative Medicine* by Andrew Stanway and *Awareness through Movement* by Moshe Feldenkrais; also my American cousin Myron Winick's *Growing up Healthy: A Parent's Guide to Good Nutrition.* Winick, one of the leading nutritionists in the USA, lent the wright of his imprimatur to Weight Watchers for a few years. He was invited to check out a health menu for the now defunct Four Seasons Restaurant (of Rothko fame) and when asked what his fee was, proposed a year's season ticket to the restaurant. My sister Mary Krom has co-authored (as Mary Rudolf) a textbook, *Paediatrics and Child Health.* Closer to home, historically speaking, is an influential book from the 1980s by Penelope Leach. My copy of *Who Cares?: A New Deal for Mothers and Their Small Children* is inscribed 1979, when my children Nathaniel and Naomi were five and three. I well remember reading it carefully and gratefully, and finding that it chimed with my own expectations and experience. Naomi tells me she has a copy. So Charlie is getting the treatment, just as Naomi did thirty years ago. What goes round comes round.

I have tried to lose weight at certain turns in the spiral of my life. At other times I have tried to keep fit. These days my exercise regime is at best a minimum of thirty minutes on my cross-trainer bike three or four times a week, and a long walk once or twice a week now that I have abandoned swimming. The cross-trainer is perfect for Radio Four listening, something I rarely do at other times, being a 'fearful tuner', that is a one-station person. Today, I learnt what should have been obvious: diet involves eating as little as possible at lunchtime to compensate for evening greed and evening drinking. Lately, in general, I have been drinking less and eating more. *Physical Fitness*, the regime of the Royal Canadian Air Force, is an excellent guide I followed at one time. All you need is eleven minutes a day. As the daughter, who is a physiotherapist, says, do anything for twenty-eight days, and it becomes a habit.

After reading F. M. Alexander's book, *The Alexander Technique*, I was encouraged by a friend, to make an appointment with Peggy Williams, the last surviving practitioner trained by Alexander himself, at her flat in High Point, Highgate. I had always wanted to visit High Point, a classic modernist building designed by Berthold Lubetkin and pointed it out to American visitors after a trip to London Zoo in August 1976, the hottest summer on record, with Brenda about to have Naomi, and all of us wishing we were penguins in the house built by the same Lubetkin. After one lesson, Peggy passed me on to a colleague she had trained. According to Alexander, one is a student learning a technique from a teacher, not a patient or client. I like the attitude. The late Carola Grindea pioneered similar ideas about posture and direction to help musicians and other performing artists relax, and Naomi Gerecht's work with singers in Jerusalem draws on similar insights. Naomi told me she could help someone like Paula to breathe in such a way at the easel that it would add three years to her working life.

Rudolf Nassauer, author of a fine and neglected novel *The Hooligan*, once in exasperation described Hampstead as North West Shit, not what Maxine Kumin had in mind when she wrote 'I honour shit for saying: We go on' in 'The Excrement Poem' (see her fine book *The Retrieval System*). Two books on shit, source material, compost even, for a story I want to write, are: Ralph Lewin's *Merde* and the entertainingly illustrated *Histoire et Bizarreries Sociales des Excréments* by Martin Monestier, which Paula bought me in St Jean de Luz, close to Biarritz, where she participated, appropriately enough, in a show on the theme of Carnival.

Astronomy (Michael Rowan Robinson)

A battered Puffin Book I read as a child has survived: *Discovery*, an introduction to science by the astronomer Sir Richard Gregory. I wrote about Michael Rowan Robinson in the nuclear section just now. Our mutual friend Richard Berengarten introduced us in the 1980s, Michael and I never having met at Cambridge. Richard felt that our political concerns about nuclear weapons as well as a shared passion for certain writers would make our interaction productive. Michael is a former president of the Royal Astronomical Society. An asteroid has been named after him and, thanks to his initiative, one has also been named after Paula. Any thoughts of it having a direct impact on Planet Earth are virtual, nominal in the best sense of the word. Here are his *Ripples in the Cosmos*, *Cosmic Landscape* and *Universe*. In *Universe*, he thanks me for reading an early draft, evidently valuing the opinion of a man in the street. Michael has a gift for making complex ideas comprehensible to someone like me, whom C. P. Snow would have rightly condemned for scientific illiteracy. In *The Physicists*, Snow suggests that Einstein's God was the God of Spinoza, which suits me very well indeed. One summer, Michael phoned up all excited. The appropriate people to confide in were away and he had, like King Midas, to share his story: there was a blip on his computer. Something was there that should not have been; it was probably a technical glitch but if it wasn't and turned out to be a planet or star or something (I forget), then glittering prizes beckoned. It wasn't and they didn't. Not true, he gets plenty of awards. On top of all this, he's a poet of quality, although virtually unpublished. Not the least of his achievements is to have been acknowledged by George Seferis, one of the greatest of European poets, whose collected prose contains an account of a visit from the young Rowan Robinson. Seferis, understandably, liked the association of cosmology and poetry within one individual's purview. Michael and his wife Mary, among all my friends, are the most radically anti-religious, the most Dawkinsesque post-Darwinist rationalists, even more than Kotowicz: it is not enough to be an agnostic; one must be an atheist. Michael and Mary get impatient when I say that some of the most glorious creations in the world, Bach's music, the poems of Hopkins, the Song of Songs, were made for the glory of God. And yet, when Michael speaks or writes of the stars, or talks about the poets he loves (we once drew up a list and our top ten were nearly identical and, of course, included Seferis), he is deeply aware of what is mysterious, wondrous and awesome (would he allow words like spiritual and numinous?) in human existence and finitude. But there I go, apparently and wrongly buying into the idea that such awareness is more likely to be found among religious believers.

World War II

Murderous Science by Benno Muller-Hill and *Hunger Disease* are disturbing to read. The latter, edited by Myron Winick, contains all the data from medical experiments conducted in the Warsaw Ghetto during the Nazi occupation of Poland. Unlike the 'elimination by scientific selection of Jews, Gypsies and others' in Germany, as described by Muller-Hill, what went on in Warsaw was morally legitimate science, for the doctors were as hungry as their patients. Indeed, everyone—doctors and patients alike—was on the brink of starvation while at the same time caught up in an epidemic of infectious disease. Obedient to the dictates of their high calling as physicians, the doctors realized that the tragic situation—brought about by an evil regime that, not far away in Auschwitz, was torturing people during so-called medical experiments—could be of benefit to mankind. The chapters include clinical, medical and patho-physiological accounts of hunger in adults and children. One of the doctors, Julian Fliederbaum, must be related to Jack Fleiderbaum, a survivor of the Warsaw Ghetto married to a cousin of mine, Orna Urman; she lived in Stanislawow, next door to the future first mayor of Jerusalem, Daniel Auster, a relative of Paul Auster. Myron Winick has fictionalized the Warsaw Ghetto doctors in his novel *Final Stamp*. Quite apart from the emotions his treatment triggers, I have to confess that I understand the science much better in this popularized account. It is an astonishing story and would make an incredible film.

Antonio Damasio

Here are Antonio Damasio's *The Feeling of What Happens* and *Descartes' Error*. I read these important books on the insistence of the late Arnold Feinstein. He, along with my Uncle Jack and Michael Rowan Robinson, fought the good fight, namely to shame me into understanding and caring about science, without which one cannot claim to be a serious intellectual. I took Kotowicz to meet Arnold but my memory is now confused as to the parameters of the argument that took place. Probably it came down to differing positions concerning the epistemology of mind in terms of the brain. Feinstein, a formidable albeit latterly frustrated mind (or should I say brain?), was certainly more 'right wing' than Kotowicz, who rejects the claim that mental illness can be explained or will ever be explained in neurological terms. One reason why Damasio has had so much influence on current thinking in these areas is that, like Oliver Sacks, he is an excellent writer and eloquent proponent of his own views. I find in my copy of *Descartes' Error* a letter I wrote Damasio in which I explained that I was enclosing a sort of aide-memoire to myself consisting of forty-eight short quotes from his book, some of which I had commented on.

Using the example of an imaginary Aunt Maggie, Damasio writes: 'What dispositional representations hold in store in their little commune of synapses is not a picture per se, but a means to reconstitute a "picture" . . . The same arrangement would hold in the auditory realm . . . Most of the words we use in our inner speech . . . exist as auditory or visual images in our consciousness.' My comment: 'Aunt Maggie's face/Aunt Maggie's voice: is it possible that writers/painters are wired up differently, with neurological predispositions to represent auditory/visual images? Certainly my own imagination is more auditory than visual, compared with Paula's.' And the second text and commentary: 'Understanding how we see or speak does not debase what is seen or spoken, what is painted or woven into a theatrical line. Understanding the biological mechanisms behind emotions and feelings is perfectly compatible with a romantic view of their value to human beings.' My comment: 'This assertion of compatibility feels true but it *is* an assertion. It does your heart credit, but it requires an essay to demonstrate it.'

'There ain't half been some clever bastards'

Here are two books by great scientists: the classic account of *The Double Helix* by James Watson and Francis Crick and *Elementary Particles and the Laws of Physics* by Richard Feynman and Steven Weinberg. The latter gave me a headache. At least with philosophy I often feel that the headache is a symptom of headway, but here I was out of my depth, on my way, yes, but heading nowhere. Alan Wall sent me extracts from the book on science he was working on with Goronwy Tudor Jones, a senior particle physicist. That bids fair to make waves, perhaps as a result of supplying the paddle that will save me while plonked in my leaky canoe, up the creek. The science fed into his novel, *Sylvie's Riddle*. Before I start making even more heavy weather of a nautical metaphor worthy of Monsieur Teste, I had better move on. Alan, as it happens, phoned when I was about to close the shop and talked me into giving him this book as a present. In return, he is going to send me Victor Weiskopf's *Knowledge and Wonder*, which I am ordered to read forthwith.

'There ain't half been some clever bastards': Ian Dury's song rings true and there are none cleverer or, as he might have said, more cleverer than Jean-Jacques Rousseau, whose *Botany: A Study of Pure Curiosity* was a Christmas present from Jonathan and Kate Griffin. This is a translation of the 1805 edition illustrated by P.-J. Redouté. 'O Nature, O my mother,' Rousseau wrote in *The Confessions*, in a passage about the delights of botany. Redouté too was a clever bastard, as the introduction tells us, although the following quotation begins in a slightly odd way; maybe it's a joke: 'People, plant lovers included, closely linked to the *ancien régime*, had little reason to expect favours during the Revolution . . . In 1792, Redouté worsened his case by yielding to a request from the bored Marie-Antoinette . . . to come and paint a cactus of which she was fond. Yet he survived in excellent shape. During the Terror he was appointed to the staff of the former Royal Botanical Garden which had become the Jardin des Plantes . . .' He prospered under the Directory and of course under Bonaparte. The transitions were well managed: 'Luck and a knack for time-serving can partly explain this success. So can hard work and a personality that seems to have been all the more attractive because of a lack of physical grace.'

Nightingale

Aldous Huxley was a big influence on a previous generation of autodidacts, men like my father and Paula's father. Beginning his *Literature and Science* with an account of the famous and infamous Leavis–Snow controversy,

611

Huxley rejects both 'the bland scientism' of C. P. Snow 's lecture *The Two Cultures* (see the naturally sympathetic account of the affair in *Stranger and Brother*, the biography by Philip Snow) and 'the violent and ill-mannered, the one-track moralistic literarism' of F. R. Leavis in his Richmond Lecture. Huxley argues for the middle way associated with his grandfather T. H. Huxley and great-uncle Matthew Arnold and, more recently, Lionel Trilling and Robert Oppenheimer, although he finds the sympathetic arguments of his contemporaries too generalizing and abstract to be enlightening. Huxley himself concludes that 'the words of the tribe and of the textbook must be purified into a many-meaninged language capable of expressing simultaneously the truth about nightingales, as they exist in their world of caterpillars . . . endocrine glands and territorial possessiveness, and the truth about the human beings who listen to the nightingale's song.'

It is said that Keats wrote his second greatest ode at Spaniard's Inn in Hampstead, where I was inspired to take Paula on our first date. The poet, walking there by road or footpath from Wentworth Place in what is now Keats Grove, would have passed the site of Paula's apartment block after about ten minutes; another five minutes and he would have passed the house (if already built) where Katharine Mansfield would live a century later, as well as the road leading to the Vale of Health (home of Byron and Lawrence); five more minutes would bring him to Whitestone Pond (then known as Leg o'Mutton Pond), on past Jack Straw's Castle—close to where Bill Sikes runs after murdering Nancy—and ten minutes later he would have arrived at Spaniard's Inn; unless, of course, he had cut across the heath, a route which it is no longer possible to recreate, since there is housing by the road across from the inn. Al Alvarez doubts the Spaniard's Inn story. He also says that the last sighting of Keats in England was of him weeping on a bench in Well Walk.

Science writing has come a long way since 1963, the year Huxley's book was published, and the many-meaninged language Huxley called for can be found in large numbers of books written for the general public, such as those by Michael Rowan Robinson or Stephen Jay Gould (*Rock of Ages*) or Nicholas Humphrey, whose *Soul Dust* I finally read after lending it to my Uncle Jack. It was characteristic of him to read it six times before handing it back. Arthur Koestler's seventieth birthday festschrift *Astride the Two Cultures* makes an obvious point with its title and, indeed, he, along with Primo Levi, was an early member of that select band of people who have written in depth and breadth about science for the educated general reader: popularization or as the French say more accurately, haute vulgarization. Thanks to the educated intervention of my Genevan friend the Hungarian Swiss writer and economist Judit Kiss (author of a fine memoir *The Summer My Father Died*), George Klein, ex-Budapest Holocaust survivor, cell biologist and writer, sent me three books from Stockholm: *Pieta*, *The Atheist at the Holy City* and *Live Now*. Klein, like Levi, whom he resembles in many ways, writes essays on the uses and abuses of science and medicine out of a profound and educated humanism. Having seen the worst, he wants to move forward and help create a humane world in which insights derived from the human and natural sciences can counter the evils which will never go away. His stance is that of an atheist Jewish Buddhist, generating a personal synthesis I find deeply attractive.

Pebble

'Pebble' has been a favourite word of mine ever since I read Christopher Middleton's poem 'Climbing a Pebble' and Francis Ponge's prose poem back in the 1960s. 'They were pebbles but I called them stones,' wrote Beckett in *Molloy*, that classic reference to cricket in a literary work. On a beach in Devon, I improvised for my young children a character called Pebble; they asked for more. A generation later, my daughter Naomi suggested that I resuscitate Pebble for my grandson Charlie. Yes, I shall take Pebble out of his casket and release him to the elements: I shall certainly be in mine. The very word asks for one's tongue to roll round it, but that thought may have been influenced by the famous story of Demosthenes. All this to introduce a book I have here, inscribed with my name and 'June 1965, London': *The Pebbles on the Beach*, a history by top pebbelista Clarence Ellis. To the best of my knowledge, this is his only book. He and the rhythm of his prose are inspired by the very subject matter: 'The cycle goes endlessly and steadily on. The finest grains become compacted into solid rock. Millions of years later the encroaching sea, aided by sun, wind and rain, breaks up the rock. A pebble is born. The waves roll it along the beaches from Cornwall to Sussex. It is resolved into sand grains and then the whole process starts again and another cycle of millions of years begins once more.' Long ago I typed this out as a found poem on my twenty-first birthday present Olivetti portable typewriter. Even better are the pebbles on my 'treasure shelf' in this very room, the only shelf without books on it. A pebble, like a shell, is a found poem in nature.

Afterword

(*Excerpts from a diary kept during early drafts*)

From 2006

I always read the early pages of a book, especially a novel, very slowly. Then I attain (literary?) critical mass and speed up. Towards the end, I slow down again. The thought of finishing the book engenders a quasi-sexual deceleration in order to postpone the climax. This rhythm interacts with other books I am reading during the same phase, although each phase has ragged edges since I don't reach the finishing lines on the same day. Why do many of us have more than one book on the go, perhaps four or five? To say it has something to do with attention span does not explain the phenomenon. Nor, in my case, does it derive from my writerly obsession with small units. Perhaps it is a way of getting more reading done: never mind the quality, feel the width. If I put down a novel, the act of picking up a poetry book or an autobiography seems to re-fire the brain cells. Late at night, the practice can involve staving off sleep, but this means I am not fresh in the morning. This, in turn, means I have less psychic energy to concentrate properly and work hard. Obsession with units, impulse towards fragmentation and minimalism, is that so unusual? Perhaps my drawing attention to these drives is a rationalization of my anxieties concerning a large-scale integrated work of greater structural complexity than usual; it also ignores the fact that work on whatever scale entails the integration of fragments and minimal units, constructed in such a way that the joins don't show, that the codes are unrevealed.

* * *

My non-computer reading is done first thing in the morning or last thing at night. Nor am I talking about 'professional reading' such as the dipping and rereading required for the present work, let alone manuscripts by friends. I'm talking about reading in general. I have an instinct which book will be right for the current mood and the energy available. Usually there comes a point when the psychic need to finish a particular book takes over and then I stay with it to the end: unfinished books have their mana, and whisper their siren calls into the ear of the newly faithful lover, devoting himself entirely to the newly senior wife in the harem. When the belatedly solo book has been completed, I feel the need to start one or two new books, and so the cycle begins again. Let's be specific: on the day of writing, apart from the aforementioned 'professional reading', I have on the go John Ruskin's autobiography *Praeterita*; non-Menard books by two Menard authors: Anthony Howell's *Oblivion*, a tango thriller set in Buenos Aires, and Will Stone's fine book of poems *Glaciation*; Philip Davis' exceptionally sympathetic biography *Bernard Malamud* and Ted Hughes' *Letters*. Sometimes, a book comes out by a writer, whether or not a personal friend or acquaintance, which one cannot wait to read, so significant, however briefly, is he or she to one's life as a reader, which is to say, to one's life: a new book of poems by Yves Bonnefoy, for example.

* * *

Today I talked at some length with my sister Annie's partner, Jack Chalkley. He is one of nature's list-makers, his latest being the hundred books that have meant the most to him. I told him about my (now abandoned) category of talismanic books/authors, which began with a list. Jack, a retired clinical psychologist, has spent every spare moment for years working on two projects that one day will end up as books: a directory of imaginary countries and a detailed study of the phenomenon. By definition, he will never know if the directory is complete but the hindsight wisdom of eventual reviewers who know some of the rightly forgotten formulaic literature—mainly late Victorian and Edwardian—is not the problem. The fear is that some famous and widely read book containing an imaginary country may escape his notice: *Nostromo, Bleak House, Naked Lunch*; a reviewer would have a fine time pointing out that he had missed one or more of these. I love the idea of his project: it is a Borgesian folly, like Lynn Holden's *Forms of Deformity*, a scholarly directory of deformed animals in folklore, that the great man himself would have appreciated. I have already reported a few countries to Jack, including indeed *Naked Lunch*, and these he has graciously accepted.

* * *

Around midnight, I was feeling kind of miserable and, if truth be told, annoyed with Paula. I was annoyed because something she said about my new long poem 'Zigzag' was spot on, and I badly wanted her to be wrong. I then spent a few hours revisiting the poem and, acting on a comment by Michael Schmidt, finally forced myself or rather forced the poem to lose a quarter of the words while somehow increasing the number of lines. The movement of the lines now plays better against the sense, creating a tension which helps shift the reader's neurones into the right side of the brain. I should now send both versions to a third party for a second opinion. I'll let it stew for a few days. I don't know why I condensed my teaching notes into a poem. Perhaps because, like Paul Celan, who himself translated Emily Dickinson, one agrees with her that 'to gather paradise' you should 'dwell in possibility / A fairer House than Prose', possibility being what she identified poetry with, just as Yves Bonnefoy identifies it with hope, even as it recalls the irrevocable.

* * *

Brian Coffey told Augustus Young, who had complained he was short of time, that busy people—Coffey had in mind himself, committed poet and active father with nine children and a serious day job teaching maths to schoolchildren—cannot find time for everything, so they have to make time by reducing the amount of the only commodity available, namely sleep. You want to write? Sleep less. Now that I no longer commute to day jobs but work mainly from home, I have no excuse for not fitting everything in; it should not be necessary to break into sleep hours—do I really need eight hours (bad) sleep a night? Resolution: sleep better and less and/or get organized; that is, save time by adopting sensible administrative procedures. A common-sense formula . . .

* * *

Walter Benjamin: a book made up entirely of quotations; how many times have I scribbled down quotations for future use? This is yet another reason to tidy up the flat. So many of my projects cannot be completed or even

617

begun until the papers are pre-sorted into dedicated folders: my unpublished poems, my notes on the family tree, my quotations.

* * *

I have been reading or rereading or dipping into essays and texts by the Bs: the one I am least familiar with, in recent years, is Michel Butor, but I have promised myself to pay closer attention to this writer who, like Francis Ponge (a major precursor of the nouveau roman) and Roland Barthes, looms large in the reading of radical writers and critics in France. Butor has a great gift, born of desire in the manner of all great gifts, which is to conduct his critical explorations in the language and domain of the general reader (like Barthes, if not Ponge). I have been looking at his poems in *A la frontière* and his essays in *Répertoires*, including those about the space of the novel and the novel as research. Long ago I read his complex and challenging *L'Emploi du temps* and the compelling and beautiful *La Modification*, which is written not in the first or third person but, famously, the second person singular, like Apollinaire's poem 'Zone'.

* * *

Typing 'Butor' into Find and Replace in order to reach the previous paragraph quickly, I was directed to 'contributor' and 'distributor' before arriving at 'Michel Butor', which only 'works' in English, not in French ('collaborateur'). I don't know how I would cope without Find and Replace, given the length of the electronic manuscript, which is expanding all over the place— preposterously, you could say—rather than being extended at the end in a linear fashion. When I turn up, say, an interesting aspect of Rilke, I go, courtesy of F/R, to one of the many references to 'Rilke' or 'Rilke's' (although he has no dedicated subsection to himself) and choose where the new one seems to belong. However, the book, already a field of force, a firmament of stars, will never be finished if I write everything that enters into its spirit. How will it read when I print out the manuscript in order to prepare a second draft in the traditional manner?

* * *

By one of those synchronicities that make you almost believe in coincidence, Paul Buck turns out to have been rereading the same Walter Benjamin essay during the same week, perhaps on the same day as me. Augustus Young, who lives in Port-Vendres, only fifteen miles on the corniche from Benjamin's last resting place at Port Bou, swears by Benjamin and draws on the master in his corruscatingly funny memoir, *Story Time*. Today, yet again, I have dipped into Barthes's autobiography. As ever, he is insistent that the facts, such as they were, survive only in language. We had better take good care of them. Subjective truth and fantasy are not one and the same thing. I roughed out a translation of two sentences and then, on a whim, checked Richard Howard's translation of the book. The versions were identical, suggesting that Barthes is one of those writers whose prose is transparent and not difficult to translate, something that had not needed to occur to me before. It is certainly less difficult than Jean Clair's or Yves Bonnefoy's.

From 2007

Eighteen months after I began this work in progress, the first draft is very long and I have no way of knowing what percentage I have completed. What I did in previous books was mould the writing as I went along. Pursuing that metaphor, I shall carve out the shape of the book during the second draft: writing as sculpture rather than writing as painting or writing as music. Perhaps I thought of that because Auguste Rodin has been on my mind lately, partly thanks to his links with Rainer Maria Rilke, who is one of my tutelary spirits, and partly because of his show at the Royal Academy. All the same, the rhythm, shape, energy, symbolism, feeling and thought in my book still end up with words, words, words, words. Yeats, like the devil citing Scripture, can always be quoted to serve a nefarious purpose, so here goes: 'Words alone are certain good.' Except, this is not true; nor are words even the best or most important thing in the world, but they are all I know how to work with. The reason the draft is so long and is taking so long is that I am having fun dipping into my books every so often and trying to reconstruct my original virtue, my innocent reading, from long ago: today, for example, James Agee and Walker Evans' *Now Let Us Praise Famous Men*. I need to finish this draft (or rather this book: how many drafts to go?), if I am to return to my other projects, provided life is granted unto me both as an individual ageing man and as a citizen of a planet which has not many years to turn itself round on the matter of climate change and the economy. Yes, all this dipping could prove fatal because at this rate I shall end my days a mad old man, a Borgesian cartographer making a map of the world that is the same size as the world. If I do not read myself the riot act, men in white coats will take me away, still at my desk, amidst the latest draft, years hence.

* * *

It is about six months since I wrote the above paragraph. I am on the point of making a big decision: to move faster in my inspection of books, not in my selection of what to write about but in the preselection of books from which the final choice will be made. I offer a prayer to the ghosts of books that will never be named, lost and gone forever, like my darling Clementine. They took their chances. That is, I took their chances and they lost, in some cases without even fighting the good fight. Yes, I am plucking up the courage to put on one side books I should have chucked out long ago:

> vanity press novels sent to me for one reason or another;
> unreadable memoirs sent ditto;
> retail therapy purchases of alternative health books;
> outdated political and ecological manifestos;
> signed copies of foreign poetry books sent by well-meaning third parties with a view to translation;
> remainder books I was sure I would read one day;
> second-hand books bought for a few coppers or shillings that had little chance of being read;
> old restaurant and wine and other guides;
> outdated computer manuals;
> book-length prospectuses;
> duplicates of books I am keeping;
> old yearbooks;
> books in languages I cannot understand;
> books from academic sales;
> and so on.

* * *

There is, in theory, a case for listing every single book in this flat—echoing Canetti's Peter Kien—if not for writing about each one, in order to obtain a taxonomical overview of a lifetime in books. However, the table of contents provides a broad-brush outline, and sympathetic readers of this book will have no difficulty in imagining what has been rejected (taken to the charity shop or thrown away or sold or given as a present), or what has been kept and not mentioned. This is quite a moment: I am about to administer the last rites on hundreds of books, each doubtless the product of love and commitment and effort. If the present work has a patron saint, it is either Isidore of Seville or Jude, and although I am not a Catholic, I call upon them to bless the lost souls—terminally abandoned books—floating round the country of old moons, that accursed site of the predawn reveries of an insomniac obsessional hoarder. I apologize now to the many hundreds of books that will not be mentioned: rest assured, you have played your part in my life; you will be the death of me, but not yet.

* * *

Tomorrow, Ivor Sherman is coming over with a new computer and printer. This has got me thinking again about technology and the rhetorical question I addressed J. Hillis Miller in the introduction to this book and which I touched on just now. Does the metaphor from sculpture about carving and moulding tell us anything about books whose first draft was written directly on to a computer? Thanks to delete and cut and paste, as well as find and replace, one can shape the writing far earlier than one did with a typewriter or in longhand. These days, the first draft incorporates aspects of the second draft. If I had succeeded in mastering additional techniques, this book would be a hypertext. Having experimented with asterisks, brackets and footnotes, surely I could have managed arrows and different colours and boxes to enrich synchronically imbricated material scattered throughout the book. Perhaps it's just as well I did not succeed.

* * *

I have not worked on the book for two months. It is no use Musa Farhi saying that one is working on a book even when one is not working on it: that is only true when the writing is done on a regular basis. In that state of being, yes, the pages of the book are turned in the mind, forth and back, and worked over in reverie at times of the day and night. But the last few weeks have seen me so deeply preoccupied with matters (political and personal) which have

621

unsettled me, that I have lost the plot, lost the habit. Well, today is day one (of the daughter's twenty-eight required to create a habit), and it is a test of character to nail one's arse to the chair—as Z. Kotowicz puts it—and do the work. The flat, however, has returned to the primordial chaos my sister Annie tried to rescue me from about three months ago and I no longer know the rationale of the piles of chosen books on the floor surrounding my desk. What a clutter. I am the master of clutter, associated so closely with side-tracking. Adam Phillips' typically elegant and brilliant essay on clutter in *Promises Promises* hurts me with its insights. He cites Winnicott's 'false-self personality . . . who 'collects' demands to clutter up his life'. At the current rate of (non-)exchange between myself and my material, I estimate I am not much more than half way through the processing. 'The greater part of any library,' says Virginia Woolf, 'is nothing but the record of . . . fleeting moments in the lives of men, women and donkeys.' I have three options: first, tell myself that the books I have already processed are representative of all my books, announce the end of the first draft, and start revising. Second, continue the processing until the first draft is completed heaven knows when. Third, hold a strategy summit with myself, and find a way of speeding up. Three is the best solution, followed by One, but no doubt I shall continue with Two.

* * *

The last few weeks have been a time of death: Menard author, ornament of the lost world of Jewish Central Europe and friend, Jakov Lind passed away in February 2007, not long after Evy Vigée died. Around the same time as Lind, another friend Mai Ghoussoup, Musa Farhi's intime and publisher at Saqi Books, died aged fifty-four, entirely unexpectedly. Then a friend of her husband Hazem came to London from Beirut to be with him, and died during the first night. The doctor-sister of someone I know who is another intime of Musa and Nina threw herself from a high building. And the daughter of Paula's former print dealer died in a bus crash in Uganda aged twenty-four, a trainee doctor working there for idealistic reasons. To complete the troubles, the sister of a good friend of mine has died under tragic circumstances.

I had only one morning to write the funeral speech for Jakov, one of the last of my living heroes. 'Don't die on me,' said Musa last night, who has been deeply distressed by the three deaths. My personal fear is that I shall die before completing my life's work, such as it (life/work) is. Published and unpublished poems, published and unpublished stories, published and unpublished non-fiction are buried, like memories or dreams, in the pre-computer chaos of this apartment, and only I can trace or track them. Forget the unwritten books! Shall I finish this very book? On a bad day I imagine a death 'before my time', from prostate cancer or stress-related heart attack, in a nuclear war or climate disaster. Tomorrow morning, my sister Annie is coming over yet again to sort me out (haha!). And now, it is time to do some tidying up and then perhaps work on a subsection of the book.

* * *

I glance at the latest and extraordinary long poem by my epistolary friend John Taggart, *Unveiling/ Marianne Moore*, which I had read in manuscript and which has now been published as a chapbook by a small press. Section twenty-one contains a prose passage from Anne Carson about reading: '. . . as an individual reads and writes he gradually learns to close or inhibit the input of his senses, to inhibit or control the responses of his body, so as to train energy and thought upon the written words. He resists the environment outside him by distinguishing and controlling the one inside him . . .' This feels right, both for oneself and also for Marianne Moore, for whom the word control was invented.

* * *

The other day, Gabriel Josipovici gave a public lecture on 'Whatever Happened to Modernism' [later: it has been incorporated into the eponymous book]. He was on the warpath: there are three kinds of writers, exemplified by Beckett (modernist), Gordimer (realist) and Rowling (beyond the pale). Provocatively, he conflated the second and third categories as 'tosh'. At the dinner afterwards, I found myself sitting next to a leading Eliot scholar, Ronald Schuchard. We swapped anecdotes about Christopher Ricks and Craig Raine (who turns out to be Valerie Eliot's literary executor) and Ted Hughes. I was moved to learn that the last thing Ted ever read was *Measure for Measure*, the page open at one of Shakespeare's profoundest meditations on mortality: 'Be absolute for death . . .' Later in the same scene Claudio avers: 'If I must die, / I will encounter darkness as a bride, / And hug it in mine arms.' If Hughes' brief candle was snuffed out at that very moment, if

623

he had to leave us to continue our strutting and fretting without him when he still had so much to give and receive, I cannot think of a more appropriate exit line for a bridegroom.

* * *

Yesterday I dropped Paula at her flat after her honorary degree ceremony at the University of Surrey. I didn't feel like going home, so I drove the short distance from the Heath to Hampstead High Street and parked at the top of Gayton Road. For some reason I was restless, edgy, frazzled, and began mulling over my thoughts for yet another unsent letter to *The Guardian*. Furthermore, rush-hour traffic was building up, so I decided to hang round Hampstead for a couple of hours. In any case, I am rarely in a hurry to return to the chaos of my flat. I wandered into Waterstones to buy a book to read in a local wine bar, having forgotten I had in the car John Carey's *What Good Are the Arts?* Once in the shop, I remembered Carey but was too lazy to retrace my footsteps and, besides, I was already hooked.

I went to the poetry shelves and delved and browsed and finally chose Ciaran Carson's version of Dante's *Inferno*, to accompany those I own by Jacqueline Risset, Laurence Binyon, Henry W. Longfellow, C. H. Sisson, Henry F. Cary, Robert Pinsky and T. A. Sinclair: already in Carson's first line ('Half way through the story of my life') something has been changed. I like the work of this Belfast writer, poetry—*Opera Etcetera* and *The Twelfth of Never*—and translations: his versions of Baudelaire, Rimbaud and Mallarmé (*The Alexandrine Plan*) constitute the most brilliant deployment of that metre in English for non-comic effect I have read. They challenge Bonnefoy's influential view, namely that the central metre in one language should be used to translate the central metre of another. We shall see what Carson makes of Dante's *terza rima*. I dip into his introduction and learn something new to me: Dante's name is a shortened version of Durante. Imagine that. Did Jimmy 'Schnozzle' Durante know? I have little cash on me. As so often when one is paying by credit card, it seems ridiculous to buy only one book. So I make amends for a long-standing foolishness and get the new Penguin edition of Babel's stories, *Red Cavalry*, translated by David McDuff and edited with notes by Efraim Sicher, having made do for years with the old and much loved *Collected Stories* introduced by Lionel Trilling.

My wine bar agenda is decided: Carson's introduction and Canto Five of *The Inferno*—with Primo Levi's Ulysses chapter in mind—and my latest rereading of Babel's wondrous story, 'Gedali', a favourite of my late friend the old Russian-born Hebrew poet Avraham Shlonsky. I begin with 'Gedali' and find the sentences 'Oh Talmuds of my childhood, turned to dust! Oh, dense sadness of memories!' One of the notes by Sicher, a Babel scholar who edited an encyclopaedia of Holocaust novelists and commissioned me to write the entry on Piotr Rawicz, tells us that this evocative image was dropped by Babel from later editions; in the context it was perhaps too easily earned. I doubt that it was expurgated or that Babel feared it went too far, for other equally resonant Jewish sentences survive. There is no doubt that Babel is a short-story writer of genius, the equal of Kipling and Hemingway. Carson's Dante introduction is typically robust. His Canto Five pulls me up with a start. This is the most vernacular, streetwise Dante I have read. It shocks me. I detect the Irish lilt. And suddenly I think of Martin McDonagh, and I am back in Paula's studio, and her Pillowman series based on his play. Every sentence you write generates countless outlets, countless strings.

* * *

When I return to a book that I love and that has deeply influenced my understanding of literature and therefore of life, for example Yves Bonnefoy's *Rimbaud*, I can, thanks to annotations and marginalia, go straight to the passages that moved me during my first reading of it back in 1964. For example: '. . . poetic utterance is at once a hope and a threat'. Annotation is but one way that the reader completes the work of the writer. I have no doubt that I would have underlined some, but not all, of those passages, had I first come to the book today. Conversely, certain unannotated passages strike me with the force of revelation. Counter-factual thought: postulate I had elected a different mentor by the accident of picking up a book by another French poet in Bowes and Bowes bookshop back in 1963. The conversion of my inner yearnings into the proactive process of translation of this poet— probably Dupin or du Bouchet—would have led me to another but not unrelated version of the inner life, another way of accessing the life of my mind and thus enabling me to regenerate it from within, deploying my own resources. Postulate too that I found Bonnefoy's *Rimbaud* twenty-five years later: I am in a different place on the flowchart. We move through life as the same person, ever changing, ever unchanging, a theme of my long poem 'Zigzag'. And I return to the idea of the mobile, the object invented by Alexander Calder that changes and does not change. Yes, like people, art objects change and do not change—pre-Raphaelite paintings look and therefore are completely different to me now that I have Paula's admiration for them hooked into my *imaginaire*, just as it has been shown that water at the same temperature in winter and summer feels different to the dipper. But let me not sidetrack myself. 'Ho ho, that last sentence is a bit rich coming from you, Rudolf, side-tracker extraordinary, stellar digressionary, grand master of deferral.'

* * *

A moment of truth has arrived. I have already spent two and a half years dipping into hundreds of books. I am surrounded by books I haven't read (half of which I shall never read) and by books I have read or part read and, on dipping anew, wonder why I read (some of) them in the first place. There are works of literary criticism, biography, fiction, poetry and, indeed, books from many of the categories into which I have divided the present work, such as the visual arts. Some are French translations of books I have read in English, gifted to me by the translator at the request of a third party. Some are associated with abandoned or unbegun or even completed editorial (or other) projects, for example books about Pierre de Ronsard associated with the unpublished translations of Ronsard by Sylvia Plath that I brought out in 1992. Enough already! As Rabbi Tarphon said in *Ethics of the Fathers*: 'The day is short, the task is great, the labourers are lazy.' I am alone. At least Bouvard and Pécuchet had each other.

Interesting how many strands in future literature emerged from different sides of Flaubert. Thus, tell me that you love *Bouvard and Pécuchet* and I will have a shrewd suspicion that you take a certain pleasure in Georges Perec on the one hand and conceptual art—Sophie Calle, Michael Landy, for example—on the other. What purpose other than a kind of sentimental and indolent perfectionism would have been achieved by attempting to do something as foolish as list all the thousands of books surrounding me? Or even to select samples for inspection? The categories of books found in the table of contents have been long established and already contain a whole range of likes and dislikes. No, after two and a half years, I have earned the right to jettison books without naming them. Theirs not to reason why, nor mine. No one will ever know. Nobody cares, with the exception of myself. See, I have given myself permission to speed up. I'm returning to the scene of the crime, owning up to my failure to read books I bought or was given. Stop this now, you have made your point. Think, if you speed up and quietly pack away books you cannot write about because, whether read or not, they are not of significance to your life or to this book (which is your life right now), you could change your life. Enough already! *Basta*! *Assez*! *Dostatochno*! *Chega*!

* * *

I had dinner with my dear daughter-in-law Helen, temporarily working in Leicester, at a good Italian restaurant in Market Harborough and returned to St Pancras with a book by Juan Ramon Jimenez for company. Its title, *The Complete Perfectionist: A Poetics of Work*, promises more than it delivers, perhaps because I am not well enough acquainted with the poetry by this Spaniard so admired by James Wright and Robert Bly. The poet's prose, mainly aphorisms, is embedded in a warm and intelligent meditation by the editor Christopher Maurer, but in a way that involves too much repetition. However, I relate strongly to Maurer's comment that Jimenez 'struggled endlessly against his own desire to be done in a hurry and against his longing to be working on something else'. The solution of Jimenez?: 'When you're working on one thing and start to yearn for another, imagine that the thing you're working on would be the one you would be yearning for if you were working on the other.' The editor then quotes Tchaikovsky: 'Inspiration does not visit the lazy.' Later, Jimenez strikes a chord: 'Friend, do not think about what has been lost of what you have written, but about what you have not written, which is much more lost for you.' On my desk is his 'poetic autobiography' *Time and Space*, which I read on the beach in Spain while on holiday in 1992 with my daughter Naomi and niece Amy. The back cover portrait of Jimenez, aged twenty-two, reveals an intense *fin de siècle* poet's elongated face that could have come straight out of El Greco.

* * *

I have found more books which will make perfect gifts for certain people, in particular those, friends or acquaintances, who have been interlocutors during the present composition. Having gone through all my books, I have a clear idea what I will not consult again in this life as a reader. I even have some idea what I will consult again, although that is necessarily open to change. At my age, it is, as ever, a question of priority. I shall give *La Vie familiale et sociale des indiens Nambikwara*, Lévi-Strauss' first book, to Bruce Ross-Smith. I shall give Jennie Feldman the photographic memorial volume of Bialik made in Tel-Aviv in 1935, the year after he died. Victor Segalen's *Chine* is for Mike Heller, whose translation of a Segalen poem I published on a MenCard to mark his seventieth birthday.

* * *

Last night I dreamt I was in a long queue outside the railway station in a strange city, waiting for a taxi to take me to a library for some research purpose (a dream which seems to exemplify Foucault's concepts of heterotopia and heterochronia all in one). Once I reached the front of the queue, no taxi came along. So, after taking directions from two people in the queue who stroked me affectionately, I set off on foot. But try as I might, I could not locate the library. I therefore attempted to find my way back to the station, only to get completely lost in this town which seemed like something out of a Dickensian phantasmagoria, with Gustave Doré's *Inferno* and Giovanni Battista Piranesi's geometry thrown in. I never did find the station and I woke up. Who knows if this dream was trying to tell me something, perhaps to make a quick getaway from libraries, or in my case, these books in my flat?

* * *

I have finished reading *Dubin's Lives* by Malamud, a novel which awaited my attentions long enough. Sipping a whiskey, I entered a reverie and emerged with the realization that I have been deeply privileged to serve as a go-between for nearly half a century. I thought of friends now dead, all of whom I met through literature, as publisher or editor: Amichai, Davie, Silkin, Hamburger, Smith, Levi, Lind, all from the generation following my older dead: Gascoyne, Prince, Griffin, Rakosi, Oppen, Jabès, Paz, Raine, Olsen. To spend a lifetime as a go-between was necessarily to store up regrets that one did not give enough time to one's own writing. Would I live long enough to make good all the time spent on others, however willingly and, perhaps, usefully? And even if I did, would political imperatives of climate change take me away from writing books, as the nuclear issue did nearly thirty years ago? I felt honour bound to strive for a world in which my grandchildren could live a decent life, free from fear and disease and hatred. Only a radical synthesis of the green tradition and liberal socialism, I thought, could save us, but deep down I know that no nation state is about to implement or even promise this utopian vision. I picked up the 'finished' novel and focused on its author, on his insistent aching demand that we pose the questions: what do we mean by a good life, and why do we spend so much time reading the best literature, and what is the connection between the two, which brought me full circle to the politics about which I had been musing.

I swallowed my sleeping pill and as I drifted off I remembered an evening round a campfire in the USA in 1964, and singing 'We shall overcome' in the company of like-minded contemporaries, full of hope: today, we owe it to the young to live as if we have hope. That is what I understand by a good life and, with luck, a good death, if such a thing exists. Reality and the imagination pre-suppose each other. Books deepen the past of the young and the future of the old. The literary imagination, in all its ways and means, creates worlds where true witness is our bond.

Bibliography

Note

The bibliography is in sections and subsections, as per the contents pages.

Standard and/or very well-known authors, as regularly discussed in the book, are not always listed here.

Conversely some books not named in my text may be listed under the author's name.

Sometimes the title of the book is given in the text without the subtitle, which, however, is always added in the bibliography.

My apartment is in chaos, inevitably, given that I went through thousands of my books to write the present work. Works listed, therefore, are not always in the edition I possess or consulted.

I sent authors' names and book titles to my bibliography assistant, Bethan Roberts, who could not know which edition I used. She is not responsible for any confusions arising from the situation.

For convenience, an author's collected poems or works are sometimes listed, rather than the separate books sometimes quoted or named in the text.

Books mentioned more than once throughout the book are listed only once, usually on first mention.

I am deeply grateful to Bethan Roberts for her exemplary assistance in the compiling of this bibliography, which has been included at the request of the publisher.

INTRODUCTION

AUSTER, Paul. 1982. *The Art of Hunger, and Other Essays*. London: Menard.

BARTHES, Roland. 1975. *Roland Barthes par lui-même*. Paris: Seuil.

BENJAMIN, Walter. 1970. *Illuminations*. Edited and introduced by Hannah Arendt. Translated by Harry Zohn. London: Jonathan Cape.

————. 1999. *The Arcades Project*. Translated by Howard Eiland and Kevin McLaughlin. London: Belknap.

BONNEFOY, Yves. 1961. *Rimbaud par lui-même*. Paris: Seuil. [The entire book is included in Yves Bonnefoy. 2009. *Notre besoin de Rimbaud*. Paris: Seuil.]

————. 1973. *Rimbaud*. Translated by Paul Schmidt. New York and London: Harper & Row.

BRESSON, Robert. 1986. *Notes on the Cinematographer*. Translated by Jonathan Griffin. London: Quartet.

CALVINO, Italo. 1977. *The Castle of Crossed Destinies*. Translated by William Weaver. London: Secker & Warburg.

————. 1979. *Invisible Cities*. Translated by William Weaver. London: Pan Books.

————. 1981. *If on a Winter's Night a Traveller*. Translated by William Weaver. London: Secker & Warburg.

————. 1985. *Mr Palomar*. Translated by William Weaver. London: Secker & Warburg.

COLLINGWOOD, R. G. 1978. *An Autobiography*. Oxford: Clarendon.

DAHLBERG, Edward. 1950. *The Flea of Sodom*. London: P. Nevill.

————. 1967. *The Leafless American*. Edited by Harold Billings. Sausalito, CA: Beacham.

————. 1970. *The Carnal Myth: A Search into Classical Sensuality*. London: Calder & Boyars.

————. 1970. *The Sorrows of Priapus*. London: Calder & Boyars.

DAIVE, Jean. 1967. *Décimale blanche*. Paris: Mercure de France.

————. 1999. *Sous la coupole*. Paris: P.O.L.

FELSTINER, John. 1995. *Paul Celan: Poet, Survivor, Jew*. New Haven, CT, and London: Yale University Press.

FUSTEL DE COULANGES, Numa Denis. 1980. *The Ancient City: A Study of the Religion, Laws, and Institutions of Greece and Rome*. Translated by Willard Small. Garden City, NY: Doubleday.

MILLER, Henry. 1950. *The Colossus of Maroussi*. Harmondsworth: Penguin.

———. 1966. *Quiet Days in Clichy*. London: Calder & Boyars.

———. 1984. *The Time of the Assassins: A Study of Rimbaud*. London: Quartet

MILLLER, J. Hillis. 1990. *Versions of Pygmalion*. Cambridge, MA, and London: Harvard University Press.

———. 1992. *Illustration*. London: Reaktion Books.

———. 2002. *On Literature*. London: Routledge.

NICHOLLS, Peter. 2002. *George Oppen and the Fate of Modernism*. Oxford and New York: Oxford University Press.

OPPEN, George. 1972. *Collected Poems*. London: Fulcrum.

———. 1990. *Selected Letters*. Edited by Rachel Blau DuPlessis. Durham, NC: Duke University Press.

PODRO, Michael. 1998. *Depiction*. New Haven, CT, and London: Yale University Press.

QUIGNARD, Pascal. 2002. *Sur le jadis*. Paris: Grasset.

REED, Jeremy. 1989. *Madness: The Price of Poetry*. London: Peter Owen.

———. 1991. *Delirium*. London: Peter Owen.

RICKWORD, Edgell. 1963. *Rimbaud: The Boy and the Poet*. Castle Hedingham: Daimon.

RIDING, Laura. 1938. *Collected Poems*. London: Cassell.

———. 1992. *First Awakenings: The Early Poems*. Edited by Elizabeth Friedmann, Alan J. Clark and Robert Nye. Manchester: Carcanet.

RILKE, Rainer Maria. 1997. *Diaries of a Young Poet*. Translated by Edward Snow and Michael Winkler. New York and London: W. W. Norton.

———. 2005. *The Book of Hours: Love Poems to God*. Translated by Anita Barrows and Joanna Macy. New York: Riverhead Books.

ROBB, Graham. 2000. *Rimbaud*. London: Picador.

RUDOLF, Anthony, ed. 2005. *Life in Books: T. G. Rosenthal*. London: Menard.

———. 2010. *Zigzag*. Manchester: Carcanet/Northern House.

SEFERIS, George. 1990. *South African Diaries, Poems and Letters*. Edited and translated by Roy Macnab. Cape Town: Carrefour.

STRAVINSKY, Igor. 1970. *Poetics of Music: In the Form of Six Lessons*. Translated by Arthur Knodel and Ingolf Dahl. Cambridge, MA, and London: Harvard University Press.

SYLVESTER, David. 1987. *Interviews with Francis Bacon*. 3rd edn. London: Thames & Hudson.

WILSON, Edmund. 1972. *To the Finland Station: A Study in the Writing and Acting of History*. London: Macmillan.

FRANCE AND FRENCH LITERATURE
Twentieth-Century French Prose

ADLER, Laure. 1998. *Marguerite Duras*. Paris: Gallimard.

ARONSON, Ronald. 2004. *Camus and Sartre: The Story of a Friendship and the Quarrel That Ended It*. Chicago and London: University of Chicago Press.

BEAUVOIR, Simone de. 1985. *Adieux: A Farewell to Sartre*. Translated by Patrick O'Brian. Harmondsworth: Penguin.

BLANCHOT, Maurice. 1955. *L'Espace littéraire*. Paris: Gallimard.

———. 1971. *L'Amitié*. Paris: Gallimard.

BONNEFOY, Yves. 2006. *Goya: Les peintures noires*. Bordeaux: William Blake et cie.

COETZEE, J. M. 2007. *Diary of a Bad Year*. London: Harvill Secker.

COURCEL, Martine de, ed. 1976. *Malraux: Life and Work*. London: Weidenfeld & Nicolson.

DURAS, Marguerite. 1960. *Practicalities: Marguerite Duras Speaks to Jérôme Beaujour*. Translated by Barbara Bray. London: Collins.

———. 2006. *Wartime Writings: 1943–1949*. Edited by Sophie Bogaert and Olivier Corpet. Translated by Linda Coverdale. New York and London: New Press.

———, and Xavière Gauthier. 1987. *Woman to Woman*. Translated by Katharine A. Jensen. Lincoln: University of Nebraska Press.

FOREST, Philippe. 2007. *Tous les enfants sauf un*. Paris: Gallimard.

FORÊTS, Louis-René des. 1963. *The Children's Room*. Translated by Jean Stewart. London: Calder.

———. 1978. *Le Bavard*. Paris: Gallimard.

————. 1988. *Les Poèmes de Samuel Wood*. Saint-Clément-la-Rivière: Fata Morgana.

————. 2000. *Ostinato*. Paris: Gallimard.

————. 2001. *Pas à pas jusqu'au dernier*. Paris: Gallimard.

————. 2011. *Poems of Samuel Wood*. Translated by Anthony Barnett. Lewes: Allardyce, Barnett.

KING, Adele. 1964. *Camus*. Edinburgh: Oliver & Boyd.

LABRO, Philippe. 2002. *Je connais gens de toutes sortes*. Paris: Gallimard.

MALRAUX, André. 1968. *Anti-memoirs*. Translated by Terence Kilmartin. New York: Holt, Rinehart & Winston.

MALLARMÉ, Stéphane. 1962. *Pour un tombeau d'Anatole*. Paris: Seuil.

————. 1983. *A Tomb for Anatole*. Translated by Paul Auster. San Francisco: North Point Press.

————. 2003. *For Anatole's Tomb*. Translated by Patrick McGuinness. Manchester: Carcanet.

MARTIN DU GARD, Roger. 1953. *Notes on André Gide*. Translated by John Russell. London: Andre Deutsch.

MILLER, David. 2005. *The Dorothy and Benno Stories*. Hastings: Reality Street Editions.

NABOKOV, Vladimir. 1980. *Lectures on Russian Literature*. Edited by Fredson Bowers. London: Weidenfeld & Nicolson.

NAUGHTON, John. 1993. *Louis René des Forêts*. Amsterdam and Atlanta, GA: Rodopi.

NOCHLIN, Linda, and Tamar Garb, eds. 1995. *The Jew in the Text: Modernity and the Construction of Identity*. London: Thames & Hudson.

RUDOLF, Anthony. 2007. *Engraved in Flesh: Piotr Rawicz and His Novel 'Blood from the Sky'*. Rev. edn. London: Menard.

SARRAUTE, Nathalie. 1976. *Tropismes*. Edited by Sheila M. Bell. Paris: Minuit.

SARTRE, Jean-Paul. 1954. *Réflexions sur la question juive*. Paris: Gallimard.

SONTAG, Susan. 2003. *Regarding the Pain of Others*. London: Hamish Hamilton.

WILLIAMS, Raymond. 1971. *Orwell*. Glasgow: Fontana Books/Collins.

French Poetry

INTRODUCTION

BONNEFOY, Yves. 1958. *Hier régnant désert*. Paris: Mercure de France.

CEPPÈDE, Jean de la. 1983. *From the Theorems of Master Jean de La Ceppède: LXX Sonnets*. Selected and translated by Keith Bosley. Ashington: Mid Northumberland Arts Group

SCÈVE, Maurice. 1961. *Poésies de Maurice Scève*. Lausanne: Mermod.

NINETEENTH-CENTURY FRENCH POETRY

BAUDELAIRE, Charles. 1968. *Twenty Prose Poems*. Translated by Michael Hamburger. London: Jonathan Cape.

———. 1986. *The Complete Verse*. Edited and translated by Francis Scarfe. London: Anvil Press Poetry.

———. 1989. *Intimate Journals*. Translated by Christopher Isherwood. London: Black Spring.

———. 1989. *The Poems in Prose, with La Fanfarlo*. Edited and translated by Francis Scarfe. London: Anvil Press Poetry.

BRETON, André, ed. 1950. *Anthologie de l'humour noir*. Paris: Sagittaire.

CÉSAIRE, Aimé. 1969. *Return to My Native Land*. Translated by John Berger and Anna Bostock. Harmondsworth: Penguin.

CLANCIER, Georges-Emmanuel. 1953. *De Rimbaud au surrealisme: Panorama critique*. Paris: Seghers.

FAIRLIE, Alison. 1960. *Baudelaire: Les fleurs du mal*. London: Arnold.

GOETHE, J. W. 1983. *Poems and Epigrams*. Selected and translated by Michael Hamburger. London: Anvil Press Poetry.

HAMBURGER, Michael. 1969. *The Truth of Poetry: Tensions in Modernist Poetry since Baudelaire*. London: Weidenfeld & Nicolson.

MALLARMÉ, Stéphane. 1977. *Mallarmé: The Poems*. Translated by Keith Bosley. Harmondsworth: Penguin.

———. 1995. *Correspondance complete, 1867–1871: Suivi de Lettres sur la poesie*. Edited by Bertrand Marchal. Paris: Gallimard.

————. 1996. *Collected Poems*. Translated by Henry Weinfield. Berkeley: University of California Press.

MAYER, Peter, ed. 1978. *Alphabetical and Letter Poems: A Chrestomathy*. London: Menard.

NERVAL, Gérard de. 1999. *Les Chimères*. Translated by Will Stone. With accompanying texts by Michael Hamburger and others. London: Menard.

PAZ, Octavio. 1975. *Conjunctions and Disjunctions*. Translated by Helen R. Lane. London: Wildwood House.

PRAZ, Mario. 1970. *The Romantic Agony*. Translated by Angus Davidson. 2nd edn. London: Oxford University Press.

REYES Alina. 2002. *Politique de l'amour*. Cadeilhan: Zulma.

SENGHOR, Léopold Sédar. 1981. *Poems of a Black Orpheus*. Translated by William Oxley. London: Menard.

SOWERBY, Benn. 1973. *The Disinherited: The Life of Gérard de Nerval, 1808–1855*. London: Peter Owen.

VERLAINE, Paul. 1979. *Women/Men; Femmes/hombres*. Translated by Alastair Elliott. London: Anvil Press Poetry.

TWENTIETH-CENTURY FRENCH POETRY

ADLARD, John. 1980. *One Evening of Light Mist in London: The Story of Annie Playden and Guillaume Apollinaire*. Edinburgh: Tragara.

ALBIACH, Anne-Marie. 1991. *Figure vocative*. Paris: Fourbis.

————. 1992. *Vocative Figure*. Translated by Anthony Barnett and Joseph Sima. 2nd edn. Lewes: Allardyce, Barnett.

APOLLINAIRE, Guillaume. 1965. *Selected Poems*. Translated by Oliver Bernard. Harmondsworth: Penguin.

AUSTER, Paul, ed. 1982. *The Random House Book of Twentieth-Century French Poetry, with Translations by American and British Poets*. New York: Random House.

BAYARD, Pierre. 2007. *How to Talk about Books You Haven't Read*. Translated by Jeffrey Mehlman. London: Granta.

BONNEFOY, Yves. 1959. *L'Improbable*. Paris: Gallimard.

————. 1991. *Giacometti: Biographie d'une oeuvre*. Paris: Flammarion.

BOUCHET, André du. 1996. *Where Heat Looms* [*Dans la Chaleur Vacante*]. Translated by David Mus. Los Angeles: Sun & Moon Press.

CHAR, René. 1956. *Hypnos Waking: Poems and Prose*. Translated by J. Mathews, with the collaboration of William Carlos Williams and others. New York: Random House.

COHEN, Leonard. 1969. *Poems, 1956–1968*. London: Jonathan Cape.

———. 1973. *Flowers for Hitler*. London: Jonathan Cape.

COHEN, Marcel. 1980. *Du désert au livre*. Paris: Belfond.

COHEN-HALIMI, Michèle. 2006. *Seul le renversement*. Bordeaux: Attente.

———, and Francis Cohen. 1999. *Je te continue ma lecture: Mélanges pour Claude Royet-Journoud*. Paris: P.O.L.

COUTURIER, Michel. 1975. *L'Ablatif absolu*. Paris: Maeght.

COWLEY, Malcolm, and Hannah Josephson, eds. 1946. *Aragon Poet of Resurgent France*. London: Pilot Press.

DEGUY, Michel. 1973. *Poèmes, 1960–1970*. Paris: Gallimard.

———. 1983. *Poèmes II, 1970–1980*. Paris: NRF/Gallimard.

———. 1988. *Le Comité: Confessions d'un lecteur de grande maison*. Seyssel: Champ Vallon.

———. 1999. *Gisants: Poèmes III, 1980–1995*. Paris: Gallimard.

———. 2002. *Un homme de peu de foi*. Paris: Bayard.

———. 2006. *Le Sens de la visite*. Paris: Stock.

———, and Jacques Roubaud, eds. 1980. *Vingt poètes américains*. Paris: Gallimard.

DUPIN, Jacques. 1992. *Selected Poems*. Translated by Paul Auster, Stephen Romer and David Shapiro. Newcastle-upon-Tyne: Bloodaxe Books.

———. 2011. *Of Flies and Monkeys*. Translated by John Taylor. Fayetteville, NY: Bitter Oleander.

FAINLIGHT, Ruth. 2010. *New and Collected Poems*. Tarset: Bloodaxe Books.

FRÉMON, Jean. 1991. *Le Singe mendiant*. Paris: P.O.L.

———. 2000. *La Vraie nature des ombres*. Paris: P.O.L.

———. 2005. *La Gloire des formes*. Paris: P.O.L.

FRÉNAUD, André. 1979. *Notre inhabileté fatale*. Paris: Gallimard.

———. 1996. *La Sorcière de Rome/Rome the Sorceress*. Translated by Keith Bosley. Tarset: Bloodaxe Books.

GENET, Jean. 2007. *L'Atelier d'Alberto Giacometti*. Paris: Gallimard.

GIROUX, Roger. 1987. *Time and the Tree*. Translated by Anthony Barnett. Hebden Bridge: Open Township.

———. 2001. *Blank: The Invisible Poem*. Translated by Anthony Barnett. Lewes: Allardyce, Barnett.

GUPPY, Shusha. 1988. *The Blindfold Horse: Memoirs of a Persian Childhood*. London: Heinemann.

———. 1991. *A Girl in Paris*. London: Heinemann.

HACKETT, C. A., ed. 1952. *Anthology of Modern French Poetry, from Baudelaire to the Present Day*. Oxford: Blackwell.

———. 1973. *New French Poetry: An Anthology*. Oxford: Blackwell.

JABÈS, Edmond. 1975. *Je bâtis ma demeure: Poèmes, 1943–1957*. Paris: Gallimard.

———. 1976. *The Book of Questions*. Translated by Rosmarie Waldrop. Middletown, CT: Wesleyan University Press.

———. 1979. *A Share of Ink*. Translated by Anthony Rudolf. London: Menard

———. 1990. *Book of Resemblances*. Translated by Rosmarie Waldrop. Middletown, CT: Wesleyan University Press.

———. 1991. *From the Book to the Book: An Edmond Jabès Reader*. Translated by Rosmarie Waldrop, with additional translations by Pierre Joris, Anthony Rudolf and Keith Waldrop. Middletown, CT: Wesleyan University Press.

JACCOTTET, Philippe. 1988. *Selected Poems*. Selected and translated by Derek Mahon. London: Penguin.

———. 1997. *Landscapes with Absent Figures*. Translated by Mark Treharne. London: Menard.

———. 2011. *And Nonetheless: Selected Prose and Poetry, 1990–2009*. Translated by John Taylor. New York: Chelsea Editions.

JACOB, Max. 1976. *Advice to a Young Poet*. Translated by John Adlard. London: Menard.

JARON, Steven. 2003. *Edmond Jabès: The Hazard of Exile*. Oxford: Legenda, European Humanities Research Centre.

———, ed. 2003. *Lettres de Max Jacob à Edmond Jabès*. Pessac: Opales.

KOESTLER, Arthur. 1969. *Arrival and Departure*. London and New York: Penguin.

LÉLY, Gilbert. 1977. *Oeuvres poétiques*. Paris: Difference.

LORD, James. 1981. *A Giacometti Portrait*. London: Faber & Faber.

———. 2004. *Mythic Giacometti*. New York: Farrar, Straus & Giroux.

MOUSSARON, Jean-Pierre. 1992. *La Poésie comme avenir: Essai sur l'œuvre de Michel Deguy*. Grenoble: Presses Universitaires de Grenoble.

PRESS, Alan, ed. and trans. 1971. *Anthology of Troubadour Lyric Poetry*. Edinburgh: Edinburgh University Press.

QUIGNARD, Pascal. 1993. *Le Nom sur le bout de la langue*. Paris: P.O.L.

REVERDY, Pierre. 1949. *Main d'oeuvre*. Paris: Mercure de France.

ROBBE-GRILLET, Alain. 2005. *Préface à une vie d'écrivain*. Paris: Seuil/France Culture.

ROUBAUD, Jacques, ed. 1971. *Les Troubadours: Anthologie bilingue*. Paris: Seghers.

ROYET-JOURNOUD, Claude. 1972. *Le Renversement*. Paris: Gallimard.

———. 2006. *Theory of Prepositions*. Translated by Keith Waldrop. Iowa City: La Presse.

———. 2007. *La Poésie entière est préposition*. Marseille: Pesty.

———. 2007. *Théorie des prépositions*. Paris: P.O.L.

RUDOLF, Anthony. 1991. *Wine from Two Glasses*. London: Adam Archive.

TAYLOR, John. 2004. *Paths to Contemporary French Literature*. 3 VOLS. London and New Brunswick, NJ: Transaction.

VIGÉE, Claude. 2006. *Etre poète pour que vivent les hommes: Choix d'essais, 1950–2005*. Paris: Parole et silence.

WALDROP, Rosmarie. 2002. *Lavish Absence: Recalling and Rereading Edmond Jabès*. Middletown, CT: Wesleyan University Press.

ZUKOFSKY, Louis. 1967. *Prepositions: The Collected Critical Essays of Louis Zukofsky*. London: Rapp & Carroll.

Visit to Paris

AGAMBEN, Giorgio. 2007. *Profanations.* Translated by Jeff Fort. New York: Zone Books.

ASSOULINE, Pierre. 2006. *Rosebud.* Paris: Gallimard.

CELAN, Paul, and Ilana Shmueli. 2006. *Correspondance 1965–1970.* Edited by Ilana Shmueli and Thomas Sparr. Paris: Seuil.

———. 2010. *The Correspondence of Paul Celan and Ilana Shmueli.* Translated by Susan Gillespie. New York: Sheep Meadow.

GENETTE, Gérard. 2006. *Bardadrac.* Paris: Seuil.

MIŁOSZ, Czesław. 1980. *Selected Poems.* New York: Ecco.

———. 2001. *Miłosz's ABC's.* Translated by Madeline G. Levine. New York: Farrar, Straus, and Giroux.

MOUNIC, Anne. 2005. *La poésie de Claude Vigée: Danse vers l'abîme et connaissance par joui-dire.* Paris: L'Harmatttan.

———. 2010. *Mille étoiles en mémoire.* Paris: Encre Vives.

———. 2010. *(X) de nom et prénom inconnu. Quatre nouvelles.* Paris: Orizons.

OUAKNIN, Marc-Alain. 1998. *Méditations érotiques: Essai sur Emmanuel Levinas.* Paris: Payot & Rivages.

RENARD, Jules. 1960. *Journal, 1887–1910.* Edited by Léon Guichard and Gilbert Sigaux. Paris: Gallimard.

ROBBE-GRILLET, Alain. 1939. *Dans le labyrinthe.* Paris: Minuit.

ROTH, Joseph. 2004. *The White Cities: Reports From France, 1925–1939.* Translated by Michael Hofmann. London: Granta.

SAINT-CHERON, Michaël de, 2006. *Entretiens avec Emmanuel Levinas, 1992–1994: Suivis de Levinas entre philosophie et pensée juive.* Paris: Livre de poche.

JEWISH WORLDS
Introduction/Writings of the Disaster

AINSZTEIN, Reuben. 1974. *Jewish Resistance in Nazi-Occupied Eastern Europe: With a Historical Survey of the Jew as Fighter and Soldier in the Diaspora.* London: Elek.

AMÉRY, Jean. 1999. *At the Mind's Limits: Contemplations by a Survivor on Auschwitz and Its Realities.* London: Granta

ANGIER, Carole. 2002. *The Double Bond: Primo Levi; A Biography.* London: Viking.

ANISSIMOV, Myriam. 1997. *Primo Levi: Tragedy of an Optimist.* Translated by Steve Cox. London: Aurum.

ANTELME, Robert. 1992. *The Human Race.* Translated by Jeffrey Haight and Annie Mahler. Marlboro, VT: Marlboro Press.

BAR-ON, Dan. 1995. *Fear and Hope: Three Generations of the Holocaust.* Cambridge, MA, and London: Harvard University Press.

BLADY SZWAJGER, Adina. 1990. *I Remember Nothing More: The Warsaw Children's Hospital and the Jewish Resistance.* Translated by Darowska and Danusia Stok. London: Collins Harvill.

BLANCHOT, Maurice. 1980. *L'Ecriture du désastre.* Paris: Gallimard.

———. 1986. *The Writing of the Disaster.* Translated by Ann Smock. Lincoln: University of Nebraska Press.

———. 2000. *The Instant of My Death.* Translated by Elizabeth Rottenberg. Stanford, CA: Stanford University Press.

BORWICZ, Michel. 1973. *Ecrits des condamnés à mort sous l'occupation nazie, 1939–1945.* Paris: Gallimard.

CANETTI, Elias. 1974. *Kafka's Other Trial: The Letters to Felice.* Translated by Christopher Middleton. London: Calder & Boyars.

CIXOUS, Hélène. 2004. *Portrait of Jacques Derrida as a Young Jewish Saint.* Translated by Beverley Bie Brahic. New York: Columbia University Press.

COHEN, Elie. 1988. *Human Behaviour in the Concentration Camp.* Translated by M. H. Braaksma. London: Free Association.

CZECH, Danuta. 1990. *The Auschwitz Chronicle, 1939–1945.* London: Tauris.

DANON BRACO, Cadik. 2002. *The Smell of Human Flesh: A Witness of the Holocaust; Memories of Jasenovac.* Beograd: Mašič.

DEKOVEN EZRAHI, Sidra. 2000. *Booking Passage: Exile and Homecoming in the Modern Jewish Imagination.* Berkeley: University of California Press.

DERRIDA, Jacques. 1994. 'Shibboleth: For Paul Celan', translated by Joshua Wilner. In *Word Traces: Readings of Paul Celan*, edited by Aris Fioretos. London and Baltimore, MD: Johns Hopkins University Press.

DES PRES, Terrence. 1976. *The Survivor: An Anatomy of Life in the Death Camps*. Oxford and New York: Oxford University Press.

DWORK, Deborah. 1991. *Children with a Star*. New Haven, CT, and London: Yale University Press.

FAYE, Jean-Pierre. 1974. *Migrations du récit sur le peuple juif*. Paris: Belfond.

FLINKER, Moshe. 1965. *Young Moshe's Diary: The Spiritual Torment of a Jewish Boy in Nazi Europe*. Jerusalem: Yad Vashem.

FRIEDRICH, Otto. 1996. *The Kingdom of Auschwitz*. London: Penguin.

HEIDELBERGER-LEONARD, Irène. 2010. *The Philosopher of Auschwitz: Jean Améry and Living with the Holocaust*. London: Tauris.

HEIMLER, Eugene. 1959. *Night of the Mist*. London: Bodley Head.

———. 1967. *Mental Illness and Social Work*. Harmondsworth: Penguin.

———. 1976. *The Storm: The Tragedy of Sinai*. Translated by Anthony Rudolf. London: Menard.

HILLESUM, Etty. 1987. *Letters from Westerbork*. Translated by Arnold J. Pomerans. London: Jonathan Cape.

HUGHES, H. Stuart. 1983. *Prisoners of Hope: The Silver Age of the Italian Jews, 1924–1974*. Cambridge, MA, and London: Harvard University Press.

KA-TZETNIK 135633. 1956. *House of Dolls*. Translated by Moshe M. Kohn. London: Muller.

———. 1972. *Star Eternal*. Translated by Nina De-Nur. London: Allen.

———. 1977. *Sunrise over Hell*. Translated by Nina De-Nur. London: Allen.

———. 1989. *Shivitti: A Vision*. Translated by Eliyah Nike De-Nur and Lisa Herman. San Francisco: Harper & Row.

KLARSFELD, Serge. 1996. *French Children of the Holocaust: A Memorial*. Edited by Susan Cohen, Howard M. Epstein and Serge Klarsfeld. Translated by Glorianne Depondt and Howard M. Epstein. New York and London: New York University Press.

KLONICKI, Aryeh. 1973. *The Diary of Adam's Father: The Diary of Aryeh Klonicki (Klonymus) and His Wife Malwina, with Letters Concerning the Fate of Their Child Adam*. Tel Aviv: Ghetto Fighters' House.

LANGER, Lawrence. 1991. *Holocaust Testimonies: The Ruins of Memory*. New Haven, CT, and London: Yale University Press.

LEVI, Carlo. 1982. *Christ Stopped at Eboli*. Translated by Frances Frenaye. Harmondsworth: Penguin.

LEVI, Primo. 1976. *Shema: Collected Poems of Primo Levi*. Translated by Ruth Feldman and Brian Swann. London: Menard.

———. 1979. *If This Is a Man; and, The Truce*. Translated by Stuart Woolf. Harmondsworth: Penguin.

———. 1986. *Moments of Reprieve*. Translated by Ruth Feldman. London: Joseph.

———. 1988. *The Drowned and the Saved*. Translated by Raymond Rosenthal. London: Joseph.

LIFTON, Betty Jean. 1988. *The King of Children: A Biography of Janusz Korczak*. London: Chatto & Windus.

LIND, Jakov. 1964. *Soul of Wood*. Translated by Ralph Manheim. London: Jonathan Cape.

———. 1966. *Landscape in Concrete*. Translated by Ralph Manheim. London: Methuen.

———. 1996. *The Stove: Short Stories*. London: Menard.

LÖWENTHAL, Zdenko, ed. 1957. *The Crimes of the Fascist Occupants and Their Collaborators against Jews in Yugoslavia*. Belgrade: Federation of Jewish Communities of the Federative People's Republic of Yugoslavia.

MODIANO, Patrick. 1972. *Night Rounds*. Translated by Patricia Wolf. London: Gollancz.

———. 1974. *Ring Roads: A Novel*. Translated by Caroline Hillier. London: Gollancz.

———. 2004. *Dora Bruder*. Paris: Gallimard.

NEUSNER, Jacob. 1973. *Understanding Jewish Theology: Classical Issues and Modern Perspectives*. New York: Ktav.

643

OPPENHEIMER, Paul. 1996. *Evil and the Demonic: A New Theory of Monstrous Behaviour*. London: Duckworth.

PAGIS, Dan. 1981. *Points of Departure*. Translated by Stephen Mitchell. Philadelphia, PA: Jewish Publication Society of America.

———. 1991. *Hebrew Poetry of the Middle Ages and the Renaissance*. Berkeley and Oxford: University of California Press.

PELEG-MARIANSKA, Miriam, and Mordecai Peleg. 1991. *Witnesses: Life in Occupied Krakow*. London: Routledge.

PERECHODNIK, Calel. 1996. *Am I a Murderer? Testament of a Jewish Ghetto Policeman*. Edited and translated by Frank Fox. Boulder, CA: Westview.

PRESSER, Jacques. 1992. *The Night of the Girondists*. Translated by Barrows Mussey. London: Harvill.

RAWICZ, Piotr. 2004. *Blood from the Sky*. Edited by Anthony Rudolf. Translated by Peter Wiles. London: Elliott and Thompson. [Copies taken over by Menard.]

RUBINOWICZ, Dawid. 1981 *The Diary of David Rubinowicz*. Translated by Derek Bowman. Edinburgh: Blackwood.

SCHEVILL, James. 1964. *Stalingrad Elegies*. Denver, CO: Swallow.

SCHNEIDER, Franz, and Charles Gullans, trans. 1974. *Last Letters from Stalingrad*. Westport, CT: Greenwood.

SEBALD, W. G. 2003. *On the Natural History of Destruction*. Translated by Anthea Bell. London: Hamish Hamilton.

———. 2006. *Campo Santo*. Edited by W. G. Sebald. Translated by Anthea Bell. London: Penguin.

SPECTOR PERSON, Ethel. 1989. *Love and Fateful Encounters: The Power of Romantic Passion*. London: Bloomsbury.

SPERBER, Manès. 1987. *All Our Yesterdays*. Translated by Joachim Neugroschel. New York and London: Holmes & Meier.

———. 1988. *Like a Tear in the Ocean*. Translated by Constantine Fitzgibbon. New York and London: Holmes & Meier.

STECKEL, Charles, W. 1973. *Destruction and Survival*. Los Angeles: Delmar.

STEINBERG, Lucien. 1974. *Not as a Lamb: The Jews against Hitler*. Translated by Marion Hunter. Farnborough: Saxon House.

SUHL, Yuri, ed. and trans. 1968. *They Fought Back: The Story of the Jewish Resistance in Nazi Europe*. London: MacGibbon & Kee.

SUTZKEVER, Abraham. 1981. *Burnt Pearls: Ghetto Poems of Abraham Sutzkever*. Translated by Seymour Mayne. Oakville, Ont.: Mosaic/Valley Editions.

THOMSON, Ian. 2002. *Primo Levi: A Life*. London: Vintage.

URMAN, Jerzy Feliks. 1991. *I'm Not Even a Grown-Up: The Diary of Jerzy Feliks Urman*. Edited by Anthony Rudolf. Translated by Anthony Rudolf and Joanna Voit. London: Menard.

VIDAL-NAQUET, Pierre. 1992. *Assassins of Memory: Essays on the Denial of the Holocaust*. Translated by Jeffrey Mehlman. New York and Oxford: Columbia University Press.

WEIL, Jiri. 1989. *Life with a Star*. Translated by Rita Klimová with Roslyn Schloss. London: Collins.

———. 1992. *Mendelssohn Is on the Roof*. Translated by Marie Winn. London: HarperCollins.

WELICZKER WELLS, Leon. 1966. *The Janowska Road*. London: Jonathan Cape. [Reissued in 1978 as *The Death Brigade*. New York: Holocaust Library.]

WIESENTHAL, Simon. 1976. *The Sunflower: On the Possibilities and Limits of Forgiveness*. New York: Schocken.

YOUNG, James. 1990 *Writing and Rewriting the Holocaust: Narrative and the Consequences of Interpretation*. Bloomington: Indiana University Press.

ZUCKERMAN, Solly. 1978. *From Apes to Warlords: The Autobiography (1904–1946) of Solly Zuckerman*. London: Hamish Hamilton.

ZUCKERMAN, Yitzhak. 1993. *A Surplus of Memory: Chronicle of the Warsaw Ghetto Uprising*. Berkeley and Oxford: University of California Press.

Politics

ARENDT, Hannah. 1963. *Eichmann in Jerusalem: A Report on the Banality of Evil*. London: Faber & Faber.

———. 1978. *The Jew as Pariah: Jewish Identity and Politics in the Modern Age.* Edited by Ron H. Feldman. New York: Grove.

BARENBOIM, Daniel. 2008. *Everything Is Connected: The Power of Music.* Edited by Elena Cheah. London: Weidenfeld & Nicolson.

BROWN, George. 1971. *In My Way: The Political Memoirs of Lord George-Brown.* London: Gollancz.

BURG, Avraham. 2010. *The Holocaust Is Over: We Must Rise From Its Ashes.* Basingstoke: Palgrave Macmillan.

GOLDMANN, Nahum. 1970. *Memories: The Autobiography of Nahum Goldmann; The Story of a Lifelong Battle by World Jewry's Ambassador at Large.* Translated by Helen Sebba. London: Weidenfeld & Nicolson.

———. 1978. *The Jewish Paradox.* Translated by Steve Cox. London: Weidenfeld & Nicolson.

LEHRMAN, S. M. 1948. *The Jewish Festivals.* 4th edn. London: Shapiro, Vallentine.

———. 1951. *The Jewish Design for Living.* London: Bachad Fellowship.

LEON, Dan. 1964. *The Kibbutz: A Portrait from Within.* Tel Aviv: Israel Horizons, in collaboration with World Hashomer Hatzair.

TIMERMAN, Jacobo. 1981. *Prisoner without a Name, Cell without a Number.* Translated by Toby Talbo. London: Weidenfeld & Nicolson.

———. 1982. *The Longest War.* London: Chatto & Windus.

History

ABRAHAMS, Beth Zion. 1950. *The Jews in England: A History for Jewish Children.* London: Anscombe.

BARNES, Julian. 2011. *The Sense of an Ending.* London: Jonathan Cape.

BENGUIGUI, Lucien-Gilles. 1995. *Racine et les sources juives d'Esther et Athalie.* Paris: L'Harmattan/Pavillon.

BIERMAN, John. 1981. *Righteous Gentile: The Story of Raoul Wallenberg, Missing Hero of the Holocaust.* London: Allen Lane.

BLOOM, Harold. 2011. *The Shadow of a Great Rock: A Literary Appreciation of the King James Bible.* New Haven, CT, and London: Yale University Press.

BRERETON, Geoffrey. 1951. *Jean Racine: A Critical Biography*. London: Cassell.

COHEN, Arthur. 1951. *Martin Buber*. London: Bowes & Bowes.

COHN, Norman. 1967. *Warrant for Genocide: The Myth of the Jewish World-Conspiracy and the Protocols of the Elders of Zion*. London: Eyre & Spottiswoode.

CORNWALL, Mark, ed. 1990. *The Last Years of Austria-Hungary: A Multi-national Experiment in Early Twentieth-Century Europe*. Exeter: University of Exeter Press.

DOCKER, John. 2001. *1492: The Poetics of Diaspora*. London and New York: Continuum.

FISHMAN, W. J. 1975. *East End Jewish Radicals, 1875–1914*. London: Duckworth.

FRIEDLANDER, Saul. 1979. *When Memory Comes*. Translated by Helen R. Lane. New York: Farrar, Straus & Giroux.

———. 1984. *Reflections of Nazism, Essay on Kitsch and Death*. Translated by Thomas Weyr. New York: Harper & Row.

GILBERT, Martin. 1979. *The Arab-Israeli Conflict: Its History in Maps*. 3rd edn. London: Weidenfeld & Nicolson.

———. 1986. *The Holocaust: The Jewish Tragedy*. London: Collins.

———. 1994. *First World War*. London: Weidenfeld & Nicolson.

GOLDMANN, Lucien. 1955. *Le Dieu caché: Etude sur la vision tragique dans les Pensées de Pascal et dans le théâtre de Racine*. Paris: Gallimard.

———. 1970. *Racine: Essai*. Paris: L'Arche.

GRUNBERGER, Richard. 1973. *Red Rising in Bavaria*. London: Barker.

HINDUS, Milton, ed. 1969. *The Old East Side: An Anthology*. Philadelphia, PA: Jewish Publication Society of America.

HOWE, Irving, with the assistance of Kenneth Libo. 1976. *The Immigrant Jews of New York: 1881 to the Present*. London: Routledge & Kegan Paul.

KELLER, Werner. 1971. *Diaspora: The Post-biblical History of the Jews*. Translated by Richard and Clara Winston. London: Pitman.

KOLITZ, Zvi. 1999. *Yosl Rakover Talks to God*. Translated by Carol Brown Janeway. London: Jonathan Cape.

LACOUE-LABARTHE, Philippe, and Jean-Luc Nancy. 1991. *Le Mythe nazi*. La Tour d'Aigues: Editions de l'Aube.

MAURIAC, François. 1928. *La Vie de Jean Racine*. Paris: Plon.

OCHS, Vanessa. 2005. *Sarah Laughed: Modern Lessons from the Wisdom and Stories of Biblical Women*. New York and London: McGraw-Hill.

PRINZ, Joachim. 1974. *The Secret Jews*. London: Vallentine, Mitchell.

ROTH, Cecil. 1932. *A History of the Marranos*. Philadelphia, PA: Jewish Publication Society of America.

———. 1934. *A Life of Menasseh ben Israel, Rabbi, Printer, and Diplomat*. Philadelphia, PA: Jewish Publication Society of America.

———. 1936. *Short History of the Jewish People*. London: Macmillan.

STERN, J. P. 1975. *Hitler: The Führer and the People*. London: Fontana Books.

TRAVEN, B. 1934. *The Treasure of the Sierra Madre*. Translated by Basil Creighton. London: Chatto & Windus.

WISTRICH, Robert. 1976. *Revolutionary Jews from Marx to Trotsky*. London: Harrap.

———. 1979. *Trotsky: Fate of a Revolutionary*. London: Robson.

———. 1995. *Weekend in Munich: Art, Propaganda and Terror in the Third Reich*. London: Pavilion.

Religion and Theology

BAUMAN, Zygmunt. 1999. *Culture as Praxis*. London: Sage.

BENJAMIN, Walter. 1998. *The Origin of German Tragic Drama*. Translated by John Osborn. London and New York: Verso.

BERGMAN, Samuel H. 1963. *Faith and Reason: An Introduction to Modern Jewish Thought*. Edited and translated by Alfred Jospe. New York: Schocken.

BESSERMAN, Perle. 1997. *Owning It: Zen and the Art of Facing Life*. New York: Kodansha International.

———. 2005. *A New Kabbalah for Women*. New York: Palgrave Macmillan.

———. 2007. *A New Zen for Women*. New York: Palgrave Macmillan.

BIERMAN, Michael, ed. 2003. *Memories of a Giant: Eulogies in Memory of Rabbi Dr. Joseph B. Soloveitchik*. Jerusalem: Urim.

BLOOM, Harold. 1975. *Kabbalah and Criticism*. New York: Seabury.

BRONER, E. M. 1994. *Mornings and Mourning: A Kaddish Journal*. San Francisco: Harper & Row.

BUBER, Martin. 1956. *Tales of Rabbi Nachman*. Translated by Maurice Friedman. New York: Horizon.

CAYGILL, Howard. 2001. *Levinas and the Political*. London and New York: Routledge.

CIORAN, Emil. 1986. *Des Larmes et des saints*. Translated from the Romanian by Sanda Stolojan. Paris: L'Herne.

COHEN, Arthur A. 1974. *Osip Emilievich Mandelstam: An Essay in Antiphon*. Ann Arbor, MI: Ardis.

———. 1981. *The Tremendum: A Theological Interpretation of the Holocaust*. New York: Crossroad.

———. 1985. *An Admirable Woman*. Manchester: Carcanet.

———. 1987. *Artists and Enemies: Three Novellas*. Boston, MA: Godine.

———, and Mordecai Kaplan. 1973. *If Not Now, When? Towards a Reconstitution of the Jewish People*. New York: Schocken.

DANBY, Herbert, trans. 1933. *The Mishnah*. London: Oxford University Press.

DERRIDA, Jacques. 1999. *Adieu to Emmanuel Levinas*. Translated by Pascale-Anne Brault and Michael Naas. Stanford, CA: Stanford University Press.

ELIACH, Yaffa. 1982. *Hasidic Tales of the Holocaust*. New York: Oxford University Press.

EPSTEIN, Perle. 1979. *Pilgrimage of a Wandering Jew*. Boston, MA: Houghton Mifflin.

FARHI, Moris. 1989. *Journey through the Wilderness*. London: Macmillan.

———. 2011. *Songs from Two Continents: Poems*. London: Saqi.

GILMAN, Sander. 1995. *Franz Kafka: The Jewish Patient*. New York and London: Routledge.

GOLDSTEIN, Rebecca. 1985. *The Mind–Body Problem: A Novel*. London: Andre Deutsch.

———. 1989. *The Late-Summer Passion of a Woman of Mind*. London: Vintage.

———. 2006. *Betraying Spinoza: The Renegade Jew Who Gave Us Modernity*. New York: Nextbook/Schocken.

———. 2010. *Thirty-Six Arguments for the Existence of God: A Work of Fiction*. London: Atlantic.

GRAYSTON, D., and M. Higgins. 1983. *Thomas Merton: Pilgrim in Process*. Toronto: Griffin House.

HESCHEL, Rabbi Abraham Joshua. 1950. *The Earth Is the Lord's: The Inner World of the Jew in East Europe*. New York: Schuman.

———. 1951. *The Sabbath: Its Meaning for Modern Man*. New York: Farrar, Straus & Giroux.

———. 1954. *Man's Quest for God: Studies in Prayer and Symbolism*. New York: Scribner.

———. 1974. *A Passion for Truth*. London: Secker & Warburg.

———. 1976. *Man Is Not Alone: A Philosophy of Religion*. New York: Farrar, Straus & Giroux.

JABÈS, Edmond. 1983. *The Book of Questions*. Translated by Rosmarie Waldrop. Middletown, CT: Wesleyan University Press.

KAPLAN. Edward. 1996. *Holiness in Words: Abraham Joshua Heschel's Poetics of Piety*. West Fulton: State University of New York Press.

———. 2007. *Spiritual Radical: Abraham Joshua Heschel in America, 1940–1972*. New Haven, CT, and London: Yale University Press.

KITAJ, R. B. 2007. *Second Diasporist Manifesto*. New Haven, CT, and London: Yale University Press.

KOCHAN, Lionel. 1997. *Beyond the Graven Image: A Jewish View*. Basingstoke: Macmillan.

LARUELLE, François, ed. 1980. *Textes pour Emmanuel Levinas*. Paris: Place.

LEVINAS, Emmanuel. 1982. *Ethique et infini: Dialogues avec Philippe Nemo*. Paris: Fayard/French Culture.

LONGWORTH, Philip. 1967. *Confrontations with Judaism: A Symposium*. London: Blond.

LÖWY, Michael. 1992. *Redemption and Utopia: Jewish Libertarian Thought in Central Europe*. Translated by Hope Heaney. London: Athlone.

MAYBAUM, Ignaz. 1946. *The Jewish Home*. London: Clarke.

———. 1960. *Jewish Existence*. London: Valentine, Mitchell.

———. 1969. *Creation and Guilt: A Theological Assessment of Freud's Father–Son Conflict*. London: Vallentine, Mitchell.

———. 1973. *Trialogue Between Jew, Christian and Muslim*. London: Routledge & Kegan Paul.

———. 1980. *Happiness Outside the State: Judaism, Christianity, Islam: Three Ways to God*. Stocksfield: Oriel.

MENDES-FLOHR, Paul, and Arthur A. Cohen, eds. 1988. *Contemporary Jewish Thought*. London: Collier Macmillan.

O'BRIEN, Michael. 2007. *Sleeping and Walking*. Chicago: Flood Editions.

OSHRI, Rabbi Ephraim. 1983. *Responsa from the Holocaust*. Edited by B. Goldman. Translated by Y. Leiman. New York: Judaica.

RAYNER, John. 1997. *An Understanding of Judaism*. Providence, RI: Berghahn.

ROSE, Gillian. 1992. *The Broken Middle: Out of Our Ancient Society*. Oxford: Blackwell.

———. 1993. *Judaism and Modernity: Philosophical Essays*. Oxford and Cambridge, MA: Blackwell.

———. 1995. *Love's Work*. London: Chatto & Windus.

———. 1996. *Mourning Becomes the Law: Philosophy and Representation*. Cambridge: Cambridge University Press.

———. 1999. *Paradiso*. London: Menard.

ROSEN, Jonathan. 2000. *The Talmud and the Internet: A Journey Between Worlds*. London: Continuum.

SCHOLEM, Gershom. 1955. *Major Trends in Jewish Mysticism*. 3rd edn. London: Thames & Hudson.

———. 1971. *The Messianic Idea in Judaism, and Other Essays on Jewish Spirituality*. London: Allen & Unwin.

———. 1980. *From Berlin to Jerusalem: Memories of My Youth*. Translated by Harry Zohn. New York: Schocken.

———. 1982. *Walter Benjamin: The Story of a Friendship*. London: Faber & Faber.

SOLOVEITCHIK, Rabbi Joseph. 1991. *Halakhic Man.* Translated by Lawrence Kaplan. Philadelphia, PA: Jewish Publication Society of America.

———. 1986. *The Halakhic Mind.* Ardmore and New York: Seth.

STONE, I. F. 2006. *The Best of I .F. Stone.* Edited by Karl Weber. New York: Public Affairs.

STYRON, William. 1979. *Sophie's Choice.* London: Jonathan Cape.

WIESEL, Elie. 1960. *Night.* Translated by Stella Rodway. London: MacGibbon & Kee.

———. 1982. *Legends of Our Time.* New York: Schocken.

WIESELTIER, Leon. 1999. *Kaddish.* London: Picador.

WILLIAMS, Rowan. 2002. *The Poems of Rowan Williams.* Oxford: Perpetua.

———. 2005. *Grace and Necessity.* London: Continuum, Morehouse.

———. 2009. *Dostoevsky: Life, Faith and Fiction:* London: Continuum.

Folklore and Humour

ALTER, Robert. 1992. *The World of Biblical Literature.* London: SPCK.

———, and Frank Kermode, eds. 1987. *The Literary Guide to the Bible.* London: Collins.

AUSUBEL, Nathan, ed. 1951. *A Treasury of Jewish Humour.* Garden City, NY: Doubleday.

———, ed. 1972. *A Treasury of Jewish Folklore: Stories, Traditions, Legends, Humor, Wisdom and Folk Songs of the Jewish People.* London: Vallentine, Mitchell.

BOROWSKI, Tadeusz. 1967. *This Way for the Gas, Ladies and Gentlemen, and Other Stories.* Selected and translated by Barbara Vedder. London: Jonathan Cape.

CONNOLLY, Cyril. 1981. *The Rock Pool.* Oxford: Oxford University Press.

CURZON, David, ed. 1994. *Modern Poems on the Bible: An Anthology.* Philadelphia, PA: Jewish Publication Society.

———, ed. 1995. *The Gospels in Our Image: An Anthology of Twentieth-Century Poetry Based on Biblical Texts.* New York: Harcourt Brace & Co.

FROMM, Erich. 1967. *You Shall Be as Gods: A Radical Interpretation of the Old Testament and Its Tradition.* London: Jonathan Cape.

JACOBSON, Dan. 1982. *The Story of Stories: The Chosen People and Its God*. London: Secker & Warburg.

JOSIPOVICI, Gabriel. 1988. *The Book of God: A Response to the Bible*. New Haven, CT, and London: Yale University Press.

LANG, Berel, ed. 1988. *Writing and the Holocaust*. New York and London: Holmes & Meier.

LIPMAN, Steve. 1991. *Laughter in Hell: The Use of Humor during the Holocaust*. Northvale, NJ, and London: Aronson.

MACCOBY, Hyam, trans. 1987. *The Day God Laughed: Sayings, Fables and Entertainments of the Jewish Sages*. London: Robson.

MIKES, George. 1969. *The Prophet Motive: Israel Today and Tomorrow*. London: Andre Deutsch.

SCHWARTZ, Howard, ed. 1976. *Imperial Messages. One Hundred Modern Parables*. New York: Avon.

———. 1979. *Gathering the Sparks: Poems, 1965–1979*. St Louis, MI: K. M. Gentile.

———. 1983. *The Captive Soul of the Messiah: New Tales About Reb Nachman*. New York: Schocken.

———, ed. 1983. *Gates to the New City: A Treasury of Modern Jewish Tales*. New York: Avon.

———. 1987. *Elijah's Violin and Other Jewish Folk Tales*. Harmondsworth: Penguin.

———. 1988. *Lilith's Cave: Jewish Tales of the Supernatural*. San Francisco: Harper & Row.

———. 1988. *Miriam's Tambourine*. Oxford: Oxford University Press.

———. 1993. *Gabriel's Palace: Jewish Mystical Tales*. New York and Oxford: Oxford University Press.

———. 1998. *Reimagining the Bible: The Storytelling of the Rabbis*. New York and Oxford: Oxford University Press.

———. 2004. *Tree of Souls: The Mythology of Judaism*. Oxford and New York: Oxford University Press.

————, and Anthony Rudolf, eds. 1980. *Voices within the Ark: The Modern Jewish Poets*. New York: Avon.

SONZOGNI, Marco, ed. 2011. *This Way: Covering/Uncovering Tadeusz Borowski's 'This Way for the Gas, Ladies and Gentlemen'*. Wellington: Dunmore.

SPIEGELMAN, Art. 2003. *Maus: A Survivor's Tale*. London: Penguin.

VONNEGUT, Kurt. 1968. *Mother Night*. London: Jonathan Cape.

Literature

ALTER, Robert. 2004. *The Five Books of Moses: A Translation with Commentary*. New York and London: W. W. Norton.

————. 2007. *The Book of Psalms: A Translation with Commentary*. New York and London: W. W. Norton.

————. 2010. *The Wisdom Books: Job, Proverbs, and Ecclesiastes; A Translation with Commentary*. New York and London: W. W. Norton.

ANSKY, S. 1992. *The Dybbuk, and Other Writings*. Edited by David G. Roskies. Translated by Golda Werman. New York: Schocken.

DAVIE, Donald, ed. 1996. *The Psalms in English*. London: Penguin.

FOX, Everett. 1995. *The Five Books of Moses: A New Translation with Introductions, Commentary, and Notes*. London: Harvill.

GORDIS, Robert. 1951. *Koheleth: The Man and His World*. New York: Jewish Theological Seminary of America.

KLEIN, A. M. 1987. *Literary Essays and Reviews*. Edited by Usher Caplan and M. W. Steinberg. Toronto: University of Toronto Press.

LEVI, Peter, trans. 1976. *Psalms*. Harmondsworth: Penguin.

MANDELSTAM, Osip. 1988. *The Noise of Time, and Other Prose Pieces*. Translated by Clarence Brown. London: Quartet.

OBENZINGER, Hilton. 1989. *New York on Fire*. Seattle, WA: Real Comet.

————. 1999. *American Palestine: Melville, Twain and the Holy Land Mania*. Princeton and Chichester: Princeton University Press.

STAVANS, Ilan, ed. 1994. *Tropical Synagogues: Short Stories*. Edited by Ilan Stavans. New York: Holmes & Meier.

TOBIAS, Henry. 1972. *The Jewish Bund in Russia from Its Origins to 1905*. Stanford: Stanford University Press.

WAIFE-GOLDBERG, Marie. 1968. *My Father, Sholom Aleichem*. London: Gollancz.

Memoirs/Fiction

APPELFELD, Aharon. 1981. *The Age of Wonders*. Boston, MA: Godine.

———. 1981. *Badenheim 39*. Translated by Dalya Bilu. London: Dent.

———. 1985. *The Retreat*. Translated by Dalya Bilu. London: Quartet.

———. 1986. *To the Land of the Cattails*. Translated by Jeffrey M. Green. New York: Grove.

———. 1988. *The Immortal Bartfuss*. Translated by Jeffrey M. Green. New York: Weidenfeld & Nicolson.

———. 1989. *For Every Sin*. Translated by Jeffrey M. Green. New York: Weidenfeld & Nicolson.

———. 1990. *The Healer*. Translated by Jeffrey M. Green. London: Weidenfeld & Nicolson.

———. 1992. *Katerina*. Translated by Jeffrey M. Green. New York: Random House.

———. 1994. *Beyond Despair: Three Lectures and a Conversation with Philip Roth*. Translated by Jeffrey M. Green. New York: Fromm International.

———. 1994. *Unto the Soul*. Translated by Jeffrey M. Green. New York: Random House

———. 2005. *A Table for One: Under the Light of Jerusalem*. Translated by Aloma Halter. London and New Milford, CT: Toby.

ARIKHA, Alba. 2011. *Major/Minor: A Memoir*. London: Quartet.

BARON, Alexander. 1948. *From the City, From the Plough*. London: Jonathan Cape.

———. 1963. *The Lowlife*. London: Collins.

CHEEVER, Susan. 1984. *Home before Dark*. London: Weidenfeld & Nicolson.

FICOWSKI, Jerzy. 2003. *Regions of the Great Heresy: Bruno Schultz, A Biographical Portrait*. New York and London: W. W. Norton.

GOLDING, Judy. 2011. *The Children of Lovers: A Memoir of William Golding by His Daughter*. London: Faber & Faber.

GROSSMAN, David. 1988. *The Yellow Wind*. Translated by Haim Watzman. London: Jonathan Cape.

———. 1990. *See Under: Love*. Translated by Betsy Rosenberg. London: Jonathan Cape.

———. 1991. *The Smile of the Lamb*. Translated by Betsy Rosenberg. London: Jonathan Cape.

———. 1993. *Sleeping on a Wire: Conversations with Palestinians in Israel*. Translated by Haim Watzman. London: Jonathan Cape.

———. 2008. *Writing in the Dark*. Translated by Jessica Cohen. London: Bloomsbury.

KANIUK, Yoram. 1988. *His Daughter*. Translated by Seymour Simckes. London: Halban

KOSINSKI, Jerzy. 1967. *The Painted Bird*. London: Corgi.

———. 1970. *Being There*. London: Bodley Head.

———. 1988. *The Hermit of 69th Street: The Working Papers of Norbert Kosky*. New York: Seaver.

———. 1992. *Passing By: Selected Essays, 1962–1991*. New York: Random House.

KREITMAN, Esther. 1983. *Deborah*. Translated by Maurice Carr. London: Virago.

MAIMON, Solomon. 1954. *Solomon Maimon: Autobiography*. Translated by J. Clark Murray. London: East and West Library.

MALAMUD, Bernard. 1983. *Pictures of Fidelman: An Exhibition*. London: Chatto & Windus.

MARKS, Dennis,. 2011. *Wandering Jew: The Search for Joseph Roth*. London: Notting Hill Editions.

MAYER, Musa. 1991. *Night Studio: A Memoir of Philip Guston*. London: Thames & Hudson

MEGGED, Aharon. 1970. *The Living on the Dead*. Translated by Misha Louvis. London: Jonathan Cape.

———. 2003. *Foiglman*. Translated by Marganit Weinberger-Rotman. London and New Milford, CT: Toby.

MICHAEL, Sami. 1995. *Victoria*. Translated by Dalya Bilu. London: Macmillan.

OZ, Amos. 1985. *The Hill of Evil Counsel: Three Stories*. Translated by Nicholas de Lange, in collaboration with the author. London: Flamingo.

———. 1995. *Don't Call It Night*. Translated by Nicholas de Lange. London: Chatto & Windus.

———. 2004. *Tale of Love and Darkness*. Translated by Nicholas de Lange. London: Chatto & Windus.

OZICK, Cynthia. 1987. *The Messiah of Stockholm*. London: Andre Deutsch.

RAFFEL, Burton, trans. 2004. *Pure Pagan: Seven Centuries of Greek Poems and Fragments*. New York: Modern Library.

RAPHAEL, Chaim [Jocelyn Davey, pseud.]. 1956. *The Undoubted Deed*. London: Chatto & Windus.

———. 1962. *Memoirs of a Special Case*. London: Chatto & Windus.

———. 1972. *A Feast of History: The Drama of Passover through the Ages*. Weidenfeld & Nicolson.

———. 1979. *A Coat of Many Colours: Memoirs of a Jewish Experience*. London: Chatto & Windus.

———. 1992. *Minyan: Ten Jewish Lives in 20 Centuries of History*. Malibu: Simon/Pangloss.

ROTH, Joseph. 1974. *The Radetzky March*. Translated by Eva Tucker, based on an earlier translation by Geoffrey Dunlop. London: Allen Lane.

———. 1983. *Job: The Story of a Simple Man*. Translated by Dorothy Thompson. London: Chatto & Windus.

SCHULZ, Bruno. 1980. *Sanatorium under the Sign of the Hourglass*. Translated by Celina Wieniewska. London: Pan Books.

———. 1988. *The Booke of Idolatry*. Edited by Jerzy Ficowski. Translated by Bogna Piotrowska. Warsaw: Interpress.

———. 1988. *The Street of Crocodiles*. Translated by Celina Wieniewska. London: Picador.

SINCLAIR, Clive. 1983. *The Brothers Singer*. London: Allison & Busby.

———. 1987. *Diaspora Blues: A View of Israel*. London: Heinemann.

SINGER, Isaac Bashevis. 1972. *Enemies: A Love Story*. Translated by Aliza Shevrin and Elizabeth Shub. London: Jonathan Cape.

————. 1973. *The Slave*. Translated by the author and Cecil Hemley. London: Jonathan Cape.

————. 1976. *A Little Boy in Search of God: Mysticism in a Personal Light*. Garden City, NY: Doubleday.

————. 1978. *A Young Man in Search of Love*. Garden City, NY: Doubleday.

————. 1980. *Old Love*. London: Jonathan Cape.

————. 1981. *Gimpel the Fool, and Other Tales*. Harmondsworth: Penguin.

————. 1981. *Lost in America*. Garden City, NY: Doubleday.

SMITH, Janna Malamud. 2006. *My Father Is a Book: A Memoir of Bernard Malamud*. Boston, MA: Houghton Mifflin.

STYRON, Alexandra. 2011. *Reading My Father: A Memoir*. New York and London: Scribner.

WILKOMIRSKI, Binjamin. 1996. *Fragments: Memories of a Childhood, 1939–1948*. Translated by Carol Brown Janeway. London: Picador.

YEHOSHUA, A. B. 1988. *The Continuing Silence of a Poet*. London: Halban.

Poetry/Film

ABSE, Dannie. 2007. *The Presence*. London: Hutchinson.

————. 2009. *New Selected Poems, 1949–2009*. London: Hutchinson.

BARTHES, Roland. 2009. *Journal de deuil*. Paris: Seuil.

CHAPMAN, Abraham, ed. 1974. *Jewish-American Literature: An Anthology of Fiction, Poetry, Autobiography, and Criticism*. New York and London: New American Library.

DEGUY, Michel. 1993. *Aux heures d'affluence: Poèmes et proses*. Paris: Seuil.

————, Bernard Cuau, Rachel Ertel, et al. 1990. *Au sujet de shoah: Le film de Claude Lanzmann*. Paris: Belin.

DRACHLER, Rose. 1983. *The Collected Poems of Rose Drachler*. Edited by Jacob Drachler. New York: Assembling Press.

KERTÉSZ, Imre. 1992. *Fateless*. Translated by Christopher C. Wilson and Katharina M. Wilson. Evanston, IL: Northwestern University Press.

————. 2010. *Kaddish for an Unborn Child*. Translated by Tim Wilkinson. London: Vintage.

LANZMANN, Claude. 1985. *Shoah*. Paris: Gallimard.

LUSTIG, Arnost. 1990. *A Prayer for Katerina Horovitzova*. Translated by J. Němcová. London: Quartet.

ROTHENBERG, Jerome. 1971. *A Book of Testimony*. Bolinas, CA: Tree Books.

————. 1974. *Esther K. Comes to America*. Greensboro, NC: Unicorn.

————. 1974. *Poland/1931*. New York: New Directions.

————. 1976. *The Notebooks*. Milwaukee, WI: Membrane.

————. 1989. *Khurbn*. New York: New Directions.

————. 1994. *Gematria*. Los Angeles: Sun & Moon Press.

————, and Harris Lenowitz, eds. 1989. *Exiled in the Word: Poems and Other Visions of the Jews from Tribal Times to Present*. Port Townsend, WA: Copper Canyon.

————, Harris Lenowitz and Charles Doria, eds. 1978. *A Big Jewish Book: Poems and Other Visions of the Jews from Tribal Times to Present*. Garden City, NY: Anchor.

RUKEYSER, Muriel. 1996. *The Life of Poetry*. Williamsburg, MA: Paris Press.

SIMONOVIC, Ifigenija. 1996. *Striking Root*. Translated by Anthony Rudolf and the author. London: Menard.

SULEIMAN, Susan Rubin, and Éva Forgács, eds. 2003. *Contemporary Jewish Writing in Hungary: An Anthology*. Lincoln: University of Nebraska Press.

POETRY

Introduction (1), (2), (3)

CANETTI, Elias. 1998. *Notes from Hampstead*. Translated by John Hargraves. New York: Farrar, Straus & Giroux.

CLARK, Tom. 1969. *Stones: Poems*. New York and London: Harper & Row.

DOUGLAS, Keith. 1966. *Collected Poems*. Edited by John Waller, G. S. Fraser and J. C. Hall. London: Faber & Faber.

————. 1992. *Alamein to Zem Zem*. Edited by Desmond Graham. London: Faber & Faber.

GRAHAM, Desmond. 1974. *Keith Douglas, 1920–1944: A Biography*. London: Oxford University Press.

HESSE, Hermann. 1971. *Poems*. Translated by James Wright. London: Jonathan Cape.

———. 1972. *Wandering: Notes and Sketches*. Translated by James Wright. London: Jonathan Cape.

JOSEPH, Jenny. 1997. *Extended Similes*. Newcastle-upon-Tyne: Bloodaxe Books.

ROETHKE, Theodore. 1965. *On the Poet and His Craft: Selected Prose of Theodore Roethke*. Edited by Ralph J. Mills. Seattle and London: University of Washington Press.

———. 1968. *Collected Poems*. London: Faber & Faber.

———. 1970. *Selected Letters*. Edited by Ralph J. Mills. London: Faber & Faber.

———. 1972. *Straw for the Fire: From the Notebooks of Theodore Roethke, 1943–63*. Selected and arranged by David Wagoner. Garden City, NY: Doubleday.

RUDOLF, Anthony. 1999. *The Arithmetic of Memory*. London: Bellew.

WRIGHT, James. 1972. *Collected Poems*. Middletown, CT: Wesleyan University Press.

British Poets: Inscriptions and Other Memories

AUSTER, Paul. 1988. *The Invention of Solitude*. London: Faber & Faber.

BARNETT, Anthony. 2012. *Poems &*. Lewes, East Sussex: Tears in the Fence/Allardyce Book.

———. 2012. *Translations*. Lewes, East Sussex: Tears in the Fence/Allardyce Book.

BARRELL, John. 1972. *The Idea of Landscape and the Sense of Place, 1730–1830: An Approach to the Poetry of John Clare*. Cambridge: Cambridge University Press.

———. 1988. *Poetry, Language and Politics*. Manchester: Manchester University Press.

BENSON, Judi. 2006. *The Thin Places*. Ware, Herts: Rockingham.

BERENGARTEN, Richard. 1972. *Avebury*. London: Anvil Press Poetry

———. 1981. *Keys to Transformation: Ceri Richards and Dylan Thomas*. London: Enitharmon.

———. 2001. *The Manager: A Poem*. London: Elliott & Thompson.

———. 2006. *The Blue Butterfly*. Cambridge, MA: Salt.

BONNEFOY, Yves. 1958. *Du Mouvement et de l'immobilité de Douve*. Paris: Mercure de France.

———. 1998. *L'Arrière-pays*. Paris: Gallimard.

———. 2012. *The Arrière-pays*. Translated with an introduction and notes by Stephen Romer. London: Seagull Books.

BORGES, Jorge Luis. 1998. *Conversations*. Edited by Richard Burgin. Jackson: University Press of Mississippi.

BRETON, André. 1964. *Nadja*. Paris: Gallimard.

———. 1966. *L'Amour fou*. Paris: Gallimard.

———. 1971. *Arcane 17*. Paris: Pauvert.

———, and Philippe Soupault. 1985. *The Magnetic Fields*. Translated by David Gascoyne. London: Atlas.

BURNSIDE, John. 1992. *Feast Days*. London: Secker & Warburg.

COXHEAD, David. 1968. *Run Come See Jerusalem: A Novel*. London: Peter Owen.

CROZIER, Andrew. 1985. *All Where Each Is*. Edinburgh: Agneau 2.

———. 2008. *Star Ground*. Lewes: Silver Hounds.

DAVIE, Donald. 1955. *Articulate Energy: An Enquiry into the Syntax of English Poetry*. London: Routledge & Kegan Paul.

———, ed. 1958. *The Late Augustans: Longer Poems of the Later Eighteenth Century*. London: Heinemann.

———. 1965. *Ezra Pound: Poet as Sculptor*. Oxford and New York: Oxford University Press.

———, trans. 1965. *Poems of Doctor Zhivago*. Manchester: Manchester University Press.

———. 1967. *Purity of Diction in English Verse*. London: Routledge & Kegan Paul.

———. 1975. *Pound*. London: Fontana Books.

———. 1982. *These the Companions: Recollections.* Cambridge: Cambridge University Press.

———. 2002. *Collected Poems.* Edited by Neil Powell. Manchester: Carcanet.

DICK, John-Paul. 1983. *Homing: Poems.* London: Menard.

DUTTON, Geoffrey. 1994. *Harvesting the Edge: Some Personal Explorations from a Marginal Garden.* London: Menard.

FEINSTEIN, Elaine. 2001. *Ted Hughes: The Life of a Poet.* London: Weidenfeld & Nicolson.

———. 2008. *Russian Jerusalem.* Manchester: Carcanet.

FISHER, Roy. 1969. *Collected Poems.* London: Fulcrum.

FORREST-THOMSON, Veronica. 1990. *Collected Poems and Translations.* London: Allardyce, Barnett.

GASCOYNE, David. 1965. *Collected Poems.* Translated by Robin Skelton. Oxford and New York: Oxford University Press

———. 1970. *Collected Verse Translations.* London and New York: Oxford University Press.

———. 1982. *A Short Survey of Surrealism.* 2nd edn. San Francisco: City Lights.

———. 2001. *Existential Writings.* Oxford: Amate.

GLAZE, Andrew. 1998. *Someone Will Go On Owing: Selected Poems, 1966–1992.* Montgomery, AL: Black Belt.

GLOVER, Jon. 1994. *To the Niagara Frontier: Poems New and Selected.* Manchester: Carcanet.

———. 2008. *Magnetic Resonance Imaging.* Manchester: Carcanet.

———. 2012. *Glass Is Elastic.* Manchester: Carcanet.

GRAHAM, W. S. 1979. *Collected Poems, 1942–1977.* London: Faber & Faber.

GRAVES, Robert. 1961. *The White Goddess: A Historical Grammar of Poetic Myth.* London: Faber & Faber.

GUEST, Harry. 2010. *Some Times.* London: Anvil Press Poetry.

GUNN, Thom. 1993. *Collected Poems.* London: Faber & Faber.

HAMBURGER, Michael, trans. 1981. *An Unofficial Rilke: Poems, 1912–1926.* London: Anvil Press Poetry.

———. 1984. *Collected Poems*. Manchester: Carcanet.

———, trans. 1988. *Poems of Paul Celan*. London: Anvil Press Poetry.

HILL, Geoffrey. 1985. *Collected Poems*. London: Penguin.

———. 2006. *Without Title*. London and New York: Penguin.

HOLMES, Richard, ed. 1996. *Coleridge: Selected Poems*. London: Penguin.

HOWELL, Anthony. 2000. *Selected Poems*. London: Anvil Press Poetry.

———. 2001. *Spending: Poems*. London: Menard/Medames.

HUGHES, Ted, 1968. *The Iron Man*. London: Faber & Faber.

———. 1971. *A Choice of Shakespeare's Verse*. London: Faber & Faber.

———. 1992. *Shakespeare and the Goddess of Complete Being*. London: Faber & Faber.

———. 2003. *Collected Poems*. Edited by Paul Keegan. London: Faber & Faber.

———. 2006. *Selected Translations*. Edited by Daniel Weissbort. London: Faber & Faber.

———. 2007. *Letters of Ted Hughes*. Edited by Christopher Reid. London: Faber & Faber.

JACKSON, H. J. 2001. *Marginalia: Readers Writing in Books*. New Haven, CT, and London: Yale University Press.

JACKSON, W. D. 2002. *Then and Now: Words in the Dark*. London: Menard.

———. 2005. *From Now to Then*. London: Menard in association with School of Humanities, King's College.

LAFITTE, Nicholas. 1992. *Near Calvary: Selected Poems 1959–1970*. London: Many Press.

LOWENSTEIN, Tom. 1973. *Eskimo Poems from Canada and Greenland*. London: Allison & Busby.

———, trans. 1977. *The Death of Mrs Owl*. London: Anvil Press Poetry.

LYNCH, Brian. 2005. *The Winner of Sorrow*. Dublin: New Island.

MACSWEENEY, Barry. 1970. *Elegy for January*. London: Menard.

MIDDLETON, Christopher. 2004. *Palavers: Christopher Middleton in Conversation with Marius Kociejowski; and, A Nocturnal Journal*. Exeter: Shearsman Books.

———. 2008. *Collected Poems*. Manchester: Carcanet.

MOORE, Nicholas. 1944. *The Glass Tower*. London: Poetry London.

———. 1950. *Recollections of the Gala: Selected Poems, 1943–1948*. London: Editions Poetry.

———. 1988. *Longings of the Acrobat: Selected Poems*. Edited by Peter Riley. Manchester: Carcanet.

———. 1990. *Spleen (Le Roi Roi Bonhomme): 31 Versions of Baudelaire's 'Je suis comme le roi'*. Edited by Anthony Rudolf. London: Menard.

MURRAY, Nicholas. 2010. *The Sweet Red Wine of Youth*. London: Little, Brown.

PLATH, Sylvia. 1965. *Ariel*. London: Faber & Faber.

———. 1967. *The Bell Jar*. London: Faber & Faber.

———. 1967. *The Colossus*. London: Faber & Faber.

PORTER, Peter. 1983. *Collected Poems*. Oxford: Oxford University Press.

POUND, Ezra. 1951. *ABC of Reading*. London: Faber & Faber.

PRINCE, F. T. 1962. *The Italian Element in Milton's Verse*. Oxford: Clarendon.

———. 1993. *Collected Poems*. Manchester: Carcanet.

PYBUS, Rodney. 1973. *In Memoriam Milena*. London: Chatto & Windus.

———. 2012. *Darkness Inside Out*. Manchester: Carcanet.

READ, Herbert, ed. 1936. *Surrealism*. London: Faber & Faber.

REED, Henry. 1946. *A Map of Verona*. London: Jonathan Cape.

RUSSELL, Peter. 1996. *The Elegies of Quintilius*. London: Anvil Press Poetry.

RUDOLF, Anthony, ed. 1976. *Poems for Shakespeare 4*. London: Globe Playhouse Trust.

SEBALD, W. G. 1999. *The Rings of Saturn*. Translated by Michael Hulse. London: Harvill.

SILKIN, Jon. 1972. *Out of Battle: The Poetry of the Great War*. London: Oxford University Press.

———, ed. 1973. *Poetry of the Committed Individual: A 'Stand' Anthology of Poetry*. Harmondsworth: Penguin.

———, ed. 1979. *Penguin Book of First World War Poetry*. Harmondsworth: Penguin.

———. 1980. *The Psalms and Their Spoils*. London: Routledge & Kegan Paul.

———. 1986. *The Ship's Pasture*. London: Routledge & Kegan Paul.

———. 2002. *Making a Republic*. London: Routledge & Kegan Paul.

———, and Jon Glover, eds. 1989. *The Penguin Book of First World War Prose*. London: Penguin.

SMITH, Ken. 1982. *The Poet Reclining: Selected Poems, 1962–1980*. Newcastle-upon-Tyne: Bloodaxe Books.

———. 1989. *Inside Time*. London: Harrap.

———. 1990. *Berlin: Coming in from the Cold*. London: Hamish Hamilton.

———. 2002. *Shed: Poems, 1980–2001*. Tarset: Bloodaxe Books.

———. 2004. *You Again: Last Poems and Tributes*. Tarset: Bloodaxe Books.

———, and Judi Benson, eds. 1993. *Klaonica: Poems for Bosnia*. Newcastle-upon-Tyne: Bloodaxe Books.

———, and Matthew Sweeney, eds. 1997. *Beyond Bedlam: Poems Written out of Mental Distress*. London: Anvil Press Poetry.

STEAD, C. K. 2006. *My Name Was Judas*. London: Harvill Secker.

STEINER, George. 2003. *Lessons of the Masters*. Cambridge, MA: Harvard University Press.

TOMLINSON, Charles. 1972. *Words and Images*. London: Covent Garden Press.

———. 1976. *In Black and White: The Graphics of Charles Tomlinson*. Cheadle: Carcanet.

———. 1985. *Collected Poems*. Oxford: Oxford University Press.

———. 2003. *Metamorphoses: Poetry and Translation*. Manchester: Carcanet.

TURNBULL, Gael. 1965. *A Very Particular Hill*. Edinburgh: Wild Hawthorn.

———. 2006. *There Are Words*. Edinburgh: Mariscat.

WAINWRIGHT, Jeffrey. 2008. *Clarity or Death*. Manchester: Carcanet.

WARREN, Rosanna. 2008. *Fables of the Self: Studies in Lyric Poetry*. New York and London: W. W. Norton.

WEISSBORT, Daniel. 2011. *Ted Hughes and Translation*. Nottingham: Five Leaves.

American Poets

ALEXANDER, Michael. 1979. *The Poetic Achievement of Ezra Pound*. London: Faber & Faber.

ALLEN, Donald. 1960. *The New American Poetry, 1945–1960*. New York: Grove.

BAKER, Deborah. 1993. *In Extremis*: *The Life of Laura Riding*. London: Hamish Hamilton.

BATES, Milton. 1985. *Wallace Stevens*: *A Mythology of Self.* Berkeley and London: University of California Press.

BERRYMAN, John. 1973. *Recovery*. London: Faber & Faber.

———. 1990. *Collected Poems, 1937–1971*. London: Faber & Faber.

BISHOP, Elizabeth. 1969. *Complete Poems*. London: Chatto & Windus.

———. 2006. *Edgar Allan Poe and The Jukebox*: *Uncollected Poems, Drafts and Fragments*. Manchester: Carcanet.

BRANDON, Ruth. 1999. *Surreal Lives*: *The Surrealists, 1917–1945*. London: Macmillan

BUNTING, Basil. 1978. *Collected Poems*. 2nd edn. Oxford: Oxford University Press.

———. 1991. *Uncollected Poems*. Oxford: Oxford University Press.

CARVER, Raymond. 1982. *What We Talk about When We Talk about Love*. London: Collins.

———. 1991. *No Heroics, Please*: *Uncollected Writings*. Edited by William L. Stull. London: Harvill.

———. 1996. *All of Us*: *The Collected Poems*. London: Harvill.

CREELEY, Robert. 1964. *The Island*. London: Calder.

———. 1965. *The Gold Diggers, and Other Stories*. London: Calder.

———. 2006. *The Collected Poems of Robert Creeley*. Berkeley and London: University of California Press.

DORN, Edward. 1961. *The Newly Fallen*. New York: Totem.

———. 1964. *Hands Up*. New York: Totem.

———. 1965. *Geography*. London: Fulcrum.

———. 1970. *Gunslinger*. BOOKS 1 and 2. London: Fulcrum.

DUNCAN, Robert. 1960. *The Opening of the Field*. New York: Grove.

———. 1966. *The Years as Catches: First Poems*. Berkeley, CA: Oyez.

———. 1968. *The Truth and Life of Myth: An Essay in Essential Autobiography*. Fremont, MI: Sumac.

———. 1970. *Roots and Branches: Poems*. London: Jonathan Cape.

———. 1971. *Bending the Bow*. London: Jonathan Cape.

DUPLESSIS, Rachel Blau, and Peter Quatermain, eds. 1999. *The Objectivist Nexus: Essays in Cultural Poetics*. Tuscaloosa and London: University of Alabama Press.

ELIOT, T. S. 1971. *The Waste Land: A Facsimile and Transcript of the Original Drafts, including the Annotations of Ezra Pound*. Edited by Valerie Eliot. London: Faber & Faber.

———. 1996. *Inventions of the March Hare*. Edited by Christopher Ricks. London: Faber & Faber.

FEINSTEIN, Elaine. 1986. *Badlands*. London: Hutchinson.

FIELD, Edward. 1998. *A Frieze for a Temple of Love*. Santa Rosa, CA: Black Sparrow.

FORCHÉ, Caroline. 1994. *The Angel of History*. Newcastle-upon-Tyne: Bloodaxe Books.

GINZBURG, Natalia. 1973. *Never Must You Ask Me*. Translated by Isabel Quigly. London: Joseph.

HAMMARSKJOLD, Dag. 1964. *Markings*. Translated by Leif Sjöberg and W. H. Auden. London: Faber & Faber.

HAWLEY, Beatrice. 1989. *The Collected Poems of Beatrice Hawley*. Edited by Denise Levertov. Cambridge, MA: Zoland.

HELLER, Michael. 1985. *Conviction's Net of Branches: Essays on the Objectivist Poets and Poetry*. Carbondale: Southern Illinois University Press.

———. 2008. *Speaking the Estranged: Essays on the Work of George Oppen*. Cambridge, MA: Salt.

HINDUS, Milton. 1977. *Charles Reznikoff: A Critical Essay*. London: Menard.

JONES, David. 1937. *In Parenthesis: Seinnyessit e Gledyf ym Penn Mameu*. London: Faber & Faber.

———. 1959. *Epoch and Artist: Selected Writings*. Edited by Harman Grisewood. London: Faber & Faber.

———. 1972. *The Anathemata: Fragments of an Attempted Writing*. London: Faber & Faber.

KALSTONE, David. 1989. *Becoming a Poet: Elizabeth Bishop with Marianne Moore and Robert Lowell*. Edited by Robert Hemenway. London: Hogarth.

KENNER, Hugh. 1959. *Art of Poetry*. New York: Rinehart.

LEAVIS, F. R. 1963. *New Bearings in English Poetry: A Study of the Contemporary Situation*. Harmondsworth: Penguin.

———. 1969. *Lectures in America*. London: Chatto & Windus.

LEVERTOV, Denise. 1959. *With Eyes at the Back of Our Heads*. New York: New Directions.

———. 1965. *The Jacob's Ladder*. London: Jonathan Cape.

———. 1968. *The Sorrow Dance*. London: Jonathan Cape.

———. 1970. *Relearning the Alphabet*. London: Jonathan Cape.

———. 1971. *To Stay Alive*. New York: New Directions.

———. 1972. *Footprints*. New York: New Directions.

———. 1975. *The Freeing of the Dust*. New York: New Directions.

———. 1986. *Oblique Prayers*. Newcastle-upon-Tyne: Bloodaxe Books.

———. 2001. *This Great Unknowing: Last Poems*. Tarset: Bloodaxe Books.

LOWELL, Robert. 2003. *Collected Poems*. Translated by Frank Bidart and David Gewanter. London: Faber & Faber.

———. 2005. *The Letters of Robert Lowell*. Translated by Saskia Hamilton. London: Faber & Faber.

LOWENFELS, Walter, ed. 1967. *Where Is Vietnam?: American Poets Respond; An Anthology of Contemporary Poems*. Garden City, NY: Anchor.

MAILER, Norman. 1971. *Armies of the Night: History as a Novel, the Novel as History*. Harmondsworth: Penguin.

MARITAIN, Jacques. 1945. *Art and Poetry*. London: Poetry London.

MONTAGUE, John. 1989. *The Figure in the Cave and Other Essays*. Edited by Antoinette Quinn. Dublin: Lilliput.

MOORE, Marianne. 1951. *Collected Poems*. London: Faber & Faber.

———. 1955. *Selected Fables of La Fontaine*. London: Faber & Faber.

O'BRIEN, Geoffrey, ed. 2004. *Bartlet's Poems for Occasions.* New York: Little, Brown.

OLSON, Charles. 1960. *The Maximus Poems.* London: Cape Goliard.

———. 1967. *Call Me Ishmael.* London: Jonathan Cape.

———. 1968. *Mayan Letters.* Edited by Robert Creeley. London: Jonathan Cape.

———. 1969. *Letters for Origin, 1950–1956.* Edited by Albert Grover. London: Jonathan Cape Goliard.

———. 1970. *Archaeologist of Morning.* London: Cape Goliard.

———, and Robert Creeley. 1980–1990. *Charles Olson and Robert Creeley: The Complete Correspondence.* Edited by George F. Butterick. 10 VOLS. Santa Barbara, CA: Black Sparrow.

OPPEN, George. 1981. *George Oppen: Man and Poet.* Edited by Burten Hatlen. Orono, ME: National Poetry Foundation.

———. 2003. *New Collected Poems.* Edited by Michael Davidson. Manchester: Carcanet.

OPPENHEIMER, Joel. 1962. *The Love Bit, and Other Poems.* New York: Totem in association with Corinth.

PICKARD, Tom. 2010. *More Pricks than Prizes.* Boston, MA: Pressed Wafer.

POUND, Ezra. 1951. *The Letters of Ezra Pound, 1907–1941.* Edited by D. D. Paige. London: Faber & Faber.

———. 1953. *The Translations of Ezra Pound.* Edited by Hugh Kenner. London: Faber & Faber.

———. 1954. *Literary Essays of Ezra Pound.* Edited by T. S. Eliot. London: Faber & Faber.

RAKOSI, Carl. 1986. *The Collected Poems of Carl Rokosi.* Orono: National Poetry Foundation, University of Maine.

———. 1995. *Poems, 1923–1941.* Edited by Andrew Crozier. Los Angeles: Sun & Moon Press.

REXROTH, Kenneth. 1971. *American Poetry in the Twentieth Century.* New York: Herder & Herder.

REZNIKOFF, Charles. 1944. *The Lionhearted: A Story about the Jews in Medieval England.* Philadelphia, PA: Jewish Publication Society of America.

———. 1967–77. *Complete Poems of Charles Reznikoff.* Edited by Seamus Cooney. 2 VOLS. Santa Barbara, CA: Black Sparrow.

———. 1969. *Family Chronicle.* London: Norton Bailey.

———. 1975. *Holocaust.* Los Angeles: Black Sparrow.

———. 1977. *The Manner Music.* Santa Barbara, CA: Black Sparrow.

RICH, Adrienne. 1970. *Snapshots of a Daughter-in-Law.* London: Chatto & Windus.

———. 1986. *Your Native Land, Your Life: Poems.* New York and London: W. W. Norton.

———. 2004. *The School among the Ruins.* New York and London: W. W. Norton.

———. 2009. *A Human Eye: Essays on Art in Society, 1996–2008.* New York and London: W. W. Norton.

SCHWARTZ, Delmore. 1978. *In Dreams Begin Responsibilities and Other Stories.* London: Secker & Warburg.

SEPTEMBER, Dee. 1979. *Making Waves.* Toronto: Unfinished Monument Press.

SEXTON, Anne. 1967. *Live or Die.* London: Oxford University Press.

———. 1976. *45 Mercy Street: Poems.* London: Secker & Warburg.

———. 1979. *Love Poems.* London: Oxford University Press.

SIMPSON, Eileen. 1982. *Poets in Their Youth: A Memoir.* London: Faber & Faber.

SIMPSON, Louis. 1968. *An Introduction to Poetry.* London: Macmillan.

———. 1978. *A Revolution in Taste: Studies of Dylan Thomas, Allen Ginsberg, Sylvia Plath, and Robert Lowell.* New York: Macmillan.

SNYDER, Gary. 1970. *Earth House Hold: Technical Notes and Queries to Fellow Dharma Revolutionaries.* London: Jonathan Cape.

———. 1972. *Regarding Wave.* London: Fulcrum.

SORRENTINO, Gilbert. 1964. *Black and White.* New York: Totem.

SPAAR, Lisa Russ. 2008. *Satin Cash: Poems.* New York: Persea.

SPICER, Jack. 1975. *The Collected Books of Jack Spicer.* Edited by Robin Blaser. Los Angeles: Black Sparrow.

STEIN, Gertrude. 1933. *The Autobiography of Alice B. Toklas.* London: Allen Lane.

————. 1995. *The Geographical History of America; or, The Relation of Human Nature to the Human Mind*. Baltimore, MD: Johns Hopkins University Press.

————. 1971. *Look at Me Now and Here I Am*. Edited by Patricia Meyerovitz. Harmondsworth: Penguin.

STEVENS, Wallace. 1955. *The Collected Poems of Wallace Stevens*. London: Faber & Faber.

————, and José Rodriguez Feo. 1986. *Secretaries of the Moon: The Letters of Wallace Stevens and Jose Rodriguez Feo*. Edited by Beverly Coyle and Alan Filreis. Durham, NC: Duke University Press.

STRAND, Mark. 1968. *Reasons for Moving: Poems*. New York: Atheneum.

————. 1970. *Darker: Poems*. New York: Atheneum.

————. 2006. *Man and Camel: Poems*. New York: Alfred A. Knopf.

SULLIVAN, J. P. 1964. *Ezra Pound and Sextus Propertius: A Study in Creative Translation*. London: Faber & Faber.

WARREN, Rosanna. 2011. *Ghost in a Red Hat: Poems*. New York: W. W. Norton.

WESTON, Susan. 1977. *Wallace Stevens: An Introduction to the Poetry*. New York and Guildford: Columbia University Press.

WIENERS, John. 1958. *The Hotel Wentley Poems*. San Francisco: Auerhahn.

————. 1964. *Ace of Pentacles*. New York: Carr & Wilson.

————. 1990. *Nerves*. London: Cape Goliard.

————. 1996. *The Journal of John Wieners Is to Be Called 707 Scott Street for Billie Holiday, 1959*. Los Angeles: Sun & Moon Press.

————. 2011. *Strictly Illegal*. Yapton: Artery Editions.

WILLIAMS, William Carlos. 1957. *Kora in Hell: Improvisations*. San Francisco: City Lights.

————. 1967. *I Wanted to Write a Poem: The Autobiography of the Works of a Poet*. Edited by Edith Heal. London: Jonathan Cape.

————. 1987–1988. *The Collected Poems of William Carlos Williams*. Edited by A. Walton Litz and Christopher MacGowan. 2 VOLS. Manchester: Carcanet.

ZUKOFSKY, Louis. 1952. *A Test of Poetry*. London: Routledge & Kegan Paul.

———. 1966. *All: The Collected Short Poems, 1923–1958*. London: Jonathan Cape.

———. 1993. *A*. Baltimore, MD, and London: Johns Hopkins University Press.

Anthologies

BRIDGES, Robert. 1921. *The Spirit of Man: An Anthology in English and French*. London: Longmans, Green & Co.

FERNANDEZ, Pablo Armando. 2011. *Parables: Selected Poems*. Oakville and Niagara Falls: Mosaic.

FORCHÉ, Caroline, ed. 1993. *Against Forgetting: Twentieth-Century Poetry of Witness*. New York and London: W. W. Norton.

READ, Herbert, ed. 1939. *The Knapsack: A Pocket-Book of Prose and Verse*. London: Routledge.

RIVERO, Isel. 2003. *Relato del Horizonte*. Madrid: Ediciones Endymion.

ROTHENBERG, Jerome, ed. 1969. *Technicians of the Sacred: A Range of Poetries from Africa, America, Asia, and Oceania*. Garden City, NY: Doubleday.

———. 1974. *Revolution of the Word: A New Gathering of American Avant Garde Poetry, 1914–1945*. New York: Seabury.

———, and George Quasha, eds. 1974. *America a Prophecy: A New Reading of American Poetry from Pre-Columbian Times to the Present*. New York: Vintage.

SIMPSON, Louis. 1972. *Air with Armed Men*. London: London Magazine Editions.

———. 1988. *Collected Poems*. New York: Paragon House.

SINGH, G., ed. 1994. *The Sayings of Ezra Pound*. London: Duckworth.

TARN, Nathaniel, ed. 1969. *Con Cuba*. London: Cape Goliard.

Small Presses

BATE, Jonathan. 2000. *The Song of the Earth*. London: Picador.

CARDENAL, Ernesto. 1988. *Nicaraguan New Time*. Translated by Dinah Livingstone. London: Journeyman.

CHILDISH, Billy. 1983. *Ten No Good Poems of Slavery Buggery Boredom and Disrespect*. Chatham: Hangman.

FELSTINER, John. 2009. *Can Poetry Save the Earth? A Field Guide to Nature Poems*. New Haven, CT, and London: Yale University Press.

LEWIS, Bill. 2003. *Blackberry Ghosts: Collected Poems*. Chatham: Urban Fox.

LIVINGSTONE, Dinah. 1993. *Second Sight: 33 Poems*. London: Katabasis.

———. 2000. *Poetry of Earth*. London: Katabasis.

MILLER, David. 1997. *Collected Poems*. Salzburg and Oxford: University of Salzburg.

UPTON, Lawrence. 2003. *Wire Sculptures*. London: Reality Street Street.

WALDROP, Rosmarie, and Keith Waldrop. 1973. *Words Worth Less*. Providence, RI: Burning Deck.

———. 2002. *Ceci n'est pas Keith—Ceci n'est pas Rosmarie: Autobiographies*. Providence, RI: Burning Deck.

WELCH, John. 1991. *Blood and Dreams*. London: Reality Studios.

Ireland and Scotland

DURCAN, Paul. 1985. *The Berlin Wall Café*. Belfast: Blackstaff.

HEANEY, Seamus. 1975. *North*. London: Faber & Faber.

———. 1999a. *Diary of One Who Vanished: A Song Cycle by Leos Janacek*. London: Faber & Faber.

———, trans. 1999b. *Beowulf*. London: Faber & Faber.

———. 2002. *Finders Keepers: Selected Prose, 1971–2001*. London: Faber & Faber.

KINSELLA, Thomas. 1972. *Notes from the Land of the Dead: Poems*. Dublin: Cuala.

LONGLEY, Michael. 1991. *Poems, 1963–1983*. London: Secker & Warburg.

MACDIARMID, Hugh. 1962. *Collected Poems of Hugh MacDiarmid*. New York: Macmillan.

MACGREEVY, Thomas. 1971. *Collected Poems*. Edited by Thomas Dillon Redshaw. Dublin: New Writers' Press.

MACLEAN, Sorley. 1971. *Poems to Eimhir*. Translated by Iain Crichton Smith. London: Gollancz.

———. 1989. *From Wood to Ridge: Collected Poems*. Manchester: Carcanet.

MONTAGUE, John. 1984. *The Rough Field*. 4th edn. Dublin: Dolmen.

————. 2001. *Company*. London: Duckworth.

MULDOON, Paul. 1994. *The Prince of the Quotidian*. Oldcastle, Ire.: Gallery.

O'DRISCOLL, Dennis. 1999. *Weather Permitting*. London: Anvil Press Poetry.

PAULIN, Tom. 2002. *The Invasion Handbook*. London: Faber & Faber.

SMYTH, Cherry. 2001. *When the Lights Go Up*. Belfast: Lagan.

SQUIRES, Geoffrey. 1975. *Drowned Stones*. Dublin: New Writers' Press.

————. 1978. *Figures*. Belfast: Ulsterman Publications.

YOUNG, Augustus. 1977. *Tapestry of Animals*. London: Menard.

————. 1980. *Danta Gradha*: *Love Poems from the Irish*. London: Menard.

————. 1986. *The Credit*. Southampton: Advent.

————. 1986. *The Credit*: *Book Two, Book Three*. London: Menard.

————. 1994. *Lampion and his Bandits*: *The Literature of Cordel in Brazil*. London: Menard.

————. 1999. *Lightning in Low Places*. Coleraine: Cranagh.

————. 2002. *Days and Nights in Hendon*: *Elegies Written in the Last Months of a Five-Year Sojourn in the High Down (Heandun)*. London: Menard.

————. 2002. *Light Years*. London: LME & Menard.

————. 2005. *Storytime*. London: Elliot & Thompson.

————. 2009. *Diversifications*: *Mayakovsky, Brecht and Me*. Exeter: Shearsman Books.

————. 2009. *The Nicotine Cat and Other People*. Dublin: Duras, in association with New Island.

————. 2009. *Secret Gloss*: *A Film Play on the Life and Work of Søren Kierkegaard*. London: Elliott & Thompson.

Poetry Translation

INTRODUCTION

ALEXANDER, Michael, trans. 1966. *The Earliest English Poems*. Harmondsworth: Penguin.

————, trans. 1973. *Beowulf*. Harmondsworth: Penguin.

COOPER, Arthur, trans. 1973. *Li Po and Tu Fu*. Harmondsworth: Penguin.

DUPIN, Jacques. 1974. *Fits and Starts: Selected Poems of Jacques Dupin*. Translated by Paul Auster. Salisbury: Compton.

GRAHAM, Angus, trans. 1965. *Poems of the Late T'ang*. Harmondsworth: Penguin.

HOWELL, Anthony, and W. G. Shepherd, trans. 2007. *Statius: Silvae: A Selection*. London: Anvil Press Poetry.

MOORE, Marianne. 1987. *The Complete Prose of Marianne Moore*. Edited by Patricia C. Willis. London: Faber & Faber.

PORTER, John, trans. 1975. *Beowulf: Anglo-Saxon Text with Modern English Parallel*. London: Pirate Press.

RADICE, William, and Barbara Reynolds, eds. 1987. *The Translator's Art: Essays in Honour of Betty Radice*. Harmondsworth: Penguin.

RILKE, R. 1939. *Duino Elegies*. Translated by Stephen Spender and J. B. Leishman. London: Hogarth.

ROTHENBERG, Jerome. 1993. *The Lorca Variations: I–XXXIII*. New York: New Directions.

WALEY, Arthur, trans. 1946. *Chinese Poems: Selected from 170 Chinese Poems, More Translations from the Chinese, The Temple and The Book of Songs*. London: Allen & Unwin.

FRANCE

ELIOT, T. S. 1976. *Poésie: Edition bilingue*. Translated by Pierre Leyris. Paris: Seuil.

———. 1992. *Quatre Quatuors*. Translated by Claude Vigée. London: Menard.

SPENDER, Stephen. 1975. *Eliot*. London: Fontana Books.

SPAIN AND SPANISH AMERICA

HERNANDEZ, Miguel. 1972. *Songbook of Absences: Selected Poems of Miguel Hernández*. Translated by Thomas Jones. Washington, DC: Charioteer Press.

———. 2001. *The Selected Poems of Miguel Hernandez*. Edited and translated by Ted Gennoways, with additional translations by Timothy Baland and others. Chicago and London: University of Chicago Press.

HIRSCH, Edward. 2002. *The Demon and the Angel: Searching for the Source of Artistic Inspiration*. San Diego, CA and London: Harcourt, Inc.

GIBBONS, Reginald, ed. 1979. *The Poet's Work: 29 Poets on the Origins and Practice of their Art*. Chicago and London: University of Chicago Press.

———. 1960. *Lorca*. Edited and translated by J. L. Gili. Harmondsworth: Penguin.

OTERO, Blas de. 1964. *Twenty Poems*. Chosen and translated by Hardie St Martin. Madison: Sixties Press.

TRAKL, Georg. 2005. *To the Silenced: Selected Poems*. Translated by Will Stone. Todmorden: Arc Publications.

VALLEJO, Cesar. 1976. *Selected Poems*. Selected and translated by Ed Dorn and Gordon Brotherston. Harmondsworth: Penguin.

———. 1995. *The Black Heralds*. Translated by Barry Fogden. Lewes: Allardyce, Barnett.

PORTUGAL

GRIFFIN, Jonathan. 1995. *In Earthlight: Selected Poems*. London: Menard.

KOTOWICZ, Z. 1996. *Fernando Pessoa: Voices of a Nomadic Soul*. London: Menard.

———. 2008. *Fernando Pessoa: Voices of a Nomadic Soul*. Rev. edn. Bristol/London: Shearsman Books/Menard.

LANCASTRE, Maria José de. 1981. *Fernando Pessoa: uma fotobiografia*. Lisbon: Imprensa Nacional-Casa da Moeda/Centro de Estudos Pessoanos.

PESSOA, Fernando. 1974. *Selected Poems*. Translated by Jonathan Griffin. Harmondsworth: Penguin.

———. 1986. *The Surprise of Being: Twenty-Five Poems*. Translated by James Greene and Clara de A. Mafra. London: Angel Books.

———. 1991. *The Book of Disquiet: A Selection*. Translated by Iain Watson. London: Quartet.

———. 1992. *Message*. Translated by Jonathan Griffin. London: Menard/King's College London.

———. 1995. *A Centenary Pessoa*. Edited by Eugenio Lisboa and H. Macedo. Translated by Keith Bosley and others. Manchester: Carcanet, in association with the Calouste Gulbenkian Foundation, the Instituto Camoes, Instituto da Biblioteca Nacional e do Livro.

————. 2001. *The Book of Disquiet*. Translated by Richard Zenith. London: Allen Lane.

————. 2007. *Poesia Inglesa*. Edited by Richard Zenith. Lisbon: Assírio & Alvim.

————. 2008. *Lisbon: What the Tourist Should See*. Bristol: Shearsman Books.

TABUCCHI, Antonio. 1992. *Requiem: un'allucinazione*. Milano: Feltrinelli.

————. 1995. *Pereira Declares: A Testimony*. Translated by Patrick Creagh. New York: New Directions.

ITALY

BODINI, Vittorio. 1980. *The Hands of the South*. Translated by Ruth Feldman and Brian Swann. Washington, DC: Charioteer Press.

GUIDACCI, Margherita. 1989. *A Book of Sibyls: Poems*. Translated by Ruth Feldman. Boston, MA: Rowan Tree.

————. 1992. *Landscape with Ruins: Selected Poetry of Margerita Guidacci*. Translated by Ruth Feldman. Detriot, MI: Wayne State University Press.

LEOPARDI. 1998. *Canti: With a Selection of His Prose*. Translated by J. G. Nicholls. Manchester: Carcanet.

————. 2010. *Canti*. Translated and annotated by Jonathan Galassi. London: Penguin.

MONTALE, Eugenio. 1969. *Selected Poems*. Translated by George Kay. Harmondsworth: Penguin.

————. 1978. *The Storm and Other Poems*. Translated by Charles Wright. Oberlin, OH: Oberlin College Press.

————. 1984. *Otherwise: Last and First Poems of Eugenio Montale*. Translated by Jonathan Galassi. New York: Random House.

————. 2004. *Selected Poems*. Edited by David Young. Oberlin, OH: Oberlin College Press.

PICCOLO, Lucio. 1972. *Collected Poems*. Edited and translated by Ruth Feldman and Brian Swann. Princeton, NJ: Princeton University Press.

PILLING, John. 1982. *An Introduction to Fifty Modern European Poets*. London: Pan Books.

QUASIMODO, Salvatore. 1983. *Complete Poems*. Translated by Jack Bevan. London: Anvil Press Poetry.

SCOTELLARO, Rocco. 1980. *The Dawn Is Always New: Selected Poetry of Rocco Scotellaro*. Translated by Ruth Feldman and Brian Swann. Princeton, NJ: Princeton University Press.

UNGARETTI, Giuseppe. 1971. *Selected Poems*. Edited and translated by Patrick Creagh. Harmondsworth: Penguin.

ZANZOTTO, Andrea. 1975. *Selected Poetry*. Edited and translated by Ruth Feldman and Brian Swann. Princeton, NJ, and Guildford: Princeton University Press.

————. 1993. *Poems*. Translated by Anthony Barnett. Lewes: Allardyce, Barnett.

GREECE

CAVAFY, Constantine. 1951. *Poems by C. P. Cavafy*. Translated by John Mavrogordato. London: Chatto & Windus.

————. 1958. *Presentation critique de Cavafy, 1863–1933*. Translated by Marguerite Yourcenar. Paris: Gallimard.

————. 1961. *Complete Poems of Cavafy*. Translated by Rae Dalven. London: Hogarth.

————. 1975. *Collected Poems*. Translated by Edmund Keeley and Philip Sherrard. London: Hogarth.

ELYTIS, Odysseus. 1980. *The Axion Esti*. Translated by Edmund Keeley and George Savidis. London: Anvil Press Poetry.

KAZANTZAKIS, Nikos. 1958. *Odyssey: A Modern Sequel*. Translated by Kimon Friar. London: Secker & Warburg.

MELEAGER. 1975. *Poems of Meleager*. Translated by Peter Whigham and Peter Jay. London: Anvil Press Poetry.

RITSOS, Yannis. 1974. *Selected Poems*. Translated by Nikos Stangos. Harmondsworth: Penguin.

SAPPHO. 1984. *Poems and Fragments*. Translated by Josephine Balmer. London: Brilliance.

Bibliography

AUSTRIA, GERMANY AND HOLLAND

BIENEK, Horst, and Johannes Bobrowski. 1971. *Selected Poems*. Translated by Ruth and Matthew Mead. Harmondsworth: Penguin.

BOBROWSKI, Johannes. 1984. *Shadow Lands*. Translated by Ruth and Matthew Mead. London: Anvil Press Poetry.

BOSLEY, Keith, trans. 1997. *Eve Blossom Has Wheels: German Love Poetry*. London: Libris.

ENZENSBERGER, Hans Magnus. 1976. *Mausoleum*. Translated by Joachim Neugroschel. New York: Urizen.

———. 1994. *Selected Poems*. Translated by Hans Magnus Enzensberger & Michael Hamburger. Newcastle-upon-Tyne: Bloodaxe Books.

FRIED, Erich. 1969. *On Pain of Seeing*. Translated by Georg Rapp. London: Rapp and Whiting.

HAMBURGER, Michael, ed. 1972. *East German Poetry: An Anthology*. Cheadle: Carcanet.

———, and Christopher Middleton, eds. 1962. *Modern German Poetry, 1910–1960: An Anthology with Verse Translations*. London: MacGibbon & Kee.

HEISE, Hans Jurgen. 1972. *Underseas Possessions: Selected Poems*. Translated by Ewald Osers. Harrow: Oleander.

HERZBERG, Judith. 1968a. *Beemdgras*. Amsterdam: Van Oorschot.

———. 1968b. *Zeepost*. Amsterdam: Van Oorschot.

———. 1988. *But What: Selected Poems*. Translated by Shirley Kaufman. Oberlin, OH: Oberlin College Press.

KIRSCH, Sarah. 1991. *The Brontës Hats*. Translated by Wendy Mulford and Anthony Vivi. Cambridge: Reality Street Editions.

KUHNER, Herbert, trans. 1992. *If the Walls between Us Were Made of Glass: Austrian Jewish Poetry*. Edited by Peter Daniel, Johannes Diethart and Herbert Kuhner. Vienna: Apfel.

———, and Peter Tyran, trans. 1983 *Hawks and Nightingales: Current Burgenland Croatian Poetry*. Edited by Peter Tyran. Vienna: Braumüller.

MIDDLETON, Christopher, ed. 1967. *German Writing Today*. Harmondsworth: Penguin.

679

SABAIS, Heinz Winfried. 1968. *Generation*. Translated by Ruth and Matthew Mead. Northwood: Anvil Press Poetry.

CENTRAL AND EASTERN EUROPE

BARNSTONE, Willis, ed. 1970. *Modern European Poetry*. Toronto and London: Bantam.

BARTUSEK, Antonin. 1975. *The Aztec Calendar and Other Poems*. Translated by Ewald Osers. London: Anvil Press Poetry.

BIALOSZEWSKI, Miron. 1974. *The Revolution of Things: Selected Poems of Miron Bialoszewski*. Translated by Andrzej Busza and Bogdan Czaykowski. Washington, DC: Charioteer Press.

FICOWSKI, Jerzy. 1981. *A Reading of Ashes: Poems*. Translated by Keith Bosley with Krystyna Wandycz. London: Menard.

HERBERT, Zbigniew. 1977. *Selected Poems*. Translated by John and Bogdana Carpenter. Oxford and New York: Oxford University Press.

———. 1985. *The Barbarian in the Garden*. Translated by Michael March and Jaroslav Anders. Manchester: Carcanet.

———. 1987. *Report from the Besieged City and Other Poems*. Translated by John and Bogdana Carpenter. Oxford: Oxford University Press.

HOLAN, Vladimir. 1971. *Selected Poems*. Translated by Jarmila and Ian Milner. Harmondsworth: Penguin.

HOLUB, Miroslav. 1967. *Selected Poems*. Translated by George Theiner and Ian Milner. Harmondsworth: Penguin.

———. 1984. *On the Contrary and Other Poems*. Translated by Ewald Osers. Newcastle-upon-Tyne: Bloodaxe Books.

JOHNSON, Bernard, ed. 1970. *New Writing in Yugoslavia*. Harmondsworth: Penguin.

JOZSEF, Attila. 1973. *Selected Poems*. Translated by John Batki. Manchester: Carcanet.

———. 1966. *Poems*. Translated by Michael Hamburger and others. London: Danubia Books

LALIC, Ivan. 1981. *The Works of Love*. Translated by Francis R. Jones. London: Anvil Press Poetry.

LYSOHORSKY, Ondra. 1971. *Selected Poems.* Translated by Ewald Osers and others. London: Jonathan Cape.

MIŁOSZ, Czesław, ed. 1970. *Post-War Polish Poetry.* Harmondsworth: Penguin.

PAVLOVIC, Miodrag. 1985. *The Slavs Beneath Parnassus: Selected Poems.* Translated by Bernard Johnson. London: Angel Books.

PILINSZKY, János. 1976. *Selected Poems.* Translated by Ted Hughes and Janos Csokits. Manchester: Carcanet.

———. 1978. *Crater: Poems, 1974–1975.* Translated by Peter Jay. London: Anvil Press Poetry.

———. 2011. *Passio.* Translated by Clive Wilmer and George Gömöri. Tonbridge: Worple.

POPA, Vasko. 1978. *Collected Poems, 1943–1976.* Translated by Anne Pennington. Manchester: Carcanet.

RADNOTI, Miklos. 1980. *The Golden Apple.* Translated by Andrew Harvey and Anne Pennington. London: Anvil Press Poetry.

———. 2000. *Camp Notebook.* Translated by Francis Jones. Todmorden: Arc Publications.

SWIR, Anna. 1985. *Happy as a Dog's Tail.* Translated by Czesław Miłosz and Leonard Nathan. San Diego, CA: Harcourt Brace Jovanovich.

WAT, Aleksander. 1977. *Mediterranean Poems.* Edited and translated by Czesław Miłosz. Ann Arbor, MI: Ardis.

———. 1990. *My Century: The Odyssey of a Polish Intellectual.* Translated by Richard Lourie. New York and London: W. W. Norton.

WIENIEWSKA, Celina, ed. 1967. *Polish Writing Today.* Harmondsworth: Penguin.

HEBREW POETRY (INCLUDING YIDDISH)

ALTERMAN, Natfan. 1978. *Selected Poems.* Translated by Robert Friend. Tel Aviv: Hakibbutz Hameuchad.

AMICHAI, Yehuda. 1971. *Selected Poems.* Translated by Assia Gutmann and Harold Schimmel, with the collaboration of Ted Hughes. Harmondsworth: Penguin.

———. 1977. *Travels of a Latter-Day Benjamin of Tudela.* Translated by Ruth Nevo. London: Menard.

————. 1978. *Amen*. Translated by Yehuda Amichai and Ted Hughes. Oxford: Oxford University Press.

————. 1988. *Selected Poetry*. Translated by Chana Bloch and Stephen Mitchell. Harmondsworth: Penguin.

————. 2000. *Yehuda Amichai: Selected Poems*. Edited by Ted Hughes and Daniel Weissbort. London: Faber & Faber.

BLOCH, Chana. 1980. *The Secrets of the Tribes: Poems*. New York: Sheep Meadow.

————, and Ariel Bloch. 1998. *Song of Songs: A New Translation with an Introduction and Commentary*. Berkeley and London: University of California Press.

CARMI, T. 1964. *The Brass Serpent: Poems*. Translated by Dom Moraes. London: Andre Deutsch.

————. 1971. *Somebody Like You*. Translated by Stephen Mitchell. London: Andre Deutsch.

————. 1983. *At the Stone of Losses*. Translated by Grace Schulman. Manchester: Carcanet.

COHEN, Joseph, ed. 1990. *Voices of Israel: Essays on and Interviews with Yehuda Amichai, A. B. Yehoshua, T. Carmi, Aharon Applefeld, and Amos Oz*. Albany: State University of New York Press.

GOLDBERG, Leah. 1976. *Selected Poems*. Translated by Robert Friend. London: Menard.

MAYNE, Seymour, ed. 1996. *Jerusalem: An Anthology of Jewish Canadian Poetry*. Montreal: Véhicule.

MITCHELL, Stephen. 1979. *Into the Whirlwind: A Translation of the Book of Job*. Garden City, NY: Doubleday.

PREIL, Gabriel. 1985. *Sunset Possibilities and Other Poems*. Translated by Robert Friend. Philadelphia, PA: Jewish Publication Society.

RA'HEL. 1994. *Flowers of Perhaps: Selected Poems of Ra'hel*. Translated by Robert Friend. London: Menard

ROSENBERG, David. 1977. *Job Speaks: Interpreted from the Original Hebrew Book of Job*. New York: Harper & Row.

————. 1991. *A Poet's Bible: Rediscovering the Voices of the Original Text*. New York: Hyperion.

STENCL, A. N. 2007. *All My Young Years: Yiddish Poetry from Weimar Germany*. Translated by Haike Beruriah Wiegand and Stephen Watts. Nottingham: Five Leaves.

WEISSBORT, Daniel, ed. 1990. *The Poetry of Survival: Post-War Poets of Central and Eastern Europe*. London: Anvil Press Poetry.

ZACH, Nathan. 2011. *The Countries We Live In: Selected Poems Natan Zach, 1955–1979*. Translated by Peter Everwhine. Portland, OR: Tavern.

ARABIC AND PERSIAN POETRY

AL-UDHARI, Abdullah, ed. and trans. 1986. *Modern Poetry of the Arab World*. Harmondsworth: Penguin.

———, trans. 1974. *Fireflies in the Dark: Classical Arab Poetry*. London: Menard.

———. 1974. *Voice without Passport*. London: Menard.

———. 1997. *The Arab Creation Myth*. Prague: Archangel.

POUND, Omar Shakespear. 1970. *Arabic and Persian Poems*. London: Fulcrum.

RUSSIAN LITERATURE

AKHMATOVA, Anna. 1974. *Poems of Akhmatova*. Translated by Stanley Kunitz and Max Hayward. London: Collins Harvill.

———. 1978. *White Flock*. Translated by Geoffrey Thurley. London: Oasis.

———. 1989. *Selected Poems*. Translated by Richard McKane. Newcastle-upon-Tyne: Bloodaxe Books.

ALVAREZ, Al, ed. 1992. *The Faber Book of Modern European Poetry*. London: Faber & Faber.

BERMAN, Marshall. 1988. *All That Is Solid Melts into Air: The Experience of Modernity*. Harmondsworth: Penguin.

BLAKE, Patrica, and Max Hayward, eds. 1964. *Half-Way to the Moon*. New York: Holt Rinehart and Winston.

BLOK, Aleksandr. 1974. *Selected Poems*. Translated by Jon Stallworthy and Peter France. Harmondsworth: Penguin.

BLOOM, Harold. 2011. *The Anatomy of Influence: Literature as a Way of Life*. New Haven, CT, and London: Yale University Press.

BRETON, André. 1928. *Nadja*. Paris: Gallimard.

BROWN, Clarence, ed. and trans. 1965. *The Prose of Osip Mandelstam*. Princeton, NJ: Princeton University Press.

BRUFORD, W. H. 1957. *Anton Chekhov*. London: Bowes & Bowes.

CASSOU, Jean. 2002. *Thirty-Three Sonnets of the Resistance and Other Poems*. Todmorden: Arc Publications.

CHEKHOV, Anton. 2003. *Seven Short Novels*. Translated by Barbara Makanow-itzky. New York and London: W. W. Norton.

DAVIE, Donald, and Angela Livingstone. 1969. *Pasternak*. Translated by Donald Davie. London: Macmillan.

FEINSTEIN, Elaine. 1998. *Pushkin*. London: Weidenfeld & Nicolson.

———. 2008. *The Russian Jerusalem*. Manchester: Carcanet.

FORD, R. A. D. 1969. *The Solitary City: Poems and Translations*. Toronto: McClelland & Stewart.

———. 1979. *Holes in Space*. Toronto: Hounslow Press.

———. 1983. *Needle in the Eye: Poems New and Old*. Oakville: Mosaic.

———, trans. 1984. *Russian Poetry: A Personal Anthology*. Oakville: Mosaic.

———. 1985. *Doors, Words and Silence*. Oakville: Mosaic.

———. 1988. *Dostoyevsky and Other Poems*. Oakville: Mosaic.

———. 1989. *Our Man in Moscow: A Diplomat's Reflections on the Soviet Union*. Toronto and London: University of Toronto Press.

———. 1995. *A Moscow Literary Memoir: Among the Great Artists of Russia from 1946 to 1980*. Toronto and London: University of Toronto Press.

HINGLEY, Ronald. 1982. *Nightingale Fever: Russian Poets in Revolution*. London: Weidenfeld & Nicolson.

HOWE, Irving. 1961. *Politics and the Novel*. London: Stevens.

MAGARSHACK, David. 1980. *Chekhov the Dramatist*. London: Methuen.

MANDELSTAM, Nadezhda. 1971. *Hope against Hope: A Memoir*. Translated by Max Hayward. London: Collins Harvill.

———. 1973. *Chapter Forty-Two and the Goldfinch*. London: Menard.

———. 1974. *Hope Abandoned: A Memoir*. Translated by Max Hayward. London: Collins Harvill.

————. 1974. *Mozart and Salieri*. Ann Arbor, MI: Ardis.

MAYAKOVSKY, Vladimir. 1970. *How Are Verses Made?* Translated by G. M. Hyde. London: Jonathan Cape.

————. 1971. *Electric Iron*. Translated by Jack Hirschman and Victor Erlich. Berkeley, CA: Maya.

MEDVEDEV, Zhores. 1975. *Ten Years after Ivan Denisovich*. Translated by Hilary Sternberg. Harmondsworth: Penguin.

NABOKOV, Vladimir. 1973. *Nikolay Gogol*. London: Weidenfeld & Nicolson

————, and Edmund Wilson. 1979. *The Nabokov–Wilson Letters: Correspondence between Vladimir Nabokov and Edmund Wilson, 1940–1971*. Edited by Simon Karlinsky. London: Weidenfeld & Nicolson.

NAYMAN, Anatoly. 1991. *Remembering Akhmatova*. Translated by Wendy Rossyln. London: Halban.

PASTERNAK, Boris. 1983. *My Sister, Life and a Sublime Malady*. Translated by Mark Rudman. Ann Arbor, MI: Ardis.

PASTERNAK, Evgeny. 1990. *Boris Pasternak: The Tragic Years, 1930–60*. Translated by Michael Duncan. London: Collins Harvill.

PAZ, Octavio. 1972. *Le Singe grammairien*. Translated from Spanish by Claude Esteban. Geneva: Skira.

————. 1989. *The Monkey Grammarian*. Translated by Helen R. Lane. London: Peter Owen.

PUSHKIN, Aleksandr. 1936. *Poems, Prose and Plays of Pushkin*. Edited by Avrahm Yarmolinsky. New York: Modern Library.

————. 1945. *Pushkin's Poems*. Translated by Walter Morison. London: Prague Press/Allen & Unwin.

————. 1963. *Poems of Pushkin*. Translated by Henry Jones. Riding Mill: Henry Jones.

————. 1964. *Eugene Onegin: A Novel in Verse*. Translated by Vladimir Nabokov. 4 VOLS. London: Routledge & Kegan Paul.

————. 1964. *Pushkin*. Translated by John Fennell. Harmondsworth: Penguin.

————. 1972. *Pushkin Threefold*. Translated by Walter Arndt. London and New York: Dutton.

———. 1982. *The Bronze Horseman and Other Poems*. Translated by D. M. Thomas. Harmondsworth: Penguin.

———. 1982. *Mozart and Salieri: The Little Tragedies*. Translated by Antony Wood. London: Angel Books.

———. 1999. *Eugene Onegin: A Novel in Verse*. Translated by Douglas Hofstadter. New York: Basic Books.

———. 2000. *The Little Tragedies*. Translated by Nancy Anderson. New Haven, CT, and London: Yale University Press.

ROBINSON, Peter, ed. 2012. *A Mutual Friend: Poems for Charles Dickens*. Reading: Two Rivers.

SCAMMELL, Michael, ed. 1970. *Russia's Other Writers*. London: Longmans, Green & Co.

SICHER, Efraim. 2006. *Jews in Russian Literature after the October Revolution: Writers and Artists between Hope and Apostasy*. Cambridge and New York: Cambridge University Press.

SOLZHENITSYN, Aleksandr. 1963. *One Day in the Life of Ivan Denisovich*. Translated by Ralph Parker. Harmondsworth: Penguin.

STEINER, George. 1959. *Tolstoy or Dostoevsky: An Essay in the Old Criticism*. New York: Alfred A. Knopf.

TERTZ, Abram [Aleksandr Sinyavsky]. 1960. *The Trial Begins*. Translated by Max Hayward. London: Collins Harvill.

———. 1963. *Fantastic Stories*. New York: Pantheon.

———. 1966. *Thought Unaware = Mysli vrasplokh*. New York: Rausen.

———. 1976. *A Voice from the Chorus*. Translated by Kyril Fitzlyon and Max Hayward. London: Collins Harvill.

TSVETAYEVA, Marina. 1974. *Selected Poems*. Translated by Elaine Feinstein. Harmondsworth: Penguin.

———. 1992. *Black Earth*. Translated by Elaine Feinstein. London: Menard.

TURGENEV, Ivan. 1945. *Poems in Prose*. Translated by Evgenia Schimanskaya. London: Drummond.

———. 1961. *Five Short Novels*. Translated by Franklin Reeve. New York: Bantam.

———. 1994. *The Essential Turgenev.* Edited by Elizabeth Cheresh Allen. Evanston, IL: Northwestern University Press.

TVARDOVSKY, Alexander. 1974. *Tyorkin and the Stovemakers.* Translated by Anthony Rudolf. Manchester: Carcanet.

VINOKUROV, Yevgeny. 1976. *The War Is Over: Selected Poems.* Translated by Anthony Rudolf and Daniel Weissbort. Cheadle: Carcanet.

VOZNESENSKY, Andrei. 1964. *Selected Poems.* Translated by Anselm Hollo. New York: Grove.

———. 1967. *Antiworlds.* Edited by Patricia Blake and Max Hayward. Translated by W. H. Auden and others. London: Oxford University Press.

WEISSBORT, Daniel. 1974. *Post-War Russian Poetry.* Harmondsworth: Penguin.

———, ed. 1998. *What Was All the Fuss About.* London: Anvil Press Poetry.

YESENIN-VOLPIN, Aleksandr. 1961. *A Leaf of Spring.* Bilingual edition. Translated by George Reavey. London: Thames & Hudson.

YEVTUSHENKO, Yevgeny. 1962. *Selected Poems.* Translated by Peter Levi. Baltimore, MD, and London: Penguin.

ZABOLOTSKY, Nikolai. 1971. *Scrolls: Selected Poems.* Translated by Daniel Weissbort. London: Jonathan Cape.

———. 1999. *Selected Poems.* Translated by Daniel Weissbort. Manchester: Carcanet.

ZINIK, Zinovy. 2011. *History Thieves.* London: Seagull Books.

(AUTO)BIOGRAPHIES, LETTERS, JOURNALS AND MEMOIRS
Autobiographies

AMERICAN

APPLE, Max. 1994. *Roommates: My Grandfather's Story.* London: Little, Brown.

BAMFORTH, Iain, ed. 2003. *The Body in the Library: A Literary Anthology of Modern Medicine.* London: Verso.

BELLI, G. G. 1974. *The Roman Sonnets of G. G. Belli.* Translated by Harold Norse. London: Perivale.

DAHLBERG, Edward. 1929. *Bottom Dogs.* London: G. P. Putnam's Sons.

———. 1965. *Because I Was Flesh: The Autobiography of Edward Dahlberg*. London: Methuen.

DAICHES, David. 1997. *Two Worlds: An Edinburg Jewish Childhood; and, Promised Lands: A Portrait of My Father*. Edinburgh: Canongate.

HELLER, Michael. 2000. *Living Root*. Albany: State University of New York Press.

———. 2005. *Uncertain Poetries: Selected Essays on Poets, Poetry and Poetics*. Cambridge, MA: Salt.

———. 2012. *This Constellation Is a Name: Collected Poems, 1965–2010*. Callicoon: Nightboat.

HEMINGWAY, Ernest. 1964. *A Moveable Feast*. London: Jonathan Cape.

JACOBSON, Dan. 1998. *Heshel's Kingdom*. London: Hamish Hamilton.

KAZIN, Alfred. 1952. *A Walker in the City*. London: Gollancz.

———. 1978. *New York Jew*. London: Secker & Warburg.

———. 1995. *Writing Was Everything*. Cambridge, MA, and London: Harvard University Press.

MAILER, Norman, with Michael Lennon. 2007. *On God: An Uncommon Conversation*. London: Continuum.

WILLIAMS, William Carlos. 1951. *Autobiography*. New York: Random House.

———. 1982. *Yes, Mrs Williams: A Personal Record of My Mother*. New York: New Directions.

ENGLISH

ARONSON, Ronald. 2008. *Living without God: New Directions for Atheists, Agnostics, Secularists, and the Undecided*. Berkeley, CA: Counterpoint.

BARTHES, Roland. 1979. *A Lover's Discourse: Fragments*. Translated by Richard Howard. London: Jonathan Cape.

BERNAL, J. D. 1970. *The World, the Flesh and the Devil: An Inquiry into the Future of the Three Enemies of the Rational Soul*. London: Jonathan Cape.

CUMMINGS, E. E. 1953. *I: Six Non-Lectures*. Cambridge, MA, and London: Harvard University Press.

DISKI, Jenny. 1986. *Nothing Natural*. London: Methuen.

———. 1987. *Rainforest*. London: Methuen.

EAGLETON, Terry. 2007. *The Meaning of Life: A Very Short Introduction*. Oxford and New York: Oxford University Press.

GARDINER, Margaret. 1982. *Barbara Hepworth: A Memoir*. Edinburgh: Salamander.

———. 1984. *Footprints on Malekula: A Memoir of Bernard Deacon*. Edinburgh: Salamander.

———. 1988. *A Scatter of Memories*. London: Free Association.

GOLDSMITH, Maurice. 1980. *Sage: A Life of J. D. Bernal*. London: Hutchinson.

GORDON, Giles. 1974. *About a Marriage*. Harmondsworth: Penguin.

GORDON, Hattie. 2003. *The Café after the Pub after the Funeral*. London and New York: Continuum.

JOSIPOVICI, Gabriel. 2001. *A Life*. London: London Magazine Editions, in association with the European Jewish Publication Society.

KAVANAGH, P. J. 1973. *A Perfect Stranger*. London: Quartet.

LEHMANN, Rosamond. 1967. *Swan in the Evening: Fragments of an Inner Life*. London: Collins.

RABINOVITCH, Sacha. 1982. *Heroes and Others*. Canterbury: Yorick.

RAINE, Kathleen. 1973. *Farewell Happy Fields: Memories of Childhood*. London: Hamish Hamilton.

———. 1975. *The Land Unknown*. London: Hamish Hamilton.

———. 1977. *The Lion's Mouth: Concluding Chapters of Autobiography*. London: Hamish Hamilton.

———. 1990. *India Seen Afar*. Bideford: Green.

RICKS, Christopher. 1974. *Keats and Embarrassment*. Oxford: Clarendon.

SUARÈS, Carlo. 1973. *Genesis Rejuvenated*. Translated by Edouard Roditi. London: Menard.

FRAGMENTARIANS

ARENDT, Hannah. 1970. *Men in Dark Times*. London: Jonathan Cape.

BAILEY, Paul. 2004. *An Immaculate Mistake: Scenes from Childhood and Beyond*. London: Penguin.

BENJAMIN, Walter. 1973. *Understanding Brecht.* Translated by Anna Bostock. London: NLB.

———. 1978. *Reflections: Essays, Aphorisms, Autobiographical Writings.* Edited by Peter Demetz. Translated by Edmund Jephcott. New York: Harcourt Brace Jovanovich.

———. 1985. *One-Way Street, and Other Writings.* Translated by Edmund Jephcott and Kingsley Shorter. London: Verso.

———. 1986. *Moscow Diary.* Edited by Gary Smith. Translated by Richard Sieburt. Cambridge, MA, and London: Harvard University Press.

———. 2006. *Berlin Childhood around 1900.* Translated by Howard Eiland. Cambridge, MA, and London: Belknap.

BERG, Leila. 1998. *Flickerbook.* London: Granta.

BISHOP, John Peale. 1960. *Selected Poems.* London: Chatto &Windus.

COOPER, William. 1990. *From Early Life.* London: Macmillan.

EAGLETON, Terry. 1981. *Walter Benjamin; or, Towards a Revolutionary Criticism.* London: NLB.

FITZGERALD, F. Scott. 1965. *The Crack-Up, with Other Pieces and Stories.* Harmondsworth: Penguin.

KOBAYASHI, Issa. 1972. *The Year of My Life: A Translation of Issa's Oraga Haru by Nobuyuki Yuasa.* Berkeley and London: University of California Press.

LEIRIS, Michel. 1968. *Manhood; preceded by The Autobiographer as Torero.* Translated by Richard Howard. London: Jonathan Cape.

LEVERTOV, Denise. 1996. *Tesserae: Memories and Suppositions.* Newcastle-upon-Tyne: Bloodaxe Books.

MASON, Raymond. 2003. *At Work in Paris: Raymond Mason on Art and Artists.* London: Thames & Hudson.

NEHER, André. 1981. *The Exile of the Word: From the Silence of the Bible to the Silence of Auschwitz.* Translated by David Maisel. Philadelphia, PA: Jewish Publication Society of America.

SARRAUTE, Nathalie. 1995. *Enfance.* Paris: Gallimard.

———. 1995. *Ici.* Paris: Gallimard.

TAUSSIG, Michael. 2006. *Walter Benjamin's Grave*. Chicago and London: University of Chicago Press.

Letters

ALTER, Robert. 1979. *A Lion for Love: A Critical Biography of Stendhal*. In collaboration with Carol Cosman. New York: Basic Books.

BARTHES, Roland. 1971. *Essais critiques*. 2nd edn. Paris: Seuil.

———. 1971. *Sade, Fourier, Loyola*. Paris: Seuil.

BENJAMIN, Walter and Gershom Scholem. 1992. *The Correspondence of Walter Benjamin and Gershom Scholem, 1932–1940*. Edited by Gershom Scholem. Translated by Gary Smith and Andre Lefevere. Cambridge, MA, and London: Harvard University Press.

BISHOP, Elizabeth. 1994. *One Art: Letters*. Edited by Robert Giroux. London: Chatto & Windus.

BUCK, Paul. 2004. *Spread Wide: An Encounter Between Kathy Acker and Paul Buck*. Paris: Editions Dis Voir.

———. 1968. *Pimot*. London: Latimer.

———. 1972. *A Cunt Not Fit for the Queen*. Amsterdam: Suppressed Limitations.

———. 1981. *No Lettuces for Miss Lush*. Stokesmead: Stingy Artist.

———. 2011. *A Public Intimacy: (A Life Through Scrapbooks)*. London: Book Works.

CELAN, Paul, and Nelly Sachs. 1995. *Paul Celan, Nelly Sachs: Correspondence*. Edited by Barbara Wiedemann. Translated by Christopher Clark. New York and Paris: Sheep Meadow.

———, and Gisèle Celan-Lestrange. 2001. *Correspondance, 1951–1970; avec un choix de lettres de Paul Celan a son fils Eric*. Paris: Seuil.

———, and Ingeborg Bachmann. 2010. *Correspondence*. Edited by Bertrand Badiou. Translated by Wieland Hoban. London: Seagull Books.

CHEKHOV, Anton. 1974. *Letters of Anton Chekhov*. Edited by Avrahm Yarmolinsky. Translated by Bernard Guilbert Guerney and Lynn Solotaroff. London: Jonathan Cape.

GREENE, Graham. 1961. *In Search of a Character: Two African Journals*. London: Bodley Head.

———. 2007. *A Life in Letters*. Edited by Richard Greene. London: Little, Brown.

GUTMAN, Robert W. 2001. *Mozart: A Cultural Biography*. London: Pimlico.

KEATS, John. 1952. *The Letters of John Keats*. Edited by Maurice Buxton Forman. London and New York: Oxford University Press.

LEVERTOV, Denise, and William Carlos Williams. 1998. *The Letters of Denise Levertov and William Carlos Williams*. Edited by Christopher MacGowan. New York: New Directions.

LUNZER, Heinz, and Victoria Lunzer-Talos. 1994. *Joseph Roth: Leben und Werk in Bildern*. Cologne: Kiepenheuer & Witsch.

———. 2008. *Joseph Roth im Exil in Paris 1933 bis 1939*. Vienna: Dokumentationsstelle für neuere österreichische Literatur.

MANDELSTAM, Osip. 1989. *The Eyesight of Wasps*. Translated by James Greene. London: Angel Books.

———. 1991. *The Collected Critical Prose and Letters*. Edited by Jane Gary Harris. Translated by Jane Gary Harris and Constance Link. London: Collins Harvill.

———. 1992. *A Necklace of Bees: Selected Poems*. Translated by Maria Enzensberger. London: Menard/King's College London.

MANN, Thomas. 1970. *Letters of Thomas Mann, 1889–1955*. Edited and translated by Richard and Clara Winston. London: Secker & Warburg.

MOORE, Marianne. 1998. *The Selected Letters of Marianne Moore*. Edited by Bonnie Costello, Celeste Goodridge and Cristanne Miller. London: Faber & Faber.

MOZART, Wolfgang. 1938. *The Letters of Mozart and His Family*. Translated by Emily Anderson. 3 VOLS. London: Macmillan.

NAIDITCH, Larissa. 2004. *Paul Celan: Materials, Investigations, Memoirs*. Jerusalem: Gesharim.

PASTERNAK, Boris, Marina Tsvetayeva and Rainer Maria Rilke. 1986. *Letters, Summer 1926*. Edited by Yevgeny Pasternak, Yelena Pasternak and Konstantin M. Azadovsky. Translated by Margaret Wettlin and Walter Arndt. London: Jonathan Cape.

REZNIKOFF, Charles. 1997. *Selected Letters of Charles Reznikoff, 1917–1976*. Edited by Milton Hindus. Santa Rosa, CA: Black Sparrow.

RILKE, Rainer Maria. 1988. *Selected Letters, 1902–1926*. Translated by R. F. C. Hull. London: Quartet.

VAN GOGH, Vincent. 1958. *The Complete Letters of Vincent Van Goch*. 3 VOLS. London: Thames & Hudson.

STENDHAL. 1952. *To the Happy Few: Selected Letters of Stendhal*. Translated by Norman Cameron. London: Lehmann.

Diaries/Journals

BABEL, Isaac. 1995. *1920 Diary*. Edited by Carol J. Avins. Translated by H. T. Willetts. New Haven, CT, and London: Yale University Press.

BLECHER, Max. 2008. *Scarred Hearts*. Translated by Henry Howard. London: Old Street.

CALVINO, Italo. 1987. *The Uses of Literature*. Translated by Patrick Creagh. Boston, MA: Houghton Mifflin Harcourt.

CANETTI, Elias. 1962. *Crowds and Power*. Translated by Carol Steward. London: Gollancz.

CLAIR, Jean. 2006. *Journal atrabilaire*. Paris: Gallimard.

EHRENBURG, Ilya. 1962. *Chekhov, Stendhal and Other Essays*. Translated by Anna Bostock, in collaboration with Yvonne Kapp. London: MacGibbon & Kee.

HARE, David. 1998. *Via Dolorosa; and, Where Shall We Live?* London: Faber & Faber.

———. 1999. *Acting Up*. London: Faber & Faber.

GASCOYNE, David. 1991. *Collected Journals, 1936–1942*. London: Skoob.

———. 1998. *Selected Prose, 1934–1996*. Edited by Roger Scott. London: Enitharmon.

IGNATOW, David. 1961. *Say Pardon*. Middletown, CT: Wesleyan University Press.

———. 1973. *Notebooks*. Edited by Ralph J. Mills. Chicago: Swallow.

JOUVE, Pierre Jean. 1968. *An Idiom of Night: Poems*. Translated by Keith Bosley. London: Rapp & Whiting.

———. 2007. *Despair Has Wings: Selected Poems of Pierre Jean Jouve*. Edited by Roger Scott. Translated by David Gascoyne. London: Enitharmon.

KLEMPERER, Victor. 2000. *Language of the Third Reich: Lingua Tertii Imperii; a Philologist's Notebook*. Translated by Martin Brady. London: Athlone.

———. 2004. *The Lesser Evil: The Diaries*. Translated by Martin Chalmers. London: Weidenfeld & Nicolson.

ODETS, Clifford. 1988. *The Time Is Ripe: The 1940 Journal of Clifford Odets*. New York: Grove.

ROTH, Joseph. 1988. *The Spider's Web*. Translated by John Hoare. London: Chatto & Windus.

SEBASTIAN, Mihail. 2001. *Journal, 1935–1944*. Translated by Patrick Camiller. London: Heinemann.

SEFERIS, George. 1973. *Collected Poems, 1924–1955*. Edited and translated by Edmund Keeley and Philip Sherrard. London: Jonathan Cape.

———. 1974. *A Poet's Journal: Days of 1945–1951*. Translated by Athan Anagnostopoulos. Cambridge MA: Belknap.

———. 2007. *A Levant Journal*. Edited and translated by Roderick Beaton. Jerusalem: Ibis Editions.

SHER, Antony. 2005. *Primo*. London: Nick Hern.

Memoirs

CHEEVER, John. 1977. *Falconer*. London: Jonathan Cape.

———. 1990. *Collected Stories*. London: Vintage.

———. 1991. *The Journals*. Translated by Robert Gottlieb. London: Jonathan Cape.

ECHENOZ, Jean. 2001. *Jérôme Lindon*. Paris: Minuit.

KAZIN, Alfred. 2011. *Alfred Kazin's Journals*. Selected and edited by Richard M. Cook. New Haven, CT, and London: Yale University Press.

KENNAWAY James, and Susan Kennaway. 1981. *The Kennaway Papers*. London: Jonathan Cape.

McEWAN, Ian. 2007. *On Chesil Beach*. London: Jonathan Cape.

Biographies

ANDREAS-SALOMÉ, Lou. 2004. *You Alone Are Real to Me: Remembering Rainer Maria Rilke*. Translated by Angela von der Lippe. Manchester: Carcanet.

APPIGNANESI, Lisa, and John Forrester. 1992. *Freud's Women*. London: Weidenfeld & Nicolson.

BELY, Andrey. 1964. *Reminiscences of Alexander Blok*. Letchworth: Bradda.

———. 1986. *The Dramatic Symphony*. Edinburgh: Polygon.

CHOPIN, Kate. 1976. *The Awakening*. Edited by Margaret Culley. New York and London: W. W. Norton.

CRANE, Stephen. 1960. *The Red Badge of Courage, and Other Stores*. London: Oxford University Press.

———. 1972. *Complete Poems of Stephen Crane*. Edited by Joseph Katz. Ithaca, NY: Cornell University Press.

DELBANCO, Nicholas. 1982. *Group Portrait: Joseph Conrad, Stephen Crane, Ford Madox Ford, Henry James and H. G. Wells*. London: Faber & Faber.

DIXON, Richard Watson. 1978. *Christ's Company, and Other Poems*. New York: Garland.

DOUGLAS, Keith. 1985. *A Prose Miscellany*. Edited by Desmond Graham. Manchester: Carcanet.

HOBDAY, Charles. 1989. *Edgell Rickword: A Poet at War*. Manchester: Carcanet.

HOFFMAN, Daniel. 1957. *The Poetry of Stephen Crane*. New York: Columbia University Press.

LACOUTURE, Jean. 1977. *Léon Blum*. Paris: Seuil.

LEVI, Peter. 1976. *Collected Poems, 1955–1975*. London: Anvil Press Poetry.

———. 1977. *The Noise Made by Poems*. London: Anvil Press Poetry.

———. 1990. *Boris Pasternak*. London: Hutchinson.

LIVINGSTONE, Angela. 1984. *Lou Andreas Salomé*. London: Gordon Fraser Gallery.

LOGUE, William. 1973. *Léon Blum: The Formative Years, 1872–1914*. DeKalb: Northern Illinois University Press.

MORGENSTERN, Soma. 1997. *Fuite et fin de Joseph Roth: Souveniers*. Paris: Levi.

Oppenheimer, Paul. 1967. *Before a Battle and Other Poems.* New York: Harcourt, Brace & World.

———. 1999. *Blood Memoir; or, the First Three Days of Creation.* New York: Marsilio.

———. 1999. *Rubens: A Portrait; Beauty and the Angelic.* London: Duckworth.

———. 2011. *A Life beyond Ideology.* London: Continuum.

Pasternak, Boris. 1959. 'Safe Conduct'. In *Prose and Poems,* edited by Stefan Schimanski, pp. 11–126. London: Ernest Benn.

———. 1960. *The Last Summer.* Translated by George Reavey. Harmondsworth: Penguin.

———. 1971. *Letters to Georgian Friends.* Translated by David Magarshack. Harmondsworth: Penguin.

———. 1983. *I Remember: Sketch for an Autobiography.* Translated by David Magarshack. Cambridge, MA, and London: Harvard University Press.

———. 1986. 'Safe Conduct'. In *The Voice of Prose,* VOL. 1, edited by Christopher Barnes. Edinburgh: Polygon.

Rickword, Edgell. 1947. *Collected Poems.* London: Bodley Head.

Rilke, Rainer Maria. 1951. *Letters to Merline, 1919–1922.* Translated by Violet M. Macdonald. London: Methuen.

———, and Lou Andréas-Salomé. 2006. *Rilke and Andréas Salomé: A Love Story in Letters.* Translated by Edward Snow and Michael Winkler. New York: W. W. Norton.

Roith, Estelle. 1987. *The Riddle of Freud: Jewish Influences on His Theory of Female Sexuality.* London: Tavistock.

Sambrook, Jeremy. 1962. *A Poet Hidden: The Life of Richard Watson Dixon, 1833–1900.* London: University of London.

———. 1980. *The Colonist.* London: Muller.

———. 1998. *Lives of the Poets.* London: Weidenfeld & Nicolson.

———. 2009. *Collected Poems.* Sheffield: Smith/Doorstop.

Schmidt, Michael. 1998. *Lives of the Poets.* London: Phoenix.

———. 2013. *Lives of the Novel.* Cambridge, MA, and London: Harvard University Press.

————, and Edward Kissam, ed. and trans. 1977. *Flower and Song: Poems of the Aztec Peoples*. London: Anvil Press Poetry.

WARNER, Val. 1998. *Tooting Idyll*. Manchester: Carcanet.

WILLIAMS, Hugo. 1979. *Love Life*. London: Whizzard.

————. 1989. *Selected Poems*. Oxford: Oxford University Press.

LITERARY CRITICISM, READING AND TRANSLATION, ESSAYS, ETC.

Literary Criticism

ALVAREZ, Al. 1958. *The Shaping Spirit: Studies in Modern English and American Poets*. London: Chatto & Windus.

————. 1961. *The School of Donne*. London: Chatto & Windus.

————. 1965. *Under Pressure: The Writer in Society; Eastern Europe and the U.S.A.* Baltimore, MD: Penguin.

————, ed. 1966. *The New Poetry: An Anthology*. Harmondsworth: Penguin.

————. 1974. *The Savage God: A Study of Suicide*. Harmondsworth: Penguin.

————. 1982. *Life after Marriage: Scenes from Divorce*. London: Macmillan.

————. 1984. *The Biggest Game in Town*. London: Fontana Books.

————. 2001. *Poker: Bets, Bluffs and Bad Beats*. London: Bloomsbury.

————. 2002. *New and Selected Poems*. London: Waywiser.

CHATMAN, Seymour. 1965. *A Theory of Meter*. The Hague: Mouton.

DIAMANT, Kathi. 2003. *Kafka's Last Love: The Mystery of Dora Diamant*. London: Secker & Warburg.

ELLISON Ralph. 2000. *Juneteenth: A Novel*. Edited by John F. Callahan. London: Penguin.

————. 2001. *Invisible Man*. Edited by John F. Callahan. London: Penguin.

JACOBS, A. C. 1996. *Collected Poems and Selected Translations*. Edited by John Rety and Anthony Rudolf. London: Menard.

JOSIPOVICI, Gabriel. 1976. *The Modern English Novel: The Reader, the Writer, and the Work*. London: Open.

————. 1977. *Four Stories*. London: Menard.

———. 1977. *The Lessons of Modernism and Other Essays*. London: Macmillan.

———. 1986. *Contre-Jour: A Triptych After Pierre Bonnard*. Manchester: Carcanet.

———. 1994. *Moo Pak: A Novel*. Manchester: Carcanet.

———. 1996. *Touch: An Essay*. New Haven, CT, and London: Yale University Press.

———. 2006. *The Singer on the Shore: Essays 1991–2004*. Manchester: Carcanet.

NADLER, Stephen. 2003. *Rembrandt's Jews*. Chicago and London: University of Chicago Press.

OLSEN, Tillie. 1980. *Tell Me a Riddle*. London: Virago.

———. 1975. *Yonnondio: From the Thirties*. London: Faber & Faber.

———. 1980. *Silences*. London: Virago.

RICKS, Christopher. 1993. *Beckett's Dying Words: The Clarendon Lectures, 1990*. Oxford: Oxford University Press.

———, ed. 1996. *Inventions of the March Hare: Poems, 1909–1917, by T. S. Eliot*. London: Faber & Faber.

———. 2003. *Decisions and Revisions in T. S. Eliot*. London: British Library/Faber & Faber.

STAROBINSKI, Jean. 1999. *La Poésie et la guerre: Chroniques, 1942–1944*. Geneva: Zoé.

TSUR, Reuven. 1977. *A Perception-Oriented Theory of Metre*. Tel Aviv: Porter Israeli Institute for Poetics and Semiotics.

WEBER, Myles. 2005. *Consuming Silences: How We Read Authors Who Don't Publish*. Athens: University of Georgia Press.

Reading and Translation

MACÉ, Marielle. 2011. *Façons de lire, manières d'être*. Paris: Gallimard.

SHERINGHAM, Michael. 1993. *French Autobiography: Devices and Desires; Rousseau to Perec*. Oxford: Clarendon.

———. 2006. *Everyday Life: Theories and Practices from Surrealism to the Present*. Oxford: Oxford University Press.

Bibliography

READING

BÉGUIN, Albert. 1946. *L'Âme romantique et le rêve: Essai sur le romantisme allemand et la poésie française*. Paris: Corti.

BERENSON, Bernard. 1960. *One Year's Reading for Fun*. London: Weidenfeld & Nicolson.

BUZZATI, Dino. 1985. *Tartar Steppe*. Translated by Stuart C. Hood. Manchester: Carcanet.

CHATWIN, Bruce. 1988a. *The Songlines*. London: Picador.

———. 1988b. *Utz*. London: Jonathan Cape.

———. 1996. *Anatomy of Restlessness: Uncollected Writings*. Edited by Jan Borm. London: Jonathan Cape.

COWAN, James. 1992. *Mysteries of the Dream-Time: The Spiritual Life of Australian Aborigines*. Bridport: Prism.

DAVIS, Philip. 1983. *Memory and Writing: From Wordsworth to Lawrence*. Liverpool: Liverpool University Press.

———. 1992. *The Experience of Reading*. London and New York: Routledge.

———. 1995. *Experimental Essays on the Novels of Bernard Malamud: Malamud's People*. Lewiston: Mellen.

———. 1997. *Real Voices: On Reading*. Basingstoke: Macmillan.

FADIMAN, Anne. 2000. *Ex Libris: Confessions of a Common Reader*. London: Penguin.

GRIGSON, Geoffrey, ed. 1970. *A Choice of Southey's Verse*. London: Faber & Faber.

HALPERN, Daniel, ed. 1990. *Literature as Pleasure*. London: Collins Harvill.

KUPIEC, Anne, and Miguel Abensour. 2008. *Emmanuel Levinas: La question du livre*. Saint-Germain-la-Blanche-Herbe: IMEC.

MICHAUX, Henri. 1968. *Ecuador: Journal de voyage*. Paris: Gallimard.

PROSE, Francine. 2007. *Reading Like a Writer: A Guide for People Who Love Books and for Those Who Want to Write Them*. New York and London: Harper Perennial.

RAPHAEL, Frederic, ed. 1975. *Bookmarks*. London: Jonathan Cape.

———. 2001. *Personal Terms*. Manchester: Carcanet.

————. 2004. *Rough Copy: Personal Terms 2.* Manchester: Carcanet.

————. 2006. *Cuts and Bruises: Pesonal Terms 3.* Manchester: Carcanet.

REES-JONES, Deryn. 2012. *Burying the Wren.* Bridge End: Seren.

SCARRY, Elaine. 2006. *On Beauty and Being Just.* London: Duckworth.

ZANE, Peder, ed. 2007. *The Top Ten: Writers Pick Their Favourite Books:* New York and London: W. W. Norton.

TRANSLATION

ARROWSMITH, William, and Roger Shattuck. 1961. *The Craft and Context of Translation: A Symposium.* Austin: Texas University Press.

BLY, Robert. 1975. *Leaping Poetry: An Idea with Poems and Translations.* Boston, MA: Beacon.

————. 1983. *The Eight Stages of Translation: With a Selection of Poems and Translations.* Boston, MA: Rowan Tree.

BROWER, Reuben, ed. 1966. *On Translation.* Oxford and New York: Oxford University Press.

DESAI, Anita. 2011. *The Artist of Disappearance: Three Novellas.* London: Chatto & Windus.

FELDMAN, Jennie. 2005. *The Lost Notebook.* London: Anvil Press Poetry.

GASS, William. 1999. *Reading Rilke: Reflections on the Problems of Translation.* New York: Alfred A. Knopf.

HOLMES, James, ed. 1970. *The Nature of Translation: Essays on the Theory and Practice of Literary Translation.* The Hague: Mouton.

JASPER, David, ed. 1993. *Translating Religious Texts: Translation, Transgression and Interpretation.* Introduced by George Steiner. Basingstoke: Macmillan.

RÉDA, Jacques. 2005. *Treading Lightly.* Translated by Jennie Feldman. London: Anvil Press Poetry.

STEINER, George. 1964. *Anno Domini.* London: Faber & Faber.

————, ed. 1966. *Penguin Book of Modern Verse Translation.* [Later reissued as *Poem into Poem*]. Harmondsworth: Penguin.

————. 1975. *After Babel: Aspects of Language and Translation.* London: Oxford University Press.

————. 1997. *Errata: An Examined Life.* London: Weidenfeld & Nicolson.

————. 2008. *My Unwritten Books.* London: Weidenfeld & Nicolson.

WEISSBORT, Daniel, ed. 1989. *Translating Poetry: The Double Labyrinth.* Basingstoke: Macmillan.

Essays, etc.

INTERVIEWS AND CONVERSATIONS

BARNES, Djuna. 1985. *Interviews.* Translated by Alyce Barry. Washington, DC: Sun & Moon Press.

————. 1974. *Nightwood.* 2nd edn. London: Faber & Faber.

BIALIK, H. N. 1969. *Bialik Speaks.* Ramat Gan: Massada.

————. 1981. *Selected Poems.* Translated by Ruth Nevo. Tel Aviv: Dvir/Jerusalem Post.

JANOUCH, Gustav. 1985. *Conversations with Kafka.* Translated by Goronwy Rees. London: Quartet.

VORAGINE, Jacobus de. 1998. *Golden Legend: Selections.* London and New York: Penguin.

ESSAYS

AUDEN, W. H. 1963. *The Dyer's Hand and Other Essays.* London: Faber & Faber.

————. 1971. *A Certain World: A Commonplace Book.* London: Faber & Faber.

————. 1973. *Forewords and Afterwords.* London: Faber & Faber.

BALLARD, J. G. 1970. *The Atrocity Exhibition.* London: Jonathan Cape.

BRADBROOK, Muriel and Ronald Hayman. 1977. *My Cambridge.* London: Robson.

BRODSKY, Joseph. 1986. *Less Than One: Selected Essays.* London: Viking.

————. 1995. *On Grief and Reason: Essays.* London: Hamish Hamilton.

BRONK, William. 1956. *Light and Dark.* Ashland: Origin Press.

————. 1964. *The World, the Worldless: Poems.* New York: New Directions.

————. 1975. *Silence and Metaphor.* New Rochelle: Elizabeth Press.

————. 1983. *Vectors and Smoothable Curves: Collected Essays.* San Francisco: North Point Press.

DAVENPORT, Guy. 1984. *The Geography of the Imagination: Forty Essays*. London: Picador.

DAVIES, Robertson. 1990. *A Voice from the Attic: Essays on the Art of Reading*. New York and London: Penguin.

FRANKEL, William, and Harvey Miller. 1989. *Gown and Tallith: In Commemoration of the Fiftieth Anniversary of the Founding of the Cambridge University Jewish Society*. London: Harvey Miller.

GLUCK, Louise. 1999. *Proofs and Theories: Essays on Poetry*. Manchester: Carcanet.

HAMILTON, Ian. 1999. *Another Round at the Pillars: Essays, Poems, and Reflections on Ian Hamilton*. Edited by David Harsent. Manaccan: Cargo.

———. 2009. *Collected Poems*. Edited by Alan Jenkins. London: Faber & Faber.

JENNINGS, Humphrey. 1985. *Pandaemonium, 1660–1886: The Coming of the Machine as Seen by Contemporary Observers*. Edited by Mary-Lou Jennings and Charles Madge. London: Andre Deutsch.

KIŠ, Danilo. 1996. *Homo Poeticus: Essays and Interviews*. Translated by Susan Sontag. Manchester: Carcanet.

MONTALE, Eugenio. 1976. *Poet in Our Time*. Translated by Alastair Hamilton. London: Boyars.

———. 1982. *The Second Life of Art: Selected Essays of Eugenio Montale*. Edited and translated by Jonathan Galassi. New York: Ecco.

OLSON, Charles. 1997. *Collected Prose*. Edited by Donald Allen and Benjamin Friedlander. Berkeley: University of California Press.

PHILLIPS, Adam. 2002. *Promises, Promises: Essays on Literature and Psychoanalysis*. London: Faber & Faber.

PINSKY, Robert. 1988. *Poetry and the World*. New York: Ecco.

SONTAG, Susan. 1967. *Against Interpretation and Other Essays*. London: Eyre & Spottiswoode.

———. 1979. *On Photography*. Harmondsworth: Penguin.

———. 1983. *Illness as Metaphor*. Harmondsworth: Penguin.

TODD, Ruthven. 1946. *Tracks in the Snow: Studies in English Science and Art*. London: Grey Walls.

VANSITTART, Peter, ed. 1981. *Voices from the Great War*. London: Jonathan Cape.

———. 1984. *Voices, 1870–1914*. London: Jonathan Cape.

———. 1992. *London: A Literary Companion*. London: Murray.

WEINFIELD, Henry. 2008. *Without Mythologies: New and Selected Poems and Translations*. Loveland: Dos Madres.

———. 2009. *The Music of Thought in the Poetry of George Oppen and William Bronk*. Iowa City: University of Iowa Press.

WOOLF, Virginia. 1925. *The Common Reader*. London: Hogarth.

———. 1989. *Moments of Being*. Edited by Jeanne Schulkind. London: Grafton.

ZANGWILL, Israel. 1896. *Without Prejudice*. London: Allen & Unwin.

———. 1898. *Dreamers of the Ghetto*. London: Heinemann.

———. 1977. *Children of the Ghetto: A Study of Peculiar People*. Leicester: Leicester University Press.

———. 1987. *The King of the Schnorrers*. London: Halban.

HOMAGES AND FESTSCHRIFTS

BARRY, Peter. 2006. *The Poetry Wars: British Poetry of the 1970s and the Battle of Earls Court*. Cambridge, MA: Salt.

CAREY, John, ed. 1986. *William Golding: The Man and His Books*. London: Faber & Faber.

SHEPPARD, Robert. 2011. *When Bad Times Made for Good Poetry: Episodes in the History of the Poetics of Innovation*. Exeter: Shearsman Books.

SKELT, Peterjon, and Yasmin Skelt, eds. 1994. *Alive in Parts of This Century: Eric Mottram at 70*. Twickenham: North & South.

FICTION

Introduction

BERGER, John. 2005. *Here Is Where We Meet*. London: Bloomsbury.

ECHENOZ, Jean. 2006. *Ravel*. Paris: Minuit.

SEBALD, W. G. 1996. *The Emigrants*. Translated by Michael Hulse. London: Harvill.

———. 1999. *Vertigo*. Translated by Michael Hulse. London: Harvill.

———. 2001. *Austerlitz*. Translated by Anthea Bell. London: Penguin.

Writers I Have Neglected

BALDWIN, James. 1963. *Go Tell It on the Mountain*. London: Corgi.

———. 1964. *The Fire Next Time*. London: Penguin.

———. 1965. *Notes of a Native Son*. London: Corgi.

———. 1972. *No Name in the Street*. London: Joseph.

———. 1976. *Another Country*. London: Corgi.

———. 1977. *Giovanni's Room*. London: Corgi

———, and Margaret Mead. 1971. *A Rap on Race*. London: Joseph.

BASSANI, Giorgio. 1974. *The Garden of the Finzi-Continis*. Translated by Isabel Quigly. London: Quartet.

———. 1993. *The Heron*. Translated by William Weaver. London: Quartet.

BUZZATI, Dino. 1987. *A Love Affair*. Translated by Joseph Green. Manchester: Carcanet.

BOYD, Brian. 1990. *Vladimir Nabokov: The Russian Years*. London: Chatto & Windus.

———. 1992. *Vladimir Nabokov: The American Years*. London: Chatto & Windus.

CAPOTE, Truman. 1978. *Other Voices, Other Rooms*. Harmondsworth: Penguin.

———. 1998. *Breakfast at Tiffany's*. London: Penguin.

———. 2000. *In Cold Blood*. London: Penguin.

CLEAVER, Eldridge. 1969. *Soul on Ice*. London: Jonathan Cape.

FONTANE, Theodor. 1976. *Effi Briest*. Translated by Douglas Parmée. Harmondsworth: Penguin.

GOMBROWICZ, W. 1979. *Ferdydurke*. Translated by Lillian Vallee. London: Boyars.

———. 1988. *Diary*. Translated by Lillian Vallee. London: Quartet.

LAJOLO, Davide. 1983. *An Absurd Vice*. Translated by Mario and Mark Pietralunga. New York: New Directions.

MIŁOSZ, Czesław. 1955. *The Seizure of Power*. Translated by Celina Wieniewska. London: Faber & Faber.

———. 1983. *The Witness of Poetry*. Cambridge, MA, and London: Harvard University Press.

————. 1988. *Collected Poems*. London: Viking.

NABOKOV, Vladimir. 1951. *Speak, Memory: A Memoir*. London: Gollancz.

PAVESE, Cesare. 1964. *Festival Night, and Other Stories*. Translated by A. E. Murch. London: Peter Owen.

————. 1965. *Dialogues with Leuco*. Translated by William Arrowsmith and D. S. Carne-Ross. London: Peter Owen.

————. 1966. *Summer Storm, and Other Stories*. Translated by A. E. Murch. London: Peter Owen.

————. 1969. *Selected Letters, 1924–1950*. Translated by A. E. Murch. London: Peter Owen.

————. 1971. *Selected Poems*. Translated by Margaret Crosland. Harmondsworth: Penguin.

————. 1978. *The Moon and the Bonfire*. Translated by Louise Sinclair. London: Quartet.

————. 2009. *This Business of Living: Diary, 1935–1950*. Edited by John Taylor. Translated by A. E. Murch. Somerset, NJ, and London: Transaction.

RUDNICKI, Adolf. 1966. *Les Fenêtres d'or et autres récits: Traduit du polonaise*. Paris: Gallimard.

————. 1968. *Feuillets bleus*. Paris: Gallimard.

————. 1969. *Le Marchand de Lodz*. Paris: Gallimard.

SEMPRUN, Jorge. 1997. *Literature or Life*. Translated by Linda Coverdale. London: Viking.

ZUPAN, Vitomil. 1988. *Minuet for Guitar: 25-Shot*. Translated by Harry Leeming. Ljubljana: Društvo slovenskih pisateljev.

Shorter Fiction

BERNHARD, Thomas. 1992. *Wittgenstein's Nephew: A Friendship*. Translated by Ewald Osers. London: Vintage.

————. 1993. *On the Mountain*. Translated by Russell Stockman. London: Quartet.

————. 1997. *The Voice Imitator: One Hundred and Four Stories*. Translated by Kenneth J. Northcott. Chicago: University of Chicago Press.

————. 2003. *Three Novellas*. Translated by Peter Jansen and Kenneth J. Northcott. Chicago: University of Chicago Press.

BOLANO, Roberto. 2011. *Antwerp*. London: Picador.

COETZEE, J. M. 1987. *Foe*. London: Penguin.

COHEN, Marcel. 2002. *Faits: Lecture courante à l'usage des grands débutants*. Paris: Gallimard.

————. 2007. *Faits, II*. Paris: Galllimard.

————. 2010. *Faits, III: Suite et fin*. Paris: Galllimard.

DAVIS, Lydia. 2010. *The Collected Stories of Lydia Davis*. London: Hamish Hamilton.

GANGEMI, Kenneth. 1969. *Olt: A Novel*. London: Calder & Boyars.

GILOT, Françoise. 1966. *Life with Picasso*. Harmondsworth: Penguin.

HANDKE, Peter. 1977. *The Goalie's Anxiety at the Penalty Kick*. Translated by Michael Roloff. London: Methuen.

————. 1980. *The Left-Handed Woman*. Translated by Ralph Manheim. London: Methuen.

————. 1985. *Slow Homecoming*. Translated by Ralph Manheim. London: Methuen.

————. 1989. *The Afternoon of a Writer*. Translated by Ralph Manheim. London: Methuen.

————. 1998. *Once Again for Thucydides*. Translated by Tess Lewis. New York: New Directions.

HRABAL, Bohumil. 1991. *Too Loud a Solitude*. London: Andre Deutsch.

JAUFFRET, Régis. 2007. *Microfictions*. Paris: Gallimard.

KEILSON, Hans. 2010. *Comedy in a Minor Key*. Translated by Damion Searls. London: Hesperus.

KERTÉSZ, Imre. 2006. *Liquidation*. Translated by Tim Wilkinson. London: Harvill Secker.

MARQUEZ, Gabriel Garcia. 2005. *Memories of My Melancholy Whores*. Translated by Edith Grossman. London: Jonathan Cape.

NOOTEBOOM, Cees. 1993. *The Following Story*. Translated by Ina Rilke. London: Harville.

PYNCHON, Thomas. 2000. *The Crying of Lot Forty Nine*. London: Vintage.

STENDHAL. 1952. *Romans et nouvelles*. Paris: Gallimard.

Americans

BALDWIN, James. 1991. *Nobody Knows My Name: More Notes of Native Son*. London: Penguin.

BURGESS, Anthony. 1981. *Earthly Powers*. Harmondsworth: Penguin.

FITZGERALD, F. Scott. 1958. *Afternoon of an Author: A Selection of Uncollected Stories and Essays*. London: Bodley Head.

MAILER, Norman. 1965. *An American Dream*. London: Andre Deutsch.

——. 1968. *Advertisements for Myself*. London: Panther.

——. 1968. *The Presidential Papers*. Harmondsworth: Penguin.

——. 1969. *Cannibals and Christians*. London: Sphere.

——. 1971. *Barbary Shore*. London: Jonathan Cape.

——. 1988. *Why Are We in Vietnam?* Oxford: Oxford University Press.

——. 1991. *The Deer Park*. London: Paladin.

PENNAC, Daniel. 1994. *Reads Like a Novel*. London: Quartet.

ROTH, Henry. 1976. *Call It Sleep*. Harmondsworth: Penguin.

SALINGER, J. D. *Catcher in the Rye*. 1951. London: Hamish Hamilton.

——. 1953. *For Esme with Love and Squalor*. London: Hamish Hamilton.

——. 1962. *Franny and Zooey*. London: Heinemann.

——. 1964. *Raise High the Roof Beam, Carpenters; and, Seymour: An Introduction*. Harmondsworth: Penguin.

WELTY, Eudora. 1955. *A Curtain of Green: A Volume of Stories*. London: Hamish Hamilton.

Europeans (Extending to Persia)

BOVE, Emmanuel. 1986. *My Friends*. Translated by Janet Louth. Manchester: Carcanet.

HEDAYAT, Sadegh. 1971. *The Blind Owl*. Translated by D. P. Costello. London: Calder & Boyars.

LUSTIG, Arnost. 2001. *Lovely Green Eyes*. Translated by Ewald Osers. London: Harvill.

———. 2004. *Waiting for Leah*. Translated by Ewald Osers. London: Harvill.

OSERS, Ewald. 2007. *Snows of Yesteryear: A Translator's Story*. London: Elliot & Thompson.

WALSER, Robert. 1957. *The Walk and Other Stories*. Translated by Christopher Middleton. London: Calder.

———. 2002. *Selected Stories*. Introduced by Susan Sontag. Translated by Christopher Middleton and others. New York: New York Review of Books.

Europe: British Writers

AMIS, Kingsley. 1953. *Lucky Jim: A Novel*. London: Gollancz.

———. 1986. *Old Devils*. London: Hutchinson.

AMIS, Martin. 1984. *Money: A Suicide Note*. London: Jonathan Cape.

———. 1991. *Time's Arrow; or, the Nature of the Offence*. London: Jonathan Cape.

BAKER, Nicholson. 2009. *The Anthologist*. London: Simon & Schuster.

BARNES, Julian. 1985. *Flaubert's Parrot*. London: Picador.

———. 1989. *The History of the World in Ten and a Half Chapters*. London: Jonathan Cape.

———. 1999. *Nothing to Be Frightened Of*. London: Vintage.

———. 2002. *Something to Declare*. London: Picador.

———. 2005. *Arthur and George*. London: Jonathan Cape.

CARTER, Angela. 1977. *The Passion of New Eve*. London: Gollancz.

———. 1979. *The Sadeian Woman: An Exercise in Cultural History*. London: Virago.

CONNOLLY, Cyril. 1945. *The Unquiet Grave: A Word Cycle*. London: Hamish Hamilton.

———. 1947. *The Rockpool*. London: Hamish Hamilton.

———. 1961. *Enemies of Promise*. Harmondsworth: Penguin.

COOPER, William. 1953. *The Ever-Interesting Topic*. London: Jonathan Cape.

———. 1982. *Scenes from Metropolitan Life*. London: Macmillan.

———. 1991. *Immortality at Any Price*. London: Sinclair-Stevenson.

———. 1999. *Scenes from Death and Life*. Oxford: Smaller Sky.

DAUDET, Alphonse. 2002. *In the Land of Pain*. Edited and translated by Julian Barnes. London: Jonathan Cape.

ELLMANN, Lucy. 1988. *Sweet Desserts*. London: Virago.

———. 1991. *Varying Degrees of Hopelessness*. London: Hamish Hamilton.

———. 2006. *Doctors and Nurses*. London: Bloomsbury.

JACOBSON, Howard. 2010. *The Finkler Question*. London: Bloomsbury.

TOYNBEE, Philip. 1981. *Part of a Journey: An Autobiographical Journal, 1977–1979*. London: Collins.

———. 1988. *End of a Journey: An Autobiographical Jounral, 1979–1981*. Edited by John Bullimore. London: Bloomsbury.

Friends

FEINSTEIN, Elaine. 1973. *The Glass Alembic*. London: Hutchinson.

———. 1984. *The Border*. London: Hutchinson.

———. 1991. *All You Need*. London: Arrow.

———. 1992. *Loving Brecht*. London: Hutchinson.

———. 1994. *Dreamers*. London: Macmillan.

———. 1995. *Lady Chatterley's Confession*. London: Macmillan.

———. 2000. *Gold*. Manchester: Carcanet.

———. 2007. *Talking to the Dead*. Manchester: Carcanet.

GEE, Maggie. 1981. *Dying in Other Words*. Brighton: Harvester.

———. 1983. *The Burning Book*. London: Faber & Faber.

———. 2005. *My Cleaner*. London: Saqi.

MARTIN, Chip. 1979. *The Jew-Hater: A Kunstlerroman*. La Jolla, CA: Starhaven.

———. 1997. *A Journeyman in Bohemia*. La Jolla, CA: Starhaven.

———. 2005. *South: Two Novellas*. London: Starhaven.

McCARTHY, Cormac. 2010. *No Country for Old Men*. London: Picador.

MOORCOCK, Michael. 1981. *Byzantium Endures*. London: Secker & Warburg.

———. 1984. *The Laughter of Carthage*. London: Secker & Warburg.

———. 1992. *Jerusalem Commands*. London: Jonathan Cape.

———. 2006. *The Vengeance of Rome*. London: Jonathan Cape.

SERRE, Anne. 1993. *Un voyage en ballon: Nouvells*. Seyssel: Champ Vallon.

———. 2002. *Le Cheval blanc d'uffington: Roman*. Paris: Mercure de France.

———. 2005. *Le-Mat*. Lagrasse: Verdier.

———. 2008. *Un chapeau leopard: Roman*. Paris: Mercure de France.

SINCLAIR, Clive. 1973. *Bibliosexuality: A Novel*. London: Allison & Busby.

———. 1985. *Blood Libels*. London: Allison & Busby.

———. 1989. *Cosmetic Effects*. London: Andre Deutsch.

———. 1991. *For Good or Evil: The Collected Stories of Clive Sinclair*. London: Penguin.

———. 1993. *Augustus Rex*. London: Penguin.

———. 1996. *The Lady with the Laptop, and Other Stories*. London: Picador.

———. 2008. *Clive Sinclair's True Tales of the Wild West*. London: Picador.

TUCKER, Eva. 1966. *Contact*. Calder & Boyars.

———. 1969. *Drowning: A Novel*. London: Calder & Boyars.

———. 2005. *Berlin Mosaic* . London and La Jolla, CA: Starhaven.

———. 2009. *Becoming English*. London: Starhaven.

WALL, Alan. 1993. *Jacob*. London: Bellew.

———. 1994. *Curved Light*. London: Bellew.

———. 1997. *Bless the Thief*. London: Secker & Warburg.

———. 1999. *The Lightning Cage*. London: Secker & Warburg.

———. 1999. *Richard Dadd in Bedlam*. London: Secker & Warburg.

———. 2003. *China*. London: Secker & Warburg.

———. 2008. *Sylvie's Riddle*. London: Quartet.

Fiction I Don't Read

DISCH, Thomas M. 1969. *Camp Concentration*. London: Panther.

FREEBORN, Richard. 1987. *The Russian Crucifix: A Victorian Mystery*. London: Macmillan.

HOUSEHOLD, Geoffrey. 1939. *Rogue Male*. London: Chatto & Windus.

———. 1965. *A Rough Shoot*. Harmondsworth: Penguin.

———. 1984. *Rogue Justice*. Harmondsworth: Penguin.

LURIE, Alison, ed. 1993. *Oxford Book of Modern Fairy Tales*. Oxford: Oxford University Press.

McMAHON, Katharine. 1999. *Confinement*. London: Flamingo.

———. 2000. *After Mary*. London: Flamingo.

MILLER, Walter M. 1960. *A Canticle for Leibowitz*. London: Weidenfeld & Nicolson.

NADELSON, Reggie. 1995. *Red Mercury Blues*. London: Faber & Faber.

RAYMOND, Derek. 2000. *The Crust on Its Uppers*. London: Serpent's Tail.

STEIN, Gertrude. 1985. *Blood on the Dining-Room Floor*. London: Virago.

SCHOOL BOOKS, REFERENCE BOOKS, PROOF COPIES AND SUCH

Children's Books

BATHURST, David. 1994. *Six of the Best! Being an Affectionate Tribute to Six of the Most Significant School Story Writers of the 20th Century*. Chichester: Romansmead.

BELOFF, Max. 1948. *History: Mankind and His Story*. London: Odhama.

BRIGGS, Raymond. 1983. *When the Wind Blows*. London: Penguin.

GOMBRICH, Ernst. 2005. *A Little History of the World*. New Haven, CT, and London: Yale University Press.

JUSTER, Norton. 1962. *The Phantom Tollbooth*. London: Collins.

MEHLMAN, Jeffrey. 1993. *Walter Benjamin for Children: An Essay on His Radio Years*. Chicago: University of Chicago Press.

POWER, Rhoda. 1952. *Redcap Runs Away*. London: Jonathan Cape.

SENDAK, Maurice. 1970. *In the Night Kitchen*. London: Bodley Head.

———. 1981. *Outside Over There*. London: Bodley Head.

———. 1993. *Where the Wild Things Are*. London: Bodley Head.

THOMPSON, Eric. 1998. *The Adventures of Brian*. London: Bloomsbury.

711

WALKER, Rowland. 1924. *Shandy of Ringmere School.* London: Partridge.

YORK, Susannah. 1973. *In Search of Unicorns.* London: Hodder & Stoughton.

———. 1976. *Lark's Castle.* London: Hodder & Stoughton.

'A'-Level Set Texts and Other School Books

FELDMAN, Gene, and Max Gartenberg, eds. 1959. *Protest: A Selection of Writings by the Beat Generation and the Angry Young Men.* London: Souvenir.

FORSTER, E. M. 1936. *Abinger Harvest.* London: Arnold.

———. 1972. *Two Cheers for Democracy.* London: Arnold.

HEPPENSTALL, Rayner, ed. 1986. *The Master Eccentric: The Journals of Rayner Heppenstall, 1969–1981.* London: Allison & Busby.

HUGHES, Ted. 1969. *Poetry in the Making: An Anthology of Poems and Programmes from Listening and Writing.* London: Faber & Faber.

ZAMYATIN, Yevgeny. 1980. *We.* Translated by Bernard Guilbert Guerney. Harmondsworth: Penguin.

Education

BERG, Leila. 1968. *Risinghill: Death of a Comprehensive School.* Harmondsworth: Penguin.

BRUNER, Jerome S. 1960. *The Process of Education.* Cambridge, MA: Harvard University Press.

———. 1979. *On Knowing: Essays for the Left Hand.* Cambridge, MA, and London: Belknap.

DEWEY, John. 1997. *Experience and Education.* New York: Touchstone.

DIXON, John. 1969. *Growth through English: A Report Based on the Dartmouth Seminar, 1966.* London: Oxford University Press.

DRUCE, Robert. 1965. *The Eye of Innocence: Children and Their Poetry.* Leicester: Brockhampton Press.

HOLBROOK, David. 1964. *The Secret Places: Essays on Imaginative Work in English Teaching and on the Culture of the Child.* London: Methuen.

HOLT, John. 1970. *How Children Learn.* Harmondsworth: Penguin.

———. 1971. *The Underachieving School.* Harmondsworth: Penguin.

————. 1978. *How Children Fail*. Harmondsworth: Penguin.

HORDER, John. 1981. *Meher Baba and the Nothingness*. London: Menard.

————. 1981. *A Sense of Being*. 2nd edn. London: Menard.

KOHL, Herbert. 1970. *The Open Classroom: A Practical Guide to a New Way of Teaching*. London: Methuen.

KOZOL, Jonathan. 1968. *Death at an Early Age: The Destruction of the Hearts and Minds of Negro Children in the Boston Public Schools*. Harmondsworth: Penguin.

PETERS, R. S. 1966. *Ethics and Education*. London: Allen & Unwin.

————, ed. 2010. *The Concept of Education*. London: Routledge.

STEVENS, Don. 1980. *Man's Search for Certainty*. New York: Dodd, Mead.

Reference Books

BONNEFOY, Yves. 1981. *Dictionnaire des mythologies et des religions des societés traditionnelles et du monde antique*. Paris: Flammarion.

CARR, J. L. 2002. *Dictionary of English Kings, Consorts, Pretenders, Usurpers, Unnatural Claimants and Royal Athelings*. Bury St Edmunds: Quince Tree.

KLOSSOWSKI, Pierre. 1971. *Roberte ce soir; and, the Revocation of the Edict of Nantes*. Translated by Austryn Wainhouse. London: Calder & Boyars.

ROSTEN, Leo. 1971. *The Joys of Yiddish: A Relaxed Lexicon of Yiddish, Hebrew and Yinglish Words Often Encountered in English . . . From the Days of the Bible to Those of the Beatnik*. Harmondsworth: Penguin.

————, ed. 1972. *Leo Rosten's Treasury of Jewish Quotations*. New York and London: McGraw-Hill.

VAUGHAN, David. 2008. *Battle for the Airwaves: Radio and the 1938 Munich Crisis*. Prague: Radioservis/Cook Communications.

WELTMAN, G., and M. S. Zuckerman. 2009. *Yiddish Sayings Mama Never Taught You*. New York: iUniverse.

Proof Copies, Review Copies and Rare Books

ALVAREZ, Al. 1999. *Where Did It All Go Right?* London: Cohen.

AMICHAI, Yehuda. 1979. *Time*. Translated by Ted Hughes. Oxford: Oxford University Press.

ATHILL, Diana. 2011. *Instead of a Book: Letters to a Friend*. London: Granta.

BOSLEY, Keith. 1987. *A Chiltern Hundred*. London: Anvil.

———, trans. 1999. *The Kalevala*. Oxford: Oxford University Press.

BRIDSON, D. G. 1943. *Aaron's Field*. London: Pendock.

———. 1950. *The Christmas Child*. London: Falcon.

———. 1971. *Prospero and Ariel: The Rise and Fall of Radio*. London: Gollancz.

———. 1972. *Quest of Gilgamesh*. Cambridge: Rampart Lions.

BUCK, Paul. 1990. *The Honeymoon Killers*. London: Xanadu.

CUNNINGHAM, J. V. 1960. *The Exclusions of a Rhyme: Poems and Epigrams*. Denver, CO: Swallow.

FIELD, Edward. 1977. *A Full Heart*. New York: Sheep Meadow.

———. 2005. *The Man Who Would Marry Susan Sontag, and Other Intimate Literary Portraits of the Bohemian Era*. Madison: University of Wisconsin Press.

FRIEND, Robert. 2003 *Dancing with a Tiger: Poems, 1941–1998*. London: Menard.

GINSBERG, Allen. 1961. *Kaddish, and Other Poems, 1958–1960*. San Francisco: City Lights.

———. 1966. *Wichita Vortex Sutra*. London: Housmans.

———. 1982. *Howl, and Other Poems*. San Francisco: City Lights.

HAGUE, René. 1977. *Commentary on the Anathemata of David Jones*. Wellingborough: Skelton.

HALL, Donald. 1975. *The Town of Hill*. Boston, MA: Godine.

JONES, David. 1969. *The Tribune's Visitation*. London: Fulcrum.

KELLY, Robert. 1970. *Kali Yuga*. London: Cape Goliard.

KEROUAC, Jack. 1971. *Scattered Poems*. San Francisco: City Lights.

LAMANTIA, Philip. 1967. *Selected Poems, 1943–1966*. San Francisco: City Lights.

MCCLURE, Michael. 1974. *Rare Angel (Writ with Raven's Blood)*. Los Angeles: Black Sparrow.

MENASHE, Samuel. 1973. *Fringe of Fire*. London: Gollancz.

SKELTON, Christopher. 1983. *The Engravings of Eric Gill*. Wellingborough: Skelton.

SMITH, Stevie. 1962. *Selected Poems*. London: Longmans, Green & Co.

———. 1969. *Novel on Yellow Paper; or, Work It Out for Yourself.* London: Jonathan Cape.

WURLITZER, Rudolph. 1971. *Flats: A Novel*. London: Gollancz.

PAINTING AND OTHER ARTS
Painters, Their Work and Their Writers

VISUAL ART

BENJAMIN, Walter. 1973. *Charles Baudelaire: A Lyric Poet in the Era of High Capitalism*. Translated by Harry Zohn. London: NLB.

GAYFORD, Martin. 2010. *Man with a Blue Scarf: On Sitting for a Portrait by Lucian Freud*. London: Thames & Hudson.

QUENEAU, Raymond. 2011. *Connaissez-vous Paris?* Paris: Gallimard.

QUEIROS, Eça de. 2002. *The Crime of Father Amaro*. Translated by Nan Flanagan. Manchester: Carcanet.

ROSENBERG, Harold. 1976. *Art on the Edge: Creators and Situations*. London: Secker & Warburg.

VASARI, Giorgio. 1965. *Lives of the Artists*. Edited and translated by George Bull. Harmondsworth: Penguin.

BOOKS BY ARTISTS

ARIKHA, Avigdor. 1995. *On Depiction: Selected Writings on Art, 1965–1994*. London: Bellew.

ATIK, Anne. 1991. *Offshore*. London: Enitharmon.

DIGBY, John, and Joan Digby. 1985. *The Collage Handbook*. London: Thames & Hudson.

GOLUB, Leon. 1997. *Do Paintings Bite? Selected Texts, 1948–1996*. Edited by Hans-Ulrich Obrist. Ostfildern: Cantz.

HERMAN, Josef. 1975. *Related Twilights: Notes from an Artist's Diary*. London: Robson.

MCKEEVER, Ian. 2005. *In Praise of Painting*. Edited by Michael Tucker. Brighton: Centre for Contemporary Visual Arts, University of Brighton.

WRITERS

BONNEFOY, Yves. 2002. *Remarques sur le regard: Picasso, Giacometti, Morandi; L'art en France entre les deux guerres*. Paris: Calmann-Lévy.

———. 2004. *Le Sommeil de personne*. Bordeaux: Blake.

———. 2006. *Dans un débris de miroir*. Paris: Galilee.

———. 2010. *La Communauté des critiques*. Strasbourg: Presses Universitaires de Strasbourg.

CLAIR, Jean. 1996. *Balthus: Les Métamorphoses d'Eros*. Paris: Réunion des musées nationaux/Adagp.

CLARK, T. J. 2006. *The Sight of Death: An Experiment in Art Writing*. New Haven, CT, and London: Yale University Press.

DAVENPORT, Guy. 1989. *A Balthus Notebook*. New York: Ecco.

———. 1998. *Objects on a Table: Harmonious Disarray in Art and Literature*. Washington, DC: Counterpoint.

DIJKSTRA, Bram. 1969. *Cubism, Stieglitz and the Early Poetry of William Carlos Williams: The Hieroglyphics of a New Speech*. Princeton, NJ: Princeton University Press.

DURCAN, Paul. 1994. *Give Me Your Hand*. London: Macmillan, in association with National Gallery Publications.

FARRÉS, Ernest. 2010. *Edward Hopper*. Translated by Lawrence Venuti. Manchester: Carcanet.

GOODRICH, Lloyd. 1949. *Edward Hopper*. Harmondsworth: Penguin.

LEVIN, Gail, ed. 1985. *Hopper's Places*. New York: Alfred A. Knopf.

———. 1995. *The Poetry of Solitude: A Tribute to Edward Hopper*. New York: Universe.

PÉGUY, Charles. 1932. *Clio*. Paris: Gallimard.

RILKE, Rainer Maria. 1955. *Letters to Frau Gudi Nölke During His Life in Switzerland*. Edited by Paul Obermüller. Translated by Violet M. Macdonald. London: Hogarth.

ROMER, Stephen. 2008. *The Yellow Studio*. Manchester: Carcanet.

STEVENS, Wallace. 1959. *Opus Posthumous*. Edited by Samuel French Morse. London: Faber & Faber.

————. 1960. *The Necessary Angel: Essays on Reality and Imagination.* London: Faber & Faber.

TAGGART, John. 1991. *Loop.* Los Angeles: Sun & Moon Press.

————. 1993. *Remaining in Light: Ant Meditations on a Painting by Edward Hopper.* Albany: State University of New York Press.

————. 1999. *And When the Saints.* Jersey City: Talisman House.

————. 2004. *Pastorelles.* Chicago: Flood Editions.

————. 2005. *Crosses: Poems, 1992–1998.* London: Stop Press.

THOMAS, R. S. 1985. *Ingrowing Thoughts.* Bridgend: Poetry Wales.

LIVRES D'ARTISTES, ILLUSTRATED BOOKS, ETC.

BONNEFOY, Yves. 2010. *Poésie et photographie.* Torino: Nino Aragno.

HOOG, Michel. 1994. *Cézanne: The First Modern Painter.* London: Thames & Hudson.

KHALFA, Jean, ed. 2001. *The Dialogue between Painting and Poetry: Livres d'artistes, 1874–1999.* Cambridge: Black Apollo.

PICON, Gaëtan. 1960. *L'Usage de la lecture.* Paris: Mercure de France.

————. 1968. *Un champ de solitude.* Paris: Gallimard.

————. 1968. *Lecture de Proust.* Paris: Gallimard.

————. 1970. *Admirable tremblement du temps.* Geneva: Skira.

————. 1970. *L'Oeuil double.* Paris: Gallimard.

————. 1971. *La Chute d'Icare.* Geneva: Skira.

————. 1974. *1863: Naissance de la peinture modern.* Geneva: Skira.

————. 1978. *The Birth of Modern Painting.* Geneva: Skira.

WALTER, Georges. 1991. *Enquête sur Edgar Allan Poe, poète américain.* Paris: Flammarion.

ART CRITICISM

BRINGHURST, Robert. 2008. *Everywhere Being Is Dancing: Twenty Pieces of Thinking.* Berkeley, CA: Counterpoint.

CASSOU, Jean. 1965. *Chagall.* Translated by Alisa Jaffa. London: Thames & Hudson.

CLARK, Kenneth. 1956. *Landscape into Art*. Harmondsworth: Penguin.

———. 1969. *Civilisation: A Personal View*. London: British Broadcasting Corporation.

DICKSON, Rachel, Jean Liddiard and Sarah MacDougall, eds. 2008. *Whitechapel at War: Isaac Rosenberg and His Circle*. London: Ben Uri Gallery/London Jewish Museum of Art.

FISCHER, Ernst. 1963. *The Necessity of Art: A Marxist Approach*. Translated by Anna Bostock. Harmondsworth: Penguin.

FRIEDLÄNDER, Max J. 1969. *Reminiscences and Reflections*. Edited by Rudolf M. Heilbrunn. London: Evelyn, Adams & Mackay.

GOMBRICH, Ernst. 1995. *The Story of Art*. London: Phaidon.

LIPKE, William. 1967. *David Bomberg: A Critical Study of His Life and Work*. London: Evelyn, Adams & Mackay.

READ, Herbert. 1931. *The Meaning of Art*. London: Faber & Faber.

ROSENBERG, Harold. 1962. *Arshile Gorky: The Man, the Time, the Idea*. New York: Horizon.

ROTHENSTEIN, John. 1945. *Edward Burra*. Harmondsworth: Penguin.

SACKVILLE-WEST, Edward. 1943. *Graham Sutherland*. Harmondsworth: Penguin.

SWEENEY, James Johnson. 1941. *Joan Miro*. New York: Museum of Modern Art.

WILSON, Jonathan. 1995. *The Hiding Room*. London: Secker & Warburg.

———. 2007. *Marc Chagall*. New York: Nextbook-Schocken.

———. 2007. *A Palestine Affair*. Nottingham: Five Leaves.

VISUAL AND VERBAL

ALBERT-BIROT, Pierre. 1964. *Grabinoulor*. Paris: Gallimard.

APOLLINAIRE, Guillaume, and Louis Aragon. 2000. *Flesh Unlimited: Surrealist Erotica*. Translated by Alexis Lykiard. London: Creation Books.

BATAILLE, Georges. 1963. *Le petit*. Paris: Pauvert.

———. 1966. *Ma mère: Roman*. Paris: Pauvert.

———. 1972. *L'Erotisme*. Paris: Union Generale d'Editions.

———. 1988. *Blue of Noon*. Translated by Harry Mathews. London: Paladin.

——. 1999. *Poèmes et nouvelles érotiques*. Paris: Mercure de France.

BÉHAR, Henri, ed. 1972. *Dada en verve*. Paris: Horay.

BOWIE, Malcolm. 1973. *Henri Michaux: A Study of His Literary Works*. Oxford: Clarendon.

CLARK, Thomas A. 2000. *Poets Poems*. Belper: Aggie Weston's Editions.

CLARK, Thomas A., and Laurie Clark. 1978. *A Meadow Voyage*. Nailsworth: Moschatel.

——. 1983. *Pauses and Digressions*. Nailsworth: Moschatel.

EISNER, Will. 2005. *The Plot: The Secret Story of the Protocols of the Elders of Zion*. New York and London: W. W. Norton.

FORD, Mark. 2005. *A Driftwood Altar: Essays and Reviews*. London and Baltimore, MD: Waywiser.

FRIEDMAN, Donald. 2007. *The Writer's Brush: Paintings, Drawings, and Sculpture by Writers*. Minneapolis, MN: Mid-List.

JACOBS, Amber. 2007. *On Matricide: Myth, Psychoanalysis, and the Law of the Mother*. New York and Chichester: Columbia University Press.

JOUFFROY, Alain. 1963. *Un rêve plus long que la nuit*. Paris: Gallimard.

PAZ, Octavio. 1974. *Alternating Current*. Translated by Helen R. Lane. London: Wildwood House.

RÉAGE, Pauline. 1954. *Histoire d'O*. Sceaux: Pauvert.

SORELL, Walter. 1977. *Three Women: Lives of Sex and Genius*. London: Wolff.

STEIN, Gertrude. 1938. *Everybody's Autobiography*. London: Heinemann.

TZARA, Tristan. 1987. *Chanson Dada: Selected Poems of Tristan Tzara*. Translated by Lee Harwood. Boston, MA: Black Widow.

WILLIAMS, James. 2006. *Jean Cocteau*. Manchester and New York: Manchester University Press.

Architecture

DELEUZE, Gilles. 1993. *The Fold: Leibniz and the Baroque*. London: Athlone.

WILSON, Colin St John, and M. J. Long. 2008. *Kitaj: The Architects*. London: Black Dog.

Photography

AGEE, James, and Walker Evans. 1965. *Let Us Now Praise Famous Men: The American Classic, in Words and Photographs, of Three Tenant Families in the Deep South*. London: Peter Owen.

BARTHES, Roland. 2008. *La Chambre claire: Note sur la photographie*. Paris: Gallimard.

BERGER, John. 1972. *Selected Essays and Articles: The Look of Things*. Harmondsworth: Penguin.

————. 1975. *The Seventh Man: A Book of Images and Words about the Experience of Migrant Workers in Europe*. Harmondsworth: Penguin.

————. 1984. *And Our Faces, My Heart, Brief as Photos*. London: Writers and Readers.

————. 2005. *Here Is Where We Meet*. London: Bloomsbury.

————. 2008. *Hold Everything Dear: Dispatches on Survival and Resistance*. London and New York: Verso.

LACEY, Peter, ed. 1969. *The History of the Nude in Photography*. London: Corgi Books.

BURGIN, Victor. 1996. *Some Cities*. London: Reaktion Books.

CALVINO, Italo. 1986. *The Uses of Literature: Essays*. Translated by Patrick Creagh. San Diego, CA: Harcourt Brace Jovanovich.

————. 1992. *Six Memos for the Next Millennium*. Translated by Patrick Creagh. London: Jonathan Cape.

DEAKIN, John. 1949. *London Today: A Selection of Photographs*. London: Saturn Press.

EVANS, Walker. 2000. *Unclassified: A Walker Evans Anthology*. Edited by Douglas Eklund, Walker Evans and Jeff L. Rosenheim. Zurich: Scalo in association with the Metropolitan Museum of Art.

FISHMAN, W. J. 1970. *The Insurrectionists*. London: Methuen.

————. 1975. *East End Jewish Radicals, 1875–1914*. London: Duckworth.

————. 1979. *The Streets of East London*. London: Duckworth.

————. 2005. *East End, 1888: A Year in a London Borough among the Labouring Poor*. Nottingham: Five Leaves Publications.

720

————. 2008. *Into the Abyss: The Life and Work of G.R. Sims*. London: Menard.

GRUŠA, Jīri. 1983. *Franz Kafka of Prague*. Translated by Eric Mosbacher. London: Secker & Warburg.

KERTÉSZ, André. 1982. *On Reading*. Harmondsworth: Penguin.

LEWIS, Chaim. 1965. *A Soho Address*. London: Gollancz.

LINDSAY, Paul. 1993. *The Synagogues of London*. London and Portland: Vallentine-Mitchell.

MAVOR, Carol. 2007. *Reading Boyishly: Roland Barthes, J. M. Barrie, Jacques Henri Lartigue, Marcel Proust, and D. W. Winnicott*. Durham, NC, and London: Duke University Press.

MITCHELL, W. J. T. 2005. *What Do Pictures Want? The Lives and Loves of Images*. Chicago and London: University of Chicago Press.

MORAES, Henrietta. 1994. *Henrietta*. London: Hamish Hamilton.

ROBBE-GRILLET, Alain. 2011. *Why I Love Roland Barthes*. Translated by Andrew Brown. Cambridge and Malden, MA: Polity.

SHAPIRO, Aumie, and Michael Shapiro, eds. 1985. *Memories of the Jewish East End*. London: Springboard Educational Trust.

SINCLAIR, Iain, and Rachel Lichtenstein. 1999. *Rodinsky's Room*. London: Granta.

WARNER, Marina. 2006. *Phantasmagoria: Spirit Visions, Metaphor and Media into the Twenty-First Century*. Oxford and New York: Oxford University Press.

Cinema

AGEL, Henri. 1962. *Esthétique du cinema*. Paris: Presses Universitaires de France.

BUÑUEL, Luis. 2000. *An Unspeakable Betrayal: Selected Writings of Luis Buñuel*. Translated by Garrett White. Berkeley and London: University of California Press.

————. 1983. *My Last Sigh*. Translated by Abigail Israel. New York: Alfred A. Knopf.

CHATEAUBRIAND, François-René. 1980. *Pensées, réflexions et maximes suivies de premières po'sies tableaux de la nature*. Edited by Alain Coelho. Nantes: Le Temps Singulier.

COCTEAU, Jean. 1930. *La Voix humaine: Pièce en un acte*. Paris: Stock.

COLLET, Jean. 1963. *Jean-Luc Godard*. Paris: Seghers.

DUCA, Lo. 1963. *Technique du cinema*. 6th edn. Paris: Presses Universitaires de France.

EDWARDS, Gwynne. 1982. *The Discreet Art of Luis Buñuel*. London: Boyars.

JARSKI, Rosemarie. 2001. *Hollywood Wit: Classic Off-Screen Quips and Quotes*. London: Prion.

KELLY, Linda. 1976. *The Young Romantics: Paris, 1827–1837*. London: Bodley Head.

MITRY, Jean. 1978. *S. M. Eisenstein*. Paris: Delarge.

MORIN, Edgar. 1956. *Le Cinéma; ou, L'Homme imaginaire: Essai d'anthropologie sociologique*. Paris: Minuit.

———. 1960. *The Stars*. Translated by Richard Howard. New York: Grove.

———. 1983. *L'Esprit du temps*. Paris: Grasset.

PHILIPE, Anne. 1963. *Le Temps d'un soupir*. Paris: Julliard.

QUEENAN, Joe. 1994. *If You're Talking to Me Your Career Must Be in Trouble: Movies, Mayhem and Malice*. London: Picador.

ROTHA, Paul. 1949. *The Film till Now: A Survey of World Cinema*. London: Vision.

SHIPMAN, David. 1979. *The Great Movie Stars: The Golden Years*. London: Angus and Robertson.

Drama

BAMFORTH, Iain. 2006. *The Good European: Essays and Arguments*. Manchester: Carcanet.

BROOK, Peter. 1990. *The Empty Space*. Harmondsworth: Penguin.

BÜCHNER, Georg. 1987. *The Complete Plays*. Edited and translated by Michael Patterson. London: Methuen.

CELAN, Paul. 1999. *Collected Prose*. Translated by Rosmarie Waldrop. Manchester: Carcanet.

———. 2011. *The Meridian: Final Version—Drafts—Materials*. Edited by Bernhard Böschenstein and Heino Schull. Translated by Pierre Joris. Stanford, CA: Stanford University Press.

COE, Richard. 1961. *Ionesco*. Edinburgh and London: Oliver & Boyd.

Cole, Toby, ed. 1980. *Playwrights on Playwrighting: The Meaning and Making of Modern Drama from Ibsen to Ionesco*. New York: Hill & Wang.

Esslin, Martin. 1962. *The Theatre of the Absurd*. London: Eyre & Spottiswoode.

———. 1984. *Brecht: A Choice of Evils*. London: Methuen.

Heaney, Seamus, and Ted Hughes, eds. 1982. *The Rattle Bag*. London: Faber & Faber.

Howell, Anthony. 1999. *The Analysis of Performance Art: A Guide to Its Theory and Practice*. Amsterdam: Harwood Academic.

———. 2001. *Serbian Sturgeon: A Journal of a Visit to Belgrade*. Amsterdam: Harwood Academic.

Kleist, Heinrich von. 1969. 'The Prince of Homburg', translated by Jonathan Griffin. In *Plays of the Year*, VOL. 36, edited by J. C. Trewin, London: Elek/Menard.

Pinter, Harold. 1979. *I Know the Place: Poems*. Warwick: Greville.

Tynan, Kenneth. 1964. *Tynan on Theatre*. Harmondsworth: Penguin.

———. 1994. *Letters*. Edited by Kathleen Tynan. London: Weidenfeld & Nicolson.

Updike, John. 1972. *Seventy Poems*. Harmondsworth: Penguin.

Welwarth, George. 1964. *The Theater of Protest and Paradox*. New York: New York University Press.

Wesker, Arnold. 1959. *Roots*. Harmondsworth: Penguin.

Williams, Tennessee. 2002. *Collected Poems*. Edited by David Roessel and Nicholas Moschovakis. New York and London: New Directions.

Music

Ansen, Alan. 1991. *The Table Talk of W. H. Auden*. Edited by Nicholas Jenkins. London: Faber & Faber.

Bernstein, Leonard. 1968. *The Joy of Music*. London: Weidenfeld & Nicolson.

Burgess, Anthony. 1982. *This Man and Music*. London: Hutchinson.

Burt, Dan. 2012. *We Look Like This*. Manchester: Carcanet.

Cooke, Deryck. 1989. *The Language of Music*. Oxford: Oxford University Press.

COTT, Jonathan. 1984. *Conversations with Glenn Gould.* Boston, MA: Little, Brown.

DILLON, Brian. 2010. *Tormented Hope.* Dublin: Penguin.

FELDMAN, Morton. 1985. *Essays.* Kerpen: Beginner.

HILL, Ralph, ed. 1949. *The Symphony.* Harmondsworth: Penguin.

———, ed. 1952. *The Concerto.* Harmondsworth: Penguin.

HOFFMAN, Eva. 2009. *Illuminations.* London: Vintage.

KAUFMAN, Louis, and Annette Kaufman. 2003. *A Fiddler's Tale: How Hollywood and Vivaldi Discovered Me.* Madison and London: University of Wisconsin Press.

MACPHERSON, Stewart. 1910. *Music and Its Appreciation; or, the Foundations of True Listening.* London: Williams.

———. 1930. *Form in Music: With Special Reference to the Designs of Instrumental Music.* London: Williams.

ROBERTSON, Alec, ed. 1957. *Chamber Music.* Harmondsworth: Penguin.

ROSEN, Charles. 2004. *Piano Notes: The Hidden World of the Pianist.* London: Penguin.

———. 2010. *Music and Sentiment.* New Haven, CT, and London: Yale University Press.

SCHOLES, Percy. 1942. *The Listener's Guide to Music: With a Concert-Goer's Glossary.* London: Oxford University Press.

Sport

ARLOTT, John. 1955. *The Picture of Cricket.* Harmondsworth: Penguin.

BAKER, William, and Stephen Ely Tabachnik. 1973. *Harold Pinter.* Edinburgh: Oliver & Boyd.

BARNA, Victor. 1962. *Table Tennis Today.* London: Barker.

CARR, J. L. 2005. *Carr's Dictionary of Extraordinary Cricketers.* London: Aurum.

CHARYN, Jerome. 2002. *Sizzling Chops and Devilish Spins: Ping-Pong and the Art of Staying Alive.* London: Souvenir.

CLEMENTS, Roy. 1992. *The Alternative Wisden on Samuel Barclay Beckett, 1906–1989.* London: Daripress.

GILLER, Norman. 2002. *Billy Wright: A Hero for All Seasons*. London: Robson.

GOLOMBEK, Harry. 1954. *The Game of Chess*. Harmondsworth: Penguin.

JACOBSON, Howard. 1993. *Roots Schmoots: Journeys Among Jews*. London: Penguin.

———. 1999. *The Mighty Walzer*. London: Jonathan Cape.

STEINER, George. 1973. *The Sporting Scene: White Knights of Reykjavik*. London: Faber & Faber.

SYNGE, Allen, ed. 1974. *Strangers' Gallery: Some Foreign Views of English Cricket*. London: Lemon Tree.

VENNER, Harry. 1960. *Instructions in Table Tennis*. London: Museum Press.

WARNER, Rex, and Lyle Blair. 1951. *Ashes to Ashes: A Post-mortem on the 1950 to 51 Tests*. London: MacGibbon & Kee.

HUMAN SCIENCES AND SCIENCE
Social Anthropology and Sociology

BAUDRILLARD, Jean. 2002. *The Spirit of Terrorism*. Translated by Chris Turner. London: Verso.

BENDIX, Reinhard. 1960. *Weber: An Intellectual Portrait*. London: Heinemann.

BENEDICT, Ruth. 1949. *Patterns of Culture*. London: Routledge & Kegan Paul.

BENOIST, Jean-Marie. 1994. *Marx est mort*. Paris: PUF.

BORGES, Jorge Luis. 2000. *Collected Fiction*. Translated by Andrew Hurley. London: Penguin.

BOTTOMORE, Tom. 1965. *Classes in Modern Society*. London: Allen & Unwin.

———. 1966. *Elites and Society*. Harmondsworth: Penguin.

———, and M. Rubel, eds. 1956. *Karl Marx: Selected Writings in Sociology and Social Philosophy*. London: Watts.

CAILLOIS, Roger. 1988. *L'Homme et le sacré*. Paris: Gallimard.

DAMASIO, Antonio. 2003. *Looking for Spinoza: Joy, Sorrow and the Feeling Brain*. London: Heinemann.

DOUGLAS, Mary. 1966. *Purity and Danger: An Analysis of Concepts of Pollution and Taboo*. London: Routledge & Kegan Paul.

———. 1996. *Natural Symbols: Explorations in Cosmology*. London: Routledge.

DURKHEIM, Emile. 1952. *Suicide: A Study in Sociology*. Edited by G. Simpson. Translated by A. Spaulding and G. Simpson. London: Routledge & Kegan Paul.

———. 1953. *Sociology and Philosophy*. Translated by D. F. Pocock. London: Cohen & West.

———. 1962. *Socialism*. Edited by Alvin W. Gouldner. Translated by Charlotte Sattler. London: Collier.

———. 1968. *The Elementary Forms of the Religious Life*. Translated by Joseph Ward Swain. London: Allen & Unwin.

———. 1984. *The Division of Labour in Society*. Translated by W. D. Halls. Basingstoke: Macmillan.

———, and M. Mauss. 1970. *Primitive Classification*. Edited and translated by Rodney Needham. London: Cohen & West.

EAGLETON, Terry. 2011. *Why Marx Was Right*. New Haven, CT, and London: Yale University Press.

ÉLIADE, Mircea. 1959. *Cosmos and History: The Myth of the Eternal Return*. Translated by Willard R. Trask. New York: Harper & Row.

———. 1959. *The Sacred and the Profane*. Translated by Willard R. Trask. New York: Harcourt Brace Jovanovich.

———. 1963. *Aspects du mythe*. Paris: Gallimard.

EVANS-PRITCHARD, E. E. 1940. *The Nuer: A Description of the Modes of Livelihood and Political Institutions of a Nilotic People*. Oxford: Clarendon.

———. 1956. *Nuer Religion*. Oxford: Clarendon.

———. 1962. *Essays in Social Anthropology*. London: Faber & Faber.

FORDE, Daryll. 1954. *African Worlds: Studies in the Cosmological Ideas and Social Values of African Peoples*. Oxford: Oxford University Press, for the International African Institute.

FORTUNE, R. F. 1935. *Manus Religion: An Ethnological Study of the Manus Natives of the Admiralty Islands*. Philadelphia, PA: The American Philosophical Society.

————. 1963. *Sorcerers of Dobu: The Social Anthropology of the Dobu Islanders of the Western Pacific*. London: Routledge & Kegan Paul.

GERTH, H., and C. Wright Mills, eds. 1948. *From Max Weber: Essays in Sociology*. London: Routledge & Kegan Paul.

GLUCKMAN, Max, ed. 1962. *Essays on the Ritual of Social Relations*. Manchester: Manchester University Press.

————, ed. 1964. *Closed Systems and Open Minds: The Limits of Naivety in Social Anthropology*. Edinburgh: Oliver & Boyd.

GOFFMAN, Erving. 1968. *Asylums: Essays on the Social Situation of Mental Patients and Other Inmates*. Harmondsworth and New York: Penguin.

————. 1969. *The Presentation of Self in Everyday Life*. London: Allen Lane.

————. 1972. *Interaction Ritual and Stigma: Essays on Face-to-Face Behaviour*. Harmondsworth: Penguin.

————. 1990. *Stigma: Notes on the Management of Spoiled Identity*. Harmondsworth: Penguin.

HALBWACHS, Maurice. 1992. *On Collective Memory*. Translated by Lewis A. Coser. Chicago: University of Chicago Press.

HARRIS, Marvin. 1979. *Cultural Materialism: The Struggle for a Science of Culture*. New York: Random House.

HERTZ, Robert. 1960. *Death and the Right Hand*. Translated by Rodney and Claudia Needham. Aberdeen: Cohen & West.

HUBERT, H., and M. Mauss. 1964. *Sacrifice: Its Nature and Function*. Translated by W. D. Halls. London: Cohen & West.

HYDE, Lewis. 1999. *The Gift: Imagination and the Erotic Life of Property*. London: Vintage.

KOTOWICZ, Z. 2012. *Psychosurgery: The Birth of a New Scientific Paradigm: Egas Moniz and the Present Day*. Lisbon: Centre for Philosophy of Science.

KROEBER, A. L., and C. Kluckhohn. 1952. *Culture: A Critical Review of Concepts and Definitions*. Cambridge, MA: Peabody Museum of Archaelogy and Ethnology.

LEACH, Edmund. 1961. *Rethinking Anthropology*. London: Athlone.

————, ed. 1967. *The Structural Study of Myth and Totemism*. London: Tavistock.

————. 1969. *Genesis as Myth and Other Essays*. London: Jonathan Cape.

————. 1970. *Lévi-Strauss*. London: Fontana Books/Collins.

LEIRIS, Michel. 1992. *Brisées*. Paris: Gallimard.

LÉVI-STRAUSS, Claude. 1948. *La Vie familiale et sociale des indiens Nambikwara*. Paris: Société des Américanistes.

————. 1956. *Tristes tropiques*. Paris: Plon.

————. 1962. *La Pensée sauvage*. Paris: Plon.

————. 1962. *Le Totémisme aujourd'hui*. Paris: Presses Universitaires de France.

————. 1963. *Tristes tropiques*. Translated by John Russell. New York: Atheneum.

————. 1964a. *Le Cru et le cuit*. Mythologies. Paris: Plon.

————. 1964b. *Totemism*. Introduced by Roger Poole. Translated by Rodney Needham. London: Merlin.

————. 1967. *The Scope of Anthropology*. Translated by Sherry Ortner Paul and Robert A. Paul. London: Jonathan Cape.

————. 1968. *Structural Anthropology*. Translated by Claire Jacobson and Brooke Grundfest Schoepf. Harmondsworth: Penguin.

————. 1989. *Myth and Meaning*. London: Routledge.

————. 1997. *Look, Listen, Read*. Translated by Brian C. J. Singer. New York: Basic Books.

————, with Georges Charbonnier. 1961. *Entretiens avec Claude Lévi-Strauss*. Paris: Plon-Julliard.

LINCOLN, Bruce. 1991. *Death, War and Sacrifice*: *Studies in Ideology and Practice*. Chicago: University of Chicago Press.

LINDSAY, Maurice, ed. 1946. *Modern Scottish Poetry*: *An Anthology of the Scottish Renaissance, 1920–1945*. London: Faber & Faber.

MACCOBY, Hyam. 1982. *The Sacred Executioner*: *Human Sacrifice and the Legacy of Guilt*. London: Thames & Hudson.

————. 1996. *A Pariah People*: *The Anthropology of Antisemitism*. London: Constable.

———. 2001. *The Disputation*. London: Calder.

———. 2006. *Antisemitism and Modernity: Innovation and Continuity*. London and New York: Routledge.

MacRae, Donald. 1974. *Weber*. London: Fontana Books/Collins.

Malinowski, B. 1922. *Argonauts of the Western Pacific: An Account of Native Enterprise and Adventure in the Archipelagoes of Melanesian New Guinea*. London: Routledge.

———. 1963. *Sex, Culture and Myth*. London: Hart-Davis.

———. 1968. *The Sexual Life of Savages in North-Western Melanesia: An Ethnographic Account of Courtship, Marriage, and Family Life among the Natives of the Trobriand Islands, British New Guinea by Bronislaw Malinowski*. 3rd edn. London: Routledge & Kegan Paul.

———. 1974. *Magic, Science and Religion, and Other Essays*. London: Souvenir.

Mauss, Marcel. 1950. *Sociologie et anthropologie*. Paris: Presses Universitaires de France.

———. 1998. *Marcel Mauss: A Centenary Tribute*. Edited by Wendy James and N. J. Allen. New York and Oxford: Berghahn.

McLellan, David. 1975. *Marx*. London: Fontana Books.

McLuhan, Marshall. 1962. *The Gutenberg Galaxy: The Making of Typographic Man*. London: Routledge & Kegan Paul.

———. 1964. *Understanding Media: The Extensions of Man*. Routledge & Kegan Paul.

———. 1970. *Counterblast*. London: Rapp & Whiting.

———. 2008. *The Medium Is the Massage*. Co-ordinated by Jerome Agel. London: Penguin.

———, and Quentin Fiore. 1968. *War and Peace in the Global Village*. Coordinated by Jerome Agel. New York and London: Bantam.

Meighan, Roland. 1986. *A Sociology of Educating*. 2nd edn. London: Holt, Rinehart & Winston.

Meyer, Alfred G. 1954. *Marxism: The Unity of Theory and Practice*. Cambridge, MA: Harvard University Press.

Mills, C. Wright. 1970. *The Sociological Imagination*. Harmondsworth: Penguin.

PAZ, Octavio. 1971. *Claude Lévi-Strauss: An Introduction*. Translated by J. S. Bernstein and Maxine Bernstein. London: Jonathan Cape.

POOLE, Roger. 1972. *Towards Deep Subjectivity*. London: Allen Lane.

RUNCIMAN, W. G. 1963. *Social Science and Political Theory*. Cambridge: Cambridge University Press.

SEBEOK, Thomas, ed. 1965. *Myth: A Symposium*. Bloomington and London: Indiana University Press.

SEMPRUN, Jorge. 1964. *The Long Voyage*. Translated by Richard Seaver. London: Weidenfeld & Nicolson.

———. 1997. *Literature or Life*. Translated by Linda Coverdale. London: Viking.

———. 1997. *Mal et modernité*. Paris: Seuil.

———. 1983. *What a Beautiful Sunday*. Translated by Alan Sheridan. London: Secker & Warburg.

———. 2001. *Le Mort qu'il faut*. Paris: Gallimard.

———, with Elie Wiesel. 1995. *Se taire est impossible*. Paris: Arte.

SIMMEL, George. 1964. *Conflict; and, the Web of Group-Affiliations*. Translated by Kurt H. Wolff. Glencoe, IL: Free Press.

STEINER, Franz. 1967. *Taboo*. Harmondsworth: Penguin.

———. 1992. *Poems*. Translated by Michael Hamburger. London: Modern Poetry in Translation.

TARN, Nathaniel. 2007. *The Embattled Lyric: Essays and Conversations in Poetics and Anthropology*. Stanford, CA: Stanford University Press.

TITMUSS, Richard. 1970. *The Gift Relationship: From Human Blood to Social Policy*. London: Allen & Unwin.

TRASK, Willard, ed. 1969. *The Unwritten Song: Poetry of the Primitive and Traditional Peoples of the World*. London: Jonathan Cape.

TURNER, Victor. 1969. *The Ritual Process: Structure and Anti-Structure*. London: Routledge & Kegan Paul.

VAN GENNEP, Arnold. 1960. *Rites of Passage*. Translated by Monika B. Vizedom and Gabrielle L. Caffe. London: Routledge & Kegan Paul.

WHEEN, Francis. 2000. *Karl Marx*. London: Fourth Estate.

WRIGHT, Charles R. 1961. *Mass Communication: A Sociological Perspective.* New York: Random House.

Philosophy

BERKELEY, Bishop. 1998. *A Treatise Concerning the Principles of Human Knowledge.* Edited by Jonathan Dancy. Oxford: Oxford University Press.

DESCARTES, Réne. 1937. *Descartes' Discourse on Method.* Oxford: Clarendon.

DIDEROT, Denis. 1972. *La Religieuse.* Paris: Gallimard.

———. 1999. *Thoughts on the Interpretation of Nature.* Edited by David Adams. Manchester: Clinamen.

FUENTES, Carlos. 1988. *Myself with Others: Selected Essays.* London: Andre Deutsch.

HART, Kevin. 2004. *The Dark Gaze: Maurice Blanchot and the Sacred.* Chicago and London: University of Chicago Press.

HEIDEGGER, Martin. 1975. *Poetry, Language and Thought.* Translated by Albert Hofstadter. New York and London: Harper & Row.

KAUFMANN, Walter, ed. 1957. *Existentialism from Dostoevsky to Sartre.* London: Thames & Hudson.

KIERKEGAARD, S. 1958. *The Journals, 1834–1854.* Edited and translated by Alexander Dru. London: Collins.

———. 1965. *The Last Years: Journals, 1853–1855.* Edited and translated by Ronald Gregor Smith. London: Collins.

MOORE, G. E. 1976. *Principia Ethica.* Cambridge: Cambridge University Press.

NIETZSCHE, F. 1982. *Daybreak: Thoughts on the Prejudices of Morality.* Translated by R. J. Hollingdale. Cambridge: Cambridge University Press.

———. 1988. *Ecce Homo: How One Becomes What One Is.* Translated by R. J. Hollingdale. London: Penguin.

PAULHAN, Jean. 1941. *Les Fleurs de Tarbes; ou, La Terreur dans les lettres.* Paris: Gallimard.

RUSSELL, Bertrand. 1959. *The Problems of Philosophy.* London: Oxford University Press.

SCARRY, Elaine. 2001. *Dreaming by the Book*. Princeton, NJ: Princeton University Press.

STEINER, George. 1978. *Heidegger*. Glasgow: Fontana Books/Collins.

STOKES, Adrian. 1973. *A Game That Must Be Lost: Collected Papers*. Cheadle: Carcanet.

WEIL, Simone. 1952. *Gravity and Grace*. Translated by Emma Craufurd. London: Routledge & Kegan Paul.

Psychoanalysis, etc.

BAKAN, David. 1990. *Sigmund Freud and the Jewish Mystical Tradition*. London: Free Association.

BETTELHEIM, Bruno. 1983. *Freud and Man's Soul*. London: Chatto & Windus.

BIALE, David. 1997. *Eros and the Jews: From Biblical Israel to Contemporary America*. Berkeley and London: University of California Press.

BLY, Robert. 1990. *A Little Book on the Human Shadow*. Edited by William Booth. Shaftesbury: Element.

BROWN, J. A. C. 1964. *Freud and the Post-Freudians*. Harmondsworth: Penguin.

BROWN, Norman O. 1959. *Life Against Death: The Psychoanalytical Meaning of History*. London: Routledge & Kegan Paul.

———. 1973. *Closing Time*. New York: Random House.

———. 1990. *Love's Body*. Berkeley: University of California Press.

———. 1991. *Apocalypse and/or Metamorphosis*. Berkeley: University of California Press.

COOPER, David. 1971. *The Death of the Family*. London: Allen Lane.

———. 1974. *Grammar of Living: An Examination of Political Acts*. London: Allen Lane.

CROWCROFT, Andrew. 1967. *The Psychotic: Understanding Madness*. Harmondsworth: Penguin.

DERRIDA, Jacques. 1996. *Archive Fever: A Freudian Impression*. Translated by Eric Prenowitz. Chicago and London: University of Chicago Press.

DOLITTLE, Hilda (HD). 1985. *Tribute to Freud; Writing on the Wall; Advent*. Manchester: Carcanet.

ESTERSON, Aaron. 1972. *The Leaves of Spring: A Study in the Dialectics of Madness.* Harmondsworth: Penguin.

FRANKL, George. 1974. *The Failure of the Sexual Revolution.* London: Kahn & Averill.

FREUD, Sigmund. 1928. *The Future of an Illusion.* Translated by W. D. Robson-Scott. London: Hogarth/Institute of Psycho-analysis.

———. 1938. *The Psychopathology of Everyday Life.* Edited by A. A. Brill. Harmondsworth: Penguin.

———. 1938. *Totem and Taboo: Resemblances Between the Psychic Lives of Savages and Neurotics.* Translated by A. A. Brill. Harmondsworth: Penguin.

———. 1961. *Beyond the Pleasure Principle, and Other Writings.* Translated by John Reddick. London: Hogarth.

———. 1962. *Two Short Accounts of Psycho-analysis.* Edited and translated by James Strachey. Harmondsworth: Penguin.

———. 1963. *Civilisation and its Discontents.* Edited by James Strachey. Translated by Joan Riviere. London: Hogarth/Institute of Psycho-analysis.

———. 1974. *Moses and Monotheism.* Edited and translated by James Strachey. London: Hogarth/Institute of Psycho-analysis.

———. 1974. *New Introductory Lectures on Psychoanalysis.* Edited and translated by James Strachey. London: Hogarth/Institute of Psycho-analysis.

HERMAN, Nini. 1987. *Why Psychotherapy.* London: Free Association.

———. 1988. *My Kleinian Home: A Journey Through Four Psychotherapies.* London: Free Association.

HILLMAN, James. 1985. *Anima: The Anatomy of a Personified Notion.* Dallas: Spring.

HUDSON, Liam. 1966. *Contrary Imaginations: A Psychological Study of the English Schoolboy.* London: Methuen.

———. 1968. *Frames of Mind: Ability, Perception and Self-Perception in the Arts and Sciences.* London: Methuen.

JUNG, Carl Gustave. 1971. *Psychological Reflections.* Edited by Jolande Jacobi. 2nd edn. London: Routledge & Kegan Paul.

KELLMAN, Steven. 2005. *Redemption: The Life of Henry Roth.* New York and London: W. W. Norton.

KOTOWICZ, Z. 1997. *Laing and the Paths of Anti-psychiatry*. London and New York: Routledge.

LAING, R. D. 1965. *The Divided Self: An Existential Study in Sanity and Madness*. Harmondsworth: Penguin.

———. 1967. *The Politics of Experience and The Bird of Paradise*. Harmondsworth: Penguin.

———. 1970. *Knots*. London: Tavistock.

———. 1976. *The Facts of Life*. London: Allen Lane.

———. 1977. *Do You Love Me? An Entertainment in Conversation and Verse*. London: Allen Lane.

———. 1990. *The Self and Others*. 2nd edn. Harmondsworth: Penguin.

———, and David Cooper. 1964. *Reason and Violence: A Decade of Sartre's Philosophy, 1950–1960*. London: Tavistock.

LEVINSON, Daniel J. 1978. *The Seasons of a Man's Life*. New York: Alfred A. Knopf.

MACINTYRE, Alasdair. 1970. *Marcuse*. London: Fontana Books.

MALCOLM, Janet. 1984. *In the Freud Archives*. London: Jonathan Cape.

MARCUSE, Herbert. 1972. *Eros and Civilisation*. London: Abacus.

MILLER, Alice. 1987. *The Drama of Being a Child: The Search for the True Self*. Translated by Ruth Ward. London: Virago.

———. 1990. *The Untouched Key: Tracing Childhood Trauma in Creativity and Destructiveness*. Translated by Hildegarde and Hunter Hannum. London: Virago.

———. 1991. *Breaking Down the Wall of Silence: To Join the Waiting Child*. Translated by Simon Worrall. London: Virago.

———. 1995. *Pictures of a Childhood: Sixty-Six Watercolours and an Essay*. Translated by Hildegarde Hannum. London: Virago.

PHILLIPS, Adam, ed. 2006. *The Freud Reader*. London: Penguin.

PONTALIS, Jean-Bertrand. 2002. *En marge des jours*. Paris: Gallimard.

———. 2010. *En marge des nuits*. Paris: Gallimard.

———. 2012. *Avant*. Paris: Gallimard.

REICH, Wilhelm. 1972. *Mass Psychology of Fascism*. Edited by Mary Higgins and Chester M. Raphael. Translated by Vincent R. Carfagno. London: Souvenir.

RIEFF, Philip. 1975. *Fellow Teachers*. London: Faber & Faber.

————. 2006. *Life among the Deathworks: Illustrations of the Aesthetics of Authority*. Charlottesville: University of Virginia Press.

ROBERT, Marthe. 1977. *From Oedipus to Moses: Freud's Jewish Identity*. Translated by Ralph Manheim. London: Routledge & Kegan Paul.

SALMON, Phillida. 1985. *Living in Time: A New Look at Personal Development*. London: Dent.

SCHATZMAN, Morton. 1973. *Soul Murder: Persecution in the Family*. London: Allen Lane.

SMAIL, David. 1987. *Taking Care: An Alternative to Therapy*. London: Dent.

STEIN, Murray. 1983. *In Midlife: A Jungian Perspective*. Dallas, TX: Spring.

STEINER, George. 1971. *In Bluebeard's Castle: Some Notes Towards the Re-definition of Culture*. London: Faber & Faber.

————. 1989. *Real Presences: Is There Anything in What We Say?* London: Faber & Faber.

WEBSTER, Richard. 1995. *Why Freud Was Wrong: Sin, Science and Psychoanalysis*. London: HarperCollins.

WELCH, John. 2008. *Dreaming Arrival*. Exeter: Shearsman Books.

YERUSHALMI, Yosef Hayim. 1982. *Zakhor: Jewish History and Jewish Memory*. Seattle and London: University of Washington Press.

————. 1991. *Freud's Moses: Judaism Terminable and Interminable*. New Haven, CT, and London: Yale University Press.

Language

BLOOMFIELD, Leonard. 1935. *Language*. London: Allen & Unwin.

BROWN, Roger. 1973. *A First Language: The Early Stages*. London: Allen & Unwin.

CASSIRER, Ernst. 1946. *Language and Myth*. Translated by Susanne K. Langer. New York and London: Harper & Brothers.

CHOMSKY, Noam. 1957. *Syntactic Structures*. The Hague: Mouton.

————. 1964. *Current Issues in Linguistic Theory.* The Hague: Mouton.

————. 1968. *Language and Mind.* New York: Harcourt, Brace & World.

CULLER, Jonathan. 1975. *Structuralist Poetics: Structuralism, Linguistics and the Study of Literature.* London: Routledge & Kegan Paul.

————. 1976. *Saussure.* Glasgow: Fontana Books/Collins.

FIXEL, Lawrence. 1979. *Book of Glimmers.* London: Menard.

————. 1991. *Truth, War and the Dream-Game: Selected Prose Poems and Parables, 1966–1990.* Minneapolis: Coffee House.

GIMSON, A. C. 1962. *An Introduction to the Pronunciation of English.* London: Arnold.

GLEASON, H. A. 1955. *An Introduction to Descriptive Linguistics.* London: Holt, Rinehart & Winston.

GOODMAN, Paul. 1973. *Speaking and Language: Defence of Poetry.* London: Wildwood House.

HARRIS, Zellig. 1951. *Structural Linguistics.* Chicago: University of Chicago Press.

HOCKETT, C. F. 1958. *A Course in Modern Linguistics.* New York: Macmillan.

JAKOBSON, Roman. 1963. *Essais de linguistique génerale.* Translated from English by Nicolas Ruwet. Paris: Minuit.

————, and Maurice Halle. 1956. *Fundamentals of Language.* The Hague: Mouton.

JESPERSEN, Otto. 1959. *Language: Its Nature, Development and Origin.* London: Allen & Unwin.

LYONS, John. 1970. *Chomsky.* London: Fontana Books.

PEYROLLAZ, Marguerite. 1954. *Manuel de phonétique et de diction françaises à l'usage des étrangers.* Paris: Larousse.

SAPIR, Edward. 1956. *Culture, Language and Personality: Selected Essays.* Edited by David G. Mandelbaum. Berkeley: University of California Press.

SAUSSURE, F. de. 1967. *Cours de linguistique générale.* Edited by Rudolf Engler. Wiesbaden: Harrassowitz.

SEBEOK, Thomas. 1968. *Style in Language.* Cambridge, MA: MIT Press.

STEINER, George. 1978. *On Difficulty, and Other Essays.* Oxford: Oxford University Press.

ULLMANN, Stephen. 1964. *Language and Style: Collected Papers*. Oxford: Blackwell.

WHORF, Benjamin. 1956. *Language, Thought and Reality: Selected Writings*. Edited by John B. Carroll. Cambridge, MA: MIT Press.

WILLIAMS, Raymond. 1976. *Keywords: A Vocabulary of Culture and Society*. London: Fontana Books.

History

BARTHES, Roland. 1954. *Michelet*. Paris: Seuil.

BERNSTEIN, Michael André. 1994. *Foregone Conclusions: Against Apocalyptic History*. Berkeley and London: University of California Press.

BROWN, Cynthia Stokes. 1988. *Like It Was: A Complete Guide to Writing Oral History*. New York: Teachers & Writers Collaborative.

CANARY, Robert, and Henry Kozicki, eds. 1978. *The Writing of History: Literary Form and Historical Understanding*. Madison: University of Wisconsin Press.

CARR, E. H. 1964. *What Is History? The George Macaulay Trevelyan Lectures Delivered in the University of Cambridge, January–March 1961*. Harmondsworth: Penguin.

GOLDEMBERG, Isaac. 1978. *The Fragmented Life of Don Jacobo Lerner*. Translated by Robert S. Picciotto. London: Sidgwick & Jackson.

HOBSBAWM, Eric. 1962. *The Age of Revolution: Europe 1789–1848*. London: Weidenfeld & Nicolson.

LEIGH, Martha. 2008. *'Couldn't Afford the Eels': Memories of Wapping, 1900–1960*. Stroud: History Press.

MICHELET, Jules. 1984. *Mother Death: The Journal of Jules Michelet, 1815–1850*. Edited and translated by Edward K. Kaplan. Amherst: University of Massachusetts Press.

MORSE, Jonathan. 1990. *Word by Word: Language of Memory*. Ithaca, NY: Cornell University Press.

REZNIKOFF, Charles. 1978. *Testimony: The United States, 1885–1915*. Santa Barbara, CA: Black Sparrow.

SEED, John. 2005. *Pictures from Mayhew: London 1850*. Exeter: Shearsman Books.

———. 2007. *That Barrikins: Pictures from Mayhew II—London 1850*. Exeter: Shearsman Books.

SINCLAIR, Iain, ed. 2006. *London: City of Disappearances*. London: Hamish Hamilton.

THOMPSON, E. P. 1993. *Witness against the Beast: William Blake and the Moral Law*. Cambridge: Cambridge University Press.

———. 1997. *The Romantics: England in a Revolutrionary Age*. Woodbridge: Merlin.

———. 1999. *Collected Poems*. Edited by Fred Inglis. Newcastle-upon-Tyne: Bloodaxe Books.

VERNADSKY, George. 1929. *A History of Russia*. New Haven, CT, and London: Yale University Press.

WELLS, H. G. 1945. *Mind at the End of Its Tether*. London: Heinemann.

———. 1961. *Axel's Castle: A Study in the Imaginative Literature of 1870–1930*. London: Collins.

WHITE, Hayden. 1973. *Metahistory: The Historical Imagination in Nineteenth Century Europe*. Baltimore, MD: Johns Hopkins University Press.

———. 1978. *Tropics of Discourse: Essays in Cultural Criticism*. Baltimore, MD, and London: Johns Hopkins University Press.

———. 1987. *The Content of the Form: Narrative Discourse and Historical Representation*. Baltimore, MD, and London: Johns Hopkins University Press.

Travel Books

BOND, Robert. 2005. *Iain Sinclair*. Cambridge, MA: Salt.

BRODSKY, Joseph. 1965. *Stikhotvoreniya i Poemi*. Washington, DC: Inter-Language Literary Associates.

———. 1966. *Collines et autres poèmes*. Translated by J.-J. Marie. Paris: Seuil.

———. 1973. *Selected Poems*. Translated by George Kline. Harmondsworth: Penguin.

———. 1992. *Watermark*. London: Hamish Hamilton.

BUCK, Paul. 2002. *Lisbon: A Cultural and Literary Companion*. Oxford: Signal.

FOXELL, Nigel. 2005. *Sardinia without Lawrence*. London: Hearing Eye.

JULIEN, Green. 1989. *Paris*. Paris: Seuil.

HAMPTON, Christopher. 1970. *The Etruscan Survival*. Garden City, NY: Doubleday.

———. 1972. *An Exile's Italy*. Leiston: Thonnesen.

HARRISON, Robert Pogue. 2003. *The Dominion of the Dead*. Chicago: University of Chicago Press.

HEATHFIELD, John. 1994. *Around Whetstone and North Finchley in Old Photographys*. Stroud: Sutton.

HOFFMAN, Eva. 1993. *Exit into History: A Journey through the New Eastern Europe*. London: Heinemann.

HYLAND, Paul. 1996. *Backwards Out of the Big World: A Voyage into Portugal*. London: HarperCollins.

JAMES, Henry. 1995. *Italian Hours*. Edited by John Auchard. London: Penguin.

LAWRENCE, D. H. 1932. *Etruscan Places*. London: Secker.

MAGRIS, Claudio. 1990. *Inferences from a Sabre*. Translated by Mark Thompson. Edinburgh: Polygon.

———. 1993. *A Different Sea*. Translated by M. S. Spurr. London: Harvill.

———. 1999. *Danube: A Sentimental Journey from the Source to the Black Sea*. Translated by Patrick Creagh. London: Harvill.

MOORCOCK, Michael. 1988. *Mother London*. London: Secker & Warburg.

SARAMAGO, José. 2000. *Journey to Portugal*. Translated by Amanda Hopkinson and Nick Caistor. London: Harvill.

SINCLAIR, Iain. 1997. *Lights Out for the Territory: 9 Excursions in the Secret History of London*. London: Granta.

———. 1997. *Slow Chocolate Autopsy: Incidents from the Notorious Career of Norton, Prisoner of London*. London: Phoenix House.

———. 1999. *Liquid City*. London: Reaktion Books.

———. 1999. *Sorry Meniscus: Excursions to the Millenium Dome*. London: Profile in association with the London Review of Books.

———, and Marc Atkins. 1999. *Dark Lanthorns: David Rodinsky's A–Z Walked Over by Iain Sinclair*. Uppingham: Goldmark.

ZWEIG, Stefan. 2010. *Journeys*. Translated by Will Stone. London: Hesperus.

Politics

ACLAND, Richard. 1974. *The Next Step*. Exeter: Privately printed.

ANDERSON, Perry, and Robert Blackburn, eds. 1965. *Towards Socialism*. London: Fontana Library.

ARONSON, Ronald. 1980. *Jean-Paul Sartre: Philosophy in the World*. London: Verso.

———. 1983. *The Dialectics of Disaster: A Preface to Hope*. London: Verso.

———. 1995. *After Marxism*. New York and London: Guilford.

———. 2008. *Living without God*. Berkeley, CA: Counterpoint.

BENN, Tony, ed. 1984. *Writings on the Wall: A Radical and Socialist Anthology, 1215–1984*. London: Faber & Faber.

BOLD, Alan, ed. 1970. *Penguin Book of Socialist Verse*. Harmondsworth: Penguin.

BREMAN, Paul, ed. 1973. *You Better Believe It: Black Verse in English from Africa, the West Indies and the United States*. Harmondsworth: Penguin.

BRUNSKILL, Ian, ed. 2007. *Great Victorian Lives: An Era in Obituaries*. London: Times.

BUTLER, Robin. 2004. *Lord Butler's Report: Espionage and the Iraq War; Extracts from the Report*. Edited by Tim Coates. London and New York: Coates.

CALDICOTT, Helen. 2004. *The New Nuclear Danger: George W. Bush's Military–Industrial Complex*. New York and London: New Press.

CHOMSKY, Noam. 1983. *The Fateful Triangle: The United States, Israel and the Palestinians*. London: Pluto.

CRANKSHAW, Edward. 1963. *The New Cold War: Moscow v. Pekin*. Harmondsworth: Penguin.

CROSSMAN, Richard, ed. 1965. *The God That Failed*. New York: Bantam.

DELLAR, Geoffrey, ed. 1983. *Attlee as I Knew Him*. London: London Borough of Tower Hamlets, Directorate of Community Services, Library Service.

DYSON, Freeman. 1979. *Disturbing the Universe*. New York: Harper & Row.

———. 1984. *Weapons and Hope*. New York: Harper & Row.

ELDER, Robert. 2010. *Last Words of the Executed*. Chicago and London: University of Chicago Press.

ELLIOTT, Geoffrey, and Harold Shukman. 2002. *Secret Classrooms: A Memoir of the Cold War*. London: St Ermin's Press.

FOOT, Michael. 1964. *Harold Wilson: A Pictorial Biography*. Compiled and edited by John Parker and Eugene Prager. Oxford and New York: Pergamon.

FREMANTLE, Anne. 1960. *This Little Band of Prophets: The Story of the Gentle Fabians*. London: Allen & Unwin.

FROMM, Erich, ed. 1967. *Socialist Humanism: An International Symposium*. London: Allen Lane/Penguin.

GOODMAN, Paul. 1969. *Five Years: Thoughts during a Useless Time*. New York: Vintage.

———. 1973. *Little Prayers and Finite Experience*. London: Wildwood House.

———. 1974. *Collected Poems*. Edited by Taylor Stoehr. New York: Random House.

GORDON, Robert. 2001. *Primo Levi's Ordinary Virtues: From Testimony to Ethics*. Oxford: Oxford University Press.

GRASS, Günter. 1969. *Poems of Günter Grass*. Translated by Michael Hamburger and Christopher Middleton. Harmondsworth: Penguin.

———. 1974. *From the Diary of a Snail*. Translated by Ralph Manheim. London: Secker & Warburg.

———. 1974. *The Tin Drum*. Translated by Ralph Manheim. London: Secker & Warburg.

———. 1978. *In the Egg, and Other Poems*. Translated by Michael Hamburger and Christopher Middleton. London: Secker & Warburg.

———. 1978. *The Flounder*. Translated by Ralph Manheim. London: Secker & Warburg.

———. 1982. *Headbirths; or, the Germans Are Dying Out*. Translated by Ralph Manheim. London: Secker & Warburg.

———. 1985. *On Writing and Politics, 1967–1983*. Translated by Ralph Manheim. London: Secker & Warburg.

———. 1990. *Two States—One Nation?* Translated by Krishna Winston with A. S. Wensinger. London: Secker & Warburg.

———. 2007. *Peeling the Onion*. Translated by Michael Henry Heim. London: Harvill Secker.

HALE, Leslie. 1961. *Hanged in Error*. Harmondsworth: Penguin.

HARRINGTON, Michael. 1963. *The Other America: Poverty in the United States*. Harmondsworth: Penguin.

———. 1966. *The Accidental Century*. London: Weidenfeld & Nicolson.

HARTMAN, Geoffrey, ed. 1986. *Bitburg in Moral and Political Perspective*. Bloomington: Indiana University Press.

HAVEL, Václav. 1989. *Letters to Olga: June 1979–September 1982*. Translated by Paul Wilson. London: Faber & Faber.

———. 1989. *Living in Truth: Twenty-Two Essays Published on the Occasion of the Award of the Erasmus Prize to Václav Havel*. London: Faber & Faber.

———. 1990. *Disturbing the Peace: A Conversation with Karel Hvíæzædala*. Translated by Paul Wilson. London: Faber & Faber.

———. 1991. *Open Letters: Selected Prose, 1964–1990*. Edited by Paul Wilson. London: Faber & Faber.

———. 1992. *Summer Meditations: On Politics, Morality and Civility in a Time of Transition*. Translated by Paul Wilson. London: Faber & Faber.

HOGGART, Richard. 1957. *The Uses of Literacy: Aspects of Working-Class Life, with Special Reference to Publications and Entertainments*. London: Chatto & Windus.

HUGO, Victor. 1992. *Last Days of a Condemned Man, and Other Prison Writings*. Translated by Geoff Woollen. Oxford: Oxford University Press.

JOLL, James. 1977. *Gramsci*. London: Fontana Books/Collins.

KOESTLER, Arthur, and C. H. Rolph. 1961. *Hanged by the Neck: An Exposure of Capital Punishment in England*. Harmondsworth: Penguin.

LIFTON, Robert Jay, and Eric Markusen. 1990. *The Genocidal Mentality: Nazi Holocaust and Nuclear Threat*. London: Macmillan.

MANDER, John. 1962. *Berlin: Hostage for the West*. Harmondsworth: Penguin.

———. 1963. *Great Britain or Little England*. Harmondsworth: Penguin.

MARGOLIUS, Heda. 1973. *I Do Not Want to Remember: Auschwitz 1941–Prague 1968*. Translated by Erazim Kohak. London: Weidenfeld & Nicolson.

MEEROPOL, Robert, and Michael Meeropol. 1975. *We Are Your Sons: The Legacy of Ethel and Julius Rosenberg*. Boston, MA: Houghton Mifflin.

NEVILLE, Richard. 1970. *Play Power*. London: Jonathan Cape.

NUTTALL, Jeff. 1968. *Bomb Culture*. London: MacGibbon & Kee.

PINTO-DUSCHINSKY, Michael. 1967. *The Political Thought of Lord Salisbury, 1854–1868*. London: Constable.

———. 1981. *British Political Finance, 1830–1980*. Washington, DC, and London: American Enterprise Institute for Public Policy Research.

———, and David Butler. 1971. *The British General Election of 1970*. London: Macmillan.

ROBERTSON, James. 1983. *The Same Alternative: A Choice of Futures*. Ironbridge: Robertson.

ROSSELLI, Carlo. 1994. *Liberal Socialism*. Edited by Nadia Urbinati. Translated by William McCuaig. Princeton, NJ: Princeton University Press.

ROWAN-ROBINSON, Michael. 1985. *Fire and Ice: The Nuclear Winter*. Harlow: Longman.

ROWE, Dorothy. 1992. *Wanting Everything: The Art of Happiness*. London: Fontana Books/HarperCollins.

RUBENSTEIN, Richard. 1966. *After Auschwitz: Radical Theology and Contemporary Judaism*. New York: Macmillan.

———. 1983. *The Age of Triage: Fear and Hope in an Over-Crowded World*. Boston, MA: Beacon.

———. 1987. *The Cunning of History: The Holocaust and the American Future*. New York: Harper & Row.

SAKHAROV, Andrei. 1968. *Progress, Co-existence and Intellectual Freedom*. London: Andre Deutsch.

SCHEER, Robert. 1983. *With Enough Shovels: Reagan, Bush and Nuclear War*. London: Secker & Warburg.

SCHELL, Jonathan. 1982. *The Fate of the Earth*. New York: Alfred A. Knopf.

SIMMONS, Michael. 1991. *The Reluctant President: A Political Life of Václav Havel*. London: Methuen.

SISSONS, Michael, and Philip French, eds. 1964. *The Age of Austerity, 1945– 1951*. Harmondsworth: Penguin.

SMITH, Jeff. 1989. *Unthinking the Unthinkable: Nuclear Weapons and Western Culture*. Bloomington: Indiana University Press.

SOLNIT, Rebecca. 2005. *Hope in the Dark: The Untold History of People Power*. Edinburgh: Canongate.

SOYINKA, Wole. 1972. *The Man Died: Prison Notes of Wole Soyinka*. London: Rex Collings.

TAWNEY, R. H. 1931. *Equality*. London: Allen & Unwin.

THOMPSON, Denys, ed. 1964. *Discrimination and Popular Culture*. Harmondsworth: Penguin.

TURGENEV, Ivan. 1959. *Literary Reminiscences and Autobiographical Fragments*. Translated by David Magarshack. London: Faber & Faber.

VISSER, Margaret. 2009. *The Gift of Thanks: The Roots and Rituals of Gratitude*. Boston, MA: Houghton Mifflin Harcourt.

WALZER, Michael. 1985. *Exodus and Revolution*. New York: Basic Books.

WILLIAMS, Raymond. 1961. *The Long Revolution*. London: Chatto & Windus.

———. 1963. *Culture and Society, 1780–1950*. Harmondsworth and New York: Penguin.

———. 1966. *Communications*. London: Chatto & Windus.

———, ed. 1968. *May Day Manifesto, 1968*. Harmondsworth: Penguin.

WILSON, Angus. 1963. *The Wild Garden; or, Speaking of Writing*. London: Secker & Warburg.

WOLF, Christa. 1984. *Cassandra: A Novel and Four Essays*. Translated by Jan Van Heurck. London: Virago.

YGLESIAS, José. 1968. *In the Fist of the Revolution: Life in Castro's Cuba*. London: Allen Lane/Penguin.

ŽIŽEK, Slavoj, Eric Santner and Kenneth Reinhard. 2005. *The Neighbour: Three Inquiries in Political Theory*. Chicago: University of Chicago Press.

FEMINISM

CHERNIN, Kim. 1981. *The Obsession: Reflections on the Tyranny of Slenderness*. New York: Harper & Row.

————. 1982. *The Hunger Song*. London: Menard.

————. 1985. *In My Mother's House*. London: Virago.

————, and Renate Stendhal. 1989. *Sex and Other Sacred Games: Love, Desire, Passion and Position*. New York: Times Books.

DWORKIN, Andrea. 1981. *Pornography: Men Possessing Women*. London: Women's Press.

————. 1990. *Mercy*. London: Secker & Warburg.

GRIFFIN, Susan. 1984. *Woman and Nature: The Roaring Inside Her*. London: Women's Press.

LEE, Carol. 1986. *The Ostrich Position: Sex, Schooling and Mystification*. London: Unwin.

MILLETT, Kate. 1971. *Sexual Politics*. London: Hart-Davis.

————. 1975. *The Prostitution Papers: A Candid Dialogue*. St Albans: Paladin.

MORGAN, Robin. 1982. *Depth Perception*. Garden City, NY: Anchor/Doubleday.

————. 1983. *The Anatomy of Freedom: Feminism, Physics and Global Politics*. Oxford: Robertson.

————. 1989. *The Demon Lover: On the Sexuality of Terrorism*. London: Methuen.

NELSON, Sharon. 1993. *Grasping Men's Metaphors*. Quebec: Muses' Company.

OLIVER, Douglas. 2005. *Whisper 'Louise': A Double Historical Memoir and Meditation*. Hastings: Reality Street Editions.

RADCLIFFE RICHARDS, Janet. 1982. *The Sceptical Feminist: A Philosophical Enquiry*. Harmondsworth: Penguin.

Science and Medicine

ALEXANDER, F. M. 1974. *The Alexander Technique: The Essential Writings of F. Matthias Alexander*. Selected by Edward Maisel. London: Thames & Hudson.

DAMASIO, Antonio. 1995. *Descartes' Error: Emotion, Reason and the Human Brain*. London: Picador.

————. 2000. *The Feeling of What Happens: Body and Emotion in the Making of Consciousness*. London: Heinemann.

ELLIS, Clarence. 1954. *The Pebbles on the Beach*. London: Faber & Faber.

FELDENKRAIS, Moshe. 1980. *Awareness through Movement: Health Exercises for Personal Growth*. Harmondsworth: Penguin.

FEYNMAN, Richard, and Steven Weinberg. 1987. *Elementary Particles and the Laws of Physics*. Compiled by Richard Mackenzie and Paul Doust. Cambridge: Cambridge University Press.

GOMEZ, Joan. 1970. *Dictionary of Symptoms*. London: Paladin.

GOULD, Stephen Jay. 2001. *Rocks of Ages: Science and Religion in the Fullness of Life*. London: Jonathan Cape.

GREGORY, Richard. 1916. *Discovery; or, the Spirit and Service of Science*. London: Macmillan.

HARRIS, Harold, ed. 1975. *Astride the Two Cultures: Arthur Koestler at 70*. London: Hutchinson.

HUMPHREY, Nicholas. 2011. *Soul Dust: The Magic of Consciousness*. London: Quercus.

HUXLEY, Aldous. 1963. *Literature and Science*. London: Chatto & Windus.

KLEIN, George. 1990. *The Atheist at the Holy City*. Translated by Theodore and Ingrid Friedmann. Cambridge, MA, and London: MIT Press.

———. 1992. *Pietà*. Translated by Theodore and Ingrid Friedmann. Cambridge, MA, and London: MIT Press.

———. 1997. *Live Now: Inspiring Accounts of Overcoming Adversity*. Translated by Clas von Sydow. Amherst, NY: Prometheus.

KUMIN, Maxine. 1979. *The Retrieval System: Poems*. Harmondsworth: Penguin.

LEACH, Penelope. 1979. *Who Cares? A New Deal for Mothers and Their Small Children*. Harmondsworth: Penguin.

LEROI, Armand Marie. 2005. *Mutants: On the Form, Varieties and Errors of the Human Body*. London: Harper Perennial.

LEWIN, Ralph A. 1999. *Merde: Excursions into Scientific, Cultural and Socio-Historical Coprology*. London: Aurum.

MONESTIER, Martin. 1997. *Histoire et bizarreries sociales des excréments: Des origines à nos jours*. Paris: Cherche midi.

MULLER-HILL, Benno. 1988. *Murderous Science: Elimination by Scientific*

Selection of Jews, Gypsies, and Others; Germany, 1933–1945. Translated by George R. Fraser. Oxford: Oxford University Press.

NASSAUER, Rudolf. 1960. *The Hooligan*. London: Peter Owen.

OLSEN, Danielle, and Hildi Hawkins, eds. 2003. *The Phantom Museum and Henry Wellcome's Collection of Medical Curiosities*. London: Profile.

ROUSSEAU, Jean-Jacques. 1979. *Botany: A Study of Pure Curiosity; Botanical Letters, and Notes Towards a Dictionary of Botanical Terms*. Letters translated by Kate Ottevanger. London: Joseph.

ROWAN-ROBINSON, Michael. 1979. *Cosmic Landscape: Voyages Back along the Photon's Track*. Oxford: Oxford University Press.

———. 1990. *Universe*. London: Longmans, Green & Co.

———. 1993. *Ripples in the Cosmos: A View Behind the Scenes of the New Cosmology*. Oxford: Freeman/Spektrum.

ROYAL CANADIAN AIRFORCE. 1978. *Exercise Plans for Physical Fitness*. Prentice Hall & IBD.

RUDOLF, Mary, and Malcolm Levene. 1999. *Paediatrics and Child Health*. Oxford: Blackwell Science.

SNOW, C. P. 1964. *The Two Cultures; and, a Second Look*. Cambridge: Cambridge University Press.

———. 1981. *The Physicists*. London: Macmillan.

SNOW, Philip. 1982. *Stranger and Brother: A Portrait of C. P. Snow*. London: Macmillan.

STANWAY, Andrew. 1982. *Alternative Medicine: A Guide to Natural Therapies*. Harmondsworth: Penguin.

WATSON, James, and Francis Crick. 1968. *The Double Helix: A Personal Account of the Discovery of the Structure of DNA*. London: Weidenfeld & Nicolson.

WEISKOPF, Victor. 1979. *Knowledge and Wonder*. 2nd edn. Cambridge, MA, and London: MIT Press.

WINICK, Myron. 1979. *Hunger Disease: Studies by the Jewish Physicians in the Warsaw Ghetto*. Translated by Martha Osnos. New York and Chichester: Wiley.

———, ed. 1982. *Growing Up Healthy: A Parent's Guide to Good Nutrition*. New York: Morrow.

———. 2007. *Final Stamp: The Jewish Doctors in the Warsaw Ghetto*. Bloomington, IN: Authorhouse.

AFTERWORD

BABEL, Isaac. 2005 *Red Cavalry, and Other Stories*. Edited by Efraim Sicher. Translated by David Macduff. London: Penguin.

BUTOR, Michel. 1957. *La Modification*. Paris: Minuit.

———. 1960–82. *Répertoires*. Paris: Minuit.

———. 1995. *L'Emploi du temps*. Paris: Minuit

———. 1996. *A la frontière: Poèmes*. Paris: Différence.

CAREY, John. 2005. *What Good Are the Arts?* London: Faber & Faber.

CARSON, Ciaran. 1996. *Opera Et Cetera*. Newcastle-upon-Tyne: Bloodaxe Books.

———. 1998. *The Alexandrine Plan*. Loughcrew: Gallery.

———. 1998. *The Twelfth of Never*. Oldcastle: Gallery.

———, trans. 2002. *Dante's Inferno*. London: Granta.

DAVIS, Philip. 2007. *Bernard Malamud: A Writer's Life*. Oxford: Oxford University Press.

HOLDEN, Lynn. 1991. *Forms of Deformity*. Sheffield: JSOT Press.

HOWELL, Anthony. 2006. *Oblivion*. London: Grey Suit Editions.

JIMENEZ, Juan Ramon. 1997. *The Complete Perfectionist: A Poetics of Work*. Edited and translated by Christopher Maurer. New York and London: Doubleday.

———. 2000. *Time and Space: A Poetic Autobiography*. Translated by Antonio de Nicolas. Bloomington, IN: Iuniverse

JOSIPOVICI, Gabriel. 2010. *Whatever Happened to Modernism*. New Haven, CT, and London: Yale University Press.

MALAMUD, Bernard. 1979. *Dubin's Lives*. London: Chatto & Windus.

SEGALEN, Victor. 1978. *Chine; ou, Le Pouvoir dans l'etendue*. London: Taranman.

STONE, Will. 2007. *Glaciation*. Cambridge, MA: Salt.

TAGGART, John, 2007. *Unveiling Marianne Moore*. Buffalo, NY: Atticus/Finch.